The Oxford Dictionary of Allusions

The Oxford Dictionary of

Allusions

Andrew Delahunty,
Sheila Dignen, and
Penny Stock

OXFORD
UNIVERSITY PRESS

OXFORD

UNIVERSITY PRESS

Great Clarendon Street, Oxford OX2 6DP

Oxford University Press is a department of the University of Oxford.
It furthers the University's objective of excellence in research, scholarship,
and education by publishing worldwide in

Oxford New York

Athens Auckland Bangkok Bogotá Buenos Aires Calcutta
Cape Town Chennai Dar es Salaam Delhi Florence Hong Kong Istanbul
Karachi Kuala Lumpur Madrid Melbourne Mexico City Mumbai
Nairobi Paris São Paulo Shanghai Singapore Taipei Tokyo Toronto Warsaw

with associated companies in Berlin Ibadan

Published in the United States
by Oxford University Press Inc., New York

British Library Cataloguing in Publication Data
Data available

Library of Congress Cataloging in Publication Data
Data available

ISBN 0-19-860031-3

1 3 5 7 9 10 8 6 4 2

Designed by Jane Stevenson
Typeset in Photina and Quay Sans
by Interactive Sciences Ltd
Printed in Great Britain by
T. J. International, Padstow

Contents

Introduction   vii

List of Themes   xi

List of Special Entries   xiii

Dictionary   **1**

Index   423

Introduction

An allusion may be defined as the mention of the name of a real person, historical event, or literary character which is not simply a straightforward reference (as in 'Hercules was an ancient Greek hero') but which conjures up some extra meaning, embodying some quality or characteristic for which the word has come to stand. So, we can describe a miser as a Scrooge, a strong man as a Hercules, a beautiful woman as a Venus. *The Oxford Dictionary of Allusions* aims to identify and explain many such allusions used in English and to illustrate their use by quotations from a variety of literary works and other texts. In the style of a thesaurus the entries are grouped thematically under such headings as **Anger, Change, Dreams, Explorers**, and **Revenge**.

Writers use allusions in a variety of ways. They can be used as a kind of shorthand, evoking instantly a complex human experience embedded within a story or dramatic event. For example, in this passage from *Jude the Obscure*,

> Arabella ascended the stairs, softly opened the door of the first bedroom, and peeped in. Finding that her shorn Samson was asleep she entered to the bedside and started regarding him,

Thomas Hardy's phrase 'shorn Samson' succinctly expresses Arabella's quiet triumph at finally having Jude in her power. Allusions can convey powerful visual images, as Robertson Davies does in his reference to the tangled limbs and snakes of the classical statue of Laocoön (described in the theme **Struggle**) in *Leaven of Malice*:

> 'And seeing it's you, I'll give you a hint: the way the string's tied, you can get loose at once if he lies down flat and you crawl right up over his head; then the string drops off without untying the knots. Bye now.' And she was off to encourage other strugglers, who lay in Laocoön groups about the floor.

It is often possible to pack more meaning into a well-chosen allusion than into a roughly equivalent descriptive term from the general language either because an allusion can carry some of the connotations of the whole story from which it is drawn, or because an individual's name can be associated with more than one characteristic. Some authors can even use a multiplicity of allusive terms to entertaining effect, as in this quotation from *The Scold's Bridle* by Minette Walters:

> I watched Duncan clipping his hedge this afternoon and could barely remember the handsome man he was. If I had been a charitable woman, I would have married him forty years ago and saved him from himself and Violet. She

has turned my Romeo into a sad-eyed Billy Bunter who blinks his passions quietly when no one's looking. Oh, that his too, too solid flesh should melt. At twenty, he had the body of Michelangelo's David, now he resembles an entire family group by Henry Moore.

The majority of allusions in English derive from classical mythology and the Bible, particularly the Old Testament. These ancient stories—the Wooden Horse of Troy, the protracted return home of Odysseus, David and Goliath, the banishment of Adam and Eve from the Garden of Eden—remain very much alive in our collective consciousness. Other fertile sources include folklore and legend (for example, Robin Hood, Lancelot, and Faust); Shakespeare (Romeo, Othello, and Lady Macbeth); Dickens (Micawber, Scrooge, and Pecksniff); the visual style of great artists (Rembrandt and Modigliani); and children's stories (Cinderella, Pinocchio, and Eeyore). The modern visual media of cinema, television and cartoons are also represented in the book (Orphan Annie, Superman, and Jurassic Park). Some individual works, such as *Gulliver's Travels*, *Alice's Adventures in Wonderland*, and *The Pilgrim's Progress*, are particularly rich sources of characters and situations subsequently used as allusions.

The book is largely based on the evidence of the quotations collected as its source material. Its thematic structure evolved during the writing as it became clear how individual entries clustered together in concept. As a result, the themes vary in treatment and coverage. Some strongly supported themes do not have opposing counterparts. There are several instances of **Betrayal** but no examples of pure loyalty, the nearest equivalent being **Friendship**. While **Deserted Places** are included here, busy or bustling places are not. There are several examples of **Arrogance and Pomposity** but few of **Humility**, and none at all of modesty. The theme **Curse** accounts for unlucky individuals, but there seem to be no archetypal allusions for someone who is very lucky. Many themes reflect the stereotypes entrenched in our culture over the centuries. All three of the adulterers in the theme **Adultery** (Emma Bovary, Anna Karenina, and Hester Prynne) are women; **Courage** is illustrated entirely by males; while the theme **Grief and Sorrow** is expressed only by female figures such as Niobe and Rachel. Some of the themes are illustrated entirely or mainly from classical sources while others are more modern. Entries in the theme **Fertility**, for example, are mythological; in both **Avarice** and **Despair** they are biblical; whilst in **Comedy and Humour** they tend to be more recent in origin. **Guilt** is almost entirely exemplified by biblical characters, with no allusions from classical sources, while **Punishment** includes

Prometheus, Sisyphus, and Tantalus, as well as Adam and Eve and Jezebel.

The themes vary considerably in length. Some are quite extensive, usually those which deal with a broad semantic area such as **Goodness**. Others, such as **Disclosure**, are much shorter, often because they deal with a relatively narrower concept, though the paucity of entries at **Cowardice** is curious.

In some themes, one individual provides the most typical or powerful instance of the concept being illustrated. Judas is by far the most frequently cited exponent of betrayal. Narcissus stands so strongly for excessive self-adulation that his name has given us the term we use for this characteristic in the general language. In other cases, allusions have changed their meaning over time. Solomon used to represent not only wisdom but also fabulous wealth, and Midas was remembered not only for his golden gift but also for his ass's ears (see the theme **Disclosure**, at which this story is recounted). Occasionally, the character who most typically represents a characteristic changes over time. For instance, in the nineteenth century Jack Sheppard represented the archetype of the person who successfully escaped. In the twentieth century he was replaced by Houdini (see the theme **Escape and Survival**).

Some individual characters or stories allude not just to one characteristic or concept but to several, and as a consequence appear in several different themes. Don Quixote, for example, is associated with thinness, insanity, illusion, and idealism, and is found under each of these themes. Other characters from *Don Quixote de la Mancha*, such as Rosinante and Sancho Panza, also appear (in **Horses** and **Friendship** respectively). For convenience, and to avoid undue repetition, in such cases a full account of the whole story or event has been given as a special boxed entry. Cross-references to a special entry are given in the entries for characters or events taken from the relevant story.

The themes and special entries appear in alphabetical order, and a list of each is given at the beginning of the book. In addition, there is a full index of entries at the end of the book showing under which theme or themes a particular entry is to be found. Closely related themes are cross-referred to each other enabling the reader to compare linked or overlapping semantic areas. For example, at **Abundance and Plenty** there are cross-references to **Fertility** and **Idyllic Places**.

This book is based on a database of quotations gleaned from an extensive and diverse reading programme and the authors would like to thank the following readers who contributed generously to the task: Kendall Clarke, Ian Clarke, Robert Grout, Ruth Loshak, Duncan Marshall, Camilla Sherwood, Peggy Tout, and Brigit Viney. In particular, we would like to thank Jane McArthur for her substantial contribution. Special additional thanks are due to Mark Grout for his support.

We would also like to thank the staff of Oxford University Press. The book has passed through a number of hands at OUP: Rob Scriven, Kendall Clarke, Kate Wandless, Susie Dent, Vicki Rodger, Alysoun Owen, and Helen Cox have all been involved at different stages. Their support and encouragement have been greatly appreciated. We are particularly grateful to Elizabeth Knowles, from whose advice and detailed attention to successive drafts of the text the book has greatly benefited.

List of Themes

Abundance and Plenty
Actors
Adultery
Adventure
Ambition
Anger
Animals, Love of
Appearing
Arrogance and Pomposity
Artists
Ascent and Descent
Avarice

Baldness
Bargain
Beauty: Female Beauty
Beauty: Male Beauty
Betrayal
Blindness

Captives
Change
Chaos and Disorder
Chastity and Virginity
Comedy and Humour
Communication
Complexity
Concealment
Conflict
Conformity
Courage
Cowardice
Craftsmen
Criminals

Cunning
Curse

Dancing
Danger
Darkness
Death
Defeat
Departure
Deserted Places
Despair
Destiny and Luck
Destruction
Detectives
Devil
Dictators and Tyrants
Difficulty
Disappearance and Absence
Disapproval
Disclosure
Disguise
Distance
Doubt
Dreams
Duality

Enemy
Envy
Escape and Survival
Evil
Explorers

Failure
Fatness
Fear
Fertility
Fierce Women
Food and Drink

Forgiveness
Freedom
Friendship

Generosity
Gesture
Gluttony
Goodness
Grief and Sorrow
Guarding
Guilt

Hair
Happiness
Hatred
Height
Heroes
Honesty and Truth
Horror
Horses
Humility
Hunters
Hypocrisy

Idealism
Idyllic Places
Illusion
Immobility
Importance
Indifference
Innocence
Insanity
Inspiration
Intelligence
Invisibility

Jealousy
Judgement and Decision

Knowledge

Lack of Change
Large Size
Leaders
Life: Generation of
  Life
Light
Love and Marriage
Lovers
Lying

Macho Men
Magic
Medicine
Memory
Messengers
Mischief
Miserliness
Modernity
Monsters
Moustaches
Movement
Murderers
Music
Mystery

Naivety
Nakedness
Nonconformity
Noses

Old Age
Optimism
Oratory
Outdatedness
Outlaws

Past
Patience

Peace
Perseverance
Pessimism
Poverty
Power
Pride
Prisons
Problem
Prophecy
Prostitutes
Punishment

Quest

Realization
Rebellion and
  Disobedience
Rebirth and
  Resurrection
Rescue
Returning
Revenge
Ruthlessness

Safety
Sculptors
Seducers and Male
  Lovers
Sex and Sexuality
Silence
Similarity
Sirens
Sleep
Small Size
Smiles
Soldiers
Solitude
Sound

Speech
Speed
Sternness
Storytellers
Strangeness
Strength
Struggle
Stupidity
Success
Suffering
Superiority

Teachers
Temperature
Temptation
Thinness
Thirft
Time
Travellers and
  Wanderers

Ugliness
Unpleasant or
  Wicked Places

Vanity
Victory

Walk
War
Water
Weakness
Wealth
Wholesomeness
Wisdom
Writers

Youth

List of Special Entries

Achilles	3
Adam and Eve	5
Alice in Wonderland	10
Apollo	15
Cain	44
Cinderella	56
Daniel	86
David	90
Dionysus	117
Don Quixote	128
Gulliver's Travels	171
Hades	172
Hercules	182
Jason and the Argonauts	220
Jesus	223
Joseph	224
Moses and the Book of Exodus	264
Noah and the Flood	279
Odysseus	283
Prometheus	311
Samson	336
Trojan War	392

Abundance and Plenty

The biblical allusions **EDEN, GOSHEN**, and the **LAND OF MILK AND HONEY** represent places of plenty. While the idea of plentifulness can also be symbolized by the classical image of the **CORNUCOPIA**, scarcity can be suggested by **MOTHER HUBBARD** and her empty cupboard. This theme is closely related to the theme **Fertility**. ▶ *See also* **Idyllic Places**.

Johnny Appleseed Johnny Appleseed was the nickname of John Chapman (1774–1847) because he planted orchards for settlers in Pennsylvania, Ohio, Indiana, and Illinois. He was known for his woodcraft and the help that he gave to pioneer settlers.

> What about the doctor down in Hillsborough? The one with the runaway daughter and the fistful of amphetamines he's scattering around like Johnny goddam Appleseed?
> MAX BYRD *Finders Weepers*, 1983

Cornucopia In Greek mythology, Amalthea was a she-goat or goat-nymph, whose milk Zeus drank when he was first born. In gratitude, Zeus placed Amalthea's image among the stars as the constellation Capricorn. Zeus also took one of Amalthea's horns, which resembled a cow's horns, and gave it to the daughters of Melisseus, a Cretan king. It became the famous Cornucopia, the Horn of Plenty which was always filled with whatever food or drink its owner desired. It is usually represented as a goat's horn spilling over with fruit, flowers, and stalks of corn.

> There was a cornucopia of food and drink almost forbidding in its plentitude.
> FRED CHAPPELL *Farewell I'm Bound to Leave You*, 1997

Garden of Eden The Garden of Eden is the home of Adam and Eve in the biblical account of the Creation. It is imagined as a place of lush beauty, in which grows 'every tree that is pleasant to the sight and good for food' (Gen. 2: 9). ▶ *See special entry* □ **ADAM AND EVE** *on p. 5*.

> His eyes rested happily on the spreading green of the bread-fruit trees. 'By George, it's like the garden of Eden.'
> W. SOMERSET MAUGHAM 'Mackintosh' in *The World Over*, 1951

> For the first seven thousand feet it is the Garden of Eden, a luxuriance of orchids, humming-birds, and tiny streams of delicious water that run by miracle alongside every path.
> LOUIS DE BERNIÈRES *The War of Don Emmanuel's Nether Parts*, 1990

> Flowers, shrubs, saplings had been brought here with their roots and earth, and set in baskets and makeshift cases. But many of the containers had rotted; the earth had spilled out to create, from one container to the next, a layer of damp humus, where the shoots of some plants were already taking root. It was like being in an Eden sprouting from the very planks of the Daphne.
> UMBERTO ECO *The Island of the Day Before*, 1994

Goshen Goshen was the fertile region of Egypt inhabited by the Israelites from the time of Joseph until the Exodus. The name Goshen can be applied to a place of plenty and comfort. ▶ *See special entry* ☐ **MOSES AND THE BOOK OF EXODUS** *on p. 264.*

> It's a bleak and barren country there, not like this land of Goshen you've been used to.
> GEORGE ELIOT *Adam Bede,* 1859

> 'As to my clothes—simply I will not have any', replies Belinda, with a look of impera-tive decision. 'I should have thought them the one Goshen in your desert', says Sarah, with an annoyed laugh; 'them and the presents'.
> RHODA BROUGHTON *Belinda,* 1883

Horn of Plenty ▶ *See* CORNUCOPIA.

land of milk and honey In the Bible, God promised to Moses to deliver the Israelites from slavery in Egypt to a land of plenty: 'And I am come down to deliver them out of the hand of the Egyptians, and to bring them up out of that land unto a good land and a large, unto a land flowing with milk and honey' (Exod. 3: 8). The term is now applied to any imagined land of plenty and happiness.

Mother Hubbard In the nursery rhyme, Old Mother Hubbard

'went to the cupboard,
To fetch her poor dog a bone.
But when she got there
The cupboard was bare,
And so the poor dog had none.'

> I stepped over an' looked down the other rows. They were bare as Mama Hubbard's cubbard.
> CHESTER HIMES 'Let Me at the Enemy—an' George Brown' (1944) in *The Collected Stories of Chester Himes,* 1990

> I drove back home, changed into leggings and a baggy white T-shirt and took a look in the fridge. Mother Hubbard would have been right at home there. I dumped out a slice of ham that had curled up to die and settled for a meal of pasta and pesto.
> SARAH LACEY *File under: Arson,* 1995

Pomona Pomona was the Roman goddess of fruit, married to Vortumnus, the god of orchards and fruit.

> Down in the heart of the apple-country nearly every farmer kept a cider-making apparatus and wring-house for his own use, building up the pomace in great straw 'cheeses', as they were called; but here, on the margin of Pomona's plain, was a debatable land neither orchard nor sylvan exclusively, where the apple-produce was hardly sufficient to warrant each proprietor in keeping a mill of his own.
> THOMAS HARDY *The Woodlanders,* 1887

Achilles

Achilles was one of the greatest Greek heroes of the Trojan War. According to legend, he was the son of the mortal Peleus and the sea-nymph Thetis. During his infancy his mother dipped him in the waters of the River Styx, thus making his body invulnerable except for the heel by which she held him. This vulnerable spot would later prove fatal.

The young Achilles received his education from the wise centaur Chiron, who taught him the arts of war and fed him on the entrails of wild animals in order to instil courage in him. Chiron also made Achilles practise running, and he subsequently became the swiftest of all men. When Achilles was young the Fates offered him the choice between a long life of ease and obscurity, or a young death and fame and glory. He chose the latter.

Thetis knew from a prophecy that if Achilles joined the Greek campaign to fight against the Trojans he would not come back alive and, in an attempt to save his life, she disguised him as a girl on the island of Scyros. He was discovered by Odysseus, Nestor, and Ajax, who had been sent to find him. They arranged for a war trumpet to sound, at which Achilles revealed himself by reaching for a shield and spear.

The *Iliad* relates how Achilles quarrelled with his commander, Agamemnon, because of Agamemnon's slight in taking from him his war-prize, the concubine Briseis. Achilles retired in anger to his tent, refusing to fight any longer. Later, after the death of his friend Patroclus, clad in Achilles' own armour, at the hand of the Trojan hero Hector, he did emerge, filled with grief and rage. In revenge, Achilles killed Hector and dragged his body behind the wheels of his chariot round the walls of Troy. Achilles himself was wounded in the heel by a poisoned arrow shot by Paris, Hector's brother, and died of this wound.

Ajax and Odysseus vied for the armour of the dead Achilles. When Agamemnon awarded the armour to Odysseus, Ajax went mad with rage, slaughtered a flock of sheep, and then committed suicide in shame.

Various aspects of the Achilles story are dealt with throughout the book.

▶ *See* **Anger, Disguise, Friendship,** *and* **Weakness**.

Actors

Below are some of the actors whose names have come to represent the acting profession or the theatre.

....

David Garrick David Garrick (1717–79) was regarded as the foremost Shakespearean actor of 18th-century England and manager of Drury Lane Theatre for nearly thirty years (1747–76). According to Oliver Goldsmith he was 'an abridgement of all that was pleasant in man'.

> 'Is the play up to viewing, Mr Garrick?' one or other of the gentlemen would periodically ask Ralph, and Ralph was ecstatic for this merely whimsical comparison of himself to the great actor-manager.
> THOMAS KENEALLY *The Playmaker*, 1987

Roscius Quintus Roscius Gallus (d. 62 BC), known as Roscius, was the most celebrated of Roman comic actors, who later became identified with all that was considered best in acting. Many great actors, notably David Garrick, were nicknamed after him. The child actor William Betty (1791–1874) was known as 'the young Roscius'.

> The celebrated provincial amateur of Roscian renown.
> CHARLES DICKENS *Great Expectations*, 1860

Stanislavsky Stanislavsky (1863–1938), the great Russian actor, director, and teacher, was born Konstantin Sergeevitch Alekseev. He founded the Moscow Art Theatre in 1898 and was known for his productions of Chekhov and Gorky. His theories about technique, in particular in paying attention to the characters' backgrounds and psychology, eventually formed the basis for the US movement known as 'method acting'.

> 'What? I didn't! That's absurd!' he protested, emoting surprise and shock in a sub-Stanislavskian style.
> REGINALD HILL *Child's Play*, 1987

Thespis Thespis was a Greek dramatic poet of the 6th century BC and generally regarded as the founder of Greek tragedy, having introduced the role of the actor in addition to the traditional chorus. The word 'Thespian', which derives from his name, means 'relating to drama or acting'.

> If Mrs. Caesar Augustus Conquergood's name might appear, alone, at the top of an otherwise double column of patrons of the Salterton Little Theatre then, in Nellie's judgment, the drama had justified its existence, Thespis had not rolled his car in vain.
> ROBERTSON DAVIES *Tempest-Tost*, 1951

Adam and Eve

According to the Book of Genesis, God, having created the world and everything in it, 'formed man from the dust of the ground, and breathed into his nostrils the breath of life; and man became a living soul'. This first man was Adam, and at first he lived alone in the Garden of Eden, imagined as a place of lush beauty, in which grew 'every tree that is pleasant to the sight and good for food'. To give Adam a companion, God took one of Adam's ribs and made it into the first woman, Eve. They lived together in innocence, knew nothing of good and evil, and were not ashamed of their own nakedness.

The tree of the knowledge of good and evil grew in the Garden of Eden, the only tree whose fruit Adam and Eve were expressly forbidden by God to eat. The Serpent, which was 'more subtil than any beast of the field which the Lord God had made', used cunning to persuade Eve to eat the forbidden fruit, saying 'in the day ye eat thereof, then your eyes shall be opened, and ye shall be as gods, knowing good and evil'. Thus tempted, Eve did eat the fruit and then in turn persuaded Adam to do the same: 'And the eyes of them both were opened, and they knew that they were naked.' As a punishment for disobeying God's command, they were banished from the garden of Eden. Because Eve had eaten first and then tempted Adam, God told her that as a punishment women would henceforth always suffer in childbirth: 'I will greatly multiply thy sorrow and thy conception; in sorrow thou shalt bring forth children.' Man for his part would be forced to toil for his livelihood: 'In the sweat of thy face thou shalt eat bread, till thou return unto the ground.'

Throughout this book there are references to Adam and Eve and to the story of the Fall.

▶ *See* ADAM *at* **Sex and Sexuality** *and* **Solitude**
　　ADAM AND EVE *at* **Happiness, Innocence, Life: Generation of Life, Nakedness, Past, Punishment,** *and* **Rebellion and Disobedience**
　　EDEN *at* **Abundance and Plenty** *and* **Idyllic Places**
　　EVE *at* **Betrayal, Evil,** *and* **Temptation**
　　FORBIDDEN FRUIT *at* **Temptation**
　　PARADISE *at* **Idyllic Places**
　　SERPENT *at* **Cunning** *and* **Problems**
　　TREE OF KNOWLEDGE *at* **Knowledge**.

Adultery

Famous adulterers appear to be female and the two most celebrated accounts of adultery in world literature, created by Flaubert and Tolstoy, seem to suggest that its inevitable consequence is suicide.

....

Emma Bovary Emma Bovary, in Flaubert's novel *Madame Bovary* (1857), is married to a country doctor in provincial Normandy. Aspiring to a more romantic and sophisticated life, she is drawn into first one affair and then a second. When the second affair ends because her lover, Léon, has tired of her, she kills herself with arsenic.

Anna Karenina In Tolstoy's novel, *Anna Karenina* (1873–7), Anna is married to a government official, Karenin. Anna has a love affair with Count Vronsky, and when she becomes pregnant she confesses her adultery to her husband, who insists she choose between himself and her lover. She chooses Vronsky but, unable to tolerate the social isolation that this leads to, eventually kills herself by throwing herself under a train.

> It was one thing reading Tolstoy in class, another playing Anna and Vronsky with the professor.
> PHILIP ROTH *My Life as a Man*, 1970

Hester Prynne Hester Prynne is the adulteress in Nathaniel Hawthorne's novel *The Scarlet Letter* (1850) set in 17th-century Boston. Hester is sent by her ageing English husband to Boston, where he joins her two years later. He arrives to find her in the pillory, with her illegitimate baby in her arms. She refuses to name her lover and is sentenced to wear a scarlet 'A', for 'adulteress', on her bosom. Her husband, taking on the assumed name of Roger Chillingworth, sets out to discover the identity of her lover and eventually identifies him as Arthur Dimmesdale, a young and much-respected church minister. Hester, ostracized by the community, brings up her child on the outskirts of the town, and eventually wins back the respect of the townsfolk by her good works.

> 'You would have surely seen . . . I mean, you were . . . ' Tristan was finding it difficult to meet Hannah's eyes. He glanced away from her. 'Weren't you and Lucas . . . I mean, that's what I assumed from what you—' 'That I was sleeping with Lucas, do you mean?' A kind of cold embarrassment dropped over Hannah, as though she were the woman taken in adultery, a latter-day Hester Prynne.
> SUSAN MOODY *The Italian Garden*, 1994

Adventure

This theme comprises both writers of adventure stories (e.g. **BOY'S OWN**, **ARTHUR CONAN DOYLE**, **WALTER SCOTT**) and fictional adventurers (e.g. **JAMES BOND** and **ALLAN QUATERMAIN**). Where the main element of a story is a quest, voyage, or other journey, it may be covered at **Quest** or **Travellers and Wanderers**.

....

007 ▶ *See* JAMES BOND.

Bilbo Baggins Bilbo Baggins is the main character in *The Hobbit* (1937) by J. R. R. Tolkien. He is a hobbit, a small imaginary creature who lives in a burrow. Accompanied by a party of dwarves and the wizard Gandalf, Bilbo travels a great distance and experiences many adventures before finally winning his share of the dwarves' lost treasure. He is a somewhat reluctant adventurer, often wishing himself back in his nice, warm hobbit-hole.

James Bond James Bond is the secret agent 007 in the novels by Ian Fleming and a series of highly successful films. His 'double oh' code number indicates that he is licensed to kill. Bond is a suave and resourceful hero, with a taste for fast cars and beautiful women, who likes his vodka dry martini to be 'shaken and not stirred'. Allusions to James Bond often refer to the many sophisticated gadgets that he uses, especially in the films.

> He was still lightheaded, and grew more so as he sipped his Bintang. Then he realised, he said, that she had managed to put something in his beer: some drug. I laughed at this. Too much James Bond, I suggested.
> CHRISTOPHER J. KOCH *The Year of Living Dangerously*, 1978

> But forget flashy cars with ejector seats, or fountain pens packed with explosives. The real-life 007s in Robin Cook's 'refocused' SIS may find a bottle of mosquito repellent more useful in their new mission: to combat Asia's ruthless drug traffickers.
> *The Independent*, 1997

Boy's Own *The Boy's Own Paper* was a popular boys' magazine sold in the late 19th and early 20th century. Founded by W. H. G. Kingston and published from 1879 until 1967, the magazine contained exciting adventure stories with titles such as *From Powder Monkey to Admiral* and *How I Swam the Channel*.

> But Jack Keane had always been the stuff of *Boy's Own Paper*; fearless, handsome, acclaimed for defending the rights of ordinary people against the big battalions of the rich and powerful.
> MICHAEL MALLOY *Cat's Paw*, 1993

> Pointless his journey may have been, but it is still an exhilarating Boys' Own adventure story.
> SEBASTIAN SHAKESPEARE in *Literary Review*, 1994

John Buchan John Buchan (1875–1940) was a Scottish novelist, chiefly remembered for his adventure stories, often featuring elaborate cross-country chases. Of these, the five thrillers featuring his hero Richard Hannay are per-haps the most popular, particularly *The Thirty-Nine Steps* (1915).

> At other times, Mary would have enjoyed the circumstances of their departure: they had elements of romantic adventure, as if lifted from a novel by John Buchan or Dornford Yates.
> ANDREW TAYLOR *Mortal Sickness*, 1995

> In the old days it was Salt Lake Flats, Utah, now it's the Nevada desert. If you are British, and in the John Buchan tradition, you have to go abroad to enjoy the true spirit of speedy adventure.
> *The Observer*, 1997

Arthur Conan Doyle Arthur Conan Doyle (1859-1930) was a Scottish novelist, remembered for his exciting adventure stories such as *The Lost World*, and for his creation of the character of Sherlock Holmes.

> I told the story well, . . . I described an attack on my life on the voyage home, and I made a really horrid affair of the Portland Place murder. 'You're looking for adven-ture,' I cried; 'well, you've found it here. The devils are after me, and the police are after them. It's a race that I mean to win.' 'By God!' he whispered, drawing his breath in sharply, 'it is all pure Rider Haggard and Conan Doyle.'
> JOHN BUCHAN *The Thirty-Nine Steps*, 1915

Phileas Fogg In Jules Verne's novel *Around the World in Eighty Days* (1873), the Englishman Phileas Fogg wagers other members of his London club that he can travel around the world in eighty days. He just manages it, travelling with his French valet Passepartout by many forms of transport including train, boat, sledge, and elephant.

> Decker thumbed through Yalom's passport—pages of stamped entries back into the States, Yalom's residing country. Then there were many other pages of foreign ink—Canada, Mexico, countries of Western and Eastern Europe including Russia, entries from the Far East, Latin America, and Africa. Lots from Africa—Egypt, South Africa, Kenya, Namibia, Liberia, Angola, Sudan, Ethiopia, Zaire, plus a host of other coun-tries Decker didn't know existed. . . . Marge said, 'Yalom was quite the Phileas Fogg.'
> FAYE KELLERMAN *Sanctuary*, 1994

Rider Haggard Henry Rider Haggard (1856-1925) was an English writer of thrilling adventure novels. Many of his novels are set in Africa, drawing on the time he spent in South Africa in the 1870s. His best-known novels are *King Solomon's Mines* (1885) and *She* (1889).

> There is something of the contemporary 'boys book'—or say of the spirit of Rider Haggard.
> HENRY JAMES *America Writers*, 1865–1912

Homeric Homer (8th century BC) was a Greek epic poet, to whom the *Odyssey* and the *Iliad* are traditionally attributed. The adjective 'Homeric' can be used to describe an epic adventure, particularly one involving a long perilous jour-ney or voyage, and perhaps a shipwreck.

> The story of the yachtsman's rescue—with its primal Homeric resonances of ship-wreck and mythic rebirth—delighted the world.
> The *Guardian*, 1997

Jason In Greek mythology, Jason was the leader of the Argonauts, who set off on a dangerous quest to retrieve the Golden Fleece, having many adventures along the way. ▶ *See special entry* ❑ **JASON AND THE ARGONAUTS** *on p. 220.*

Indiana Jones Indiana Jones is the whip-cracking archaeologist-explorer hero of the film *Raiders of the Lost Ark* (1981) and its sequels. The films are set in the 1930s and all feature hair-raising chase sequences.

> 'What about you?' I said crossly. 'If you hadn't been behaving like some sexagenarian Indiana Jones, we wouldn't have got into this mess in the first place.'
> MICHÈLE BAILEY *Haycastle's Cricket*, 1996

Allan Quatermain Allan Quatermain is a principal character in several of Rider Haggard's adventure stories, including *King Solomon's Mines* (1885) and *Allan Quatermain* (1887). In the former novel, Quatermain sets off with two other men to find George Curtis, who has gone missing while looking for the treasure of King Solomon's mines in the lost land of the Kukuanas. After a perilous journey across deserts and over freezing mountains, they find the missing man and return safely home with enough of the lost treasure to make them wealthy men. Their servant also turns out to be the rightful king of the Kukuanas and, after a battle, they restore him to his throne.

Walter Scott The Scottish poet and novelist Sir Walter Scott (1771-1832) is sometimes mentioned in connection with the romantic heroes and heroines of many of his poems and novels. During his lifetime and for nearly a century after his death he was a hugely popular writer.

> The girl was romantic in her soul. Everywhere was a Walter Scott heroine being loved by men with helmets or with plumes in their caps. She herself was something of a princess turned into a swine-girl in her own imagination. And she was afraid lest this boy, who, nevertheless, looked something like a Walter Scott hero, who could paint and speak French, and knew what algebra meant, and who went by train to Nottingham every day, might consider her simply as the swine-girl, unable to perceive the princess beneath; so she held aloof.
> D. H. LAWRENCE *Sons and Lovers*, 1913

> The truth is, he mistook me for a knight out of Walter Scott, because I once fished him out of a scrape in a gaming hell.
> KATE ROSS *Cut to the Quick*, 1993

Sinbad Sinbad the Sailor is the hero of one of the tales in the *Arabian Nights*, a rich young man who relates how he gained his wealth from his seven remarkable voyages. He tells how on each of the voyages he was shipwrecked or separated from his ship in some way and met with many strange adventures, including an encounter with the Old Man of the Sea.

Alice in Wonderland

Lewis Carroll's children's story *Alice's Adventures in Wonderland* (1865) is an account of a young girl's experiences in a surreal, illogical, dream-like world. At the beginning of the story Alice follows a white rabbit down a rabbit-hole and finds herself apparently tumbling down a very deep well. At the bottom she finds a little door that is too small for her to fit through until she drinks from a bottle labelled 'Drink me' and immediately starts to shrink, becoming ten inches high. Not long after this she is required to eat a cake labelled 'Eat me', to make her grow taller. Further strange incidents occur, with Alice greeting each development with the words 'Curiouser and curiouser!'. In addition to the White Rabbit, who looks at his watch as he hurries along, muttering to himself about how late he is, Alice encounters a succession of other outlandish creatures. A huge Caterpillar sits on a leaf, smoking a hookah. The Duchess nurses a pig-baby and has a Cheshire Cat, a large cat with a broad fixed grin. Alice watches as the Cheshire Cat's body gradually disappears 'beginning with the end of the tail, and ending with the grin, which remained some time after the rest of it had gone'.

Alice attends a bizarre tea party in the company of the Hatter, the March Hare and the Dormouse. The Hatter and the March Hare engage in nonsensical conversation, full of non sequiturs and strange riddles. The dormouse snoozes all through the tea party, despite attempts to wake it by pinching it. Later the Queen of Hearts, who is given to shouting 'Off with her head!', plays croquet with hedgehogs for balls and flamingos for mallets. Many of the characters, including Alice herself, give evidence at the trial to establish who stole the Queen's tarts. Finally Alice wakes from what has apparently been a dream.

Throughout this book there are references to characters and episodes from *Alice's Adventures in Wonderland*.

▶ *See* ALICE *at* **Ascent and Descent**, **Hair**, **Height**, *and* **Small Size**
  ALICE IN WONDERLAND *at* **Strangeness**
  CHESHIRE CAT *at* **Disappearance and Absence** *and* **Smiles**
  DORMOUSE *at* **Sleep**
  FATHER WILLIAM *at* **Old Age**
  MAD HATTER *at* **Insanity**
  MAD HATTER'S TEA PARTY *at* **Chaos and Disorder**
  MARCH HARE *at* **Insanity**
  WHITE RABBIT *at* **Speed** *and* **Time**.

Ambition

This theme covers ambition for power and aspiration for social status. The myth of **ICARUS** can be used to symbolize the fall of one who overreaches.
▶ *See also* **Success**.

....

Mrs Bennet In Jane Austen's *Pride and Prejudice* (1813), the vulgar, gossipy Mrs Bennet is preoccupied with finding wealthy husbands for her five un-married daughters.

> So, by some mysterious transference, the children's birthday party has turned into a battleground of social ambitions, ripe for the attention of a contemporary Jane Austen. No one considers the embarrassment of the mother who can't afford to keep up, or the danger of turning our children into spoilt little brats. Or is it merely a harmless indulgence in parental pride? After all, today's Mrs Bennets aren't trying to marry off their five-year-olds, they just want the fun of dressing them up and cluck-ing over them.
> *The Independent*, 1996

Icarus In Greek mythology, Icarus and Daedalus flew on wings which Dae-dalus had constructed, in an attempt to escape from Crete. However, Icarus flew too close to the sun, the wax which held the wings in place melted, and Icarus fell to his death in the sea. Icarus can be alluded to as someone who fails because of excessive ambition.

> He was Icarus now, and on the very verge of challenging gravity, or God, depending how one looked at it.
> JENNY DISKI *Happily Ever After*, 1991

Lady Macbeth In Shakespeare's play *Macbeth* (1623), Lady Macbeth, am-bitious for her husband's advancement, spurs him on to murder King Duncan so that Macbeth will seize the throne. Wives who appear to display a cold-blooded ruthlessness in furthering their husband's career are often compared to Lady Macbeth.

> 'Why don't you get her to play in the shop? A personal appearance? You've never done one of those before. . . . And you'd probably sell a few of her tapes, and probably a couple of extra things besides. And you could get it put into the *Time Out* gigs list.'
> 'Ooer, Lady Macbeth. Calm down and listen to the music.'
> NICK HORNBY *High Fidelity*, 1995

Lady Would-Be Lady Would-Be and her husband, Sir Politic Would-Be, are characters in Ben Jonson's comedy *Volpone* (1606), both pompous, foolish, and, as their name suggests, socially ambitious.

> And whomsoever you are to go to, will excuse you, when they are told 'tis *I* that command you not to go; and *you* may excuse it too, young Lady *Would-be*, if you recollect, that 'tis the unexpected arrival of your late lady's daughter, and your master's sister, that requires your attendance on her.
> SAMUEL RICHARDSON *Pamela*, 1740

Anger

This theme is chiefly concerned with expressions of rage on a god-like or at least heroic scale (**AGAMEMNON, AHASUERUS**), but also covers ill-temper and moodiness (**HOTSPUR, ACHILLES**). ▶ *See also* **Fierce Women, Macho Men, Revenge**.

....

Achilles In Greek mythology, Achilles was the greatest Greek warrior in the Trojan War. According to Homer's *Iliad*, he quarrelled with his commander, Agamemnon, and retired in anger to his tent, refusing to participate further in the war. After the death of his beloved friend Patroclus, Achilles did finally emerge, killed the Trojan hero Hector, and was himself killed by Hector's brother, Paris. The *Iliad* opens with the words: 'Sing, goddess, of the anger of Achilles, son of Peleus, that accursed anger which brought uncounted anguish on the Achaians.' Achilles can typify anger, and in particular angry sulkiness.
▶ *See special entries* ❏ **ACHILLES** *on p. 3 and* ❏ **TROJAN WAR** *on p. 392.*

> There was every temporal reason for leaving: it would be entering again into a world which he had only quitted in a passion for isolation, induced by a fit of Achillean moodiness after an imagined slight.
> THOMAS HARDY *The Woodlanders*, 1887

Agamemnon In Greek mythology, Agamemnon was the King of Mycenae and brother of Menelaus. The *Iliad* refers to the wrath of Agamemnon on being told that he must return a captive Trojan girl to her father to appease the god Apollo: 'Then there stood up in the assembly the hero son of Atreus, wide-ruling Agamemnon, in deep anger: fury filled his dark heart full, and his eyes were like blazing fire.' Agamemnon agreed to return the girl, but demanded that Achilles hand over to him his concubine Briseis to take her place, which led to the furious quarrel between the two men. Agamemnon typically represents terrible wrath. ▶ *See special entry* ❏ **TROJAN WAR** *on p. 392.*

> The frogs and the mice would be nothing to them, nor the angers of Agamemnon and Achilles.
> ANTHONY TROLLOPE *Barchester Towers*, 1857

Ahasuerus Ahasuerus was a Persian king who appears in the Old Testament Book of Esther, and is usually identified with Xerxes (486–465 BC). The wrath of Ahasuerus was aroused when his first wife, Vashti, would not submit to his commands. As a result of this, he banished Vashti, and in her place married Esther, a Jew.

Later, Haman, one of the courtiers of Ahasuerus, angered by the refusal of the Jew Moredecai to bow down to him, persuaded Ahasuerus to allow the extermination of all Jews. Haman prepared a gallows fifty cubits high on which to hang the Jews, including Mordecai, who was the former guardian of Esther. On hearing of this, Esther went to Ahasuerus to plead for the life of Mordecai and all the Jews: 'And Esther spake yet again before the king, and fell down at his feet, and besought him with tears to put away the mischief of Haman the Agagite, and his device that he had devised against the Jews' (Esther 8: 3).

Ahasuerus, realizing that Haman was wicked, ordered him to be hanged on his own gallows. Ahasuerus is alluded to as a man whose wrath is to be feared or appeased, or a man who should be approached with trepidation.

> 'Utter it, Jane: but I wish that instead of a mere inquiry into, perhaps, a secret, it was a wish for half my estate.' 'Now, king Ahasuerus! What do I want with half your estate?'
> CHARLOTTE BRONTË *Jane Eyre*, 1847

> Presently my mother went to my father. I know I thought of Queen Esther and King Ahasuerus; for my mother was very pretty and delicate-looking, and my father looked as terrible as King Ahasuerus.
> ELIZABETH GASKELL *Cranford*, 1851–3

Capulet In Shakespeare's *Romeo and Juliet* (1599), Capulet is Juliet's quick-tempered father. He flies into a rage when his daughter refuses to marry Count Paris, violently berating her for her disobedience and threatening to drag her to the church if necessary.

Basil Fawlty Basil Fawlty is the highly irascible hotelier, played by John Cleese, in the BBC television series *Fawlty Towers*, which ran from 1975 until 1979. He is temperamental, rude to the guests, and loses his temper uncontrollably with the slightest provocation.

> To reprise his Basil Fawlty schtick as a curmudgeonly hotel-owner.
> *Sunday Herald (Glasgow)*, 1999

Hotspur 'Hotspur', or 'Harry Hotspur', was a name given to Sir Henry Percy (1364-1403), son of the 1st Earl of Northumberland. He is a character in Shakespeare's *Henry IV, Part I* (1598). Known for his fiery, uncontrolled temper and impetuousness, he is described as a 'wasp-stung and impatient fool' in the play.

> I must say anger becomes you; you would make a charming Hotspur.
> THOMAS LOVE PEACOCK *Crotchet Castle*, 1831

Juno In Roman mythology, Juno was the wife and sister of Jupiter, and Queen of Heaven, equivalent to the Greek Hera. In many stories she is depicted as jealously enraged by the philanderings of her husband. The Trollope quotation below refers to the wrath of Juno, or Hera, at being slighted by Paris when he chose Aphrodite instead of her as the fairest of three goddesses.

> Not allowed to dispose of money, or call any thing their own, they learn to turn the market penny; or, should a husband offend, by staying from home, or give rise to some emotions of jealousy—a new gown, or any pretty bawble, smooths Juno's angry brow.
> MARY WOLLSTONECRAFT *A Vindication of the Rights of Women*, 1792

> We know what was the wrath of Juno when her beauty was despised. We know too what storms of passion even celestial minds can yield. As Juno may have looked at Paris on Mount Ida, so did Mrs Proudie look on Ethelbert Stanhope when he pushed the leg of the sofa into her lace train.
> ANTHONY TROLLOPE *Barchester Towers*, 1857

Poseidon Poseidon was the Greek god of the sea, water, earthquakes, and horses, often depicted with a trident in his hand. Poseidon was frequently portrayed as both irritable and vengeful. He corresponds to the Roman god Neptune.

Mandras was too young to be a Poseidon, too much without malice. Was he a male sea-nymph, then? Was there such a thing as a male Nereid or Potamid?
LOUIS DE BERNIÈRES *Captain Corelli's Mandolin*, 1994

Vesuvius Vesuvius is an active volcano near Naples, in southern Italy. It erupted violently in AD 79, burying the towns of Pompeii and Herculaneum.

She also became more and more irascible and violent, something of a terror in the neighbourhood; and visitors had to keep a safe distance. Her eruptions were vesuvian.
ANDRÉ BRINK *Imaginings of Sand*, 1996

Animals, Love of

These allusions all express an empathy with animals, particularly reflected in concern for their welfare and the ability to communicate with them.

....

Brigitte Bardot Brigitte Bardot (born Camille Javal, 1934) is a French actress whose appearance in *And God Created Woman* (1956) established her reputation as an international sex symbol. After retiring from acting she became an active supporter of animal welfare and the cause of endangered animal species.

As one might have guessed from the mountains of dogs and cats they destroy every year (and sometimes exhibit in Benetton-style adverts), the RSPCA is no Brigitte Bardot. No mushy rescuing of cats from burning Malibu beach houses here.
The Independent, 1993

Walt Disney Walt Disney (1901–66), the creator of Donald Duck and Mickey Mouse, is sometimes associated with the 'cute' portrayal of animals, both in such full-length animated cartoons as *Snow White* and *Bambi* and in his nature documentaries.

There are a lot of animals slaughtered in his books. He isn't Walt Disney, no. He was interested in cruelty, I agree.
JULIAN BARNES *Flaubert's Parrot*, 1984

Doctor Dolittle In Hugh Lofting's books (1920–52), Doctor John Dolittle is an animal-loving doctor whose human patients desert his practice because his house resembles a menagerie. Dolittle decides that he would much prefer to treat animals instead, and his parrot Polynesia helps him to learn all the animal languages, starting with the ABC of birds.

St Francis of Assisi St Francis (c.1181–1226), born Giovanni di Bernardone, was an Italian monk who founded the Franciscan order of friars. He is said to have had a great love for nature and an empathy with birds and animals. St Francis is often depicted in art, sometimes preaching to birds or holding wild animals.

> Sure he could get under your skin but so would St Francis of Assisi on a job like this. He'd have spent all his time looking at the bloody birds in the Jungle instead of reading his cue-cards.
> JULIAN BARNES *A History of the World in 10½ Chapters*, 1989

James Herriot James Herriot, the pseudonym of James Alfred Wight (1916–95), used his experiences working as a veterinary surgeon in north Yorkshire as the source for a series of short stories, collected in *If Only They Could Talk* (1970), *All Creatures Great and Small* (1972), and *The Lord God Made Them All* (1981). His amusing and extremely popular stories were made into a British TV series as well as a number of films.

Jain Jainism is a non-theistic religion founded in India in the 6th century BC by the Jina Vardhamana Mahavira. One of its central doctrines is non-injury to any living creatures.

> The total abstainer from all forms of animal product enjoys a clear, Jain-like conscience to parade before the rest of us. He or she can claim that his presence on earth hurts no other creature.
> JEREMY PAXMAN in *The Observer*, 1995

Apollo

In Greek mythology, Apollo was the son of Zeus and Leto and the twin brother of Artemis. He was born on the island of Delos, the site of his most important cult festival. The other main shrine for the worship of Apollo was the oracle at Delphi. While a boy he had travelled to Delphi, killed a huge snake called Python, and taken control of the oracle there. He came to be associated with the sun and was sometimes given the epithet Phoebus ('the bright one'). Apollo later usurped Helios' place as the god of the sun who drove the sun's chariot across the sky each day. He had a wide range of other attributes such as music (his instrument was a seven-stringed lyre), medicine (he was the father of Aesculapius, or Asclepius, the god of medicine and healing), poetic inspiration, archery, prophecy, and pastoral life (he protected herdsmen). Apollo, representing order, reason, and self-discipline, is often contrasted with Dionysus, representing creativity, sensuality, and lack of inhibition. In art Apollo is represented as a beautiful young male. Apollo had numerous affairs with nymphs, mortal women, and also young men. Among his unsuccessful encounters were those with Daphne, who chose to be transformed into a laurel tree rather than submit to his advances, and Cassandra, whose rejection of Apollo he punished by causing her prophecies thereafter to be disbelieved.

A number of Apollo's attributes are dealt with in this book.

▶ *See* **Beauty: Male Beauty**, **Inspiration**, **Light**, **Medicine**, *and* **Music**.

Appearing

This theme encompasses a number of different ideas. First, there are the allusions that suggest the sudden and unexpected materialization of something (**BURNING BUSH, WITCH OF ENDOR**). There is also the idea of creation or birth (**ATHENE, GALATEA**). Some of the quotations below exploit the specific image of a figure emerging from the sea (**PROTEUS, VENUS**). ▶ *See also* **Disappearance and Absence**.

....

Aphrodite ▶ *See* VENUS.

Athene In Greek mythology, Athene was the goddess of wisdom, also known as Pallas or Pallas Athene, corresponding to the Roman goddess Minerva. She is said to have sprung fully grown and fully armed from the brain of her father Zeus.

> Darwin was a passionate anti-saltationist, and this led him to stress, over and over again, the extreme gradualness of the evolutionary changes that he was proposing. The reason is that saltation, to him, meant what I have called the Boeing 747 macromutation. It meant the sudden calling into existence, like Pallas Athene from the head of Zeus, of brand-new complex organs at a single stroke of the genetic wand.
> RICHARD DAWKINS *The Blind Watchmaker*, 1986

> And the old man replied that once he had freed himself from those underpants, he had only to slash the hide with his knife, and he would emerge like Minerva from Jove's head.
> UMBERTO ECO *The Island of the Day Before*, 1994

Banquo's ghost In Shakespeare's *Macbeth* (1623), the victorious Scottish generals Macbeth and Banquo meet three witches who prophesy that Macbeth will be king and that Banquo's heirs will sit on the throne. Macbeth murders the king and takes his crown and then, in an attempt to defeat the prophecy, hires three murderers to kill Banquo and his son. At the start of a banquet held by the Macbeths, the first murderer arrives to inform Macbeth that they have killed Banquo but that his son, Fleance, has escaped. On returning to the banqueting table Macbeth finds his place taken by Banquo's ghost. None of the guests present can see the ghost, but Macbeth is so distressed that Lady Macbeth brings the banquet to a hasty close.

> One night, however, during one of our orgies—one of our high festivals, I mean—he glided in, like the ghost in Macbeth, and seated himself, as usual, a little back from the table, in the chair we always placed for 'the spectre', whether it chose to fill it or not.
> ANNE BRONTË *The Tenant of Wildfell Hall*, 1848

> I was closeted with our Head of Chambers who rose, on my arrival, with the air of a somewhat more heroic Macbeth who is forcing himself to invite Banquo's ghost to take a seat, and would he care for a cigarette.
> JOHN MORTIMER *Rumpole's Return*, 1980

Hovering like Banquo's ghost around the conference will be the former Chancellor Kenneth Clarke.
The Observer, 1997

burning bush According to the story in the Bible, God appeared to Moses in the form of a burning bush: 'And the angel of the Lord appeared to him in a flame of fire out of the midst of a bush; and he looked, and lo, the bush was burning, yet it was not consumed' (Exod. 3: 2). ▶ *See special entry* □ **MOSES AND THE BOOK OF EXODUS** *on p. 264.*

> 'She has revelations. All this stuff about Darcy's Utopia is dictated to her, she claims, by a kind of shining cloud.' I laughed. I couldn't help it. 'Like God appearing to Moses in a burning bush, or the Archangel Gabriel to Mohammed as a shining pillar?' I asked.
> FAY WELDON *Darcy's Utopia*, 1990

Gabriel In Jewish and Christian tradition, Gabriel is an archangel and messenger of God. According to the Bible, he appears to Daniel, to Zacharias, and to the Virgin Mary in the Annunciation. In Islamic tradition, Gabriel revealed the Koran to the prophet Muhammad, becoming the angel of truth.

Galatea In Greek mythology, Galatea was the name given to the ivory statue of a woman carved by the sculptor Pygmalion. Revolted by the imperfections of living women, Pygmalion had resolved never to marry, but he fell in love with his own creation. When Aphrodite brought the beautiful statue to life, he married her.

> And with a sudden motion she shook her gauzy covering from her, and stood forth in her low kirtle and her snaky zone, in her glorious radiant beauty and her imperial grace, rising from her wrappings, as it were, like Venus from the wave, or Galatea from her marble.
> H. RIDER HAGGARD *She*, 1887

Hydra In Greek mythology, the Hydra was a many-headed snake of the marshes of Lerna in the Peloponnese, whose heads grew again as they were cut off. One of Hercules' labours was to kill the Hydra, and he accomplished this by having his companion Iolaus sear each neck as Hercules cut off the head. ▶ *See special entry* □ **HERCULES** *on p. 182.*

> The footnotes engulfed and swallowed the text. They were ugly and ungainly, but necessary, Blackadder thought, as they sprang up like the heads of the Hydra, two to solve in the place of one solved.
> ANTONIA BYATT *Possession*, 1990

> Yet, it had no real effect. The supplies of cocaine from Columbia remained constant, and as one of the Hydra's heads was cut off, another dozen sprang up to replace it.
> MEL STEIN *White Lines*, 1997

Minerva ▶ *See* **ATHENE.**

Moses ▶ *See* **BURNING BUSH.**

Proteus In Greek mythology, Proteus was a minor sea-god who had been given the power of prophecy by Poseidon. When consulted, he would avoid answering questions by changing his shape at will. His name is sometimes used to mean a changing or inconstant person or thing. Proteus was sometimes depicted as emerging from the sea, almost like a male Venus, and resting on the seashore.

> So might I, standing on this pleasant lea,
> Have glimpses that would make me less forlorn;
> Have sight of Proteus rising from the sea;
> Or hear old Triton blow his wreathed horn.
> WILLIAM WORDSWORTH *The World is too much with us*, 1807

> And suddenly, like a crew-cut Proteus rising from the sea, Ron Patimkin emerged from the lower depths we'd just inhabited and his immensity was before us.
> PHILIP ROTH *Goodbye, Columbus*, 1959

Venus Venus was the Roman goddess of love, corresponding to the Greek Aphrodite. She is said to have been born from the sea-foam and is often portrayed rising from the sea in art. She is sometimes depicted (as in Botticelli's painting *Birth of Venus*) emerging from a large sea-shell.

> She ducked gracefully to slip into the lacy fabric which her mother held above her head. As she rose Venus-like above its folds there was a tap on the door, immediately followed by its tentative opening.
> EDITH WHARTON *The Custom of the Country*, 1913

> 'I mean give us a hand!' snapped Cutangle, rising from the wavelets like a fat and angry Venus.
> TERRY PRATCHETT *Equal Rites*, 1987

Witch of Endor In the Book of Samuel, the Witch of Endor was the woman consulted by Saul when he was threatened by the Philistine army. At his request she summoned up the ghost of the prophet Samuel, who prophesied the death of Saul and the destruction of his army by the Philistines (1 Sam. 28). Rudyard Kipling associates Endor with spiritualism in his poem 'The Road to Endor':

> 'Oh, the road to Endor is the oldest road
> And the craziest road of all!
> Straight it runs to the Witch's abode
> As it did in the days of Saul.'

> I merely lit that fire because I was dull, and thought I would get a little excitement by calling you up and triumphing over you as the Witch of Endor called up Samuel. I determined you should come; and you have come!
> THOMAS HARDY *The Return of the Native*, 1880

Arrogance and Pomposity

This theme covers feelings of arrogance or self-importance. Superiority in rank or status is dealt with at the theme **Superiority**.

Coriolanus Coriolanus is the main character in Shakespeare's play *Coriolanus* (1623). He is a proud, courageous soldier who shows in an arrogant outburst in the Forum his contempt for the Roman rabble and resentment at having to solicit their votes.

> There was just a hint of Coriolanus going before the plebs as Lord Irvine defended his choice of wallpaper to the select committee.
> *BBC Radio 4*, 1998

Louis XIV Louis XIV (1638–1715), also known as the Sun King, was 5 years old when he succeeded to the throne. He appointed himself to be his own chief minister, and kept tight control over government and policy. He is said to have coined the phrase 'L'état c'est moi' ('I am the state'). His reign was a period of magnificence in terms of art and literature and represented a time of great power for the French in Europe.

> Dixon was not unconscious of this awed reverence which was given to her; nor did she dislike it; it flattered her much as Louis the Fourteenth was flattered by his courtiers shading their eyes from the dazzling light of his presence.
> ELIZABETH GASKELL *North and South*, 1854–5

> Michael came in soaked to the skin—his taxi had broken down and he'd walked the rest of the way—but still behaving as if he was Louis XIV making a grand entrance at a court ball.
> PETER DICKINSON *The Yellow Room Conspiracy*, 1995

Malvolio In Shakespeare's *Twelfth Night* (1623), Malvolio is Olivia's pompous and puritanical steward, 'the best persuaded of himself, so cramm'd, as he thinks, with excellencies that it is his grounds of faith that all that look on him love him'.

> He smiled on me in quite a superior sort of way—such a smile as would have become the face of Malvolio.
> BRAM STOKER *Dracula*, 1897

Marie Antoinette Marie Antoinette (1755–93) was the wife of Louis XVI and queen of France. Her extravagance combined with a much-quoted response 'Qu'ils mangent de la brioche' (traditionally translated as 'Let them eat cake'), supposedly made on being told that the poor people of Paris were unable to afford bread, have led to her being regarded as a figure of arrogance.

> 'You? Fraternising with the working classes? What on earth came over you?' He scowled. 'You talk as though I'm Marie Antoinette.' 'Sometimes you behave like Marie Antoinette. Let's face it, Claude: you are not a man of the people.'
> HILARY WHELAN *Frightening Strikes*, 1995

Podsnap Mr Podsnap is a character in Dickens's *Our Mutual Friend* (1864–5) who is self-satisfied, complacent, and has a high opinion of his own importance: 'Mr Podsnap . . . stood very high in Mr. Podsnap's opinion.'

> Masochists may get their kicks from national self-denigration, but for the rest of us there is neither much fun nor much enlightenment in such bouts of inverted Podsnappery.
> *The Independent*, 1992

Pooh-Bah Pooh-Bah is the Lord-High-Everything-Else, a character in Gilbert and Sullivan's *The Mikado* (1885). His name can be applied to a self-important person or to a person holding many offices at once.

> *None is too many*, is what some Canadian government pooh-bah said about the Jews, during the war.
> MARGARET ATWOOD *The Robber Bride*, 1993

> 'Ben, look at this ... What do you see?'
> Same thing I had seen at our earlier viewing, a shot of King and four former State Department poohbahs exiting a helicopter at a luxurious Aspen, Colorado non-profit think-tank mountain ranch maintained by our tax dollars.
> JUSTIN SCOTT *Frostline*, 1997

Queen of Sheba In the Bible, the Queen of Sheba, having heard about the famous Solomon, went to visit him taking with her a magnificent caravan 'with camels that bare spices, and very much gold, and precious stones' (1 Kgs. 10: 2). The name can be used to typify a women or girl who is conscious of her own superiority.

Thraso Thraso is a boastful soldier in the Roman writer Terence's comedy *Eunuchus*. His name, and the related adjective 'Thrasonical', can be used to denote someone who is vain and boastful.

> Mr O'Rourke, surely you are not so Thrasonical as to declare yourself a genius?
> TIMOTHY MO *An Insular Possession*, 1986

Artists

An effective way of describing the appearance of something, or indeed a mood or situation, is to do so in terms of a famous artist's work or even an individual painting. In the quotations below, the reader is reminded of an artist's characteristic style by a **BOTTICELLI** or **RUBENS** figure, a **HOPPER** or **DUFY** scene, a **TURNER** or **CLAUDE** landscape. Artists may also be covered under other themes: for instance, Correggio is included under **Happiness** and Rembrandt under **Darkness**.

Beardsley Aubrey Beardsley (1872–98) was an English artist and illustrator who worked in the Art Nouveau style. He is chiefly known for his stylized black-and-white illustrations for such works as Oscar Wilde's *Salome* (1894) and Pope's *The Rape of the Lock* (1896) and for the periodical *The Yellow Book*, of which he became artistic director in 1894. Beardsley's work, often dealing with grotesque or erotic subjects, epitomized the 'decadence' of the 1890s.

> He kept a bevy of boys himself, over whom he ruled with great severity, jealous and terrible as a Beardsleyan queen.
> JOHN BANVILLE *The Book of Evidence*, 1989

Blake William Blake (1757–1827) was an English artist and poet. His intensely imaginative and visionary watercolours and engravings include illustrations for *The Book of Job* (1826), for works by Dante and Shakespeare, and for his own *Prophetic Books* (1783–1804). His figures are usually heavily muscled and the colours in pale pastel tones. Blake's writings and visual work were largely ignored during his lifetime.

> And the people in the streets, it seemed to him, whether milling along Oxford Street or sauntering from lion to lion in Trafalgar Square, formed another golden host, beautiful in the antique cold-faced way of Blake's pastel throngs.
> JOHN UPDIKE *Bech: A Book*, 1970

Botticelli Sandro Botticelli (1445–1510), born Alessandro di Mariano Filipepi, was a Florentine painter of religious and mythological subjects, whose work includes such paintings as *Primavera*, 'Springtime' (c.1478) and *Birth of Venus* (c.1480). Botticelli is known for the delicate beauty of his Madonnas and goddesses and for his gracefulness of line.

> As Miriam sang her mouth seemed hopeless. She sang like a nun singing to heaven. It reminded him so much of the mouth and eyes of one who sings beside a Botticelli Madonna, so spiritual.
> D. H. LAWRENCE *Sons and Lovers*, 1913

> With great gentleness he moved towards the hospitable regions of her being, towards the peaceful fields of her interior landscape, where white flowers placed themselves against green backgrounds as in Botticelli paintings of spring.
> A.S. NIN *Children of the Albatross*, 1947

Bruegel Pieter Bruegel (c.1525–69), known as Pieter Bruegel the Elder and nicknamed 'Peasant Bruegel', was a Flemish artist. Bruegel produced landscapes, religious allegories, and satirical paintings of peasant life, such as *Peasant Wedding Feast* (1566). His work displays a real interest in village customs combined with a satirical view of folly, vice, and the sins of the flesh. His name is sometimes spelt Breughel or Brueghel.

> Daniel was without his uniform, in the fisherman's sweater and a vast shapeless black duffel coat, hooded and toggled, that he had bought at an army surplus store. It made him look, the enormous man, something like a Brueghel peasant.
> A. S. BYATT 'The Human Element' in *The Virgin in the Garden*, 1978

Burne-Jones Edward Burne-Jones (1833–98) was an English painter and designer whose work was largely inspired by medieval legends and other literary themes. His paintings, in subdued tones and peopled by pale knights and damsels, evoke a romantic mythical dream world. He also produced many tapestry and stained-glass designs for William Morris's firm.

> A silly woman would say he looked romantic. He reminded you of one of the knights of Burne-Jones though he was on a larger scale and there was no suggestion that he suffered from the chronic colitis that afflicted those unfortunate creatures.
> W. SOMERSET MAUGHAM 'The Human Element' in *The World Over*, 1951

Claude Claude Lorraine (1600–82), originally named Claude Gellée, was a French landscape painter, celebrated for his subtle and poetic treatment of light. His paintings lead the eye into the expansive panoramas through variations of colour: dark greenish-brown in the foreground, light green in the middle distance, and blue in the far distance.

> The sea and the mountains floated in the steady evening sunshine. It was all peace,

elements and void, golden air and mute blue distances, like a Claude.
JOHN FOWLES *The Magus*, 1966

Degas Edgar Degas (1834–1917) was a French painter and sculptor associated with Impressionism. He is best known for his drawings, paintings, and pastels of ballet dancers, cabaret artistes, and women dressing and bathing.

She was a big, sexy brunette—as Garcia said, 'Something straight out of Degas.'
JACK KEROUAC *On the Road*, 1957

Dufy Raoul Dufy (1877–1953) was a French painter and textile designer, whose chief subjects were racecourses, boating scenes, and society life. Dufy's style is characterized by bright colours and lively calligraphic draughtsmanship.

There was a bright wind, it was a Dufy day, all bustle, movement, animated colour.
JOHN FOWLES *The Magus*, 1966

El Greco El Greco (1541–1614) was a Spanish painter, born in Crete as Domenikos Theotokopoulos. His portraits and religious works are characterized by elongated and distorted figures, solemn facial expressions, and vibrant use of colour (blues, lemons, livid pinks). Among his famous works are the altarpiece *The Assumption of the Virgin* (1577–9) and the painting *The Burial of Count Orgaz* (1586).

Mrs Overend had recently got rid of her black-and-orange striped divans, cushions and sofas. In their place were curiously cut slabs, polygons, and three-legged manifestations of Daisy Overend's personality, done in El Greco's colours.
MURIEL SPARK *The Collected Stories*, 1958

His face was as gloomy as an El Greco; insufferably bored, decades of boredom, and probably, I decided, insufferably boring.
JOHN FOWLES *The Magus*, 1977

Etty William Etty (1787–1849) was an English artist best known for his sensual paintings of the nude.

She was his passive victim, her head resting on his shoulder, marble made warmth, an Etty nude, the Pygmalion myth brought to a happy end.
JOHN FOWLES *The French Lieutenant's Woman*, 1969

Giotto Giotto di Bondone (*c*.1267–1337) was an Italian painter, generally recognized as the founder of Florentine painting and the initiator of a more naturalistic and dramatic style in contrast to the rather stiff, two-dimensional design of Byzantine art. According to the story in Vasari's *Lives of the Artists* (1550), when the Pope sent for an example of Giotto's work before commissioning him to paint in St Peter's he drew a perfect circle with one turn of his hand.

To keep his heart high and yet out of his throat, he made a song . . .

Full Ringing Round
As the Belly of Silenus
Giotto Painter of Perfect Circles
NATHANAEL WEST *The Dream Life of Balso Snell*, 1931

Goya Francisco Jose de Goya y Lucientes (1746–1828) was a Spanish painter and etcher. He became official portrait painter to the Spanish court, producing portraits of extraordinary, sometimes brutally frank, realism. Goya also painted society portraits, many of women dressed in the style of a *maja*, in traditional black Spanish dress with black lace mantilla. His etchings include the series *The Disasters of War*, depicting the French occupation of Spain (1808-14).

> Gladys de Grey is a black-haired beauty straight off a Goya canvas, all passion and fire.
> PETER LOVESEY *Bertie and the Tinman*, 1987

> The wounded bicycle stood in the dim light from the stable, like a victim in a Goya engraving of a casualty of war.
> FRANK PARRISH *Voices from the Dark*, 1993

Hogarth William Hogarth (1697-1764) was an English painter and engraver. His series of engravings on 'modern moral subjects', such as *A Rake's Progress* (1735) and *Marriage à la Mode* (1743-5), satirized the vices of both high and low life in 18th-century England.

> [They were] dressed up in a strange old livery—long great-coats, with small capes, coeval with the sedan, and similar to the dress of the class in Hogarth's pictures.
> ELIZABETH GASKELL *Cranford*, 1851-3

> That evening Lord Marchmain was in good spirits; the room had a Hogarthian aspect, with the dinner-table set for the four of us by the grotesque, *chinoiserie* chimney-piece, and the old man propped among his pillows sipping champagne, tasting, praising, and failing to eat, the succession of dishes which had been prepared for his homecoming.
> EVELYN WAUGH *Brideshead Revisited*, 1945

Hopper Edward Hopper (1882-1967) was an American realist painter. Works such as *Early Sunday Morning* (1930) and *Nighthawks* (1942) depict scenes from everyday American city life in which static figures appear in bleak settings such as motel rooms and diners, conveying an atmosphere of loneliness and isolation.

> Childcott's balding head gleamed briefly as he turned his head to stare out of the window at the Edward-Hopper-type starkness of suburban London after the shops have closed.
> SUSAN MOODY *Grand Slam*, 1994

Ingres Jean Auguste Dominique Ingres (1780-1867) was a French painter whose elegant portraits and sensuous female nudes, including *La Grande Baigneuse* (1808), demonstrate his brilliant draughtsmanship.

> But when I see her in dreams . . . it is not with that terrible aspect she wore the last time I saw her, when her face could hardly be called a face at all, but with the look of a portrait by Ingres or Goya, a full pale face, with dark, lustrous eyes, a fixed, unchanging regard, and two or three black curls, or crescents of curls, stealing down over her forehead.
> L. P. HARTLEY *The Go-Between*, 1953

Klimt Gustav Klimt (1862-1918) was an Austrian painter and designer, the greatest of Art Nouveau painters. He achieved a jewelled effect in his work similar to mosaics, combining stylized human forms with decorative and ornate clothing or backgrounds in elaborate patterns, often using gold leaf. One of his most famous paintings is *The Kiss* (1909).

She was pale, and looked tired and distracted. I noticed for the first time how she had aged. The woman I knew fifteen years ago was still there, but fixed inside a coarser outline, like one of Klimt's gem-encrusted lovers.
JOHN BANVILLE *The Book of Evidence*, 1989

Lautrec ▶ See TOULOUSE-LAUTREC.

Leonardo Leonardo da Vinci (1452-1519) was an Italian painter, sculptor, scientist, and engineer, generally celebrated as the supreme example of the Renaissance genius. He painted two versions of *The Virgin of the Rocks*, one (1483-5) now in the Louvre, Paris and the other (c.1508) now in the National Gallery, London. Both depict the Virgin Mary with the infant St John adoring the infant Christ, grouped in front of a background of strange rocks. The subject of the *Mona Lisa* (1504-5) is also positioned above a landscape of rocks and a winding stream. These paintings demonstrate Leonardo's careful use of sfumato, the technique of achieving a transition from light to shadow by gradually shading one into the other.

She reminded him of a Leonardo more than ever; her sunburnt features were shadowed by fantastic rocks; at his words she had turned and stood between him and the light with immeasurable plains behind her.
E. M. FORSTER *A Room with a View*, 1908

Michelangelo Michelangelo Buonarroti (1475-1564) was an Italian sculptor, painter, architect, and poet. A leading figure of Renaissance art, his celebrated works include the sculpture *Pietà* (c.1497-1500) in Rome, the huge marble *David* (1501-4) in Florence, the spectacular fresco that decorates the ceiling of the Sistine Chapel in Rome (1508-12) and *The Last Judgement* (1536-41) on the same chapel's altar wall. Many of Michelangelo's works depict heroically muscular male nudes.

Primitive yet complex, elephantine but delicate; as full of subtle curves and volumes as a Henry Moore or a Michelangelo.
JOHN FOWLES *The French Lieutenant's Woman*, 1969

Millet Jean François Millet (1814-75) was a French painter, etcher, and draughtsman, known especially for his scenes of peasants at work such as *The Gleaners* (1857) and *The Angelus* (1858-9). Such paintings express the artist's immense sympathy for the simplicity of the rural life.

I found myself possessed of a surprising interest in the shepherdess, who stood far away in the hill pasture with her great flock, like a figure of Millet's, high against the sky.
SARAH ORNE JEWETT *A Dunnet Shepherdess*, 1899

Picasso Pablo Picasso (1881-1973) was a Spanish painter, sculptor, and graphic artist, one of the most versatile and influential artists of the 20th century. His melancholy 'blue period' (1901-4) depicting the poor and suffering gave way to his 'rose period' (1904-6) depicting circus life. Among Picasso's masterpieces are *Les Demoiselles d'Avignon* (1907), an important work in the development of Cubism, and *Guernica* (1937), which expresses the artist's condemnation of the bombing of civilians in the Spanish Civil War. In the early 1920s Picasso went through a classical period, in which he painted monumental figures inspired by antique sculpture.

For all his size and shape, he looked neither strong nor fertile. He was like one of

Picasso's great sterile athletes, who brood hopelessly on pink sand, staring at veined marble waves.
NATHANAEL WEST *The Day of the Locust*, 1939

Pollock Jackson Pollock (1912–56) was a US abstract expressionist painter, the foremost exponent of 'action painting' In 1947 he abandoned the use of brushes, adopting a technique in which he vigorously dribbled or hurled the paint straight onto the canvas. These works, sometimes referred to as his 'drip paintings', are made up of complicated laceworks of swirling coloured lines.

The ENT Man treated his victims' blood like it was paint and he was Jackson Pollock.
PAUL JOHNSTON *Body Politic*, 1997

Rembrandt Rembrandt Harmenszoon van Rijn (1606–69) was the greatest Dutch painter of the 17th century, particularly celebrated for his portraits and self-portraits and for his dramatic use of chiaroscuro (treatment of light and shade), contrasting highlights and half-lights with deep shadows. Of all the artists grouped here, Rembrandt is the one whose name is most often used as shorthand for the idea of 'a great painter'.

Now a man's head was lit as with a light of Rembrandt.
G. K. CHESTERTON *The Man Who Was Thursday*, 1908

Reynolds Joshua Reynolds (1723–92) was an English painter who was regarded as the leading portraitist of his day and became the first president of the Royal Academy in 1768. Many of his portraits consciously borrow poses from classical statues and Renaissance paintings.

Her youngest brother was only five. He was a frail lad, with immense brown eyes in his quaint fragile face—one of Reynolds's 'Choir of Angels', with a touch of elf.
D. H. LAWRENCE *Sons and Lovers*, 1913

Rivera Diego Rivera (1886–1957) was a Mexican painter whose monumental murals for public buildings in the 1920s and 1930s were influenced by Aztec art and deal with political and revolutionary subjects.

'Ms Ochoa?' The face that looked up was out of a mural by Rivera. Reddish-brown skin stretched tightly over sharply defined but delicately constructed bones; liquid lips and melting black eyes gabled by full, dark brows. Her hair was long and sleek, parted in the middle, hanging down her back. Part Aztec, part Spanish, part unknown.
JONATHAN KELLERMAN *When the Bough Breaks*, 1992

Rothko Mark Rothko was a Russian-born US painter (1903–70), an abstract expressionist. His most characteristic works are enormous canvases consisting of rectangles or horizontal bands of subtly related colour with blurred edges.

Rousseau Henri Rousseau (1844–1910), known as 'le Douanier' ('the customs officer'), was a French naive painter. Self-taught, he is best known for his paintings of exotic jungle landscapes and haunting dream-like scenes, including *Tiger in a Tropical Storm* (1891), *The Sleeping Gypsy* (1897), and *The Snake Charmer* (1907). These pictures are bold and colourful, and painted with a painstakingly detailed technique.

An island with a happy name lay opposite, and on it stood a row of prim, tight

buildings, naive as a painting by Rousseau.
DOROTHY PARKER *The Custard Heart*, 1944

Rubens Peter Paul Rubens (1577–1640) was the foremost Flemish painter of
the 17th century, an exuberant master of the baroque. Rubens painted portraits and religious works but is perhaps best known for his mythological
paintings featuring voluptuous female nudes, such as *Venus and Adonis*
(*c.*1635). These sumptuous paintings display the artist's love of rich colour,
sensual feeling for the tactile, and sheer delight in fleshy women. Indeed, the
word 'Rubenesque' can be used to describe a woman's attractively plump and
rounded figure.

> Or take the blond darling of the football team with the permanent blush in his full
> cheeks, the distrustful smile of someone hard of hearing and the smooth, fleshy body
> and incipient beer belly resplendent with quivering health, feminine on a Rubens
> scale.
> EDMUND WHITE *A Boy's Own Story*, 1982

> She put down the paper. 'An artist's model?' 'Right.' 'With your figure?' 'My figure is
> simply crying out to be captured in charcoal, according to my new friend. I have a
> Rubenesque form and challenging contours.'
> PETER LOVESEY *The Summons*, 1995

Steen Jan Steen (1626–79) was a Dutch painter of humorous subjects, espe-
cially crowded tavern scenes and social gatherings in middle-class households.
His prolific output includes such works as *The World Upside-Down* (*c.*1663),
Interior of a Tavern with Cardplayers and a Violin Player (1665–8), and *The
Wedding Party* (1667). The term 'Jan Steen household' is still used today by the
Dutch to describe a boisterous and chaotic family.

> As I went past, a drunk stumbled out, and for a second, before the door swung shut
> again, I had a glimpse inside. I walked on without pausing, carrying the scene in my
> head. It was like something by Jan Steen: the smoky light, the crush of red-faced
> drinkers, the old boys propping up the bar, the fat woman singing, displaying a
> mouthful of broken teeth.
> JOHN BANVILLE *The Book of Evidence*, 1989

Titian Titian (*c.*1488–1576), whose Italian name was Tiziano Vecellio, was a
Venetian painter and one of the greatest artists of the High Renaissance. He is
known particularly for his sumptuous mythological works, such as *Bacchus
and Ariadne* (1522–3) and *Diana Surprised by Actaeon* (1556–9), noted for their
brilliant colours, especially glowing reds and deep blues.

> Miss Templeman deposited herself on the sofa in her former flexuous position, and
> throwing her arm above her brow—somewhat in the pose of a well-known con-
> ception of Titian's—talked up at Elizabeth-Jane invertedly across her forehead and
> arm.
> THOMAS HARDY *The Mayor of Casterbridge*, 1886

> How odd that bones, reminders of old mortality, should be considered essential to
> beauty in this perverse age. What of Titian and Rubens?
> ALICE THOMAS ELLIS *The 27th Kingdom*, 1982

Toulouse-Lautrec Henri de Toulouse-Lautrec (1864–1901) was a French
painter and lithographer. His reputation largely rests on his colour lithographs
from the 1890s, depicting scenes of Parisian low life, actors, music-hall
singers, circus artists, prostitutes, and waitresses in Montmartre. The Moulin

Rouge series of posters (1894) is particularly well known. His work is characterized by strong silhouettes, large areas of flat garish colour, and theatrical lighting. The artist broke both his legs in childhood, as a result of which he was stunted in growth, and the appearance of Toulouse-Lautrec himself is sometimes alluded to.

> My mother arrived in the kitchen barefoot. The sight of her bunions and her big yellow toenails annoyed me. She had wrapped herself in an impossible, shot-silk teagown. She had the florid look of one of Lautrec's ruined doxies.
> JOHN BANVILLE *The Book of Evidence*, 1989

Turner Joseph Mallord William Turner (1775–1851) was an English painter who became interested in capturing the effects of atmospheric light in his pictures. His best-known paintings, such as *The Fighting Téméraire* (1838), depict dramatic skies using yellows, oranges, and reds in an impressionistic style.

> 'Look . . . ' Barton nodded up towards the slope and the wood, to where they could just see Queronne in the lemon-white light. 'It's like a Turner canvas.'
> SUSAN HILL *Strange Meeting*, 1971

Van Dyck Anthony Van Dyck (also Vandyke) (1599–1641) was a Flemish painter chiefly famous for his portraits of the English aristocracy and royalty, including a number of Charles I. Van Dyck's refined and languidly elegant portrait style determined the course of English portraiture for at least 200 years. The term Vandyke is also applied to a broad white collar which has the edge cut into deep points and to a neat pointed beard, both of which commonly appear in Van Dyck's portraits. Vandyke brown is a deep rich brown colour.

> One was a young man, in the Vandyke dress common to the time of Charles I.
> WALTER SCOTT *The Bride of Lammermoor*, 1819

> Well, I see this rather like a portrait by Van Dyck, with a good deal of atmosphere, you know, and a certain gravity, and with a sort of aristocratic distinction.
> W. SOMERSET MAUGHAM *Cakes and Ale*, 1930

Van Gogh Vincent Van Gogh (1853–90) was a Dutch Post-Impressionist painter. The bright colours (especially the vivid yellows) and thick, frenzied, swirling brushwork give his paintings a passionate intensity. Among his best-known works are several studies of sunflowers and landscapes such as *A Starry Night* (1889). Van Gogh suffered from depression, and after a violent quarrel with Gauguin he cut off part of his own ear. He eventually committed suicide. Among his portraits is *Self-portrait with Bandaged Ear* (1889).

> I went in search of Randolph. He wore a large lint pad pressed to the left side of his head, held in place by a rakishly angled and none-too-clean bandage. . . . he bore a striking resemblance to poor, mad Vincent in that self-portrait made after he had disfigured himself for love.
> JOHN BANVILLE *The Book of Evidence*, 1989

Velasquez Diego Rodriguez de Silva y Velazquez (1599–1660) was the foremost Spanish artist of the 17th century. In 1623 he was appointed court painter to Philip IV in Madrid, where he painted many notable portraits of the royal family. He produced several portraits of the king's daughter, the doll-like Infanta Margareta Teresa, including *Las Meninas* (1656), which portrays her with her retinue of maid-servants and dwarfs, and *The Infanta Margareta in*

Blue (1659). Velasquez's works also include a number of impressive equestrian portraits.

> Style? Why, she had the style of a little princess; if you couldn't see it you had no eye. It was not modern, it was not conscious, it would produce no impression in Broadway; the small, serious damsel, in her stiff little dress, only looked like an Infanta of Velazquez.
> HENRY JAMES *Portrait of a Lady*, 1881

> He was a beautiful horse that looked as though he had come out of a painting by Velasquez.
> ERNEST HEMINGWAY *For Whom the Bell Tolls*, 1941

Veronese Paulo Veronese (*c.*1528–88) was an Italian painter, born in Verona as Paolo Caliari and later named after his birthplace. He specialized in biblical, allegorical, and historical subjects, and is particularly known for his richly coloured feast and banquet scenes such as *The Marriage at Cana* (1562) and *The Feast in the House of Levi* (1573). The latter, originally titled *The Last Supper*, was the subject of a trial by the Inquisition, which objected to Veronese's habit of inserting profane details (dogs, soldiers, drunkards, etc.) into his sacred pictures.

> Let me set the scene. There were ten of us . . . at the back of the restaurant, at a long table in a slight alcove—a touch Last Supper after Veronese.
> JULIAN BARNES *Talking It Over*, 1991

Zeuxis Zeuxis (5th century BC) was a Greek painter known for creating extremely lifelike paintings. One anecdote relates how birds flew to his painting of a bunch of grapes, taking them to be real.

> Is she pretty? More—beautiful. A subject for the pen of Nonnus, or the pencil of Zeuxis.
> THOMAS LOVE PEACOCK *Crotchet Castle*, 1831

Ascent and Descent

The allusions grouped here can be used to describe rising, falling, and climbing up or down. Where some kind of metaphorical fall is being expressed, the stories of **ICARUS** and **LUCIFER** are often called to mind.

Alice At the beginning of Lewis Carroll's children's story *Alice's Adventures in Wonderland*, Alice follows a white rabbit down a rabbit hole and finds herself apparently tumbling down a very deep well: 'Down, down, down. Would the fall *never* come to an end? "I wonder how many miles I've fallen by this time?" she said aloud.' She eventually lands with a thump in Wonderland. ▶ *See special entry* □ **ALICE IN WONDERLAND** *on p. 10*.

> The plane was unmistakably going down, down, down, like Alice in the rabbit hole.
> F. SCOTT FITZGERALD *The Last Tycoon*, 1941

Elijah   Elijah (9th century BC) was a Hebrew prophet who maintained the worship of Jehovah against that of Baal and other pagan gods. According to the Bible, he was carried to heaven in a chariot of fire: 'And as they still went on and talked, behold, a chariot of fire and horses of fire separated the two of them. And Elijah went up by a whirlwind into heaven' (2 Kgs. 2: 11-13).

Ganymede   In Greek mythology, Ganymede was a Trojan youth who was so beautiful that he was carried off by an eagle to be cup-bearer to Zeus.

> What little child ever refused to be comforted by that glorious sense of being seized strongly and swung upwards? I don't believe Ganymede cried when the eagle carried him away, and perhaps deposited him on Jove's shoulder at the end.
> GEORGE ELIOT *Adam Bede*, 1859

Icarus   In Greek mythology, Icarus was the son of Daedalus. He escaped from Crete on wings made by his father but plunged to his death in the Aegean Sea when he flew too near the sun, whose heat melted the wax which held the feathers on his wings.

> Of outside influences, Marian's favour had been the Jacob's ladder of my ascent; had the balance of my feelings for her been disturbed by a harsh look, I should have fallen, like Icarus.
> L. P. HARTLEY *The Go-Between*, 1953

> The spyglass allowed him to see spindles, feathery bullets, black shudders or other shudders of indistinct hue, who flung themselves from a taller tree aiming at the ground with the insanity of an Icarus eager to hasten his own destruction.
> UMBERTO ECO *The Island of the Day Before*, 1994

Jacob's ladder   In the Bible, Jacob was a Hebrew patriarch, the son of Isaac and Rebecca. At a place that he named Bethel he had a dream: 'And he dreamed that there was a ladder set up on the earth, and the top of it reached to heaven; and behold, the angels of God were ascending and descending on it!' (Gen. 28: 12).

> In our dreams we sometimes struggle from the oceans of desire up Jacob's ladder to that orderly place. Then human voices wake us and we drown.
> JEANETTE WINTERSON *The Passion*, 1987

Lucifer   Lucifer, the Devil, was traditionally regarded as the chief of the fallen angels, hurled out of heaven for rebelling against God: 'How art thou fallen from heaven, O Lucifer, son of the morning! how art thou cut down to the ground, which didst weaken the nations!' (Isa. 14: 12). As can be seen from the quotations below, Lucifer is closely identified with the idea of falling.

> I had no exultation of triumph, still less any fear of my own fate. I stood silent, the half-remorseful spectator of a fall like the fall of Lucifer.
> JOHN BUCHAN *Prester John*, 1910

> It was her face that did it. I didn't know at the time. I thought I was just a bit hyper, like everyone else. But I was gone, sunk. Unimaginable change had happened. Fallen, like Lucifer; fallen . . . like the stock market in 1929.
> JULIAN BARNES *Talking It Over*, 1991

> Up in the thin blue air Gordon was free, it was only when he came down to earth that the problems began. Falling to earth in flames like some metal-bound Lucifer was easier than facing the narrow future that lay ahead of him if he survived the war.
> KATE ATKINSON *Human Croquet*, 1997

Avarice

This theme covers the idea of financial greed. Other aspects of materialism are explored within the themes **Miserliness** and **Wealth**.

Mammon Mammon, deriving from the Aramaic word for 'riches', is the personification of wealth, seen as greedy and selfish materialism. The saying 'Ye cannot serve God and mammon' comes from the New Testament (Matt. 6: 24 and Luke 16: 13). Milton used the name Mammon for a wealth-loving fallen angel in his *Paradise Lost*. Someone who is said to serve Mammon puts their desire for money and material wealth above all other things.

> I said I was not one to go and serve Mammon at that rate; that I knew when I'd got a good missus.
> ELIZABETH GASKELL *Cranford*, 1851–3

> Mr Crimsworth . . . frequented no place of worship, and owned no God but Mammon.
> CHARLOTTE BRONTË *The Professor*, 1857

> Hucknall, it transpires, is no fan of out-of-town shopping: 'invariably a planning error'. He fears for the future of the city-centre mall—where he has interests in a bar and a hotel. 'A city centre is about the buzz of people and great buildings; the Trafford Centre is about the supremacy of Mammon and bad taste', he said.
> The *Independent*, 1998

Midas Midas was the King of Phrygia, a country in what is now part of Turkey. In Greek legend, Midas was granted his wish that everything he touched should be turned to gold. However, when the food in his mouth and, according to some versions, even his beloved daughter, turned to gold, he begged to be released from his gift, and was allowed to do so by bathing in the River Pactolus. Midas is sometimes mentioned as someone who suffers on account of his greed for money.

> 'All I saw was the money. I just didn't want to look down that road. If I had . . . It's like some story I heard once. Some guy, Greek I think, was so greedy he begged the gods to give him a gift—everything he touched would turn to gold. Only thing is, these gods, they zap you: they always give you what you ask for but it turns out not to be what you want. Well, this guy was like me: he had a daughter that he loved more than life. But he forgot to look down the road. And when he touched her, she turned to gold, too. That's what I've done, haven't I?' 'King Midas', I said.
> SARA PARETSKY *Indemnity Only*, 1982

Naboth's vineyard The Old Testament Book of Kings (1 Kgs. 21) relates how Ahab, King of Samaria, coveted the vineyard of Naboth a Jezreelite because it was close to his palace. He asked Naboth to give it to him, offering him either another vineyard or money in return. When Naboth refused, saying that the Lord had forbidden him to give away his father's inheritance, Ahab's wife, Jezebel, plotted Naboth's death so that her husband could take over the vineyard. Ahab and Jezebel were both punished by God for their greed. Allusions to

Naboth's Vineyard are usually in the context of a possession that is coveted and obtained by dishonest means.

Canada, where Biblical references are still understood by quite a few people, sees itself suddenly as Naboth's Vineyard.
ROBERTSON DAVIES *Merry Heart*, 1998

Baldness

The image here tends to be that of a prematurely hairless (perhaps shaved) head rather than baldness that is the result of the normal ageing process. As with other aspects of a person's appearance covered in this book, cinema and television have provided us with visual icons. ▶ *See also* **Hair**.

....

Aeschylus Aeschylus (*c.*525–*c.*456 BC) was a Greek dramatist, best known for his trilogy dealing with the story of Orestes, the *Oresteia* (458 BC), consisting of *Agamemnon*, *Choephoroe*, and *Eumenides*. According to legend, an eagle, mistaking his bald head for a rock, dropped a tortoise on it (to break the shell), thus killing him.

Yul Brynner Yul Brynner (1915–85) was a US film star whose films include *The King and I* (1956) and *The Magnificent Seven* (1960), but he is probably remembered chiefly for his shaved head.

A tall, cheerful man with a Yul Brynner hairstyle (he jokes of being 'follicley challenged'), a keen intellect and a penchant for icon-smashing, Mr. Braiden has become the guru of a back-to-basics movement that advocates turning conventional police culture and organization on its head.
Globe & Mail, 1994

Kojak Kojak was the bald-headed police detective played by Telly Savalas in the American TV series *Kojak* (1973–77). His catchphrase was 'Who loves ya, baby?'

Many of the sallies were aimed at his lack of hair. He was called Kojak at first, but this was a gross slander; Farmer's hair receded at the temples and was less than luxuriant on the crown, that was all.
MAX MARQUIS *Written in Blood*, 1995

Mekon The Mekon is Dan Dare's arch-enemy in the comic strip by Frank Hampson which appeared in the *Eagle* comic between 1950 and 1967. He originates from the planet Venus, is green-skinned, and has a small body and an enormous bald head. A person with a large dome-like head can sometimes be referred to as a Mekon.

Crash bade farewell to another student, a rich teenage boy with the good build and space-ranger short-back-and-sides and Mekon cranium of the future.
MARTIN AMIS *The Information*, 1995

Bargain

Literature provides various examples of bargain, pact, or agreement that involve harsh terms or regrettable consequences. The pact between **FAUST** and the Devil is probably the most resonant of these.

....

Esau and Jacob In the Bible, Esau and Jacob were the twin sons of Isaac and Rebecca, Esau being the first-born. When faint with hunger one day, he begged his brother for some of the food Jacob was preparing. Jacob gave him a 'mess of pottage' (lentil stew) in exchange for the sale of Esau's birthright. This phrase is now used to describe a material comfort gained at the expense of something more valuable.

> As for those benighted creatures who are disgracefully happy with their chains, they must be prevented from bartering their birthrights, like female Esaus, for a mess of pottage in the guise of a bribe to stay at home.
> *The Glasgow Herald*, 1998

Faust Johann Faust was a 16th-century German magician and astrologer who became associated with the legend that he sold his soul to the devil in exchange for knowledge and power. The legend has inspired numerous literary works, notably the dramas *Dr Faustus* (1604) by Marlowe and *Faust* (1808, 1832) by Goethe. In Marlowe's play, Faustus sells his soul to Mephistopheles in exchange for 24 years during which Mephistopheles will grant him whatever he desires. To enter a Faustian pact is to sacrifice one's spiritual or moral values for material gains.

> [If] I had been offered the chance to play for Liverpool as a child . . . on condition that I agreed to die on my 30th birthday. I would have signed this Faustian contract in a twinkling.
> *Radio Times*, 1997

> The story of how Hazar, 31, became involved with what is reputed to be one of the deadliest terrorist organisations in the world has elements of the classic Faustian bargain.
> *The Observer*, 1997

Herod and Salome Salome was the daughter of Herodias, wife of King Herod Antipas. She danced for her stepfather the king 'whereupon he promised with an oath to give her whatsoever she would ask.' Salome was instructed by her mother to demand the head of John the Baptist, as a punishment for John's condemning her marriage. 'And the king was sorry: nevertheless for the oath's sake, and them which sat with him at meat, he commanded it to be given her' (Matt. 14: 6–9).

> I remembered that he considered all this to be pleasure, as Herod thought Salome's dance was fun until he heard what she wanted as a reward.
> EDMUND WHITE *A Boy's Own Story*, 1982

mess of pottage ▶ *See* **ESAU AND JACOB**.

pound of flesh ▸ *See* SHYLOCK.

Shylock In Shakespeare's *The Merchant of Venice* (1600), Shylock is a Jewish moneylender who lends the sum of 3,000 ducats to the merchant Antonio on condition that a pound of Antonio's own flesh will be forfeited to him should the debt not be repaid within three months. 'A pound of flesh' has thus come to mean an agreed payment or penalty which is strictly due but which is harsh or inhuman to demand.

Beauty: Female Beauty

Most of the allusions explained below denote a beautiful woman. Many refer to goddesses or other figures from classical mythology. Some are the names of artists associated with portraying a particular image of female beauty. Female beauty as the trigger for disaster or tragedy is an enduring theme—witness the stories of **BATHSHEBA** and **HELEN**.

Aglaia ▸ *See* GRACES.

Aphrodite In Greek mythology, Aphrodite was the goddess of beauty, fertility, and sexual love, identified by the Romans with Venus. She was supposed to have been born from the sea-foam on the shores of the island of Cythera, and references to Aphrodite sometimes exploit this feature of the myth. One of the names under which she was worshipped was Cytherea.

> Ah, there is beauty! beauty in perfection. What a cloud of sable curls about the face of a houri! What fascinating lips! What glorious black eyes! Your Byron would have worshipped her, and you—you cold, frigid islander!—you played the austere, the insensible in the presence of an Aphrodite so exquisite?
> CHARLOTTE BRONTË *The Professor*, 1857

> Eighteen he remembered her, and not too tall, with almost masculine features below short chestnut hair: brown eyes, full cheeks and proportionate lips, like Aphrodite his inward eye had commented time and time again, only a little sweeter.
> ALAN SILLITOE *The Loneliness of the Long Distance Runner*, 1959

Artemis ▸ *See* DIANA.

Bathsheba In the Bible, Bathsheba was the beautiful wife of Uriah the Hittite (2 Sam. 11) whom King David took as his mistress after he had seen her bathing. David caused her husband to be killed in battle and subsequently married her. Bathsheba became the mother of Solomon. ▸ *See special entry* □ DAVID *on p. 90.*

Beauty and the Beast *Beauty and the Beast* is the title of a fairy tale in which a beautiful young woman, Beauty, is forced to live with the Beast, an ugly monster, in order to save her father's life. Having come to pity and love the Beast, she finally consents to marry him. Her love frees the Beast from the enchantment he is under and he is restored to the form of a handsome prince. Any couple of widely contrasting physical attractiveness can be described as the Beauty and the Beast.

> Therefore, she looked even younger than he was, almost like a very young girl; and the effect of this was to make Ellis, who was so much shorter than she, look older than he was, and more corrupt. They became an odd and unprecedented beauty and the beast.
> JAMES BALDWIN *Another Country*, 1963

> Attorney Callender handed the writ of habeas corpus to the Lieutenant and Fats said, 'Come on, Katy', and took the tall mini-skirted, naked-looking, hot-skinned, cold sex-pot by the elbow and marched her toward the door. They looked like Beauty and the Beast.
> CHESTER HIMES *Blind Man with a Pistol*, 1969

Botticelli   Sandro Botticelli (1445–1510), the Florentine Renaissance painter, is best known for such paintings as *The Birth of Venus* and *Mars and Venus*, in which he endows the goddess with a serene and delicate classical beauty. Botticelli's women usually have pale skin and long wavy fair hair.

> There was not a soul about at that time save Clea, who was on the far beach in a blue bathing-costume, her marvellous hair swinging about her like a blonde Botticelli.
> LAWRENCE DURRELL *Clea*, 1960

> She had, yes, I suppose a Botticelli beauty, long fair hair, grey violet eyes.
> JOHN FOWLES *The Magus*, 1966

> Anthea had a face like a Botticelli Venus, a Beauty Queen's body, and a dignified manner.
> ANTONIA BYATT *The Virgin in the Garden*, 1978

Cleopatra   Cleopatra (69–30 BC) was the Queen of Egypt 47–30 BC. She is usually remembered for her beauty, for her affairs with Julius Caesar and Mark Antony, and for committing suicide by allowing herself to be bitten by an asp. Her relationship with Antony is the subject of Shakespeare's *Antony and Cleopatra* (1623) and Dryden's *All for Love* (1678), while her relationship with Caesar is the subject of Shaw's *Caesar and Cleopatra* (1907). The name Cleopatra can be used to typify a woman of exotic beauty and allure.

> In a word, all Cleopatra—fierce, voluptuous, passionate, tender . . . and full of . . . rapturous enchantment.
> NATHANIEL HAWTHORNE *The Marble Faun,* 1860

Diana   In Roman mythology, Diana was identified with the Greek goddess Artemis and was associated with hunting, virginity, and, in later literature and art, with the moon. She was the personification of feminine grace and vigour.

> There have been plenty of young heroes, of middle stature and feeble beards, who have felt quite sure they could never love anything more insignificant than a Diana, and yet have found themselves in middle life happily settled with a wife who waddles.
> GEORGE ELIOT *Adam Bede*, 1859

> In her dress of white and silver, with a wreath of silver blossoms in her hair, the tall

girl looked like a Diana just alighting from the chase.
EDITH WHARTON *The Age of Innocence*, 1920

Esther In the Old Testament book that bears her name, Esther was a woman who was chosen on account of her beauty by King Ahasuerus of Persia to be his queen in place of the deposed Queen Vashti. Esther used her influence with him to save the Israelites in captivity from persecution. She is one of the most popular Jewish heroines.

Presently my mother went to my father. I know I thought of Queen Esther and King Ahasuerus; for my mother was very pretty and delicate-looking, and my father looked as terrible as King Ahasuerus.
ELIZABETH GASKELL *Cranford*, 1951–3

Euphrosyne ▶ *See* GRACES.

Gibson Girl Charles Dana Gibson (1867–1944) was an American artist and illustrator whose drawings popularized the fashionable ideal of American womanhood in the 1890s and early 1900s: well-built, wasp-waisted, and dressed in tailored Edwardian style.

The young girl in the picture had a massed pile of light hair, and a sharp waist, and that plump-softness of skin and slightly heavy Gibson-girl handsomeness of feature that the age so much admired.
JOHN FOWLES *The Magus*, 1966

Graces In Greek mythology, the Graces were three beautiful goddesses, Aglaia, Thalia, and Euphrosyne, daughters of Zeus, who personified charm, grace, and beauty, which they bestowed upon the world as physical, intellectual, artistic, and moral qualities.

How incongruous it seemed to be telephoning a woman like that. The Graces assembling seemed to have joined hands in meadows of asphodel to compose that face.
VIRGINIA WOOLF *To the Lighthouse*, 1927

Hamadryad Hamadryads were nymphs in Greek and Roman mythology, beautiful maidens who lived in trees and died when the tree died.

'I shall be sitting for my second portrait then,' she said, smiling. 'Will it be larger than the other?' 'Oh, yes, much larger. It is an oil-painting. You will look like a tall Hamadryad, dark and strong and noble, just issued from one of the fir-trees, when the stems are casting their afternoon shadows on the grass.'
GEORGE ELIOT *The Mill on the Floss*, 1860

Perhaps, too, she had at last recognized herself in the Hamadryad of the popular sapling; the slim Hamadryad whose movements were like the swaying of a young tree in the wind. 'The Woman who was a Tree' was what he had called the poem.
ALDOUS HUXLEY *Crome Yellow*, 1921

Hebe In Greek mythology, Hebe was the daughter of Zeus and Hera and was the goddess of youth. She was cup-bearer to the gods before she was replaced by Ganymede.

Olivia, now about eighteen, had that luxuriancy of beauty with which painters generally draw Hebe; open, sprightly, and commanding.
OLIVER GOLDSMITH *The Vicar of Wakefield*, 1766

I went to look at the pretty butter-maker, Hetty Sorrel. She's a perfect Hebe; and if

I were an artist, I would paint her. It's amazing what pretty girls one sees among the farmer's daughters, when the men are such clowns.
GEORGE ELIOT *Adam Bede*, 1859

Helen In Greek mythology, Helen was the daughter of Zeus and Leda who grew into the most beautiful woman in the world. She married Menelaus, and her abduction by the Trojan prince, Paris, led to the Trojan war.

Doctor Faustus, in Marlowe's play of that title (1604), calls up the spirit of Helen of Troy and addresses her with these well-known lines:

'Was this the face that launch'd a thousand ships
And burnt the topless towers of Ilium?'

▶ *See special entry* □ **TROJAN WAR** *on p. 392.*

I, whose loveliness is more than the loveliness of that Grecian Helen, of whom they used to sing, and whose wisdom is wider, ay, far more wide and deep than the wisdom of Solomon the Wise.
H. RIDER HAGGARD *She*, 1887

Who's love is given over-well
Shall look on Helen's face in hell,
Whilst they whose love is thin and wise
May view John Knox in paradise.
DOROTHY PARKER 'Partial Comfort' in *Sunset Gun*, 1928

Madonna The Madonna (literally 'my lady') is a name for the Virgin Mary, the mother of Jesus Christ, used especially when she is represented in a painting or sculpture, usually as a woman of serene and saintly beauty.

The expression of the countenance was in the last degree gentle, soft, timid, and feminine, and seemed rather to shrink from the most casual look of a stranger, rather than to court his admiration. Something there was of the Madonna cast, perhaps the result of delicate health, fiercer, more active, and energetic, than her own.
WALTER SCOTT *The Bride of Lammermoor*, 1819

But Holly was asleep, and lay like a miniature Madonna, of that type which the old painters could not tell from Venus, when they had completed her.
JOHN GALSWORTHY *A Man of Property*, 1906

Wynonna was pretty because she was twenty-something, but Naomi was something out of a Renaissance painting, a mountain Madonna.
SHARYN MCCRUMB *The Hangman's Beautiful Daughter*, 1996

Marilyn Monroe The American film actress Marilyn Monroe (born Norma Jean Mortenson, later Baker, in 1926) became the definitive Hollywood sex symbol, a breathy-voiced blonde who combined sex appeal with innocence and vulnerability. She starred in such films as *Gentlemen Prefer Blondes* (1953) and *Some Like It Hot* (1959) before her death from an overdose of sleeping pills in 1962.

A small, curvaceous woman with platinum blonde hair sashayed towards us across the newsroom like some latter-day Marilyn Monroe.
ANNIE ROSS *Moving Image*, 1995

The people protecting you have morticians who made Boris Karloff look like Marilyn Monroe.
TOM SHARPE *Grantchester Grind*, 1995

Nefertiti Nefertiti (14th century BC) was an Egyptian queen, the wife of

Akhenaten. She is best known from the painted limestone portrait bust of her, now in Berlin, that depicts her as a woman of slender regal beauty.

> She had a beautiful neck; the throat of a Nefertiti.
> JOHN FOWLES *The Magus*, 1966

> They stayed very late, all except Mrs Max, who left directly dinner was over. I watched as she was driven away, sitting up very straight in the back of one of the black limousines, a ravaged Nefertiti.
> JOHN BANVILLE *The Book of Evidence*, 1989

> The girls watched mesmerised as Kate wiped the make-up off her face. And Kate watched them in the mirror. Maisie, tall now, with pale translucent skin, narrow limbs, and an aureole of reddish fair hair, an Arthur Rackham girl. Alison, even taller, a Nefertiti head and an easy athletic grace. The puma and the butterfly.
> MAUREEN O'BRIEN *Dead Innocent*, 1999

Nymph   Nymphs were mythological semi-divine spirits represented as beautiful maidens and associated with aspects of nature, especially with rivers and woods. The corresponding adjective is 'Nymphean'.

> Without throwing a Nymphean tissue over a milkmaid, let it be said that here criticism checked itself as out of place, and looked at her proportions with a long consciousness of pleasure.
> THOMAS HARDY *Far from the Madding Crowd*, 1874

> Nymph? Goddess? Vampire? Yes, she was all of these and none of them. She was, like every woman, everything that the mind of a man . . . wished to imagine.
> LAWRENCE DURRELL *Clea*, 1960

Pocahontas   Pocahontas (*c.*1595–1617) was a beautiful American Indian princess who is alleged to have saved the life of the English colonist John Smith when he was captured by her father Powhatan.

> Then go to America, and drown your sorrows on the bosom of some charming Pocahontas.
> JOHN FOWLES *The French Lieutenant's Woman*, 1969

Rubens   Peter Paul Rubens (1577–1640) was a Flemish painter perhaps best known for his mythological and biblical paintings featuring female nudes with voluptuously rounded figures.

> She had none of that dazzling brilliancy, of that voluptuous Rubens beauty.
> ANTHONY TROLLOPE *Barchester Towers*, 1857

Snow White   The heroine of the traditional fairy tale *Snow White and the Seven Dwarfs* is 'as white as snow, as red as blood and had hair as black as ebony', and her name can be applied to a beautiful girl or woman with pale skin, black hair, and red lips.

Thalia   ▶ *See* GRACES.

Venus   Venus was the Roman goddess identified with the Greek Aphrodite, the goddess of beauty, fertility, and sexual love. She was supposed to have been born from the sea-foam, though she is sometimes depicted (as in Botticelli's painting *The Birth of Venus*) emerging from a large sea-shell.

With that glow in her pale face, her breast heaving, her eyes so large and dark and soft, she looked like Venus come to life!
JOHN GALSWORTHY *A Man of Property*, 1906

Here was beauty. It silenced all comment except that of eager praise. A generation that had admired piquante women, boyish women, ugly, smart, and fascinating women was now confronted by simple beauty, pure and undeniable as that of the young Venus whom the Greeks loved to carve.
STELLA GIBBONS *Cold Comfort Farm*, 1932

Beauty: Male Beauty

Writers have traditionally turned to classical myth or art for archetypes of (often youthful) male beauty, with **ADONIS** serving as probably the most durable representative of masculine attractiveness. ▶ *See also* **Beauty: Female Beauty** *and* **Youth**.

Adonis   In Greek mythology, Adonis was a beautiful youth who was loved by both Aphrodite and Persephone. He was killed by a wild boar, but Aphrodite begged Zeus to restore him to life. Zeus decreed that Adonis should spend the winter months of each year in the underworld with Persephone and the summer months with Aphrodite. As the quotations below suggest, a man described as an Adonis usually has not only a handsome face but also a gorgeous body.

I really can't see any resemblance between you, with your rugged strong face and your coal-black hair, and this young Adonis, who looks as if he was made out of ivory and rose-leaves.
OSCAR WILDE *The Picture of Dorian Gray*, 1891

I suppose a very calculating man would keep his shirt on to the last, getting rid of his socks and shorts as fast as possible, and then cast off the shirt, revealing himself as an Adonis. But I was a schoolboy undresser, and had never stripped to enchant.
ROBERTSON DAVIES *The Manticore*, 1972

The funny thing about David was that though he was absolutely not an Adonis and pretty wet in most ways, he was rather good in bed—fairly simple, but enjoying himself a lot and seeing that you did too.
PETER DICKINSON *The Yellow Room*, 1995

Apollo   Apollo was a Greek god, the son of Zeus and Leto and the twin brother of Artemis. He was sometimes given the epithet Phoebus ('the bright one'), and in later poetry is associated with the sun. In art Apollo is represented as an ideal type of male beauty, for example in the famous statue the Apollo Belvedere, now in the Vatican. ▶ *See special entry* ☐ **APOLLO** *on p. 15*.

Your words have delineated very prettily a graceful Apollo; he is present to your imagination,—tall, fair, blue-eyed, and with a Grecian profile.
CHARLOTTE BRONTË *Jane Eyre*, 1847

The little priest was not an interesting man to look at, having stubbly brown hair and a round and stolid face. But if he had been as splendid as Apollo no one would have looked at him at that moment.
G. K. CHESTERTON 'The Hammer of God' in *The Innocence of Father Brown*, 1911

He was the finest young man that ever trod this planet: beautiful, like young Apollo.
JOHN MASEFIELD *The Box of Delights*, 1935

Endymion Endymion was a beautiful young man in Greek mythology who was loved by the moon goddess Selene. According to one version of his story, Zeus caused him to sleep forever so that he would remain eternally young and handsome.

Ganymede In Greek mythology, Ganymede (or Ganymedes) was a Trojan youth who was so beautiful that he was carried off by an eagle to be Zeus's cup-bearer. He is the archetype of a youth of extraordinary beauty.

Her chair being a far more comfortable one than his she still slept on inside his great-coat, looking warm as a new bun and boyish as Ganymedes.
THOMAS HARDY *Jude the Obscure*, 1895

Now listen: were it by any chance the case that Oliver's radiant sexuality occasionally put aside the workaday, and were his heliotropic gaze to turn towards Stoke Newington's unlikely Ganymede, then, to enlist a vernacular which my accuser herself will be able to grasp, *I wouldn't have any trouble there, mate.*
JULIAN BARNES *Talking It Over*, 1991

Heathcliff Heathcliff is the passionate gipsy hero of Emily Brontë's romantic novel *Wuthering Heights* (1847). He has long dark hair and a rugged, wild attractiveness.

She had grown agreeably used to breakfast with Ken Cracknell, who looked this morning, with his dark hair and smouldering eyes, like a young Heathcliff of the legal aid system.
JOHN MORTIMER *Rumpole's Return*, 1980

Dominic, as always, had positioned himself slightly back from the family group, his black suit and darkly brooding eyes giving him a touch of Heathcliff.
LAUREN HENDERSON *The Black Rubber Dress*, 1997

Michelangelo Michelangelo (1475-1564, full name Michelangelo Buonarroti) was an Italian sculptor, painter, architect, and poet. A leading figure during the High Renaissance, he established his reputation in Rome with sculptures such as the *Pietà* (c.1497-1500) and then in Florence with his marble *David* (1501-4). In his portrayal of the nude, Michelangelo depicted the beauty and strength of the human body. He is probably best known for painting the ceiling of the Sistine Chapel in Rome (1508-12).

I have seldom seen a more splendid young fellow. He was naked to the waist and of a build that one day might be over-corpulent. But now he could stand as a model to Michelangelo!
WILLIAM GOLDING *Rites of Passage*, 1980

At twenty, he had the body of Michelangelo's David, now he resembles an entire family group by Henry Moore.
MINETTE WALTERS *The Scold's Bridle*, 1994

Narcissus In Greek mythology, Narcissus was a youth of extraordinary beauty who cruelly spurned many admirers, including the nymph Echo. On bending down to a pool one day to drink, he fell in love with his own reflection. Narcissus is alluded to as an example of excessive physical vanity, and his name has given us the word 'narcissism'.

Betrayal

By far the most frequently used archetype of treachery is **JUDAS**. Other figures commonly mentioned in this context are **BRUTUS** (betrayer of a friend), **DELILAH** (betrayer of a lover), and **BENEDICT ARNOLD** (betrayer of one's country). Of the allusions covered below, only **URIAH** is a victim rather than a perpetrator of treachery.

Benedict Arnold Benedict Arnold (1741–1801) was an American general in the American Revolution, chiefly remembered as a traitor who in 1780 plotted, with the British army major John André, to betray the American post at West Point to the British. When the plot was discovered, Arnold escaped and later fought on the side of the British.

> He had carried Mark O'Meara's clubs in the 1997 matches before switching to the young Spaniard. On an alcoholic high after his country's win, a burly American fan no doubt saw him as a golfing Benedict Arnold.
> *The Guardian*, 1999

> I hold the glass for Beth, bending the straw to her lips. 'You were lucky Lyle was there. To explain.'
> 'That Benedict Arnold?' She takes a couple of sips. 'He told them. Betrayed my confidence.'
> SUSAN SUSSMAN with SARAJANE AVIDON *Audition for Murder*, 1999

Ascalaphus In Greek mythology, Ascalaphus, the son of Acheron, was an inhabitant of the underworld. After Persephone had been abducted by Hades to be his queen in the underworld, she was granted the opportunity to return to the earth on condition that she had eaten nothing in the underworld. However, she had eaten some pomegranate seeds from a tree, and this fact was revealed by Ascalaphus. Persephone was ordered by Zeus to remain six months with Hades and to spend the rest of the year on the earth with her mother Demeter. Persephone turned Ascalaphus into an owl for his act of betrayal.

Brutus Marcus Junius Brutus (85–42 BC) was a Roman senator who, with Cassius, was a leader of the conspirators who assassinated Julius Caesar in AD 44. Caesar's dying words as he was stabbed by his friend Brutus are supposed to have been: 'Et tu, Brute?' ('You too, Brutus?'). Brutus subsequently committed suicide after being defeated by Antony and Octavian at Philippi.

> I rose to my feet with some of the emotions of a man who has just taken the Cornish Express in the small of the back. She was standing looking at me with her hands on

her hips, grinding her teeth quietly, and I gazed back with reproach and amazement, like Julius Caesar at Brutus.
P. G. WODEHOUSE *Laughing Gas*, 1936

I heard the woman yell, 'Gaston! Get out here!' and then a man appeared and engulfed them both with bearlike arms. I had a sinking feeling as I watched them, like Brutus might've felt just before he stabbed Caesar.
JOHN DUNNING *The Bookman's Wake*, 1995

Caesar ▶ *See* BRUTUS.

Delilah In the Bible, Delilah betrayed her lover Samson to the Philistines by revealing to them the secret of his prodigious strength. 'And the lords of the Philistines came to her and said to her, "Entice him, and see wherein his great strength lies, and by what means we may overpower him, that we may bind him to subdue him; and we will each give you eleven hundred pieces of silver" ' (Judg. 16: 5). Delilah discovered that Samson's strength lay in his long hair and had it cut off while he slept, after which she delivered him up to the Philistines. Any treacherous woman can consequently be described as a Delilah. ▶ *See special entry* ☐ SAMSON *on p. 336.*

Ay, and I fancy I've baited the hook right. Our little Delilah will bring our Samson.
ANTHONY HOPE *The Prisoner of Zenda*, 1894

'Lassiter!' Jane whispered, as she gazed from him to the black, cold guns. Without them he appeared shorn of strength, defenseless, a smaller man. Was she Delilah? Swiftly, conscious of only one motive—refusal to see this man called craven by his enemies—she rose, and with blundering fingers buckled the belt round his waist where it belonged.
ZANE GREY *Riders of the Purple Sage*, 1912

Eve In the Bible, Eve was the first woman, wife of Adam. Eve first ate the forbidden fruit from the Tree of Knowledge, tempted to do so by the serpent, and then persuaded Adam to eat the fruit too, thus ensuring their expulsion from Eden. ▶ *See special entry* ☐ ADAM AND EVE *on p. 5.*

You are welcome to all my confidence that is worth having, Jane: but for God's sake, don't desire a useless burden! Don't long for poison—don't turn out a downright Eve on my hands!
CHARLOTTE BRONTË *Jane Eyre*, 1847

Joanna the faithless, the betrayer: Joanna who mocked him, whispered about him behind his back, trapped and tortured him. Joanna Eve.
FAY WELDON *The Cloning of Joanna May*, 1989

Judas Judas Iscariot was the disciple who, in return for thirty pieces of silver, betrayed Jesus to the Jewish authorities with a kiss of identification: 'Now the betrayer had given them a sign, saying, "The one I shall kiss is the man; seize him." And he came up to Jesus at once and said, "Hail, Master!" And he kissed him. Jesus said to him, "Friend, why are you here?" Then they came up and laid hands on Jesus and seized him' (Matthew 26: 48–50). Overcome with remorse, Judas later hanged himself. The term 'Judas' can be used to refer to a person who treacherously betrays a friend. A 'Judas kiss' is an act of betrayal. ▶ *See special entry* ☐ JESUS *on p. 223.*

Was not Stephen Guest right in his decided opinion that this slim maid of eighteen was quite the sort of wife a man would not be likely to repent of marrying?—a woman who was loving and thoughtful for other women, not giving them Judas-

kisses with eyes askance on their welcome defects, but with real care and vision for their half-hidden pains and mortifications, with long ruminating enjoyment of little pleasures prepared for them?
GEORGE ELIOT *The Mill on the Floss*, 1860

Everybody, when he spoke, listened attentively to him as if he was addressing them in church. He wondered where the inevitable Judas was sitting now, but he wasn't aware of Judas as he had been in the forest hut.
GRAHAM GREENE *The Power and the Glory*, 1940

Are we to watch our words and stick out our necks to the knives of potential traitors here in this place where we meet to put our minds and hearts in the struggle . . . are we to sit with Judas in our midst?
NADINE GORDIMER *My Son's Story*, 1990

Lady in Red The mysterious 'Lady in Red' was the mistress of the bank robber and murderer John Dillinger (named the FBI's 'public enemy number one' in 1933). She betrayed Dillinger's whereabouts to the FBI, whose agents shot him dead in Chicago in 1934.

'But what about the money?' she asked. China hooted. 'She's makin' like she's the Lady in Red that told on Dillinger. Dillinger wouldn't have come near you lessen he was going hunting in Africa and shoot you for a hippo.'
TONI MORRISON *The Bluest Eye*, 1970

Thirty Pieces of Silver ▶ *See* JUDAS.

Uncle Tom Uncle Tom is a loyal and ever-patient black slave, the main character of Harriet Beecher Stowe's anti-slavery novel *Uncle Tom's Cabin* (1852). The term can be applied to a black man whose behaviour to white people is regarded as submissively servile, and by extension can refer to anyone regarded as betraying his or her cultural or social allegiance.

'Ignore his lying tongue,' Ras shouted. 'Hang him up to teach the black people a lesson, and theer be no more traitors. No more Uncle Toms. Hang him up theer with them blahsted dummies!'
RALPH ELLISON *Invisible Man*, 1952

Uriah Uriah the Hittite was an officer in David's army, the husband of Bathsheba. David sent Uriah to his death in the front line of battle so that he could marry Bathsheba. Uriah was given a letter to carry to his commanding officer, Joab, which was in fact Uriah's own death-warrant: 'Set Uriah in the forefront of the hardest fighting, and then draw back from him, that he may be struck, and die' (2 Sam. 11: 15). ▶ *See special entry* □ DAVID *on p. 90.*

Blindness

In a number of the stories in this theme, blindness is inflicted as a punishment for a crime or offence.

Blind Pew In R. L. Stevenson's *Treasure Island* (1883), Blind Pew is the sinister blind pirate, the 'horrible, soft-spoken, eyeless creature', whose approach is signalled by the tapping of his stick along the road. It is Pew who delivers the dreaded 'Black Spot' to the old captain at the *Admiral Benbow* inn, and who leads the pirates' attack on the inn. He is abandoned by his companions, however, and is trampled to death by a horse.

Gloucester In Shakespeare's *King Lear* (1623), the Earl of Gloucester, whose pity for Lear has led him to assist the old king's escape to Dover, has his eyes put out by the Duke of Cornwall. The blinding of Gloucester is one of the most gruesome scenes in Shakespeare.

Homer Homer (8th century BC) was a Greek epic poet, held to be the author of the *Iliad* and the *Odyssey*, though it is probable that these were based on much older stories which had been passed on orally. He is traditionally supposed to have been blind, sometimes referred to as 'the Blind Bard'.

Nelson Admiral Horatio Nelson (1758–1805), lost his right eye at Calvi in Corsica in 1794. According to tradition, at the battle of Copenhagen in 1801 Nelson put his telescope to his blind eye to look at the approaching Danish fleet, and, with the words 'I see no ships', ignored the order to withdraw the English navy. To 'turn the eye of Nelson' to something is the same as 'turn a blind eye' to it, in other words to pretend not to notice.

> No longer will a cumshaw ensure that the captains of the revenue cruisers turn the blind eye of Lord Nelson to the nefarious trade.
> TIMOTHY MO *An Insular Possession*, 1986

Oedipus In Greek mythology, Oedipus was the son of Jocasta and of Laius, king of Thebes. Growing up in ignorance of his parentage, Oedipus unwittingly quarrelled with and killed his father and then married his mother. On discovering the truth, Oedipus put out his own eyes in a fit of madness. The image of the blinded Oedipus is a familiar one from the plays of Sophocles.

> I hit him where I wanted, plug in his right eye . . . Demetriades stood like a parody of Oedipus with his hands over his eyes.
> JOHN FOWLES *The Magus*, 1977

Peeping Tom According to legend, Tom the tailor was said to have peeped at Lady Godiva when she rode naked through the streets of Coventry, as a result of which he was struck blind. He was thereafter known as 'Peeping Tom'.

Samson As a result of his betrayal by Delilah, the Israelite leader Samson was captured by the Philistines who 'put out his eyes, and brought him down to Gaza, and bound him with fetters of brass' (Judg. 16: 21). The phrase 'eyeless in Gaza', the title of a novel by Aldous Huxley, comes originally from Milton's *Samson Agonistes* (1671):

'Ask for this great deliverer now, and find him
Eyeless in Gaza, at the mill with slaves.'
▶ *See special entry* □ **SAMSON** *on p. 336.*

> The door opened; Miss Nellie and her music-master stood behind it, but blind Samson, . . . did not know they were there.
> WILLA CATHER *My Antonia*, 1918

Tiresias In Greek mythology, Tiresias was a soothsayer from Thebes who was renowned for his wisdom. In his youth, he was blinded by Athene as a punishment for seeing her bathing naked. Later, relenting somewhat, she gave him the gift of prophecy in compensation.

> The eyes of Lucian Freud's sitters as they stare out from his pictures suggest that, like the blind Tiresias, they 'have foresuffered all'.
> *New York Review of Books,* 1993

Cain

....

In the Book of Genesis, Cain was the first-born son of Adam and Eve who murdered his younger brother Abel. Cain was a tiller of the ground and Abel a keeper of sheep. When they brought their offerings to God, Abel's lamb was accepted but Cain's offering from his harvest was not. In jealous anger Cain killed his brother. God demanded an explanation for Abel's absence, to which Cain responded 'Am I my brother's keeper?' Once his crime was revealed, Cain was cursed by God for ever. He was cast out from his homeland and forced to live a life of vagrancy as an outcast for the rest of his life. God branded him with a mark, to indicate that no one should kill him and shorten his nomadic punishment.

Various aspects of the Cain story are dealt with throughout the book.

▶ *See* **Curse, Guilt, Murder, Solitude,** *and* **Travellers and Wanderers**.

Captives

Most of the figures in this theme are either historical or fictional victims of incarceration. **ANDROMEDA, GULLIVER,** and to some extent **SAMSON,** focus more on the idea of physical restraint. ▶ *See also* **Prisons**.

....

Andromeda In Greek mythology, Andromeda was the daughter of Cepheus and Cassiopeia, King and Queen of Ethiopia. Cassiopeia boasted that her daughter was more beautiful even than the Nereids, or sea nymphs, which angered Poseidon. As a punishment, Poseidon sent a sea monster to destroy the land and agreed to end the punishment only if Andromeda was sacrificed to the sea monster. Andromeda was therefore chained to a rock and left to her fate. She was rescued by Perseus, who flew to her rescue on the winged horse, Pegasus, and slew the sea monster.

> I mean, it's bad enough being forced to appear on a television programme in the

first place, let alone chained to a series like Andromeda to a rock.
JOHN MALCOLM *Into the Vortex*, 1996

Gulliver In a famous episode at the beginning of Jonathan Swift's *Gulliver's Travels* (1726), the shipwrecked Gulliver wakes on the shore of Lilliput to find himself unable to move: 'I found my arms and legs were strongly fastened on each side to the ground; and my hair, which was long and thick, tied down in the same manner. I likewise felt several slender ligatures across my body, from my armpits to my thighs.'

> Having stabbed one leader in the back, he felt he could not do it again. Besides, he owed Margaret Thatcher no loyalty—and he feels genuine loyalty to Major. Bound by Lilliputian cords, the great Gulliver could do nothing but hope.
> *The Observer*, 1995

Man in the Iron Mask During the reign of Louis XIV (1643–1715), 'the Man in the Iron Mask' was the name given to a mysterious state prisoner held for over forty years in various prisons until he died in the Bastille in November 1703. Whenever he travelled between different prisons he wore a black mask, made not in fact of iron, but of velvet. Although his identity was never revealed, he was buried under the name of 'M. de Marchiel'. It has been suggested that he was an illegitimate son or an illegitimate elder brother of Louis XIV.

> At all times the privileged prisoner's cell was in semi-darkness. . . . The other prisoners nicknamed him 'The Man in the Iron Mask' . . . No one knew his real name.
> M. GUYBON tr. ALEXANDER SOLZHENITSYN *First Circle*, 1968

Count of Monte Cristo The Count of Monte Cristo is the hero of a novel of the same name by Alexandre Dumas published in 1844. The novel relates how Edmond Dantès is betrayed by enemies and incarcerated in the Château d'If. After fourteen years he finally manages to escape, having been told by a fellow prisoner of buried treasure on the island of Monte Cristo. Dantès finds the treasure, assumes the title of Count of Monte Cristo, and sets about taking revenge on those who had brought about his imprisonment.

> Digween held his breath, suddenly fearful that his world might be about to dissolve beneath his feet.
> But what Wield had said was, 'He's not going back there. He escaped!'
> Hiding his relief, Digween exclaimed, 'He . . . it . . . is a monkey, not the Count of bloody Monte Cristo. All right, we can't send him . . . it . . . back to that place, but the proper place for him . . . it . . . is a zoo!'
> REGINALD HILL *On Beulah Height*, 1998

Princes in the Tower The Princes in the Tower were Edward, Prince of Wales (born 1470) and Richard, Duke of York (born 1472), the two young sons of Edward IV. When Edward IV died in 1483, the young Edward reigned briefly as Edward V, but soon afterwards he and his brother were sent to the Tower of London by their uncle, the future Richard III. It is generally assumed that they were murdered in the tower at the instigation of Richard, although some argue that the culprit was his successor, Henry VII. Two skeletons discovered in the Tower in 1674 are thought to be theirs.

Prisoner of Chillon The *Prisoner of Chillon* is the title of a poem by Byron, published in 1816, which describes the imprisonment of François de

Bonnivard (1496–1570) in the castle of Chillon, on Lake Geneva.

Prisoner of Zenda *The Prisoner of Zenda* is the title of a book by Anthony Hope, published in 1894. The novel follows the adventures of Rudolf Rassendyll, an Englishman who bears a striking resemblance to the King of Ruritania. When the King is kidnapped, Rassendyll impersonates him, helps to rescue him from his imprisonment in the castle of Zenda, and thwarts a plot to usurp him.

> Edna: Oh, I'm dead chokka! Cook, wash, clean—that's all I do—I never go anywhere. I'm like the bleeding Prisoner of Zenda.
> TERENCE DAVIES *A Modest Pageant*, 1992

Samson In the Old Testament, the Book of Judges relates how Samson, known for his great strength, was betrayed by his lover, Delilah, who discovered that the secret of his strength lay in his hair and had it cut off while he slept. As a result of this betrayal, Samson was captured by the Philistines, blinded, and taken to Gaza. During his captivity, his hair grew back and, being brought out to make sport for the Philistines during a religious celebration, he called on God for strength and pulled down the pillars of the Philistines' temple, destroying himself and a large number of Philistines. ▶ *See special entry* ☐ **SAMSON** *on p. 336*.

> Like imprisoned Samson, I would rather remain all my life in the mill-house, grinding for my very bread, than be brought forth to make sport for the Philistine lords and ladies
> WALTER SCOTT *The Bride of Lammermoor*, 1819

> I fell to plotting ways of short-circuiting the machine. Perhaps if I shifted my body about so that the two nodes would come together—No, not only was there no room, but it might electrocute me. I shuddered. Whoever else I was, I was no Samson. I had no desire to destroy myself even if it destroyed the machine; I wanted freedom, not destruction.
> RALPH ELLISON *Invisible Man*, 1952

Oscar Wilde The Irish writer Oscar Wilde (1854–1900) was imprisoned for two years in Reading gaol (1895–7) for homosexual offences. His poem *The Ballad of Reading Gaol* (1898), concerning the trial and execution of the murderer Charles Thomas Wooldridge, is based on his experiences there and criticizes the prison's harsh conditions.

> Should I extend the week's grace to a fortnight? Convince myself that the poor woman would need more than a week to prepare for the biggest culture-shock since Oscar Wilde had gone inside?
> RICHARD HALEY *Thoroughfare of Stones*, 1995

Change

Classical mythology is rich in tales of physical transformation, many of which were retold by Ovid in his *Metamorphoses*. This theme is illustrated mainly by such shape-changers, both voluntary and involuntary, but also by transformations of status or circumstances. ▶ *See also* **Duality, Lack of Change**.

....

Arachne Arachne was a weaver who lived in Lydia in ancient Greece. She challenged the goddess Athene to a weaving contest and wove a piece of cloth representing the loves of the gods. When Athene could find no flaw in the cloth she refused to admit that Arachne had won the contest, destroying the cloth and changing Arachne into a spider.

Cinderella In the fairy story, Cinderella's life is made miserable by her step-mother and stepsisters. She is dressed in rags and is forced to do menial tasks. When her stepsisters go off to a royal ball leaving Cinderella behind, she is found weeping by her fairy godmother, who waves her wand, turning a pump-kin into a coach, six mice into horses to pull it, and a rat into a coachman. Cinderella's rags are turned into beautiful clothes and glass slippers appear on her feet. The name Cinderella can be used to describe a transformation from poverty or plainness to prosperity or glamour, while the fairy godmother can represent the agent of transformation. ▶ *See special entry* ☐ CINDERELLA *on p. 56.*

> She had acquired such wonderful arts, that the woman and girl who formed the staff of domestics regarded her as quite a Sorceress, or Cinderella's Godmother: who would send out for a fowl, a rabbit, a vegetable or two from the garden, and change them into anything she pleased.
> CHARLES DICKENS *A Tale of Two Cities*, 1859

Damascus (the road to) The road to Damascus was the site for the sudden and dramatic conversion to Christianity undergone by Saul of Tarsus. With a reputation as a committed persecutor of Christians, he had set out planning to take prisoner any Christians he found in Damascus. On the way he suddenly found himself the centre of a blinding light and, falling to the ground, heard God's voice crying 'Saul, Saul, why persecutest thou me?' (Acts 9: 4). Saul, later known as Paul, became a powerful and influential Christian. References to the road to Damascus are usually in the context of a sudden conversion to a belief, opinion, or cause.

> Richard underwent some sort of religious conversion—the full road-to-Damascus number, so I heard. When he came out of gaol, he couldn't cope with the real world. He didn't have any support, I suppose that was the problem: no job to go back to, no family—he wasn't married and in all the years I knew him I never heard him men-tion any relatives. Jesus was probably all he had.
> HILARY WHELAN *Frightening Strikes*, 1995

Daphne In Greek mythology, Daphne was a nymph, daughter of Peneus, with whom the god Apollo fell in love. In attempting to escape his pursuit, Daphne called upon the gods for help and was turned into a laurel tree.

fairy godmother ▶ *See* CINDERELLA.

frog prince In the fairy story *The Frog Prince*, a princess, playing with a golden ball, inadvertently drops it into a fountain. A frog offers to retrieve the ball if she will, in return, love him and let him be her companion. The princess promises without any intention of keeping her word but her father, the King, insists that the promise be honoured, and she reluctantly complies. However, when the frog demands to sleep in her bed, she throws it against the wall. As the frog falls, he turns into a handsome prince. By later fairy tale convention, a frog is transformed into a prince after being kissed by a princess.

> The princess had started to kiss the frog, and chickened out. The transformation was only half complete. The man's wide, lipless mouth was Batrachian, and so were his eyes—small and protuberant, set back in a sloping forehead. His sleek shining black hair looked like a satin skullcap. His figure was upright but frog-shaped; even the skillful tailoring of his navy blazer and gray slacks could not conceal a barrel-shaped torso and short, stubby limbs.
> ELIZABETH PETERS *Naked Once More*, 1989

> I don't mean I've done a sudden transformation. I'm not a frog that's been kissed by a princess or whatever the fairy tale is.
> JULIAN BARNES *Talking It Over*, 1991

Io In Greek mythology, Io was a mortal woman and priestess of Hera with whom Zeus fell in love. In order to protect Io from the jealousy of his wife, Hera, Zeus turned her into a heifer. Hera was not deceived, and sent a stinging insect to goad the heifer, which fled to Egypt where Zeus returned her to human form.

Jekyll and Hyde In Robert Louis Stevenson's *The Strange Case of Dr Jekyll and Mr Hyde* (1886), Dr Jekyll discovers a drug that allows him to create a separate personality, Mr Hyde, through which he can express the evil side of his character. Periodically, he changes from the worthy physician into the evil Hyde, and eventually Hyde gains the upper hand over Jekyll. The term 'Jekyll and Hyde' can thus be used to refer to someone whose personality appears to undergo an abrupt transformation, particularly from gentleness to aggressiveness or violence.

> I just said a double thing. I said I would rob a bank. And then I said I hate corruption. Hmmm. Jekyll and Hyde.
> STUDS TERKEL *American Dreams: Lost and Found*, 1980

> I told her that she had had a lucky escape from my father, but she defended him, saying, 'He is another person when he is on his own with me. He is so sweet and kind'. Yes, and so was Dr Jekyll.
> SUE TOWNSEND *The Growing Pains of Adrian Mole*, 1984

> Under normal circumstances Bruce was a happy drinker, not one of those sad Jekyll and Hyde characters who turn into social psychopaths with their third glass.
> BEN ELTON *Popcorn*, 1996

Clark Kent and Superman Clark Kent appears to be a shy bespectacled reporter for the *Daily Planet* newspaper. However, when trouble threatens he transforms himself into Superman, a superhero from the planet Krypton who is able to fly and has superhuman strength. Originally a US comic book character, Superman has also appeared in a series of successful films. Clark Kent's transformation takes place out of sight and typically in a telephone box, from which he emerges fully garbed in cape and tights as Superman.

> 'Fire away', he said, all business. We might just have met. I was impressed by this Clark Kent-like transformation: from admirer to news hound in half a minute, and no need to pop into a telephone booth.
> LAUREN HENDERSON *The Black Rubber Dress*, 1997

Lot's wife According to Gen. 19: 24, God destroyed the towns of Sodom and

Gomorrah by fire and brimstone as a punishment for the depravity and wickedness of their inhabitants. Lot, the nephew of Abraham, was allowed to escape from the destruction of Sodom with his family. His wife disobeyed God's order not to look back at the burning city and she was turned into a pillar of salt.

> Don't ever look back, kid. . . . You turn into some old cow's salt lick.
> WILLIAM BURROUGHS *The Naked Lunch*, 1959

> Pokler, billeted at a fisherman's cottage, came in from his evening walks behind a fine mask of salt. Lot's wife. What disaster had he dared to look back on?
> THOMAS PYNCHON *Gravity's Rainbow*, 1973

> I tell you, if you look back, you will get turned, like Lot's wife, to a pillar of salt; Lot's wife, nostalgic for the past.
> FAY WELDON *Darcy's Utopia*, 1990

Pauline Paul's conversion to Christianity on the road to Damascus can be referred to as the Pauline conversion. ▶ *See* **DAMASCUS (THE ROAD TO)**.

> 'I appreciate your feelings. But I felt I must come to tell your wife that I now believe her to be innocent and want to do what I can to put the record straight.' He did not unbend. 'It would certainly have been welcome if you had experienced this Pauline conversion at the time. Now, when my wife is trying to put it all behind her, I cannot see that disinterring the past will serve any useful purpose.'
> ALINE TEMPLETON *Last Act of All*, 1995

Proteus In Greek mythology, Proteus, the son of Oceanus and Tethys, was given by Poseidon the power to prophesy the future. He also had the power to change his shape, which he would exploit in order to escape those seeking his predictions. In an episode recounted in the *Odyssey*, Proteus changes himself in rapid succession into a lion, a serpent, a panther, a wild boar, a torrent of water, and a tree. The name Proteus has come to refer to changeability, along with the adjective 'protean'.

> Donald appeared not to see her at all, and answered her wise little remarks with curtly indifferent monosyllables, his looks and faculties hanging on the woman who could boast of a more Protean variety in her phases, moods, opinions, and also principles, than could Elizabeth.
> THOMAS HARDY *The Mayor of Casterbridge*, 1886

> Compared with Molloy's Protean performance hers was the merest shadow, but it was far beyond anything that she had ever dreamed she might achieve.
> ROBERTSON DAVIES *A Mixture of Frailties*, 1951

> Well, it was a virtuoso performance, and obscured for those few hours all shadows of the other Lennys, the cold, the cruel, the distant ones. And so I learnt a lesson for times to come. That my battle was not so much with a dragon breathing fire, as with Proteus changing shapes, and that whatever magic was woven around me, I should always be on my guard.
> SARAH DUNANT *Snow Storms in a Hot Climate*, 1988

Rubicon In 49 BC, Julius Caesar, having defeated the Gauls in the Gallic Wars, brought his troops south to fight a civil war against Pompey and the Roman Senate. When he crossed the Rubicon, a stream marking the boundary between Italy and Gaul, he was committed to war, having violated the law that forbade him to take his troops out of his province. To 'cross the Rubicon' is to commit oneself to changing to a new course, leaving no possibility of turning back.

> He had crossed his Rubicon—not perhaps very heroically or dramatically, but then it is only in dramas that people act dramatically.
> SAMUEL BUTLER *The Way of All Flesh*, 1903

> Another depressing development for Laurence is that his children know about the split now. I think that's a kind of Rubicon as far as he's concerned. As long as they didn't know, there was always the possibility that he and Sally might get back together again with no serious damage done, no embarrassment, no loss of face.
> DAVID LODGE *Therapy*, 1995

Rumpelstiltskin In the Grimms' fairy story, a miller claims that his daughter can spin straw into gold. The king locks the girl into a room with a pile of straw and a spinning wheel, promising to marry her if she can accomplish the task. Rumpelstiltskin appears and spins the straw into gold, asking for her necklace in payment. He performs this feat for the girl twice more, requiring in payment first her ring and then, when she has no more jewellery, her first child.

> If his father had been a demonstrative man, if he had been able to show the affection for Sonny that he almost certainly felt, it would have been easier. But for Alex, affection was swamped, always, by the apprehension that something Sonny did might diminish the standing of his father in the eyes of the school. Like Rumpelstiltskin, Sonny spun gold out of straw. He developed a charm and an assurance—not to mention a talent for cricket—that eventually won the other boys' respect.
> MICHELLE SPRING *Running for Shelter*, 1994

> He always arrived fifteen minutes ahead of the agreed time because he knew she'd be early. It didn't matter which time he'd chosen, she'd turn up ahead of schedule because she was convinced he was Rumpelstiltskin, the man who could spin twenty-four-carat gold out of the dry straw of her life.
> VAL MCDERMID *The Wire in the Blood*, 1997

Saul/Paul Saul of Tarsus, a persecutor of the Christians, became known as Paul after his conversion to Christianity on the road to Damascus. ▶ *See* **DAMASCUS (THE ROAD TO)**.

> 'You start Saul, and end up Paul,' my grandfather had often said. 'When you're a youngun, you Saul, but let life whup your head a bit and you starts to trying to be Paul—though you still Sauls around on the side.'
> RALPH ELLISON *Invisible Man*, 1952

> I remember a dramatic scene. I was Paul on the road to Damascus . . . I was walking towards the museum along Fifth Avenue, thirty blocks, because there was a victory parade . . . I kept walking, and there was a long-haired kid, nearer the bleachers, being assailed by this guy. The guy was yelling from the top of the bleachers: 'You guys ought to be eliminated. In a democracy like this, you're not fit.' I stopped and thought: If this is what Vietnam is doing to us, it's time it was over. I was anti-war from that day on.
> STUDS TERKEL *American Dreams: Lost and Found*, 1980

Superman ▶ *See* **CLARK KENT**.

Ugly Duckling In Hans Christian Andersen's fairy story *The Ugly Duckling* (1846), a cygnet in a brood of ducklings is mocked by the other ducks and hens for his drab appearance. He runs away, struggles through the winter, and in the spring meets three swans. Looking at his reflection in the water, he discovers that he too has turned into a beautiful swan. The term 'ugly duckling' can be applied to a person, initially thought ugly, who turns out to be extremely beautiful.

> She was a fairy princess who had taken a fancy to a little boy, clothed him, petted him, turned him from a laughing stock into an accepted member of her society, from an ugly duckling into a swan.
> L. P. HARTLEY *The Go-Between*, 1953

Vicar of Bray The Vicar of Bray is the subject of an anonymous 18th-century song in which he boasts that he has been able to adapt to the differing religious regimes of, successively, Charles, James, William, Anne, and George. 'The Vicar of Bray' stands for someone who will change their opinions in order to retain power.

> The Ashleys have always had a talent for retaining just what they wanted to retain, while adapting immediately and without effort to the winning side. The Vicar of Bray must have been a close relation. We were Catholics right up to Henry VIII, then when the Great Whore got him we built a priest's hole and kept it tenanted until we saw which side the wafer was buttered, and then somehow there we were under Elizabeth, staunch Protestants and bricking up the priest's hole, and learning the Thirty-nine Articles off by heart, probably aloud.
> MARY STEWART *Touch Not the Cat*, 1976

> Inevitably, his success had encouraged sniping and his detractors claimed that, amongst political turncoats, he made the Vicar of Bray look like a model of constancy.
> MARTIN EDWARDS *Yesterday's Papers*, 1994

Zeus Zeus, the supreme ruler of the Olympian gods in Greek mythology, had many amorous liaisons with goddesses, nymphs, and mortal women. He often disguised himself to accomplish seductions, encountering Danae in the form of a shower of gold, Leda as a swan, and Europa as a bull.

> 'You never slept with Oupa?' I repeat, inanely. 'Yet you had six children.'
> 'Nine. Three died.'
> 'So the Holy Ghost got going on you too?' I say sarcastically.
> 'Like Zeus, the Holy Ghost has been known to assume many shapes.'
> ANDRÉ BRINK *Imaginings of Sand*, 1996

Chaos and Disorder

This theme encompasses both the idea of confusion or chaos and that of disorder or lawlessness. Most of the quotations below express the idea of noisy confusion.

Babel According to the Book of Genesis in the Bible, the descendants of Noah moved to the plain of Shinar where they settled and decided to build a city and a tower, the tower of Babel, 'whose top may reach unto heaven' (Gen. 11: 4). On seeing the tower, God was concerned that man was becoming too powerful and so decided to thwart him by introducing different languages: 'Go to, let us go down, and there confound their language, that they may not understand one another's speech' (Gen. 4: 6–7). Having caused them to be mutually incomprehensible, God then dispersed and scattered them. The Tower of Babel has come to symbolize a noisy confusion of voices or a chaotic mixture of languages.

> Everyone seemed eager to talk at once, and the result was Babel.
> H. G. WELLS *The Invisible Man*, 1897

> The crew's mess on board the Kronos is a Tower of Babel of English, French, Filipino, Danish, and German.
> PETER HØEG *Miss Smilla's Feeling for Snow*, 1992

Bacchante In Greek mythology, the Bacchantes or Maenads were the female devotees of the cult of Dionysus, also known as Bacchus. They took part in frenzied, orgiastic, and ecstatic celebrations at the festivals of Dionysus.

Bedlam Bedlam was the popular name of the Hospital of St Mary of Bethlehem in London, founded as a priory in 1247 at Bishopsgate and by the 14th century a mental hospital. In 1675 a new hospital was built in Moorfields, and this in turn was replaced by a building in the Lambeth Road in 1815 (now the Imperial War Museum) and transferred to Beckenham in Kent in 1931. The word 'Bedlam' now denotes a state of wild disorder or noisy uproar.

> There was a muleteer to every donkey and a dozen volunteers beside, and they banged the donkeys with their goad-sticks, and pricked them with their spikes, and shouted something that sounded like 'Sekki-yah!' and kept up a din and a racket that was worse than Bedlam itself.
> MARK TWAIN *The Innocents Abroad*, 1869

> Their usual scene of operations, Meridian's billiard-room, is tonight rowdy beyond all previous nights, and it has been a Bedlam in the past.
> TIMOTHY MO *An Insular Possession*, 1986

Dionysus In Greek mythology, Dionysus (also called Bacchus) was the son of Zeus and Semele and the god of wine. His cult was celebrated at various festivals throughout the year, some of which included orgies and ecstatic rites. Dionysus, representing creativity, sensuality, and lack of inhibition, is often contrasted with Apollo, representing order, reason, and self-discipline. ▶ *See special entry* ☐ **DIONYSUS** *on p. 117.*

> Wilkie told Marina Yeo that he would create a true Apollonian order from a Dionysiac cacophony.
> A. S. BYATT *The Virgin in the Garden*, 1978

Dodge City Dodge City, in Kansas, USA, had a reputation as a rowdy frontier town until Wyatt Earp became chief deputy marshal in 1876 and introduced order. Dodge City can be alluded to as a place characterized by lawless or unregulated conflict, particularly involving gun fights.

> An 'off-duty' gun. It was the first thing they all did twenty-two years ago, those slick-sleeved, scrubbed, and hard-muscled rookies with their big eyes and crewcuts and bags full of hope. They ran out and bought 'off-duty' guns. Dodge City. The John Wayne syndrome.
> JOSEPH WAMBAUGH *The Glitter Dome*, 1981

Sometimes I don't feel like a very nice person anymore. We grow up with these little, safe notions about the lives we want to lead, the people we want to love, the work we want to do, and how we'll be rewarded for our hard work. Then we get out there in twentieth century urban America and it's Dodge City all over again. The spoils go to the ones with the best aim, the quickest draw, the biggest guns.

STEVEN WOMACK *Dead Folks' Blues*, 1992

Sally handed me the translation of the coded message and looked around. 'I thought there'd be wanted posters on the walls and gun racks filled with shotguns.'

'This isn't Dodge City,' Lula said, 'We got some class here. We keep the guns in the back room with the pervert.'

JANET EVANOVICH *Four to Score*, 1998

wreck of the Hesperus 'The Wreck of the Hesperus' is the title of a poem by H. W. Longfellow (1840), which tells of the destruction of a schooner, the *Hesperus*, which was caught in a storm and wrecked on the reef of Norman's Woe, off the coast of Massachusetts, in 1839.

When he went back to the room it was filled with the slight but offensive smell of face powder and there were clothes everywhere. Miserably, he dressed. 'The wreck of the blasted Hesperus,' he said.

V. S. NAIPAUL *A House for Mr Biswas*, 1961

And he would certainly have said I looked like the Wreck of the Hesperus; it was one of his few literary allusions.

ROBERTSON DAVIES *The Manticore*, 1972

Mad Hatter's Tea Party The Mad Hatter is a character in Lewis Carroll's *Alice's Adventures in Wonderland* (1865) and one of the participants at a strange tea party where the Hatter and the March Hare talk nonsense and the Dormouse falls asleep. ▶ *See special entry* ☐ **ALICE IN WONDERLAND** *on p. 10.*

Staff meetings at Rummidge had been bad enough under Master's whimsically despotic regime. Since his departure they made the Mad Hatter's Tea Party seem like a paradigm of positive decision-making.

DAVID LODGE *Changing Places*, 1975

Maenad ▶ *See* **BACCHANTES**.

Pan In Greek mythology, Pan was a god of nature, fecundity, flocks, and herds, usually represented with the horns, ears, and legs of a goat on a man's body. He lived in Arcadia and was said to be responsible for sudden, irrational fears (the origin of our word 'panic'). His name can also denote general commotion and disorder. News of Pan's death is said to have been brought by a divine voice shouting across the sea to a sailor, Thamus: 'When you reach Palodes, take care to proclaim that the great god Pan is dead!'

Mr Beebe . . . was bidden to collect the factions for the return home. There was a general sense of groping and bewilderment. Pan had been amongst them - not the great god Pan, who has been buried these two thousand years, but the little god Pan, who presides over social contretemps and unsuccessful picnics.

E. M. FORSTER *A Room with a View*, 1908

She sank down on to her knees, on to the carpet of golden leaves and Gordon ran off through the trees, wildly, like a mad disciple of the great god Pan.

KATE ATKINSON *Human Croquet*, 1997

Pandemonium Pandemonium, meaning 'all the demons', was the name given by John Milton to the capital of Hell in his poem *Paradise Lost* (1667). The word 'pandemonium' is usually now applied to a place of utter confusion and uproar.

> It was dreadful to be thus dissevered from his dryad, and sent howling back to a Barchester pandemonium just as the nectar and ambrosia were about to descend on the fields of asphodel.
> ANTHONY TROLLOPE *Barchester Towers*, 1857

Chastity and Virginity

The biblical stories of **DAVID**, **JEPHTHAH'S DAUGHTER**, and **JOSEPH** are each colourful variations on the theme of sexual abstinence.

....

St Agnes St Agnes (d. *c.*304) was a Roman martyr and is the patron saint of virgins. Said to have been a Christian virgin who refused to marry, she was martyred during the reign of Diocletian. Her emblem is a lamb.

Artemis In Greek mythology, Artemis was the twin sister of Apollo and the virgin goddess of chastity, the hunt, and the moon. She was believed to protect virgins and women in childbirth. Diana is her Roman name.

> The purity of his nature, his freedom from the grosser passions, his scrupulous delicacy, had never been fully understood by Grace till this strange self-sacrifice in lonely juxtaposition to her own person was revealed. The perception of it added something that was little short of reverence to the deep affection for him of a woman who, herself, had more of Artemis than of Aphrodite in her constitution.
> THOMAS HARDY *The Woodlanders*, 1887

Britomart ▶ *See* SPENSER.

Daphne Daphne in Greek mythology was a nymph who chose to be turned into a laurel tree to save herself from the amorous pursuit of Apollo. She is often represented in art, for example in Bernini's marble sculpture *Apollo and Daphne* (1622–25).

> A spasm passed through Grace. A Daphnean instinct, exceptionally strong in her as a girl, had been revived by her widowed seclusion; and it was not lessened by her affronted sentiments towards the comer, and her regard for another man.
> THOMAS HARDY *The Woodlanders*, 1887

David In an episode described in the Old Testament, the elderly King David chastely shared his bed with a young woman called Abishag in order that she could warm his body with hers: 'So they . . . found Abishag the Shunammite, and brought her to the king. The damsel was very fair and cherished the king; but the king knew her not' (1 Kgs. 1: 1–4). ▶ *See special entry* □ **DAVID** on p. 90.

> Poor man, he's so sad. His wife dead. I only stayed to comfort him, and he couldn't

anyway. He said he was like King David, and could I just warm him all night.
FAY WELDON *Life Force,* 1992

Jephthah's daughter In the Bible, Jephthah was a judge of Israel who sacrificed his daughter to fulfil a rash vow he had made that if victorious in battle
he would sacrifice the first living thing that he met on his return home. He
consented to her request to go into the mountains to bewail the fact that she
was dying a virgin. At the end of two months, 'she returned to her father, who
did with her according to his vow which he had vowed: and she knew no
man' (Judg. 11).

> 'Well,' said he, 'I will not be too urgent; but the sooner you fix, the more obliging I
> shall think you. Mr Andrews, we must leave something to these Jeptha's daughters,
> in these cases. I suppose, the little bashful folly, which, in the happiest circumstances,
> may give a kind of regret to a thoughtful mind, on quitting the maiden state, is a
> reason with Pamela; and so she shall name her day.'
> SAMUEL RICHARDSON *Pamela,* 1740

Joseph In the Bible, Joseph was a Hebrew patriarch, son of Jacob. A famous
episode took place while he was overseer in the house of Potiphar, an Egyptian
officer. Potiphar's wife tried to seduce him but Joseph repeatedly refused her
advances because of his loyalty to his master. Finally when she found herself
alone in the house with Joseph, she siezed hold of him, saying 'Lie with me'.
Joseph fled from the house, leaving a piece of his clothing in her hand.
Potiphar's wife subsequently made a false accusation that he had attempted to
rape her (Gen. 39). ▶ *See special entry* □ JOSEPH *on p. 224.*

> I don't believe you ever knew what a sore touch it was with Boy that you were such
> a Joseph about women. He felt it put him in the wrong. He always felt that the best
> possible favour you could do a woman was to push her into bed.
> ROBERTSON DAVIES *The Manticore,* 1972

Lysistrata Lysistrata is the heroine of a comic play of the same name by
Aristophanes, first produced in 411 BC. The play was both written and set
during the Peloponnesian War between Athens and her empire and Sparta
and the Peloponnesian states. Lysistrata decides that the men are not serious
about negotiating for peace, so she assembles women from both sides of the
conflict and persuades them to refuse to have sex with their husbands until
there is peace. The play ends with Lysistrata and the women triumphant and
a banquet for both sides in the Acropolis.

> Although she declined an offer to live in a glass coffin in a shark-filled pool, she
> made regular headlines by stunts such as offering sex to striking car workers whose
> wives had adopted Lysistrata tactics to get them back to work.
> *The Guardian,* 1998

Spenser Edmund Spenser (*c.*1552–99) was an English poet, best known for
his allegorical romance *The Faerie Queene* (1590; 1596). In Book III of this
work, Spenser celebrates the courtly virtue of chastity, 'that fairest virtue, far
above the rest', as embodied in the character of Britomart, the female knight of
chastity.

> I get the impression that Trevor believes in a version of Mediaeval Chastitie, sort of
> Spenserian you know.
> MARGARET ATWOOD *The Edible Woman,* 1969

Cinderella

In the fairy story, Cinderella's life is made miserable after her father's remarriage by her stepmother and stepsisters. She is kept in poverty, dressed in rags, and forced to do menial tasks. When her stepsisters go off to a royal ball leaving Cinderella behind, she is found weeping by her fairy godmother, who waves her wand, turning a pumpkin into a coach, six mice into horses to pull it, and a rat into a coachman. Cinderella's rags are turned into beautiful clothes and glass slippers appear on her feet. She is instructed by her fairy godmother to leave the ball by midnight, because on the stroke of midnight her beautiful clothes and coach and horses will revert to their normal forms. At the ball she meets the prince. Rushing away from the ball at the stroke of midnight, she leaves behind a glass slipper. The prince announces that he will marry whoever can wear the slipper, and he eventually discovers that it fits only Cinderella.

Various aspects of the Cinderella story are dealt with throughout the book.

▶ *See* CINDERELLA *at* **Change, Conformity, Poverty,** *and* **Success**
CINDERELLA AND THE PRINCE *at* **Lovers**
UGLY SISTERS *at* **Ugliness** *and* **Vanity**.

Comedy and Humour

Most of the entries below epitomize a particular style of comedy or humour, for example bawdy, surreal, or slapstick. Humourlessness is represented here by QUEEN VICTORIA, famously 'not amused'. ▶ *See also* **Smiles**.

Carry On films The Carry On films were a series of British films, the first of which, *Carry On, Sergeant*, was made in 1958 and the last in 1974. Starring comedians such as Sid James, Kenneth Williams, Barbara Windsor, and Hattie Jacques, the films were characterized by a combination of bawdy humour, bad puns, and slapstick comedy.

Chaucer The poet Geoffrey Chaucer (*c.*1343–1400) is best known for his *Canterbury Tales* (*c.*1387), in which twenty-nine pilgrims who have met at the Tabard inn in Southwark agree to each tell a story to pass the time. The collection's reputation for coarse or ribald humour is based on some of the better-known stories, such as 'The Miller's Tale'.

He could also break wind at will, with a prolonged whining note of complaint, and when he did so in class and then looked around with an angry face, whispering, 'Who done that?' our mirth was Chaucerian, and the teacher was reduced to making a refined face, as if she were too good for a world in which such things were possible.
ROBERTSON DAVIES *Fifth Business*, 1970

Goons *The Goon Show* was an extremely popular BBC radio comedy series which ran from 1952 to 1960. The Goons were originally Peter Sellers, Harry Secombe, Spike Milligan, and Michael Bentine, and the off-beat humour was expressed through a set of regular characters, including Eccles and Bluebottle, who spoke in silly voices and were involved in absurd plots.

Keystone Kops The Keystone Kops were a troupe of film comedians led by Ford Sterling who, between 1912 and 1920, made a number of silent comedies at the Keystone Studios in Hollywood. Dressed in oversized police uniforms, the bumbling Keystone Kops took part in chaotic chase scenes involving daring comic stunts.

Once the Keystone Kops-like operation was in the air, another failing of the Canadian device was noted: it did not adjust well to altitude-induced air pressure differences.
LAURIE GARRETT *Coming Plague*, 1995

Laurel and Hardy Arthur Stanley Jefferson (1890–1965), known as Stan Laurel, and Norvell Hardy Junior (1892–1957), known as Oliver Hardy, became one of the most famous comic film duos of all time. The thin Stan, often looking confused, scratching his head, and bursting into tears, and the fat, blustering, bossy Ollie appeared in many films together from the 1920s until the 1940s, and their simple slapstick humour and disaster-prone adventures have enjoyed enduring popularity.

Marx Brothers The Marx Brothers were a family of American film comedians, consisting of the brothers Chico (Leonard 1886–1961), Harpo (Adolph 1888–1964), Groucho (Julius Henry 1890–1977) and Zeppo (Herbert 1901–79). Their films are characterized by an anarchic humour and madcap zaniness, and include *Duck Soup* (1933) and *A Night at the Opera* (1935).

Monty Python *Monty Python's Flying Circus* was a British TV comedy series which was first broadcast between 1969 and 1974 and is remembered for its combination of satire, bad taste, and surrealist sense of the absurd. Sketches tended either to end abruptly or to run illogically into the next one.

She had only, after all, meant the thing as a sort of English—as a sort of *Monty Python*-esque—joke.
REBECCA GOLDSTEIN *Strange Attractors*, 1993

Rabelais The French writer François Rabelais (c.1494–1553) is chiefly known for his two satires *Pantagruel* and *Gargantua* which, through their larger-than-life characters, express an exuberantly bawdy humour combined with a biting satirical wit and a philosophy of enjoying life to the full.

Married or not, I could fancy Paula, were I prepared to wave goodbye to a modestly

successful career. Early thirties, unmarried, generous curves and a sense of humour that could have stopped Rabelais in his tracks.
RAYMOND FLYNN *A Public Body*, 1996

What disturbs us is ageing *women* having children. There's something ribald, Rabelaisian, about old fathers—'a man is as old as the woman he feels', as Groucho Marx put it—while old mothers are seen as selfish and unnatural.
The Observer, 1997

Thalia Thalia was the Muse of comedy in Greek mythology.

Queen Victoria The famous line 'We are not amused' is attributed to Queen Victoria (1819-1901) in Caroline Holland's *Notebooks of a Spinster Lady* (1919), though whether she actually uttered these words is not at all certain. The quotation is so well known, though, that Queen Victoria can be alluded to in the context of a lack of a sense of humour or an inability to see the funny side of a situation.

His smile was wide, about three-quarters of an inch. 'I don't amuse easy', he said. 'Just like Queen Victoria', I said.
RAYMOND CHANDLER *The High Window*, 1943

Communication

This theme covers various aspects of communication, from the ability to interpret messages from the gods to the inability to communicate encapsulated in the story of the **TOWER OF BABEL**. ▶ *See also* **Messengers**, **Oratory**.

Babel ▶ *See* **TOWER OF BABEL**.

Delphic Oracle Delphi was one of the most important religious sites in the ancient Greek world. It was the seat of the Delphic Oracle, which was consulted on a wide range of religious, political, and moral questions and whose answers, delivered in a state of ecstasy by the priestess known as the Pythia, were often ambiguous and riddle-like.

She could utter oracles of Delphian ambiguity when she did not choose to be direct.
THOMAS HARDY *The Return of the Native*, 1880

She had a turn for improvising and phrasing ambiguous but startling messages that

would have done credit to the Oracle at Delphi.
ROBERTSON DAVIES *Fifth Business*, 1970

This really is very pleasant—to escape. I'm not sure why it is, but I find that a roomful of 'scholars' tends to bring on an attack of mental indigestion. That Delphic tone they love to take. And something chilly and unhelpful about them too.
CAROL SHIELDS *Mary Swann*, 1990

Doctor Dolittle Doctor Dolittle is the hero of a series of children's books written by Hugh Lofting, the first of which, *The Story of Doctor Dolittle*, was published in 1920. An animal-lover who changes from being a doctor of people to a doctor of animals, John Dolittle is taught the language of animals by his parrot, Polynesia, and learns to communicate with all animals.

McLuhan Marshall McLuhan (1911–80) was a Canadian writer and thinker who was particularly interested in the ways in which different communication media affect societies. He claimed that electronic forms of communication had turned the world into a 'global village'. McLuhanite openness is thus complete openness and good communication.

Sibyl The Sibyls were prophetesses in ancient Greece. They included the Cumaean Sibyl who guided Aeneas through the underworld. Sibyls gave their prophecies in an ecstatic state, when they were believed to be possessed by a god, and their utterances were often ambiguous and riddle-like.

When Ken Cracknell asked me about our strategy, I would utter such Sibylline phrases as 'I propose to play it largely by ear', or 'Sufficient unto the day, my dear fellow', or 'Let's just deny everything and then see where we go from there'.
JOHN MORTIMER *Rumpole's Return*, 1980

Tower of Babel According to the Book of Genesis in the Bible, the descendants of Noah decided to build a city and a tower, the tower of Babel, 'whose top may reach unto heaven' (Gen. 11: 4). On seeing the tower, God was concerned that man was becoming too powerful and so decided to thwart him by introducing different languages: 'Go to, let us go down, and there confound their language, that they may not understand one another's speech' (Gen. 4:6–7). Having caused the people to be mutually incomprehensible, God then dispersed and scattered them. The story can be mentioned in the context of linguistic diversity, particularly when this severely hampers communication.

'This is the original Tower of Babel', Harris said. 'West Indians, Africans, real Indians, Syrians, Englishmen, Scotsmen in the office of Works, Irish priests, French priests, Alsatian priests'.
GRAHAM GREENE *The Heart of the Matter*, 1948

writing on the wall Belshazzar, King of Babylon, gave a great banquet for 1,000 of his lords (Dan. 5: 1–28). During the banquet they drank from goblets taken from the temple and praised the gods of gold, silver, bronze, iron, wood, and stone. Suddenly the fingers of a human hand appeared and wrote on the wall the words 'Mene, Mene, Tekel, Upharsin'. Daniel translated the words, explaining to Belshazzar that his reign was over, that he had been weighed in the balance and found wanting, and that his kingdom would be divided and given to the Medes and the Persians. ▶ *See special entry* □ **DANIEL** *on p. 86.*

Complexity

The idea of complexity illustrated within this theme is generally a somewhat negative one, viewed as either unnecessary (**RUBE GOLDBERG, HEATH ROBINSON**) or sinister (**BYZANTINE, LABYRINTH**). The entry for **BACH** demonstrates a more admiring view.

Ariadne In Greek mythology, Ariadne was the daughter of King Minos of Crete and Pasiphae. She fell in love with Theseus and helped him escape from the labyrinth of the Minotaur by giving him a ball of thread, which he unravelled as he went in and followed back to find his way out again after killing the Minotaur. Such a ball of thread used to be called a clew, and it is from this idea of its being used to trace a path through a maze (and by extension being applied to anything that guides through perplexity, a difficult investigation, etc.) that we derive the modern word 'clue'. ▶ *See also* **LABYRINTH**.

> Her body muffled in furs, her heart muffled like her steps, and the pain of living muffled as by the deepest rich carpets, while the thread of Ariadne which led everywhere, right and left, like scattered footsteps in the snow, tugged and pulled within her memory and she began to pull upon this thread . . . as one pulls upon a spool, and she heard the empty wooden spool knock against the floor of different houses.
> ANAÏS NIN *Children of the Albatross*, 1947

Bach Johann Sebastian Bach (1685-1750) was a German composer and organist, the outstanding representative of German baroque music. Bach was a master of counterpoint and developed the fugue form (in which a succession of parts or voices are interwoven) to a high art.

> The music of our Lord's skin sliding over His flesh!—more exact than the fugues of Bach.
> NATHANAEL WEST *The Dream Life of Balso Snell*, 1931

Byzantine The Byzantine Empire between the 4th and 15th centuries was characterized by highly ritualized politics and complex bureaucratic structures. The word 'Byzantine' has therefore come to be used to mean extremely convoluted and devious.

> Now they saw each other a dozen times a month, if that. Their schedules created Byzantine complications of timing.
> BARBARA PARKER *Suspicion of Guilt*, 1995

> [They are] trying to cut 'bureaucracy' and claw power away from the Byzantine layers of local education administration.
> *The Observer*, 1997

Escher M. C. Escher (1902-72) was a Dutch graphic artist, whose prints often exploit puzzling visual paradoxes and illusions. Many of his works play with perspective to create examples of impossible architecture. One of his most famous images is the lithograph *Ascending and Descending* (1960), in which hooded figures endlessly walk up (or down) a staircase.

The house was taking on the appearance of an Escher drawing—lots of steps leading nowhere.
FAYE KELLERMAN *Sanctuary*, 1994

Rube Goldberg Reuben Goldberg (1883–1970) was a US comic strip artist known for his drawings of ludicrously complex machinery designed to perform simple everyday tasks. His name has become a byword for any unnecessarily complicated and inefficient machine, structure, or system.

Orchids are Rube Goldberg machines; a perfect engineer would certainly have come up with something better.
STEPHEN JAY GOULD *Ever Since Darwin*, 1978

Gordian knot Gordius was a peasant who was chosen King of Phrygia, whereupon he tied the pole of his wagon to the yoke with an intricate knot. An oracle prophesied that whoever undid it would become the ruler of all Asia. Alexander the Great is said to have simply cut through the knot with his sword. Hence a 'Gordian knot' is a complex problem or task.

One can only guess at the purposes of our Creator, in fashioning of Humanity such a complex and Gordian knot.
MARGARET ATWOOD *Alias Grace*, 1996

Heath Robinson William Heath Robinson (1872–1944) was an English cartoonist who drew humorous cartoons of absurdly ingenious and complicated machines which performed simple everyday tasks. Like that of Rube Goldberg, his name has become synonymous with any device or system that seems unnecessarily complicated.

You remember that kid's game, Mousetrap? That ludicrous Heath Robinson machine you had to build, where silver balls went down chutes, and little men went up ladders, and one thing knocked into another to set off something else, until in the end the cage fell on to the mouse and trapped it?
NICK HORNBY *High Fidelity*, 1995

Labyrinth In Greek legend, the Labyrinth was a huge maze constructed by Daedalus at Knossus (also Cnossos or Cnossus) in Crete for King Minos. It was designed as a home for the Minotaur, a creature with a man's body and a bull's head. The Labyrinth was such a complex network of passages and chambers that it was thought no one could escape from it. The term can be applied to any intricate or complicated arrangement. ▶ *See also* **ARIADNE**.

Such an elaborately developed, perplexing, exciting dream was certainly never dreamed by a girl in Eustacia's situation before. It had as many ramifications as the Cretan labyrinth, as many fluctuations as the Northern Lights, as much colour as a parterre in June, and was as crowded with figures as a coronation.
HERMAN MELVILLE *Moby Dick*, 1851

The pattern of His veins!—more intricate than the Maze at Cnossos.
NATHANAEL WEST *The Dream Life of Balso Snell*, 1931

She remembered the sadness she had earlier noticed in his eyes. He was a man who had known both good and evil. She was sure of it now. His mind was a dark labyrinth, intricate and convoluted, with a Minotaur of some kind crouching at the core. There was something frightening as well as fascinating about him.
JOHN SPENCER HILL *The Last Castrato*, 1995

Concealment

This theme addresses the notion of concealing one's presence, identity, or intentions. It includes a trio of famously masked men, the **LONE RANGER**, the **MAN IN THE IRON MASK**, and **ZORRO**. ▶ *See also* **Disclosure, Disguise, Mystery.**

....

Ali Baba In the story of *Ali Baba and the Forty Thieves* (one of the stories in the *Arabian Nights*), the captain of the forty thieves conceals his men in leather oil jars outside the house of Ali Baba, intending to kill him during the night.

> Blue Ali Baba oil jars were dotted around, big enough to keep tigers.
> RAYMOND CHANDLER *The Lady in the Lake*, 1943

Black Hander The name Black Hand has been used by a number of secret societies, most notably a group of terrorists and blackmailers, composed mainly of Sicilians active in the United States in the late 19th and early 20th centuries. The name was also used for a secret society which aimed at the unification of the southern Slavs at the beginning of the 20th century.

> He became the Black Hander once more. He looked this way and he looked that. He peeped hither and peered thither. Then he lowered his voice to such a whisper that I couldn't hear a damn word.
> P. G. WODEHOUSE *Laughing Gas*, 1936

Arthur Dimmesdale The Reverend Arthur Dimmesdale is a character in Nathaniel Hawthorne's *The Scarlet Letter* (1850). A young and much-respected church minister, he keeps secret the fact that he is the father of Hester Prynne's illegitimate baby while she is ostracized by the community and condemned to wear a scarlet 'A', for 'adulteress', on her bosom. Hester's husband, under the assumed name of Roger Chillingworth, discovers his secret and tortures him mentally with it until he finally confesses publicly and dies in Hester's arms.

> In all, the doctor he reminded me of most was Dr. Roger Chillingworth in Hawthorne's *Scarlet Letter*. Appropriate enough, because I sat facing him as full of shameful secrets as the Reverend Arthur Dimmesdale.
> PHILIP ROTH *My Life as a Man*, 1970

Lone Ranger The Lone Ranger is a masked law-enforcer in the American West, created in 1933 by George W. Trendle and Fran Striker for a radio series and popularized in a later TV series (1956–62). His true identity remains concealed and he is known only as the 'masked man' or 'masked rider'.

Polonius In Shakespeare's play *Hamlet* (1604), Polonius is the court chamberlain who hides behind an arras (a tapestry screen) in Gertrude's bedchamber to eavesdrop on Hamlet's conversation with the queen. Hamlet, believing it is the King, Claudius, he can hear behind the arras, runs his sword through it and mistakenly stabs Polonius to death.

Mrs Rochester During the course of Charlotte Brontë's *Jane Eyre* (1847), it is revealed that the existence of the 'insane' wife of Edward Rochester has been kept secret and that she has been kept in seclusion in an upper room at Thornfield Hall. The early life of Bertha Rochester is imagined by Jean Rhys in her novel *Wide Sargasso Sea* (1966).

> 'You saw her once, didn't you?' said Nancy. 'That's right. I just happened to look up and caught her peering at me from an upper window, like the first Mrs Rochester or something, though she kept well back from the window.'
> SUSAN MOODY *The Italian Garden*, 1994

Zorro Zorro is the masked hero of Hollywood films of the 1930s to 1960s, who first appeared in a comic strip in 1919. In reality he is Don Diego de la Vega, a member of a wealthy Spanish family, but his true identity remains a secret and in his disguise as Zorro (The Fox) he rights wrongs and protects the weak, leaving as his calling-card a letter Z cut into the clothing or body of his enemies.

> Milo knocked softly just before midnight. He was carrying a hard-shell case the size of an attaché and had on a polo shirt, twill pants, and windbreaker. All in black. Regular-guy parody of the L.A. hipster ensemble. I said, 'Trying to fade into the night, Zorro?'
> JONATHAN KELLERMAN *Devil's Waltz*, 1993

Conflict

Disagreement or conflict is often suggested in terms of a feud (**BORGIAS, MONTAGUES AND CAPULETS**) or a quarrel (**APPLE OF DISCORD, PUNCH AND JUDY**). ▶ *See also* **Enemy, Hatred**.

Apple of Discord The Apple of Discord was a golden apple marked with the words 'for the fairest' that Eris, the Greek goddess of discord, threw among the guests at the wedding of Peleus and Thetis, causing disagreement between three goddesses, Hera, Athene, and Aphrodite. The goddesses asked Paris to judge which of them was the fairest and Aphrodite won the contest by offering him Helen of Troy as a bribe. Paris's abduction of Helen led to the Trojan War.
▶ *See special entry* ▢ **TROJAN WAR** *on p. 392.*

> Macedonia . . . became the apple of discord between the newly forming nation-states that were destined to replace the Ottoman Empire.
> *New York Review of Books*, 1995

Big-Endians and Little-Endians In Jonathan Swift's *Gulliver's Travels* (1726) the Big-Endians are a group of people in Lilliput who believe that eggs should be broken at the big end rather than at the little end, as commanded by the Emperor of Lilliput. The Big-Endians have taken refuge in the neighbouring land of Blefuscu, and as a result of this disagreement Lilliput and Blefuscu have 'been engaged in a most obstinate war for six and thirty moons past'.

Borgias The Borgias were a Neapolitan family with Spanish origins. Alfonso de Borgia (1378–1458) became Pope as Calixtus III in 1455 and his nephew, Rodrigo, succeeded him as Alexander VI in 1492. Cesare and Lucrezia (or Lucretia) Borgia were two of Alexander's children, born before he became Pope. Cesare was suspected of murdering his brother and killed his sister's second husband, Alfonso of Aragon. The Borgias have acquired a popular reputation for treachery, incest, and using poison to dispose of enemies.

> All cabinets are riddled with frictions, but this lot seem to be consumed with more feuds than the Borgias, and to have a similar penchant for poisoning as the preferred method of bumping off rivals.
> *The Observer*, 1997

Eris Eris was the Greek goddess of discord. ▶ *See* **APPLE OF DISCORD**.

Montagues and Capulets The Montagues and the Capulets are warring Veronese families in Shakespeare's *Romeo and Juliet* (1599). Juliet is a Capulet and Romeo a Montague, and their love and secret marriage are doomed when Romeo reluctantly becomes embroiled in the bitter hatred and fighting between the families.

> And they were freighted, apparently, with an internal feud of Montague and Capulet proportions.
> *Post (Denver)*, 1994

> I told them I liked it when things were vast and made of iron. And I described a courtyard I went into where there was an iron girder strung between two houses. It seemed to be holding the two buildings apart, as if one was the Capulet house and the other was the house of the Montagues.
> ROSE TREMAIN *The Way I Found Her*, 1998

Punch and Judy Punch and Judy are characters in a traditional English seaside puppet show presented to children on a stage in a collapsible booth. Punch strangles his baby, is beaten by his wife whom he then beats to death, and has various violent encounters with other characters including a doctor and a policeman.

> That was how they came to find themselves together on a journey which threw up a sort of ludicrous shadow-image of a love-relationship, like a clever magic-lantern picture of a landscape, created by, strangely—not Justine at all—but a worse mischief-maker—the novelist himself. 'It was Punch and Judy all right!' said Pursewarden ruefully afterwards.
> LAWRENCE DURRELL *Balthazar*, 1958

> Edie Iden . . . was built on the same substantial lines as her husband. She came through from the shut public bar to take up position leaning on the bar beside Charlie, and rest her bosom on her forearms. Jonathan Cade, drinking his coffee a yard away in the empty lounge, pictured Mr Punch bobbing up beside them to crack a cudgel across their heads. Edie even sounded, with her breathy squeak, like someone in a puppet show.
> STAYNES AND STOREY *Dead Serious*, 1995

Conformity

Different aspects of conformity are expressed here, from the unquestioning obedience of the **STEPFORD WIVES** to the strict compliance with rules, instructions, or standards suggested by **CINDERELLA**'s clock striking midnight or **PROCRUSTES**' bed. ▶ *See also* **Rebellion and Disobedience, Nonconformity**.

....

Cinderella In the traditional fairy story, Cinderella is instructed by her fairy godmother to leave the royal ball by midnight, because on the stroke of midnight her beautiful clothes and coach and horses that the fairy godmother has magically transformed for her will revert to their normal forms. This aspect of the story is sometimes mentioned in the context of an instruction that must be followed precisely, or more specifically when referring to a late-night deadline that must be adhered to. ▶ *See special entry* ☐ CINDERELLA *on p. 56.*

> Quarter of an hour to midnight. Poor Cinderella. I must get my father home before the clock strikes or he'll lose his beauty-sleep.
> LAWRENCE DURRELL *Balthazar,* 1958

> [The house] had a triple garage and hard-standing for half a dozen cars, but tonight was clearly party night. Richard's hot pink Volkswagen Beetle convertible looked as out of place as Cinderella at a minute past midnight.
> VAL MCDERMID *Clean Break,* 1995

Gradgrind Thomas Gradgrind is the chief character in Dickens's *Hard Times* (1854). He believes in 'facts and calculations', thinking he is following the precepts of utilitarianism. He brings these principles to the task of raising his five children, ruling out their imagination and creativity. A 'Gradgrind' is thus someone who adheres too strictly to a set of rules or principles.

> Obviously the ideal of education for its own sake, which is at the heart of every civilised society, will suffer as businesses demand a utilitarian curriculum. No business believes poets are more important than accountants. The loss would matter less if the new Gradgrinds were providing Britain with coherent and demanding vocational education to replace the widely ridiculed NVQs.
> *The Observer,* 1997

> Women and children—especially in one-parent families—haven't had a lot to cheer about since the Government began its Gradgrind benefits review.
> *The Big Issue,* 1998

Pavlov Ivan Petrovich Pavlov (1849–1936) was a Russian physiologist and director of the Institute of Experimental Medicine in St Petersburg, winning a Nobel prize for work on digestion in 1904. He is best known for his later work on conditioned reflexes using dogs. He showed that, by linking food with the sound of a bell over a period of time, the salivation response associated with food could become a conditioned response to the sound of the bell alone.

Pavlov's dogs have come to stand for automatic or unconscious obedience to a signal, while a Pavlovian response is any automatic unthinking response.

> The shop-bell rang and, behaving exactly like a Pavlov dog, Stamp got up and began, elaborately, to put on his coat.
> KEITH WATERHOUSE *Billy Liar*, 1959

> Obviously continual response to the music had developed within them an almost Pavlovian response to the noise, a response which they believed was pleasure.
> JOHN KENNEDY TOOLE *A Confederacy of Dunces*, 1980

> I've obviously got some sort of Pavlov reflex to men. . . . If a bloke asks me the time of day often enough, after a while I only have to look at my watch to imagine myself saying 'I do' and driving a Volvo estate filled with children dressed in Baby Gap clothes.
> ARABELLA WEIR *Does My Bum Look Big in This*, 1997

Procrustes In Greek mythology, Procrustes was a brigand who forced travellers who fell into his hands to lie on an iron bed. If they were longer than the bed, he cut off the overhanging length of leg; if they were shorter than the bed, he stretched them until they fitted it. He was eventually killed by Theseus, who attached him to his own bed and then, as he was too long for it, cut off his head. References to Procrustes usually suggest someone who attempts to enforce uniformity or conformity by forceful or ruthless methods. The adjective 'Procrustean' comes from his name.

> I do not say that people don't judge their neighbours' conduct, sometimes, doubtlessly, unfairly. But I do say that there is no unvarying conventional set of rules by which people are judged; no bed of Procrustes to stretch or cramp their minds and lives.
> WILLIAM MORRIS *News From Nowhere*, 1886

> Procrustes in modern dress, the nuclear scientist will prepare the bed on which mankind must lie.
> ALDOUS HUXLEY *Brave New World*, 1946

Stepford Wives *The Stepford Wives* is the title of a film made in 1974, based on a book by Ira Levin, which tells the story of a young couple who move into the commuter village of Stepford, near New York. The wife is shocked that the other wives she meets are interested only in trivial domestic issues and in serving their husbands' needs, to the point that they seem incapable of even thinking about anything else. It gradually emerges that the men of the village, in their chauvinistic search for ideal wives, have in fact killed their real wives and replaced them with androids programmed to behave in this way. A 'Stepford wife' is therefore a dutiful wife who is mindlessly devoted to the minutiae of domestic life and blindly obeys her husband, seeming to have no mind or wishes of her own. More generally, the term can be applied to anyone who unthinkingly supports another person or behaves according to a set pattern.

> She went off without a word, as obedient and unquestioning as a Stepford wife.
> RICHARD HALEY *Thoroughfare of Stones*, 1995

> He leaned over and kissed me. 'Mmmmmm, you smell nice,' then offered me a cigarette. 'No thank you, I have found inner poise and given up smoking,' I said, in a pre-programmed, Stepford Wife sort of way, wishing Daniel wasn't quite so attractive when you found yourself alone with him.
> HELEN FIELDING *Bridget Jones's Diary*, 1996

Courage

There are two main groupings within this theme: individuals who cour-ageously face a dangerous situation (**DANIEL, HORATIUS**) and examples of valiant defences (**ALAMO, THERMOPYLAE**), especially against overwhelming odds. ▶ *See also* **Cowardice, Danger**.

Alamo The Alamo was a fort (formerly a Christian mission) in San Antonio, Texas, which in 1836 was besieged by the Mexican army during the war between Texas and Mexico. It was defended by a small group of soldiers and civilians all of whom (including the frontiersman and politician Davy Crockett) died. The phrase 'Remember the Alamo' was later used as a rallying-cry by the Texan army.

Bunker Hill Bunker Hill in Boston was the site of the first pitched battle of the American Revolution in 1775, where the American colonists were forced to retreat by superior British weaponry. Although the victory was British, the colonists' tenacity and the losses they inflicted on the British boosted the Americans' morale.

Gary Cooper The American film actor Gary Cooper (1901–61) is often associ-ated with his role as the small-town marshal Will Kane in the film *High Noon* (1952). In an iconic scene at the climax of the film, Cooper walks alone down the street to confront several outlaws single-handedly.

> As I passed along the bar the men on the stools eyed me narrowly, then fidgeted uneasily in their seats. I felt like Gary Cooper making that solitary walk down Main Street.
> SARA PARETSKY *Tunnel Vision*, 1994

Custer's last stand George Armstrong Custer (1839–76) was an American cavalry general who was sent to Dakota to protect gold miners and railway surveyors against the Sioux after gold had been found in what had been Sioux tribal lands. In 1876, while scouting, his regiment, the 7th cavalry, came upon a large encampment of Sioux and Cheyenne in the Little Bighorn valley in southern Montana. Custer and his men were surrounded and killed by the Sioux under their leader, Sitting Bull, in a battle subsequently known as 'Custer's last stand'.

> 'If I sneak out of here before the debt is paid off, I won't be worth a goddamned thing to myself.' 'Custer's last stand.' 'That's it. The old put-up-or-shut-up routine.'
> PAUL AUSTER *Music of Chance*, 1990

Daniel In the Bible, Daniel was a Hebrew prophet and interpreter of dreams and visions who spent his life in captivity with the Jewish people in Babylon. When, after a successful career, he was appointed sole administrator over various princes and other administrators, they plotted to have him thrown into the lions' den. Daniel was sealed into the den and left for the night but in the morning was discovered by the King, unscathed. Daniel explained 'My God hath sent his angel, and hath shut the lions' mouths, that they have not hurt me' (Dan. 6: 22). Daniel has come to represent the courage of someone who faces great danger alone without any material protection. ▶ *See special entry* □ **DANIEL** *on p. 86.*

> Don't you feel like Daniel setting off for the lion's den, going back there? If you really think one of the Fontclairs is a murderer, how can you sit down to dinner with them, sleep under their roof?
> KATE ROSS *Cut to the Quick*, 1993

> He watched her walk firmly towards the Incident Room, where all lights were on. At the entrance, she turned and waved. She wouldn't be welcome in that room, as she well knew. Daniel into the lion's den.
> JENNIE MELVILLE *Baby Drop*, 1994

Dunkirk Dunkirk (Dunkerque) is a port on the north French coast from where over 335,000 Allied soldiers were evacuated under German fire during the Second World War by a mixture of naval and ordinary civilian vessels. Although from a military point of view this represented a defeat, the soldiers having been forced to retreat to the shore, Dunkirk is remembered by the British as something of a triumph and the 'Dunkirk spirit' has come to refer to a stubborn refusal to admit defeat no matter how dangerous or difficult the circumstances.

> Technical lighting and electronic glitches reduced Glyndebourne's new smash hit to a concert performance, in costume, against plain black drapes, relying on music, text and everybody's Dunkirk spirit.
> *The Oxford Times*, 1994

> The Metro was crowded but a Dunkirk spirit reigned. On personal observation, passengers were unusually polite to one another and almost chatty.
> *The Independent*, 1997

Greatheart Greatheart, a character in Part 2 of *Pilgrim's Progress* by John Bunyan (1684), escorts and guards Christiana and her children on their pilgrimage. He slays Giant Despair and overcomes various other monsters.

> He may be stern; he may be exacting; he may be ambitious yet; but his is the sternness of the warrior Greatheart, who guards his pilgrim convoy from the onslaught of Apollyon.
> CHARLOTTE BRONTË *Jane Eyre*, 1847

Horatius Horatius Cocles (530–500 BC) was a Roman hero who volunteered to be one of the last three defenders of a bridge over the Tiber river against an Etruscan army under Lars Porsena intent on invading Rome. Initally, he and two others, Herminius and Lartius, fought on the bank while the Roman army crossed back to Rome and prepared to destroy the bridge. His companions darted across to Rome just before the bridge fell but Horatius swam back across the Tiber in full armour. The story of Horatius' defence of the bridge is retold in the poem 'Horatius at the Bridge' in *Lays of Ancient Rome* (1842) by Macaulay.

> To the abuse in front and the coaxing behind she was equally indifferent. How long she would have stood like a glorified Horatius, keeping the staircase at both ends, was never to be known. For the young lady whose sleep they were disturbing awoke, and opened her bedroom door, and came out onto the landing.
> E. M. FORSTER *Where Angels Fear to Tread*, 1905

Perhaps I would have taken the easy way. I am only a man, but Carlo was like one of those heroes in our old stories, like Horatius Cocles, or whoever it was who held the bridge of Porsenna [sic] against a whole army.
LOUIS DE BERNIÈRES *Captain Corelli's Mandolin*, 1994

But who will be the brave Horatio in the House of Commons and move the Bill and seek the support and withstand the hounding that could well come from the press, and the scolding that might proceed from Their Lordships and Their Ladyships and the full gale force 10 of the Brits in a high puff of morality?
The Independent, 1996

Little Dutch boy The tale of the little Dutch boy is recounted as a story entitled 'The Hero of Haarlem' in Mary Mapes Dodge's children's classic *Hans Brinker or the Silver Skates* (1865). The boy is returning from a visit when he hears the sound of trickling water and sees a small hole in the dyke. He climbs up the dyke and plugs the hole with his finger in order to stop it becoming enlarged and leading to flooding. The boy undergoes a terrible ordeal alone all night and unable to move before being rescued and relieved at daybreak the following morning.

'Watch. Call me if you see anybody. Don't let them wander by, Howard. Don't let them get lost.' The crew boss made it sound as if he was addressing Horatio on the bridge or the little boy with his finger in the dike.
NEVADA BARR *Firestorm*, 1996

But now that president sometimes looks rather like the boy with his hand in the dyke, behind which the water is building up pressure.
The Observer, 1997

Mafeking Mafeking (now Mafikeng) is a town in South Africa which was attacked by Boers at the start of the Boer War. It was defended by British troops during a seven month siege before they were relieved by the British army. The success of the defence was a boost to national morale at a time when the course of the war was turning against the British.

Thermopylae Thermopylae was a narrow pass in ancient Greece which was along the main route into southern Greece taken by armies invading from the north and consequently an important site for defence. The most famous battle fought at the pass was between invading Persians, commanded by Xerxes, and an army of approximately 6,000 Greeks, including 300 Spartans, under the leadership of Leonidas, King of Sparta. The Persians found an alternative mountain pass and were able to come upon the Greeks from behind. Many of the Greek allies departed before the battle but Leonidas, his Spartans, and many Thespians and Thebans died in defence of the pass. Simonides' epitaph on the battle read:

'Go, tell the Spartans, thou who passest by,
That here obedient to their laws we lie.'

He would much prefer not to die. He would abandon a hero's or a martyr's end gladly. He did not want to make a Thermopylae, not be Horatius at any bridge, nor be the Dutch boy with his finger in that dyke.
ERNEST HEMINGWAY *For Whom the Bell Tolls*, 1941

He shivered and then stood erect. He had made a decision; it would be another Thermopylae. If three hundred Spartans could hold out against five million of the

bravest Persians, what could he not achieve with twenty divisions against the Italians?
LOUIS DE BERNIÈRES *Captain Corelli's Mandolin*, 1994

Cowardice

Cowardice is typically revealed behind a front of bluster or belligerence.
▶ *See also* **Courage**, **Fear**.

....

Bob Acres Bob Acres is a ridiculous but mild character in Sheridan's *The Rivals* (1775) who believes himself to be a rival for the hand of Lydia Languish. He is persuaded to fight a duel with her preferred suitor but on his arrival at the location for the fight his courage disappears rapidly, 'oozing out at the palms of his hands'.

> 'If you are busy, another time will do as well', continued the bishop, whose courage like Bob Acres' had oozed out, now that he found himself on the ground of battle.
> ANTHONY TROLLOPE *Barchester Towers*, 1857

Cowardly Lion The Cowardly Lion is one of the companions of Dorothy in her journey to find Oz in the children's story *The Wizard of Oz* by L. Frank Baum (1900). The lion roars very loudly to frighten other creatures away and to disguise the fact that he is scared of them himself. He hopes that the Wizard of Oz will give him courage, although, in fact, he acts bravely to protect his companions throughout their travels.

> Mr. Perot transformed a tale about fistfights during a union-certification campaign (which the union won) into the 20th-century equivalent of the Haymarket riot. This small-minded appeal to jingoism not only batters facts, it also makes the U.S. look like the Cowardly Lion of world politics.
> *New York Times*, 1993

Scaramouch Scaramouch (literally 'skirmish') was a stock character in old Italian farce, portrayed as a cowardly braggart. He was usually represented as a Spanish don, wearing a black costume.

> He swore no scaramouch of an Italian robber would dare to meddle with an Englishman.
> WASHINGTON IRVING *Tales of a Traveller*, 1824

Craftsmen

The makers, builders, and inventors listed below are all drawn from classical mythology. Of these, the figure most strongly associated with the idea of craftsmanship is probably **DAEDALUS**. ▶ *See also* **Sculptors**.

....

Argus In Greek mythology, Argus was the craftsman who built the ship, *Argo*, on which Jason and the Argonauts voyaged to recover the Golden Fleece. ▶ *See special entry* ☐ **JASON AND THE ARGONAUTS** *on p. 220*.

Athene Athene (also called Pallas Athene) was the Greek goddess of wisdom, and also the patroness of arts and crafts, especially spinning and weaving. She is identified with the Roman goddess Minerva.

Daedalus In Greek mythology, Daedalus was an Athenian craftsman. He fled from Athens to Crete after jealously killing his pupil Talos, whose skills threatened to outdo his own. In the service of King Minos of Crete, Daedalus designed and built the labyrinth in which the Minotaur was kept. When Minos later refused to allow him to leave Crete, he escaped by making wings for himself and his son, Icarus. Although Daedalus escaped and flew to safety, Icarus flew too high and the sun melted the wax holding his wings together, so that he plunged to his death. Daedalus can be alluded to as a clever craftsman or maker of clever or complicated devices.

> It was a dirty reeking room into which we entered, with men and women idling upon stools and cushions—I know not if Daedalus would have made a labyrinth for such monsters.
> PETER ACKROYD *The House of Dr Dee*, 1993

Epeius In Greek mythology, Epeius, a skilled craftsman, built the Trojan Horse with the help of Athene. ▶ *See special entry* ☐ **TROJAN WAR** *on p. 392*.

Hephaestus ▶ *See* **VULCAN**.

Minerva In Roman mythology, Minerva was the goddess of arts and crafts, identified with the Greek Athene.

> She started the pen in an elephantine march across the sheet. It was a splendid round, bold hand of her own conception, a style that would have stamped a woman as Minerva's own in more recent days.
> THOMAS HARDY *The Mayor of Casterbridge*, 1886

Vulcan Vulcan was the Roman god of fire and metalworking, identified with the Greek Hephaestus. He is said to have made Pandora (the first woman on earth), the thunderbolts of Zeus, and the armour of Achilles. Vulcan is often depicted at the forge.

> A Vulcan guarding the flames, he gives us instructions about which doors to keep closed or opened for proper distribution of heat, lays kindling by, discusses qualities of coal, and teaches us how to rake, feed, and bank the fire.
> TONI MORRISON *The Bluest Eye*, 1970

Criminals

The figures below are thieves, robbers, and gangsters. Other criminals are covered at the themes **Murderers** and **Outlaws**. ▶ *See also* **Evil**.

....

Al Capone Al (Alphonse) Capone (1899–1947) was notorious for his involvement in organized crime in Chicago in the 1920s. Though it was never possible to find sufficient evidence to convict him of his crimes, he was eventually imprisoned in 1931 for tax evasion. Capone died in prison.

> The Greek's muscles were dough-colored. You wouldn't have wanted him to take a headlock on you. That's the kind of man the Organization hired. The Capone people were now in charge.
> SAUL BELLOW *Something to Remember Me By*, 1991

> 'There's no shortage of smart operators like Heriot 07 who get what they can from the city. They cover their arses. If they're spotted, they pay people off. Or arrange a good kicking.' 'Sounds like Chicago under Al Capone.'
> PAUL JOHNSTON *Body Politic*, 1997

Arthur Daley Arthur Daley was a character in the ITV series *Minder* (1979–94), a shady wheeler-dealer always full of schemes to make money quickly, usually involving selling goods of dubious origin. Daley always managed to avoid being arrested, but never actually made any money from his schemes.

> Burglars are being encouraged by the public's 'Arthur Daley' mentality to crime and willingness to turn a blind eye to stolen goods, one of Britain's most senior police officers said yesterday.
> *The Independent*, 1994

John Dillinger John Dillinger (1903–34) was an armed bank robber based in Indiana, named the FBI's 'public enemy number one' in 1933. He was shot dead by FBI agents in Chicago acting on information given by his girlfriend, now popularly known as the 'Lady in Red'.

> 'You always wanted it that way, Jess. You changing your mind?' 'No. It's just . . . ' He sighed. 'Spring.' 'Don't feel bad. It turns even the best of us to mush.' 'Leave it to Tark—more Diogenes than Dillinger these days—to understand that.'
> MEG O'BRIEN *Eagles Die Too*, 1993

Fagin In Charles Dickens's novel *Oliver Twist* (1838), Fagin is the leader of the gang of pickpockets into whose hands the runaway Oliver falls.

> When I tried to shoo them away one of them knocked my hat off, while another deftly snatched out of my hand the carrier bag containing my new jacket . . . I did not care about the jacket . . . but I would have liked to see where those girls would go. I imagined a lean-to made of rags and bits of galvanised iron on a dusty patch of waste ground . . . Or perhaps there was a Fagin somewhere waiting for them, skulking in the shadows in some derelict tenement.
> JOHN BANVILLE *The Book of Evidence*, 1989

> Of course this is true. All good writers, if they are honest, will acknowledge that

when they come across a good thing in someone else's work, either consciously or unconsciously they store it away for the day when inspiration fails. And if writers are pickpockets, then Shakespeare is our Fagin, always on the look out for a shiny new phrase.
The Observer, 1999

Godfather 'The Godfather' is the term used to denote the head of a Mafia family, popularized by Mario Puzo in his novel *The Godfather* (1968) and by the 1972 film which, together with two sequels, was based on it. The original Godfather, Don Corleone (played by Marlon Brando in the film), is succeeded by his son, Michael Corleone (played by Al Pacino). The book and films document the power struggles and vendettas between Mafia families.

Moriarty In Arthur Conan Doyle's Sherlock Holmes stories, the fiendish Professor Moriarty is the detective's greatest enemy, 'the Napoleon of crime'.

I tried Ralph again. This time he answered on the fourth ring. 'What's up, Miss Marple?' he asked. 'I thought you were out after Professor Moriarty until tomorrow.'
SARA PARETSKY *Indemnity Only,* 1982

She no longer paled or trembled at the idea of sudden death. The renowned John Goss, with all the cool skill, clever thinking and iron fists of detectives in novels, would get her safely past every Moriarty going. She finished the last of her sandwich with obvious pleasure.
RICHARD HALEY *Thoroughfare of Stones,* 1995

Cunning

The figures below are tricksters and schemers, whose displays of guile range from **TOM SAWYER** with his ploy to avoid a domestic chore, through the political cunning of **MACHIAVELLI,** to the murderous plotting of the **BORGIAS** and **LADY MACBETH.** The **DEVIL,** often simply the epitome of evil, can more specifically be mentioned as the embodiment of craftiness, especially when represented in the form of the **SERPENT.** ▶ *See also* **Mischief.**

Artful Dodger In Dickens's *Oliver Twist* (1837–8), 'the Artful Dodger' is the nickname of Jack Dawkins, a clever young pickpocket and a member of Fagin's gang of thieves. He is known especially for his quick-wittedness.

Dozens of little Artful Dodgers hustling the white men who invaded their parents' country.
ARMISTEAD MAUPIN *Babycakes,* 1984

Autolycus In Greek mythology, Autolycus, the son of Chione, was a cunning thief who stole animals from the herds of Sisyphus. He had the power to change the appearance of whatever beasts he stole and so, although Sisyphus noticed that his own herds were growing smaller and those of Autolycus were growing larger, he was unable to make any accusations. Sisyphus finally caught Autolycus by marking the hooves of his cattle. Autolycus is also the name of a character in Shakespeare's *Winter's Tale*, a light-fingered rogue, 'a snapper-up of unconsidered trifles'.

Borgias The Borgias were a Neopolitan family with Spanish origins. Cesare (1476-1507) and Lucrezia or Lucretia (1480-1519) Borgia were children of Pope Alexander VI. Although they were patrons of the arts, they are chiefly remembered for their alleged plotting against and murder of their enemies, especially by poisoning.

> I watched her recoiling from that poulet en casserole, as if it had been something dished up by the Borgias.
> P. G. WODEHOUSE *Cocktail Time*, 1958

> [This is] a party whose personal hatreds and plotting make Lucretia Borgia and Machiavelli look tame.
> *The Observer*, 1997

Delilah According to the Old Testament Book of Judges, Delilah used her guile to extract from Samson the secret of his great strength so that she could betray him to the Philistines in return for money. She repeatedly asked Samson the secret of his strength and when he had given her three false answers said: 'How canst thou say, I love thee, when thine heart is not with me? Thou hast mocked me these three times, and hast not told me wherein thy great strength lieth' (Judg. 16: 15). Samson finally relented and told her that his great strength lay in his long hair and that if it were cut short he would 'become weak, and be like any other man'. ▶ *See special entry* ☐ **SAMSON** *on p. 336.*

> Ay, and I fancy I've baited the hook right. Our little Delilah will bring our Samson.
> ANTHONY HOPE *The Prisoner of Zenda*, 1894

Devil The Devil, also referred to as Satan or Lucifer, is the supreme spirit of evil in the Christian and Jewish religions, thought of as scheming to tempt people into wickedness.

> I dare say he knew me as soon as he saw my face; but was as cunning as Lucifer. He came up to meet me, and took me by the hand, and said, 'Whose pretty maiden are you?'
> SAMUEL RICHARDSON *Pamela*, 1740

Iago Iago is the villainous ensign in Shakespeare's *Othello* (1622) who schemes against Othello himself, deceiving him into believing that his wife, Desdemona, has been unfaithful to him. This ultimately leads to the tragic deaths of Othello and Desdemona.

> 'And you say Mathilda was evil-minded?' Furiously, she ground into gear. 'Compared with you she was a novice. Juliet to your Iago.'
> MINETTE WALTERS *The Scold's Bridle*, 1994

> Politicians who peddle their sincerity between whiles become transparent liars. Men who trade on integrity turn Iagos.
> PETER PRESTON in The *Guardian*, 1995

Jacob Jacob and Esau were the twin sons of Isaac and Rebecca in the Bible, Esau being the first born. Esau used to go on hunting expeditions and, return-ing from one of these famished, begged Jacob for some of the food Jacob was preparing, 'red pottage of lentils'. Jacob refused him food until Esau sold Jacob his birthright. Later, when Isaac was on his deathbed, he promised Esau, his favoured son, his blessing if he would bring him some game prepared in the way he liked. Rebecca and Jacob tricked Isaac into blessing Jacob. When Isaac and Esau discovered the deception, Esau said 'Is not he rightly named Jacob? for he hath supplanted me these two times: he took away my birthright; and, behold, now he hath taken away my blessing.'

Loki In Scandinavian mythology, Loki was the god of mischief and discord. He was instrumental in the death of Balder. Loki discovered that mistletoe was the only substance that had not been asked by Balder's mother, Frigga, to swear that it would not harm her son and so was the only thing to which Balder was vulnerable. Loki shaped a dart from the wood and tricked the blind god Hod into throwing it at Balder, who immediately fell dead to the ground. For this Loki was punished by the gods by being bound beneath the earth.

> But God, thank goodness includes both Loki and Odin, the comedian and the scholar, the jester and the saint. God did not fashion a very regular universe after all. And we poor sods of his image are therefore condemned to struggle with calendrical questions till the cows come home, and Christ comes round again to inaugurate the millennium.
> STEPHEN J. GOULD *Questioning the Millennium*, 1997

Lucifer ▶ *See* DEVIL.

Lady Macbeth In Shakespeare's play *Macbeth* (1623), Lady Macbeth plots with her husband to have King Duncan killed so that her husband can assume the throne in his place. She persuades him to commit the murder despite his hesitation and reluctance. She is thus alluded to as a cold-blooded and scheming woman.

> The little girls with their assessing eyes, their slippery deceitful smiles, tartaned up like Lady Macbeth.
> MARGARET ATWOOD *Cat's Eye*, 1988

> Maria . . . took to interviewing Mandalari's clients during his absence, gradually becoming the Lady Macbeth of Palermo's money launderers, yet all the while protesting her ignorance of the Mafia's wider operators.
> *The Observer*, 1997

Machiavelli Niccolò di Bernardo dei Machiavelli (1469–1527) was an Italian statesman and political philosopher. His best-known work is *The Prince* (1532), in which he argues that rulers may have to resort to methods that are not in themselves desirable in order to rule effectively. His name has come to represent the use of deceit and cunning in the pursuit of personal power, and the adjective 'Machiavellian' has entered the language meaning 'elaborately cunning and scheming'.

> Sidney talked for the same reason as the hunted sepia squirts ink, to conceal his movements. Behind the ink-cloud of the Ancient Indians he hoped to go jaunting up to town unobserved. Poor Sidney! He thought himself so Machiavellian. But his ink was transparent, his cunning like a child's.
> ALDOUS HUXLEY *Point Counter Point*, 1928

> Beware of that Machiavel of a policeman. If he gets wind of the plot, we're lost.
> JOHN KENNEDY TOOLE *A Confederacy of Dunces*, 1980

> 'Who was Iago?' Jack grinned. 'You didn't come here to ask me that.' 'You're quite

right, but I'd still like to know.' 'He's a character from Othello. A Machiavelli who manipulated people's emotions in order to destroy them.'
MINETTE WALTERS *The Scold's Bridle*, 1994

Prometheus In Greek mythology, Prometheus was a demigod, one of the Titans, seen in many legends as the champion of humankind against the gods. Various stories attest to his cunning, usually in the service of man. Zeus asked him to arbitrate in a dispute between men and gods over which portion of a sacrificial bull should be given to the gods and which portion should be kept by men. Prometheus divided the carcass into two bags, one containing the flesh, the other containing the bones, then tricked Zeus into choosing the bag containing the bones, which would thereafter be the gods' portion. In another episode, he stole fire from Mount Olympus by hiding it in a stalk of fennel. ▶ *See special entry* ☐ **PROMETHEUS** *on p. 311.*

Ruritania Ruritania is an imaginary central European kingdom used as the setting for Anthony Hope's novels of courtly intrigue and romance, such as *The Prisoner of Zenda* (1894) and *Rupert of Hertzau* (1898). The name has become synonymous with political scheming.

Satan ▶ *See* **DEVIL**.

Tom Sawyer Tom Sawyer is the hero of Mark Twain's novel *The Adventures of Tom Sawyer* (1876). In a famous episode, Tom is asked by his Aunt Polly to whitewash a fence, a monotonous chore. When one by one his friends come along, Tom pretends to be enjoying the work so much that his friends beg to be allowed to have a go. Tom therefore has 'a nice, good, idle time all the while— plenty of company—and the fence had three coats of whitewash on it!'

At other times, Tom Sawyer-like, she led the way in mischief, as when she decided that they should have a dog, despite a school rule prohibiting pets.
LEONARD S. MARCUS *Margaret Wise Brown*, 1992

Scheherazade Scheherazade is the narrator of the *Arabian Nights*. Married to King Shahriyar, who has a habit of killing his new brides the morning after their wedding night, she staves off her fate with an ingenious scheme. She tells her husband a tale every evening, stopping it at an exciting point before the end and concluding the tale the following evening. Eventually, he is persuaded to abandon his murderous plan.

Serpent In the Bible, the Serpent, which was 'more subtil than any beast of the field which the Lord God had made', persuaded Eve to eat the forbidden fruit from the tree of the knowledge of good and evil in the Garden of Eden, saying that 'in the day ye eat thereof, then your eyes shall be opened, and ye shall be as gods, knowing good and evil' (Gen. 3). ▶ *See special entry* ☐ **ADAM AND EVE** *on p. 5.*

By his original constitution aided by the co-operating influences of his lot, Billy in many respects was little more than a sort of outright barbarian, much such perhaps as Adam presumably might have been ere the urbane Serpent wriggled himself into his company.
HERMAN MELVILLE *Billy Budd, Foretopman*, 1924

It is necessary . . . to be innocent as the dove with Monsieur de Toiras, but also sly as the serpent in the event that his king wishes them to sell Casale.
UMBERTO ECO *The Island of the Day Before*, 1994

Becky Sharp Becky Sharp and Amelia Sedley are the main characters in Thackeray's satirical novel *Vanity Fair* (1847–8). Becky starts out penniless and orphaned unlike the comfortably-off Amelia. However, she harnesses her charm and wits in her relentless pursuit of her own comfort and wealth.

> But there was a minute tilt at the corner of her eyelids, and a corresponding tilt at the corner of her lips . . . that denied, very subtly but quite unmistakably, her apparent total obeisance to the great god Man. An orthodox Victorian would perhaps have mistrusted that imperceptible hint of a Becky Sharp; but to a man like Charles she proved irresistible.
> JOHN FOWLES *The French Lieutenant's Woman*, 1969

Trojan Horse In Greek mythology, the Trojan Horse, also known as the Wooden Horse of Troy, was a device used by the Greeks after the death of Achilles to capture the city of Troy. The Greek craftsman Epeius constructed a large wooden horse and left it outside the walls of the city. The Greeks then sailed out of sight, leaving behind just one man, Sinon, who pretended to be a Greek deserter. Sinon reported to the Trojans that the horse was an offering to Athene, which, if brought within the city walls, would render Troy impregnable. The horse was in fact full of Greek soldiers, and once it had been brought into Troy and night had fallen, these soldiers came out and took the city. ▶ *See special entry* □ **TROJAN WAR** *on p. 392.*

Volpone Volpone is the main character in Ben Jonson's comedy of the same name (printed 1607). Volpone, a childless man, lures potential heirs to his bedside where he pretends he is about to die imminently. His sidekick, Mosca, persuades each of these suitors that a suitable expensive present will confirm that he is the heir, and Volpone gloats gleefully over the gifts. Eventually Mosca engineers a position in which he can blackmail Volpone. Rather than lose his wealth to him, Volpone confesses to the authorities and the two are punished for their scheme.

Curse

The most striking of those whose names have come to be linked allusively to the idea of being cursed are whole families such as the house of **ATREUS** and, less commonly, the family of **JEROBOAM**, in which not only more than one person but more than one generation is involved. The allusion is thus to a family who seem to have considerably more than their fair share of misfortune or tragedy. Cursed individuals include **CAIN**, who can stand for a disastrous and doomed person, and **JONAH**, for one who brings bad luck (particularly at sea). ▶ *See also* **Guilt**, **Punishment**.

Albatross ▶ *See* **ANCIENT MARINER**.

Ancient Mariner In Samuel Coleridge's poem 'The Rime of the Ancient Mariner' (1798), a mariner shoots an albatross at sea and as a result of this 'hellish thing', killing a bird of good omen, a curse falls on his ship. As a penance, he is forced to wear the albatross hung round his neck. The ship is becalmed near the Equator and everyone except the mariner perishes.

> Must go and see how Bert is getting on. God! I wish I'd never got involved with him; he is like an Ancient Mariner around my neck.
> SUE TOWNSEND *The Growing Pains of Adrian Mole*, 1984

> In my weaker moments I have often longed to cast myself on your mercy. How lucky, for both our sakes, that I have held out! You do not need an albatross from the old world around your neck.
> J. M. COETZEE *Age of Iron*, 1990

Atreus In Greek mythology, Atreus was the progenitor of a family known as the House of Atreus. His brother Thyestes laid a curse on it after Atreus had tricked him into eating the flesh of Thyestes' own sons at a feast. The family were subsequently involved in mutual murder and betrayal for several generations. One of Atreus' sons, Agamemnon, leader of the forces who besieged Troy, was murdered by his wife, Clytemnestra. The other son, Menelaus, was married to Helen of Troy, whose abduction by Paris led to the Trojan War.
▶ *See special entry* ☐ **TROJAN WAR** *on p. 392.*

> 'I'm trying to protect my sister. That's all I'm concerned about. You're not helping.' 'You can't hide things for ever. The Mordifords should know that by now.' 'What's left of us. Beatrice would say it's a family curse, like the House of Atreus. A bit above our mercantile station, wouldn't you say?'
> GILLIAN LINSCOTT *Widow's Peak*, 1994

Cain In the Bible, Cain, the elder son of Adam and Eve, murdered his brother, Abel, and as a consequence was cursed to wander the earth for the rest of his life (Gen. 4: 1–16). God branded him with a mark, identifying him as not to be killed but instead left to live out his nomadic punishment. ▶ *See special entry* ☐ **CAIN** *on p. 44.*

> In this manner, Hester Prynne came to have a part to perform in the world. With her native energy of character and rare capacity, it could not entirely cast her off, although it had set a mark upon her, more intolerable to a woman's heart than that which branded the brow of Cain.
> NATHANIEL HAWTHORNE *The Scarlet Letter*, 1850

> However the unjust discrimination against him had begun earlier; it had begun the day after Boxing Day. It seemed that since that business in the Market Square when that silly bitch fell off her horse and cracked her head open, the mark of Cain was on him. No one wanted him around. Others felt they could not drink in comfort knowing he was there, ill-omened, accursed.
> ANN GRANGER *A Season for Murder*, 1991

Flying Dutchman *The Flying Dutchman* was a legendary ghost ship supposed to be seen in the region of the Cape of Good Hope and presaging disaster. It was said to haunt the seas eternally as a result of a murder that had been committed on board. The term is sometimes applied to the ship's captain. In Wagner's opera of the same name (1843), Captain Vanderdecken is freed from a curse when he finds a woman willing to sacrifice herself for him.

Jeroboam In the Bible, Jeroboam rebelled against Solomon and, after

Solomon's death, encouraged the Israelites to rebel against Solomon's successor, Rehoboam. Jeroboam incited the Israelites to commit the sin of idolatry, encouraging them to worship two golden calves as gods. He also established a priesthood and, even though warned against it, continued to appoint priests. In punishment God decreed that Jeroboam's entire family be destroyed. 'Therefore, behold, I will bring evil upon the house of Jeroboam . . . And will take away the remnant of the house of Jeroboam, as a man taketh away dung, till it be all gone' (I Kgs. 14: 10).

> 'How horrid that story was last night! It spoiled my thoughts of today. It makes me feel as if a tragic doom overhung our family, as it did the house of Atreus.' 'Or the house of Jeroboam,' said the quondam theologian.
> THOMAS HARDY *Jude the Obscure*, 1894

Jonah In the Bible, Jonah was a Hebrew minor prophet, who was commanded by God to 'go to Nineveh, that great city, and cry against it; for their wickedness is come up before me' (Jonah 1: 2). However, Jonah was afraid and ran away, boarding a ship bound for Tarshish. God responded by sending a violent storm to threaten the ship. Eventually, acknowledging that he was the cause of the tempest, Jonah told the sailors to throw him overboard, whereupon the storm abated. Jonah lived to comply with God's instructions, but his disobedience had endangered the unwitting sailors with whom he had sailed and his name has subsequently stood for a bringer of ill luck.

> His presence was a perpetual reminder of bad luck, and soon he was suffering the cold shoulder that had been my lot when Happy Hannah first decided I was a Jonah.
> ROBERTSON DAVIES *World of Wonders*, 1975

Tutankhamun The tomb of Tutankhamun, in the Valley of the Kings in Egypt, was discovered by Howard Carter (1874–1939) and the Earl of Carnarvon (1866–1923) in November 1922. Carnarvon died in Luxor shortly after the discovery from a mosquito bite which led to a blood infection and pneumonia. Carter died seventeen years later but before he was able to provide a final report on the find, having spent the intervening years conserving the contents of the tomb and sending them to the Cairo Museum. The association of the two deaths gave rise to a popular tradition that the tomb was cursed.

Dancing

Most of the dancers included here are modern, drawn from ballet and the cinema. The frenzied dancing associated with the worship of Dionysus is covered at **Chaos and Disorder**.

Fred Astaire Fred Astaire (1899–1987), who was born Frederick Austerlitz, was an American actor, singer, and dancer. His first partner was his sister Adele, who starred with him in Broadway shows such as *Lady Be Good* in the 1920s. When his sister married he moved to Hollywood, where he paired up with Ginger Rogers. Together they made many successful film musicals including *Top Hat* (1935) and *Shall We Dance?* (1937). Astaire starred without Rogers in later films such as *Easter Parade* (1948) and *The Band Wagon* (1953).

> Lucifer sank his teeth into a woman's nose, anointed a teenaged boy's hair with brown slickum, and leaped from pew to pew like a demonic little version of Fred Astaire.
> ROBERT R. MCCAMMON *Boy's Life*, 1991

Isadora Duncan The American dancer Isadora Duncan (1878–1927) developed a new style of fluid barefoot dancing derived from classical Greek art. She travelled widely in Europe, and founded several dancing schools there. She was strangled accidentally when her trailing scarf became entangled in the wheel of a car.

> The girl, on her knees, arms thrown back, was a dancer. She was effecting some kind of Isadora Duncan, swan-raped, *Noh* swoon: demonstrating both her 'inner stillness' and the power she exercised over her body.
> IAIN SINCLAIR *Downriver*, 1991

Margot Fonteyn Margot Fonteyn was the stage name of the English classical ballet dancer Margaret Hookham. She danced for the company that became the Royal Ballet and was trained by Ninette de Valois. She started her partnership with Rudolph Nureyev in 1962 and created many roles with notable choreographers such as Frederick Ashton and Kenneth MacMillan. Fonteyn was named 'prima ballerina assoluta' in 1979, a title that has only been awarded three times.

> 'That's Bella on the terrace of our hotel.' Featherstone had produced his wallet, from which he proudly drew a number of creased and faded snaps from the space between his credit cards and his cheque book. 'What's she doing?' said Miss Trant, giving a cursory look, 'The Dying Swan?' 'Oh, yes,' said Featherstone proudly. 'Quite a little Margot Fonteyn, isn't she?'
> JOHN MORTIMER *Rumpole's Return*, 1980

Rita Hayworth Rita Hayworth (1918–87), born Margaret Carmen Cansino, was an American film actress, star of such films as *Gilda* (1946) and *The Lady from Shanghai* (1948). A cousin of Ginger Rogers, she was an accomplished dancer.

> Brenda, who'd been drinking champagne like her Uncle Leo, did a Rita Hayworth tango with herself.
> PHILIP ROTH *Goodbye, Columbus*, 1959

Nijinsky Vaslav Nijinsky (1890–1950), the legendary Russian dancer, trained at the Imperial Ballet School in St Petersburg and became one of the leading dancers in Diaghilev's Ballet Russe. He appeared in the first performance of Stravinsky's *Petrouchka* (1911) and danced in Fokine's ballets as well as in the classical repertoire. His own choreography included *L'Après-midi d'un Faune* (1912) and *Sacre du Printemps* (1913). His career ended when he was diagnosed as having paranoid schizophrenia in 1917.

> It is said of the same puppets . . . that they are *antigrav*, that they can rise and leap, like Nijinsky, as if no such thing as gravity existed for them.
> PAUL DE MAN *Rhetoric of Romanticism*, 1983

Rudolph Nureyev Rudolph Nureyev (1939–93) was a Russian ballet dancer who defected to Paris in 1961. His partnership with Margot Fonteyn, dancing for the Royal Ballet, was inspired. In addition to his wide range of roles in classical and modern ballet, he choreographed *La Bayadère* (1963) and other ballets, performed in films such as *Don Quixote* (1975), and was artistic director of the Paris Opera Ballet 1983–9.

> So I Nureyeved the front steps and flowed through the door in a single motion of Yale and Chubb.
> JULIAN BARNES *Talking It Over*, 1991

Pavlova Anna Pavlova (1881–1931) was a Russian ballerina who became famous for her roles in Fokine's ballets, in particular in his solo dance for her, *The Dying Swan*. She lived in Britain from 1912 and formed her own company with which she toured Europe and the world.

> Her office was hardly larger than the interior of my car . . . and she had to squeeze between the edge of her desk and the wall to get up to greet me. It was a maneuver that would have looked clumsy performed by Pavlova and Margaret Dopplemeier turned it into a lurching stumble.
> JONATHAN KELLERMAN *When the Bough Breaks*, 1992

> Johnnyboy draped himself across the workbench like Pavlova in the closing moments of the 'Dying Swan'.
> JOYCE HOLMS *Bad Vibes*, 1998

Red Shoes *The Red Shoes* was a Powell and Pressburger film released in 1948 starring Moira Shearer as a student who becomes a famous ballerina. When she falls in love and has to choose between love and career, she commits suicide.

Ginger Rogers Ginger Rogers (1911–95), born Virginia Katherine McMath, was an American actress and dancer. Best known for her dancing partnership with Fred Astaire, she also won an Oscar for her performance as an actress in *Kitty Foyle* (1940). ▶ *See also* **FRED ASTAIRE**.

> I put my hand in his and followed. He was one of those men who can make you feel like Ginger Rogers on the dance floor, conveying an entire set of suggestions in the way he applied pressure to the small of my back.
> SUE GRAFTON *H Is for Homicide*, 1991

Salome According to the Bible (Matt. 14: 6-9), Salome, the stepdaughter of King Herod Antipas, danced for her stepfather the king and 'pleased him'. He then 'promised with an oath to give her whatsoever she would ask' and Salome, instructed by her mother, demanded the head of John the Baptist.

Terpsichore Terpsichore (literally 'delighting in dance') was the Muse of dancing, particularly choral dancing and its accompanying song. The adjective derived from her name is 'Terpsichorean'.

> The old-fashioned fronts of these houses . . . rose sheer from the pavement, into which the bow-windows protruded like bastions, necessitating a pleasing *chassez-déchassez* movement to the time-pressed pedestrian at every few yards. He was bound also to evolve other Terpsichorean figures in respect of door-steps, scrapers, cellar-hatches, church buttresses.
> THOMAS HARDY *The Mayor of Casterbridge*, 1886

St Vitus St Vitus (died *c.*300) was a Christian martyr, said to have died during the reign of Diocletian. He was the patron of those who suffered from epilepsy and certain nervous disorders, including St Vitus's dance (Sydenham's chorea). St Vitus is sometimes alluded to in the context of violent physical movement.

> Not a limb, not a fibre about him was idle; and to have seen his loosely hung frame in full motion, and clattering about the room, you would have thought Saint Vitus himself, that blessed patron of the dance, was figuring before you in person.
> WASHINGTON IRVING *The Legend of Sleepy Hollow*, 1819–20

West Side Story Bernstein and Sondheim's film musical *West Side Story* (1961) relocates the story of Romeo and Juliet to 20th-century New York. Shakespeare's feuding families the Montagues and the Capulets are represented as rival gangs, the Jets and the Sharks. Among several memorable dance sequences featuring fast, aggressive, athletic movements in the film is the 'rumble', danced as a stylized gang fight.

> The sweating, red-faced cops in their blue uniforms and white helmets slashed the hot night air with their long white billies as though dancing a cop's version of West Side Story.
> CHESTER HIMES *Blind Man with a Pistol*, 1969

Zorba In the 1964 film of Nikos Katantzakis' novel *Zorba the Greek*, Anthony Quinn plays Zorba, a larger-than-life Cretan much given to exuberant solo dancing.

> Michael was already imagining the scenario. Ol' frizzy-haired Mona, sullen and horny in some smoky taverna. Mrs Madrigal holding court in her oatmeal linen caftan, doing that Zorba dance as the spirit moved her.
> ARMISTEAD MAUPIN *Sure of You*, 1990

Danger

The idea of danger is represented here by three main types of allusion: dangerous places (**BLUEBEARD'S CASTLE**, **CAPE HORN**), dangerous creatures (**CIRCE**, **SIRENS**), and dangerous situations (**SWORD OF DAMOCLES**, **TITANIC**).

Bluebeard's castle Bluebeard is the main character in a story by Charles Perrault in the collection *Histoires et Contes du Temps Passé* (1697). In the story, Bluebeard kills several wives and keeps their remains in one room of his castle, the door of which is always locked. Bluebeard's Castle is referred to as a place of danger, where grisly deeds are performed.

> It slides easily into the serrated slit of the lock, and I cannot suppress the light thrill that runs down my spine. It is like entering a story, something by Grimm, Bluebeard's Castle.
> ANDRÉ BRINK *Imaginings of Sand*, 1996

Calypso In Greek myth, Calypso was a nymph who lived on the island of Ogygia. When Odysseus was shipwrecked on the island, Calypso took him for her lover, offering him immortality if he would become her husband. She kept him on her island for seven years until Zeus intervened and ordered her to release him. Like the sirens, Calypso can represent a woman who is dangerously attractive to men. ▶ *See special entry* ☐ **ODYSSEUS** *on p. 283.*

> Perhaps he had too fixed an idea of what a siren looked like and the circumstances in which she appeared—long tresses, a chaste alabaster nudity, a mermaid's tail, matched by an Odysseus with a face acceptable in the best clubs. There were no Doric temples in the Undercliff; but here was a Calypso.
> JOHN FOWLES *The French Lieutenant's Woman*, 1969

Cape Horn Cape Horn is the extreme tip of South America. Bad weather and dangerous sea currents mean that it is very difficult to navigate safely round the cape.

> 'Did the sugar on the raspberry tarts you ate in your mouth taste the worse for being sweetened with the tear of slavery—for it should have tasted salt, but it did not. Did you think of the nigger who cut the cane? You did not. Merely to exist is to be involved in the system others have created to tend your daily needs.' 'Monstrous, Walter, monstrous.' 'There is a Cape Horn of the mind, too, which is as difficult to double as the real. Monstrous? Yes, I would allow that its waves are monstrous.'
> TIMOTHY MO *An Insular Possession*, 1986

Circe In Greek mythology, Circe was a sorceress who lived on the island of Aeaea. She turned Odysseus' men into swine but Odysseus managed to protect himself from this fate using the mythical herb moly, and he was able to make her restore his men to their human form. Circe represents a person or place that, though attractive and fascinating, is dangerous. ▶ *See special entry* ☐ **ODYSSEUS** *on p. 283.*

> The dog has not warmed to me. Too much cat-smell. Cat-woman: Circe.
> J. M. COETZEE *Age of Iron*, 1990

Daniel in the lions' den Daniel was a Hebrew prophet (6th century BC). The Old Testament Book of Daniel relates how he was cast into the lions' den for continuing to pray to God when it had been forbidden. He survived for a night unharmed by the lions, saying in the morning: 'My God hath sent his angel, and hath shut the lions' mouths, that they have not hurt me' (Dan. 6: 22). ▶ *See special entry* ☐ **DANIEL** *on p. 86.*

> Older than the crew, in their thirties. They were two lost little lamb-i-kins who had wandered into the lions' den.
> CHARLES HIGSON *Full Whack*, 1995

Jurassic Park *Jurassic Park* is the title of a film (1993) based on a book of the same name by Michael Crichton (1991). The plot features a theme park inhabited by dinosaurs which have been created from DNA taken from ancient mosquitoes preserved in amber. The dinosaurs are not supposed to be able to breed, but it is discovered that one particularly dangerous species, the carnivorous velociraptor, is able to reproduce. At the end of the film the velociraptors are moving out of the confines of the park.

> For prison is like Jurassic Park, but infinitely more dangerous: a single-sex society where some specimens, through a freak of genes, can mutate to the opposite sex.

> And others, through an excess of libido, willingly lose the ability to differentiate.
> PAUL BENNETT *False Profits*, 1998

Lorelei In Germanic folklore, Lorelei is the name of a rock at the edge of the Rhine, held to be the home of a siren with long blonde hair whose song lures boatmen to destruction. The name can also be applied to the siren herself, so a 'Lorelei' is a dangerously fascinating woman.

Scylla and Charybdis In Greek mythology, Scylla was a ferocious sea monster with many heads. She lived in a cave opposite the whirlpool Charybdis. Sailors had to steer very carefully to avoid the two dangers. If they steered too hard to avoid one, they would become victims of the other. Scylla and Charybdis represent two dangers which are to be avoided equally.

> Goodenough did not answer immediately but concentrated on finding a spot as equidistant as possible from the Scylla of the roaring fire and the Charybdis of the pulsating radiator.
> REGINALD HILL *Child's Play*, 1987

Sirens In Greek mythology, the Sirens were sea creatures, usually portrayed as bird-women, whose singing had the power to lure sailors to their deaths on dangerous rocks. In the *Odyssey*, when Odysseus had to sail past the island of the Sirens, he ordered his crew to plug their ears with wax so that they would not hear the singing of the Sirens. He had himself lashed to the mast of his ship so that he would not be able to respond to their call. The word is now used to suggest someone or something that lures a person away from a safe course to danger or uncertainty. ▶ *See special entry* ☐ **ODYSSEUS** *on p. 283*.

> Charles and his father sometimes disagreed. But they always parted with an increased regard for one another, and each desired no doughtier comrade when it was necessary to voyage for a little past the emotions. So the sailors of Ulysses voyaged past the Sirens, having first stopped one another's ears with wool.
> E. M. FORSTER *Howards End*, 1910

sword of Damocles Damocles was a legendary courtier of Dionysius I of Syracuse, who had talked openly of how lucky Dionysius was. To show him how precarious this happiness was, Dionysius invited Damocles to a sumptuous banquet, and seated him under a sword which was suspended by a single thread. 'The sword of Damocles' thus refers to a danger that is always present and might strike at any moment.

> True, in old age we live under the shadow of Death, which, like a sword of Damocles, may descend at any moment.
> SAMUEL BUTLER *The Way of All Flesh*, 1903

> A reduction in international armaments is impossible; by virtue of any number of fears and jealousies. The burden grows worse as science advances, for the improvements in the art of destruction will keep pace with its advance and every year more and more will have to be devoted to costly engines of war. It is a vicious circle. There is no escape from it—that Damocles sword of a war on the first day of which all the chartered covenants of princes will be scattered like chaff.
> FAY WELDON *Darcy's Utopia*, 1990

> Daphne took another call. I knew even before I had registered her hushed and respectful tone that the sword of Damocles was suspended above me.
> BEN ELTON *Inconceivable*, 1999

Symplegades In Greek mythology the Symplegades, literally 'clashing ones', were rocks at the north end of the Bosporus which were believed to clash together, crushing ships that passed between them. When Jason and the Argo-nauts had to pass between them a bird was released to fly ahead of the ship. The rocks came together and nipped off the bird's tail feathers, and as they recoiled again the Argonauts rowed through with all speed and lost only the ornament on the stern of the ship. After this, in accordance with a prophecy, the rocks remained still. ▶ *See special entry* ☐ **JASON AND THE ARGONAUTS** *on p. 220.*

Titanic The *Titanic* was a British passenger liner which was claimed to be unsinkable. On her maiden voyage in 1912, the ship struck an iceberg in the North Atlantic and sank with the loss of 1,490 lives. The scale of the loss of life, mainly men, was a consequence of the over-confidence of the owners of the liner, the White Star Line. The company was so sure of the ship's design and engineering it they provided only a few lifeboats, believing that they would never be needed. The *Titanic* is often alluded to as an example of a foolish belief in the ability of modern science to eliminate danger, or more frequently as an unavoidable disaster.

> Jane Collingswood looked at Rachel for a second, then said, 'I think you're being very brave. I don't know how I'd hold up if I were in your shoes.' I did. Jane Collingswood could survive the sinking of the Titanic.
> STEVEN WOMACK *Dead Folks' Blues,* 1992

> Janey had it right, Ben. Booze. Dope. Just different seats on the Titanic.
> JUSTIN SCOTT *Stone Dust,* 1995

Typhoid Mary Mary Mallon (d. 1938), known as 'Typhoid Mary', was an Irish-born American cook who transmitted typhoid fever in the USA.

> He's dying, man, and what do they do? The assholes wear surgical masks and stand back ten feet from his bed like he's Typhoid Mary while they're asking him shit.
> PATRICIA CORNWELL *Body of Evidence,* 1991

> 'Deirdre?' The Head of Sixth Form forced his vocal cords into action. 'You threaten me—my sixth form—with Deirdre Lessing, the Typhoid Mary of West Sussex?'
> M. J. TROW *Maxwell's Flame,* 1995

Daniel

According to the Book of Daniel, Daniel was a devout Jew who spent his life as one of those taken into exile in Babylon. He had a gift for interpreting visions and dreams. He was able to explain the meaning of a strange dream that Nebuchadnezzar, the king of Babylon, had had, for which he was made the king's chief adviser. Later, Daniel interpreted a second dream of Nebuchadnezzar to foretell his insanity, which immediately came to pass.

In a famous episode during Nebuchadnezzar's reign, the king set up a golden idol and commanded all to worship it. When three of Daniel's fellow Jews, Shadrach, Meshach, and Abednego, refused to do so, the king ordered some of his soldiers to throw them into a 'fiery furnace'. Although the soldiers were consumed by the flames, Shadrach, Meshach, and Abednego miraculously came out unharmed: 'these men, upon whose bodies the fire had no power, nor was an hair of their head singed, neither were their coats changed, nor the smell of fire had passed on them.'

Belshazzar, who held power after Nebuchadnezzar, gave a great banquet with wine for a thousand of his lords. During the banquet they drank wine from the gold and silver goblets taken from the temple in Jerusalem and praised the gods of gold, silver, bronze, iron, wood, and stone. Suddenly the fingers of a human hand appeared and wrote on the wall the words 'Mene, Mene, Tekel, Upharsin'. Daniel translated the words, explaining to Belshazzar that his reign was over, that he had been weighed in the balance and found wanting, and that his kingdom would be divided and given to the Medes and the Persians. That night Belshazzar was killed and the Persian army, led by Darius, captured Babylon.

King Darius appointed Daniel sole administrator, over all the other officials and princes. In an attempt to bring about Daniel's downfall, the other officials and princes asked the king to establish a decree saying that for thirty days no one should pray to any God or man except the king. Daniel ignored this command. As a result of this disobedience, he was cast into the lions' den and left for the night. In the morning he was discovered by the king, unscathed. Daniel explained, 'My God hath sent his angel, and hath shut the lions' mouths, that they have not hurt me.'

In the apocryphal Book of Susanna, Daniel is portrayed as a wise judge, proving the falsely accused Susanna to be innocent.

Throughout this book there are references to Daniel and to episodes from the Book of Daniel.

▶ *See* DANIEL *at* **Courage, Danger, Rebellion and Disobedience,** *and* **Wisdom**
　　BELSHAZZAR *at* **Food and Drink** *and* **Prophecy**

Daniel *continued*

▶ *See* **NEBUCHADNEZZAR** *at* **Dreams, Hair,** *and* **Insanity**
　　SHADRACH, MESHACH AND ABEDNEGO *at* **Temperature**
　　WRITING ON THE WALL *at* **Communication.**

Darkness

It is striking that the idea of darkness has commonly been linked with that of the underworld, the land of the dead. **CIMMERIAN, PLUTONIAN,** and **STYGIAN** can all be used as synonyms for 'gloomy'. An obscurely lit interior is sometimes described with reference to **CARAVAGGIO** and **REMBRANDT**.

Caravaggio Michelangelo Merisi da Caravaggio (*c.*1571–1610) was an Italian painter whose paintings are distinctive in their dramatic use of light and shade (chiaroscuro), often showing figures against a very dark background with light shining from one side or from below onto their faces.

> [The table] was lit by one tall lamp with a dark shade; the light flowed downwards, concentrated on the white cloth, and was then reflected up, lighting our faces strangely, Caravaggio fashion, against the surrounding darkness.
> JOHN FOWLES *The Magus*, 1966

Cimmerian In Greek mythology, the Cimmerians were people who lived in a land on the edge of the world which was perpetually covered with mist and cloud and where the sun never shone. In Homer's *Odyssey* the land of the Cimmerians is the place nearest to Hades, the land of the dead. It contains Persephone's grove, to which Odysseus goes to make contact with the spirits of the dead.

> A kind of landscape and weather which leads travellers from the South to describe our island as Homer's Cimmerian land, was not, on the face of it, friendly to women.
> THOMAS HARDY *The Return of the Native*, 1880

Erebus In Greek mythology, Erebus was the primeval god of darkness, born from Chaos right at the beginning of the world. The name was later identified with Hades, and is used with this meaning in the *Iliad* and the *Odyssey*. ▶ *See special entry* ☐ **HADES** *on p. 172.*

Ginnungagap In Scandinavian mythology, Ginnungagap (also spelt Ginnung-Gap) was the Great Void, the space between Niflheim, the land of the dead, and Muspelheim, the region of intense heat. It had no beginning or end and no night and day.

> She wrapped round her a long red woollen cravat and opened the door. The night in

all its fulness met her flatly on the threshold, like the very brink of an absolute void, or the antemundane Ginnung-Gap believed in by her Teuton forefathers. For her eyes were fresh from the blaze, and here there was no street lamp or lantern to form a kindly transition between the inner glare and the outer dark.

THOMAS HARDY *The Woodlanders*, 1887

Hades In Greek mythology Hades, also known as Pluto, was the brother of Zeus and Poseidon and the lord of the underworld, the land of the dead. Those who died were said to have gone to the house of Hades. The name Hades later came to refer to the place itself, a place of perpetual darkness and gloom. ▶ *See special entry* □ **HADES** *on p. 172.*

Niflheim In Scandinavian mythology, Niflheim was the underworld, a place of eternal cold, darkness, and mist. While those who died in battle were believed to go to Valhalla and feast with Odin, those who died of old age or illness were believed to go to Niflheim.

But he continued motionless and silent in that gloomy Niflheim or fogland which involved him, and she proceeded on her way.

THOMAS HARDY *The Woodlanders*, 1887

Ninth Plague of Egypt The Book of Exodus in the Old Testament relates how Pharaoh refused to allow Moses to lead the Israelites out of Egypt to the Promised Land. To punish Pharaoh, God sent ten plagues to Egypt, the ninth of which was 'a thick darkness in all the land of Egypt three days' (Exod. 10: 22). The Israelites in Goshen were spared this darkness. ▶ *See special entry* □ **MOSES AND THE BOOK OF EXODUS** *on p. 264.*

By reason of the density of the interwoven foliage overhead, it was gloomy there at cloudless noontide, twilight in the evening, dark as midnight at dusk, and black as the ninth plague of Egypt at midnight.

THOMAS HARDY *Far from the Madding Crowd*, 1874

Pluto In Greek mythology, Pluto was an alternative name for Hades, lord of the underworld. It was considered unwise to mention Hades by his true name, so the name Pluto, meaning literally 'the rich one', was often used instead. The realm of Pluto is therefore the underworld, a land of perpetual darkness and gloom. ▶ *See special entry* □ **HADES** *on p. 172.*

Ghastly, grim, and ancient Raven, wandering from the nightly shore,
Tell me what thy lordly name is on the night's Plutonian shore?

EDGAR ALLEN POE *The Raven*, 1845

The ravine now expandingly descends into a great, purple, hopper-shaped hollow, far sunk among many Plutonian, shaggy-wooded mountains.

HERMAN MELVILLE *The Paradise of Bachelors and the Tartarus of Maids*, 1856

I don't want to die on the Sicilian plains—to be snatched away, like Proserpine in the same locality, to the Plutonian shades.

HENRY JAMES *Portrait of a Lady*, 1881

Rembrandt Rembrandt Harmenszoon van Rijn (1606–69) was a Dutch painter known for his subtle use of light and shadow, or chiaroscuro, and especially for the obscure lighting and brown-and-black palette of his later paintings.

The interior was shadowy with a peculiar shade. The strange luminous semi-

opacities of fine autumn afternoons and eves intensified into Rembrandt effects.
THOMAS HARDY *Far from the Madding Crowd*, 1874

The dim gold lamplight and the restless firelight made Rembrandt shadows in the remoter corners of the kitchen.
STELLA GIBBONS *Cold Comfort Farm*, 1932

Stygian In Greek mythology, the River Styx was the main river of Hades, the underworld, across which the souls of the dead were said to be ferried by Charon. Any deep, gloomy, or foggy darkness can be described as 'Stygian'.
▶ *See special entry* □ **HADES** *on p. 172.*

A beam from the setting sun pierced the Stygian gloom.
H. RIDER HAGGARD *She*, 1887

It was a Stygian night. Outside the rain drifted in drapes and an east wind was gusting.
LOUIS DE BERNIÈRES *Captain Corelli's Mandolin*, 1994

Tartarus In Greek mythology, Tartarus was the lowest region of Hades, a place of perpetual gloom reserved for the punishment of those who had committed some outrage against the gods.

David

In the Bible, David was the youngest son of Jesse. He was noted as a musician and is traditionally regarded as the author of the Psalms. The young David relieved King Saul's melancholy by playing the lyre. When still a shepherd boy, David accepted the challenge from the Philistine champion Goliath to single combat. Although Goliath was nine feet tall and wore full armour including a brass helmet, David went to fight him armed only with a sling and five pebbles. Using the sling, he struck Goliath on the forehead and killed him. David's success was greeted by the women coming out to meet Saul and singing: 'Saul hath slain his thousands, and David his ten thousands.' From this time on Saul became jealous of David's popularity and on a number of occasions tried to kill him. David and Saul's son Jonathan had become bosom friends and had sworn a compact of love and mutual protection. Jonathan repeatedly tried to intercede on David's behalf with his father but eventually David was forced to escape to the mountains.

Saul and Jonathan were killed in battle against the Philistines. On Saul's death David was made king of Judah and later he was chosen as ruler of the whole of Israel. He made Jerusalem his capital and reigned there for thirty-three years.

King David had many wives, including Bathsheba. While she was still the wife of Uriah the Hittite, an officer in David's army, Bathsheba had been seen bathing by David from the roof of the palace. David sent for her and slept with her and she later let him know that she was pregnant. The Israelites were at the time laying seige to Rabbah, and David arranged for Uriah to be sent into the front line, where the city's defenders were strongest and where he was killed. After her period of mourning was over, David married Bathsheba.

David's later years were darkened by the rebellion and death of his favourite son, Absalom. The ambitious Absalom killed David's oldest son, Amnon, and later raised an army and rose against his father, chasing David out of Jerusalem. In the subsequent battle, David ordered his men to deal gently with Absalom, but his commander, Joab, ignored this command and killed Absalom. On hearing of the death of his son, David wept, 'O my son, Absalom, my son, my son Absalom! Would God I had died for thee, O Absalom, my son, my son!'

Throughout this book there are references to David and to most of the figures and episodes mentioned in the above account.

▶ *See* ABSALOM *at* **Death** *and* **Rebellion and Disobedience**
  BATHSHEBA *at* **Beauty: Female Beauty**
  DAVID *at* **Chastity and Virginity, Music,** *and* **Victory**
  DAVID AND BATHSHEBA *at* **Lovers**

David *continued*

▶ *See* DAVID AND JONATHAN *at* **Friendship**
   GOLIATH *at* **Large Size** *and* **Weakness**
   URIAH *at* **Betrayal**.

Death

Most of the entries below personify or represent a generalized idea of
death. By contrast, a reference to **ABSALOM**, **MARAT**, or **OPHELIA** is intended
to bring to mind a particular way of meeting one's death.

Absalom Absalom was the favourite son of King David, who led a rebellion
against his father but was eventually defeated in battle and killed by Joab, one
of David's officers. According to the biblical account (2 Sam. 18), Absalom was
fleeing on a mule, but was caught by his long hair in the branches of an oak
tree, and 'he was taken up between the heaven and the earth'. Joab took three
darts in his hand 'and thrust them through the heart of Absalom, while he
was yet alive in the midst of the oak'. David subsequently lamented the loss of
his son: 'O my son Absalom, my son, my son Absalom! Would God I had died
for thee, O Absalom, my son, my son!' ▶ *See special entry* ☐ **DAVID** *on p. 90.*

> Well, doctor, 'tis a mercy you wasn't a-drowned, or a-splintered, or a-hanged up to a
> tree like Absalom—also a handsome gentleman like yourself, as the prophets say!
> THOMAS HARDY *The Woodlanders*, 1887

Angel of Death Death is sometimes personified as a winged messenger, often
cloaked and in the form of a skeleton, called the Angel of Death. The term can
also be applied to a number of angels including Apollyon, Azrael, and Michael.
▶ *See* **AZRAEL**.

> Some day soon the Angel of Death will sound his trumpet for me.
> BRAM STOKER *Dracula*, 1897

> When Staunton died . . . his death was reported at some length in our Neue Zurcher
> Zeitung. That paper, like the London Times, recognizes only the most distinguished
> achievements of the Angel of Death.
> ROBERTSON DAVIES *World of Wonders*, 1975

> Every so often I thought: What if the engine dies on us—what then? And saw a
> skinny man, like the Angel of Death, watching us from the rag of a cactus's shade.
> PAUL THEROUX *The Old Patagonian Express*, 1978

Anubis Anubis was the Egyptian god of the dead and the protector of tombs,
who conducted the souls of the dead to their judgement. Anubis was the son of
Osiris and is often represented with the head of a jackal.

Azrael In Jewish and Islamic mythology, Azrael (literally 'help of God') was the angel who severed the soul from the body at death.

Black Death The Black Death is the name commonly given to the great epidemic of bubonic plague that killed between a third and a half of the population of Europe in the mid-14th century. The plague originated in central Asia and China and spread rapidly through Europe, transmitted by the fleas of black rats.

'What we need is a cataclysm,' Fish was saying. . . . 'A cataclysm. Another Black Death, a vast explosion, millions wiped from the face of the earth, civilization as we know it all but obliterated, then Birth would be essential again.'
MARGARET ATWOOD *The Edible Woman*, 1969

Charon In Greek mythology, Charon was the ferryman who ferried the souls of the dead across the rivers Styx and Acheron into Hades.

So there I was at Bush Hill, where Rush had assigned me with my brother, to bury the flow of dead that did not ebb just because the Charon who was their familiar could no longer attend them.
JOHN EDGAR WIDEMAN *Fever*, 1989

Death Death was one of the Four Horsemen of the Apocalypse: 'And I looked, and behold, a pale horse, and his name that sat on him was Death' (Rev. 6: 8). The other horsemen were Pestilence, War, and Famine.

Not knowing whether to expect friend or foe, prudence suggested that he should cease his whistling and retreat among the trees till the horse and his rider had gone by, a course to which he was still more inclined when he found how noiselessly they approached, and saw that the horse looked pale, and remembered what he had read about Death in the Revelation.
THOMAS HARDY *The Woodlanders*, 1887

Grim Reaper The Grim Reaper, a cloaked figure wielding a scythe, is the personification of death.

Virginia is the No 1 source-state for handguns on the East Coast . . . We must stop the trafficking or become known as the Grim Reaper State.
The Independent, 1993

Holocaust The Holocaust is the name given to the mass murder of Jews and other persecuted groups under the German Nazi regime. In the period 1941-5 more than 6 million European Jews were killed in concentration camps such as Auschwitz, Dachau, and Treblinka as part of Adolf Eichmann's 'final solution'.

Baroness Thatcher stepped up the political pressure for a military crackdown on the Serbs last night—with a call for air strikes, a suggestion that Western inaction had 'given comfort' to the aggressor and a warning of a 'second Holocaust'.
The Independent, 1992

Lethe In Greek mythology, Lethe was one of the rivers of the underworld Hades, whose water caused those who drank it to lose all memory of their past life on earth. Lethe thus represents oblivion or forgetfulness and, occasionally, death. ▶ *See special entry* □ **HADES** *on p. 172.*

Abused river! You bear upon your face wares as deadly and soporiferous as the very
waters of Styx or Lethe.
TIMOTHY MO *An Insular Possession*, 1986

Marat Jean Paul Marat (1743–93) was a French revolutionary politician and
journalist. He founded a radical newspaper which supported the French Revolution and criticized the moderate Girondists, contributing to their overthrow.
Earlier forced into hiding, he had hidden in the Paris sewers, where he contracted a skin disease which meant he spent much of his later life sitting in his
bath. It was here that he was stabbed to death by the Girondist Charlotte
Corday. There is a famous painting called *The Death of Marat* by Jacques-Louis
David.

On moving my hand above the surface of the water, I experienced the greatest fright
I ever received in the whole course of my life; for imagine my horror on discovering
my hand, as I thought, full of blood. My first thought was that I had ruptured an
artery, and was bleeding to death, and should be discovered, later on, looking like a
second Marat, as I remember seeing him in Madame Tussaud's.
GEORGE AND WEEDON GROSSMITH *The Diary of a Nobody*, 1892

Ophelia In Shakespeare's *Hamlet* (1604), Ophelia is the daughter of Polonius
whose grief after her father's murder at Hamlet's hands drives her out of her
mind. Later it is reported that, while making garlands of flowers by the side of
a stream, she fell in and drowned. Ophelia's death scene is the subject of a
famous painting (1851–2) by John Everett Millais, which depicts her floating
face-upwards in the stream, surrounded by flowers, and about to slip beneath
the water.

How do you know that Hetty isn't floating at the present moment in some star-lit
pond, with lovely water-lilies round her, like Ophelia?
OSCAR WILDE *The Picture of Dorian Gray*, 1891

I just hoped there was no way he could trace back to my connection with Tim.
Otherwise my lifeless corpse would probably be found floating down the river on
Sunday evening after the river cruise, an Ophelia in polluted waters.
LAUREN HENDERSON *The Black Rubber Dress*, 1997

Styx In Greek mythology, the Styx was the dark, gloomy river that flowed
around the underworld Hades, across which Charon ferried the souls of the
dead. Other rivers in Hades were the Acheron, Lethe, Cocytus, and
Phlegethon. ▶ *See special entry* □ **HADES** *on p. 172.*

The report Dr. Fraker had dictated effectively reduced Rick's death to observations
about the craniocerebral trauma he'd sustained, with a catalogue of abrasions, con-
tusions, small-intestine avulsions, mesenteric lacerations, and sufficient skeletal
damage to certify Rick's crossing of the River Styx.
SUE GRAFTON *C is for Corpse*, 1990

Research had assured Jonathan that although some of these intruders from the past
were not fussy about requiring darkness or any particular ambiance in which to
operate, some of them appeared to work to a species of timetable not discernible
from this side of the Styx.
STAYNES AND STOREY *Dead Serious*, 1995

Tower Hill The scaffold on Tower Hill was the place where traitors imprisoned in the Tower of London, often high-ranking state prisoners, were executed by beheading. The first such execution there was in 1388 and the last in 1747, though the site was also used for public hangings until 1780.

> His execution was a hole-and-corner affair. There was no high scaffolding, no scarlet cloth (did they have scarlet cloth on Tower Hill? They should have had), no awe-stricken multitude to be horrified at his guilt and be moved to tears at his fate—no air of sombre retribution.
> JOSEPH CONRAD *Lord Jim*, 1900

Tyburn Tyburn was a place in London, near Marble Arch, where public hangings were held from 1388 to 1783. The triangular gallows there were often referred to as 'Tyburn Tree'.

> She didn't deserve to die. Perhaps none of us do, not like that. We don't even hang the Whistler now. We've learned something since Tyburn, since Agnes Poley's burning.
> P. D. JAMES *Devices and Desires*, 1989

Valley of (the Shadow of) Death The phrases 'the valley of the shadow of death' and 'the valley of death' have various literary sources. Psalm 23 contains the lines: 'Yea, though I walk through the valley of the shadow of death, I will fear no evil.' In John Bunyan's allegory *Pilgrim's Progress*, Christian passes through the Valley of the Shadow of Death, with a dangerous bog on one side and a deep ditch on the other, and the mouth of Hell close by. Alfred, Lord Tennyson's poem *The Charge of the Light Brigade* (1854) contains the famous refrain

'Into the valley of Death
Rode the six hundred'.

> But after a time he fell silent, and there was only the sound of Charley's hooves on the road, and the rustling of the slight wind. I thought I might jump down from the wagon, and run off into the woods; but knew I would not get far, and even if I did, I would then be eaten by the bears and wolves. And I thought, I am riding through the Valley of the Shadow of Death, as it says in the Psalm; and I attempted to fear no evil, but it was very hard, for there was evil in the wagon with me, like a sort of mist.
> MARGARET ATWOOD *Alias Grace*, 1996

Defeat

Over the centuries various famous military defeats, from **ACTIUM** to **WATERLOO** to **VIETNAM**, have each come to epitomize a decisive or humiliating defeat. ▶ *See also* **Failure**, **Victory**.

Actium Actium, a promontory in Ancient Greece, was in 31 BC the scene of a sea and land battle in which the forces of Mark Antony and Cleopatra were decisively defeated by the fleet of Octavian (the future Emperor Augustus).

> Soon he would be overtaken; but warm in the circle of Leila's arms, as if he were Antony at Actium, he could hardly bring himself to feel fear.
> LAWRENCE DURRELL *Mountolive*, 1958

Alamo The Alamo was a fort (formerly a Christian mission) in San Antonio, Texas, which in 1836 was besieged by the Mexican army during the war between Texas and Mexico. It was defended by a small group of soldiers and civilians all of whom (including the frontiersman and politician Davy Crockett) died. 'The Alamo' can refer to a last stand that fails.

> He still had what Donald once described as that 'last Texican at the Alamo look': ready, willing, and able to go down fighting.
> TOM CLANCY and STEVE PIECZENIK *Op-Center*, 1995

Austerlitz The battle of Austerlitz took place in 1805 near the village of Austerlitz (now Slavkov in the Czech Republic). It was a victory for Napoleon but a serious defeat for the allied Austrians and Russians.

> That dinner at the King's Arms with his friends had been Henchard's Austerlitz: he had had his successes since, but his course had not been upward.
> THOMAS HARDY *The Mayor of Casterbridge*, 1886

Little Bighorn The Battle of Little Bighorn, also referred to as 'Custer's last stand', was a defeat for George Custer and his troops at the hands of Sioux warriors. The battle took place in the valley of the Little Bighorn river in what is now Montana.

Vietnam The Vietnam War was a lengthy conflict between South Vietnam and the Communist North Vietnam. The US became militarily involved on the side of the South in the 1960s, but the war became unpopular and the US withdrew its troops in 1973 under the presidency of Richard Nixon, ceding victory to the North. References to Vietnam often suggest the idea of a worsening disaster.

> *Anderson Country* is Forgan's Vietnam: she's committed to it and can't get out.
> *The Independent*, 1994

Waterloo The battle between the French on one side and the British, Dutch, and Prussians on the other near the village of Waterloo (now in Belgium) in 1815 was the final battle in the Napoleonic wars and marked the end of Napoleon's rule in Europe. The name can allude to a decisive defeat from which recovery is impossible.

> He frowned and flipped the cigaret against the wall at the back of the cell. He was conscious of a dull burning resentment at having been sold by a lousy frail. He didn't claim to be smart but he didn't usually act that dumb. Well, a jane had been many a con's Waterloo, but that didn't ease the choking, self-contemptuous intensity of the chagrin.
> CHESTER HIMES *His Last Day*, 1933

Departure

This theme concentrates on the act of leaving a place, either individually or in numbers. Vanishing from a place, especially mysteriously, is covered at **Disappearance and Absence.** ▶ *See also* **Appearing**.

....

Exodus Exodus is the second book of the Bible, relating the departure of the Israelites under the leadership of Moses from their slavery in Egypt and their journey towards the promised land of Canaan. This journey is ascribed by scholars to various dates within the limits *c.*1580–*c.*1200 BC. An exodus is a mass departure of people, especially emigrants. ▶ *See special entry* ◻ **MOSES AND THE BOOK OF EXODUS** *on p. 264.*

> The English Department had changed its quarters since his arrival at Rummidge. . . . The changeover had taken place in the Easter vacation amid much wailing and gnashing of teeth. Oy, oy, Exodus was nothing in comparison.
> DAVID LODGE *Changing Places*, 1975

Lot The Book of Genesis relates how Lot, seen by God to be a righteous man, was led by angels out of the city of Sodom before God destroyed it.

> What the deuce is the hurry? Just so must Lot have left Sodom, when he expected fire to pour down upon it out of burning brass clouds.
> CHARLOTTE BRONTË *The Professor*, 1857

Captain Oates Captain Lawrence Oates (1880–1912) was an English explorer on Scott's expedition to the South Pole. Believing that his severe frostbite would jeopardize his companions' survival, he deliberately went out into a blizzard to sacrifice his own life. His famous last words were: 'I am just going outside and may be some time.' His epitaph reads: 'Hereabouts died a very gallant gentleman, Captain L. E. G. Oates of the Inniskilling Dragoons. In March 1912, returning from the Pole, he walked willingly to his death in a blizzard, to try and save his comrades, beset by hardship. This note is left by the Relief Expedition. 1912.'

> He didn't believe her. But he said, 'I suppose I'm a bit of a burden on you, Dora, these days. Perhaps I ought to go off and die.' Like Oates at the south Pole.
> MURIEL SPARK 'The Father's Daughters' in *The Collected Stories*, 1961

Parthian The Parthians lived and ruled in an area of western Asia in ancient times and were governed by a military aristocracy. They held out against the encroaching Romans until the second century AD and were famous for their cavalry, who had perfected the art of shooting backwards at an enemy from whom they were in retreat, the 'Parthian shot'. The term has come to be applied to a hostile remark delivered by someone at the moment of departure.

> 'I command you to leave this room at once.' 'Very well. Since all I have ever experienced in it is hypocrisy, I shall do so with the greatest pleasure.' With this Parthian shaft Sarah turned to go.
> JOHN FOWLES *The French Lieutenant's Woman*, 1969

Deserted Places

This theme deals with the idea of deserted or abandoned places, sometimes suggested by reference to the ruins of ancient cities. ▶ *See also* **Disappearance and Absence, Illusion**.

....

Beau Geste *Beau Geste* (1924) by P. C. Wren is an adventure story dealing with the exploits of the French Foreign Legion. It contains a famous scene in which, with hardly any soldiers left alive to defend a fort, the corpses of the dead are arranged on the fort's battlements to give the illusion of a strongly armed presence.

> Caz got back to John Street for half past two. There were a couple of voices in the back office behind the front desk, but other than that, the place was still a cheap version of Beau Geste meets the Marie Celeste.
> ALEX KEEGAN *Kingfisher*, 1995

Karnac Karnac is a village in Egypt, on the Nile near Luxor. It is the site of ancient Thebes, whose ruins, including the great temple of Amun, still survive there.

> Half-past ten in the morning was about her hour for seeking this spot—a time when the town avenues were deserted as the avenues of Karnac.
> THOMAS HARDY *The Mayor of Casterbridge*, 1886

Mary Celeste The *Mary Celeste* (often erroneously referred to as the *Marie Celeste*) was an American brig that set sail from New York for Genoa and was found drifting in the North Atlantic in December 1872, abandoned but with evidence of very recent occupation. It was never discovered what had happened to the crew.

> She boarded the lift, stuffing the booklet back into the folder. By the tenth and final floor, she was alone in the lift, and she emerged into a corridor that seemed about as lively as the deck of the Marie Celeste.
> VAL MCDERMID *Union Jack*, 1993

> And, anyway, it won't always be like this, with all her things around. She'll clear it out soon, and the Marie Celestial air about the place—the half-read Julian Barnes paperback on the bedside table and the knickers in the dirty clothes basket—will vanish.
> NICK HORNBY *High Fidelity*, 1995

Petra Petra is an ancient ruined city in Jordan. It was the capital of the Nabataeans from 312 BC until 63 BC, when they became subject to Rome. The city's extensive ruins include temples and tombs carved in the sandstone cliffs. The poet John Burgon famously described Petra as 'A rose-red city—"half as old as time".'

> Think of it. Of a Sunday, Wall Street is deserted as Petra; and every night of every day it is an emptiness.
> HERMAN MELVILLE *Bartleby*, 1856

Pompeii Pompeii was an ancient city in western Italy, south-east of Naples. Following an eruption of Mount Vesuvius in AD 79, the city was completely buried beneath volcanic ash. Excavations of the site, which began in 1748, have revealed that the ruins had been extremely well preserved, giving a detailed insight into the everyday life in Roman times.

> He was rather glad that they were all out; it was amusing to wander through the house as though one were exploring a dead, deserted Pompeii.
> ALDOUS HUXLEY *Crome Yellow*, 1921

Typhoid Mary Typhoid Mary was the name given to Mary Mallon (d. 1938), an Irish-born American cook who transmitted typhoid fever in the USA. Her name can be used to suggest someone whose presence can instantly empty a place of people.

> Archie Young looked round the canteen which was almost empty, all the tables near them had cleared with speed. It was like being Typhoid Mary, he thought.
> GWENDOLINE BUTLER *The Coffin Tree*, 1994

Despair

Loss or absence of hope are covered here. The tendency to expect things to turn out badly is covered at **Pessimism**. ▶ *See also* **Optimism**.

....

Aegeus In Greek mythology, Theseus had promised his father, Aegeus, that if he successfully destroyed the Minotaur he would signal this on his return to Athens by hoisting white sails, rather than the customary black ones. This he forgot to do and Aegeus, believing his son to be dead, threw himself to his death from a cliff.

Faust Faust is the subject of a medieval legend and subsequently of dramas by Marlowe, *Dr Faustus* (1604), and Goethe, *Faust* (1808, 1832). In Marlowe's version, Dr Faustus sells his soul to Mephistopheles in return for a period during which he can have anything he desires. In Goethe's version, Faust becomes Mephistopheles' servant and again is to have what he desires. For much of the time he is despairing and dissatisfied, although he is finally redeemed. Marlowe's Dr Faustus experiences the agony of utter despair as his contract with Mephistopheles ends and his life and soul are forfeit.

> Farfrae's character was just the reverse of Henchard's, who might not inaptly be described as Faust has been described—as a vehement gloomy being who had quitted the ways of vulgar men, without light to guide him on a better way.
> THOMAS HARDY *The Mayor of Casterbridge*, 1886

Giant Despair Giant Despair is a character in the *Pilgrim's Progress* by John Bunyan (1678, 1684). The giant finds Christian and his companion Hopeful sleeping in the grounds of his castle, Doubting Castle, and puts them in the castle dungeon where 'they lay from Wednesday morning till Saturday night, without one bit of bread, or drop of drink, or light, or any to ask how they did'. Giant Despair beats them and advises them to kill themselves. Eventually, they escape using 'the key called Promise' which opens all the locks in the castle.

Slough of Despond The Slough of Despond is a bog into which Christian and his fellow traveller, Pliable, fall because they were not paying attention to the path, in Bunyan's religious allegory *Pilgrim's Progress* (1678, 1684). Christian sinks deeply into the mire because he carries a burden on his back but manages to struggle through to the other side, where he is helped out. Pliable is quickly discouraged, manages to struggle out of the bog on the side he entered, and gives up the journey. The term 'Slough of Despond' is sometimes used for a state of utter hopelessness and despondency.

> We were in the Slough of Despond tonight, and Mother came and pulled us out as Help did in the book.
> LOUISA M. ALCOTT *Little Women*, 1868

> Burdens fell, darkness gave place to light, Marjorie apocalyptically understood all the symbols of religious literature. For she herself had struggled in the Slough of Despond and had emerged; she too had climbed laboriously and without hope and had suddenly been consoled by the sight of the promised land.
> ALDOUS HUXLEY *Point Counter Point*, 1928

> Brussels he sees as 'utterly complacent, and a negative force of great influence', but not quite the Slough of Despond.
> *The Observer*, 1996

Tristram In one version of the medieval legend of Tristram and Iseult, Tristram, when dying, sends for Iseult. He arranges a signal from the boat in which she would be travelling to let him know whether she is on board. If she is coming, a white flag will be flown; a black flag will be flown if she is not. When the boat arrives, the white flag is flying but his wife tells him it is black and he dies in despair, believing that Iseult has not come.

Destiny and Luck

The entries below cover both the idea of predestination and that of fortune, whether good or bad. ▶ *See also* **Punishment**.

Fate Fate is the name given to a goddess who controls people's destinies, especially one of the Fates or one of the Norns.

> Not only is the hand of Fate discernible in this affair; Fate has been leaving fingerprints all around the place ever since Higgins got his bright idea.
> ROBERTSON DAVIES *Leaven of Malice*, 1954

> In many subtle ways, but mainly by her silence, she showed that Mr Biswas, however grotesque, was hers and that she had to make do with what Fate had granted her.
> V. S. NAIPAUL *A House for Mr. Biswas*, 1961

> Kenneth Cracknell, Esq. . . . was the learned judge whom Fate had selected to

preside over the trial of the unhappy Revenue official.
JOHN MORTIMER *Rumpole's Return*, 1980

Fates In Greek and Roman mythology, the Fates were three sisters, daughters of Night, who presided over the destiny of every mortal individual. Clotho spun the thread of a person's life, Lachesis determined the luck that a person would have, and Atropos decided when each individual would die by cutting the thread of their life. They were also called, by the Greeks, the Moirae and, by the Romans, the Parcae.

The Fates had unexpectedly (and perhaps just a little officiously) removed an obstacle from his path.
SAKI 'Cross-Currents' in *Reginald in Russia*, 1910

Fortuna In Roman mythology, Fortuna was the goddess of fortune.

Fortuna's wheel had turned on humanity, crushing its collarbone, smashing its skull, twisting its torso, puncturing its pelvis, sorrowing its soul.
JOHN KENNEDY TOOLE *A Confederacy of Dunces*, 1980

Karma In Buddhist philosophy, Karma is the doctrine that the sum total of all a person's actions and experiences in all their incarnations determines the fate of their next incarnation.

Nemesis In Greek mythology, Nemesis was the goddess responsible for retribution, either for a person who had transgressed the moral code or for a person who had taken too much pride in their success or luck (hubris). Nemesis can now be used to refer to a person's doom or terrible but unavoidable fate.

She refused to put so much as a piece of thread into a needle in anticipation of her confinement and would have been absolutely unprepared, if her neighbours had not been better judges of her condition than she was, and got things ready without telling her anything about it. Perhaps she feared Nemesis, though assuredly she knew not who or what Nemesis was.
SAMUEL BUTLER *The Way of All Flesh*, 1903

It was six a.m. and Bruce's appointment with nemesis was well under way. His old life was already over. Even if he survived his ordeal, nothing would ever be the same again.
BEN ELTON *Popcorn*, 1996

Norns In Nordic mythology, the Norns were three goddesses who spun the fate of both people and the gods. They were named Urd (the past), Verdandi (the present), and Skuld (the future), and gathered under the ash tree Yggdrasil.

Yonder float the white swans—an Icelandic story-teller would say they are Norns, presiders over destiny.
F. METCALFE *Oxonian in Iceland*, 1861

Odysseus Odysseus, the King of Ithaca in Greek mythology and hero of Homer's *Odyssey*, spent ten years returning home to his wife Penelope after the Trojan War was over. During this period he encountered numerous obstacles and dangers that he had to overcome. He can thus be associated with a long period of bad luck. ▶ *See special entry* ☐ **ODYSSEUS** *on p. 283.*

Woeps was on the phone. Cook heard him say, 'Is it bad?' and he suspected his friend was talking to his wife about yet another domestic calamity. Woeps' only serious fault—and it could hardly be called a fault—was his Odyssean attraction for bad luck.

DAVID CARKEET *Double Negative*, 1980

Oedipus In Greek mythology, Oedipus was left on a mountain to die because of a prophecy that he would kill his father. He was rescued by a shepherd and grew up in ignorance of his own parentage. Oedipus subsequently quarrelled with and killed his father, Laius, and then unwittingly married his own mother, Jocasta, with whom he had four children. When they discovered the truth, Oedipus blinded himself and Jocasta hanged herself. Oedipus can be alluded to as someone who is predestined to act in a particular way and is powerless to act otherwise.

> Mr. Tulliver's prompt procedure entailed on him further promptitude in finding the convenient person who was desirous of lending five hundred pounds on bond. 'It must be no client of Wakem's,' he said to himself; and yet at the end of a fortnight it turned out to the contrary; not because Mr. Tulliver's will was feeble, but because external fact was stronger. Wakem's client was the only convenient person to be found. Mr. Tulliver had a destiny as well as Oedipus, and in this case he might plead, like Oedipus, that his deed was inflicted on him rather than committed by him.
>
> GEORGE ELIOT *The Mill on the Floss*, 1860

Polycrates Polycrates was the ruler of Samos and was extraordinarily lucky. So much luck put him in danger of retribution from Nemesis, and in order to appease her he threw away a very valuable ring. The ring was found by a fisherman in the belly of a fish and returned to Polycrates, who was subsequently killed.

Destruction

A number of these entries describe the end of the world according to various mythologies. There are also several accounts of cities being levelled, whether by trumpet blast, fire and brimstone, or atomic bomb.

Abaddon Abaddon (literally 'destruction' or 'abyss') is 'the angel of the bottomless pit' in the Book of Revelation, sometimes identified with the Devil.

> Some red-liveried, sulphur-scented imp of Abaddon.
>
> AUGUSTA J. WILSON *Vashti*, 1869

Apocalypse The Apocalypse is a name given to the Book of Revelation, the last book of the New Testament. The book recounts a divine revelation of the future to St John, including the total destruction of the world: 'And, lo, there was a great earthquake; and the sun became black as sackcloth of hair, and the moon became as blood' (Rev. 6: 12). Following this comes the last battle between the forces of good and evil, the final defeat of Satan and the creation of a new heaven and earth. The four agents of destruction, personified in the

Four Horsemen of the Apocalypse, are Pestilence, Famine, War, and Death. The word 'apocalypse' has now come to mean any event of great or total destruction, in more recent times especially a nuclear holocaust.

> The land about them was laid to waste in a small but extravagant apocalypse; bushes were uprooted and leafless, the ground was littered with little pieces of bridge.
> LOUIS DE BERNIÈRES *The War of Don Emmanuel's Nether Parts*, 1990

> For a year I had lived with the possibility of Liam Brady's transfer to another club in the same way that, in the late fifties and early sixties, American teenagers had lived with the possibility of the impending Apocalypse.
> NICK HORNBY *Fever Pitch*, 1993

Armageddon According to the Book of Revelation, Armageddon is the site of the last battle between the forces of good and evil before the Day of Judgement. The term is often used to describe a destructive conflict on a huge scale, latterly especially a nuclear war.

> I had a long drink, and read the evening papers. They were full of the row in the Near East, and there was an article about Karolides, the Greek Premier. . . . I gathered that they hated him pretty blackly in Berlin and Vienna, but that we were going to stick by him, and one paper said that he was the only barrier between Europe and Armageddon.
> JOHN BUCHAN *The Thirty Nine Steps*, 1915

> He has read somewhere that eighty per cent of all aircraft accidents occur at either take-off or landing. . . . By taking the non-stop polar flight to London, in preference to the two stage journey via New York, Zapp reckons that he has reduced his chances of being caught in such an Armageddon by fifty per cent.
> DAVID LODGE *Changing Places*, 1975

> We expect Armageddon; the Bible has trained us well. We assume either annihilation or salvation, perhaps both. Millenarian beliefs are as old as time; the apocalypse has always been at hand.
> PENELOPE LIVELY *Moon Tiger*, 1988

Dresden Dresden is a city in eastern Germany, on the river Elbe. It was one of Germany's most beautiful cities until it was almost totally destroyed by heavy Allied bombing on the night of 13 February 1945. Dresden has been extensively rebuilt since 1945.

Goth ▶ *See* VANDAL.

Götterdämmerung In Germanic mythology, Götterdämmerung was 'the twilight of the gods', their destruction and that of the world in a final battle with the forces of evil. This is the title of the last opera in Wagner's *Ring Cycle*. The term can be used to refer to the cataclysmic downfall of a powerful organization or regime. ▶ *See also* RAGNAROK.

> That same night at the national stadium, England faced their gotterdammerung against the All Blacks.
> *Scottish Rugby*, 1991

> 'There was certainly a huge dust-up about it,' she said. 'I mean, we're talking mega here, right? Apparently it had been going on for the best part of a year and Myra was the last to know. When she did find out it was like *Götterdämmerung*. I believe Myra brandished a knife at Lara and told her to be on the next stagecoach out of

town and, according to local legend, she had Simon's balls bronzed and still wears them round her neck on a chain.'
JOYCE HELM *Foreign Body*, 1997

Hiroshima Hiroshima is a city and port on the south coast of the island of Honshu, western Japan. It was the first city to be the target of an atomic bomb, dropped by the United States on 6 August 1945, which resulted in the deaths of more than a third of the city's population of 300,000.

There was every likelihood that they would freeze on Friday, or fry, or vanish in pure energy with nothing left of them but shadows like the men of Hiroshima after the lightburst.
A. S. BYATT *The Virgin in the Garden*, 1978

Jericho Jericho is a town in Palestine, one of the world's oldest settlements and believed to have been occupied from at least 9000 BC. According to the Bible, Jericho was a Canaanite city destroyed by the Israelites after they crossed the Jordon into the Promised Land, led by Joshua. Its walls were flattened by the shout of the army and the blast of the trumpets. 'So the people shouted when the priests blew with the trumpets: and it came to pass, when the people heard the sound of the trumpet, the people shouted with a great shout, and the wall fell down flat . . . and they took the city' (Joshua 6: 20).

At that period English society was still a closed body and it was not easy for a Jew to force its barriers, but to Ferdy they fell like the walls of Jericho.
W. SOMERSET MAUGHAM *The Alien Corn*, 1951

As Jenny Long drove to the hospital the next morning she sang softly to herself. She was quite confident that it wouldn't be long before Harry gave in and said it was time they got married. After all, even Jericho fell in the end.
MAX MARQUIS *Written in Blood*, 1995

Juggernaut In Hindu mythology, Juggernaut, or Jagannath (meaning 'lord of the world'), is the name of an image of Krishna annually carried in procession on an enormous cart. Devotees of the god are said to have thrown themselves under its wheels to be crushed in the hope of going straight to paradise. The word can be used to denote a huge destructive force that crushes whatever is in its path.

That human Juggernaut trod the child down and passed on regardless of her screams.
ROBERT LOUIS STEVENSON *The Strange Case of Dr Jekyll and Mr Hyde*, 1886

And now, young Pongo, stand out of my way, or I'll roll over you like a Juggernaut.
P. G. WODEHOUSE *Cocktail Time*, 1958

The horse was terrified already by the noise and the proximity of the horse box, but horses don't altogether understand about the necessity of removing themselves pronto from under the wheels of thundering juggernauts. Frightened horses, on the whole, are more apt to run *into* the paths of vehicles, than away.
DICK FRANCIS *Trial Run*, 1978

Nineveh Nineveh was an ancient city located on the east bank of the Tigris, opposite the modern city of Mosul. It was the capital of the ancient Assyrian empire during the reign of Sennacherib until it was destroyed in 612 BC by the Babylonians and Medes. Its destruction is forecast by the Old Testament prophet Nahum. Elsewhere in the Bible, the prophet Jonah is called by God to preach to the people of Nineveh and warn them of the destruction of their city unless they reform their wicked behaviour.

> He had as much of a vested interest in the damnation of the trekkers as Jonah had had in the annihilation of Nineveh.
> ANDRÉ BRINK *Imaginings of Sand*, 1996

Pompeii The ancient city of Pompeii in western Italy was completely buried beneath volcanic ash following an eruption of Mount Vesuvius in AD 79.

> I picked up the waste-paper basket and found, among ash to equal the destruction of Pompeii, a large number of old cigar butts, and handful of unopened bills ... and an unopened cablegram.
> JOHN MORTIMER *Rumpole's Return*, 1980

Ragnarok In Norse mythology, Ragnarok (literally 'destined end of the gods' or 'twilight of the gods') is the final battle between the gods and the forces of evil that will result in the destruction of the world, the Scandinavian equivalent of the Götterdämmerung.

> An all-out race war would be triggered, a final, bloody Ragnarok of the races.
> *Time*, 1993

Sirens In Greek mythology, the Sirens were sea creatures who lured sailors to destruction on dangerous rocks by the beauty of their singing. Sirens are usually depicted as women or as half-woman and half-bird. ▶ *See special entry* □ ODYSSEUS *on p. 283.*

> She will always be the odd Japanese artist who stole Britain's greatest rock'n'roller, the wife of John Lennon, the woman who split the Beatles, the siren on whose rock the mythical innocence of the Sixties was wrecked.
> *The Independent*, 1996

Sodom and Gomorrah Sodom and Gomorrah were towns in ancient Palestine, probably south of the Dead Sea. According to Gen. 19: 24, they were destroyed by fire and brimstone from heaven as a punishment for the depravity and wickedness of their inhabitants. Lot, the nephew of Abraham, was allowed to escape from the destruction of Sodom with his family. His wife disobeyed God's order not to look back at the burning city and she was turned into a pillar of salt.

> Talk of the abuses of slavery! Humbug! The thing itself is the essence of all abuse! And the only reason why the land don't sink under it, like Sodom and Gomorrah, is because it is used in a way infinitely better than it is.
> HARRIET BEECHER STOWE *Uncle Tom's Cabin*, 1852

Vandal The Vandals were a Germanic people that overran part of Roman Europe in the 4th and 5th centuries AD. Of the various invading peoples of this period (Goths, Visigoths, Huns, etc.), it is the Vandals whose name is most closely associated with the idea of mass invasion and wanton destruction. In modern usage, a vandal is a person who maliciously destroys or damages property.

> The glittering dresses on the blank-faced or headless mannequins are no longer what they seemed, the incarnation of desire. Instead they look like party trash.

Crumpled paper napkins, the rubble left by rowdy crowds or looting armies. Although nobody saw them or could say for certain who they were, the Goths and the Vandals have been through.
MARGARET ATWOOD *The Robber Bride*, 1993

Yahoo The Yahoos are an imaginary race of brutish creatures, resembling human beings, in Jonathan Swift's *Gulliver's Travels* (1726). They embody all the baser vices and instincts of the human race. The word 'yahoo' has become a part of the language, referring to a coarse, loutish, or rowdy person, or one who engages in wanton vandalism. ▶ *See special entry* ☐ **GULLIVER'S TRAVELS** *on p. 171.*

In the main the animals would have walked along quietly enough; but the Casterbridge tradition was that to drive stock it was indispensable that hideous cries, coupled with Yahoo antics and gestures, should be used.
THOMAS HARDY *The Mayor of Casterbridge*, 1886

Hens were in attendance, quietly and unquestioningly supportive, among all the dust and rubbish. As for the two pigs, they were yahoos even by the standards of the yard.
MARTIN AMIS *London Fields*, 1989

Detectives

Famous fictional detectives are often mentioned in the context of investigation or deduction. The most commonly cited of these, as the illustrative quotations suggest, is **SHERLOCK HOLMES**. ▶ *See also* **Intelligence**.

....

Dick Barton Dick Barton, Special Agent, was the hero of a radio series broadcast between 1946 and 1951, in which he courageously pursued and defeated arch-criminals.

Nancy Drew Nancy Drew is the name of an American teenage detective created in the 1930s by Edward Stratemeyer and the heroine of a series of novels for children written by a variety of writers under the name Carolyn Greene.

He shook his head. 'What happened?' 'I fell into a yucca plant.' 'Ouch!' He flinched in sympathy. 'Just jumped up and bit you, huh?' 'What I get for playing Nancy Drew,' I said, and told him about chasing the burglar who'd broken into Andy Bynum's house.
MARGARET MARON *Shooting at Loons*, 1994

Sherlock Holmes Sherlock Holmes is an extremely perceptive private detective in a series of stories by Arthur Conan Doyle. Holmes's exceptional powers of observation and deductive reasoning enable him to solve the seemingly impenetrable mysteries that are brought to him by troubled clients. Probably the most famous fictional detective of all, Holmes plays the violin, smokes a pipe, has an opium habit, and wears a deerstalker. He is a master of disguise.

Holmes is assisted by his stalwart associate, Dr Watson, with whom he shares rooms at 221B Baker Street, London. His arch-enemy is the criminal master-mind Professor Moriarty. One story ends with Holmes and Moriarty grappling together above the Reichenbach Falls and the former apparently plunging to his death there. In fact Conan Doyle subsequently resurrected his hero for further adventures.

> They were curious. Something was fishy. They tried some amateur Sherlocking by asking the same questions twice, expecting us to make a slip.
> JACK KEROUAC *On the Road*, 1957

> At once I took up my pipe, violin and deerstalker like a veritable Sherlock. I have always been an X-marks-the-spot man. 'Let us go and revisit it,' I said briskly.
> LAWRENCE DURRELL *Clea*, 1960

> You were all right as a jockey. You should give up this pretence of being Sherlock Holmes.
> DICK FRANCIS *Come to Grief*, 1995

Philip Marlowe Philip Marlowe is the hard-boiled private detective in such novels as *The Big Sleep* (1939) and *Farewell, My Lovely* (1940) by the US writer Raymond Chandler. Tough, cynical, yet honourable, the Marlowe character is well-known from the films of Chandler's novels, notably as embodied by Humphrey Bogart and Robert Mitchum.

> 'I'm following my own leads.' She looked at Robin. 'Philip Marlowe here?' Robin gave her a helpless look. 'Is this dangerous, Alex?' 'No. I just want to look into a few things.'
> JONATHAN KELLERMAN *When the Bough Breaks*, 1992

Miss Marple Jane Marple is the elderly detective created by the crime writer Agatha Christie. She lives in the village of St Mary Mead, indulging in her hobbies of knitting and gardening. Her disarming appearance as a mildly gossipy old spinster hides a shrewdness and acuteness of observation that she uses to solve murders.

> I tried Ralph again. This time he answered on the fourth ring.
> 'What's up, Miss Marple?' he asked. 'I thought you were out after Professor Moriarty until tomorrow.'
> SARA PARETSKY *Indemnity Only*, 1982

> Would you kindly stop shining that light in my eyes? Your Miss Marple act is less polished if I may say so, than your . . . letters.
> CAROL SHIELDS *Mary Swan*, 1990

Perry Mason Perry Mason is the fictional defence lawyer in a series of novels by Erle Stanley Gardner and in a US television series of the 1960s. The stories frequently end with a dramatic courtroom scene in which Mason proves his client innocent of the crime.

> How like Denn to choose a place like this for a rendezvous. He knew perfectly well he should turn himself in to Sheriff Bo Poole and try to hire himself a Perry Mason.
> MARGARET MARON *Bootlegger's Daughter*, 1992

> 'Given that Scotty, for whatever reason, decided to murder his wife,' she began, trying a new tack, 'doesn't it seem odd that with access to a boat and hundreds of square miles of deep water, he would choose to dispose of the body by eating it?' 'Not if he was the reincarnation of Charlie Mott,' Damien said triumphantly. He and Tinker

looked at her expectantly, twin Perry Masons having delivered the coup de grace.
NEVADA BARR *A Superior Death*, 1994

Pinkerton's Pinkerton's National Detective Agency was founded in Chicago in 1850 by Allan Pinkerton, a Scottish-born US detective. This was the first American private detective agency, which became famous after solving a series of train robberies. During the American Civil War Pinkerton served as chief of the secret service on the Union side, directing espionage behind the Confederate lines.

'And you don't happen to have a friend at a courier firm, do you?' 'Guilty.' I held up my hand in submission. 'The lady from the courier firm was Mrs Bradshaw, yes?' 'Yes.' It was obvious that Pinkerton's wouldn't be the right career move for me.
MALCOLM HAMER *Dead on Line*, 1996

Hercule Poirot Hercule Poirot is the Belgian detective in many novels by Agatha Christie. He has a waxed moustache, drinks tisanes, and uses 'the little grey cells' to deduce the identity of the murderer.

It was well after midnight before Jamieson got back to the residency and heard Sue gasp when she saw the state of him. Jamieson sat down slowly in the only armchair and asked her to pour him a drink while he told her what had happened. 'So you didn't even find out what Thelwell was up to?' said Sue. There was a suggestion of 'I told you so' in her voice, but she didn't actually say it. Jamieson agreed with a shake of the head and said, 'More Clouseau than Poirot.'
KEN MCCLURE *Chameleon*, 1994

Sam Spade Sam Spade is the American private investigator in the novels written by Dashiell Hammet in the 1930s. Spade was the first in a long line of tough, hard-boiled American private detectives. Essentially an honourable man, he is willing to break the law on occasion to see justice done.

The downtown office buildings were just sparkling on their lights; it made you think of Sam Spade.
JACK KEROUAC *On the Road*, 1957

I inquired. He said that when they got ready to roll out and make an arrest, I'd know about it. Translation: 'We are no longer buddies, Sam Spade, so you can go fuck yourself.'
CAROL BRENNAN *Chill of Summer*, 1995

Dick Tracy Dick Tracy was one of the first American comic strip detectives, first appearing in 1931. Tracy joins forces with the police to find the criminals who have kidnapped his girlfriend and murdered her father, and goes on to become a tireless fighter for justice, pursuing criminals at great risk to himself.

The work I do for nonprofits is limited to writing the occasional check. Anyway, I never wanted to be Dick Tracy, running around town with a gun.
SARA PARETSKY *Tunnel Vision*, 1994

V. I. Warshawski V.I. Warshawski is the Chicago-based private investigator heroine of a series of novels by Sara Paretsky. Feisty, tough, and feminist, she is, in the American tradition, not above breaking the law herself when necessary.

She knew as well as I that a million people pass through Heathrow every week. That London's a big place. That without a point of contact, not even V. I. Warshawski

would have a hope in hell of locating Claire.
MICHELLE SPRING *Running for Shelter*, 1994

Devil

This theme is dominated by the Judaeo-Christian figure of the **DEVIL**, known as **SATAN** and by a wide variety of other names. Other evil spirits or fallen angels, some of whom can also be identified with Satan, are included. Usually the allusive force of such references is the personification of evil.

··

Abaddon Abaddon, whose name is Hebrew for 'destruction' or 'abyss', is described in Rev. 9 as 'the angel of the bottomless pit' who presides over a swarm of tormenting locusts that 'have tails like scorpions, and stings'. He is sometimes identified with the Devil and also with Hell. His Greek name is Apollyon.

> And my father preached a whole set of sermons on the occasion; one set in the morning, all about David and Goliath, to spirit up the people to fighting with spades or bricks, if need were; and the other set in the afternoons, proving that Napoleon (that was another name for Bony, as we used to call him) was all the same as an Apollyon and Abaddon.
> ELIZABETH GASKELL *Cranford*, 1851–3

Ahriman According to the dualistic cosmology of Zoroastrianism, Ahriman is the supreme evil spirit who is perpetually in conflict with the supreme good spirit, Ahura Mazda (or Ormazd). This is Bunyan's description of him: 'He was clothed with scales like a fish (and they are his pride), he had wings like a dragon, and out of his belly came fire and smoke, and his mouth was as the mouth of a lion.'

Apollyon Apollyon (meaning 'the destroyer') is the 'angel of the bottomless pit' described in Rev. 9: 11 (see **ABADDON** above). In Christian thought he is often identified with the Devil. In Bunyan's *Pilgrim's Progress*, Apollyon is the foul fiend, the personification of evil, who bars Christian's way but is ultimately defeated by the latter's virtue.

> He may be stern; he may be exacting: he may be ambitious yet; but his is the sternness of the warrior Greatheart, who guards his pilgrim convoy from the onslaught of Apollyon.
> CHARLOTTE BRONTË *Jane Eyre*, 1847

> Feeling stronger than ever to meet and subdue her Apollyon, she pinned the note inside her frock, as a shield and a reminder.
> LOUISA M. ALCOTT *Little Women*, 1868

> He anxiously descended the ladder, and started homewards at a run, trying not to

think of giants, Herne the Hunter, Apollyon lying in wait for Christian.
THOMAS HARDY *Jude the Obscure*, 1896

Beelzebub In the Old Testament, Beelzebub (literally 'the lord of the flies') is the God of the Philistine city Ekron (2 Kgs. 1). He is mentioned in several of the Gospels, where he is called 'the prince of demons'. Beelzebub is often identified with the Devil. In *Paradise Lost*, however, Milton gives the name to one of the fallen angels, next to Satan in power.

She 'spaed fortunes', read dreams, composed philtres, discovered stolen goods, and made and dissolved matches as successfully as if, according to the belief of the whole neighbourhood, she had been aided in those arts by Beelzebub himself.
WALTER SCOTT *The Bride of Lammermoor*, 1819

Winterborne was standing in front of the brick oven in his shirt-sleeves, tossing in thorn-sprays, and stirring about the blazing mass with a long-handled, three-pronged Beelzebub kind of fork.
THOMAS HARDY *The Woodlanders*, 1887

Devil In Christian and Jewish belief, the Devil is the supreme spirit of evil. He is the enemy of God and the tempter of humankind. In theological tradition he was regarded as the chief of the fallen angels, cast out of heaven for rebellion against God. He presided over those condemned to eternal fire. Popularly, the Devil is often represented as a man with horns, a forked tail, and cloven hooves, an image derived from figures of Greek and Roman mythology such as Pan and the satyrs. The Devil is known by numerous names, especially Satan and Lucifer. Other names include 'the Evil One', 'Old Harry', 'Old Nick', and 'the Prince of Darkness.'

Thus the devil, who began, by the help of an irresistible poverty, to push me into this wickedness, brought me to a height beyond the common rate, even when my necessities were not so terrifying.
DANIEL DEFOE *Moll Flanders*, 1722

But it was only a thought, put into my head by the Devil, no doubt.
MARGARET ATWOOD *Alias Grace*, 1996

Evil One The Evil One is another name for the Devil or Satan.

Sophia wandered about, a prey ripe for the Evil One.
ARNOLD BENNETT *The Old Wives' Tale*, 1908

Lucifer Lucifer (literally 'bearer of light') is another name for the Devil or Satan, particularly when regarded as the leader of the angels who rebelled against God and were hurled from heaven down to hell. Lucifer is also another name for the morning star, the planet Venus.

O black, perfidious creature! thought I, what an implement art thou in the hands of Lucifer, to ruin the innocent heart?
SAMUEL RICHARDSON *Pamela*, 1740

In literature as in life everything would go on getting less and less innocent. The rapists of the eighteenth century were the romantic leads of the nineteenth; the anarchic Lucifers of the nineteenth were the existential Lancelots of the twentieth.
MARTIN AMIS *The Information*, 1995

She was a bit too perfect, that girl. With her cast in the angelic role, lapped in

universal love and admiration, there wasn't really another starring part for her husband, except Lucifer.
ALINE TEMPLETON *Last Act of All*, 1995

Mephistopheles Mephistopheles is the evil spirit to whom Faust in German legend sold his soul, especially as represented in Marlowe's *Doctor Faustus* (*c.*1590) and Goethe's *Faust* (1808–32). Mephistopheles entraps Faust with wit, charm, and rationality. His name, and the adjective 'Mephistophelean', are often used to describe a fiendish but urbane tempter.

When it was over he pulled my head round so that he could see my face and said, 'You O.K. kid?' I can remember the tone now. He was obviously happy and the Mephistophelian smile had given place to an expression that was almost boyish.
ROBERTSON DAVIES *World of Wonders*, 1975

Old Harry Old Harry is another name for the Devil or Satan.

The old mill 'ud miss me, I think, Luke. There's a story as when the mill changes hands, the river's angry—I've heard my father say it many a time. There's no telling whether there mayn't be summat *in* the story, for this is a puzzling world, and Old Harry's got a finger in it—it's been too many for me, I know.
GEORGE ELIOT *The Mill on the Floss*, 1860

Old Nick Old Nick is another name for the Devil or Satan.

Prince of Darkness The Prince of Darkness is another name for the Devil or Satan.

Satan Satan (meaning 'the adversary') is the most common name given to the supreme evil spirit, the Devil. The name is used to suggest utter evil or wickedness.

O my poor old Harry Jekyll, if ever I read Satan's signature upon a face, it is on that of your new friend.
ROBERT LOUIS STEVENSON *The Strange Case of Dr Jekyll and Mr Hyde*, 1886

But the deeper the depression of the rest, young Rupert went about Satan's work with a smile on his eye and a song on his lip.
ANTHONY HOPE *The Prisoner of Zenda*, 1894

Dictators and Tyrants

Many of history's dictators and tyrants remain bywords for cruel and ruthless behaviour. ▶ *See also* **Evil**, **Leaders**, **Ruthlessness**.

Idi Amin Idi Amin (b. 1925) was a Ugandan soldier and head of state 1971–9. In 1971 he overthrew President Milton Obote and seized power. He presided over a regime characterized by brutality and repression, during which Uganda's Asian population was expelled and thousands of his political opponents murdered. Amin was overthrown in 1979 and fled the country.

Don't forget what I told you in the motel room. About the world getting crazier and crazier. Besides, maybe the cultists were camera shy when your professor friend studied them but not anymore. Weirdos change, like anyone else. Jim Jones was everyone's hero until he turned into Idi Amin.
JONATHAN KELLERMAN *Blood Test*, 1986

Attila the Hun Attila (406–53) was the king of the Huns 434–53. Having attacked and devastated much of the Eastern Roman Empire in 445–50, Attila invaded the Western Empire but was defeated by the Romans and the Visigoths in 451. He and his army, noted for its savagery, were the terror of Europe during his lifetime, and Attila later came to be called the 'Scourge of God'. He is supposed to have died either by poison or from a massive nose-bleed.

In the grey-green light of the Embassy he listened thoughtfully to the latest evaluations of the new Attila, and a valuable summary of the measured predictions which for months past had blackened the marbled minute-papers of [the] German Department.
LAWRENCE DURRELL *Mountolive*, 1958

'Don't deliver your publicity lecture to me,' Lotty snapped. Her thick brows contracted to a solid black line across her forehead. 'As far as I am concerned he is a cretin with the hands of a Caliban and the personality of Attila.'
SARA PARETSKY *V. I. for Short*, 1995

Colonel Gadaffi's metamorphosis from dictator to sensitive writer is as incongruous as Attila the Hun revealing a passion for Buddhist theology.
The Observer, 1996

Caligula Gaius Caesar Germanicus (AD 12–41) was a Roman emperor, the son of Germanicus Caesar and Agrippina. His nickname, 'Caligula', came from the soldier's boots (*caligulae*) that he wore as a small child. He became emperor at a young age after the death of Tiberius in 37 and his brief reign was notorious for its cruelty and tyranny. Caligula was famously supposed to have given a consulship to his horse.

'Watson, having risen to historic fame at an early age, became the Caligula of biology,' says Harvard biologist Edward Wilson in his biography *Naturalist*. 'He was given licence to say anything that came to his mind and expect to be taken seriously.'
The Observer, 1997

Genghis Khan Genghis Khan (1162–1227) was a military leader and founder of the Mongol empire, which at his death stretched from the Pacific to the Black Sea. Though a brilliant military leader and administrator, he acquired a reputation for horrific cruelty. Modern-day people holding fanatically right-wing views are sometimes humorously described as being 'to the right of Genghis Khan'.

Atkinson came slowly into the room. As so often, especially in the mornings, his demeanour seemed to imply that he was unacquainted with the other two and had, at the moment, no intention of striking up any sort of relation with them. This morning he looked more than ever like Genghis Khan meditating a purge of his captains.
KINGSLEY AMIS *Lucky Jim*, 1953

He seems to assume I'm about as liberal-minded as Ghengis Khan and the annoying

thing is, when he talks to me, I start sounding like the worst sort of reactionary. He provokes it. I take up points of view I don't actually support strongly and start defending them to the hilt.
ANN GRANGER *A Season for Murder*, 1991

What he is and what he says he is—two different things. I think the guy's a hard-nosed reactionary. To the right of Genghis Khan.
JANE STANTON HITCHCOCK *The Witches' Hammer*, 1995

Hitler Adolf Hitler (1889–1945) was the Austrian-born founder of the German Nazi Party and Chancellor of the Third Reich 1933–45. Following his appointment as Chancellor of Germany in 1933, he established a totalitarian regime, the Third Reich, proclaiming himself Führer ('leader'). His territorial aggression led to the Second World War and his anti-semitic policies to the Holocaust. His name can be applied to anyone tyrannical or despotic.

But the white man bumped into him anyway, and then turned and said, 'What's the matter with you, nigger, you want all the street?' 'Now look, white folks—' Ward began, but the white man pushed him: 'Go on, beat it, nigger, 'fore you get in trouble.' 'All right, Mr Hitler,' Ward mumbled and started off.
CHESTER HIMES *All He Needs Is Feet*, 1945

Little Hitlers, every one, Diamond thought. How does anything ever get decided these days? Maybe on the orders of a bigger Hitler, like me.
PETER LOVESEY *The Summons*, 1995

And within a few weeks, Saddam—and yes, he *is* a venal, cruel, wicked, evil man—was being transformed into the Hitler of Iraq, just as the Israelis had called Yasser Arafat the Hitler of Beirut in 1982, and just as Eden had called Nasser the Mussolini of the Nile in 1956.
The Independent, 1998

Ivan the Terrible Ivan IV, born Ivan Vasilyevich (1530–84), was the Grand Duke of Muscovy 1533–47 and proclaimed himself the first Tsar of Russia in 1547. As he grew increasingly paranoid and tyrannical, he conducted a reign of terror against the Boyars (the old Russian aristocracy), executing thousands of people. He consequently acquired the nickname 'the Terrible'.

Mussolini Benito Mussolini (1883–1945), the founder and leader of the Italian Fascists, was born in Predappio in north-east Italy, the son of a blacksmith. Initially socialist, he founded the Italian Fascist Party after the First World War, becoming known as 'Il Duce' (the leader). He organized a march on Rome by his blackshirts in 1922 and was made Prime Minister. Mussolini established himself as a dictator and allied Italy with Germany during the Second World War. He was executed by Italian Communist partisans shortly before the end of the war.

'If you've finished being funny,' said Everard, 'I'll take my leave.' Tinpot Mussolini, Illidge was thinking.
ALDOUS HUXLEY *Point Counter Point*, 1928

Herod wasn't just a tyrant and a unifier of his country, he was also a patron of the arts—perhaps we should think of him as a sort of Mussolini with good taste.
JULIAN BARNES *A History of the World in 10½ Chapters*, 1989

Nero Nero (AD 37–68) was a Roman emperor 54–68, notorious for his tyranny and cruelty. He ordered the murder of his mother Agrippina in 59, and his reign was marked by the persecution of Christians and the executions of leading Romans who had plotted against him. Nero was alleged to have started the fire that destroyed half of Rome in 64.

> 'Wicked and cruel boy!' I said. 'You are like a murderer—you are like a slave–driver—you are like the Roman Emperors!' I had read Goldsmith's History of Rome, and had formed my opinion of Nero, Caligula, &c.
> CHARLOTTE BRONTË *Jane Eyre*, 1847

Papa Doc François Duvalier (1907–71), known as 'Papa Doc' was President of Haiti 1957–71. His regime was noted for its brutality and oppressiveness. Many of his opponents were either assassinated or forced into exile by his security force, known as the Tontons Macoutes.

> As for the people, many are afraid of him and the rest admire him, not for his behaviour, you understand, but because he can get away with it. They see this as power and they admire a big man here. He spends their money on new cars and so forth for himself and his friends, they applaud that. . . . It's the old story, my friend. We will have a Papa Doc and after that a revolution or so. Then the Americans will wonder why people are getting killed.
> MARGARET ATWOOD *Bodily Harm*, 1981

Pharaoh Pharaoh was the title of a king of ancient Egypt, most associated with those mentioned in the Old Testament and Hebrew scriptures in whose time the oppression and Exodus of Israel took place. The title can be applied to any tyrant. ▶ *See special entry* ☐ **MOSES AND THE BOOK OF EXODUS** *on p. 264.*

> But going back to what's fundamental, Vic, it seems to me you guard everything you do like you were protecting baby Moses from the Pharaoh.
> SARA PARETSKY *Tunnel Vision*, 1994

Stalin Joseph Stalin (1879–1953) was born Iosif Vissarionovich Dzhugashvili and changed his name to Stalin ('man of steel') in 1912. He became a Bolshvik in 1903 and General Secretary of the Communist Party in 1924. After Lenin's death in 1924, he became increasingly powerful and was leader of the party by 1926. Stalin's attempts to collectivize agriculture led to the death of up to 10 million peasants, and his purges against anyone thought to oppose him were ruthless. After the Second World War he gained power over eastern Europe and imposed the iron curtain which divided Europe until 1989. His name is often associated with the idea of authoritarianism.

> At the same time Clemmow was addressing the massed ranks of the BBC *Newsnight* operation facing, ashen-faced, allegations of 'editorial Stalinism' and 'centralised control'.
> *The Observer*, 1997

Difficulty

The stories of **HERCULES** and **SISYPHUS** call to mind the undertaking of formidable tasks, successfully in the case of the former and unsuccessfully in the case of the latter. **ATLAS** and the **OLD MAN OF THE SEA** suggest onerous burdens. This idea of having something difficult to accomplish is obviously closely related to the theme of **Perseverance**, and to that of a **Problem**, both covered elsewhere.

....

Atlas Atlas was one of the Titans in Greek mythology, punished for rebelling against Zeus by being made to support the heavens on his shoulders. The image of Atlas holding up the sky, or sometimes the earth itself, is a common one in art and literature. The name can be applied to anyone who is forced to bear a heavy burden.

> I am like a spy who has signed a covenant of perpetual secrecy, I am like someone who is the only person in the world that knows the truth and yet is forbidden to utter it. And this truth weighs more than the universe, so that I am like Atlas bowed down forever beneath a burden that cracks the bones and solidifies the blood.
> LOUIS DE BERNIÈRES *Captain Corelli's Mandolin*, 1994

Augean stables In Greek mythology, the stables of the king of Augeas housed a very large herd of oxen and had never been cleaned out. Hercules undertook the task of cleaning them as one of his twelve labours. He achieved this task by diverting two rivers, the Alpheus and the Peneus, through the stables. The phrase 'cleaning the Augean stables' is often now used to mean not merely cleaning up a mess but putting right a corrupt or morally unacceptable situation. ▶ *See special entry* □ **HERCULES** *on p. 182*.

> 'What are you doing here, Warshawski?' 'Cleaning the Augean stables, Todd. You can call me Hercules. Although I think he had some help. In a way I've outperformed him.'
> SARA PARETSKY *Guardian Angel*, 1992

> I am convinced we need fundamental constitutional reform at all levels. We must cleanse the Augean stables at Westminster of the mess of patronage and special interests which do so much to discredit democracy.
> EMMA NICHOLSON in The *Observer*, 1995

Excalibur Excalibur was King Arthur's sword. It had been embedded in a stone and Arthur was able to draw it out when no one else could move it, thus proving himself the rightful king of England.

> The wall had a surprising grip on it. It was like the whole structure of that wall had settled down around this useless, forgotten piece of iron. I said to Valentina: 'This is like trying to extract the sword Excalibur from the stone!'
> ROSE TREMAIN *The Way I Found Her*, 1998

Hercules In Greek and Roman mythology, Hercules (called Heracles by the Greeks) was a hero of superhuman strength and courage who performed twelve immense tasks or 'labours' imposed on him by Eurystheus, King of Argos, including the cleaning of the Augean stables. He was usually depicted with a lion-skin, club, and bow. Most allusions to Hercules are in the context of performing a formidably difficult task. ▶ *See special entry* □ **HERCULES** *on p. 182*.

> He had already been at work on it for more than seven years and as yet, he would say to anyone who asked him about the progress of the book ... 'It's a labour of Hercules.'
> ALDOUS HUXLEY *Point Counter Point*, 1928

Charles produced the piece of ammonitiferous rock he had brought for Ernistina, who put down her fireshield and attempted to hold it, and could not, and forgave Charles everything for such a labour of Hercules, and then was mock-angry with him for endangering life and limb.
JOHN FOWLES *The French Lieutenant's Woman*, 1969

These cases, and thousands more in scores of other countries, are detailed in Index on Censorship, the bimonthly magazine which has just celebrated (though that hardly seems an appropriate word) its 25th anniversary. The magazine has a Lilliputian circulation and a Herculean task: winning for the people of the world one of the most basic of human rights, the freedom of expression.
The Guardian, 1997

Old Man of the Sea The Old Man of the Sea is a character in 'Sinbad the Sailor', one of the tales in the *Arabian Nights*. He persuades Sinbad to carry him on his shoulders, whereupon he twines his legs round him, so that Sinbad cannot dislodge him. Sinbad is forced to carry him on his shoulders for many days and nights, until at last he gets the Old Man drunk with wine and manages to shake him off. The term is used to denote a tiresome, heavy burden.

Well, we can't have it, so don't let us grumble but shoulder our bundles and trudge along as cheerfully as Marmee does. I'm sure Aunt March is a regular Old Man of the Sea to me, but I suppose when I've learned to carry her without complaining, she will tumble off, or get so light that I shan't mind her.
LOUISA M. ALCOTT *Little Women*, 1868

Pelion on Ossa In Greek mythology, Mount Pelion in Thessaly was held to be the home of the centaurs, and the giants were said to have piled Pelion on top of Mount Ossa (or sometimes Ossa on Pelion) in their attempt to scale Mount Olympus and destroy the gods. To 'pile Pelion on Ossa' is to add difficulty to difficulty.

Whether one thinks the relevant ministers should have gone or stayed, these have been abject performances. Their effect has been to make mountains of molehills (except in the case of the ERM, where it was more a case of piling Pelion on Ossa).
The Sunday Telegraph, 1994

That was final enough in itself, but within minutes a fax arrived from Capitaine Lapollet. If such a thing was possible, it made things worse by rubbing salt into Timberlake's near-mortal wounds. It said the late Comte de Gaillmont's group was A, which meant that he could be Jean-Louis's father. It didn't mean he was his father, but this last blow was piling Pelion upon Ossa.
MAX MARQUIS *Written in Blood*, 1995

Sisyphus In Greek mythology, Sisyphus was a king of Corinth, punished in Hades for his misdeeds in life by being condemned to the eternal task of rolling a huge stone to the top of a hill. Every time he approached the summit, the stone slipped and rolled down to the bottom again. An endless and fruitless task can be described as Sisyphean. ▶ *See special entry* □ **HADES** *on p. 172.*

Trinity College had undertaken the Sisyphean task of repairing all of its historic Front Square.
JOHN BRADY *A Stone of the Heart*, 1988

Is that the only future humanity has, to push the boulder, like Sisyphus, up to the top

of a hill, only to see it roll to the bottom again?
ISAAC ASIMOV *Forward the Foundation*, 1994

Ralph glanced round at a profusion of books and papers equalling that of the front room, and shrugged eloquently. 'You can see how things are. I feel like Sisyphus trying to keep up with the projects and my assistant only keeps the stone from backsliding a bit.'
DEBORAH CROMBIE *Dreaming of the Bones*, 1996

sorcerer's apprentice *The Sorcerer's Apprentice* is the title of an orchestral composition by Paul Dukas (1897), after a ballad by Goethe (1797). It was one of the pieces used in the 1940 Disney animated film *Fantasia*. According to the story on which Dukas's work is based, the sorcerer's apprentice finds a spell to make objects do work for him but is then unable to cancel it. In the Disney version, Mickey Mouse is the apprentice and the spell causes a broom to keep fetching buckets of water from a well. The term is used to describe a person who instigates but is unable to control a process.

How would Emily put what she felt into words? She would describe this, perhaps, in terms of that image of her sweeping, sweeping, the sorcerer's apprentice put to work in a spiteful garden against floods of dying leaves that she could never clean away no matter how hard she tried.
DORIS LESSING *Memoirs of a Survivor*, 1974

Dionysus

In Greek mythology, Dionysus (also called Bacchus) was the son of Zeus and the mortal Semele. Zeus had taken Semele as a lover and when she asked Zeus to reveal himself to her in all the splendour of a god, he acceded to this rash request. The fire of the thunderbolts which flashed about him incinerated Semele, but Zeus just had time to snatch the unborn child from her womb. He sewed it up immediately inside his own thigh for protection, from where a few months later the baby Dionysus emerged. This is why Dionysus was sometimes known as 'the twice-born god'.

Originally a god of the fertility of nature, in later traditions Dionysus is a god of wine who loosens inhibitions and inspires creativity in music and poetry. His cult was celebrated at various festivals throughout the year, some of which included orgies and ecstatic rites. His female de-votees were called the Bacchantes or Maenads. Dionysus, representing creativity, sensuality, and lack of inhibition, is often contrasted with Apollo, representing order, reason, and self-discipline.

When he had grown to adulthood, Hera drove him mad and he began a series of wanderings in the east. He was cured of his madness by the earth mother-goddess Cybele. Dionysus spread his cult, teaching man-kind the elements of civilization and the use of wine. On his travels he is frequently represented drawn in a chariot by tigers and accompanied by Pan, Silenus, and a rowdy retinue of satyrs and maenads.

According to one story, Dionysus was captured by pirates. When they tried to tie him up, the knots kept untying themselves. Wine started to flow around the ship and a vine and ivy grew up over the mast and sails. Dionysus turned himself into a fierce lion. The sailors leapt over-board and were transformed into dolphins.

A number of Dionysus' attributes are dealt with in this book.

▶ *See* **DIONYSUS** *or* **BACCHUS** *at* **Chaos and Disorder, Fertility, Food and Drink,** *and* **Travellers and Wanderers**.

Disappearance and Absence

A number of the allusions grouped here relate to mysterious disappear-ances: **BERMUDA TRIANGLE, AMELIA EARHART, JIMMY HOFFA, LORD LUCAN, MARY CELESTE**. Elusiveness can be suggested by reference to **MACAVITY** and the **SCARLET PIMPERNEL**. The other main idea is that of something visible disappearing from sight, whether gradually (**CHESHIRE CAT**) or instantly

(**PROSPERO'S BANQUET**). ▶ *See also* **Deserted Places, Invisibility, Mystery**.

....

Enoch Arden In Tennyson's poem of the same name (1864), Enoch Arden is shipwrecked and presumed dead for ten years. By the time he returns, his wife Annie has remarried and, observing from afar the couple's happiness, Enoch decides not to ruin it by making himself known.

Atlantis Atlantis was a legendary island continent in the ocean west of the Pillars of Hercules. According to Plato in the Timaeus, Atlantis was beautiful and prosperous and ruled part of Europe and Africa, but following volcanic eruptions it was swallowed up by the sea.

> Under the clouds out there it's as still, and lost, as Atlantis.
> THOMAS PYNCHON *Gravity's Rainbow*, 1973

> In those days ... the island of Britain was no island at all but part of the ancient kingdom of Atlantis, which, when it sank beneath the waves, left this western part to be our kingdom.
> PETER ACKROYD *The House of Dr Dee*, 1993

Bermuda Triangle The Bermuda Triangle is an area of the western Atlantic bounded by Bermuda, Florida, and Puerto Rico which is supposedly associated with an unusually high number of unexplained disappearances of ships and aircraft.

> I'd entered what Renée's mother calls the Bermuda Triangle of Health, which is pretty terrifying.
> SIMON GRAY *Gray's Anatomy*, 1993

Cheshire Cat In Lewis Carroll's *Alice's Adventures in Wonderland* (1865), the Cheshire Cat is a large cat with a broad fixed grin. Alice watches as the Cheshire Cat's body gradually disappears 'beginning with the end of the tail, and ending with the grin, which remained some time after the rest of it had gone'. ▶ *See special entry* □ **ALICE IN WONDERLAND** *on p. 10*.

> 'Affairs of greater moment' would occupy more and more of his attention, until gradually, like the Cheshire cat, he had faded altogether out of the world of the schoolroom and the nursery into higher and more comfortable spheres. The boys settled down again to happiness.
> ALDOUS HUXLEY *Point Counter Point*, 1928

> 'Where's the elevator?' I called out. 'Don't work.' He disappeared, leaving a cackle hanging in the air behind him like the Cheshire cat's grin.
> MIKE PHILLIPS *Point of Darkness*, 1994

> Labour policies are like the Cheshire cat: look twice and they have disappeared, leaving only Mr Blair's enduring smile.
> *The Independent on Sunday*, 1996

Amelia Earhart Amelia Earhart (1898–1937) was an American aviator, the first woman to fly the Atlantic in 1928, and the first woman to do so solo in 1932, completing the journey from Newfoundland to Londonderry in a time of 13¼ hours. The aircraft carrying Earhart and her navigator, Frederick J. Noonan, disappeared over the Pacific Ocean during a subsequent round-the-world flight in 1937.

Jimmy Hoffa Jimmy Hoffa (1913–c.1975) was a US labour leader, president of the Teamsters' Union (transport workers) from 1957. He disappeared mysteriously in 1975 and is believed to have been murdered.

> Finding first-rate outfield arms today is like searching river bottoms for Jimmy Hoffa.
> *Show*, 1990

Lord Lucan Lord Lucan (b. 1934) was a British aristocrat who mysteriously disappeared in 1974 on the night that his wife was attacked and his children's nanny was murdered. He has never been found.

> He stood beside her car. 'You're that sure he's coming back?' she said, getting in. He extended his hand. 'Bet,' he said. 'How much?' 'Why so sure?' she pressed. 'Who wants to do a Lucan? The guy's got . . . What's her name? The girlfriend? Sarah?'
> DAVID ARMSTRONG *Thought for the Day*, 1997

Macavity In T. S. Eliot's collection of poems *Old Possum's Book of Practical Cats* (1939), Macavity the Mystery Cat is the criminal mastermind, the 'fiend in feline shape', who always has an alibi and always manages to elude Scotland Yard and the Flying Squad: 'For when they reach the scene of crime—Macavity's not there!'

Mary Celeste The *Mary Celeste* (commonly, though erroneously, referred to as the *Marie Celeste*) was an American brig that set sail from New York for Genoa and was found drifting in the North Atlantic in December 1872 in perfect condition but abandoned. What happened to the crew has remained a mystery ever since.

> She vanished so swiftly and so completely that journalists of the time scented something as delicious as the lost continent of Atlantis, or the *Mary Celeste*.
> PHILIP PULLMAN *Shadow in the North*, 1988

> A quick scoping of the kitchen didn't tell me much. There were no half-eaten meals on the table, no coffee bubbling on the hotplate. This wasn't a Marie Celeste situation, this looked like somebody who'd gone on holiday in a slight rush.
> MIKE RIPLEY *Family of Angels*, 1996

Prospero's banquet In Shakespeare's *The Tempest* (1623), Prospero is the exiled Duke of Milan who practises magic on a remote enchanted island. After causing the shipwreck of his brother Antonio and his party, Prospero sends his servant, the spirit Ariel, to present a banquet to them and then to make it instantly vanish.

Scarlet Pimpernel 'The Scarlet Pimpernel' is the name assumed by the English nobleman Sir Percy Blakeney, the hero of a series of novels by Baroness Orczy, including *The Scarlet Pimpernel* (1905). Apparently a lazy fop, he daringly rescues aristocrats from the guillotine during the French Revolution and smuggles them out of France. His calling-card is the sign of the red flower from which he takes his pseudonym. The Scarlet Pimpernel's exploits inspire the famous rhyme:

'We seek him here, we seek him there,
Those Frenchies seek him everywhere.
Is he in heaven?—Is he in hell?
That demmed, elusive Pimpernel?'

His name can be applied to anyone who is difficult to find or catch.

> I'm asking Wilson, but he's gone away—to Lagos for a week or two. The damned elusive Pimpernel. Just when I wanted him.
> GRAHAM GREENE *The Heart of the Matter*, 1948

Sennacherib Sennacherib (d. 681 BC) was King of Assyria 705–681 BC, devoting much of his reign to suppressing revolts in various parts of his empire. He sacked Babylon in 689. According to the account in the Bible, when he invaded Palestine in the reign of Hezekiah, his army was destroyed by a pestilence brought by the Angel of Death: 'And the Lord sent an angel, who cut off all the mighty warriors and commanders and officers in the camp of the king of Assyria' (2 Chr. 32: 21). This episode is the subject of Byron's poem 'The Destruction of Sennacherib'.

> Max felt his suave sophistication return with the rush of elation that an ailing diva must have when she finds her voice again. A touch here, a word there, and the guests disappeared like the hosts of Sennacherib.
> SARA PARETSKY *V. I. for Short*, 1995

Disapproval

This theme is chiefly concerned with moral disapproval and condemnation. ▶ *See also* **Sternness**.

Antisthenes Antisthenes (*c.*445–*c.*365) was the founder of the Cynic school of philosophy, whose pupils included Diogenes. Antisthenes despised art and learning, and the luxuries and comforts of life, and taught that virtue consists in self-control and independence of worldly needs.

John Calvin John Calvin (1509–64) was a French Protestant theologian and reformer, a leader of the Protestant Reformation in France and Switzerland. His name is mentioned in the context of adherence to strict moral behaviour and principles.

> 'When did you get to be such a little Calvinist, anyway?' 'I'm not talking about sex; I'm talking about lying.'
> ARMISTEAD MAUPIN *Sure of You*, 1990

> 'I never agreed with all that entertainment for the tourists,' the old man added. 'At least the gambling and whoring. I'm no Calvinist, but to me that's just dirty money.'
> PAUL JOHNSTON *Body Politic*, 1997

Cato Marcus Porcius Cato (234–149 BC), known as Cato the Elder or Cato the Censor, was a Roman statesman, orator, and writer. As censor in 184 BC he was vigorously opposed to luxury and decadence and tried to restore simplicity to Roman life. He became convinced that Rome would never be safe until Carthage was destroyed, ending all his speeches in the Senate with the words

'Delenda est Carthago' ('Carthage must be destroyed'). His name is associated with severity and austerity in matters of morality.

> Seduced by an ageing libertine, Mr Quarles's mistresses were surprised to find themselves dining with a Hebrew prophet, and taking their amusements with a disciple of Cato or of Calvin.
> ALDOUS HUXLEY *Point Counter Point*, 1928

Diogenes Diogenes (*c.*400–*c.*325 BC) was a Greek philosopher, the most famous of the Cynics. He promoted self-sufficiency and the denial of physical pleasure and rejected social conventions. According to legend he lived in a barrel, to demonstrate his belief that the virtuous life was the simple life. One story told of him is that he carried a lantern out in daylight, saying that he was seeking an honest man.

> I was filled with a sour scorn that I now know was nothing but envy, but then mistook it for philosophy. I didn't really want the clothes, I didn't really want the girl or the booze, but it scalded me to see him enjoying them, and I hobbled away grumbling to myself like Diogenes.
> ROBERTSON DAVIES *Fifth Business*, 1970

> He immediately built himself a grass hut, Indian style, thatched it with palm, and to the wonder of the locals began to live like Diogenes and labour like Sisyphus, except with better results.
> LOUIS DE BERNIÈRES *The War of Don Emmanuel's Nether Parts*, 1990

Mrs Grundy Mrs Grundy is an off-stage character from Thomas Morton's play *Speed the Plough* (1798), whose name is repeatedly invoked with the words: 'What will Mrs Grundy say?' In the play she represents conventional propriety and prudery. 'Grundyism' is the narrow-minded condemnation of unconventional behaviour.

> Fastidious men do not live in pigsties, nor can they long remain in politics or business. There are nature's Greeks and nature's Mrs Grundies.
> ALDOUS HUXLEY *Point Counter Point*, 1928

> Perhaps it would turn out to be a fortuitous early warning, making Dalziel step back before he got in too deep. Shit, thought Wield with sudden self-disgust. How mealy-minded could you get! A few months of what felt like a stable partnership had turned him into Mrs Grundy!
> REGINALD HILL *The Wood Beyond*, 1996

John Knox John Knox (*c.*1505–72) was a Scottish Protestant reformer, the founder of the Presbyterian Church of Scotland. Like those of other famous Protestant figures, his name is sometimes used in the context of moral uprightness or disapproval.

> Whose love is given over-well
> Shall look on Helen's face in hell,
> Whilst they whose love is thin and wise
> May view John Knox in paradise.
> DOROTHY PARKER 'Partial Comfort' in *Sunset Gun*, 1928

> 'Camille has been famous for a whole year now,' she said dejectedly, 'and we're no nearer getting married. I thought it would be neat if I got pregnant, it would hurry

things up. But—there you are—can't get him into bed. You've no idea what Ca-mille's like when he's got one of his fits of rectitude. John Knox was merely a be-ginner.'
HILARY MANTEL *A Place of Greater Safety*, 1992

Hell and damnation: he knew about the very unofficial tapes. And Teddy with a puritan conscience that made Messrs Knox and Calvin look flexible, even soft. Not the moment to be precipitate myself. Not the occasion for the full and frank ad-mission.
RAYMOND FLYNN *Busy Body*, 1998

Savonarola Girolamo Savonarola (1452–98) was a Dominican monk and as-cetic and a zealous religious and political reformer. A puritanical opponent of the Renaissance, he gained power in Florence, where he preached against immorality, vanity, and corruption in the religious establishment. This led the Pope to excommunicate him, and he was hanged and burnt as a heretic.

Meanwhile, up at the mill, I was slogging away and trying to earn an honest bob or two in conference with the book-seller, who was describing the difficulties which face an honest vendor of adult reading material in the town of Grimble. There was, it seemed, a local Savonarola or Calvin who was a particular thorn in Mr Meacher's flesh.
JOHN MORTIMER *Rumpole's Return*, 1980

Voltaire Voltaire, the pseudonym of François-Marie Arouet (1694–1778), was a French writer, dramatist, and poet, a leading figure of the Enlighten-ment. He condemned intolerance and superstition and was an outspoken critic of religious and social institutions, his radical views earning him several periods of imprisonment and banishment. His name is particularly associated with mocking scepticism.

'Sue, you are terribly cutting when you like to be—a perfect Voltaire!'
THOMAS HARDY *Jude the Obscure*, 1895

Disclosure

The main idea here is the revealing of a secret, especially unwittingly.
▶ *See also* **Concealment**.

Freudian Sigmund Freud (1856–1939) was an Austrian neurologist and psychotherapist who was the first to draw particular attention to the role of the subconscious mind in human behaviour. A Freudian slip or accident is a remark, gesture, or action, apparently accidental, that in fact reveals sub-conscious desires or fears.

The loss of the manuscript, I thought, was a Freudian accident.
I. B. SINGER *The Lecture*, 1968

Midas Midas was a legendary king of Phrygia who was one day asked to judge a musical contest between Apollo and Pan. He unwisely chose Pan, where-upon Apollo punished him by giving him ass's ears to show his stupidity. Midas concealed his appearance from all but his barber who, unable to keep the secret but afraid to reveal it publicly, told it to a hole in the ground, which he then filled in. Reeds grew over the hole and whispered 'Midas has ass's ears' when the wind blew.

Rumpelstiltskin In the Grimms' fairy story, Rumpelstiltskin helps a miller's daughter to spin straw into gold for the king, and she in return promises to give him her first child. She becomes queen, and when her first child is born Rumpelstiltskin says that she may keep the child if she can discover his name within three days. She sends out messengers to find all the strange names they can collect, and one messenger comes across the little man dancing round a fire and chanting a rhyme that ends with the line: 'Rumpelstiltskin is my name!' When the queen confronts him with his name, Rumpelstiltskin be-comes so angry that he stamps his foot into the ground and tears himself in two when he tries to pull it out.

Disguise

In this theme, those who adopt a disguise do so in order to deceive, but for a variety of motives. ▶ *See also* **Concealment, Cunning**.

....

Achilles According to Greek mythology, Thetis, the mother of Achilles, knew from a prophecy that if Achilles sailed with the Greek fleet to fight against the Trojans he would not come back alive. In an attempt to save his life, she disguised him as a girl and entrusted him to Lycomedes, King of Scyros. Odysseus, Nestor, and Ajax were sent to find him, and did so by laying a pile of gifts, mostly jewels and fine clothes, but also a shield and spear, in the hall of Lycomedes' palace. Odysseus then ordered a sudden trumpet blast, at which one of the girls stripped to the waist and seized the shield and spear. This was Achilles, who then promised to lead his men to Troy. ▶ *See special entries* ☐ **ACHILLES** *on p. 3 and* ☐ **TROJAN WAR** *on p. 392.*

Brom Bones In Washington Irving's story *The Legend of Sleepy Hollow* (1820-21), Brom Bones impersonates a ghostly headless horseman, using a pumpkin and a hat for the head that he is supposedly carrying, to scare off his rival suitor, Ichabod Crane.

Charley's Aunt In Brandon Thomas's farce *Charley's Aunt*, which opened in London in 1892, Lord Fancourt Babberly is persuaded by two friends to assist them in their amorous endeavours by impersonating his rich aunt. He intro-duces himself with the famous line: 'I'm Charley's aunt from Brazil—where the nuts come from', but runs into difficulties when the real aunt appears.

Jacob In the Old Testament, Jacob, with his mother Rebecca's help, dressed as his older brother Esau in order to obtain the blessing of their father, Isaac, who was old and unable to see well. He put on Esau's clothes and his mother put the skins of young goats on his hands and neck so that they would feel hairy like Esau's. Despite recognizing Jacob's voice, Isaac was fooled: 'The voice is Jacob's voice, but the hands are the hands of Esau' (Gen. 27: 22). He therefore gave Jacob the blessing of the first-born, which should have belonged to Esau.

Odysseus In Greek mythology, when Odysseus returned to Ithaca after his many adventures during and after the Trojan War, Athene disguised him as an old beggar so that he could arrive secretly at his palace and challenge his wife Penelope's many suitors. The disguise was so effective that even Penelope and Telemachus, his son, failed to recognize him. The only ones who saw through his disguise were his faithful hound, Argus, whom Odysseus found dying on a dung heap, and his former nurse, Eurycleia, who was called upon to wash his feet and knew him from an old scar on his leg. ▶ *See special entry* ☐ ODYSSEUS *on p. 283.*

Portia In Shakespeare's play *The Merchant of Venice* (1600), Portia, a rich heiress, disguises herself as a male lawyer to save Antonio, a friend of her betrothed, Bassanio. Antonio had borrowed money from Shylock to help Bassanio and later, unable to pay it back, is faced with paying the bond of a pound of his flesh instead. Portia saves Antonio's life by arguing that, although Shylock has the right to take a pound of Antonio's flesh, he has no right to shed any of his blood, making it impossible for Shylock to exact his due.

Mr Toad In Kenneth Graham's story for children *The Wind in the Willows* (1908), Mr. Toad of Toad Hall, who has been thrown into jail for stealing a motor car, disguises himself as a washerwoman in order to escape.

wolf in Red Riding Hood In the fairy story *Little Red Riding Hood*, first recorded by Perrault in 1697, Little Red Riding Hood, a young girl who earns her name from her red cloak and hood, sets off one day to visit her sick grandmother. Walking through a wood on her way, she meets a wolf, who asks where she is going. On hearing the answer, the wolf runs on ahead, imitates Red Riding Hood's voice to gain entry to the grandmother's cottage, and devours the grandmother. It then puts on the grandmother's clothes and gets into the grandmother's bed to await Red Riding Hood. When she arrives, the wolf talks to her kindly, trying to disguise its voice, but Red Riding Hood is struck by the strange appearance of her grandmother, and comments on the size of her ears, eyes, and finally teeth: 'What big teeth you have, grandmother', at which point the wolf, responding 'All the better to eat you with!', leaps up and devours Red Riding Hood. The wolf can be alluded to in the context of someone disguising themselves in order to win another's confidence and hide their own dishonest or evil intentions.

> The animal itself was as peaceful and well-behaved as that father of all picture-wolves, Red Riding Hood's quondam friend, whilst seeking her confidence in masquerade.
> BRAM STOKER *Dracula*, 1897

wolf in sheep's clothing The wolf in sheep's clothing is one of the fables of Aesop, a Greek storyteller who lived in the 6th century BC. The fable relates how a wolf decides to disguise himself as a sheep in an attempt to obtain an easy meal. He spends the day with a flock of sheep, fooling sheep and shepherd alike, and in the evening is shut into the fold with the other sheep. However, when the shepherd gets hungry later in the evening he comes to the fold to choose a sheep to eat and chooses the wolf, which he proceeds to eat on the spot. A 'wolf in sheep's clothing' is anyone who uses an outward appearance of friendship or kindness to conceal underlying hostility or cruelty.

> I'm ordinarily the sweet soul, too good for this world, too kind for my own good, too gentle, a little lamb. To discover the wolf cub in lamb's skin doesn't suit my mother's preconceptions.
> EDMUND WHITE *A Boy's Own Story*, 1982

Distance

This theme includes places that are both 'far away' (e.g. **TIMBUKTU, ULTIMA THULE**) and 'widely separated' (e.g. **DAN TO BEERSHEBA, JOHN O'GROATS TO LAND'S END**).

Atlantis Atlantis was a legendary island continent in the ocean west of the Pillars of Hercules. According to Plato, Atlantis was beautiful and prosperous and ruled part of Europe and Africa, but following volcanic eruptions it was swallowed up by the sea.

> I made a serious attempt to be sensitive, culturally aware and all that. I borrowed Sanchez from Ramparts Division to translate. We brought food, kept a low profile. I got *nada*. Hear no evil, speak no evil. I honestly don't think they knew much about Elena's life. To them West L.A.'s as distant as Atlantis. But even if they did they sure as hell weren't going to tell me.
> JONATHAN KELLERMAN *When the Bough Breaks*, 1992

Dan to Beersheba Dan was a town in the north of Canaan, the Promised Land to which Moses led the people of Israel in the Bible. It marked the northern limit of the ancient kingdom of Israel. Beersheba, which still exists as a town, was the town which marked the southern limit of the kingdom. According to the Book of Judges, the people of Israel were 'gathered together as one man, from Dan even to Beersheba' (Judg. 20: 1). Something that happens from Dan to Beersheba therefore happens everywhere. ▶ *See special entry* ☐ **MOSES AND THE BOOK OF EXODUS** *on p. 264.*

> What profits it to have a covenanted State and a purified Kirk if a mailed Amalekite can hunt our sodgers from Dan to Beersheba?
> JOHN BUCHAN *Witch Woods*, 1927

Darkest Africa Before Africa had been fully explored by Europeans it was known to them as the Dark Continent. Darkest Africa was therefore an unexplored land far away from modern European life and full of potential dangers. The term may have originated from titles of works by the explorer

Henry Morton Stanley, *Through the Dark Continent* (1878) and *Through Darkest Africa* (1890).

end of the rainbow According to legend, there is a pot of gold buried at the spot where a rainbow comes down and touches the earth. The end of the rainbow is therefore a distant place where dreams come true. The idea was popularized by the song 'Over the Rainbow' from the 1939 film *The Wizard of Oz*, which begins with the words:

'Somewhere over the rainbow
Way up high,
There's a land that I heard of
Once in a lullaby.'

> The Japanese stock market was the last-but-one in a long line of Wall Street Loreleis. Like Xerox, conglomerates, and convertible debentures, it had been the legendary pot of gold at the end of some local rainbows. Those happy few blessed with foresight got more than sordid, material gain. They got brief immortality. Going into Japan at the right time was like predicting exactly when Dow-Jones would reach five- or fifteen-hundred.
> EMMA LATHEN *Sweet and Low*, 1978

Great Divide The Great Divide or Continental Divide is another name for the Rocky Mountains, a range of mountains in North America which extends from the US–Mexico border to the Yukon territory in northern Canada. It was once thought of as the epitome of a faraway place.

> Albert had then crossed the Great Divide and gone to work as a solicitor's clerk in a grey and wind-blasted town called Grimble, in the north of England.
> JOHN MORTIMER *Rumpole's Return*, 1980

John O'Groats to Land's End John O'Groats is a village at the extreme north-eastern point of the Scottish mainland. Land's End is a rocky promontory in south-west Cornwall, which forms the westernmost point of England. John O'Groats and Land's End are considered to be the two extreme ends of the British mainland.

> The sexual antics of public figures—Cecil Parkinson, Bill Clinton, Paddy Ashdown, Frank Bough, Alan Clark—never fail to send the same old-maidish frisson reverberating from John O'Groats to Land's End.
> *The Guardian*, 1993

Nineveh Nineveh was an ancient city located on the east bank of the Tigris, opposite the modern city of Mosul, Iraq. It was the oldest city of the ancient Assyrian Empire and its capital during the reign of Sennacherib until it was destroyed by the Medes and the Babylonians in 612 BC. In the opening lines of John Masefield's poem *Cargoes* (1903), Nineveh and Ophir are presented as places of far-away exoticism:

'Quinquireme of Nineveh from distant Ophir
Rowing home to haven in sunny Palestine'.

> I've been to Europe and the States but never to Nineveh and Distant Ophir.
> JULIAN BARNES *Talking it Over*, 1991

Ophir Ophir was an unidentified region in the Bible, perhaps in south-east Arabia, famous as the source of the gold and precious stones brought to King

Solomon (I Kgs. 9: 28, 10: 10). ▶ *See also* **NINEVEH**.

Outer Mongolia Mongolia in eastern Asia, bordered by Russia and China, was known formerly as Outer Mongolia and thought of as the epitome of a remote, inaccessible place.

Pillars of Hercules The Pillars of Hercules are the two promontories at the sides of the Straits of Gibraltar, one in Europe and one in North Africa, known in ancient times as Calpe and Abyla and now known as the Rock of Gibraltar and Mount Acho in Ceuta. According to Greek mythology, they were either erected by Hercules or pushed apart by him as he travelled to the island of Erytheia to complete the tenth of his twelve Labours. They were regarded in ancient times as marking the limit of the known world. ▶ *See special entry* ☐ **HER-CULES** *on p. 182.*

Siberia Siberia is a vast region of northern Russia, known for the harshness of its climate and the bleakness of its landscape, and formerly used as a place of banishment and exile.

> In the grim Siberian wastes of the Brighton Conference Centre . . . not one pro-Mandelson joke was to be heard.
> *The Observer*, 1997

Timbuktu Timbuktu or Timbuctoo is a town in northern Mali, thought of as a very faraway place.

> And he yelled at us to get out of the station before he kicked our arses to Timbuctoo.
> CHRISTOPHER HOPE *Darkest England*, 1996

Ultima Thule Thule was a land first described by the ancient Greek explorer Pytheas as being six days' sail north of Britain, thought to be either Iceland, Norway, or the Shetland Islands. To the Romans it was the northernmost extremity of the world, described by Virgil as 'Ultima Thule', literally 'farthest Thule'. It has come to denote any distant unknown region or, figuratively, the limit of what is attainable.

> Forget Marat, and the black distress he bred; he's going to create a new, Ultima Thule atmosphere, very plain, very bright, every word translucent, smooth. The air of Paris is like dried blood; he will (with Robespierre's permission and approval) make us feel that we breathe ice, silk and wine.
> HILARY MANTEL *A Place of Greater Safety*, 1992

> After a brief crawl he reached the end, striking his head against hard larch, the Ultima Thule of the *Daphne*, beyond which he could hear the water slapping against the hull.
> UMBERTO ECO *The Island of the Day Before*, 1994

Don Quixote

Don Quixote is the ageing hero of a romance *Don Quixote de la Mancha* (1605-15) by Miguel de Cervantes. He is devoted to tales of chivalry and romance, becoming so obsessed with these stories that 'the moisture of his brain was exhausted to that degree, that at last he lost the use of his reason'. Unable to distinguish the fanciful from the real, he determines to turn knight errant himself and sets out in search of adventures. Tall, lean, and thin-faced, he dons rusty armour and is accompanied by his scrawny old horse, Rosinante, and a squire, Sancho Panza. In a famous episode he attacks a group of windmills in the belief that they are giants. In Don Quixote's confused mind, a good-looking village girl, whom he names Dulcinea del Toboso, is elevated to the ideal of womanly beauty and virtue. His determination to keep to what he perceives to be a life of chivalry only ends when one of his friends disguises himself as another knight, defeats Don Quixote, and makes him end his exploits.

Various aspects of the Don Quixote story are dealt with throughout the book.

▶ *See* DON QUIXOTE *at* **Idealism, Illusion, Insanity,** *and* **Thinness**
   DULCINEA *at* **Inspiration**
   ROSINANTE *at* **Horses**.

Doubt

This theme covers the idea of doubt both in the sense of disbelief (including 'doubters' like **DOUBTING THOMAS** and the 'doubted' like **CASSANDRA**) and in the sense of uncertainty, as exemplified by **CAPTAIN CORCORAN** and **HAMLET**.

Cassandra In Greek mythology, Cassandra, the daughter of the Trojan king Priam, was loved by Apollo and given the gift of prophecy by him. When she later offended him, however, he turned the gift into a curse by ordaining that her prophecies, though true, would always be disbelieved. Her name is now applied to anyone whose warnings are doubted but eventually prove to be correct.

> But Cassandra was not believed, and even the wisdom of *The Jupiter* sometimes falls on deaf ears.
> ANTHONY TROLLOPE *Barchester Towers*, 1857

'I suppose my day wasn't as bad as yours,' Laurie said. 'But I'm beginning to understand how Cassandra felt when Apollo made sure that she was not to be heeded.'
ROBIN COOK *Blindsight*, 1993

Captain Corcoran Captain Corcoran is the captain of HMS *Pinafore* in Gilbert and Sullivan's opera of the same name (1878). He sings a song in which he proudly tells his crew of the things that he 'never, never' does. When challenged, he concedes that this is not quite true:

'What, never?'
'No, never.'
'What, never?'
'Well—hardly ever.'

Nature is so wondrously complex and varied that almost anything possible does happen. Captain Corcoran's 'hardly ever' is the strongest statement that a natural historian can make.
STEPHEN JAY GOULD *Ever Since Darwin*, 1978

Doubting Thomas Thomas, known also as Thomas Didymus, meaning 'twin' in Aramaic, was one of the twelve Apostles in the New Testament. After the Crucifixion, when Jesus appeared before the disciples to show them that he had risen from the dead, Thomas was not present. When the other disciples told Thomas that they had seen Jesus, he said he would not believe that it was true 'except I shall see in his hands the print of the nails, and put my finger into the print of the nails, and thrust my hand into his side' (John 20: 25). The expression 'Doubting Thomas' is now used to mean an incredulous or sceptical person.

Since he became news, he's been at pains to let the figures speak for themselves. 'The lab data's there in black and white.' It's also in the Vanderbilt computer system which means others can review it. When doubting Thomases from the press or the medical world come to speak to him, 'I print out the lab sheets, boom, boom, boom.'
The Observer, 1997

Hamlet Hamlet, the Prince of Denmark, is the hero of Shakespeare's tragedy of that title. Introspective and indecisive, Hamlet broods over revenge for his father's murder. The play features several famous soliloquies in which Hamlet deliberates on the course of action he should take. His name can be applied to someone who stops to ponder what to do, especially to an anxiously indecisive person.

To what extent was he, Gloster Ridley, justified in imposing his taste upon the newspaper's subscribers? Still, was it not for doing so that he drew his excellent salary and his annual bonus, reckoned upon the profits? What about the barber's chair; might there not be a few buttocks for Shillito? But he could go on in this Hamlet-like strain all day.
ROBERTSON DAVIES *Leaven of Malice*, 1954

Sadduccee The Sadducees were a Jewish sect at the time of Christ, who accepted only the written law, not oral tradition, denied the existence of angels and demons, and did not believe in the resurrection of the dead. A Sadduccee is therefore someone who refuses to believe things that are readily accepted by others.

'Law, mother! I don't doubt he thought so. I suppose he and Cack got drinking toddy

together, till he got asleep, and dreamed it. I wouldn't believe such a thing if it did happen right before my face and eyes. I should only think I was crazy, that's all.' 'Come, Lois, if I was you, I wouldn't talk so like a Sadduccee,' said my grandmother.
HARRIET BEECHER STOWE *The Ghost in the Mill*, 1872

Dreams

As the Margaret Atwood quotation below suggests, 'a dream can mean something', and the prophetic dream which can be interpreted by those gifted to do so is a recurring motif in the Bible. Oracles perform a corresponding function in classical legend. ▶ *See also* **Prophecy**, **Sleep**.

....

Joseph In the Bible, Joseph was the son of Jacob and Rachel. In his boyhood, he discovered he had a gift for prophetic dreams. As an adult in Egypt he was put in prison, where he interpreted the dreams of Pharaoh's butler and baker. Two years later Pharaoh was troubled by dreams that he could not understand and, hearing of Joseph's gift from his butler, sent for him. Joseph interpreted Pharaoh's dream of seven thin kine (or cows) devouring seven fat kine as predicting seven years of plenty followed by seven years of famine, advising Pharaoh to store grain in preparation for the long famine ahead. ▶ *See special entry* ❑ JOSEPH *on p. 224.*

Morpheus In Roman mythology, Morpheus is the god of dreams, son of Somnus, the god of sleep. To fall 'into the arms of Morpheus' is thus to fall asleep.

Nebuchadnezzar Nebuchadnezzar (*c.*630–562 BC) was King of Babylon 605–562 BC, and built the massive fortification walls of Babylon and the Hanging Gardens. He conquered and destroyed Jerusalem in 586 BC and exiled the Israelites to Babylon. The prophet Daniel had a gift for interpreting visions and dreams. He was able to explain the meaning of a strange dream of Nebuchadnezzar's, for which he was made the king's chief adviser. Later, Daniel interpreted a second dream of Nebuchadnezzar to foretell his insanity, which immediately came to pass. ▶ *See special entry* ❑ DANIEL *on p. 86.*

That night was an eventful one to Eustacia's brain, and one which she hardly ever forgot. She dreamt a dream; and few human beings, from Nebuchadnezzar to the Swaffham tinker, ever dreamt a more remarkable one.
THOMAS HARDY *The Return of the Native*, 1880

Pharaoh ▶ *See* JOSEPH.

Listen here . . . I have dreams like a Pharaoh. When I was fourteen and asleep in Fowey, I was here on this exact shore. I saw Will Bryant—it's none of a surprise to me. These days and night, I have dreams I cannot utter . . . .
THOMAS KENEALLY *The Playmaker*, 1987

I suppose he is interested in my dreams because a dream can mean something, or so

it says in the Bible, such as Pharaoh and the fat kine and the lean kine, and Jacob with the angels going up and down the ladder.
MARGARET ATWOOD *Alias Grace*, 1996

Pilate's wife In the New Testament, when Jesus was brought before Pontius Pilate for judgement, Pilate's wife reported to her husband the distress she had suffered in a dream on account of Jesus, and urged him: 'Have thou nothing to do with that just man: for I have suffered many things this day in a dream because of him.'

'All dreams mean something.' 'For Joseph and Pharaoh, or Pilate's wife, perhaps. You will have to work very hard to convince me that they mean anything here and now.'
ROBERTSON DAVIES *The Manticore*, 1972

Duality

The allusions below can be used to express the dual or divided nature of something, especially a person's personality. **JANUS** and **MR FACING-BOTH-WAYS** can both suggest two-facedness or duplicity. ▶ *See also* **Change**, **Hypocrisy**, **Similarity**.

Centaur In Greek mythology, a centaur is one of a race of creatures who has the upper body, arms, and head of a man and the body and legs of a horse.

But as he straightened and pressed ahead, care caught up with him again. Turning half-beast and half-divine, divining himself like a heathen Centaur, he had escaped his death once more.
EUDORA WELTY 'A Still Moment' in *The Collected Stories of Eudora Welty*, 1943

Cox and Box In the operetta *Cox and Box* by Burnand and Sullivan (1867), Cox and Box are two lodgers whose occupations allow their landlady to let the same room out to each of them, one using it by day and one using it by night. They discover their landlady's duplicity when Cox, who sleeps in the room at night, is given a holiday. The operetta was based on a play entitled *Box and Cox* by J. M. Morton, published in 1847.

Mr Facing-both-ways Mr Facing-both-ways is one of several characters who are relatives of Mr By-ends in the first part of Bunyan's *Pilgrim's Progress* (1678). Mr By-ends claims many rich relatives in the town of Fair-speech (not, as in the Peacock quotation, Vanity Fair) and, on being questioned by Christian as to who these relatives are, replies: 'Almost the whole town', listing a litany of names including that of Mr Facing-both-ways.

I have a great abomination of this learned friend; as author, lawyer, and politician, he is triformis, like Hecate: and in every one of his three forms he is bifrons, like Janus; the true Mr Facing-both-ways of Vanity Fair.
THOMAS LOVE PEACOCK *Crotchet Castle*, 1831

They had scarcely entered the house when they were outside it again. Harriet, feeling as peevish as the Major, said: 'Mr. Facing-both-ways stayed on.' *'Who?'* 'Your friend Phipps.' 'You're always wrong about people.' 'I don't think so. I never liked Dubedat and I was right. I was doubtful of Toby Lush.'
OLIVIA MANNING *Friends and Heroes*, 1965

Janus Janus was the ancient Roman god of gates and doorways. He was generally represented as Janus Bifrons ('with two faces') by a head with two faces looking in opposite directions.

Marian sat on one side of him, his good side: I soon came to think of him as two-sided, like Janus. Together, they looked like Beauty and the Beast.
L. P. HARTLEY *The Go-Between*, 1953

It is, of course, its essentially schizophrenic outlook on society that makes the middle class such a peculiar mixture of yeast and dough. . . . Now this Janus-like quality derives from the class's one saving virtue, which is this: that alone of the three great castes of society it sincerely and habitually despises itself.
JOHN FOWLES *The French Lieutenant's Woman*, 1969

Jekyll and Hyde Dr Jekyll is the main character in Robert Louis Stevenson's *The Strange Case of Dr. Jekyll and Mr Hyde* (1886). He discovers a drug that allows him to create a separate personality, Mr Hyde, in order to express the evil in his own character. Sometimes he is Dr Jekyll, sometimes Mr Hyde. The term 'Jekyll and Hyde' can be used to refer to someone who has two very distinct sides or personalities.

'We're the two parts of Romola Saville's dual personality.' 'I being the Dr Jekyll,' put in the portly one, and both laughed yet once more.
ALDOUS HUXLEY *Point Counter Point*, 1928

She had done all that, had her hair black, green, then braided; worn beads on her head and round her neck; scuffed round Turkey with dirty feet and sandals for a year; did Greece, Europe by train. Then she'd stopped. Now she was a copper, just about as straight and 'citizen' as you could get, but Caz still liked the smell of anarchy, of noncomformity. When she thought of herself, her character, as Jekyll and Hyde, her only problem was she didn't know which half was the bad side.
ALEX KEEGAN *Kingfisher*, 1995

Enemy

Whereas the theme **Hatred** is concerned with personal animosity, this theme deals with the concept of tribal enmity, particularly of a long-standing nature. ▶ *See also* **Conflict, Evil, Friendship.**

Amalekite The Amalekites were a nomadic tribe of Canaan and the Sinai peninsula, reputedly descended from Esau's grandson Amalek. They waged war against the Israelites, for whom the Amalekites represented perpetual treachery and hostility: 'The Lord will have war with Amalek from generation to generation' (Exod. 17: 16).

> But he, sly fox, son of Satan, seed of the Amalekite, he saw me looking at him in the church.
> OLIVE SCHREINER *The Story of an African Farm*, 1883

hosts of Midian The Midianites were a tribal group portrayed in the Bible as nomadic shepherds and traders. The Book of Judges relates the story of a battle led by Gideon against the Midianites in which he defeated the 'host of Midian'. The host of Midian can be alluded to as any unfriendly or hostile group.

> I shouldn't be surprised if Tommy and his little friend weren't still lurking in the shadows somewhere. They're like the hosts of Midian. They prowl and prowl around.
> P. G. WODEHOUSE *Laughing Gas*, 1936

> I knew which side I was on; yet the traitor within my gates felt the issue differently, he backed the individual against the side, even my own side, and wanted to see Ted Burgess pull it off. But I could not voice such thoughts to the hosts of Midian prowling round me under the shade of the pavilion verandah.
> L. P. HARTLEY *The Go-Between*, 1953

Montagues and Capulets The Montagues and the Capulets are the two feuding Veronese families to which Romeo and Juliet respectively belong in Shakespeare's *Romeo and Juliet* (1599). As the first lines of the play explain:

'Two households, both alike in dignity,
In fair Verona, where we lay our scene,
From ancient grudge break to new mutiny,
Where civil blood makes civil hands unclean.'

> The Molloys and the Timsons are like the Montagues and the Capulets.
> JOHN MORTIMER *Rumpole of the Bailey*, 1978

> There were soon two factions facing off like Montagues and Capulets.
> *Radio 4*, 1997

Philistines When in the biblical story the Philistines arrived to take Samson captive, Delilah said 'The Philistines be upon you, Samson!' (Judg. 16). These words can be used when people regarded as the enemy suddenly arrive. ▶ *See special entry* □ **SAMSON** *on p. 336.*

> 'The Philistines be upon us,' said Liddy, making her nose white against the glass.
> THOMAS HARDY *Far From the Madding Crowd*, 1874

Envy

As can be seen from the stories below, embittered envy of another's success, beauty, favour, etc. is often presented as the motive for malicious action, even murder. Curiously, there does not seem to be a strong archetype representing the quality of envy, as there is for so many of the qualities covered elsewhere in this book (e.g. Othello for jealousy, Lucifer for pride, Solomon for wisdom). ▶ *See also* **Jealousy**.

....

Calchas In Greek mythology, Calchas was the wisest of the Greek soothsayers at the time of the Trojan War. He is supposed to have died of grief and disappointment after another soothsayer, Mopsus, was shown to be better than him at prophecy.

Iago Iago is Othello's ensign in Shakespeare's play *Othello* (1622). Partly out of anger at being passed over for promotion and partly out of a general, bitter envy of Othello, Iago brings about an end to Othello's success and happiness by tricking him into believing that his wife, Desdemona, has been unfaithful to him. As a result of this, Othello kills first Desdemona and later himself.

Joseph In the Bible, Joseph was the son of Jacob and Rachel. He was his father's favourite son, and when his father gave him a coat of many colours his brothers became envious of him, and 'hated him, and could not speak peaceably unto him' (Gen. 37: 4). They attacked him, stripped him of his coat, and sold him into slavery in Egypt. The brothers then took Joseph's coat, dipped it in the blood of a kid they had killed and took it to their father to convince him that Joseph was dead. ▶ *See special entry* ☐ JOSEPH *on p. 224.*

Snow White's stepmother In the traditional fairy tale, Snow White's stepmother, proud of her own beauty, becomes envious of her stepdaughter as Snow White grows to be more beautiful than her. The stepmother orders Snow White to be taken into the forest and killed so that she will once again be 'the fairest of them all'. The men charged with Snow White's murder take pity on her and simply abandon her in the forest, where she lives for a while in the house of the Seven Dwarfs and eventually marries a handsome prince.

Escape and Survival

The idea of physical escape is frequently used figuratively to describe the extrication of oneself from a predicament. Also covered here is the notion of being spared punishment or death. In the cases of DEUCALION and his biblical counterpart, NOAH, and of LOT, they survive while all others perish. ▶ *See also* **Freedom**, **Safety**.

....

Artful Dodger The Artful Dodger is the nickname of Jack Dawkins, a clever young pickpocket and a member of Fagin's gang of thieves in Dickens's *Oliver Twist* (1837–8). He is known for his ability to use his wits to get himself out of trouble without ever being caught.

> In these supposedly rational times, the spectacle of someone repeatedly engaging in sexual behaviour which is dangerously risky, and, potentially, exceedingly self-destructive, provokes many people to resort to some psychopathological explanation. Many see President Clinton as an Artful Dodger who just got caught.
> *The Independent*, 1998

Deucalion In Greek mythology, Deucalion was the son of Prometheus. When Zeus, angered by the crimes of men, decided to destroy them by a great flood, Prometheus warned Deucalion, who built a boat for himself and his wife, Pyrrha, in which they floated until the waters subsided and they safely came to land on Mount Parnassus.

Houdini Harry Houdini (born Erik Weisz, 1874–1926) was a Hungarian-born American magician and escape artist, famous for his escapes from chains, handcuffs, padlocks, straitjackets, and numerous locked containers.

> 'I kept wondering if maybe he hadn't been there all along, hiding out somewhere on the balcony, listening to our conversation.' 'Houdini he may be, God he isn't,' I said lightly, but she didn't seem to hear.
> SARAH DUNANT *Snow Storms in a Hot Climate*, 1991

> Her wrists and ankles had been cuffed to a solid wooden chair that was bolted to the stone-flagged floor. 'How's she going to make a break?' I asked. 'Unless she happens to be related to Houdini, of course.'
> PAUL JOHNSTON *Body Politic*, 1997

Isaac In the Old Testament, God commanded Abraham to take his son, Isaac, and offer him as a burnt offering. Abraham did as he was bid: he built an altar, laid wood on it, bound his son, and laid him on the altar. Abraham took a knife and was just about to slay Isaac when the angel of the Lord appeared and said 'Lay not thine hand upon the lad, neither do any thing unto him' (Gen. 22: 12). When Abraham looked up, there was a ram caught in a thicket nearby, which Abraham took and used instead of his son for the burnt offering.

Jonah In the Bible, Jonah, a minor Jewish prophet, refused to obey God's command and preach to the Ninevites. Instead, he embarked on a ship bound for Tarshish, but God sent a storm and, to save the ship, the other sailors cast Jonah into the water as a bringer of bad luck. Jonah was then swallowed by a huge fish (traditionally a whale), and spent three days and three nights in its belly, in which time he repented and prayed to God to save him. After three days 'the Lord spake unto the fish, and it vomited out Jonah upon the dry land' (Jonah 2: 10). Jonah can be alluded to as someone who survives a very difficult or dangerous situation.

Lot In the Bible, Lot was the nephew of Abraham and an inhabitant of Sodom, who was allowed to escape from the city before it was destroyed by God because of the wickedness of its inhabitants.

> We thought a bolt had fallen in the middle of us, and Joseph swung onto his knees, beseeching the Lord to remember the Patriarchs Noah and Lot; and, as in former times, spare the righteous, though he smote the ungodly.
> EMILY BRONTË *Wuthering Heights*, 1847

Noah According to the Bible, Noah was 'a righteous man, blameless in his generation' in contrast to the wickedness and corruption of the rest of the human race. Before God sent the flood to cover the earth and destroy all humankind, he warned Noah and instructed him to build the ark in order to save his family and specimens of every kind of animal. ▶ *See special entry* □ **NOAH AND THE FLOOD** *on p. 279.*

> The world had been destroyed and only the lamp-post, like Noah, preserved from the universal cataclysm.
> ALDOUS HUXLEY *Point Counter Point*, 1928

Pegasus In Greek mythology, Pegasus was the winged horse on which Perseus came to rescue Andromeda, who had been tied to a rock and left to be devoured by a sea monster. The name Pegasus can represent a means of escape.

> Bertie, in short, was to be the Pegasus on whose wings they were to ride out of their present dilemma.
> ANTHONY TROLLOPE *Barchester Towers*, 1857

> He seemed to see her like a lovely rock-bound Andromeda, with the devouring monster Society careering up to make a mouthful of her; and himself whirling down on his winged horse—just Pegasus turned Rosinante for the nonce—to cut her bonds, snatch her up, and whirl her back into the blue.
> EDITH WHARTON *The Custom of the Country*, 1913

Jack Sheppard Jack Sheppard (1702-24) was a notorious thief who was famous for his prison escapes, including one in which he escaped from Newgate prison through a chimney. He was later captured and hanged.

> He is safe now at any rate. Jack Sheppard himself couldn't get free from the strait-waistcoat that keeps him restrained.
> BRAM STOKER *Dracula*, 1897

Teflon Teflon (®) is a material used as a non-stick coating for pans and kitchen utensils. Its name can be used in connection with criminals who always manage to avoid having criminal charges 'stuck' on them, or with politicians who seem able to shrug off scandal or misjudgement so that nothing 'sticks'.

> In their periods of melancholy, such as the day he walked from court after beating a charge of importing 1.4 tonnes of pure cocaine, they called him the 'Teflon criminal'.
> *The Observer*, 1997

Tinker Bell In J. M. Barrie's play *Peter Pan* (first performed in 1904), Tinker Bell is a fairy and a friend of Peter's. It is said in the play that every time someone says that they do not believe in fairies, a fairy dies. When Tinker Bell herself is close to death, members of the audience are invited to clap their hands to show that they do believe in fairies, and thus save Tinker Bell's life.

Evil

Most of the entries below deal with individual exemplars of villainy and wickedness. Allusions to other aspects of the idea of evil are covered elsewhere in this book. ▶ *See also* **Criminals**, **Devil**, **Dictators and Tyrants**, **Monsters**, **Ruthlessness**, **Unpleasant or Wicked Places**.

Ahab Ahab (*c*.875–54 BC) was an idolatrous king of Israel, the husband of Jezebel. With her he introduced into Israel the worship of the Phoenician god Baal, and his name thereafter became associated with wickedness, especially the offence of honouring pagan gods: 'There was none who sold himself to do what was evil in the sight of the Lord like Ahab, whom Jezebel his wife incited' (1 Kgs. 21: 25).

Cesare Borgia Cesare Borgia (1476–1507) was the son of Pope Alexander VI and the brother of Lucrezia Borgia. He was a ruthless political and military leader, and was said to be the model for the ruler in Machiavelli's *The Prince*. His father made him a cardinal in 1493 and subsequently the Duke of Romagna. His name is popularly associated with ruthless plotting and the use of poison to dispatch his enemies.

> The men of Faith, the Madmen, as I have been calling them, who believe in things unreasonably, with passion, and are ready to die for their beliefs and their desires. . . . These wild men, with their fearful potentialities for good or for mischief, will no longer be allowed to react casually to a casual environment. There will be no more Caesar Borgias, no more Luthers and Mohammeds, no more Joanna Southcotts, no more Comstocks.
> ALDOUS HUXLEY *Crome Yellow*, 1921

Lucrezia Borgia Lucrezia, or Lucretia, Borgia (1480–1519) was the daughter of Pope Alexander VI and sister of Cesare Borgia, both of whom she was alleged to have committed incest with. Although her court became a centre for Renaissance artists, poets, and scientists, she has acquired, probably unfairly, her brother's reputation as a ruthless plotter and poisoner.

> Beautiful as Pauline Borghese, she looked at the moment scarcely purer than Lucrece de Borgia.
> CHARLOTTE BRONTË *The Professor*, 1857

> She makes that helpless gesture and has that goddamned headache and you would like to slug her except that you are glad you found out about the headache before you invested too much time and money and hope in her. Because the headache will always be there, a weapon that never wears out and is as deadly as the bravo's rapier or Lucrezia's poison vial.
> RAYMOND CHANDLER *The Long Goodbye*, 1953

Borgias The Borgias were a Spanish-Italian noble family originating from Valencia, whose members included Pope Alexander VI, Cesare Borgia, and Lucrezia Borgia. They are associated with ruthlessness, murder (especially by poisoning), and incest. ▶ *See also* **CESARE BORGIA, LUCREZIA BORGIA**.

> I'm not talking hot air, my friend. I happen to know every detail of the hellish contrivance, and I can tell you it will be the most finished piece of blackguardism since the Borgias.
> JOHN BUCHAN *The Thirty Nine Steps*, 1915

Caliban Caliban is a character in Shakespeare's *The Tempest* (1623). A brutish and misshapen monster, Caliban is the son of the witch Sycorax, and was the sole inhabitant of the island before Prospero's arrival. His name can be applied to a man of savage and bestial nature, or to the brutish side of human nature in general.

> He escorted them to their box with a sort of pompous humility, waving his fat jewelled hands, and talking at the top of his voice. Dorian Gray loathed him more

than ever. He felt as if he had come to look for Miranda and had been met by Caliban.
OSCAR WILDE *The Picture of Dorian Gray*, 1891

I was wrestling with my unconscious, an immense dark brother who seeped around me when I was awake, flowed over me when I slept . . . a force with a baby's features, greedy orifices, a madman's cunning and an animal's endurance, a Caliban as quicksilver as Ariel.
EDMUND WHITE *A Boy's Own Story*, 1982

Cruella de Vil Cruella de Vil is the rich, evil, screeching villainess in Dodie Smith's *One Hundred and One Dalmations* (1956), who steals ninety-nine Dalmation puppies in order to make a spotted fur coat from their skins. Two Disney film versions have been made, an animated one in 1961 and a live-action remake in 1996.

Something terrible had happened to the toughest office manager in Manchester. Imagine Cruella De Vil transformed into one of those cuddly Dalmation puppies, only more so. It was like watching Ben Nevis grovel. 'And could you sign one, "for Ted"?' she begged.
VAL MCDERMID *Star Struck*, 1988

Darth Vader Darth Vader is the villain in the film *Star Wars* (1977) and its sequels. Formerly Anakin Skywalker, a Jedi knight who has been corrupted to 'the dark side', Darth Vader is always dressed in black and wears a helmet.

Markby looked towards the large studio portrait of the late Jack glowering handsomely from a sidetable. A dark-haired, thick-browed, lantern-jawed thug. Women often found that type attractive. Glyn didn't resemble him particularly. Perhaps he rode around on the motorbike, dressed up like Darth Vader, to compensate.
ANN GRANGER *Candle for a Corpse*, 1995

Eve According to the biblical account, Eve committed the first sin by disobeying God's command not to eat the fruit of the Tree of Knowledge and by enticing Adam to do the same. She can thus be alluded to in the context of wrongdoing or tempting another to wrongdoing. ▶ *See special entry* □ ADAM AND EVE *on p. 5.*

When the women came in they were older than I had imagined, not at all like the pictures in the priest's book of sinful things. Not snake-like, Eve-like with breasts like apples, but round and resigned, hair thrown into hasty bundles or draped around their shoulders.
JEANETTE WINTERSON *The Passion*, 1987

Herod Herod the Great (*c.*74–4 BC) was the Roman King of Judaea who, according to Matthew's Gospel, ordered the Massacre of the Innocents, hoping that by killing all male children under two he would ensure the death of the infant Jesus. Allusions to Herod are often in the context of the killing of children on a large scale.

'I think of the A4,' sez he, 'as a baby Jesus, with endless committees of Herods out to destroy it in its infancy.'
THOMAS PYNCHON *Gravity's Rainbow*, 1973

The infant Udin is dead. I mourn him as though he had been my own. I say Sukarno

killed him, as surely as though he were a Herod.
CHRISTOPHER J. KOCH *The Year of Living Dangerously*, 1978

All babies start off looking like the last tomato in the fridge, but 'cute', 'gorgeous' and 'adorable', which were the adjectives Lucy was throwing about the place with gay abandon, struck me as the ravings of an insane and blind woman. Quite frankly, I began to see King Herod in a wholly different light.
BEN ELTON *Inconceivable*, 1999

Hogarth William Hogarth (1697-1764) was an English painter, engraver, and satirist. His series of engravings on 'modern moral subjects', such as *A Rake's Progress* (1735) and *Marriage à la Mode* (1743-5), satirized the vices of both high and low life in 18th-century England. *Gin Lane* (1751), depicting a scene of drunkenness and squalor, is one of Hogarth's most famous prints.

In his intrepid trip down the stairs he encountered every sort of vice: fornication, crack smoking, heroin injection, dice games and three-card monte, and more fornication ... 'It's bloody Hogarth', said Steiner. 'Gin Lane. Except that it's vertical.'
TOM WOLFE *The Bonfire of the Vanities*, 1987

Mr Hyde In Robert Louis Stevenson's *The Strange Case of Dr Jekyll and Mr Hyde* (1886), Mr Hyde is the separate, purely evil, personality that the physician Dr Jekyll is able to assume by means of a drug he discovers. A person who reveals an unsuspected evil side to their character can be said to be changing into Mr Hyde.

Now we are getting to know Mr Hyde. Only he isn't Dr Jekyll's gaudy monster, who trampled a child; he is just a proud little boy who hurt some humble people, and knew it and enjoyed it.
ROBERTSON DAVIES *The Manticore*, 1972

'Domestic violence', said Boehlinger. 'More P.C. crap. All we do is rename things. It's wife-beating! I've been married thirty-four years, never laid a finger on my wife! First he woos her like Prince Charming then it all goes to hell in a handbasket and he's Mr Hyde—she was *frightened* of him, Miss Connor. Scared clean out of her mind. That's why she left him.'
JONATHAN KELLERMAN *Billy Straight*, 1998

Iago Iago is a character in Shakespeare's play *Othello* (1622). Although Othello believes his ensign Iago to be completely loyal and 'honest', Iago is in fact scheming against him. Iago incites Othello into believing that the latter's wife, Desdemona, has been unfaithful to him, resulting ultimately in Othello's killing first Desdemona and, later, himself. Iago has become an archetype of pure malevolence.

Sarah glared at him through the window. 'And you say Mathilda was evil-minded?' Furiously, she ground into gear. 'Compared with you she was a novice. Juliet to your Iago.'
MINETTE WALTERS *The Scold's Bridle*, 1994

She was like some Iago. Or some evil guardian angel.
CONNIE WILLIS *Bellwether*, 1996

Loki In Scandinavian mythology, Loki was the god of mischief and evil, who was responsible for the death of Balder and was punished by being bound to a rock.

Lady Macbeth In Shakespeare's play *Macbeth* (1623), Lady Macbeth plots with her husband to kill King Duncan so that her husband can assume the throne in his place. She persuades him to commit the murder despite his hesitation and reluctance. Any ambitious, scheming, or ruthless woman can be described as a Lady Macbeth.

> And, as I did so, the door burst open, and there was Miss Brinkmeyer, looking like Lady Macbeth at her worst.
> P. G. WODEHOUSE *Laughing Gas*, 1936

> Ellen is just too ruthless for comfort. Ellen and Lady Macbeth? Nothing in it!
> FAY WELDON *Darcy's Utopia*, 1990

> 'In a way her son was a much nastier character. Sophie was Lady Macbeth writ large. She pulled the trigger on Jean-Louis and Caterina Tozharska herself.' He smiled wryly. 'But even Lady Macbeth couldn't bring herself to kill.'
> MAX MARQUIS *Written in Blood*, 1995

Moloch Moloch was a Canaanite deity referred to in several books of the Old Testament to whom worshippers sacrificed their children. The Israelites, moving into the land of Canaan, were expressly forbidden to worship Moloch (Levi. 18: 21).

> Indeed ... the national education of women is of the utmost consequence, for what a number of human sacrifices are made to that Moloch prejudice!
> MARY WOLLSTONECRAFT *A Vindication of the Rights of Women*, 1792

Rasputin Grigori Rasputin (1871–1916) was a Russian monk, notorious for his debauchery, who came to exert great influence over the Tsarina Alexandra, wife of Nicholas II, by claiming miraculous powers to heal the heir to the throne, who suffered from haemophilia. Rasputin was eventually assassinated by a group of Russian noblemen loyal to the Tsar.

> Believe me, I'd much rather be by your side than poolside, where I spend most of my time these days. Which is what a 'development deal' seems to entail. ... I develop a tan while the studio develops cold feet on the project. Happily, thanks to my beloved agent, Rasputin, they still have to pay oodles of money either way, but I have to stick around awhile, just in case it's a go.
> JANE DENTINGER *Death Mask*, 1988

Whore of Babylon The Whore of Babylon is referred to in the Book of Revelation. She is described as a woman sitting on a scarlet beast with seven heads and ten horns: 'The woman was arrayed in purple and scarlet colour, and decked with gold and precious stones and pearls, having a golden cup in her hand full of abominations and filthiness of her fornication.' On her forehead was written: 'Babylon the great, mother of harlots and abominations of the earth' (Rev. 17: 3–5). The term was applied to the Roman Catholic Church by the early Puritans, and could also be used to represent sexual immorality.

> I'd marry the W— of Babylon rather than do anything dishonourable!
> THOMAS HARDY *Jude the Obscure*, 1895

> Here he was: leading foreigners over in hordes to places that were not theirs, to cause disputes, to uproot niggers, to plant the Whore of Babylon in the midst of the righteous!
> FLANNERY O'CONNOR *The Displaced Person*, 1953

Explorers

One who discovers or explores a new place, perhaps when first encountering the people who live there, can be compared to a famous explorer of the past, particularly one of the 15th- or 16th-century navigators. ▶ *See also* **Detectives**.

....

Balboa Vasco Núñez de Balboa (1475-1519) was a Spanish explorer who joined an expedition to Darien (in Panama), initially as a stowaway, later as commander. During one of his further expeditions he became the first European to sight the Pacific Ocean, in 1513.

> At last he reached the summit, and a wide and novel prospect burst upon him with an effect almost like that of the Pacific upon Balboa's gaze.
> THOMAS HARDY *Far from the Madding Crowd*, 1874

> And the man named Dick kept standing up in the car as if he were Cortez or Balboa, looking over that grey fleecy undulation.
> F. SCOTT FITZGERALD *The Last Tycoon*, 1941

St Brendan St Brendan (484-577) was an Irish abbot. The *Navigatio Brendani* (Navigation of St Brendan, *c.*1050) recounts the story of a voyage made by St Brendan and a band of monks to a land of saints far to the north and west of Ireland, possibly Orkney or the Hebrides.

Columbus Christopher Columbus (1451-1506) was an Italian explorer who, sponsored by the rulers of Spain, Ferdinand and Isabella, set out across the Atlantic Ocean in 1492 with the intention of reaching Asia and proving that the world was round. In fact, he discovered the New World, reaching the Bahamas, Cuba, and Hispaniola (now the Dominican Republic and Haiti). He made three further journeys, during which he also discovered the South American mainland.

> The disturbance was as the first floating weed to Columbus—the contemptibly little suggesting possibilities of the infinitely great.
> THOMAS HARDY *Far from the Madding Crowd*, 1874

> So, Flora mused, must Columbus have felt when the poor Indian fixed his solemn, unwavering gaze upon the great sailor's face. For the first time a Starkadder looked upon a civilized being.
> STELLA GIBBONS *Cold Comfort Farm*, 1932

Captain Cook Captain James Cook (1728-79), English navigator and explorer, led expeditions to the Pacific in the *Endeavour*, to the Antarctic in the *Resolution*, and finally to try to discover a passage round the north coast of America from the Pacific. He was forced to turn back from his last voyage and, reaching Hawaii, was killed by the islanders.

> You wave an airy adieu to the boys on shore, light your biggest pipe, and swagger

about the deck as if you were Captain Cook, Sir Francis Drake, and Christopher Columbus all rolled into one.
JEROME K. JEROME *Three Men in a Boat*, 1889

Cortés Hernando Cortés (or Cortez) (1485-1547) was a Spanish adventurer who conquered Mexico, then known as New Spain. Darien, mentioned in Keats' poem below, was the name for the isthmus of Panama.

Then felt I like some watcher of the skies
When a new planet swims into his ken;
Or like stout Cortez, when with eagle eyes
He stared at the Pacific—and all his men
Looked at each other with a wild surmise—
Silent, upon a peak in Darien.
JOHN KEATS *On First Looking into Chapman's Homer*, 1816

This was the first sign of humanity she had encountered among the Starkadders, and she was moved by it. She felt like stout Cortez or Sir James Jeans on spotting yet another white dwarf.
STELLA GIBBONS *Cold Comfort Farm*, 1932

Sir Francis Drake Sir Francis Drake (*c.*1540-96), English explorer and privateer, was the first Englishman to see the Pacific and the first to sail round the globe. He harried the Spanish, both in Spain and in South America, and took a leading part in foiling the Spanish Armada in 1588. Despite Spanish protests, he was knighted in 1581 by Queen Elizabeth I.

Amerigo Vespucci Amerigo Vespucci (1451-1512), was an Italian-born navigator in whose honour the Americas were named. He made two voyages to the New World, in which he discovered the mouth of the Amazon and explored the north-east coast of South America. His distorted and embroidered account of his travels was published in 1507 (*Four Voyages*), and based on this, the Latin version of his name, 'Americus', was given to the two American continents.

She first reached Wildeve's Patchs, as it was called, a plot of land redeemed from the heath, and after long and laborious years brought into cultivation. The man who had discovered that it could be tilled died of the labour: the man who succeeded him in possession ruined himself in fertilizing it. Wildeve came like Amerigo Vespucci and received the honours due to those who had gone before.
THOMAS HARDY *The Return of the Native*, 1878

Failure

This theme encompasses the inability to achieve a particular goal (**SISYPHUS**, **CANUTE**), a more general failure in life (**WILLY LOMAN**, **EDWIN REARDON**), and a decline in one's fortunes, a metaphorical 'fall' (**ICARUS**, **LUCIFER**). **CHAPPAQUIDDICK** can be invoked in the context of an incident

that subsequently and irrecoverably tarnishes a, usually political, career.
▶ *See also* **Defeat, Poverty, Success**.

....

Canute Canute (d. 1035) was the Danish-born King of England, Denmark, and
Norway who is traditionally believed to have reproved his flattering courtiers
by demonstrating that, although he was king, he nevertheless did not have the
power to command the advancing waves to stay back. However, it is almost
always the figure of Canute himself who is used to represent the stupidity and
futility of believing that one can halt the advance of something that is in fact
impossible to stop.

> 'Louise', he called, 'Louise'. There was no reason to call: if she wasn't in the living-room
> there was nowhere else for her to be but the bedroom . . . yet it was his habit to
> cry her name, a habit he had formed in the days of anxiety and love. The less he
> needed Louise the more conscious he became of his responsibility for her happiness.
> When he called her name he was crying like Canute against a tide—the tide of her
> melancholy and disappointment.
> GRAHAM GREENE *The Heart of the Matter*, 1948

> Two tough women. So it is not surprising they talk as tough as they are. 'The level of
> deprivation in this country goes down and down and down', Ms Morgan says. 'It
> spirals. Whatever we do. It's not even like King Canute. The water is lapping round
> our feet before we've even had the chance to order the tide to turn back'.
> *The Independent*, 1998

> The words are all so similar, so utterly useless really, that after a while they merge
> into a blur. It is not their fault; no one can say anything. Even the promise of a cross-
> border security summit, announced last night, sounds like King Canute's courtiers
> raging at the waves.
> JONATHAN FREEDLAND in The *Guardian*, 1998

Casey Casey is the eponymous hero of the late 19th-century ballad 'Casey at
the Bat' by Ernest L. Thayer. Casey was confidently expected to save the day in
a baseball game but, having not even tried to hit the first two balls, he struck
out on the third: 'There is no joy in Mudville—Mighty Casey has struck out.'
The name can be used to refer to failure when success was confidently
expected.

Chappaquiddick On July 8 1968 Edward Kennedy, at that time a likely US
presidential candidate, drove off a bridge in Chappaquiddick, Massachusetts.
His passenger, Mary Jo Kopechne, drowned, and Kennedy himself was found
guilty of leaving the scene of an accident. It is widely thought that this event
blighted his chance of becoming president. Chappaquiddick can be used to
allude to a serious error of judgement that subsequently dogs someone's career.

> Resettled in Soweto, the vast black metropolis outside Johannesburg, she set up her
> own office, built her own following, spoke her own mind and organised the now
> infamous Mandela United Football Club. Ostensibly a soccer team intended to keep
> youngsters out of trouble, it became a band of thugs who terrorised the township. By
> 1991, four members of the club had been convicted of murder. The most notorious
> case, that of the 14-year-old resistance hero, Stompie Mocketsi Seipei, became Mrs
> Mandela's Chappaquiddick.
> *The Independent*, 1995

Clouseau Inspector Clouseau was a character, played by Peter Sellers, in the comedy film *The Pink Panther* (1963) and its sequels. He was a stupid, bungling, accident-prone police detective.

Edsel The Edsel was a car launched by the Ford Motor Company in 1957 as part of a $250 million investment in an attempt to compete with General Motors and in particular with their Oldsmobile. The car was a complete flop.

> When Petra told him she was pregnant, he looked at her as if she were an Edsel.
> JONATHAN KELLERMAN *Billy Straight*, 1998

Icarus Icarus was the son of Daedalus in Greek mythology. Daedalus constructed wings which he and Icarus used to fly to freedom from Crete. However, the wings were attached by wax, and when Icarus flew too close to the sun the wax melted, and he fell to his death in the Aegean sea.

> To fly into the air on flapping wings is the goal of two North American engineers. They have already flown a radio-controlled model ornithopter on a flight lasting almost three minutes, and they believe that within three years they could create an ornithopter that would carry a person into the skies—hopefully with more success than Icarus.
> *New Scientist*, 1992

Willy Loman Willy Loman is the main character in Arthur Miller's play *Death of a Salesman* (1949), a travelling salesman for a lingerie company. He comes to realize that his life has been a complete failure, and finally commits suicide in order to help his son get a new start in life with the insurance money.

Lucifer Lucifer, whose name means 'bearer of light', was the leader of a revolt against God in heaven and was hurled down to hell as a punishment. He came to be identified with Satan. Milton describes the fallen archangel Satan, or Lucifer, in Book I of *Paradise Lost* (1667).

> I had no exultation of triumph, still less any fear of my own fate. I stood silent, the half-remorseful spectator of a fall like the fall of Lucifer.
> JOHN BUCHAN *Prester John*, 1910

> That was what had happened to Derek, too. He had been treated by the public and the press as a big name because of his part in the series, but Derek had actually been a man obsessed with failure, a star that had fallen, Lucifer-like, from a great height, after playing the major Shakespearian roles in his youth.
> CHARLOTTE LAMB *In the Still of the Night*, 1995

Phaethon In Greek mythology Phaethon, the son of Helios, the sun god, asked to drive his father's sun chariot for a day. However, he did not have the strength to control the horses and the chariot rose so high above the earth that human beings on the ground nearly froze, then plunged so close to the earth that it was scorched. Zeus intervened to save the world and killed Phaethon with a thunderbolt.

> The sun rose higher on its journey, guided, not by Phaethon, but by Apollo, competent, unswerving, divine.
> E. M. FORSTER *A Room with a View*, 1908

Edwin Reardon Edwin Reardon is a character in George Gissing's novel *New Grub Street* (1891), a gifted writer whose literary ambitions are nonetheless thwarted by poverty and by the lack of sympathy of his materialistic wife.

Unable to succeed as a writer and deserted by his wife, Reardon is driven to an early grave.

Sisyphus In Greek mythology, Sisyphus was a king of Corinth, punished in Hades for his misdeeds by being condemned endlessly to roll a rock up a hill which then always rolled back down again. His name can allude to efforts to achieve or finish something which constantly fails. ▶ *See special entry* ☐ **HADES** *on p. 172.*

> The process is something like Sisyphus: you're always falling back downhill.
> RICHARD FEYNMAN *Surely You're Joking, Mr Feynman*, 1985

> The team gets hot, threatens to win the Championship, blows it. The players move on, the side rebuilds, then it happens all over again. The club's official historians compared its existence to that of Sisyphus. Now yet again the boulder has gone all the way uphill and rolled straight back over all our toes.
> *The Guardian*, 1994

Fatness

Some of the entries below have their counterparts at the theme **Thinness**. For instance, the fat knight **FALSTAFF** contrasts with the thin knight Don Quixote. Whereas **RUBENS** is the painter most associated with depicting plump female figures, the names of El Greco and Modigliani suggest leanness. ▶ *See also* **Large Size**.

Billy Bunter Billy Bunter is the rotund bespectacled schoolboy hero of a series of stories by Frank Richards set in a boys' public school called Greyfriars. The stories first appeared in the *Magnet* comic in 1908. Known as 'the Fat Owl of the Remove', Bunter wears an enormous pair of check trousers.

> I took after my mother, and already at that age was inclined towards flab. (Yes, m'lud, you see before you a middling man inside whom there is a fattie trying not to come out. For he was let slip once, was Bunter, just once, and look what happened.)
> JOHN BANVILLE *The Book of Evidence*, 1989

> She has turned my Romeo into a sad-eyed Billy Bunter who blinks his passions quietly when no one's looking. Oh, that his too, too solid flesh should melt.
> MINETTE WALTERS *The Scold's Bridle*, 1994

Falstaff Sir John Falstaff is the fat, witty, good-humoured old knight in Shakespeare's *Henry IV* and *The Merry Wives of Windsor*. Falstaff's enormous paunch prompts the young prince Hal to ask: 'How long is't ago, Jack, since thou sawest thine own knee?' Observing Falstaff fleeing an ambush, Hal remarks:

'Falstaff sweats to death
And lards the lean earth as he walks along.'

> It was all so fine, so precise, and it was a wonder that this miracle was wrought by

a whiskered Falstaff with a fat belly and a grubby singlet showing through the layers of wet, sour hessian.
PETER CAREY *Oscar and Lucinda*, 1988

The professor was a big, jovial man of Falstaffian appearance.
MARJORIE ECCLES *A Species of Revenge*, 1996

Fat Controller In the Reverend W. Awdry's series of books about Thomas the Tank Engine (first appearing in 1946), the Fat Controller presides over the Big Station with self-important and bureaucratic officiousness.

Mr Pickwick Mr Samuel Pickwick is the central character of Charles Dickens's novel *The Pickwick Papers* (1836–7). Founder of the Pickwick Club, he is jovial, generous, and unworldly in character and short, plump, and bespectacled in appearance.

His face was round and shiny, like Mr Pickwick's.
JOHN BUCHAN *The Thirty-Nine Steps*, 1915

He was a little man, considerably less than of middle height, and enormously stout; he had a large, fleshy face, clean-shaven, with the cheeks hanging on each side in great dew-laps, and three vast chins; his small features were all dissolved in fat; and, but for a crescent of white hair at the back of his head, he was completely bald. He reminded you of Mr. Pickwick. He was a grotesque figure of fun, and yet, strangely enough, not without dignity.
W. SOMERSET MAUGHAM *Mackintosh*, 1951

Upright, he looked like Mr Pickwick, with a chubby rubicund face and a fringe of long white hair around a gleaming pink scalp.
ANABEL DONAL *The Glass Ceiling*, 1994

Miss Piggy Miss Piggy is a puppet creation of Jim Henson that has appeared in the television series *The Muppet Show* and *Sesame Street*. She is a large pink pig with long blonde hair.

I just know I've put on at least half a pound. The bus driver's going to notice and give me a pitying look, sort of saying, 'Well, hello, Miss Piggy, how do you expect to get a seat on the bus with that fat arse?'
ARABELLA WEIR *Does My Bum Look Big in This?*, 1997

Rubens Peter Paul Rubens (1577–1640) was the foremost Flemish painter of the 17th century, an exuberant master of the Baroque. Many of Rubens's paintings feature voluptuous female nudes, displaying his sheer delight in fleshy women. The word 'Rubenesque' can be used to describe a woman's attractively plump and rounded figure.

Upstairs, I took off all my clothes and had a full view of myself in the wardrobe mirror. I was getting fat all right. I turned sideways, and looked round so that I could see the reflection of my hip. It was nicely curved and white like the geranium petals in the dressmaker's window-ledge. 'What's Rubenesque?' I asked Baba. 'I don't know. Sexy, I suppose. Why?' 'A customer said I was that.'
EDNA O'BRIEN *The Country Girls*, 1960

The old couple in the room next door moved out and were replaced by two plump Rubensian nymphs whose life was a permanent party for all manner of local Romeos.
LOUIS DE BERNIÈRES *Señor Vivo and the Coca Lord*, 1991

Silenus In Greek mythology, Silenus was an old woodland spirit who was a teacher of Dionysus. He is generally represented as a fat and jolly old man, riding an ass, intoxicated, and crowned with flowers.

> She wriggled away and stared with cold judgment at his white Silenus-paunch and rosy appendages on the sheets.
> A. S. BYATT *The Virgin in the Garden*, 1978

Fear

The abstract notion of fear is personified by the mythological figures DEIMOS and PHOBOS. More specific human anxieties are associated with traditional children's stories and with certain film genres. ▶ *See also* **Cowardice, Horror, Monsters**.

....

Norman Bates ▶ *See* PSYCHO.

Deimos In Greek mythology, Deimos was one of the sons of Aphrodite and Ares. He is sometimes seen as a personification of fear.

Grimm The brothers Jacob (1785–1863) and Wilhelm (1786–1859) Grimm published their collection of traditional fairy tales between 1812 and 1822. Many of the tales, such as 'Hansel and Gretel', deal with such primitive child-like fears as being deserted by parents or being attacked by wild animals.

> It slides easily into the serrated slit of the lock, and I cannot suppress the light thrill that runs down my spine. It is like entering a story, something by Grimm.
> ANDRÉ BRINK *Imaginings of Sand*, 1996

Hansel and Gretel Hansel and Gretel are a brother and sister who appear in a traditional fairy story first published by the Brothers Grimm. Abandoned in a forest by their parents, the terrified children come across a house made of bread, cakes, and sweets. The house in fact belongs to a witch, who imprisons the children and plans to eat them. Hansel and Gretel succeed in killing the witch by pushing her into her own oven, and escape back to their parents, taking with them jewels they have found in the witch's house.

> Entering the tunnel's blackness, leaving behind the brightly lit world of sleepy readers, a tiny rush of adrenaline, like MSG after a Chinese dinner, coursed through my blood-stream. Part of it was pure reversion to childhood's fears. Hansel and Gretel. Snow White. Lost in dark woods, with enemies all around.
> CAROLYN WHEAT *Ghost Station*, 1991

Alfred Hitchcock Alfred Hitchcock (1899–1980) was an English film director chiefly associated with suspenseful thrillers such as *Psycho* (1960) and *The Birds* (1963), in which huge flocks of birds turn on people and attack them. ▶ *See also* PSYCHO.

> As I bend over to resume my pyrotechnics there is a whirring sound, as if in response to the peacock's shriek, and when I look up I see a great multicoloured cloud

descending. It's the birds, even more of them than I have seen before, covering the sky ... I hunch down to protect myself. This is pure Hitchcock.
ANDRÉ BRINK *Imaginings of Sand*, 1996

Nightmare on Elm Street *Nightmare on Elm Street* is the title of a gory horror film made in 1984 in which a killer called Freddy Krueger, who has knives for fingernails, brutally murders teenagers in their dreams. The film was followed by several sequels.

If health professionals and writers took the middle line between Never-Never Land and Nightmare on Maternity Street perhaps Life After Babies wouldn't be quite such a rude awakening.
The Independent, 1994

Phobos In Greek mythology, Phobos, one of the sons of Aphrodite and Ares, was the god of dread and alarm. He was often represented with a lion's head.

Psycho *Psycho* is the title of an Alfred Hitchcock thriller, released in 1960. The film centres on Norman Bates, a murderous psychopath who is the owner of the Bates Motel, and includes a famously shocking murder scene in which a woman is stabbed repeatedly by Bates in her shower.

The owner, whom I roused from a backroom television den, didn't look anything like Norman Bates, and treated the whole transaction as if it was just his job. It made me wonder if we Europeans are the only ones to conjure up an instant vision of *Psycho* on journeys into the unknown. Americans at least had experience of motels long before that particular highway was removed and Norman's mother slept once too often with her new lover.
SARAH DUNANT *Snow Storms in a Hot Climate*, 1988

Fertility

Fertility deities are central figures in world myth. This theme is closely related to the theme **Abundance and Plenty**.

Abraham Abraham was a biblical leader, considered to be the father of the Hebrews. All Jews claim descent from him (Gen. 11: 27–25: 10).

In the latter quarter of each year cattle were at once the mainstay and the terror of families about Casterbridge and its neighbourhood, where breeding was carried on with Abrahamic success.
THOMAS HARDY *The Mayor of Casterbridge*, 1886

Aphrodite In Greek mythology, Aphrodite was the goddess of beauty, fertility, and sexual love. Her Roman equivalent was Venus.

Her mood now was that of Aphrodite triumphing. Life—radiant, ecstatic, wonderful—seemed to flow from her and around her.
H. RIDER HAGGARD *She*, 1887

Ashtoreth Ashtoreth or Ashtaroth is the name used in the Bible for the Phoenician goddess Astarte. ▶ *See* **ASTARTE**.

Astarte Astarte was a Phoenician goddess of fertility and sexual love, the counterpart of the Greek Aphrodite. She is referred to in the Bible as Ashtoreth or Ashtaroth, and worship of her is linked with worship of Baal and similarly condemned: 'And the children of Israel did evil again in the sight of the Lord, and served Baalim, and Ashtaroth' (Judg. 10: 6).

> The bailiff was pointed out to Gabriel, who, checking the palpitation within his breast at discovering that this Ashtoreth of strange report was only a modification of Venus the well-known and admired, retired with him to talk over the necessary preliminaries of hiring.
> THOMAS HARDY *Far From the Madding Crowd*, 1874

Bacchus Bacchus is an alternative name for Dionysus. ▶ *See* **Dionysus**.

Demeter In Greek mythology, Demeter was the goddess of cornfields and fecundity, whose symbol is an ear of corn. She was the mother of Persephone, and when Persephone was abducted by Hades and taken to the underworld, Demeter wandered around looking for her daughter and swore that the earth would remain barren until Persephone was restored to her. A compromise was finally reached whereby Persephone would spend nine months of each year with her mother, the time when plants grow and produce fruit, and three months of each year with Hades in the underworld, the time when the earth is cold and barren.

Dionysus In Greek mythology, Dionysus, also called Bacchus, was the god of fertility and nature. His worship was associated with wild dancing, and he later became the god of wine, who loosened inhibitions and inspired creativity. ▶ *See special entry* □ **DIONYSUS** *on p. 117.*

Flora In Roman mythology, Flora was the goddess of flowers and spring, depicted in Sandro Botticelli's celebrated painting, *Primavera*. Anyone carrying flowers can be described by invoking her name.

> I rang the door-bell, holding my flowers spread across both outstretched forearms. I did not want to appear like a delivery man. Rather I was a simple, a frangible petitioner, assisted only by the goddess Flora.
> JULIAN BARNES *Talking It Over*, 1991

Freyja In Norse mythology, Freyja was the goddess of love and also of fertility, fecundity, peace, and plenty.

Fierce Women

The allusions to fierce, aggressive women (or she-monsters) here are considerably more negative in their connotations than are those to their male counterparts at the theme **Macho Men**. ▶ *See also* **Murder**.

Amazon In Greek mythology, the Amazons were a race of female warriors alleged to exist on the borders of the known world. Their name was explained by the Greeks as meaning 'without a breast', from a story that they cut off their right breasts to enable them to draw their bows more easily. An Amazon is thus any tall, strong, or aggressive woman, or a woman who becomes fierce once her anger has been roused.

> Save for a certain primness as she offered the tray to her sister, Sophia's demeanour gave no sign whatever that the Amazon in her was aroused.
> ARNOLD BENNETT *The Old Wives' Tale*, 1908

> The girl glared back at him, her splendid brows beetling like an Amazon's.
> EDITH WHARTON *The Custom of the Country*, 1913

harpy In Greek and Roman mythology, harpies (originally from the Greek *harpuiae*, meaning 'snatchers') were fierce monsters with the heads and bodies of women and wings and claws of vultures. The word 'harpy' has now become part of the language, meaning a cruel or grasping, unscrupulous woman.

> And all the time, as we were pitching it in red hot, we were keeping the women off him as best we could, for they were as wild as harpies.
> ROBERT LOUIS STEVENSON *The Strange Case of Dr Jekyll and Mr Hyde*, 1886

termagant Termagant was the name given in medieval morality plays to an imaginary deity of violent and turbulent character. The name now denotes an overbearing or shrewish woman.

Food and Drink

The entries below encompass not only food and drink but also feasting and revelry. ▶ *See also* **Gluttony**.

Amalthea In Greek mythology, Amalthea was a she-goat or goat-nymph, who provided the milk Zeus drank when he was first born. ▶ *See also* **HORN OF PLENTY**.

ambrosia Ambrosia was the food of the Greek gods and the source of their immortality. ▶ *See also* **NECTAR**.

> We feasted that evening as on nectar and ambrosia.
> CHARLOTTE BRONTË *Jane Eyre*, 1847

> The rolls didn't taste quite as good as they had done in the cool of the morning, but as I ate I began to feel better. The tepid water was a benison, and the fruit was ambrosia itself.
> MARY STEWART *My Brother Michael*, 1960

Bacchanalia The Bacchanalia was the name given to the annual feast and celebrations in honour of the Greek god Dionysus, also called Bacchus. The

celebrations were characterized by wild orgies and drunkenness. The corresponding adjective 'Bacchanalian' can refer to drunkenness or to wild or
drunken partying.

> The learned profession of the law was certainly not behind any other learned pro-
> fession in its Bacchanalian propensities.
> CHARLES DICKENS *A Tale of Two Cities*, 1859

> That was what she might well do, he feared, to teach him not to venture out of the
> familiar, safe dustbin of their world into the perilous world of night-time bacchanalia,
> revelry and melodrama.
> ANITA DESAI *In Custody*, 1984

> Jagger runs and cycles; Aerosmith singer Steve Tylor has banned sugar, salt, wheat,
> yeast, fat, red meat and alcohol from his band's menus. Even the Grateful Dead
> while publicly burning the Bacchanalian flame at both ends, were secretly calorie
> watching.
> *The Independent*, 1997

Bacchante In Greek mythology, the Bacchantes or Maenads were the (usually
female) followers of the god Bacchus, priestesses who indulged in drunken and
orgiastic celebration at the festivals of Bacchus.

> The praise of folly, as he went on, soared into a philosophy, and Philosophy herself
> became young, and catching the mad music of Pleasure, wearing, one might fancy,
> her wine-stained robe and wreath of ivy, danced like a Bacchante over the hills of
> life, and mocked the slow Silenus for being sober. Facts fled before her like fright-
> ened forest things. Her white feet trod the huge press at which wise Omar sits, till
> the seething grape-juice rose round her bare limbs in waves of purple bubbles.
> OSCAR WILDE *The Picture of Dorian Gray*, 1891

> She drank, and she loved, and she danced. But she never again became the Bac-
> chante, the beloved, the high priestess of her Art.
> DOROTHY PARKER in *Constant Reader*, 1928

Bacchus Bacchus was another name for Dionysus, the Greek god of fertility
and, in later traditions, wine. ▶ *See special entry* ◻ **DIONYSUS** *on p. 117.*

> Now Eastman enters Atkins's tea-room, that holy of holies, shrine—one
> supposes—of the anti-Bacchus.
> TIMOTHY MO *An Insular Possession*, 1986

Belshazzar Belshazzar, King of Babylon, gave a great banquet with wine for
1,000 of his lords (Dan. 5: 1–4, 25–8). The wine was drunk from the gold and
silver goblets that his father, Nebuchadnezzar, had taken from the temple in
Jerusalem. As they drank the wine and praised the gods of gold and silver, a
hand appeared on the wall and wrote the words 'Mene, Mene, Tekel, Upharsin', heralding the end of the kingdom. ▶ *See special entry* ◻ **DANIEL** *on p. 86.*

> A sideboard was set out . . . on which was a display of plate that might have vied
> . . . with Belshazzar's parade of the vessels of the temple.
> WASHINGTON IRVING *The Sketch-Book of Geoffrey Crayon, Gent.*, 1820

> 'I always like this room,' said Spandrell as they entered. 'It's like a scene for Bel-
> shazzar's feast.'
> ALDOUS HUXLEY *Point Counter Point*, 1928

Cornucopia ▶ *See* **HORN OF PLENTY**.

Falernian Falernian was a particularly good-quality wine made in Roman times from the grapes of the Falernian territory in Campania and praised by both Horace and Virgil.

> 'If I am to take more of the severe falernian,' said he, laying his hand on the decanter of port, 'I must know the lady's name.'
> ANTHONY TROLLOPE *The Small House at Allington*, 1862

fatted calf ▶ *See* PRODIGAL SON.

Horn of Plenty The horn of plenty was one of the horns of the she-goat or goat-nymph Amalthea, in Greek mythology. Zeus endowed the horn with the magical property of refilling itself endlessly with whatever food or drink was desired. The horn of plenty was later stylized as the Cornucopia (from the Latin words *cornu copiae*, literally 'horn of plenty'), pictured as a goat's horn spilling over with fruit, flowers, and stalks of corn.

Jacob's pottage In the Bible, Jacob and Esau were the twin sons of Isaac and Rebecca. One day, Esau, returning from the countryside, found Jacob cooking 'red pottage of lentils' or lentil stew. He was extremely hungry and asked for some of the stew. Jacob would only give Esau the food if he swore to sell Jacob his birthright as the elder of the twins. Esau sold his birthright to Jacob and had the stew (Gen. 25: 29–34).

> New Deliverance was borderline charismatic and not the sort of church I felt comfortable attending; but at lunch the day before, Nadine had caught me off guard—a fudge delight cookie has the power to cloud minds—and laid on the guilt. 'Isabel says you went to her and Haywood's church last Sunday and to Seth and Minnie's Sunday before last, but you haven't been to ours in almost two years.' With Jacob's pottage rich and chocolaty on my tongue, I had no quick words with which to resist.
> MARGARET MARON *Southern Discomfort*, 1993

Lucullus Lucius Licinius Lucullus (*c.*110–56 BC) was a wealthy Roman general who led a luxurious life and was famed for hosting spectacularly lavish feasts.

> There had been placed in the middle of each table . . . a basket woven from hardened vines in a highly rustic Appalachian Handicrafts manner. . . . Sherman stared at the plaited vines. They looked like something dropped by Gretel or little Heidi of Switzerland at a feast of Lucullus.
> TOM WOLFE *The Bonfire of the Vanities*, 1987

manna Manna was the 'bread' provided by God for the Israelites when they were crossing the desert during their flight from Egypt (Exodus 16). The manna appeared as small white flakes like frost on the desert floor and would not keep overnight except on the sixth day when enough was provided to keep for the seventh day also, the Sabbath, on which the travellers were to rest. It was white like coriander seed and tasted like wafers made with honey, and it sustained the Israelites until they arrived at the border of Canaan. ▶ *See special entry* □ MOSES AND THE BOOK OF EXODUS *on p. 264.*

> The word is not prepared beforehand; it falls on me mind like the manna fell from

heaven into the bellies of the starving Israelites.
STELLA GIBBONS *Cold Comfort Farm*, 1932

nectar Nectar was the drink of the Greek gods. ▶ *See also* **AMBROSIA**.

It was dreadful to be thus dissevered from his dryad, and sent howling back to a
Barchester pandemonium just as the nectar and ambrosia were about to descend on
the fields of asphodel.
ANTHONY TROLLOPE *Barchester Towers*, 1857

Then I say, I thank you from the bottom of my heart, Sir, this radish was like the
nectar of the Gods.
MARGARET ATWOOD *Alias Grace*, 1996

Prodigal Son The Prodigal Son, a younger son in the parable (Luke 15:
11–32), squandered his share of his inherited property in wild living and
subsequently endured great poverty when his wealth was spent and the country in which he was living endured a famine. He returned, repenting, to his
father's house where his father freely forgave him, ordered a fatted calf to be
killed, and gave a celebratory and welcoming feast.

'Two eggs,' she commanded, rapping out her solicitude. 'Two, I insist. They were made
especially for you.' 'You treat me like the prodigal son,' said Burlap. 'Or the fatted calf
while it was being fattened.'
ALDOUS HUXLEY *Point Counter Point*, 1928

Samuel In the Bible, Saul, son of Kish, went looking for some donkeys of his
father that had gone missing. After much searching, Saul was about to give up
and return home when his servant told him that there was a man of God in
the town whose prophecies always came true. Saul was concerned that he
would not have enough food with which to reward the holy man, Samuel.
When Saul found Samuel, Samuel had meat already set aside to feed Saul (1
Sam. 9: 22–4).

'May be so, Mr Henchard,' said the weather-caster. 'Ah—why do you call me that?'
asked the visitor with a start. 'Because it's your name. Feeling you'd come I've waited
for 'ee; and thinking you might be leery from your walk I laid two supper plates—
look ye here.' He threw open the door and disclosed the supper-table, at which
appeared a second chair, knife and fork, plate and mug, as he had declared. Henchard felt like Saul at his reception by Samuel.
THOMAS HARDY *The Mayor of Casterbridge*, 1886

Saturnalian The ancient Roman festival of Saturn in December, called the
Saturnalia, was characterized by general unrestrained merrymaking. The term
is often applied to a scene of wild revelry or an orgy.

Silenus In Greek mythology, Silenus was an old woodland spirit who was a
teacher of Dionysus. He is often depicted as a lascivious old drunkard.

But now, of all inappropriate beings, who should appear but Silenus? Brocklebank,
perhaps a little recovered or perhaps in some extraordinary trance of drunkenness,
reeled out of his cabin and shook off the two women who were trying to restrain
him.
WILLIAM GOLDING *Rites of Passage*, 1980

Forgiveness

Allusions carrying the idea of forgiveness seem particularly to be drawn from the New Testament. Classical mythology, which has provided us with archetypes of so many other areas of human emotion and psychology, does not appear to feature similarly forgiving characters.

Jesus The Bible relates how, when Jesus was crucified, he spoke to God from the cross saying 'Father, forgive them; for they know not what they do' (Luke 23: 34). This is sometimes cited as the greatest possible act of forgiveness. ▶ *See special entry* □ **JESUS** *on p. 223.*

Prodigal Son In the parable of the Prodigal Son told by Jesus in the Bible (Luke 15: 11-32), a father readily forgave his spendthrift son who returned home after squandering his share of the inherited property in wild living. To celebrate his homecoming the father ordered servants to 'bring hither the fatted calf, and kill it; and let us eat and be merry'.

> The wicked wolf that for half a day had paralysed London and set all the children in the town shivering in their shoes, was there in a sort of penitent mood, and was received and petted like a sort of vulpine prodigal son.
> BRAM STOKER *Dracula*, 1897

Tannhäuser Tannhäuser (*c.*1200-*c.*1270) was a German lyric poet who became a legendary figure as a knight enamoured of a beautiful woman. She takes him into the grotto of Venus, where he spends seven years in revelry and debauchery. He then repents and goes to the Pope to ask for forgiveness. The Pope answers that it is as impossible for Tannhäuser to be forgiven as it is for his dry staff to burgeon. Tannhäuser leaves in despair, but after three days the Pope's staff does in fact blossom. The Pope sends for Tannhäuser, but he has returned to the grotto of Venus. The story is the subject of an opera by Wagner.

Freedom

'Freedom' here primarily means freedom from slavery or subjugation, rather than release from captivity. ▶ *See also* **Captives**, **Escape and Survival**, **Prisons**, **Rescue**.

John Brown John Brown (1800-59) was an American abolitionist who sought to free slaves by force. He was captured in 1859 after raiding a government arsenal at Harpers Ferry in Virginia in an attempt to arm runaway slaves and start an uprising. Brown was tried and executed, and became a martyr for abolitionists. He is remembered in the song 'John Brown's Body', which was popular in the North during the American Civil War.

Patrick Henry Patrick Henry (1736-99) was an American political leader and patriot. A few weeks before the beginning of the War of American Independence he made a famous speech urging the American colonies to revolt against English rule. The speech contained the famous words: 'I know not what course others may take, but as for me, give me liberty or give me death!'

> She was very angry. Give her nails, she'd chew them up and spit tacks. 'I have a hard time respecting my parents. I have nothing but contempt for the way they were. I won't do that.' Her voice rang out. Echoes, shades of Patrick Henry. Admirable, no question.
> KAREN KIJEWSKI *Wild Kat*, 1994

Jim In Mark Twain's novel *Huckleberry Finn* (1884), Jim is a runaway slave who meets up with Huck and travels with him down the Mississippi on a raft. During the course of the book Jim is sold back into slavery and then rescued again by Huck and Tom Sawyer.

> I was trying to tell you that I know many things about you—not you personally, but fellows like you . . . With us it's still Jim and Huck Finn. A number of my friends are jazz musicians, and I've been around. I know the conditions under which you live— why go back, fellow? There is so much you could do here where there is more freedom.
> RALPH ELLISON *Invisible Man*, 1952

Abraham Lincoln Abraham Lincoln (1809-65) was an American Republican statesman and the sixteenth president of the United States from 1861 to 1865. He is sometimes referred to as 'Honest Abe' or 'The Great Emancipator' on account of his involvement in the abolition of slavery. Although not an abolitionist himself, Lincoln viewed slavery as an evil and opposed its extension. During the Civil War he managed to unite the Union side behind the anti-slavery cause, and emancipation was formally proclaimed on New Year's Day 1864.

Messiah The Messiah (from Hebrew *Masiah*, meaning 'anointed') is the promised deliverer of the Jewish nation prophesied in the Hebrew Bible. In Christianity, the term is applied to Jesus Christ, and it is used allusively to refer to any person who saves or delivers others.

> 'Why did you say in the letter that you threw up all the time?' 'I was really talking about Mickey there. I was talking *for* him. He would never write, sergeant, though I pleaded with him. He'll waste away to nothing if I don't help, sergeant . . . ' 'You're a regular Messiah, aren't you?'
> PHILIP ROTH *Defender of the Faith*, 1959

> In the gallery of the old photographs she was always the same, staring out, while everyone else seemed disgracefully protean, kaftaned Messiahs, sideburned Zapatas.
> MARTIN AMIS *The Information*, 1995

Moses Moses (*c*. 14th-13th centuries BC) was a Hebrew prophet and lawgiver. The Old Testament Book of Exodus relates how Moses led the Israelites out of slavery in Egypt and into the Promised Land. ▶ *See special entry* ☐ **MOSES AND THE BOOK OF EXODUS** *on p. 264.*

> 'And now our Prophet has arrived', he said with his eyes popping expressively. 'Our latterday Moses, who shall lead us out of the wilderness.'
> CHESTER HIMES *Blind Man With a Pistol*, 1969

Friendship

There are numerous examples in this book of a classical archetype having a direct biblical counterpart representing the same idea. Here the pairs of **DAMON AND PYTHIAS** and of **ACHILLES AND PATROCLUS** are mirrored by **DAVID AND JONATHAN**, each pair synonymous with faithful friendship. ▶ *See also* **Conflict, Enemy**.

Achates In Virgil's *Aeneid*, Achates is the companion of Aeneas whose fidelity to his friend is so exemplary as to become proverbial, hence the term *fidus Achates* ('faithful Achates').

> 'Friend!' replied Craigengelt, 'my cock of the pit? why, I am thy very Achates, man, as I have heard scholars say—hand and glove—bark and tree—thine to life and death!'
> WALTER SCOTT *The Bride of Lammermoor*, 1819

Achilles and Patroclus In Greek mythology, the Greek heroes Achilles and Patroclus were bosom friends. According to the *Iliad*, Patroclus, having prevailed on Achilles to lend him his armour, was killed by the Trojan hero Hector. Achilles returned to the battle and avenged his beloved friend's death by slaying Hector. ▶ *See* **ACHILLES** *on p. 3 and special entry* ☐ **TROJAN WAR** *on p. 392.*

> Close as Achilles and Patroclus, the two of us.
> JULIAN BARNES *Talking It Over*, 1991

Damon and Pythias Damon was a legendary Syracusan of the 4th century BC whose friend Pythias (also called Phintias) was sentenced to death by Dionysius I. Damon stood bail for Pythias, who returned from settling his affairs just in time to save him. Pythias was then reprieved.

> Papa, I am really longing to see the Pythias to your Damon. You know, I never saw him but once, and then we were so puzzled to know what to say to each other that we did not get on particularly well.
> ELIZABETH GASKELL *North and South*, 1854–5

> And, moreover, Captain Dale would not have been Damon to any Pythias, of whom it might fairly be said that he was a mere clerk.
> ANTHONY TROLLOPE *The Small House at Allington*, 1862

> 'I thought you had a bond of common interest.' 'We had', was the reply. 'But it is more than ten years since Henry Jekyll became too fanciful for me ... Such unscientific

balderdash', added the doctor, flushing suddenly purple, 'would have estranged Damon and Pythias.'
ROBERT LOUIS STEVENSON *The Strange Case of Dr Jekyll and Mr Hyde*, 1886

Of course she thinks, since I'm Fontclair's groomsman, he and I must have been Damon and Pythias for years.
KATE ROSS *Cut to the Quick*, 1993

David and Jonathan In the Old Testament (1 Sam. 18: 1–3; 20: 17) Jonathan, the son of Saul, and David, Saul's appointed successor as King of Israel, swore a compact of love and mutual protection: 'the love of Jonathan was knit with the soul of David, and Jonathan loved him as his own soul'. When Saul grew jealous of David's popularity and sought to bring about his death, Jonathan repeatedly tried to intercede on David's behalf with his father.
▶ *See special entry* ◻ **DAVID** *on p. 90.*

Among the members of his church there was one young man, a little older than himself, with whom he had long lived in such close friendship that it was the custom of their Lantern Yard brethren to call them David and Jonathan.
GEORGE ELIOT *Silas Marner*, 1861

Why should you not make friends with your neighbour at the theatre or in the train, when you know and he knows that feminine criticism and feminine insight and feminine prejudice will never come between you! Though you become as David and Jonathan, you need never enter his home, nor he yours.
E. M. FORSTER *Where Angels Fear to Tread*, 1905

After that there's an undignified struggle for possession of the gun, which Archie wins, followed by a lot of weeping, mostly by the husband, then they sit down and talk and by the time they get back to the house they're like David and Jonathan.
BARRY NORMAN *The Mickey Mouse Affair*, 1995

Don Quixote and Sancho Panza Don Quixote, the hero of a romance by Miguel de Cervantes (1605–15), is accompanied and helped in his knightly adventures by his companion and friend, Sancho Panza. ▶ *See special entry* ◻ **DON QUIXOTE** *on p. 128.*

Man Friday In Daniel Defoe's novel *Robinson Crusoe* (1719), Man Friday is the name given by Crusoe to the man that he meets on his island (on a Friday) after spending many years there alone following a shipwreck. The two become close friends and constant companions.

You're the one everybody envies, in that journalist crowd—you're not really aware of that, and you take it for granted that Billy should be your Man Friday.
CHRISTOPHER J. KOCH *The Year of Living Dangerously*, 1978

Three Musketeers Athos, Porthos, and Aramis are the three friends whose adventures with D'Artagnan are celebrated in Alexandre Dumas's novel *The Three Musketeers* (1844). They declare their comradeship with the famous rallying-cry: 'All for one, and one for all!'

And then Weary tied in with two scouts, and they became close friends immediately, and they decided to fight their way back to their own lines. They were going to travel fast. They were damned if they'd surrender. They shook hands all around. They called themselves 'The Three Musketeers'.
KURT VONNEGUT *Slaughterhouse 5*, 1969

Generosity

Other philanthropes (such as Maecenas) are included at the theme **Wealth**. ▶ *See also* **Miserliness**.

....

Lady Bountiful Lady Bountiful is a wealthy character in Farquar's comedy *The Beaux' Stratagem* (1707). Her name can be used to describe a woman whose generosity is coupled with a certain degree of condescension.

> Approaching, he heard her say in her kindly Lady Bountiful manner, 'You must come and have dinner with us one day. I've got a lot of books that might interest you.'
> GRAHAM GREENE *The Heart of the Matter*, 1948

> Lindsay arrived back with refreshments for everyone—Lord Bountiful dispensing alms to the poor, Fizz thought ungratefully—and whistled in the rest of the Am Bealach contingent to partake.
> JOYCE HELM *Foreign Body*, 1997

Father Christmas ▶ *See* SANTA CLAUS.

Robin Hood The legend of Robin Hood probably began in the 12th or 13th century and was well established by the 14th. According to the stories, he was the leader of a band of outlaws living in Sherwood Forest in Nottinghamshire who robbed the rich (most notably the Sheriff of Nottingham) and gave the spoils to the poor.

> I sit by the River Shannon near the dry docks sipping Mrs. Finucane's sherry. Aunt Aggie's name is in the ledger. She owes nine pounds. It might have been the money she spent on my clothes a long time ago but now she'll never have to pay it because I heave the ledger into the river. I'm sorry I'll never be able to tell Aunt Aggie I saved her nine pounds. . . . I wish I could tell them, I'm your Robin Hood.
> FRANK MCCOURT *Angela's Ashes*, 1997

Rockefeller John Davison Rockefeller (1839-1937) was an American oil magnate who founded the Standard Oil Company. He later used his money for philanthropic projects, giving money for medical research and educational institutions and establishing the Rockefeller Foundation in 1913 'to promote the well-being of mankind'.

> No worthy charity ever knocked and found him absent. In his limited way, having only half a million at his disposal instead of the customary millions, he was as much of a philanthropist as Rockefeller. He gave substantially to the Community Fund, aside from which he donated his time and services to many civic enterprises.
> CHESTER HIMES *A Modern Fable*, 1939

Santa Claus In the modern tradition, Santa Claus (or Father Christmas, as he is usually called in Britain) lives at or near the North Pole, where he is aided by elves in making presents for children. He is represented as wearing a red robe and having a long white beard. On the night of Christmas Eve, he sets forth in his sleigh pulled by reindeer to visit all good children, coming down the chimney of each family's house to leave the children their presents. The name Santa Claus derives from St Nicholas, honoured in Holland as the patron saint of children, and the origin of the figure of Father Christmas.

> 'Don't be any dafter than you can help. I've a proposition for you. Anyway—' he gave me one of his unexpectedly charming smiles, the hanging judge becoming a Santa Claus who would send absolutely every item on the list—'you might as well have lunch first'
> JOHN BRAINE *Room at the Top*, 1957

> 'When I give, I give to all', Mrs Tulsi said. 'I am poor, but I give to all. It is clear, however, that I cannot compete with Santa Claus'.
> V. S. NAIPAUL *A House for Mr Biswas*, 1961

> And here I am as poor as a bowl of yak—me. What do they think I am? Some kind of Sandy Claus? Well, they can just take they stocking down, 'cause it *ain't* Christmas.
> TONI MORRISON *The Bluest Eye*, 1970

Gesture

Unlike the vast majority of themes in this book, this one comprises allusions that describe not an idea or emotion but a physical gesture or action, such as carrying someone (**AENEAS**), rubbing one's hands (**URIAH HEEP, LADY MACBETH**), or striking someone and making them jump (**ITHURIEL**). ▶ *See also* **Ascent Descent, Movement**.

Aeneas In Greek and Roman mythology, Aeneas was a Trojan leader, son of Anchises and Aphrodite, and legendary ancestor of the Romans. At the end of the Trojan War, when Troy was in flames, he carried his ageing father away upon his shoulders. The story of his subsequent wanderings is told in Virgil's *Aeneid*.

> She shook her head, and he lifted her up; then, at a slow pace, went onward with his load. . . . Thus he proceeded, like Aeneas with his father.
> THOMAS HARDY *The Return of the Native*, 1880

Elisha Elisha (9th century BC) was a Hebrew prophet, disciple and successor of Elijah, whose mantle he received: 'And as they still went on and talked, behold, a chariot of fire and horses of fire separated the two of them. And Elijah went up by a whirlwind into heaven . . . And [Elisha] took up the mantle of Elijah that had fallen from him, and went back and stood on the bank of the Jordan' (2 Kgs. 2: 11–13).

> But like the prophet in the chariot disappearing in heaven and dropping his mantle to Elisha, the withdrawing night transferred its pale robe to the breaking day.
> HERMAN MELVILLE *Billy Budd, Foretopman*, 1891

Uriah Heep Uriah Heep is the dishonest clerk in Dickens's novel *David Copperfield* (1850) who gains complete control over the lawyer Mr Wickfield. Feigning humility, he describes himself as 'so very 'umble', while repeatedly wringing his hands. Eventually his crimes of forgery and theft are exposed and he is imprisoned.

> He has these annoying mannerisms—he wrings his hands, just like Uriah Heep!
> KATE CHARLES *A Dead Man Out of Mind*, 1994

Ithuriel In Milton's *Paradise Lost* (1667), Ithuriel is one of the Cherubim, 'a strong and subtle spirit', who is sent by Gabriel to search for Satan in the Garden of Eden. Touched by Ithuriel's spear, which 'no falsehood can endure', Satan starts up in his own shape and is ejected.

> Rainbarrow had again become blended with night when Wildeve ascended the long acclivity at its base. On his reaching the top a shape grew up from the earth immediately behind him. It was that of Eustacia's emissary. He slapped Wildeve on the shoulder. The feverish young innkeeper and engineer started like Satan at the touch of Ithuriel's spear.
> THOMAS HARDY *The Return of the Native*, 1880

Lady Macbeth In Shakespeare's tragedy *Macbeth* (1623), Lady Macbeth spurs her husband on to murder King Duncan and assume the crown. The first murder is followed by others and eventually Lady Macbeth loses her wits and is observed sleepwalking and rubbing her hands in an attempt to remove the spots of blood that she imagines to be on them. Finally, she commits suicide.

> Whatever else the years give me cause to forgive him for I shall never forgive him for wrecking my party and making a fool of Claude. Why am I clutching this orange, she wondered. She stared down at her hand, like lady Macbeth. What, in our house? When she returned to her guests—the perfumed blood under her nails—the performance was over.
> HILARY MANTEL *A Place of Greater Safety*, 1992

> He wasn't listening. His eyes had swivelled away from me, drawn back to the house. I looked, too, and saw that his wife had emerged. She'd upped the melodrama, wringing her hands Lady Macbeth style.
> GILLIAN SLOVO *Close Call*, 1995

> Now he was rubbing his hands like Lady Macbeth on speed.
> PAUL JOHNSTON *Body Politic*, 1996

Pontius Pilate Pontius Pilate was the Roman procurator of Judaea before whom accusations against Jesus were brought. The Jews, under the direction of the high priest, Caiaphas, wanted Jesus executed, which required him to be tried under Roman rather than Jewish law. After questioning Jesus, Pilate could find no basis for a charge against him. The Jews were insistent that Jesus be crucified and eventually Pilate gave in to them: 'When Pilate saw that he could prevail nothing, but that rather a tumult was made, he took water and washed his hands before the multitude, saying, I am innocent of the blood of this just person: see ye to it' (Matt. 27: 24). This gave rise to the phrase 'to wash your hands of something'. ▶ *See special entry* □ JESUS *on p. 223*.

> Chief Ranger Hull crossed the clearing, wiping his hands carefully on a clean white pocket hanky. . . . Hull never looked up from his hands while he talked, but continued to rub meticulously between each finger with the square of cotton. . . . Finally Norman Hull pocketed the handkerchief and Anna breathed a sigh of relief. Till it

stopped she'd not realized how much his Pontius Pilate routine was getting on her nerves.
NEVADA BARR *Endangered Species*, 1997

Gluttony

The entries below express the ideas of eating too much and having an enormous appetite. ▶ *See also* **Food and Drink**.

Sir Toby Belch Sir Toby Belch is the uncle of Olivia in Shakespeare's *Twelfth Night* (1623), known for his love of good food and drink, for 'cakes and ale'.

At present I share Balliol with one ... man ... who rather repels me at meals by his ... habit of shewing satisfaction with the food: Sir Toby Belch was not in it.
ALDOUS HUXLEY *The Letters of Aldous Huxley*, 1915

Billy Bunter Billy Bunter is the rotund schoolboy hero of a series of stories by Frank Richards set in a boys' public school called Greyfriars. The stories were first published in the *Magnet* comic in 1908, and later in book form. Known as 'the Fat Owl of the Remove' on account of his large, round spectacles, Bunter has an obsessive love of 'tuck' and is willing to do anything, even steal from his friends, in order to obtain it.

In 1953, the Tory government of Mr Churchill lifted the wartime rationing on sweets. That day I was violently sick. But not before consuming a quantity of toffee, chocolate, sherbet and gobstoppers with a Bunter-like passion.
TRISTAN GAREL-JONES in *The Observer*, 1996

Gargantua Gargantua (whose name means 'gullet') is a prince of gigantic proportions and prodigious appetite in Rabelais's satire *Gargantua* (1534). He is the father of Pantagruel. A gargantuan appetite or meal is an extremely large one.

Then the baking would begin, and in a few days there would be a party, consisting chiefly of a Gargantuan feed, with Mrs. Gall the heart and soul of it.
ROBERTSON DAVIES *A Mixture of Frailties*, 1951

Broadway followed, and marriage the same year, at the age of 19. The birth of a daughter in this first, as in his two subsequent marriages, in no way slowed down his gargantuan promiscuity.
BRENDA MADDOX in *The Observer*, 1996

Pantagruel Pantagruel (whose name means 'all-thirsty') is the son of Gargantua in Rabelais's satire *Pantagruel* (1532). A giant like his father, Pantagruel has a similarly enormous appetite, especially for wine.

Don Emmanuel, with his rufous beard, his impressive belly, and his flair for ribaldry, made pantagruelian quantities of guarapo, involving hundreds of pineapple skins, which he served with a gourd and his usual good humour.
LOUIS DE BERNIÈRES *Señor Vivo and the Coca Lord*, 1991

Winnie the Pooh Winnie the Pooh is the teddy bear of Christopher Robin in A. A. Milne's books *Winnie the Pooh* (1926) and *The House at Pooh Corner* (1928). He is a rather plump bear who is not particularly intelligent (he describes himself as 'a Bear of Very Little Brain') and has a constant craving for honey, often suggesting that it is 'time for a little something'. In one episode, he enters a rabbit's burrow, eats a considerable amount of honey, and then becomes stuck when trying to get out of the hole again.

> Charlie as crime preventer was like Winnie the Pooh as honey warden.
> SARAH LACEY *File Under Deceased*, 1992

> It had been a long day. First, there had been the inspection of the roof-space at the Chavanacs' villa: an undignified episode, in which he had almost got stuck in a very small trapdoor (like Pooh Bear wedged in a window, Hugo said later).
> HILARY WHELAN *Frightening Strikes*, 1995

Yogi Bear Yogi Bear is an American animated cartoon character who appeared on television in the 1950s and 1960s. Living in Jellystone Park, Yogi Bear considers himself 'smarter than the average bear' and with his companion, Boo Boo, spends his time trying to outwit the park ranger and steal picnic baskets from visitors to the park.

Goodness

This theme covers the idea of human goodness, particularly as manifested in acts of compassion and charity. As well as more traditional figures, several 20th-century Nobel Peace Prize laureates have become synonymous with virtue and morality. ▶ *See also* **Evil**, **Heroes**, **Wholesomeness**.

Christ ▶ *See* JESUS CHRIST.

Christian Christian is the central character of Bunyan's religious allegory *The Pilgrim's Progress* (1678, 1684) who undertakes a pilgrimage to the Celestial City, encountering on the way such adversaries as Giant Despair and Apollyon, the foul fiend.

St Francis of Assisi St Francis (c.1181–1226), born Giovanni di Bernardone, was an Italian monk who founded the Franciscan order of friars. He exemplifies humility, simple faith, and in particular a great love for, and empathy with, birds and animals.

> I shall get a job in an arts and crafts shop in Horsham and do barbola work in my spare time. I shall be all right ... and later on I can go to Italy and perhaps learn to be a little like St Francis of Assisi.
> STELLA GIBBONS *Cold Comfort Farm*, 1932

Gabriel In the Bible, Gabriel was the archangel who foretold the birth of Jesus to the Virgin Mary (Luke 1: 26–38) and who also appeared to Zacharias, father of John the Baptist, and to Daniel. In Islam, Gabriel revealed the Koran to Muhammad.

> Alida Fischer calls him Archangel Gabriel, because his true self came out of its shell when her son was arrested. I must say he disliked her son intensely, but when the trouble came he went at once to the rescue.
> ALAN PATON *Ah, But Your Land Is Beautiful*, 1981

> As far as Cassandra Swann was concerned, Charlie Quartermain, gross, unbuttoned, spehisciform, might be St Francis of Assissi and the Angel Gabriel rolled into one, with a touch of Paul Newman on the one hand and a dollop of Socrates on the other, but that still wouldn't make up for the fact that basically she just didn't fancy him.
> SUSAN MOODY *King of Hearts*, 1995

> There may be no winning the next election for the Tories, even if they could draft a new leader combining the purity of the Archangel Gabriel, the cunning of Machiavelli and the strength of Hercules.
> ANDREW RAWNSLEY in The *Observer*, 1995

Sir Galahad In Arthurian legend, Sir Galahad was one of the Knights of the Round Table, the son of Sir Lancelot and Elaine. Galahad's immaculate purity and virtue predestines him to succeed in the quest for the Holy Grail. His name is often used to describe a man who comes to the aid of a woman.

> 'You received my flowers?' he questioned. She regained some of her composure. 'Yes, Sir Galahad, but I'm a little disappointed in your eyes.'
> CHESTER HIMES *A Modern Marriage*, 1933

> 'I have to go out,' I said. 'I have to go over there and see what has happened. And she can't stay here alone. And no man, not even a doctor, is going to put her to bed. Get a nurse. I'll sleep somewhere else.' 'Phil Marlowe,' he said. 'The shop-soiled Galahad. Okay. I'll stick around until the nurse comes.'
> RAYMOND CHANDLER *The High Window*, 1943

> The thought of my unexpected Sir Galahad kept me going past the high dank brick wall, with its sprayed-on abuse and peeling posters, across the corner where the street lights were out of action, and towards my rendezvous.
> PAT SWEET *Troubled Waters*, 1994

Good Samaritan One of Jesus's parables tells of a Samaritan who stopped to help a victim of thieves left wounded by the roadside and already ignored by a priest and a Levite, both of whom passed by on the other side (Luke 10: 30–7). The Samaritan, by contrast, 'had compassion, and went to him and bound up his wounds, pouring on oil and wine; then he set him on his own beast and brought him to an inn, and took care of him.' Inhabitants of Samaria would have been regarded by the Jews as enemies and outcasts, having split from mainstream Judaism, recognizing only the Pentateuch of the Bible. The term 'Good Samaritan' is now used to describe a person who is helpful and compassionate, especially to those in adversity.

> I told her that I had had a fall—I didn't say how—and she saw by my looks that I was pretty sick. Like a true Samaritan she asked no questions, but gave me a bowl of milk with a dash of whisky in it, and let me sit for a little by her kitchen fire.
> JOHN BUCHAN *The Thirty-Nine Steps*, 1915

> 'Can I do anything for you?' 'We have been stranded a half hour,' Yusef said. 'The cars have gone by, and I have thought—when will a Good Samaritan appear?'
> GRAHAM GREENE *The Heart of the Matter*, 1948

That Brian Cassidy from the hotel, he was going to let her die right there, but a Good Samaritan in the garage, he sometimes feeds her on the sly when Mr Cassidy isn't watching, he called for an ambulance.
SARA PARETSKY *Ghost Country*, 1998

Goody Two-Shoes Little Goody Two-Shoes is the heroine of a 1765 children's book by John Newbery, published under the full title *The History of Little Goody Two-Shoes; Otherwise called, Mrs Margery Two-Shoes. With the Means by which she acquired her Learning and Wisdom, and in consequence thereof her Estate*. An orphan who is delighted with a pair of new shoes (from which she gets her nickname), Margery becomes educated and ultimately wealthy through her own virtue and industry. Her name has now come to be used for a smugly virtuous person.

Do you have to swear every other word?' 'Do you have to be such a stuck-up goody two shoes?' We carried on in silence.
SHYAMA PERERA *Haven't Stopped Dancing Yet*, 1999

Jesus Jesus Christ is the central figure of the Christian religion, a Jewish religious leader worshipped by Christians as the Son of God and the Saviour of Mankind. He is traditionally cited as the perfect model of goodness and compassion. ▶ *See special entry* □ JESUS *on p. 223.*

And Daniel—to his cousin a sort of Christ between thieves—was hurried past the privileged loafers in the corridor, and down the broad steps.
ARNOLD BENNETT *The Old Wives' Tale*, 1908

Well, he looks awfully nice. Of course you never really know someone till you've been married to them for a while and discover some of their scruffier habits. I remember how upset I was when I realized for the first time that after all Joe wasn't Jesus Christ. I don't know what it was, probably some silly thing like finding out he's crazy about Audrey Hepburn. Or that he's a secret philatelist.
MARGARET ATWOOD *The Edible Woman*, 1969

Joseph In the Bible, Joseph was the son of Jacob. When a boy, Joseph, favoured by Jacob over his brothers, was given a coat of many colours by his father. Driven by jealousy, his brothers sold him into slavery in Egypt, where Joseph became adviser to Pharaoh and rose to high office, eventually becoming governor of Egypt. He was reconciled with his family when he helped them during a famine in Canaan, showing particular compassion for his father and his youngest brother, Benjamin. Joseph is often alluded to as the archetype of a powerful person who acts with kindness and loyalty towards his own people. ▶ *See special entry* □ JOSEPH *on p. 224.*

The honour and love you bear him is nothing but meet, for God has given him great gifts, and he uses them as the patriarch Joseph did, who, when he was exalted to a place of power and trust, yet yearned with tenderness towards his parent, and his younger brother.
GEORGE ELIOT *Adam Bede*, 1859

Martin Luther King Martin Luther King (1929–68) was a US Baptist minister and civil rights leader who opposed discrimination against blacks by organizing non-violent resistance and peaceful mass demonstrations. He was awarded the 1964 Nobel Peace Prize. A brilliant and inspiring orator, his most famous speech reiterates the words 'I have a dream'. King was assassinated in Memphis, Tennessee in 1968.

Many seem to believe that you are destined to be to the unborn what Martin Luther King was to the black people of America, and the late Robert F. Charisma to the disadvantaged Chicanos and Puerto Ricans of the country.
PHILIP ROTH *Our Gang*, 1971

Madonna The Madonna (literally 'my lady') is a name for the Virgin Mary, the mother of Jesus Christ, especially when she is represented in a painting or sculpture. The name is sometimes applied to a woman of apparently perfect virtue and purity.

We were never happy. Gavin was a public schoolboy who never grew up. Like many men with that background, he was uneasy with women. Some end up treating us like whores, others decide we're madonnas. Gavin was the madonna type. Unfortunately I'm not. I found the strain of playing Mary Poppins just too much. In the end I told him to bugger off.
KEN MCCLURE *Requiem*, 1992

Florence Nightingale An English nurse and medical reformer, Florence Nightingale (1820-1910) became famous during the Crimean War for improving sanitation and medical procedures, achieving a dramatic reduction in the mortality rate. She became known as the 'Lady of the Lamp' because of her nightly rounds of the wards carrying a lamp.

'Besides, there is sure to be a lot of material I can collect for my novel; and perhaps one or two of the relations will have messes or miseries in their domestic circle which I can clear up.' 'You have the most revolting Florence Nightingale complex,' said Mrs Smiling.
STELLA GIBBONS *Cold Comfort Farm*, 1932

Every woman I've had turned to hate. First they cool the fires, all lovey-dovey, real little Florence Nightingales, darling this, darling that, then, when you think it's gone out for good, whoosh they've stoked up a blaze that would melt steel.
MIKE NICOL *The Powers That Be*, 1989

Oh and why did she give up wanting to be a social worker? Was she too fucking sensitive to the pain of the world? Wrong way round: if you ask me, the pain of the world wasn't sensitive enough to *her*. All those damaged people and fucked-up families didn't appreciate the astonishing privilege they were being granted of having their troubles treated by Miss Florence Nightingale herself.
JULIAN BARNES *Talking It Over*, 1991

Samaritan ▶ *See* GOOD SAMARITAN.

Oskar Schindler Oskar Schindler (1908-74) was a German industrialist who, during the Second World War, employed Jewish workers in his factory in Poland and managed to save many of them from certain death in concentration camps by having them relocated to a new armaments factory in Czechoslovakia. His life and role in rescuing Polish Jews are celebrated in Thomas Keneally's novel *Schindler's Ark* (1982) and the film *Schindler's List* (1993), directed by Steven Spielberg.

He eventually reached New York in 1940, with the help of a Japanese Schindler figure called Chiune Sugihara, a vice-consul in Lithuania, who gave him a transit visa and later helped some 10,000 desperate Jews.
The Observer, 1997

Albert Schweitzer Albert Schweitzer (1875-1965) was a Franco-German medical missionary, theologian, and musician, born in Alsace. In 1913 he qualified as a doctor and went as a missionary to Lambarene in French Equatorial Africa (now Gabon), where he established a hospital and spent most of his life. Schweitzer was awarded the Nobel Peace Prize in 1952. His philosophy was founded on 'reverence for life'.

> This is the guy who killed my mother, Reverend. And he's going to kill again, that's a fact. He's out there laughing at me, and laughing at the cops, and laughing at you for protecting him, and I would knock down Mother Theresa, run over Albert Schweitzer and shoot the Pope to get at this guy. Do you understand me now?
> STEPHEN BOGART *Play It Again*, 1994

Mother Teresa Mother Teresa (1910–97) was a Roman Catholic missionary, born Agnes Gonxha Bojaxhiu of Albanian parents in what is now Macedonia. She became a nun in 1928 and went to India, where she devoted herself to helping the destitute. She founded the order of Missionaries of Charity, which became noted for its work among the poor and dying in Calcutta. Mother Teresa was awarded the Nobel Peace Prize in 1979. She is often referred to as the model of saintly compassion.

> Or maybe she could go in for superhuman goodness, instead. Hair shirts, stigmata, succouring the poor, a kind of outsized Mother Teresa.
> MARGARET ATWOOD *The Robber Bride*, 1993

> Then Hawkeye said, 'Shame about Jasper Moon. I rather liked him. He might have put his pecker in peculiar places, but his heart was in the right spot. Ever since I caught those young tearaways who'd been vandalizing his street door he always gave a good Christmas bung to the Widows and Orphans fund.' Rafferty frowned as yet another witness depicted Moon as aspiring to sainthood. What was it about the man? Their child-abuser seemed to be turning into a veritable Father Teresa.
> GERALDINE EVANS *Death Line*, 1995

Archbishop Tutu Desmond Mpilo Tutu (b. 1931) is a South African clergyman. He served as general secretary of the South African Council of Churches 1979–84, and during this time he became a leading figure in the struggle against the country's apartheid policies, advocating non-violent opposition. He was awarded the Nobel peace prize in 1984. Tutu became Johannesburg's first black Anglican bishop in 1985 and was made archbishop of Cape Town in 1986.

> And I'm telling you, when Bacon gets hold of something, things happen. He's not Martin Luther King or Bishop Tutu. Okay? He's not gonna win any Nobel Prize. He's got his own way of doing things, and sometimes it might not stand close scrutiny.
> TOM WOLFE *The Bonfire of the Vanities*, 1987

Grief and Sorrow

It is striking that there is such a similarity between some of the stories below. The figure of the mother mourning the death of her children is clearly a potent symbol of grief. ▶ *See also* **Despair**, **Suffering**.

Constance In Shakespeare's *King John* (1623), Constance of Brittany is the mother of Arthur, the king's young nephew, and a claimant to the throne. Her son's death draws from her a passionate expression of grief:

Grief fills the room up of my absent child,
Lies in his bed, walks up and down with me,
Puts on his pretty looks, repeats his words.

> Few of us wish to disturb the mother of a litter of puppies when mouthing a bone in the midst of her young family. Medea and her children are familiar to us, and so is the grief of Constance.
> ANTHONY TROLLOPE *Barchester Towers*, 1857

Deirdre In Irish legend, Deirdre was the beautiful daughter of the harper to King Conchobar of Ulster. According to a prophecy her beauty would bring death and ruin to the men of Ulster. Although she was the intended bride of Conchobar, she fell in love and eloped with Naoise. When Naoise was treacherously slain by Conchobar, Deirdre took her own life, ending her misery.

Hecuba Hecuba was the wife of King Priam of Troy and mother of numerous children, including Hector, Paris, Cassandra, and Troilus. Homer's *Iliad* tells of her suffering and grief during the Trojan War as she witnesses the deaths of many of her sons at the hands of the Greeks, in particular the slaying of her eldest son, Hector, by Achilles and the desecration of his body. ▶ *See special entry* □ **TROJAN WAR** *on p. 392*.

Mary Magdalene In the New Testament, Mary Magdalene was a follower of Jesus, traditionally said to be a reformed prostitute. She is often portrayed in art weeping repentant tears, and the word 'maudlin' is derived from her name.

Niobe In Greek mythology, Niobe was the daughter of Tantalus and the mother of numerous offspring. She boasted that her large family made her superior to the goddess Leto, who only had two children, Apollo and Artemis. Angered by this, Apollo slew all Niobe's sons, and Artemis her daughters. Niobe herself was turned into a stone, and her tears into streams that eternally trickled from it. She has become a symbol of inconsolable grief. In Shakespeare's *Hamlet*, Hamlet describes his mother at his father's funeral as 'Like Niobe, all tears'.

> The Niobe of nations! there she stands,
> Childless and crownless, in her voiceless woe.
> LORD BYRON *Childe Harold*, 1818

Rachel Rachel was the second wife of Jacob, and the mother of Joseph and Benjamin. In the Book of Jeremiah, she is described as weeping for her children who were taken away in captivity to Babylon: 'Thus says the Lord: A voice is heard in Ramah, lamentation and bitter weeping. Rachel is weeping for her children; she refuses to be comforted for her children, because they are not' (Jer. 31: 15).

> She was like Rachel, 'mourning over her children, and would not be comforted.'
> WASHINGTON IRVING *The Sketch-Book of Geoffrey Crayton, Gent.*, 1820

> But by her still halting course and winding, woeful way, you plainly saw that this

ship that so wept with spray, still remained without comfort. She was Rachel, weeping for her children, because they were not.
HERMAN MELVILLE *Moby Dick*, 1851

rivers of Babylon Psalm 137, which commemorates the exile of the Jews in Babylon, opens with the words: 'By the rivers of Babylon, there we sat down, yea, we wept, when we remembered Zion.' The phrase 'the rivers of Babylon' has come to be associated with the idea of mourning for the dead.

Guarding

This theme deals not only with the idea of physically keeping guard over something but also with the more general idea of being vigilant or watchful.

....

Argus In Greek mythology, Argus was a giant with a hundred eyes, whom Hera made guardian of Io (transformed into a heifer by Zeus). Argus never slept with more than a pair of eyes at a time, so he was able to watch Io constantly. After Hermes had killed Argus on behalf of Zeus, Hera took the eyes to deck the peacock's tail. The term 'Argus-eyed' has come to mean vigilant or observant.

Well, thought I, I hope still, Argus, to be too hard for thee. Now Argus, the poets say, had an hundred eyes, and was set to watch with them all, as she does, with her goggling ones.
SAMUEL RICHARDSON *Pamela*, 1741

Cerberus Cerberus was the three-headed dog which guarded the entrance to Hades in Greek mythology. Cerberus could be appeased with a cake, as by Aeneas, or lulled to sleep, as by Orpheus, with lyre music. One of the twelve labours of Hercules was to bring him up from the underworld. Someone who guards the entrance to a place can be described as a Cerberus. ▶ *See special entries* □ HADES *on p. 172 and* □ HERCULES *on p. 182*.

She longed to mention that Claridges were looking for a doorman. He'd be perfect in the role, now he was so well-groomed and barking like Cerberus.
ALICE THOMAS ELLIS *The 27th Kingdom*, 1982

A call to his office got me as far as his secretary, Veronica, who watched over his working day like Cerberus in human form. After diligent cross-examination she allowed me to talk to her master, who was as affable as his secretary was chilly.
MALCOLM HAMMER *Shadows on the Green*, 1994

As we got out of the car I warned Vico not to talk in the stairwell. 'We don't want the dogs to hear me and wake Mr. Contreras.' 'He is a malevolent neighbor? You need me perhaps to guard you?' 'He's the best-natured neighbor in the world. Unfortunately, he sees his role in my life as Cerberus, with a whiff of Othello thrown in.'
SARA PARETSKY *V. I. for Short*, 1995

Garm Garm is the dog that guards the gates of hell in Norse mythology, a Norse equivalent of Cerberus.

Guilt

Two meanings of the word 'guilt' are dealt with here: the feeling of culpability and shame, and the fact of having committed a particular offence. The concept of guilt is central to the Judaeo-Christian tradition but appears to be rarely expressed in classical myth. ▶ *See also* **Curse**, **Innocence**.

....

Cain According to the Book of Genesis, Cain, the eldest son of Adam and Eve, murdered his own brother Abel (Gen. 4:1–16). For this crime he was cast out from his homeland and forced to live a life of vagrancy as an outcast. ▶ *See special entry* ❑ **CAIN** *on p. 44*.

> Summarized briefly, mainstream pop ethology contends that two lineages of hominids inhabited Pleistocene Africa. One, a small, territorial carnivore, evolved into us; the other, a larger, presumably gentle herbivore, became extinct. Some carry the analogy of Cain and Abel to its full conclusion and accuse our ancestors of fratricide.
> STEPHEN JAY GOULD *Ever Since Darwin*, 1978

Judas According to the Bible, Judas Iscariot was the disciple who betrayed Jesus for thirty pieces of silver. When he learned that Jesus had been condemned to death, he realized the enormity of his betrayal and repented, returned the money to the priests who had paid him, and then hanged himself (Matt. 27: 3–5). The pieces of silver were used to buy a potter's field, used as a burial place for foreigners. ▶ *See special entry* ❑ **JESUS** *on p. 223*.

> Eustacia was always anxious to avoid the sight of her husband in such a state as this, which had become as dreadful to her as the trial scene was to Judas Iscariot. It brought before her eyes the spectre of a worn-out woman knocking at a door which she would not open; and she shrank from contemplating it.
> THOMAS HARDY *The Return of the Native*, 1880

Macbeth/Lady Macbeth In Shakespeare's play *Macbeth* (1623), Lady Macbeth plots with her husband to kill King Duncan so that her husband can assume the throne in his place. After this murder, and the subsequent murder of Banquo, which Macbeth and his wife also order, they are both troubled by guilt for what they have done. Lady Macbeth sleepwalks, washing her hands in her sleep in an attempt to remove the blood which she imagines to be there. She finally goes mad and kills herself. Macbeth also suffers nightmares and visions as a result of his feelings of guilt.

> Mrs Todd rocked gently for a time, and seemed to be lost, though not poorly, like Macbeth, in her thoughts.
> SARAH ORNE JEWETT *A Dunnet Shepherdess*, 1899

Mary Magdalene In the New Testament, Mary Magdalene was one of the followers of Jesus. Although she is not explicitly described as a prostitute, she is traditionally believed to have been one. Similarly, she is often identified with the woman, a sinner ashamed of her sins, who came to Jesus in the Pharisee's house, washed his feet with her tears, dried them with her hair, and anointed them with oil (Luke 7: 38).

Pontius Pilate Pontius Pilate was the Roman procurator of Judaea from *c.*26 to *c.*36, remembered for presiding at the trial of Jesus Christ. The chief priests and elders who had brought Jesus to him demanded that Jesus be put to death. Pilate, who alone could order the death penalty, was not persuaded that Jesus had committed any crime, but gave in to popular demand and ordered that Jesus be crucified. He washed his hands before the crowd, saying: 'I am innocent of the blood of this just person: see ye to it' (Matt. 27: 24). Pontius Pilate is alluded to as someone who colludes in a crime or dishonest act but tries to distance himself from it and assume no responsibility for it. ▶ *See special entry* ☐ **JESUS** *on p. 223.*

> 'I know Hosnani was a friend of yours, sir.' Mountolive felt himself colouring slightly. 'In matters of business, a diplomat has no friends,' he said stiffly, feeling that he spoke in the very accents of Pontius Pilate.
> LAWRENCE DURRELL *Mountolive*, 1958

> The day will come when we and the British Empire will stand together and say to the world, 'It was we who made you free,' and the Americans and the Russians and the other Pontius Pilates like them will hang their heads and feel ashamed that all the glory came to us.
> LOUIS DE BERNIÈRES *Captain Corelli's Mandolin*, 1994

> 'I think I know why she left the money to Dr Blakeney.' 'Why?' 'I reckon it was a Pontius Pilate exercise. She'd done a lousy job herself bringing up her daughter and granddaughter, knew they'd destroy themselves with jealous infighting if she left the money to them, so passed the buck to the only person she'd ever got on with or respected. Namely Dr Blakeney.'
> MINETTE WALTERS *The Scold's Bridle*, 1994

scapegoat In the Bible, the scapegoat was a goat which was sent into the wilderness after a priest had symbolically laid all the sins of the Israelites upon it so that the sins would be taken away (Lev. 16: 8–22). The word 'scapegoat' has now come to refer to any person who takes the blame for the wrongdoings or failings of others.

> Last night I had looked into the heart of darkness, and the sight had terrified me. What part should I play in the great purification? Most likely that of the Biblical scapegoat.
> JOHN BUCHAN *Prester John*, 1910

Gulliver's Travels

Jonathan Swift's *Gulliver's Travels* (1726) is a satire in the form of a narrative of the travels of Lemuel Gulliver. In the course of the book Gulliver visits many strange lands. First he finds himself shipwrecked on the island of Lilliput. In a famous episode Gulliver wakes on the shore to find himself unable to move because the tiny Lilliputians have fastened his limbs, hair, and body to the ground with strings. The Lilliputians are only six inches tall and, as Gulliver discovers, are as small-minded as they are small-bodied, being petty, pretentious, and factious. One of the issues they quarrel over is the question of whether eggs should be broken at the big or the small end. In his next adventure, Gulliver visits Brobdingnag, a land inhabited by giants who are as tall as steeples. This time it is Gulliver himself who is perceived to be a moral pygmy.

In the third part of the book, Gulliver visits a number of places, notably the flying island of Laputa. Here Gulliver finds the wise men so wrapped up in their speculations that they lack all common sense or knowledge of practical affairs. He also encounters the Struldbrugs of Luggnagg, a race endowed with immortality but who become increasingly infirm and decrepit. In the fourth part, Gulliver travels to the country of the Houyhnhnms, a race of horses endowed with reason. Their simplicity and virtues are contrasted with the disgusting brutality of the Yahoos, a race of brutish creatures, resembling human beings, who embody all the baser vices and instincts of the human race.

Throughout this book there are references to characters and episodes from *Gulliver's Travels*.

▶ *See* BIG-ENDIANS AND LITTLE-ENDIANS *at* **Conflict**
    BROBDINGNAGIAN *at* **Large Size**
    GULLIVER *at* **Captives, Immobility, Large Size,** *and* **Travellers and Wanderers**
    HOUYHNHNMS *at* **Intelligence**
    LILLIPUTIAN *at* **Importance** *and* **Small Size**
    STRULDBRUG *at* **Old Age**
    YAHOO *at* **Destruction**.

Hades

Hades, sometimes also called Erebus, contained the Plain of Asphodel, where the ghosts of the dead led a vague, unsubstantial life, a shadowy continuation of their former life where 'the soul hovers to and fro' (*Odyssey*). Those who had been virtuous went on to Elysium, a happy land of perpetual day. Those who had been enemies of the gods were taken to the punishment fields of Tartarus for eternal punishment, the most famous of these being Tantalus, Ixion, and Sisyphus.

The land of the dead was separated from the land of the living by one of the rivers of Hades, the Styx or the Acheron. The dead were ferried across the River Styx by Charon. At the entrance to the underworld stood the watchdog Cerberus, who prevented any of the living from entering and any of the dead from leaving. Three other rivers intersected the underworld, Phlegethon or Pyriphlegethon, Cocytus, and Lethe. The lord of the underworld was known as Hades or Pluto. His wife was Persephone, whom he captured and took down to live with with him in the underworld.

Throughout this book there are references to Hades and to some of its features.

▶ See ACHERON *at* **Suffering** *and* **Unpleasant or Wicked Places**
   CERBERUS *at* **Guarding**
   CHARON *at* **Ugliness**
   EREBUS *at* **Darkness**
   HADES *at* **Darkness, Suffering,** *and* **Unpleasant or Wicked Places**
   IXION *at* **Punishment** *and* **Suffering**
   LETHE *at* **Death** *and* **Memory**
   PERSEPHONE *at* **Temptation**
   PLUTO *at* **Darkness**
   SISYPHUS *at* **Difficulty, Failure, Punishment,** *and* **Suffering**
   STYGIAN *at* **Darkness**
   STYX *at* **Death**
   TANTALUS *at* **Punishment** *and* **Suffering**
   TARTARUS *at* **Punishment, Suffering,** *and* **Unpleasant or Wicked Places**.

Hair

This theme mainly covers long hair, other distinctive hair styles, and hair colour. Many of the allusions derive from visual rather than literary sources, being drawn from cinema, painting, and cartoons. ▶ *See also* **Baldness**.

....

Alice Alice, the heroine of Lewis Carroll's *Alice's Adventures in Wonderland* (1865), is depicted in John Tenniel's illustrations with long blonde hair. In *Through the Looking-Glass* (1871), the illustrations show her hair held back with a wide hairband, now known as an Alice band. ▶ *See special entry* □ **ALICE IN WONDERLAND** *on p. 10.*

> What would they make of the wedding photos stuck in the back of his bureau drawer? Of Vic, with her Alice-in-Wonderland hair and pale, innocent face.
> DEBORAH CROMBIE *All Shall Be Well*, 1995

Byron George Gordon, Lord Byron (1788-1824) was an English romantic poet, famous for his passionate love affairs as much as for his poetry. His major works include *Childe Harold's Pilgrimage* (1812-18) and *Don Juan* (1819-24). One of the best-known portraits of the poet, by Richard Westall, shows Byron in profile with thick, curly, slightly tousled black hair.

> Head on, his widow's peak and the longish wavy blond hair that flowed back from it still looked . . . well, Byronic . . . rather than a bit lonely on the dome of his skull.
> TOM WOLFE *The Bonfire of the Vanities*, 1987

> Mark Underhill looked Byronic in his oversized white shirt, his dark hair curling about the collar.
> SHARYN MCCRUMB *The Hangman's Beautiful Daughter*, 1996

Esau In the Bible, Esau, the son of Isaac, is described as a red, hairy man (Gen. 25: 25). He sold his birthright to his younger twin, Jacob, for pottage (lentil stew). Esau was the ancestor of the Edomites.

Jane Fonda Jane Fonda (b. 1937) is a US film actress who won an Oscar for her performance in *Klute* (1971). She has abundant tawny hair and is known not only for her films but also for her successful fitness videos.

> At that time she assumed a long-legged, supple, Jane Fonda look; hair plentiful and curly about the head.
> FAY WELDON *Darcy's Utopia*, 1990

Greta Garbo Greta Garbo (1905-90) was a fair-haired Swedish-born US actress, born Greta Gustafsson. She had a haunting beauty and a compelling screen presence. Her films include *Queen Christina* (1933), *Anna Karenina* (1935), and *Ninotchka* (1939). After her early retirement, she also became famous for her reclusiveness.

> 'How long will it take it to grow long?' 'Really long?' 'No, I mean to thy shoulders. It

is thus I would have thee wear it.' 'As Garbo in the cinema?' 'Yes,' he said thickly.
ERNEST HEMINGWAY *For Whom the Bell Tolls*, 1941

Lady Godiva Lady Godiva (d. 1080) was an English noblewoman, wife of Leofric, Earl of Mercia. According to a 13th-century legend, she rode naked through the market-place of Coventry, clothed only in her long, golden hair, to persuade her husband to reduce the heavy taxes he had imposed on the people. All the townspeople stayed indoors and shut up their windows, except for Tom the Tailor, who looked at her through a window as she rode past and was thereafter known as Peeping Tom.

Goldilocks Goldilocks is the name of a little girl in a traditional fairy story, *Goldilocks and the Three Bears*, and the name can be applied to any person with light blonde hair. In the story, Goldilocks visits the bears' house, eats the little bear's porridge, and is eventually found by the bears asleep in his bed.

You just potter about ... while I repair to the kitchen with young Goldilocks here and show him how to cook a sausage.
P. G. WODEHOUSE *Laughing Gas*, 1936

'Fish,' he said to the beard, 'this is Goldilocks.' I smiled rigidly. I am not a blonde.
MARGARET ATWOOD *The Edible Woman*, 1969

Betty Grable Betty Grable (1916–73) was a US film actress and dancer whose 'million-dollar legs' made her the most popular pin-up of the Second World War. She was a curly-haired blonde with a peaches-and-cream appeal.

She wore her usual Betty Grable hairdo.
MARGARET ATWOOD *The Edible Woman*, 1969

Heathcliff Heathcliff is the passionate gypsy hero of Emily Brontë's romantic novel *Wuthering Heights* (1847). He has long dark hair and a brooding presence.

It was Vivaldo. He was wearing a black raincoat and his hair was wild and dripping from the rain. His eyes seemed blacker than ever, and his face paler. 'Heathcliff!' she cried, 'How nice you could come!'
JAMES BALDWIN *Another Country*, 1963

He seemed much younger than her, had Heathcliff-type hair and wore jeans.
The Independent, 1997

Judas Judas Iscariot was the disciple who betrayed Jesus to the Jewish authorities in return for thirty pieces of silver. He is traditionally depicted in art as red-headed.

Veronica Lake Veronica Lake (1919–73) was a petite US film actress who often played slinky femmes fatales in 1940s thrillers. She had a distinctive peek-a-boo hairstyle, her long blonde hair draped over one eye, a style much imitated by film-goers of the time.

I noticed that, when he remembered to, he clipped his words; he's learned that from Ronald Colman, I thought, and felt a little less impressed—it puts him on the same level as the millhand with the Alan Ladd deadpan and the millgirl with the Veronica Lake hair style.
JOHN BRAINE *Room at the Top*, 1957

Little Orphan Annie Little Orphan Annie is the heroine of a US comic strip, an orphan girl with curly red hair.

> As he eased his way around the screen door, trying not to let in any more flies, he could see her head bent over the typewriter, a mare's nest of Orphan Annie curls that made him long to duck her head in a bucket of water.
> SHARYN MCCRUMB *If Ever I Return*, 1990

> Decker shook her hand noticing long, slender fingers. Her face was grave, but childlike—waifish with big brown eyes. Her hair was auburn and bushy. Little Orphan Annie had grown up to be a doctor.
> FAYE KELLERMAN *Prayers for the Dead*, 1996

Medusa In Greek mythology, Medusa was one of the Gorgons who, like her sisters, had snakes for hair and the power to turn anyone who looked at her to stone. Medusa, the only mortal one of the sisters, was killed by Perseus, who cut off her head.

> He saw her—the marble whiteness of the sea-goddess' face, hair combed back upon her shoulders, staring out across the park where the dead autumn leaves and branches flared and smoked; a Medusa among the snows, dressed in her old tartan shawl.
> LAWRENCE DURRELL *Mountolive*, 1958

> The wind had picked up considerably, invading Anna's hair to create a sort of Medusa effect.
> ARMISTEAD MAUPIN *Sure of You*, 1990

naiad In Greek and Roman mythology, a naiad was a water-nymph, a beautiful long-haired maiden associated with lakes, rivers, and fountains.

> She remained always as Michael had first seen her: a woman who talked with her Naiad hair, her winged eyelashes, her tilted head, her fluent waist and rhetorical feet.
> ANAÏS NIN *Children of the Albatross*, 1947

Nazirite A Nazirite was an Israelite specially consecrated to the service of God, whose vows included letting his hair grow. 'All the days of his vow of separation no razor shall come upon his head; until the time is completed for which he separates himself to the Lord, he shall be holy; he shall let the locks of hair of his head grow long' (Num. 6: 1–5). The prophets Samuel and Samson were Nazirites. In the quotation below it is almost certainly Nazirite rather than Nazarene (a native of Nazareth) that is meant.

> His head was utterly concealed beneath a cascade of matted hair that seemed to have no form or colour. In places it stuck out in twisted corkscrews, and in others it lay in congealed pads like felt; it was the hair of a Nazarene or of a hermit demented by the glory and solitude of God.
> LOUIS DE BERNIÈRES *Captain Corelli's Mandolin*, 1994

Nebuchadnezzar Nebuchadnezzar (*c*.630–562 BC) was the King of Babylon 605–562 BC who built the massive fortification walls of Babylon and the Hanging Gardens. He conquered and destroyed Jerusalem in 586 BC and exiled the Israelites to Babylon. According to the prophet Daniel, he was punished for his wickedness and arrogance with insanity. 'The same hour was the thing fulfilled upon Nebuchadnezzar; and he was driven from men, and did eat the grass as oxen, and his body was wet with the dew of heaven, till his hairs were grown like eagles' feathers, and his nails like birds' claws' (Dan. 4: 29–33). There is a famous drawing by William Blake depicting the king in this condition. ▶ *See special entry* □ **DANIEL** *on p. 86.*

> You have a 'faux air' of Nebuchadnezzar in the fields about you, that is certain: your hair reminds me of eagles' feathers; whether your nails are grown like birds' claws or not, I have not yet noticed.
> CHARLOTTE BRONTË *Jane Eyre*, 1847

Peter Pan *Peter Pan*, subtitled *The Boy Who Wouldn't Grow Up* (1904), is J. M. Barrie's play for children about a boy with magical powers who, with the fairy Tinker Bell, takes the Darling children to Never-Never Land. Peter is traditionally played on stage by an actress, and so a 'Peter Pan haircut' is a short boyish one worn by a woman or girl.

> I could see why my mother was fascinated by the music. It was being pounded out by a little Chinese girl, about nine years old, with a Peter Pan haircut. The girl had the sauciness of a Shirley Temple.
> AMY TAN *Two Kinds*, 1989

Pre-Raphaelite The Pre-Raphaelite Brotherhood was a group of English 19th-century artists founded by Dante Gabriel Rossetti, John Everett Millais, and Holman Hunt. Their aim was to emulate the vivid use of colour and meticulously detailed fidelity to nature of Italian painting from before the time of Raphael. The term 'Pre-Raphaelite' is often applied to a woman who resembles the models painted by this school, especially in having wavy auburn hair and a pale complexion. The faces of these models, notably Elizabeth Siddal, Fanny Cornforth, and Jane Morris, appear in a great many of the paintings.

> Some would say her hair is her finest feature, though Robyn herself secretly hankers after something more muted and malleable, hair that could be groomed and styled according to mood—drawn back in a severe bun like Simone de Beauvoir's, or allowed to fall to the shoulders in a Pre-Raphaelite cloud.
> DAVID LODGE *Nice Work*, 1988

> Beneath the wide, full mouth, the arrogant stare of the eyes, the dark, crimped, Pre-Raphaelite hair streaming in the wind.
> P. D. JAMES *Devices and Desires*, 1989

> She has narrow sloping shoulders, and in those days a soulful pre-Raphaelite look.
> FAY WELDON *Life Force*, 1992

Rapunzel In the fairy story, Rapunzel is a beautiful long-haired girl who is locked at the top of a tall tower by a witch. The witch, and subsequently a handsome prince, are able to climb up to her after calling out 'Rapunzel, Rapunzel, let down your long hair'.

> As I understand it, a gazebo is an open structure. I spent fifteen minutes searching for something resembling a park bandstand before coming upon a round building made of piled rock, like an old New England stone fence gone berserk. The rocks rose high, into a miniature fairy-tale tower, complete with turret. Huddled by the shore of a dark lake, it looked like an illustration from a children's book. If I waited till sunrise perhaps Rapunzel would cast down hair even longer than Marissa's.
> LINDA BARNES *Cold Case*, 1997

> Vicky had the hair for it, yards of beautiful Rapunzel tresses curled and heaped and framing her delicate features like a baroque picture frame carved of chestnut.
> JUSTIN SCOTT *Frostline*, 1997

Samson In the Bible, Samson was an Israelite leader (probably 11th century BC) whose famed strength lay in his long hair (Judg. 13–16). His lover, Delilah, discovered this and had it cut off while he slept, after which she delivered him up to his enemies, the Philistines. Samson is sometimes mentioned as an example of a big, strong, long-haired man. ▶ *See special entry* □ **SAMSON** *on p. 336*.

> He ran a hand through his black Samson hair.
> PHILIP ROTH *The Conversion of the Jews*, 1959

> And Richard, who had had some bad haircuts in his time, found himself thinking: Samson and Delilah. Oh, what a haircut was that!
> MARTIN AMIS *The Information*, 1995

Satan Satan is traditionally depicted with sharp features and a V-shaped hairline in the middle of his forehead.

> The V motif was picked up again by thickish brows rising outward from twin creases above a hooked nose, and his pale brown hair grew down—from high flat temples—in a point on his forehead. He looked rather pleasantly like a blond Satan.
> DASHIELL HAMMETT *The Maltese Falcon*, 1930

Shirley Temple Blonde and curly-headed, Shirley Temple (b.1928) was a US child star of the 1930s. She appeared in such films as *Curly Top* (1935) and *Dimples* (1936).

Topsy Topsy is the mischievous little black slave girl in Harriet Beecher Stowe's novel *Uncle Tom's Cabin* (1852), whose 'woolly hair was braided in sundry little tails, which stuck out in every direction'. She says that she had neither a father nor a mother, and when she is asked if she knows who made her, Topsy replies 'I 'spect I grow'd. Don't think nobody never made me.'

> Black women in terrycloth robes with their faces greased and their straightened hair done in small tight plaits like Topsy.
> CHESTER HIMES *Blind Man with a Pistol*, 1969

Venus de Milo The Venus de Milo is a classical marble statue of the goddess Aphrodite (c.100 BC), now in the Louvre in Paris. The statue, missing its arms, was discovered on the Greek island of Melos in 1820. Aphrodite's short wavy hair is tied back with a ribbon.

> She had crisp white hair which she wore like the Venus of Milo.
> W. SOMERSET MAUGHAM *Cakes and Ale*, 1930

Woody Woodpecker Woody Woodpecker is a cartoon character with a tall comb of red hair.

> He has red hair that stands up at the top like Woody Woodpecker's.
> MARGARET ATWOOD *Cat's Eye*, 1988

Happiness

This theme largely deals with states of perfect contentment or bliss. Imaginary places that have come to stand for an idealized state of happiness can be found at the closely related theme **Idyllic Places**. ▶ *See also* **Comedy and Humour, Smiles**.

....

Adam and Eve In the Bible, Adam was the first man, created by God from the dust of the ground and God's breath, and Eve the first woman, formed from one of Adam's ribs. They lived together in innocence in the Garden of Eden until they were tempted to eat the forbidden fruit of the tree of knowledge. As a result of this original sin of disobedience, they were banished from Eden. Adam and Eve can represent a state of utter contentment, particularly when preceding the loss or destruction of such happiness. ▶ *See special entry* ❑ ADAM AND EVE *on p. 5*.

> We are Adam and Eve, unfallen, in Paradise.
> GEORGE ELIOT *The Mill on the Floss*, 1860

Correggio Antonio Allegri da Correggio (*c*.1494–1534) was an Italian painter of the High Renaissance. His best-known works are a series of frescos in the Camera di San Paolo and other Parma churches, painted in a sensual style, with a soft play of light and colour and striking use of foreshortening. These frescos often depict frolicking *putti* (cherubs) with an exuberance that captures the vitality and joyfulness of children.

> The rush of conflicting feelings was too great for Maggie to say much when Lucy, with a face breathing playful joy, like one of Correggio's cherubs, poured forth her triumphant revelation.
> GEORGE ELIOT *The Mill on the Floss*, 1860

Dionysiac ▶ *See* DIONYSIAN.

Dionysian In Greek mythology, Dionysus (also called Bacchus) was a Greek god, the son of Zeus and Semele. Originally a god of the fertility of nature, associated with wild and ecstatic religious rites, in later traditions he was a god of wine who loosened inhibitions and inspired creativity in music and poetry. 'Dionysian' and 'Dionysiac' usually describe frenzied and unrestrained abandon or ecstasy.

> He longed to be possessed by the spirit of Dionysian abandon.
> DAVID LODGE *The British Museum Is Falling Down*, 1965

> And the people in the streets, it seemed to him, whether milling along Oxford Street or sauntering from lion to lion in Trafalgar Square, formed another golden host, beautiful in the antique cold-faced way of Blake's pastel throngs, pale Dionysiacs, bare thighs and gaudy cloth, lank hair and bell-bottoms.
> JOHN UPDIKE *Bech: A Book*, 1970

> Oh, how Sir Gerald . . . would love to be able to wallow in that filth with such Dionysian abandon!
> TOM WOLFE *The Bonfire of the Vanities*, 1987

Epicurus The Greek philosopher Epicurus (341–271 BC) founded a school of philosophy that espoused hedonism, described by Epicurus in one of his letters as: 'We say that pleasure is the beginning and end of living happily.' In his philosophy, happiness is achieved by becoming free from pain and anxiety by, among other things, freeing oneself from fear of the supernatural and death. A hedonistic or supremely happy state can be described as Epicurean.

> Ten o'clock was the hour fixed for this meeting, and Wimsey was lingering lovingly over his bacon and eggs, so as to leave no restless and unfilled moment in his morning. By which it may be seen that his lordship had reached that time of life when a man can extract an Epicurean enjoyment even from his own passions—the halcyon period between the self-tormenting exuberance of youth and the fretful *carpe diem* of approaching senility.
> DOROTHY SAYERS *Have His Carcass*, 1932

Hyperboreans In Greek mythology, the Hyperboreans were a fabled race worshipping Apollo and living in a land of perpetual sunshine and happiness beyond the north wind (known as Boreas).

Lotus-eaters The Lotus-eaters, as described in Homer's *Odyssey*, are a people who live in a far-off land and eat the fruit of the lotus which puts them into a pleasant state of dreamy forgetfulness in which they lose the desire to return to their homes. ▶ *See special entry* ☐ **ODYSSEUS** *on p. 283.*

> Her presence brought memories of such things as Bourbon roses, rubies, and tropical midnights; her moods recalled lotus-eaters and the march in 'Athalie'; her motions, the ebb and flow of the sea; her voice, the viola.
> THOMAS HARDY *The Return of the Native*, 1880

> The summons to this lotus-eating existence had come from my son, Nick . . . who had crowned his academic career by becoming Head of the Department of Social Studies in the University of Miami. He had also acquired a sizeable house with a swimming bath in the garden.
> JOHN MORTIMER *Rumpole's Return*, 1980

Nirvana Nirvana is the final goal of Buddhism, a transcendent state in which there is neither suffering, desire, nor sense of self.

> He began to feel a drowsy attachment for this South—a South, it seemed, more of Algiers than of Italy, with faded aspirations pointing back over innumerable generations to some warm, primitive Nirvana, without hope or care.
> F. SCOTT FITZGERALD *The Beautiful and Damned*, 1922

Hatred

This theme covers personal feelings of hatred or dislike. Enmity involving larger groups of people is dealt with at **Enemy**. ▶ *See also* **Conflict**, **Envy**.

Captain Ahab In Herman Melville's novel *Moby Dick* (1851), the monomaniacal Captain Ahab obsessively pursues Moby Dick, a huge white whale, driven by hatred for the creature that on a previous voyage had cost him his leg.

basilisk The basilisk was a legendary monster, the king of serpents, which could reputedly strike someone dead with its stare. A 'basilisk stare' is thus a cold stare.

> *Gloucester*: Thine eyes, sweet lady, have infected mine.
> *Anne*: Would they were basilisks, to strike thee dead!
> WILLIAM SHAKESPEARE *Richard III*, 1597

> Without softening very much the basilisk nature of his stare, he said, impassively: 'We are coming to that part of my investigation, sir.'
> JOSEPH CONRAD *The Secret Agent*, 1907

Esau The Book of Genesis relates how Jacob, with his mother Rebecca's help, dressed as his older brother Esau in order to obtain the blessing of their father, Isaac. When Esau found out what Jacob had done he hated him and swore to kill him: 'And Esau hated Jacob because of the blessing wherewith his father blessed him: and Esau said in his heart, The days of mourning for my father are at hand; then will I slay my brother Jacob' (Gen. 27: 41).

> He's of a rash, warm-hearted nature, like Esau, for whom I have always felt great pity.
> GEORGE ELIOT *Adam Bede*, 1859

Dr Fell Dr John Fell (1625–86) was an Anglican divine and Dean of Christ Church, Oxford. One of his students was Thomas Brown, who later became a well-known satirist. Dr Fell asked Brown to translate one of the epigrams of Martial:

Non amo te, Sabidi, nec possum dicere quare;
Hoc tantum possum dicere, non amo te.

(I do not love you, Sabidius, and I cannot say why;
All I can say is this, that I do not love you.)

   Thomas Brown's famous translation read:

I do not love thee, Dr Fell,
The reason why I cannot tell;
But this I know, and know full well,
I do not love thee, Dr Fell.

   Dr Fell is alluded to as a person whom one dislikes for no particular reason.

> There is something more, if I could find a name for it. God bless me, the man seems hardly human! Something troglodytic, shall we say? or can it be the old story of Dr. Fell? or is it the mere radiance of a foul soul that thus transpires through, and transfigures, its clay.
> ROBERT LOUIS STEVENSON *The Strange Case of Dr Jekyll and Mr Hyde*, 1886

> Look, I don't really care for Franklin much more than you do, John, but it's a perfectly irrational dislike. He's done nothing to me at all—or to you, for that matter. It's a pure case of Dr Fell.
> SUSAN HILL *Strange Meeting*, 1971

Height

ALICE, the **TOWER OF BABEL,** and **JACK'S BEANSTALK** are all known for growing extremely tall. **SIMEON STYLITES,** on the other hand, was famously
positioned at a great height off the ground. ▶ *See also* **Large Size, Small
Size**.

....

Alice At the beginning of Lewis Carroll's children's story *Alice's Adventures in
Wonderland* (1865), Alice follows a white rabbit down a rabbit-hole and finds
herself apparently tumbling down a very deep well. Not long after drinking
from a bottle labelled 'Drink me' which makes her shrink to a height of ten
inches, she is required to eat a cake labelled 'Eat me' which makes her grow so
tall that she eventually fills a room. ▶ *See special entry* ☐ **ALICE IN WONDERLAND** *on p.
10.*

> 'Yes,' I admitted, feeling enormous, like Alice after she'd OD'd on Eat Me mushrooms.
> Size 2 women have that effect on me.
> LINDA BARNES *Cold Case*, 1997

Tower of Babel According to the Book of Genesis in the Bible, the descendants of Noah moved to the plain of Shinar where they settled and decided to
build a city and a tower, the Tower of Babel, 'whose top may reach unto
heaven' (Gen. 11: 4). God punished them for their presumption by making
their speech mutually unintelligible.

> I take it, that the earliest standers of mast-heads were the old Egyptians; because, in
> all my researches, I find none prior to them. For though their progenitors, the build-
> ers of Babel, must doubtless, by their tower, have intended to rear the loftiest mast-
> head in all Asia, or Africa either; yet (ere the final truck was put to it) as that great
> stone mast of theirs may be said to have gone by the board, in the dread gale of
> God's wrath; therefore, we cannot give these Babel builders priority over the Egyp-
> tians.
> HERMAN MELVILLE *Moby Dick*, 1851

Jack and the beanstalk In the children's fairy story of Jack and the beanstalk, Jack exchanges his mother's cow for some magic beans from which an
enormous beanstalk grows up into the clouds. Jack climbs up and steals treasure from the giant's castle, eventually cutting down the beanstalk and killing
the giant.

> The next morning, when Thomasin withdrew the curtains of her bedroom window,
> there stood the Maypole in the middle of the green, its top cutting into the sky. It
> had sprung up in the night, or rather early morning, like Jack's bean-stalk.
> THOMAS HARDY *The Return of the Native*, 1880

St Simeon Stylites St Simeon Stylites (*c.*390–459) was a Syrian monk who
is said to have become the first to practise an extreme form of asceticism which
involved living for thirty years on top of a tall pillar.

> In Saint Stylites, the famous Christain hermit of old times, who built him a lofty stone
> pillar in the desert and spent the whole latter portion of his life on its summit,

hoisting his food from the ground with a tackle; in him we have a remarkable instance of a dauntless stander-of-mast-heads; who was not to be driven from his place by fogs or frosts, rain, hail, or sleet; but valiantly facing everything out to the last, literally died at his post.

HERMAN MELVILLE *Moby Dick*, 1851

Hercules

In Greek and Roman mythology, Hercules (called Heracles by the Greeks) was a hero of superhuman strength and courage, usually depicted with a lion-skin, club, and bow. He was the son of Zeus by Alcmene, wife of Amphitryon. The jealousy that Zeus' wife, the goddess Hera, felt towards Alcmene drove her to send two serpents to kill the infant Hercules, but he seized and crushed them in his hands. Throughout his life, though, he would be persecuted by Hera. When he had grown to adulthood, Hera sent Hercules into a fit of madness during which he killed his wife, Megara, and their children. When he came to his senses and realized what he had done he went to Delphi to seek advice from the Pythian Oracle. To atone for this crime he was told he had to serve Eurystheus, king of Argos, for twelve years. Eurystheus imposed twelve immense tasks or 'labours' on him. The labours were as follows:

1. The killing of the lion of Nemea, which Hercules strangled with his bare hands, and whose skin he cut off with its own claws and afterwards wore.

2. The killing of the Lernaean Hydra, a water-serpent with many heads, each of which when cut off gave place to two new ones. With the help of his companion Iolaus, Hercules seared each neck with a burning torch as he cut off the head.

3. The capture of an incredibly swift stag, the Cerynean Hind, sacred to Artemis. Hercules had to capture it unharmed, which he did by pursuing it for a year and finally ensnaring it.

4. The capture of a destructive wild boar that lived on Mount Erymanthus. Hercules drove the boar from its lair, then chased it through the snow until it became exhausted.

5. The cleansing of the stables of Augeas, which had never been cleaned out. Hercules accomplished the task by diverting the two rivers Alpheus and Peneus so that they flowed through the stables and washed away the piles of dung.

6. The killing of the carnivorous birds near Lake Stymphalus. He drove them out of the trees by clashing bronze castanets and then shot them down with his bow.

7. The capture of the Cretan wild bull, which Hercules succeeded in bringing back alive to Eurystheus.

Hercules *continued*

8. The capture of the mares of Diomedes, which fed on human flesh. In so doing Heculcs fed Diomedes to his own mares.

9. The obtaining of the girdle of Hippolyta, the queen of the Amazons.

10. The capture of the oxen of the three-bodied monster Geryon.

11. The obtaining of the golden apples from the garden of the nymphs of the Hesperides. Hercules achieved this with the help of Atlas, the giant who bore the world on his shoulders.

12. The removal from Hades of the three-headed dog, Cerberus, which guarded the entrance to the underworld.

After he had completed these labours, Hercules married Deianira. Once, when Hercules and Deianira had to cross a river, the centaur Nessus offered to carry Deianira across while Hercules swam. However, once Hercules was in the water, Nessus made off with Deianira and attempted to rape her, and Hercules, realizing that he had been tricked, fired an arrow which pierced Nessus through the breast. As he lay dying, Nessus told Deianira to take some of his blood and use it as a love potion by smearing it onto a garment of Hercules if ever she suspected that he was being unfaithful. Some time later, Deianira became jealous of her husband's attraction towards Iole, a princess whom he had captured and was intending to bring home with him. Hercules had asked Deianira to send him some ceremonial robes and she used the opportunity to try out the supposed love potion, by smearing some of the blood of Nessus onto one of the robes in an attempt to win back his love. The blood was in fact a poison, Nessus' revenge, and caused the death of Hercules. When she realized what she had done, Deianira took her own life. The dying Hercules was carried to Mount Oeta, where a funeral pyre was built. After his death he was granted immortality among the gods.

Throughout this book there are references to Hercules and to his labours.

▶ *See* AUGEAN STABLES *at* **Difficulty**
  CERBERUS *at* **Guarding**
  DEIANIRA *at* **Jealousy**
  HERCULES *at* **Difficulty**, **Strength**, *and* **Struggle**
  HYDRA *at* **Appearing** *and* **Rebirth and Resurrection**
  PILLARS OF HERCULES *at* **Distance**.

Heroes

This theme includes not only heroes and superheroes who represent good in the fight against evil, but also romantic heroes who represent a chivalric or romantic ideal. ▶ *See also* **Adventure**, **Goodness**, **Rescue**.

....

Batman and Robin The crime-fighting superheroes Batman and Robin made their first appearance in 1939 in an American comic strip, and have since appeared both on television and in films. In normal life the two are the wealthy Bruce Wayne and his young ward Dick Grayson, but as Batman and Robin, with the aid of clever gadgets and their speedy Batmobile, they fight against cunning super-criminals such as the Joker and the Penguin in order to protect Gotham City.

Biggles Biggles is a fictional British pilot. The hero of many adventures in two world wars, created by Captain W. E. Johns and first appearing in books in the 1930s, his name is associated with British stiff-upper-lip courage and patriotism.

Modesty Blaise Modesty Blaise is the heroine of a strip cartoon created by Peter O'Donnell and first published in the *Evening Standard* in 1963. A retired gangster, she fights against crime and wrongdoing showing great courage and resourcefulness.

Rhett Butler The dashing and charming Rhett Butler is the hero of Margaret Mitchell's novel *Gone with the Wind* (1936). The book was made into an immensely popular Hollywood film in 1939, with the role of Butler played by Clark Gable. Set at the time of the American Civil War, the book tells the story of Butler's romance with southern belle Scarlett O'Hara, and he has come to represent an archetype of the romantic hero.

Byron George Gordon, Lord Byron (1788–1824), the English romantic poet, is alluded to as one who led an unconventional, romantically adventurous life. He travelled widely in Europe, and left England permanently following a series of scandals, most notably the suggestion of incest with his sister, and problems with debts. In 1824 he joined the fight for Greek independence, but died of a fever before he saw any real fighting. His name gives rise to the terms 'Byronic' and 'Byronism'.

> He's got a streak of his father's Byronism. Why, look at the way he threw up his chances when he left my office; going off like that for six months with a knapsack, and all for what?—to study foreign architecture—foreign!
> JOHN GALSWORTHY *The Man of Property*, 1906

Dan Dare Dan Dare was a comic-strip cartoon hero who appeared in the *Eagle* comic between 1950 and 1967. A commander of the Space Fleet, Dan Dare battled against his arch-enemy from Venus, the Mekon.

> The Middle East, with all its complexities and dangers and religious tension—yes, and its evils—is being turned into a comic strip in which Dan Dare will launch his

space-age high-tech at the Mekon of Baghdad.
The Independent, 1998

Mr Darcy Fitzwilliam Darcy is the hero of Jane Austen's novel *Pride and Prejudice* (1796), who courts and finally wins Elizabeth Bennet. Wealthy and extremely handsome, with a proud and rather aloof manner, he has come to represent a certain type of romantic hero.

> She was busy running her tresses through her manicured fingers and flapping her blue-mascaraed eyelashes at James Rattray-Potter, who was propped against the desk in a suave, man-of-the-world pose, ankles crossed. He was a generic Mills and Boon hero to Dominic Planchet's Mr Darcy, but I could see that his brand of florid good looks would appeal to secretaries and girls who lacked confidence.
> LAUREN HENDERSON *The Black Rubber Dress*, 1997

Bulldog Drummond Bulldog Drummond is the hero of a series of stories by 'Sapper', published from 1920 onwards. Drummond is an ex-army officer who fights against the master criminal Carl Peterson.

Flash Gordon Flash Gordon is the spaceman hero created by the American cartoonist Alex Raymond in 1934. He has many adventures in space, notably on the planet Mongo, where he combats the evil Ming the Merciless.

Errol Flynn Errol Flynn (1909–59) was an Australian-born American actor who became famous for his swashbuckling roles in such costume adventure films as *Captain Blood* (1935) and *The Adventures of Robin Hood* (1938).

> I gave him a smile. *Dawn Patrol*. Errol Flynn courageous in the face of certain doom.
> ROBERT CRAIS *Lullaby Town*, 1992

Indiana Jones Indiana Jones is the whip-cracking archeologist-explorer hero of the film *Raiders of the Lost Ark* (1981) and its sequels. The first film was promoted with the slogan 'The Hero Is Back'.

> Foreign correspondents were a revered, much romanticized group—the Indiana Joneses of journalism.
> *New Yorker*, 1995

Lancelot According to Arthurian legend, Lancelot, or Launcelot, was the most famous of King Arthur's knights. He was the lover of the Queen, Guinevere, and father of Galahad. His name has become a byword for chivalrous heroism.

> Marutha's hero was a Circassian warrior, a sort of Eastern Sir Lancelot, and every home she subsequently made with Moshe retained an Oriental flavour.
> T. PALMER *Menuhin*, 1991

Lawrence of Arabia T. E. Lawrence (1888–1935), known as 'Lawrence of Arabia', was a British soldier and writer who, from 1916 onwards, helped to organize and lead the Arab revolt against Turkey. His book *The Seven Pillars of Wisdom* (1926) was an account of the events of this period. He is sometimes alluded to as a brave, romantic adventurer.

> My Texan got back into the coach again, stowing his photographic equipment away, having preserved for posterity some *mafioso* on camel-back who brandished a

Lawrence of Arabia rifle in one hand and a string of plastic lapis lazuli beads in the other.
PENELOPE LIVELY *Moon Tiger*, 1988

Lochinvar Lochinvar, the hero of Sir Walter Scott's ballad *Marmion* (1808), is a young Highlander who goes to the wedding of the woman he loves, abducts her, and rides away with her. Young Lochinvar is the archetypal romantic hero:

'So faithful in love, and so dauntless in war,
There never was knight like the young Lochinvar'.

He had been quite shocked to learn that at the present point in time she was the only resident of the place, except for Tom away down at the stables and too far away to hear any cries for help—although Tom could get there fairly rapidly if summoned by phone. On the other hand, given Tom's reputation as the local rural Don Juan, perhaps the idea of Tom galloping up to Rose Cottage on a foaming steed looking like young Lochinvar was not exactly the sort of protection he, Markby, fancied for her.
ANN GRANGER *A Season for Murder*, 1991

Captain Marvel Captain Marvel was an American comic book hero from the 1940s, who used his superhuman powers to defeat evil villains. He transformed himself into his costumed form by uttering the magic word 'Shazam!'

Arnold Schwarzenegger The Austrian-born American actor Arnold Schwarzenegger (b.1947) began his career as a bodybuilder, becoming Mr Universe on seven occasions. As a film actor, he is best known for his role as an impassive killer in *The Terminator* (1984) and its sequel.

'Nowt better than a bit of exercise', said Dalziel, patting his gut with all the complacency of Arnold Schwarzenegger flexing his biceps.
REGINALD HILL *On Beulah Height*, 1998

Ranger was waiting under the canopy. He was dressed in a black T-shirt and black assault pants tucked into black boots. He had a body like Schwarzenegger, dark hair slicked back off his face and a two-hundred-watt smile.
JANET EVANOVICH *Four to Score*, 1998

Siegfried In Germanic legend, Siegfried (equivalent to the Sigurd of Norse legend) was a prince of the Netherlands and the hero of the first part of the *Nibelungenlied*. Having obtained a hoard of treasure by killing the dragon Fafner, Siegfried helped Gunther to win Brunhild before being treacherously slain by Hagen. Siegfried's story is also told in the opera of the same name in Wagner's *Ring Cycle*.

Luke Skywalker Luke Skywalker is the young hero of the Star Wars films, the first of which, *Star Wars*, was released in 1977. The films portray a classic struggle between good and evil, in which Luke Skywalker fights against the evil Empire and its general, Darth Vader.

Labour's chief whip versus an amiable rebel—it sounds like a battle between Torquemada and Luke Skywalker.
The Observer, 1997

Superman Superman is a US comic book superhero from the planet Krypton who possesses prodigious strength, the ability to fly, X-ray vision, and other powers which help him to battle against crime and evil. His alter ego is Clark Kent, a shy, bespectacled reporter for the *Daily Planet* newspaper.

> Kent was the TV heartthrob of the Gulf War, his Superman good looks gilding his newshawk reputation.
> *Chatelaine*, 1992

John Wayne John Wayne, born Marion Michael Morrison (1907–79), was an American film actor who specialized in westerns such as *True Grit* (1969) and became known for his portrayals of tough but honest gunfighters or lawmen.

> A mythical John Wayne America, a land of free, rugged individualists that has been progressively undermined by federal laws and regulations.
> *The Independent*, 1996

Honesty and Truth

The archetype of the honest individual is **GEORGE WASHINGTON**. It may be noted that there seem to be fewer memorable icons of truth-telling than of mendacity. ▶ *See also* **Cunning, Hypocrisy, Lying**.

Cordelia When in Shakespeare's play *King Lear* (1623) the King asks his three daughters which of them loves him the best, the two older sisters, Goneril and Regan, flatter their father with extravagant declarations of their love. The youngest daughter, Cordelia, is the only one to speak truthfully, acknowledging that she loves her father according to her duty, but refusing to say that she will always love only him, for when she marries she must also love her husband. Lear furiously denounces what he believes to be her lack of love for him: 'So young and so untender?' Cordelia replies: 'So young, my lord, and true.'

Diogenes Diogenes (*c*.400–*c*.325 BC) was a Greek philosopher, the most famous of the Cynics. A well-known story told about him is that, denouncing the corruption he saw all around him, he carried a lantern out in daylight, saying that he was seeking an honest man.

> The significance of the name will not escape you. *Lantern*—it is the lantern of Diogenes, searching for the honest, the true, and the good.
> ROBERTSON DAVIES *A Mixture of Frailties*, 1951

Galileo Galileo Galilei (1564–1642) was an Italian astronomer and physicist. Under torture he publicly recanted his view that the sun was the centre of the universe and the earth moved around the sun, but is later reported as declaring 'Eppur si muove' ('but it does move'). He is remembered as someone who stood up for a truth that others denied.

> We do not remember Galileo either because of his inventions (mostly copied), or his

astronomy (in detail often wrong), but for the great moral and philosophical stand he took against the secular and religious authorities of his time.
T. PALMER *Menuhin*, 1991

Iago Iago is Othello's ensign in Shakespeare's play *Othello* (1622). Although Iago is secretly plotting the downfall of Othello, the latter believes Iago to be completely loyal and honest, 'for I know thou'rt full of love and honesty'. Othello addresses Iago repeatedly as 'honest Iago'.

George Washington George Washington (1732–99) was the first president of the US, serving from 1789 to 1797. An early biographer of Washington, Mason Weems, recounted a fanciful story of how Washington as a boy, on receiving a new hatchet, chopped down his father's prized cherry tree. When his father asked how the tree had fallen, Washington was tempted to tell a lie, but then, 'looking at his father with the sweet face of youth brightened with the inexpressible charm of all-conquering truth, he bravely cried out, "I can't tell a lie. I did cut it with my hatchet"'. George Washington is often mentioned as an example of someone who tells the truth and admits to wrongdoing.

'You must have looked like George Washington or something.' 'If that was the old darling who never told a lie,' I had to admit, 'well really, not much.'
JOHN MORTIMER *Rumpole's Return*, 1980

She didn't trust him any more. He'd had sex with her neighbour, impregnated her, he'd lied to her, he wasn't the man she'd thought he was, the honest George Washington, incapable of telling a lie.
LISA JEWELL *Ralph's Party*, 1999

Horror

This theme includes allusions to writers and artists whose works are called to mind in the context of gruesome or horrifying sights. ▶ *See also* **Fear, Monsters, Unpleasant or Wicked Places**.

....

Hieronymus Bosch Hieronymus Bosch (*c.*1450–1516) was a Flemish painter whose allegorical works are filled with grotesque creatures and macabre images, often set in strange hell-like landscapes.

He still wasn't entirely happy about Goodenough's sexual inclinations. 'If you'd seen that gay bar,' he told Vera. 'I mean I don't care what people do but it was like a vision of Hell by Hieronymus Bosch.'
TOM SHARPE *Grantchester Grind*, 1995

Dante Dante Alighieri (1265–1321) was an Italian poet whose epic *The Divine Comedy* (1309–20) relates the poet's imagined visit to Hell, Purgatory, and Paradise. References to Dante are often in the context of a hideous or horrific sight, suggestive of the horrors of Hell depicted by the poet.

I gazed on him while unfinished; he was ugly then; but when those muscles and

joints were rendered capable of motion, it became a thing such as even Dante could not have conceived.
MARY SHELLEY *Frankenstein*, 1831

Beijing became a Dantean pit of underworld activity in the years following the country's economic expansion.
PAUL JOHNSTON *Body Politic*, 1997

It is also a timely reminder in the midst of the current Kosovo crisis of the real issues that confront us in taking on Slobodan Milosevic and his thugs; of the acts that have been perpetrated across the former Yugoslavia in the name of Serbia's most rabid nationalism. Peress's award-winning photographs, and Stover's cool, unhysterical prose, take you to the most awful place on earth, beyond even Dante's imagination.
The Observer, 1998

Goya Francisco José de Goya y Lucientes (1746–1828) was a Spanish painter and etcher. His set of sixty-five etchings *The Disasters of War* (1810–14) express the cruelty and horror of war through scenes of death, execution, pillage, and famine. One such engraving, called 'Great exploits with dead men', depicts mutilated corpses hanging from a tree.

Three bodies hung from the branches, pale in the shadow, as monstrous as Goya etchings.
JOHN FOWLES *The Magus*, 1977

Grünewald Mathias Grünewald (c.1460–1528) was a German painter whose most famous work, the nine-panel *Isenheim Altar*, contains scenes of figures suffering, with twisted limbs and contorted postures. The central panel of the altar depicts the crucifixion of Christ, with Christ's body distorted by the torture of the Cross and covered with festering wounds.

'The neighbours don't care. The children love you. Come live with us and see in the spring. You're dying of carbon monoxide down here.' 'I'd drown in flesh up there. You pin me down and the others play pile-on.' 'Only Donald. And aren't you funny about that? Rodney and I absolutely agreed, a child shouldn't be excluded from anything physical. We thought nothing of being nude in front of them.' 'Spare me the picture, it's like a Grünewald.'
JOHN UPDIKE *Bech: A Book*, 1970

Horses

PEGASUS and **SLEIPNIR** are two examples of a creature familiar in myth and fantasy, the flying horse.

....

Black Beauty Anna Sewell's novel *Black Beauty* (1877) gives an account of the life and adventures of a horse who has many different owners and experiences. The book became an enduring children's classic.

Pegasus In Greek mythology, Pegasus was a winged horse which sprang from the blood of the Gorgon Medusa when Perseus cut her head off. Pegasus was ridden by Perseus in his rescue of Andromeda, and by Bellerophon when he fought the Chimera.

> I opened them to see the deer as stunned as I was peering at me through the glass, standing utterly still, unable to move. But standing. After an interminable moment, he lifted his head and took off like Pegasus across the turnpike.
> CAROL BRENNAN *Chill of Summer*, 1995

Rosinante Rosinante or Rozinante is the name of Don Quixote's scrawny old horse in Cervantes' romance. The name can be applied to any worn-out or emaciated horse. ▶ *See special entry* □ **DON QUIXOTE** *on p. 128*.

> Plump and naked . . . they [camels] were a great contrast to our shaggy, Rosinantine beasts.
> PETER FLEMING *News from Tartary*, 1936

Sleipnir In Scandinavian mythology, Sleipnir was Odin's eight-legged horse which could outrun the wind on water or land, or through the air.

Humility

This theme covers examples of both false and true humility. ▶ *See also* **Arrogance, Pride**.

Uriah Heep Uriah Heep is the shrewd, deceitful clerk of the lawyer Mr Wickfield in Dickens's *David Copperfield* (1850). By pretending always to be 'so very 'umble' he insinuates his way into Mr Wickfield's confidence and becomes one of his partners. Heep uses this position to defraud people of money, until he is exposed, sent to prison, and condemned to transportation for life. His name is a byword for obsequiousness and false humility, and his often-repeated gesture of rubbing his hands together as he speaks is sometimes alluded to in this context.

> Under Asbery's urbane expression you could imagine a secret grimace of pleasure at Margot's confusion, at my shock. Uriah Heep's servility had disguised a lot of hate.
> MAX BYRD *Finders Weepers*, 1983

> Mr Gerald Suzman was portly, but he walked the path from the road with sprightliness that belied his considerable expanse of belly. He had a grey goatee beard and a sharp eye, and if he occasionally rubbed his hands together it was as an expression of pleasure or satisfaction, not a Heep-like tic to ingratiate himself.
> ROBERT BARNARD *A Hovering of Vultures*, 1993

Jesus The Bible portrays Jesus Christ as one from a humble background who preached a message of humility and meekness. Born in a stable, Jesus became a carpenter like his father, Joseph. Jesus described himself as 'meek and lowly in heart' (Matt. 11: 29) and in the Sermon on the Mount he stated 'Blessed are the meek: for they shall inherit the earth' (Matt. 5: 5). ▶ *See special entry* □ **JESUS** *on p. 223*.

And into this land came a humble prophet, lowly like the humble carpenter of Nazareth.
RALPH ELLISON *Invisible Man*, 1952

Job The Old Testament Book of Job relates how Job, despite the dire sufferings inflicted on him by God, remains humble and accepting: 'the Lord gave, and the Lord hath taken away; blessed be the name of the Lord' (Job 1: 21).

Hunters

Most of the hunters grouped here are drawn from classical mythology. ARTEMIS (or DIANA), the figure who most usually personifies hunting, herself plays a part in the stories of ACTAEON, ORION, and the CALYDONIAN BOAR HUNT. ▶ *See also* **Quest**.

....

Actaeon In Greek mythology, Actaeon was a hunter who, because he accidentally saw Artemis (the virgin goddess of the hunt) bathing naked, was changed into a stag and torn to pieces by his own hounds.

> Further up they saw in the mid-distance the hounds running hither and thither, as if the scent lay cold that day. Soon members of the hunt appeared on the scene, and it was evident that the chase had been stultified by general puzzle-headedness as to the whereabouts of the intended victim. In a minute, a gentleman-farmer, panting with Actaeonic excitement, rode up to the two pedestrians, and Grace being a few steps in advance he asked her if she had seen the fox.
> THOMAS HARDY *The Woodlanders*, 1887

Artemis Artemis was a Greek goddess, daughter of Zeus and Leto and twin sister of Apollo. She was a huntress often depicted with a bow and arrows, and noted for her strength and speed. The Romans called her Diana.

> 'Like a force of nature' he thought, as he watched her with bent head tunnelling her way through the damp wind. A great physical force. Such energy, such strength and health . . . Mary was a sort of berserker Diana of the moors.
> ALDOUS HUXLEY *Point Counter Point*, 1928

Atalanta In Greek mythology, Atalanta was a huntress who was extremely fleet-footed. She refused to marry any man unless he first defeated her in a race. If the runner lost, he was put to death. Many suitors tried to outrun her, but all failed until one, variously identified as Hippomenes or Melanion, asked Aphrodite for help and was given three golden apples by her. When he dropped these at intervals during the race, Atalanta was unable to resist the apples' beauty and stopped to pick them up. ▶ *See also* CALYDONIAN BOAR HUNT.

Calydonian boar hunt In Greek mythology, when Artemis sent a huge boar to devastate the land of Calydon, its ruler, Meleager, assembled a band of heroes, including Castor and Pollux, Theseus, and Jason, to hunt the boar in what became known as the Calydonian boar hunt. Meleager himself killed the boar and gave the head to Atalanta, who had first wounded it. ▶ *See also* **ATALANTA**.

Diana ▶ *See* **ARTEMIS**.

Nimrod In the Old Testament, Nimrod is named as the founder of the Babylonian dynasty and is described as 'a mighty hunter' (Gen. 10: 8–9). Thus any great or skilful hunter or sportsman can be described as a Nimrod.

> It was not so positively stated, but the consensus seemed to be that Bertha Shanklin had shown poor taste in dying so soon and thus embarrassing the local Nimrod.
> ROBERTSON DAVIES *Fifth Business*, 1970

Orion In Greek mythology, Orion was a giant and hunter who at his death was changed into a constellation by Artemis.

Tristram Tristram (also Tristan or Tristrem) was a knight of medieval legend who was the lover of Iseult. He was renowned as a skilful hunter.

> There hasna been a better hunter since Tristrem's time.
> WALTER SCOTT *The Bride of Lammermoor*, 1819

Hypocrisy

Literature has provided us with several vivid embodiments of hypocrisy. Two of the most memorable, **Pecksniff** and **Uriah Heep**, were created by Charles Dickens. ▶ *See also* **Cunning**, **Lying**.

....

Archimago Archimago is the evil enchanter in Edmund Spenser's *The Faerie Queene* (1590), who symbolizes hypocrisy and uses cunning disguises to trick and deceive people.

Uriah Heep Uriah Heep is the shrewd, deceitful clerk of the lawyer Mr Wickfield in Dickens's *David Copperfield* (1850). Under the guise of appearing 'so very 'umble', he insinuates his way into Mr Wickfield's confidence and becomes one of his partners. Heep uses this position to defraud people of money, until he is exposed, sent to prison, and condemned to transportation for life.

> He began to wonder if there wasn't something of a Uriah Heep beginning to erupt on the surface of Sam's personality; a certain duplicity.
> JOHN FOWLES *The French Lieutenant's Woman*, 1969

Pecksniff Seth Pecksniff is a character in Dickens's *Martin Chuzzlewit* (1844). An architect by profession, Pecksniff is an arch-hypocrite with a 'soft and oily' manner, who uses an outward appearance of virtue and morality to win the affection and respect of old Martin Chuzzlewit, in an attempt to inherit his money. He fails in this attempt and is exposed as the hypocrite that he really is.

> Sad for once, as Hayes had struck me as only exception to rule that 'decent Tory' is an oxymoron. Accuser looks like a pasty-faced, hard-eyed, sharp-toothed, back-stabbing, nausea-inducing, pocket-lining Pecksniff, who says he is acting in the public interest.
> *The Observer*, 1997

Pharisee The Pharisees were members of an ancient Jewish sect who strove to ensure that the state was ruled according to strict Jewish law. According to the Bible, they were denounced by Jesus for their hypocrisy in maintaining an outward appearance of morality and virtue while acting only out of self-interest: 'Woe unto you, scribes and Pharisees, hypocrites! For ye are like unto whited sepulchres, which indeed appear beautiful outward, but are within full of dead men's bones, and of all uncleanness' (Matt. 23: 27).

> They who only strive for this paltry prize, like the Pharisees, who prayed at the corners of streets, to be seen by men, verily obtain the reward they seek.
> MARY WOLLSTONECRAFT *A Vindication of the Rights of Women*, 1792

> Conventionality is not morality. Self-righteousness is not religion. To attack the first is not to assail the last. To pluck the mask from the face of the Pharisee, is not to lift an impious hand to the Crown of Thorns.
> CHARLOTTE BRONTË *Preface to Jane Eyre*, 1848

> 'Useless relatives!' he was saying. 'Thieves and gossips. Pharisees! Troublemakers! Hypocrites!'
> BEN OKRI *Dangerous Love*, 1996

Tartuffe Tartuffe is the main character of Molière's play *Le Tartuffe ou L'Imposteur*, first performed in 1664. Tartuffe is a religious hypocrite, who uses the sly pretence of virtue and religious devotion to win the admiration and friendship of an honest but foolish man, Orgon. Tartuffe cleverly persuades the wealthy Orgon to sign over all his property to him, while behind Orgon's back he makes advances to his wife and mocks his gullibility.

> 'I see it all,' said the archdeacon. 'The sly *tartufe*! He thinks to buy the daughter by providing for the father.'
> ANTHONY TROLLOPE *Barchester Towers*, 1857

Idealism

This theme embraces both the concept of idealism and that of romanticism. ▶ *See also* **Adventure, Idyllic Places**.

Arcadia A mountainous district in the Peloponnese of southern Greece, Arcadia in poetic fantasy represents an idealized region of rural contentment.

> There were no lands of sunshine, heavy with the perfume of flowers. Such things were only old dreams of paradise. The sunlands of the West and the spicelands of

the East, the smiling Arcadias and blissful Islands of the Blest—ha! ha!
JACK LONDON *In a Far Country*, 1910

I had not forgotten Sebastian. He was with me daily in Julia; or rather it was Julia I
had known in him, in those distant Arcadian days.
EVELYN WAUGH *Brideshead Revisited*, 1945

Tim had been looking for Arcadia, for poetry and love and happiness, but maybe in
the wrong place.
GWENDOLINE BUTLER *Coffin and the Paper Man*, 1990

Don Quixote Don Quixote, the hero of a romance (1605–15) by Miguel de
Cervantes, has his wits disordered by his devoted reading of chivalric romances
and sets out on his horse, Rosinante, in search of knightly adventures himself.
He attacks a group of windmills in the belief that they are giants and elevates
a good-looking village girl, whom he names Dulcinea del Toboso, to the ideal
of womanly beauty and virtue. Don Quixote can be alluded to as a foolish,
mistaken idealist or someone who naively believes that they can set the world
to rights single-handedly. ▶ *See special entry* ☐ **DON QUIXOTE** *on p. 128.*

I've been in business for myself for about six years. Before that I was an attorney
with the Public Defender in Cook County. I got tired of seeing poor innocent chumps
go off to Statevill because the police wouldn't follow up our investigations and find
the real culprits. And I got even more tired of watching clever guilty rascals get off
scot-free because they could afford attorneys who know how to tap-dance around
the law. So I thought—à La Doña Quixote perhaps—that I'd see what I could do on
my own about the situation.
SARA PARETSKY *Deadlock*, 1984

Without a win in five matches, the Cup represents the chance for Newcastle to bring
tangible reward for a once refreshing approach, just as next Sunday's home match
against Manchester United appears a last tilt at the Championship windmill.
The Independent on Sunday, 1995

Marie Antoinette Marie Antoinette (1755–93), the wife of Louis XVI of
France, is said to have had an idealized view of peasant life. At the Petit
Trianon, a small country house in the grounds of the Palace of Versailles, she
enjoyed living her version of the simple life of a poor country woman.

It was not merely tramping that Mary liked. She got almost as much enjoyment out
of the more prosaic settled life they led, when they returned to England. 'Marie-
Antoinette at the Trianon', was what Rampion called her, when he saw her cooking
the dinner; she did it with such child-like enthusiasm.
ALDOUS HUXLEY *Point Counter Point*, 1928

You sang your folksongs like a cheap Marie Antoinette pretending to be a shepherdess.
ROBERTSON DAVIES *A Mixture of Frailties*, 1951

Plato The Greek philosopher Plato (*c.*429–*c.*347 BC) was a pupil of Socrates
and a teacher of Aristotle. His *Republic* explores his ideas of a perfect and just
society. His name has become a byword for idealized perfection. Platonic love is
love that is purely spiritual and not sexual, and a Platonic vision or idea is a
perfect, idealized one.

Poor little Julie was lost in the photo-painter's Platonic idea of childhood; her tiny
humanity was smothered somewhere back of gobs of pink and white.
PHILIP ROTH *Goodbye Columbus*, 1959

Utopia Utopia (literally 'no-place') is an imaginary place or condition of ideal perfection. The word was first used as the name of an imaginary island, governed on a perfect political and social system, in the book *Utopia* (1516) by Sir Thomas More. The name has given us the adjective 'Utopian', meaning 'idealistic'.

> Oh, is it, then, Utopian
> To hope that I may meet a man
> Who'll not relate, in accents suave,
> The tales of girls he used to have?
> DOROTHY PARKER 'De Profundis' in *Enough Rope*, 1926

> Their education had taught them to judge civilization entirely by material progress and they were, in consequence, ashamed of their background and anxious to forget it. A suburbia covering the length and breadth of Iraq was the Utopia of which they dreamed.
> WILFRED THESIGER *The Marsh Arabs*, 1964

> When the students of the sixties saw the dream of a new Utopia, he quietly completed his doctoral thesis on the great vowel-shift; when the pill came and the sexual world was transformed, he promptly married a small dark girl met on a camping holiday.
> MALCOLM BRADBURY *Rates of Exchange*, 1983

Idyllic Places

The idea of the lost paradise, such as **EDEN** or **ARCADIA**, has had an enduring influence on the human imagination and is frequently found in mythology and literature. Similarly, the place of perfect happiness that is the reward in the afterlife for virtue or valour in one's earthly life is central to many beliefs. Some of the other places included here, imaginary lands like **EL DORADO** and **COCKAIGNE**, have their own specific connotations.
▶ *See also* **Abundance and Plenty, Happiness, Unpleasant or Wicked Places**.

Albion In poetic or literary contexts, the name Albion (traditionally from Latin *albus* 'white', in reference to Dover's chalk cliffs) is sometimes used to denote Britain or England, conceived of as a green paradise.

> When their keepers departed, the 400-odd rodents escaped and set up home under the green trees of Albion.
> *The Independent on Sunday*, 1993

Arcadia A mountainous district in the Peloponnese of southern Greece, Arcadia (or Arcady), represents in classical poetic fantasy an idealized region of rural contentment. It is also the setting of Philip Sidney's prose romance *Arcadia*, published posthumously in 1590. The tomb inscription *Et in Arcadia ego*, often depicted in classical paintings, is sometimes quoted as meaning 'I too once lived in Arcady', to express the idea of a perfect happiness now lost. This interpretation of the phrase is, however, disputed.

> Ah, he doesn't know in the least what he is saying. This is not what he meant to say. His arm is stealing round the waist again, it is tightening its clasp; he is bending his face nearer and nearer to the round cheek, his lips are meeting those pouting child-lips, and for a long moment time has vanished. He may be a shepherd in Arcadia for aught he knows, he may be the first youth kissing the first maiden, he may be Eros himself, sipping the lips of Psyche—it is all one.
> GEORGE ELIOT *Adam Bede*, 1859

> If Deptford was my Arcadia, Toronto was a place of no such comfort.
> ROBERTSON DAVIES *The Manticore*, 1972

> Ada told herself that Charleston, with its cadres of ancient aunts enforcing elaborate rituals of chaperonage, was perhaps some made-up place, with only a tangent relation to the world she now lived in, like Arcady.
> CHARLES FRAZIER *Cold Mountain*, 1997

Arden The Forest of Arden is the name of a former forest region of north Warwickshire in the English Midlands, the setting of most of Shakespeare's *As You Like It* (1623). It is often used to represent the ideal of rural as opposed to urban or courtly life. The Forest of Arden can be used as an equivalent of the Garden of Eden, an earthly paradise.

Avalon In Arthurian legend, Avalon was the place to which Arthur was conveyed after his death, often portrayed as a paradise.

Beulah Beulah (literally in Hebrew 'married woman') is the land of Israel: 'thou shalt be called Hephzibah, and thy land Beulah: for the Lord delighteth in thee, and thy land shall be married' (Isa. 62: 4). In Bunyan's *Pilgrim's Progress*, Beulah lies beyond the Valley of the Shadow of Death and also out of the reach of Giant Despair: Yea, here they heard continually the singing of birds, and saw every day the flowers appear in the earth . . . in this country the sun shineth night and day.'

> I thought sometimes I saw beyond its wild waters a shore, sweet as the hills of Beulah.
> CHARLOTTE BRONTË *Jane Eyre*, 1847

Canaan Canaan was the land, later known as Ancient Palestine, which the Israelites gradually conquered and occupied during the latter part of the second millennium BC. In the Bible it was the land promised by God to Abraham and his descendants (Gen. 12: 7). By extension, the name Canaan can be applied to any promised land or to heaven. ▶ *See special entry* ☐ MOSES AND THE BOOK OF EXODUS *on p. 264.*

> Fresh green of the river bank; faded terra-cotta of the dining-room wallpaper, colours of distant Canaan, of deserted Eden.
> EVELYN WAUGH *Scoop*, 1938

> Up there at the top of the hill, 161st Street and the Grand Concourse had been the summit of the Jewish dream, of the new Canaan, the new Jewish borough of New York, the Bronx!
> TOM WOLFE *The Bonfire of the Vanities*, 1987

Celestial City In Bunyan's *Pilgrim's Progress* (1678, 1684), the Celestial City is the goal of Christian's pilgrimage, representing Heaven: 'It was builded of pearls and precious stones, also the street thereof was paved with gold.' ▶ *See also* **NEW JERUSALEM.**

> Gold and purple clouds lay on the hilltops, and rising high into the ruddy light were silvery white peaks that shone like the airy spires of some Celestial City.
> LOUISA M. ALCOTT *Little Women,* 1868

Cloud Cuckoo Land Cloud Cuckoo Land (a translation of the Greek *Nephelo-kokkygia*) is the imaginary city built in the air by birds in Aristophanes' play *The Birds*. Hence any fanciful realm can be described as Cloud Cuckoo Land, a world or state of mind that exists only in a person's imagination, distanced from reality.

Cockaigne The Land of Cockaigne or Cockayne (from the Old French *pais de cocaigne*, 'fool's paradise') was in medieval legend an imaginary land of luxury and idleness, where good food and drink were plentiful.

> She watched the car drive away. It was going to Cloud Cuckoo Land; it was going to the Kingdom of Cockaigne; it was going to Hollywood.
> STELLA GIBBONS *Cold Comfort Farm,* 1932

Delectable Mountains In Bunyan's *Pilgrim's Progress*, the summit of the Delectable Mountain, 'Emmanuel's Land', is within sight of the Celestial City.

> We call this hill the Delectable Mountain, for we can look far away and see the country where we hope to live some time.
> LOUISA M. ALCOTT *Little Women,* 1868

Eden Eden (meaning 'delight'), or the Garden of Eden, was the home of Adam and Eve in the biblical account of the Creation, from which they were banished by God for their disobedience in eating the forbidden fruit of the Tree of Knowledge. The name can be used to refer to a place or state of supreme happiness, innocence, and concord.

> Versailles! It is wonderfully beautiful! You gaze, and stare, and try to understand that it is real, that it is on the earth, that it is not the Garden of Eden.
> MARK TWAIN *The Innocents Abroad,* 1869

> Yet this was—the way she relayed it—a redeemed forest and an Eden.
> THOMAS KENEALLY *The Playmaker,* 1987

El Dorado El Dorado was the fabled city (or country) of gold sought in the 16th century by Spanish conquistadors who believed it existed somewhere in the area of the Orinoco and Amazon rivers. Hence any place of fabulous wealth can be described as an El Dorado.

> They would regain the ship and sail under his orders, asking no questions. their recompense: a share of a treasure as vast as a dozen Eldorados.
> UMBERTO ECO *The Island of the Day Before,* 1994

Elysium In Greek mythology, Elysium, or the Elysian Fields, was the name of the fields at the end of the earth to which certain favoured heroes were conveyed by the gods to enjoy a life after death. The name can be used to refer to a place of perfect happiness or bliss.

> Antoine and Francoise with their children, but without ever knowing why, joined the

refugees for the sake of their vision of elysium and because of Don Emmanuel's enthusiasm.
LOUIS DE BERNIÈRES *The War of Don Emmanuel's Nether Parts*, 1990

Fortunate Isles ▶ *See* ISLANDS OF THE BLEST.

Goshen Goshen was the fertile region in Egypt allotted to Jacob and the Israelites, where there was light during the plague of darkness: 'there was thick darkness in all the land of Egypt three days ... but all the people of Israel had light where they dwelt' (Exod. 10: 23). The name Goshen can be applied to a place of plenty or a place of light. ▶ *See special entry* ☐ MOSES AND THE BOOK OF EXODUS *on p. 264*.

It's a bleak and barren country there, not like this land of Goshen you've been used to.
GEORGE ELIOT *Adam Bede*, 1859

Happy Islands ▶ *See* ISLANDS OF THE BLEST.

Islands of the Blest The Islands of the Blest, often located near where the sun sets in the west, were the place to which people in classical times believed the souls of heroes and the good were conveyed to a life of bliss. They were also known as the Fortunate Isles or the Happy Islands. Like Elysium or the Elysian Fields, the term Islands of the Blest can be applied to heaven or paradise. Tennyson's 'Ulysses' (1842) includes the lines:

'It may be we shall touch the Happy Isles,
And see the great Achilles, whom we knew.'

There were no lands of sunshine, heavy with the perfume of flowers. Such things were only old dreams of paradise. The sunlands of the West and the spicelands of the East, the smiling Arcadias and blissful Islands of the Blest—ha! ha!
JACK LONDON *In a Far Country*, 1900

Land of Promise ▶ *See* PROMISED LAND.

Never-Never Land Never-Never Land is the magical country to which Peter Pan escorts Wendy, John, and Michael Darling in J. M. Barrie's play *Peter Pan* (first performed 1904). The land is populated by staple characters from children's stories, such as mermaids and pirates, including the murderous pirate Captain Hook. Never-Never Land can be alluded to as an ideal place far from the problems encountered in the real world.

'Of course,' he added with a flash of his normal style, 'I suppose she could have had a date or something.' The photographer chuckled. 'Yeah,' he said, 'maybe her prince came and took her to Never Never Land.'
MOLLY MCKITTERICK *The Medium Is Murder*, 1991

If health professionals and writers took the middle line between Never-Never Land and Nightmare on Maternity Street perhaps Life After Babies wouldn't be quite such a rude awakening.
The Independent, 1994

New Jerusalem In Christian theology, the New Jerusalem is the abode of the blessed in heaven. The term can be used to refer to an ideal place or situation.
▶ *See also* CELESTIAL CITY.

You think Victoria is like the New Jerusalem.
G. K. CHESTERTON *The Man Who Was Thursday*, 1908

It had to come from Cape Town, a place Samuel had never seen in her life but which in her reckoning ranked with the new Jerusalem.
ANDRÉ BRINK *Imaginings of Sand*, 1996

Paradise Paradise is the Garden of Eden described in the Book of Genesis, the place of perfect happiness enjoyed by Adam and Eve before their Fall and expulsion. The term is more commonly used, however, to refer not to the biblical Eden but rather to Heaven, 'the second Eden', and to a place or state of complete happiness. ▶ *See special entry* □ ADAM AND EVE *on p. 5.*

Not a river at all, just a trickle of water choked with reeds, and mosquitoes in the evenings, and a caravan park full of screaming children and fat barefoot men in shorts braising sausages over gas cookers. Not Paradise at all.
J. M. COETZEE *Age of Iron*, 1990

The sun was shining and every stone of the wall seemed as clear as glass and lighted up like a lamp, it was like passing through the gates of Hell and into Paradise.
MARGARET ATWOOD *Alias Grace*, 1996

Promised Land In the Bible, Canaan is described as 'the Promised Land', promised by God to Abraham and his descendants as their heritage (Gen. 12: 7). The term can be applied to any desired place of expected happiness, especially heaven. ▶ *See special entry* □ MOSES AND THE BOOK OF EXODUS *on p. 264.*

Years ago, when we were in trouble, we thought we could one day go north. Well, we are north now. We are at that Promised Land.
STUDS TERKEL *American Dreams: Lost and Found*, 1980

Shangri-la Shangri-la is a Tibetan utopia depicted in James Hilton's novel *Lost Horizon* (1933), frequently used as a type of an earthly paradise, a place of retreat from the worries of modern civilization.

He gave a quick, nervous cough. 'Jesus. You can run but you can't hide. I figured that place was Shangri-la. But it's getting as bad up there as it is in the city.'
TED WOOD *A Clean Kill*, 1995

Utopia Utopia (literally 'no-place') is an imaginary place or condition of ideal perfection. The word was first used as the name of an imaginary island, governed on a perfect political and social system, in the book *Utopia* (1516) by Sir Thomas More.

The founders of a new colony, whatever Utopia of human virtue and happiness they might originally project, have invariably recognized it among their earliest practical necessities to allot a portion of the virgin soil as a cemetery, and another portion as the site of a prison.
NATHANIEL HAWTHORNE *The Scarlet Letter*, 1850

In Mr Carleton's salesman's Utopia the only reason prospective buyers ever gave for not purchasing stock was that they doubted it to be a promising investment.
F. SCOTT FITZGERALD *The Beautiful and Damned*, 1922

We got talking about the permissive sexual mores of the ancient Polynesians, which Yolande described as 'the kind of sexual Utopia we were all pursuing in the sixties— free love and nudity and communal child-rearing'.
DAVID LODGE *Paradise News*, 1992

Valhalla In Norse mythology, Valhalla was the great banqueting hall in Asgard in which heroes who had been slain in battle feasted with Odin eternally.

> 'Then why didn't you just live there happily ever after?' 'Because there's a snake in every paradise, even if it is Valhalla, or Nirvana, or whatever it was they called it in Persia.'
> ANDRÉ BRINK *Imaginings of Sand*, 1996

Xanadu Xanadu is the name of the ancient city in South-east Mongolia where Kublai Khan (1216–94), the Mongol emperor of China, had his residence. Coleridge's poem 'Kubla Khan' (1816) begins with the famous words:

'In Xanadu did Kubla Khan
A stately pleasure-dome decree'.

The name can be applied to a place of dreamlike magnificence, beauty, and luxury.

> Levy's Lodge—that was what the sign at the coast road said—was a Xanadu of the senses; within its insulated walls there was something that could gratify anything.
> JOHN KENNEDY TOOLE *A Confederacy of Dunces*, 1980

> [The film] is Hoop Dreams, a three-hour documentary about two black inner city kids who dream of playing in the NBA, the professional basketball league and Xanadu to every deprived teenager who can dribble 20 yards.
> *The Guardian*, 1995

Illusion

BARMECIDE'S FEAST and the **DEAD SEA FRUIT** are both examples of apparently delicious food not being what it seems and leading to disappointment. **DON QUIXOTE** and **WALTER MITTY** are cases of fantasists who construct alternative realities for themselves. ▶ *See also* **Honesty and Truth**, **Hypocrisy**.

Apples of Sodom ▶ *See* DEAD SEA FRUIT.

Barmecide's Feast In the *Arabian Nights*, a prince of Baghdad named Barmecide invites Schacabac, a poor beggar, to dine with him. The table is set with ornate plates and dishes, but all are empty. When, to test Schacabac's humour, Barmecide asks his guest how he finds the food, and offers him illusory wine, Schacabac declines, pretending to be already drunk, and knocks Barmecide down. Relenting, Barmecide gives Schacabac a proper meal. Barmecide's name is used to describe something, especially food or hospitality, that is in fact illusory or unreal.

> That night, on going to bed, I forgot to prepare in imagination the Barmecide supper of hot roast potatoes, or white bread and new milk, with which I was wont to amuse my inward cravings.
> CHARLOTTE BRONTË *Jane Eyre*, 1847

Your lighter boxes of family papers went up-stairs into a Barmecide room that always had a great dining-table in it and never had a dinner.
CHARLES DICKENS *A Tale of Two Cities*, 1859

It was a curious sort of a feast, I reflected, in appearance indeed, an entertainment of the Barmecide stamp, for there was absolutely nothing to eat.
RIDER HAGGARD *She*, 1887

Dead Sea Fruit The Dead Sea Fruit, also known as Apples of Sodom, were fruits reputed to grow at Sodom, near the Dead Sea. They were beautiful to look at but bitter to the taste or full of ashes, and the expression is now used of anything that promises pleasure but brings only disappointment.

Like Dead Sea fruits, that tempt the eye,
But turn to ashes on the lips!
THOMAS MORE *Lalla Rookh*, 1817

Your poor mother's fond wish, gratified at last in the mocking way in which over-fond wishes are too often fulfilled—Sodom apples as they are—has brought on this crisis.
ELIZABETH GASKELL *North and South*, 1854–5

He had looked for rapturous joy in loving this lovely creature, and he already found that he met with little but disappointment and self-rebuke. He had come across the fruit of the Dead Sea, so sweet and delicious to the eye, so bitter and nauseous to the taste.
ANTHONY TROLLOPE *Barchester Towers*, 1857

Don Quixote In Cervantes's romance *Don Quixote de la Mancha* (1605-15), Don Quixote cannot distinguish the fanciful from the real. In a famous episode he attacks a group of windmills in the belief that they are giants. In Don Quixote's confused mind, a good-looking village girl, whom he names Dulcinea del Toboso, is elevated to the ideal of womanly beauty and virtue. Don Quixote can represent someone who fights against illusory evils, or someone who does not see things as they really are. ▶ *See special entry* ◻ **DON QUIXOTE** *on p. 128*.

We are most of us like Don Quixote, to whom a windmill was a giant, and Dulcinea a magnificent princess: all more or less the dupes of our own imagination.
THOMAS LOVE PEACOCK *Nightmare Abbey*, 1818

Emperor's New Clothes Hans Christian Anderson's story of *The Emperor's New Clothes*, first published in 1836, tells the story of an emperor obsessed with beautiful clothes. He is visited by two swindlers who promise to make him the most beautiful clothes ever seen. Using an empty loom, they pretend to weave the cloth and stitch the clothes, telling the emperor that the cloth they are using is invisible to anyone who is unfit for his office or stupid. Although no one, including the emperor, can see the clothes, all collude in the deception for fear of appearing foolish or incompetent. The emperor parades naked through the streets of the town, with all the people cheering except for one small boy who cries, 'But the Emperor has nothing on at all!' 'The Emperor's New Clothes' can describe something that is promised or believed in but does not in fact exist.

Common sense is a very poor guide to scientific insight for it represents cultural prejudice more often than it reflects the native honesty of a small boy before the naked emperor.

STEPHEN JAY GOULD *Ever Since Darwin*, 1978

Walter Mitty Walter Mitty is the hero of James Thurber's short story *The Secret Life of Walter Mitty* (1939), a daydreamer who, in his imagination, transforms the dull reality of his life into a series of spectacular adventures in which he is the brave and undefeated hero. A 'Walter Mitty' is thus someone who lives in a world of his own imagination and does not face reality.

> Compulsive shoppers can ring for help when they have the urge to buy something expensive; former sufferer Lawrence Michaels will try to talk them out of it. 'A lot are Walter Mittys who need to face reality', says Michaels, who chairs self-help group Walletwatch.
> *The Observer*, 1997

Immobility

Two ideas are covered here: being immobilized (**GULLIVER, TIN MAN**) and being brought to a standstill (**JOSHUA**). ▶ *See also* **Captives, Movement**.

Daphne In Greek mythology, Daphne was a nymph, daughter of Peneus, with whom the god Apollo fell in love. In attempting to escape his pursuit, Daphne called upon the gods for help and was turned into a laurel tree. She is often depicted in art, literally rooted to the spot as she undergoes her transformation.

> Alexander slid into the seat beside her, Alexander's Old Spice smell brushed her nostrils, Alexander's soft-modulated voice murmured no, surely not muscle-bound, but with her nerves chained up in alabaster and she a statue, or as Daphne was, root-bound, that fled Apollo.
> A. S. BYATT *The Virgin in the Garden*, 1978

Gulliver In a famous episode at the beginning of Jonathan Swift's *Gulliver's Travels* (1726), the shipwrecked Gulliver wakes on the shore to find himself unable to move because the tiny Lilliputians have fastened his limbs, hair, and body to the ground with strings. ▶ *See special entry* □ **GULLIVER'S TRAVELS** *on p. 171*.

> Hypotheses pinned me down, as Gulliver was pinned by the countless threads of the Lilliputians.
> JOHN FOWLES *The Magus*, 1977

> As a great 'No!' burst from deep in his chest, he stood, not quickly, but as Gulliver might have, had he been better able to resist the ropes of the Lilliputians.
> PETER CAREY *Jack Maggs*, 1997

Joshua Joshua, Moses' successor as leader of Israel, led the Israelites in their return to the land of Canaan. The Book of Joshua includes an account of the

Israelites' victory over the Amorites during which Joshua prayed to God: '"Sun, stand thou still at Gibeon, and thou Moon in the valley of Aijalon." And the sun stood still, and the moon stayed, until the nation took vengeance on their enemies' (Josh. 10: 12–13).

> We were gaining about twenty minutes every day, because we were going east so fast—we gained just about enough every day to keep along with the moon. It was becoming an old moon to the friends we had left behind us, but to us Joshuas it stood still.
> MARK TWAIN *The Innocents Abroad*, 1869

Tin Man In L. Frank Baum's children's story *The Wizard of Oz* (1900), the Tin Woodman is one of Dorothy's companions on her journey to find Oz. When Dorothy and the Scarecrow first meet the Tin Woodman, he is frozen in position, having been caught in the rain while chopping wood. He is freed by Dorothy, who locates his oil can and oils his joints. The Tin Woodman is now more popularly known as the Tin Man, as the character was called in the 1939 film of the book starring Judy Garland.

> He stood from a crouched position, his knees cracking as he rose. He and the Tin Man—they needed oil.
> FAYE KELLERMAN *Sanctuary*, 1994

> After he'd been taken off the ventilator and was no longer being fed immobilising drugs that 'turned me into the Tin Man, forcing open one eye, twitching one little finger', and after he knew that he was, after all, going to live, the psychological reactions set in.
> *The Observer*, 1996

Importance

This theme mainly comprises ways of expressing great significance or momentousness but also includes entries that suggest the opposite idea, that of lack of importance or triviality.

Ark of the Covenant The Ark of the Covenant was a box containing tablets giving the law as revealed to Moses by God. The Ark was carried by the Israelites on their wanderings, and when they settled was placed in the temple at Jerusalem. An extremely sacred object, it was lost when Jerusalem was captured in 586 BC. ▶ *See special entry* □ **MOSES AND THE BOOK OF EXODUS** *on p. 264.*

> I had in my pocket the fetish of the whole black world; I had their Ark of the Covenant, and soon Laputa would be on my trail.
> JOHN BUCHAN *Prester John*, 1910

> He hummed as he filled the kettle, it was a good sign to use the big brown pot. They took the big pot round with them from job to job, it was their Ark of the Covenant almost.
> GWENDOLINE BUTLER *A Dark Coffin*, 1995

Book of Kells The Book of Kells is an illuminated manuscript of the Gospels kept at Trinity College, Dublin. It is thought to have been made on the island of Iona by Irish monks in the 8th or 9th century. Lavishly decorated with full-page illustrations, it is considered the most distinguished of the manuscripts of its type still extant.

> Fogarty picked up the folder and opened it and looked at it for a moment as if he were studying the Book of Kells.
> ROBERT B. PARKER *Thin Air*, 1995

Holy of Holies The Holy of Holies was a sacred inner chamber in the temple in Jerusalem in which the Ark of the Covenant was kept before it was lost.
▶ *See* **ARK OF THE COVENANT.**

> They never spoke of such things again, as it happened; but this one conversation made them peculiar people to each other; knit them together, in a way which no loose, indiscriminate talking about sacred things can ever accomplish. When all are admitted, how can there be a Holy of Holies?
> ELIZABETH GASKELL *North and South*, 1854–5

> She discerned that Mrs Wilcox, though a loving wife and mother, had only one passion in life—her house—and that the moment was solemn when she invited a friend to share this passion with her. To answer 'another day' was to answer as a fool. 'Another day' will do for brick and mortar, but not for the Holy of Holies into which Howards End had been transfigured.
> E. M. FORSTER *Howards End*, 1910

Lilliputian In Jonathan Swift's *Gulliver's Travels* (1726), Lilliput is the country visited by Lemuel Gulliver where the inhabitants are only six inches tall. The result of this reduced scale is to make the political feuding and pretensions of the inhabitants appear ridiculous. The related adjective 'Lilliputian' is used to describe something that is of little significance. ▶ *See special entry* □ **GULLIVER'S TRAVELS** *on p. 171*.

Mickey Mouse Mickey Mouse is a Walt Disney cartoon character, first appearing in 1928. His name can now be used to describe something insignificant or trivial.

> We got a Mickey Mouse educational system that doesn't teach us how things work, how the government works, who runs it.
> STUDS TERKEL *American Dreams: Lost and Found*, 1980

> I mean I'm sure they're acting like their ancestors and they're quite willing (in exchange for some Mickey Mouse presents) to build a raft and transport us upstream on it and be filmed doing this.
> JULIAN BARNES *A History of the World in 10½ Chapters*, 1989

> 'This whole case could blow up on us,' Vince said. 'We don't have a body, number one.' 'We don't have a body *yet*,' I said. 'And the two prior cases on Calvert weren't just mine, they were IAD's as well. If we failed, we both failed. And anyway, those cases were Mickey Mouse compared to the gravity of the current allegation.'
> LINDA CHASE and JOYCE ST GEORGE *Perfect Cover*, 1995

Noddy Noddy is a character in children's stories by Enid Blyton, a boy whose head nods as he speaks. His name can be used to refer to anything childlike, over-simplistic, or trivial.

Olympus Mount Olympus, in Greece, is traditionally held to be the home of the

Greek gods. The adjective 'Olympian' can refer to anyone or anything that is superior to or more important than lesser mortals.

> It was Mrs Heeny who peopled the solitude of the long ghostly days with lively anecdotes of the Van Degens, the Driscolls, the Chauncey Ellings and the other social potentates whose least doings Mrs Spragg and Undine had followed from afar in the Apex papers, and who had come to seem so much more remote since only the width of the Central Park divided mother and daughter from their Olympian portals.
> EDITH WHARTON *The Custom of the Country*, 1913

Titan The Titans were the older gods of Greek mythology who were succeeded by the Olympian gods. The corresponding adjective 'titanic' has come to refer to something that is both powerful and important.

> Oh, it all burst before the girl, and she even stretched out her gloved hands as if it was tangible. Any fate was titanic; any contest desirable; conqueror and conquered would alike be applauded by the angels of the utmost stars.
> E. M. FORSTER *Howards End*, 1910

> They respected him because he spoke English, though they could scarcely believe he had actually been to England. England they held to be a sort of paradise, the abode of titans.
> OLIVIA MANNING *The Spoilt City*, 1962

Indifference

What unites the entries below is a lack of human feeling or sympathy.
▶ *See also* **Ruthlessness**.

Ariel Ariel is a fairy or spirit in Shakespeare's *The Tempest* (1623) who has no physical form or substance and is therefore divorced from human emotions.

> She had never shown any repugnance to his tenderness, but such response as it evoked was remote and Ariel-like.
> EDITH WHARTON *The Custom of the Country*, 1913

Belle Dame Sans Merci *La Belle Dame Sans Merci* is the title of a ballad by Keats, published in 1820. It tells the story of a knight who becomes enthralled by the charms of a fairy woman who pretends to love him and care for him, as a result of which his strength fails him and he is seen 'alone and palely loitering'. The name in fact pre-dates Keats, and *La Belle Dame Sans Mercy* was the title of a French poem of 1424 by Alain Chartier.

> I imagine she was one of the few women who ever turned you down. That rankled; and having one's advances received with howls of mirth must have hurt. If she'd remained here in Pine Grove, married, turned into an ordinary aging housewife, you'd have forgotten her. But the mystery and the romance of her life, added to her

rejection, transformed her into the unattainable ideal woman. La Belle Dame sans Merci.

ELIZABETH PETERS *Naked Once More*, 1989

Fates In Greek and Roman mythology, the Fates were the three goddesses who presided over the birth, life, and death of humans. They were represented as three women spinning: Clotho, who held the distaff and spun the thread of a person's life, Lachesis, who drew off the thread, and Atropos, who cut short the thread and so determined when a person's life would end. They can be alluded to for their role in determining human life and death without emotion.
▶ *See also* PARCAE SISTERS.

fiddle while Rome burns ▶ *See* NERO.

Jolly Miller The comic opera *Love in a Village* (1762) contains a song about the jolly miller, in which the miller declares: 'I care for nobody, not I, If no one cares for me'.

> And then sometimes, very disquietingly for poor Susan, he would suddenly interrupt his emotions with an oddly cynical little laugh and would become for a while somebody entirely different, somebody like the Jolly Miller in the song. 'I care for nobody, no, not I, and nobody cares for me'.
> ALDOUS HUXLEY *Point Counter Point*, 1928

Laodicean The Laodiceans in the Bible were a group of Christians who were indifferent to religion, being 'lukewarm, and neither cold nor hot' (Rev. 3: 16). A Laodicean is thus someone who is or seems indifferent, showing no strong feeling.

> He felt himself to occupy morally that vast middle space of Laodicean neutrality which lay between the Communion people of the parish and the drunken section.
> THOMAS HARDY *Far from the Madding Crowd*, 1874

Marie Antoinette Marie Antoinette (1755–93), the wife of Louis XVI, won widespread unpopularity through her extravagant lifestyle at a time when the French people were going hungry. She is reported to have said, on being told that the poor of Paris had no bread to eat, 'Qu'ils mangent de la brioche' (traditionally translated as 'Let them eat cake'). This phrase has won her a reputation for callousness and indifference to the plight of the poor. She was beheaded during the French Revolution.

> 'He's forgotten the Marhaen', he said. 'He's forgotten them, as people. They're nothing but an extension of himself, to make speeches to. He said it himself: when he speaks to the people, it's a dialogue with his alter-ego'. His voice rose above the drunken conversation. 'What a disgusting admission, while the people starve', he said. 'The Bung's a Marie Antoinette, but *he* says, "Let them eat rats."'
> CHRISTOPHER J. KOCH *The Year of Living Dangerously*, 1978

> 'And they have such long holidays! Why can't they do two jobs, if they're short of money?'
> 'Let them eat cake', murmured Freddie.
> 'I never understood why poor Marie Antoinette got such stick for saying that', said Eleanor. 'It seems a perfectly good suggestion to me, though cake's not very good for you'.
> FAY WELDON *Darcy's Utopia*, 1990

Nero Nero (AD 37–68) was a Roman emperor who ruled AD 54–68. During his reign a huge fire destroyed half of Rome; Nero allegedly played his fiddle and simply watched while the city burned. To 'fiddle while Rome burns' is to stand by and watch while disaster occurs.

> 'I have to denounce the vacillation of the government in the strongest terms', he said. 'They fiddle while Ishmaelia burns.'
> EVELYN WAUGH *Scoop*, 1938

> When we raise our eyes, we will see that He, having become for us a Nero, not in injustice but in severity, will not console us or succor us or sympathize with us, but, rather, he will laugh with inconceivable delight!
> UMBERTO ECO *The Island of the Day Before*, 1994

> The horny young things of *And The Beat Goes On* are now the ruling elite—smug, decadent Neros who fiddle with themselves while the younger generation burns with resentment.
> *The Observer*, 1996

Parcae Sisters 'The Parcae Sisters' was the Roman name for the Fates. ▶ *See* **FATES**.

> Octavian saw his daughter slowly disappearing in the engulfing slush, her smeared face further distorted with the contortions of whimpering wonder, while from their perch on the pigsty roof the three children looked down with the cold unpitying detachment of the Parcae Sisters.
> SAKI 'The Penance' in *The Toys of Peace*, 1919

Snow Queen *The Snow Queen* is a fairy story by Hans Christian Anderson in which Kai, a young boy, is carried off by the cold and cruel Snow Queen after two splinters of glass become lodged in his eyes and heart, making him unable to feel any human emotions. He is rescued by his sister, Gerda, who melts his frozen heart with her tears. The Snow Queen has come to represent a person, especially a woman, who seems incapable of human emotions.

> I was so young I thought it didn't matter. Infatuated! His unhappiness had to be loaded on to me; that was what it was. He denied life, made me deny it too. He turned me into some sort of snow queen and when I made just one small attempt to thaw myself out he used it as an excuse to throw me out of his life.
> FAY WELDON *The Cloning of Joanna May*, 1989

> It started by describing Alice's beauty as 'a fatal thing'. It wondered if 'like Daphne she will get so tired of it, she will pray to be turned into a hedge'. It said nothing about Valentina's own fantastic snow-queen beauty.
> ROSE TREMAIN *The Way I Found Her*, 1998

Innocence

Two meanings of the word 'innocence' are dealt with here: freedom from moral wrong and the state of not being guilty of a specific crime or wrong-doing, often in the context of being falsely accused. Sexual innocence is covered at **Chastity and Virginity**. ▶ *See also* **Guilt**, **Naivety**.

Adam and Eve The Book of Genesis relates how God created Adam and Eve, the first man and woman, to live in the Garden of Eden. Before the Serpent persuaded them to eat the forbidden fruit from the tree of knowledge of good and evil they were completely innocent, knew nothing of good and evil, and were not ashamed of their own nakedness: 'And they were both naked, the man and his wife, and were not ashamed' (Gen. 2: 25). Adam and Eve can be alluded to as archetypal innocents, living in harmony with nature, and knowing nothing of human weaknesses or wickedness. ▶ *See special entry* □ ADAM AND EVE *on p. 5.*

'At least in other nations', Robbie Ross had fulminated, 'Adam and Eve arrived innocent. Here they arrived with their crimes already written all over their faces.'
THOMAS KENEALLY *The Playmaker*, 1987

Caesar's wife When it was suggested that Pompeia, wife of Julius Caesar, was having an extramarital affair, Caesar divorced her saying that, although he knew nothing of the affair, 'Caesar's wife must be above suspicion'. Caesar's wife may be invoked in the context of a person being required to behave in such a way that no suspicion of guilt can ever fall on them.

Bradley, your conduct has given rise to rumours—and I hope for your sake they are no more than that—so unspeakably distasteful that . . . I mean Caesar's wife . . . hrump . . . that is, the Department must be above suspicion . . . certainly above such suspicions as you have seemingly aroused.
WILLIAM BURROUGHS *Naked Lunch*, 1959

'You're forgetting Caesar's wife, Crosby.'
Crosby double-declutched to give himself time to think. 'Who sir?'
'Caesar's wife. She was above suspicion.'
CATHERINE AIRD *The Religious Body*, 1966

Desdemona In Shakespeare's play *Othello* (1622), Desdemona is the daughter of a Venetian senator who falls in love with and marries the Moorish general Othello. The treacherous Iago, Othello's ensign, convinces Othello that Desdemona is being unfaithful to him and, although she is completely innocent, Othello murders her in jealous rage.

Dreyfus Alfred Dreyfus (1859-1935) was a French army officer of Jewish descent who in 1894 was falsely accused of passing military secrets to the Germans. His trial, imprisonment on Devil's Island, and eventual release caused a major political crisis in France. Dreyfus can be alluded to as an innocent person falsely accused or punished.

As things stood we had an offender, a detected crime, and no demands for a second PM. The coroner had therefore released the body for burial. Not the wisest move: Klondike Bill was beginning to look about as guilty as Captain Dreyfus, and I sincerely hoped that the hierarchy had given HM Coroner an explanation, together with the lawyers' version of a frank and sincere smile.
RAYMOND FLYNN *A Public Body*, 1996

Lamb of God The lamb is a biblical symbol of innocence and meekness, and 'the Lamb of God' is a name sometimes given to Jesus, famously in the quotation from the Bible: 'The next day John seeth Jesus coming unto him, and saith, Behold the Lamb of God, which taketh away the sin of the world' (John 1: 29). The Lamb of God is the epitome of innocence and goodness.

'Why, I wonder, is he so suspicious of poor Guy?' 'Him!' Inchcape snorted in amused

contempt. 'He'd be suspicious of the Lamb of God.'
OLIVIA MANNING *The Spoilt City*, 1962

Pontius Pilate Pontius Pilate was the Roman procurator of Judaea from *c.*26 to *c.*36, remembered for presiding at the trial of Jesus Christ. The chief priests and elders who had brought Jesus to him demanded that Jesus be put to death. Pilate, who alone could order the death penalty, was not persuaded that Jesus had committed any crime, but gave in to popular demand and ordered that Jesus be crucified. He washed his hands before the crowd, saying: 'I am innocent of the blood of this just person' (Matt. 27: 24). Pontius Pilate can be mentioned in the context of someone who makes a public show of proclaiming their innocence and distancing themselves from wrongdoing, and Pilate's gesture proclaiming his innocence has given us the phrase 'to wash one's hands of something', meaning to take no further responsibility for it. ▶ *See special entry* □ JESUS *on p. 223.*

'This stuff you sent me,' Nolan barked. 'These damn research tabulations. I thought we'd settled all that. I thought I told you—' 'You told me not to concern myself with them, yes,' Mac agreed as pleasantly as he could manage. 'You also said you hadn't actually seen them. Now that you have, my hands are clean.' 'And who the fuck are you, Pontius Pilate?' 'My hands are clean.' He breathed deeply several times.
NANCY FISHER *Side Effects*, 1994

Susanna Susanna is the central character in the Book of Susanna, one of the books of the Apocrypha in the Bible. She was a beautiful young woman who aroused the lust of two of the elders. When the two elders found her alone in her garden one day, they threatened her that unless she slept with them they would accuse her of adultery with a young man, which would mean her certain death. Susanna chose the latter, saying that she preferred to suffer death than to 'sin in the sight of the Lord'. Susanna was tried and condemned to death, but, in answer to her prayer, God 'raised up the spirit of a young youth, whose name was Daniel'. Daniel cross-examined the two elders and showed that they were lying, upon which they were condemned to death and Susanna was released. Susanna is alluded to as someone who is falsely accused.

Well, we are playing rough, aren't we? And the virtuous Val presenting herself like Susannah, she who suffered from the horny-pawed Elders.
JULIAN BARNES *Talking It Over*, 1991

Insanity

A variety of literary characters are afflicted with madness. This usually takes the form of a general derangement, but in the case of **CAPTAIN AHAB** is realized as a single-minded obsession.

....

Captain Ahab Captain Ahab is the captain of the whaling ship *Pequod* in Herman Melville's *Moby Dick* (1851). The monomaniacal Ahab obsessively pursues Moby Dick, the huge white whale that on a previous voyage had cost him his leg.

I could feel the road some twenty inches beneath me, unfurling and flying and hissing at incredible speeds across the groaning continent with that mad Ahab at the wheel.
JACK KEROUAC *On the Road*, 1957

Take Ky Laffoon. Anyone with a name like that has all the potential to be as loopy as Captain Ahab, and sure enough Laffoon was potty.
The Guardian, 1997

Bedlam Bedlam was the popular name of the Hospital of St Mary of Bethlehem, founded as a priory in 1247 at Bishopsgate, London, and by the 14th century a mental hospital. In 1675 a new hospital was built in Moorfields and this in turn was replaced by a building in the Lambeth Road in 1815 (now the Imperial War Museum) and transferred to Beckenham in Kent in 1931. 'Bedlam' is an archaic word for a mental hospital or an asylum. The term 'Tom o' Bedlam' used to be applied to a person who was mentally ill.

I'm sure the child's half an idiot i' some things; for if I send her up-stairs to fetch anything, she forgets what she's gone for, an' perhaps 'ull sit down on the floor i' the sunshine an' plait her hair an' sing to herself like a Bedlam creatur', all the while I'm waiting for her down-stairs.
GEORGE ELIOT *The Mill on the Floss*, 1860

Don Quixote Don Quixote is the hero of a romance (1605–15) by Miguel de Cervantes, a satirical account of chivalric beliefs and conduct. He has his wits disordered by his devoted reading of chivalric romances and sets out on his horse, Rosinante, in search of knightly adventures himself. In a famous episode he attacks a group of windmills in the belief that they are giants. In Don Quixote's confused mind, a good-looking village girl, whom he names Dulcinea del Toboso, is elevated to the ideal of womanly beauty and virtue.
▶ *See special entry* ☐ **DON QUIXOTE** *on pp. 128.*

Is the man going mad? thought I. He is very like Don Quixote.
ELIZABETH GASKELL *Cranford*, 1851–3

No one in his senses would dream of following her. To idealize so repulsive a Dulcinea one would have to be madder than Don Quixote himself.
ALDOUS HUXLEY *Point Counter Point*, 1928

George III George III (1738–1820) reigned as king of Great Britain and Ireland from 1760 to 1820. The American colonies were lost during his reign. His political influence declined from 1788 after repeated bouts of insanity. In 1811 it became clear that the king's mental health made him unfit to rule and his son was made regent. It is now believed that the King suffered from porphyria, a rare hereditary disease.

Even we hacks live with the unspoken dread that, quite suddenly, we could become as cuckoo as King George III and be offered jobs as Daily Mail leader writers.
The Guardian, 1997

Ben Gunn Ben Gunn is a character in Robert Louis Stevenson's *Treasure Island* (1883), a pirate who has been marooned on Treasure Island and has spent three years going mad in his solitude, living off 'goats and berries and oysters', and dreaming of toasted cheese.

King Lear Lear, a legendary early king of Britain, is the central figure in Shakespeare's tragedy *King Lear* (1623). In the play, the foolish and petulant old king divides his kingdom between his two older daughters, Goneril and Regan, but is subsequently driven mad by his outrage at the grudging hospitality and ill treatment he feels he receives at their hands. His 'mad scenes' take place on a heath in a violent storm. Before his wits leaves him, Lear speaks of his fear of becoming deranged:

'O let me not be mad, not mad, sweet heaven!
Keep me in temper; I would not be mad!'.

It was, Ralph thought in a remote and detached way, better to labour for a sane king than mad Lear.
THOMAS KENEALLY *The Playmaker*, 1987

We are all scared of it, be honest. Madness. Don't tell me, as you flick through these pages in that rather airy way of yours, that you have never considered the dark, almost subliminal fear that you might awake one morning as barking as Lear, for I know better.
The Guardian, 1997

Mad Hatter In Lewis Carroll's *Alice's Adventures in Wonderland* (1865), Alice attends a bizarre tea party in the company of the Hatter, the March Hare, and the Dormouse. The Hatter's conversation consists mainly of non sequiturs and strange riddles like 'Why is a raven like a writing-desk?'. To be 'as mad as a hatter' is to be wildly eccentric, a phrase that derives from the effects of mercury poisoning that was formerly a common disease suffered by hatters. ▶ *See special entry* ☐ ALICE IN WONDERLAND *on p. 10*.

So for a while, like two mad hatters, we hunted them by torch light, topping each other's scores.
MAVIS NICHOLSON *Martha Jane and Me*, 1992

March Hare The March Hare is a character in Lewis Carroll's *Alice's Adventures in Wonderland* (1865), who is present at the Mad Hatter's tea party: 'The March Hare took the watch and looked at it gloomily: then he dipped it into his cup of tea, and looked at it again.' The term 'as mad as a March Hare' comes from the leaping and boxing and other excitable behaviour characteristic of hares in the breeding season in March. ▶ *See special entry* ☐ ALICE IN WONDERLAND *on p. 10*.

Then, mad as a bunch of March hares, yelling and hooting at the top of our voices, we rushed as fast as our legs would carry us, through the wood to home.
WINIFRED FOLEY *Child in the Forest Trilogy*, 1974

Nebuchadnezzar Nebuchadnezzar (c.630–562 BC) was a king of Babylon whose madness is described in the Book of Daniel in the Bible: 'He was driven from men, and did eat grass as oxen, and his body was wet with the dew of heaven, till his hairs were grown like eagles' feathers, and his nails like birds' claws' (Dan. 4: 33). ▶ *See special entry* ☐ DANIEL *on p. 86*.

Ophelia In Shakespeare's *Hamlet* (1604), Ophelia, the daughter of Polonius, is in love with Hamlet but rejected by him. Her grief after her father's fatal stabbing at Hamlet's hands sends her into a state of madness. Ophelia's famous 'mad scene', during which she sings several bawdy and death-obsessed songs, is soon followed by the report that she has drowned herself. According to theatrical tradition, she is often portrayed on stage with flowers entwined in her hair.

> 'My mother mentioned something about it. According to her, the name was Daisy Belford. She wouldn't accept that Arthur was dead and kept wandering round among the glaciers looking for him.' 'A kind of goat-girl Ophelia. Very picturesque, it must have been. D'you suppose she twined edelweiss in her hair?'
> GILLIAN LINSCOTT *Widow's Peak*, 1994

> She is an accomplished actress and a most practised liar. While among us, she amused herself with a number of supposed fits, hallucinations, caperings, warblings and the like, nothing being lacking to the impersonation but Ophelia's wild flowers entwined in her hair.
> MARGARET ATWOOD *Alias Grace*, 1996

Mrs Rochester The deranged wife of Edward Rochester in Charlotte Brontë's *Jane Eyre* (1847) is kept in seclusion at Thornfield Hall. Her existence is only revealed when Jane's marriage to Rochester is about to take place. The early life of Bertha Rochester is imagined by Jean Rhys in her novel *Wide Sargasso Sea* (1966). Allusions to Mrs Rochester are often to a strange or mad person who is kept locked or hidden away in an attic.

> Dropped at the comfy, modern entrance of St Pat's, the psychiatric hospital where Professor Anthony Clare does his day job, I had no choice but to make my way through the entire building to reach Clare's Georgian lair on the far side. It was oddly quiet—the Mrs. Rochesters of Dublin obviously have good sound-proofing in their attics.
> *The Sunday Telegraph*, 1999

Inspiration

This theme is dominated by the Muses and the places associated with their worship.

Aganippe In Greek mythology, Aganippe was a spring sacred to the Muses on Mount Helicon, whose waters were believed to give inspiration to those who drank from them.

> I never dranke of Aganippe well.
> PHILIP SIDNEY *Astrophel and Stella*, 1586

Apollo In Greek mythology, Apollo was the son of Zeus and Leto. Among his numerous attributes, he was the god of poetic inspiration. ▶ *See special entry* ☐ APOLLO *on p. 15.*

Calliope Calliope was one of the nine Muses in Greek mythology, associated especially with epic poetry. ▶ *See* MUSES.

Castalia In Greek mythology, the Castalian spring was a spring on Mount

Parnassus that was sacred to Apollo and to the Muses, and its waters were said to have the power of inspiring the gift of poetry in those who drank of them.

> A stream of prophecy, which rivalled the truth and reputation of the Delphic oracle, flowed from the Castalian fountain of Daphne.
> EDWARD GIBBON *History of the Decline and Fall of the Roman Empire*, 1781

Clio Clio was one of the nine Muses in Greek mythology, associated especially with history. ▶ *See* **MUSES**.

Dulcinea Dulcinea is the name of Don Quixote's love in Cervantes' picaresque romance *Don Quixote*, published 1605-15. Her real name is Aldonza Lorenzo but Don Quixote, who naively idealizes her, gives her the name Dulcinea del Toboso and finds in her inspirations for his many deeds of misplaced heroism. ▶ *See special entry* ◻ **DON QUIXOTE** *on p. 128.*

> No one in his senses would dream of following her. To idealize so repulsive a Dulcinea one would have to be madder than Don Quixote himself.
> ALDOUS HUXLEY *Point Counter Point*, 1928

Erato Erato was one of the nine Muses in Greek mythology, associated especially with the lyre and lyric love. ▶ *See* **MUSES**.

Euterpe Euterpe was one of the nine Muses in Greek mythology, associated especially with lyric poetry and flute playing. ▶ *See* **MUSES**.

Helicon In Greek mythology, Helicon was the largest mountain of Boeotia and was associated with the Muses. The spring of Aganippe and fountain of Hippocrene, believed to give inspiration to those who drank of their waters, were on its slopes.

Hippocrene In Greek mythology, Hippocrene was a fountain sacred to the Muses on Mount Helicon, created for them by the winged horse Pegasus, who stamped his moon-shaped hoof. It was believed to give the power of poetic inspiration to those who drank of it. It is alluded to in John Keats' poem *Ode to a Nightingale*. In the Huxley quotation below, the writer quotes directly from Keats.

> O for a beaker full of the warm South,
> Full of the true, the blushful Hippocrene.
> JOHN KEATS *Ode to a Nightingale*, 1820

> 'Warbling your native woodnotes wild!' said Willie. 'May I help myself to some of that noble brandy? The blushful Hippocrene.'
> ALDOUS HUXLEY *Point Counter Point*, 1928

Melpomene Melpomene was one of the nine Muses in Greek mythology, associated especially with tragedy. ▶ *See* **MUSES**.

> His face is like the tragic mask of Melpomene.
> THOMAS HARDY *Jude the Obscure*, 1895

Muses In Greek mythology, the nine Muses were the daughters of Zeus and Mnemosyne, the goddess of memory. They were the patron goddesses of intellectual and creative ability, literature, music, and dance, providing inspiration to mortals. Later, each individual Muse became associated with one particular art:

Calliope: epic poetry
Clio: history
Erato: the lyre and lyric love poetry
Euterpe: lyric poetry and flute playing
Melpomene: tragedy
Polyhymnia: songs to the gods
Terpsichore: dancing and the singing that accompanies it
Thalia: comedy and bucolic poetry
Urania: astronomy

Various places were associated with the worship of the Muses and were therefore considered to be places of inspiration, notably Pieria on Mount Olympus, Mount Helicon in Boeotia, and Mount Parnassus. Aganippe, Castalia, Hippocrene, and the Pierian spring were all waters that were associated with the Muses and supposed to give poetic inspiration to those who drank of them. Poets, writers, and musicians call on the Muses for inspiration, or refer to their inspiration as their Muse. The Muses are usually alluded to collectively, though sometimes by their individual names.

> Dinah, who required large intervals of reflection and repose, and was studious of ease in all her arrangements, was seated on the kitchen floor, smoking a short stumpy pipe, to which she was much addicted, and which she always kindled up, as a sort of censer, whenever she felt the need of an inspiration in her arrangements. It was Dinah's mode of invoking the domestic Muses.
> HARRIET BEECHER STOWE *Uncle Tom's Cabin*, 1852

> The tribute to Irving had been specially written by that favoured child of the Muses, Urban Frawley.
> ROBERTSON DAVIES *World of Wonders*, 1975

> If I am silent, it is but the tribute genius pays to art. The painter may daub to commission, but his Muse does not.
> TIMOTHY MO *An Insular Possession*, 1986

Parnassus In Greek mythology, Parnassus was a mountain a few miles north of Delphi associated with Apollo and the Muses. On its slopes was the Castalian spring, whose waters were believed to give inspiration to those who drank of them.

> If the world of literary critism knew nothing but, say, her twelve finest poems, she would have an unquestioned, uncategorized place on anyone's Parnassus.
> VICTORIA GLENDINNING *Edith Sitwell*, 1981

Pieria In Greek mythology, Pieria was a district on the slopes of Mount Olympus associated with the Muses. The Pierian spring was located there, believed to give poetic inspiration to those who drank its waters.

> A little learning is a dangerous thing;
> Drink deep, or taste not the Pierian spring
> ALEXANDER POPE *An Essay on Criticism*, 1711

> 'This is no time for blasphemy!' 'A little learning goes to the heads of fools.' 'Yes, drink deep of the Pierian spring or . . .'
> NATHANAEL WEST *The Dream Life of Balso Snell*, 1931

Polyhymnia Polyhymnia was one of the nine Muses in Greek mythology, associated especially with songs to the gods. ▶ *See* **MUSES**.

Terpsichore Terpsichore was one of the nine Muses in Greek mythology, associated especially with dancing and the singing that accompanies it. ▶ *See* **MUSES**.

> He offended her by refusing to go into a dance-hall on the grounds that the music was so bad that it was a sacrilege against St Cecilia and Euterpe and Terpsichore, when she just wanted to go in and lose her unhappiness in dancing.
> LOUIS DE BERNIÈRES *Señor Vivo and the Coca Lord*, 1991

Thalia Thalia was one of the nine Muses in Greek mythology, associated especially with comedy and bucolic poetry. ▶ *See* **MUSES**.

> Call me the Great Escapologist. Call me Harry Houdini. Hail Thalia, Muse of Comedy. Oh boy I need a round of applause.
> JULIAN BARNES *Talking It Over*, 1991

Urania Urania was one of the nine Muses in Greek mythology, associated especially with astronomy. ▶ *See* **MUSES**.

Intelligence

Famous thinkers such as **ALBERT EINSTEIN** and **STEPHEN HAWKING** can be used to represent the idea of intelligence. Some of the other names here are associated with a specific manifestation of such intelligence, namely logical reasoning. ▶ *See also* **Judgement and Decision**, **Knowledge**, **Stupidity**, **Wisdom**.

Aristotle Aristotle (384–322 BC) was a Greek philospher and scientist. A pupil of Plato and tutor to Alexander the Great, in 335 BC he founded the Peripatetic school and library (the Lyceum) outside Athens. Aristotle established the inductive method of reasoning, maintaining that systematic logic, based upon the syllogism, was the essential method of all rational inquiry and hence the foundation of all knowledge. Aristotle's philosophy was to become the basis of medieval Christian scholasticism.

> A boy's sheepishness is by no means a sign of overmastering reverence; and while you are making encouraging advances to him under the idea that he is overwhelmed by a sense of your age and wisdom, ten to one he is thinking you extremely queer. The only consolation I can suggest to you is, that the Greek boys probably thought the same of Aristotle.
> GEORGE ELIOT *The Mill on the Floss*, 1860

> 'I don't understand why you denigrate yourself so much', Charlotte said in mock desperation. 'You're a combination of Getty and Aristotle, compared to most of the management this lot will have encountered.'
> REBECCA TINSLEY *Settlement Day*, 1994

St Augustine St Augustine (354–430) was one of the early Christian leaders and writers known as the Fathers of the Church. He became bishop of Hippo (in North Africa) in 396. His influence on both Roman Catholic and Protestant theology was immense, and he is regarded as the patron saint of scholars.

Professor Challenger Professor George Edward Challenger is the distinguished zoologist and anthropologist who leads the expedition to the land of dinosaurs in Arthur Conan Doyle's *The Lost World* (1912). He also appears in other books by Conan Doyle and is a somewhat irascible and unconventional scientist, given to developing his own individual and rather unlikely theories.

> If you took a living body and cut it up into ever smaller pieces, you would eventually come down to specks of pure protoplasm. At one time in the last century, a real-life counterpart of Arthur Conan Doyle's Professor Challenger thought that the 'globigerina ooze' at the bottom of the sea was pure protoplasm. When I was a schoolboy, elderly textbook authors still wrote about protoplasm although, by then, they really should have known better.
> RICHARD DAWKINS *The Blind Watchmaker*, 1986

Darwin Charles Darwin (1809–82) was an English naturalist and geologist who formulated the theory of evolution by natural selection to explain the origin of animal and plant species. His work *On the Origin of Species* was published in 1859 and *The Descent of Man* in 1871.

Einstein Albert Einstein (1879–1955) was a German-born American mathematician and theoretical physicist who formulated the theory of relativity. He was awarded the Nobel prize for physics in 1921. He is often regarded as the greatest scientist of the 20th century and is frequently mentioned as the archetype of the extremely intelligent person. The phrase 'no Einstein' is commonly used to mean 'unintelligent'.

> Bech, rather short for his age, yet with a big nose and big feet that promised future growth, was recognized from the first by his classmates as an only son, a mother's son more than a father's, pampered and bright though not a prodigy (his voice had no pitch, his mathematical aptitude was no Einstein's); naturally he was teased.
> JOHN UPDIKE *Bech: a Book*, 1970

> He walked her to the door. They made an odd couple: he, short, slightly rumpled, inclined to corpulence; she, tall, slender elegant. Einstein and Aphrodite.
> JOHN SPENCER HILL *The Last Castrato*, 1995

> It's a neat theory, but you don't have to be Einstein to spot some serious flaws.
> *The Observer*, 1998

Stephen Hawking Stephen Hawking (b. 1942) is an English theoretical physicist whose main work has been on quantum gravity and black holes. Confined to a wheelchair because of a progressive disabling neuromuscular disease, he performs his complex mathematical calculations mentally. He is the author of *A Brief History of Time* (1988).

> On Tuesday Van Gaal issued a memo to English football: think more about the game (he has been saying that for years). English football took him up on it. In front of an ecstatic but still disbelieving crowd Newcastle out-played, out-fought and, most of all, out-thought their visitors, whose coach is supposed to be the game's Stephen Hawking, and who carry a spaniel-like sheen that speaks of endless grooming and refining.
> *The Guardian*, 1997

Sherlock Holmes Sherlock Holmes is an extremely perceptive private detective in a series of stories by Arthur Conan Doyle. Holmes's exceptional powers of observation and deductive reasoning enable him to solve many seemingly impenetrable mysteries.

> He opened the other drawers in the desk, hoping to find further clues to this eccentric character, but they were empty except for one containing a piece of chalk, an exhausted ball-point, two bent pipe-cleaners and a small, empty can that had once contained an ounce of pipe tobacco, Three Nuns Empire Blend. Sherlock Holmes might have made something of these clues.
> DAVID LODGE *Changing Places*, 1975

> This is the 'inorganic mineral' theory of the Glasgow chemist Graham Cairns-Smith, first proposed 20 years ago and since developed and elaborated in three books, the latest of which, *Seven Clues to the Origin of Life*, treats the origin of life as a mystery needing a Sherlock Holmes solution.
> RICHARD DAWKINS *The Blind Watchmaker*, 1986

> Reasoning is not a free good. As we walk down the stairs of inference, of Sherlock-Holmes style deduction, each step becomes less certain, less secure, less persuasive.
> BART KOSKO *Fuzzy Thinking*, 1993

Houyhnhnms In Jonathan Swift's *Gulliver's Travels* (1726), the Houyhnhnms are a race of intelligent talking horses, who have 'a general disposition to all virtues', have no conception of evil, and try always to 'cultivate reason, and to be wholly governed by it'. They live alongside the barbaric Yahoos, who resemble human beings but have no intelligence or reason and live entirely according to their animal instincts. ▶ *See special entry* ☐ **GULLIVER'S TRAVELS** *on p. 171.*

Jesuit A Jesuit is a member of the Society of Jesus, a Roman Catholic order of priests founded in 1534 by St Ignatius Loyola, Francis Xavier, and others to do missionary work throughout the world. The Jesuits have also been noted as educators and theologians. The term 'Jesuitical' has acquired a pejorative use to describe a person who uses over-subtle, hair-splitting arguments.

> He was as diligent as any Jesuit at arranging the arguments in every case under *Pro* and *Contra* and examining them thoroughly.
> ROBERTSON DAVIES *Tempest-Tost*, 1951

Isaac Newton Isaac Newton (1642–1727), the English mathematician and physicist, was the greatest single influence on theoretical physics until Einstein. In his work *Principia Mathematica* (1687), Newton gave a mathematical description of the laws and mechanics of gravitation. According to tradition, his insights into gravity began when he saw an apple fall from a tree.

Occam's razor Occam's razor is the principle, attributed to the English philosopher William of Occam (*c.*1285–1349), that in explaining a thing no more assumptions should be made than are necessary.

> But it was really Charles's heart of which she was jealous. That, she could not bear to think of having to share, either historically or presently. Occam's useful razor was unknown to her. Thus the simple fact that he had never really been in love became clear proof to Ernestina, on her darker days, that he had once been passionately so.
> JOHN FOWLES *The French Lieutenant's Woman*, 1969

It has been one of the blessings of my life as College Chaplain that I am no longer required to bless any babies. Looking into what I suppose must be called their faces almost convinced me that Darwin was absolutely right. I remember one particularly horrid little boy who made me think of Occam's Razor rather wistfully.
TOM SHARPE *Grantchester Grind*, 1995

Plato Plato (*c*.429–*c*.347 BC) was a Greek philosopher whose ideas had a profound influence on Western thought. The pupil of Socrates and teacher of Aristotle, he founded the Academy school of philosophy in Athens. Plato set out his views in the *Dialogues*, in which Socrates is the central character who conducts the discussions.

Socrates Socrates (469–399 BC) was a Greek philosopher whose method of inquiry (the Socratic method) was based on debating moral issues with those around him: he systematically questioned his pupils and then cross-examined them to expose inconsistencies and errors.

'I do, as it happens,' said Philip and, still skirmishing . . . in the realm of dialectic, went on like a little Socrates, with his cross-examination.
ALDOUS HUXLEY *Point Counter Point*, 1928

As far as Cassandra Swann was concerned, Charlie Quartermain, gross, unbuttoned, spehisciform, might be St Francis of Assissi and the Angel Gabriel rolled into one, with a touch of Paul Newman on the one hand and a dollop of Socrates on the other, but that still wouldn't make up for the fact that basically she just didn't fancy him.
SUSAN MOODY *King of Hearts*, 1995

Spock In the original series of the TV science fiction programme *Star Trek* (1966–9), Mr Spock is the ultra-logical science officer on the USS *Enterprise*. He has a human mother and a Vulcan father, and it is the Vulcan side of his nature that causes his actions to be governed by logical reasoning rather than by intuition or emotion.

We would like to believe we reasoned with Aristotle's logic. That's why Sherlock Holmes and Star Trek's Mr. Spock are heroes and not fictional commoners.
BART KOSKO *Fuzzy Thinking*, 1993

Invisibility

An object or garment that bestows the power of invisibility on its owner or wearer is a familiar motif in stories and myths. ▶ *See also* **Disappearance and Absence**.

Alberich's cloak In the German epic poem the *Nibelungenlied*, Alberich is a dwarf who guards the treasure of the Nibelungs, which includes a cloak of invisibility called 'tarnkappe'. He is robbed of it by Siegfried.

Bilbo Baggins In J. R. R. Tolkien's *The Hobbit* (1937), Bilbo Baggins is a hobbit, a member of an imaginary race of small, hairy-footed, burrow-dwelling people. During his adventures he acquires a magic ring that confers invisibility on the wearer. This ring, 'so powerful that in the end it would utterly overcome anyone of the mortal race who possessed it', is central to the plot of Tolkien's later work, *The Lord of the Rings* (1954–5).

> 'I'll call myself Mary,' Alison said, loudly enough to be sure of his hearing. 'That sounds nice and innocuous.' 'No one would suspect a meek, mild Mary of any skullduggery,' ... It would be like wearing a cloak of invisibility or Bilbow [sic] Baggins, stolen magic ring.
> SUSAN KELLY *Hope Will Answer*, 1992

Gyges Gyges (*c.* 685–*c.* 657 BC) was a Lydian shepherd who, according to the story told by Plato, descended into a chasm, where he found a horse made of brass. He opened its side and found inside it the body of a man of great size. Gyges removed from the man's finger a brazen ring which, when he wore it, made him invisible. He subsequently used this ring to make himself known to the queen, marry her, and usurp the crown of Lydia's king Candaules.

> What is the practical meaning of this silvery appearance which is generally absent in fishes that live in very deep and dark waters? The probable answer has been suggested several times—that the silveriness gives its possessors a Gyges' ring, a power of becoming invisible.
> J. ARTHUR THOMSON *Biology for Everyman*, 1934

Harvey Harvey is a six-foot tall rabbit created by Mary C. Chase in her 1944 comedy *Harvey* and popularized in a 1950 film of the same name. Harvey is invisible to everyone except the drunken Elwood P. Dowd.

Invisible Man *The Invisible Man* is the title of a novel by H. G. Wells, published in 1897, in which a scientist by the name of Griffin discovers a means of making himself invisible. Although he himself is completely invisible, his clothes remain visible, as do his footprints. The story was filmed in 1933 with Claude Rains as the scientist, and there have been numerous other film and television versions.

> Between the arrogant, stretched legs of that colossus ran a stringy pattern of grey footprints stamped upon the white snow. 'God!' cried Angus involuntarily; 'the Invisible Man!'
> G. K. CHESTERTON 'The Invisible Man' in *The Innocence of Father Brown*, 1911

> Black faces now melted into blackness; one saw apparently empty garments walking about, as in *The Invisible Man*.
> LAWRENCE DURRELL *Mountolive*, 1958

Mambrino's helmet In Ariosto's poem *Orlando Furioso* (1532), Mambrino is a pagan king whose golden helmet makes the wearer invisible. In Cervantes' *Don Quixote* (1605), Quixote sees a barber riding with his brass basin upon his head and, mistaking this for Mambrino's helmet, gets possession of it.

Jason and the Argonauts

In Greek mythology, Jason was the son of Aeson. Jason's uncle Pelias usurped the throne of Thessaly that was rightfully Jason's. Pelias promised that he would surrender it when his nephew brought him the Golden Fleece from Colchis at the furthest end of the Black Sea. This fleece of pure gold hung from an oak tree in a sacred grove and was guarded by an unsleeping dragon. Pelias in fact hoped that Jason would never return.

Jason accepted this challenge. First he asked the shipwright Argus to construct him a ship, which was named the *Argo* after its builder. Then he assembled a crew, the Argonauts, who included such heroes as Hercules, Orpheus, Theseus, Nestor, and Castor and Pollux. Jason set out with the Argonauts to find and recover the Golden Fleece. Among the dangers they faced on their perilous voyage were the Symplegades, or clashing cliffs, which clashed together and crushed ships as they passed between them. When the Argonauts had to pass between them, a bird was released to fly ahead of the ship. The rocks came together and nipped off the bird's tail feathers, and as they recoiled again the Argonauts rowed through with all speed, losing only the ornament on the stern of the ship. After this, in accordance with a prophecy, the rocks remained still.

At Colchis King Aeetes agreed to give Jason the fleece provided he accomplished various tasks the king set him. Jason was challenged to yoke the two fire-breathing bulls of Hephaestus, the god of fire and craftsmen. He was helped by the king's daughter Medea, who was a sorceress. She gave Jason a magic ointment to spread on his body to protect him from the bulls' fiery breath. Then Jason was required to plough and sow a field with dragon's teeth. Medea warned him that armed men would spring up from the dragon's teeth, telling him to throw a stone in their midst, at which they would ignore him and turn on one another. Having succeeded in ploughing the field, sowing the dragon's teeth, and overcoming the armed warriors, Jason seized the fleece after Medea had charmed the dragon guarding it. The Argonauts fled Colchis with Aeetes in pursuit. In order to delay her father, Medea killed her younger brother Apsyrtus and dismembered his body, throwing pieces of his corpse over the side of the ship. She knew this would slow Aeetes down as he tried to recover the pieces of his son.

Jason married Medea but later abandoned her for Glauce, the daughter of Creon, king of Corinth. Medea was so enraged that she took revenge by murdering their two children as well as Jason's young bride, sending Glauce a poisoned gown which burnt her to death. Jason himself finally met his death when a timber broke off the *Argo* and struck his head, killing him.

Jason and the Argonauts *continued*

Throughout this book there are references to Jason and the Argonauts.

▶ *See* ARGONAUTS *at* **Quest** *and* **Travellers and Wanderers**
ARGUS *at* **Craftsmen**
GOLDEN FLEECE *at* **Quest** *and* **Wealth**
JASON *at* **Adventure**
MEDEA *at* **Jealousy** *and* **Revenge**
SYMPLEGADES *at* **Danger**.

Jealousy

As can be seen from the stories below, it is common in literature for sexual jealousy (often ill-founded) to be the occasion of violent death. ▶ *See also* **Envy**.

Cephalus In Greek mythology, Cephalus, husband of Procris, was heard to speak sweet words of love to a gentle breeze that was cooling him. His wife, on hearing of this, and believing him to have a lover, crept into some nearby bushes to listen. Cephalus heard movement in the bushes and, thinking it was some wild beast, threw his spear and killed his wife.

Deianira In Greek mythology, Deianira was the wife of Hercules. When on one occasion the centaur Nessus tried to abduct her, Hercules shot him through the breast with an arrow. Nessus told Deianira to take some of his blood and use it as a love potion by smearing it onto a garment of Hercules if ever she suspected that he was being unfaithful. Some time later, Deianira became jealous of her husband's attraction towards Iole, a princess whom he had captured while away from home and was intending to bring home with him. Hercules had asked Deianira to send him some ceremonial robes and she used the opportunity to test the supposed love potion, by smearing some of the blood of Nessus onto one of the robes in an attempt to win back his love. The blood was in fact a poison, Nessus' revenge, and caused the death of Hercules. When she realized what she had done, Deianira took her own life. ▶ *See special entry* ☐ HERCULES *on p. 182.*

Leontes Leontes is the King of Sicily in Shakespeare's play *A Winter's Tale* (1623). Leontes mistakenly believes that his wife, Hermione, has been unfaithful to him with his childhood friend, Polixenes. In his jealousy he attempts unsuccessfully to have Polixenes poisoned, throws Hermione into prison, and orders that his own baby daughter, Perdita, be left on a desert shore to die.

Medea In Greek mythology, Medea, a princess of Colchis, was a sorceress who fell in love with Jason and helped him to obtain the Golden Fleece. She became jealous when Jason later abandoned her to marry the daughter of Creon, king of Corinth, and took revenge by murdering their two children as well as Jason's young bride. ▶ *See special entry* ☐ **JASON AND THE ARGONAUTS** *on p. 220.*

Oedipus In Greek mythology, Oedipus unwittingly killed his father Laius and married his mother Jocasta, not knowing who they were. His name has become associated with the idea of the incestuous love of a son for his mother and the jealousy of a son towards his father.

> Her younger brother, Basil, in his final year of Modern Greats at Oxford, spoke of going into the City when he graduated, but Robyn considered this was just talk, designed to ward off hubris about his forthcoming examinations, or an Oedipal teasing of his academic father.
> DAVID LODGE *Nice Work*, 1989

Othello Othello is the main character in Shakespeare's play *Othello* (1622). A Moor, he kills his wife, Desdemona, in a fit of jealous rage, because he mistakenly believes that she has been unfaithful to him. Othello can be referred to as the epitome of sexual jealousy.

> As we got out of the car I warned Vico not to talk in the Stairwell. 'We don't want the dogs to hear me and wake Mr. Contreras.' 'He is a malevolent neighbor? You need me perhaps to guard you?' 'He's the best-natured neighbor in the world. Unfortunately, he sees his role in my life as Cerberus, with a whiff of Othello thrown in.'
> SARA PARETSKY *V. I. For Short*, 1995

> But it is when jealousy turns into pathological jealousy, or the Othello syndrome as it is now called, that problems begin to surface and treatment becomes necessary.
> *The Independent*, 1998

Polyphemus In Greek mythology, Polyphemus was one of the Cyclops, huge one-eyed monsters, who fell in love with Galatea, a sea nymph. She did not love him, but did have a lover by the name of Acis. In a jealous rage, Polyphemus hurled a rock at Acis, crushing him to death.

Jesus

Jesus Christ is the central figure of the Christian religion, a Jewish religious leader worshipped by Christians as the Son of God and the saviour of mankind. The main sources of his life are the four Gospels of Matthew, Mark, Luke, and John.

According to these accounts, Jesus was born in Bethlehem to Mary, the wife of Joseph, a carpenter of Nazareth, having been miraculously conceived. At the age of 30 Jesus was baptized by John the Baptist in the River Jordan. He spent forty days fasting in the wilderness, where he was challenged by Satan with a series of temptations. Jesus came out of the wilderness to begin his ministry and for the next three years taught and preached in Galilee. His message was the coming of the kingdom of God. He chose a group of twelve disciples to accompany him. Jesus told parables (such as those of the Good Samaritan and the Prodigal Son), healed the sick, and performed miracles, including turning water into wine and raising Lazarus from the dead. In his Sermon on the Mount he preached love, humility, and charity. His teachings aroused the hostility of the Pharisees and the governing Romans.

In the third year of his mission, Jesus was betrayed to the authorities in Jerusalem by Judas Iscariot, one of his disciples. After sharing the Last Supper with his disciples, he went to pray in the garden of Gethsemane, where he was arrested. He was taken before the high priest, and then turned over to the Romans as a blasphemer and political agitator. Following a hurried trial and despite the misgivings of the Roman procurator, Pontius Pilate, Jesus was condemned to be crucified at Calvary, outside Jerusalem. On the third day after his death his tomb was found to be empty. According to the New Testament, he rose from the dead and ascended into heaven.

Throughout this book there are references to Jesus and to episodes from his life, particularly to the events surrounding his Crucifixion.

▶ See CALVARY *at* **Suffering**
  GETHSEMANE *at* **Suffering**
  GOLGOTHA *at* **Suffering**
  JESUS *at* **Forgiveness, Goodness, Humility, Solitude,** *and* **Temptation**
  JUDAS *at* **Betrayal** *and* **Guilt**
  LAZARUS *at* **Rebirth and Resurrection** *and* **Returning**
  PONTIUS PILATE *at* **Gesture, Guilt,** *and* **Innocence**
  SATAN *at* **Temptation**
  SERMON ON THE MOUNT *at* **Oratory.**

Joseph

Joseph was the son of Jacob and Rachel. In his boyhood, he was his father's favourite son, and when his father gave him a coat of many colours his brothers became jealous, and 'hated him, and could not speak peaceably unto him'. They also hated him for his prophetic dreams. They attacked him, stripped him of his coat, and threw him into a pit. Then they sold him into slavery to the Ishmaelites who brought him to Egypt. Taking his coat, Joseph's brothers dipped it in the blood of a kid they had killed and took it to their father to convince him that Joseph was dead.

In Egypt Joseph was bought by Potiphar, an Egyptian officer, in whose house he was soon made overseer. Potiphar's wife tried to seduce him but Joseph repeatedly refused her advances because of his loyalty to his master. Potiphar's wife subsequently made a false accusation that he had attempted to rape her and as a result Joseph was put in prison. There he interpreted the dreams of Pharaoh's butler and baker. Two years later Pharaoh was troubled by dreams that he could not understand and, hearing of Joseph's gift from his butler, sent for him. Joseph interpreted Pharaoh's dream as predicting seven years of plenty followed by seven years of famine, advising Pharaoh to store grain in preparation for the long famine ahead. Joseph became adviser to Pharaoh and rose to high office, eventually becoming governor of Egypt.

During the famine years, Jacob sent his sons to Egypt to try to buy corn. When Joseph's brothers came to him for help, Joseph at first treated them roughly but, when his brothers revealed how their father had suffered since his disappearance, he eventually revealed to them who he was. He was reconciled with his family and brought them to Egypt.

Various aspects of the story of Joseph are dealt with throughout the book.

▶ See JOSEPH at **Chastity and Virginity, Dreams, Envy,** and **Goodness**
   PHARAOH at **Dreams**
   POTIPHAR'S WIFE at **Sex and Sexuality**.

Judgement and Decision

The judgements of **SOLOMON** and **PARIS** both involve deciding in favour of a claimant over one or more rival claimants. One decision is remembered for its wisdom, the other for causing a war. ▶ See also **Wisdom**.

Paris In Greek mythology, all the gods and goddesses were invited to the wedding of Peleus and Thetis except Eris, the goddess of discord. Angered by this, Eris threw a golden apple inscribed with the words 'for the fairest' at the feet of the wedding guests, causing disagreement between three goddesses, Hera, Athene, and Aphrodite, who each claimed the prize for herself. When Zeus appointed the Trojan prince Paris, the son of King Priam, to judge them, each goddess in turn tried to bribe him. Athene promised him wisdom and victory in war; Hera promised him dominion over mankind; Aphrodite promised him the most beautiful woman on earth as his wife. Paris chose Aphrodite as the winner of the contest. His reward was to be Helen of Troy. ▶ *See special entry* ☐ **TROJAN WAR** *on p. 392.*

Rhadamanthus Rhadamanthus was the son of Zeus and Europa, and brother of Minos, who, as a ruler and judge in the underworld, was renowned for his justice. The term 'Rhadamanthine' has come to mean stern and incorruptible in judgement.

> But Tom, you perceive, was rather a Rhadamanthine personage, having more than the usual share of boy's justice in him—the justice that desires to hurt culprits as much as they deserve to be hurt, and is troubled with no doubts concerning the exact amount of their deserts.
> GEORGE ELIOT *Mill on the Floss*, 1860

Solomon Solomon, the son of David and Bathsheba, was the king of ancient Israel *c.*970–*c.*930 BC. He was famed for his wisdom and justice. The phrase 'the Judgement of Solomon' refers to his arbitration in a dispute about a baby claimed by each of two women (1 Kgs. 3: 16–28). Solomon proposed dividing the baby in half with his sword, and then gave it to the woman who showed concern for its life.

> It was beginning to dawn on me that I am the member of public to whom the public interest requirement refers. In effect, the police are saying, 'You were there. Was it bad? Do you think that person deserves to be punished?'
> But this requires the judgement of Solomon.
> *The Independent*, 1995

> I phoned my condolences to a couple of Danbury Hospital patients recovering from a River Road head-on. Ollie, it seemed, had proved Solomonic in an attempt to hasten the investigation, slapping both colliders with 'excessive speed for conditions'.
> JUSTIN SCOTT *Frostline*, 1997

Knowledge

Most entries in this theme allude to the possession of understanding or information. **TOPSY**, however, represents lack of knowledge. ▶ *See also* **Intelligence, Stupidity, Teachers, Wisdom.**

Argus In Greek mythology, Argus was a giant with a hundred eyes. He never slept with more than one pair of eyes at a time, so he was able to see what was happening around him at all times. Someone who is 'Argus-eyed' is therefore all-seeing and all-knowing.

> Woe betide the six-foot hero who escorts Mrs Proudie to her pew in red plush breeches, if he slips away to the neighbouring beer shop, instead of falling into the back seat appropriated to his use. Mrs Proudie has the eyes of Argus for such offenders.
> ANTHONY TROLLOPE *Barchester Towers*, 1857

Janus Janus was one of the earliest of the Roman gods, depicted with two faces, one facing forwards and the other facing backwards. He was thus a god of wisdom and knowledge, as he had knowledge of the past and was able to see the future. He was also the god of doorways, and of beginnings and endings.

> A friend is Janus-faced: he looks to the past and the future. He is the child of all my foregoing hours, the prophet of those to come.
> RALPH WALDO EMERSON 'Friendship' in *Essays*, 1841

Sibyl A Sibyl was a woman who in antiquity was believed to be a prophetess or oracle. The most famous was the Sibyl of Cumae in south Italy, who guided Aeneas through the underworld.

> She would lie with far-seeing eyes like a sibyl, stroking my face and repeating over and over again: 'If you knew how I have lived you would leave me. I am not the woman for you, for any man. I am exhausted.'
> LAWRENCE DURRELL *Justine*, 1957

Topsy Topsy is a young slave girl in Harriet Beecher Stowe's novel *Uncle Tom's Cabin*, published in 1852. She has been kept in complete ignorance by her owners, and knows nothing about her family. When asked who she is and who were her parents, Topsy famously replies 'Never was born, never had no father, nor mother, nor nothin'. I 'spect I growed.'

tree of knowledge According to the Book of Genesis, the tree of the knowledge of good and evil grew in the Garden of Eden and bore the forbidden fruit which Eve was tempted to eat: 'the woman saw that the tree was good for food, and that it was a delight to the eyes, and that the tree was to be desired to make one wise, she took of its fruit and ate; and she gave some to her husband, and he ate. Then the eyes of both were opened, and they knew that they were naked' (Gen. 3: 6–7). To 'eat from the tree of knowledge' is to obtain knowledge at the cost of a loss of innocence. ▶ *See special entry* □ ADAM AND EVE *on p. 5.*

> I do not actually remember the curtains of my room being touched by the summer wind although I am sure they were; whenever I try to bring to mind this detail of the afternoon sensations it disappears, and I have knowledge of the image only as one who has swallowed some fruit of the Tree of Knowledge—its memory is usurped by the window of Mrs Van der Merwe's house and by the curtains disturbed, in the rainy season, by a trifling wind, unreasonably meaning a storm.
> MURIEL SPARK 'The Curtain Blows by the Breeze' in *Collected Stories*, 1961

Lack of Change

The main idea here is the prevention of, or the opposition to, change. The theme also covers the notion of inflexibility. ▶ *See also* **Change**, **Immobility**.

....

Colonel Blimp Colonel Blimp is the name of a pompous, obese, elderly character invented by cartoonist David Low during the Second World War. His name has come to represent anyone with reactionary Establishment opinions, inflexible in his opposition to anything new.

> 'Well, he's a damn sight more interesting than Colonel Blimp,' Miriam said. 'He's a sensible generous warm-hearted man. Not a stuffed shirt trying to find something to do to fill in his retirement.'
> PHILIPPA GREGORY *Perfectly Correct*, 1997

Canute Canute (d. 1035) was a Danish-born king of England, Denmark, and Norway. According to the famous story, Canute reproved his flattering courtiers by demonstrating that, although he was king, he did not have the power to stop the incoming tide. He is traditionally remembered, however, as foolishly and obstinately attempting to stop the tide and failing. He has come to stand for an attempt to prevent change, particularly a futile attempt.

> Fifty is OK if it looks like 36 in full camera make-up—step forward, Joan Collins, Goldie Hawn—but even the most imaginative and prestigious photographers find it hard to offer us any variety of woman at that age. Following the American model, you spend a great deal of your time, money and energy attempting, Canute-like, to hold back the tide of age.
> *The Independent*, 1997

Luddites The Luddites were groups of early 19th-century English textile workers who believed that the introduction of new machinery was threatening their jobs. They responded by breaking up the machines. The name derives from a workman called Ned Ludd, nicknamed 'King Ludd', who is thought to have destroyed two stocking frames. Anybody who opposes change, especially in the form of new technology, can be referred to as a Luddite.

> Now this is most inconvenient. It is to throw a spanner into the very works of the machine—much as the Luddites at home.
> TIMOTHY MO *An Insular Possession*, 1986

> The whole apparatus of structuralist and post-structuralist thought is founded in fraudulence, speciousness, hopelessly ill-digested scientism, witting obfuscation and the hubris of a quasi-hieratic caste to whom compatriots meekly submit, lest they be reckoned intellectually Luddite.
> *The Observer*, 1997

Medes and Persians In the Book of Daniel, King Darius signed a decree saying that for thirty days no one should pray to any God or man except the king. The king's officials called for him to 'establish the decree, and sign the writing, that it be not changed, according to the law of the Medes and Persians, which altereth not' (Dan. 6: 8). Hence a law of the Medes and Persians is one that cannot be altered. It was as a punishment for ignoring Darius' command that Daniel was cast into the lion's den.

> I know what my aim is, and what my motives are; and at this moment I pass a law, unalterable, as that of the Medes and Persians, that both are right.
> CHARLOTTE BRONTË *Jane Eyre*, 1847

Jeremy Taylor Jeremy Taylor (1613–67) was an Anglican clergyman and theologian. On the royalist side during the civil war as chaplain to Charles I, he stayed true to his faith despite three periods of imprisonment.

> Well, if I were so placed, I should preach Church dogma, pure and simple. I would have nothing to do with these reconciliations. I would stand firm as Jeremy Taylor; and in consequence should have an immense and enthusiastic congregation.
> GEORGE GISSING *Born in Exile*, 1892

Tin Man The Tin Woodman is one of Dorothy's companions on her journey to find Oz in L. Frank Baum's children's story *The Wizard of Oz* (1900). When Dorothy and the Scarecrow first meet the Tin Woodman, he is frozen in position, having been caught in the rain while chopping wood. He is freed by Dorothy, who locates his oil can and oils his joints. The Tin Woodman is now more popularly known as the Tin Man, as he was rechristened in the film starring Judy Garland as Dorothy (1939). The following quotation plays on the idea of the Tin Man's inflexibility before he is returned to mobility.

> Lucy had a gift for making me feel like the Tin Man rusting in the forest. Was I becoming the rigid, serious adult I would have disliked when I was her age?
> PATRICIA CORNWELL *Cruel and Unusual*, 1993

Large Size

Most of the entries in this theme are used to describe people of huge stature. Some of them can also be used to signify something that is gigantic in scale. ▶ *See also* **Power**, **Small Size**, **Strength**.

....

Anak In the Bible, Anak was a man of great stature who founded a race of giants known as the Anakim. They were so huge they frightened the spies of Moses: 'And there we saw the giants, the sons of Anak, which come of the giants: and we were in our own sight as grasshoppers, and so we were in their sight' (Num. 13: 33).

> By some naturalists who have vaguely heard rumors of the mysterious creature, here spoken of [giant squid], it is included among the class of cuttle-fish, to which, indeed, in certain external respects it would seem to belong, but only as the Anak of the tribe.
> HERMAN MELVILLE *Moby Dick*, 1851

Brobdingnagian Brobdingnag is the land inhabited by giants in Book II of

Swift's *Gulliver's Travels* (1726). 'Brobdingnagian' can be used to describe anything that is gigantic in size or scale. ▶ *See special entry* □ **GULLIVER'S TRAVELS** *on p. 171.*

> I felt a wish to quit the high road, which I had hitherto followed, and get in among those tilled grounds—fertile as the beds of a Brobdignagian kitchen-garden—spreading far and wide even to the boundaries of the horizon.
> CHARLOTTE BRONTË *The Professor*, 1857

> It was a pleasure, except that eating among these Brobdingnags, I felt for quite a while as though four inches had been clipped from my shoulders, three inches from my height, and for good measure, someone had removed my ribs and my chest had settled meekly in towards my back.
> PHILIP ROTH *Goodbye, Columbus*, 1959

> Mighty Welsh muscleman Gary Taylor defends his title against 15 girthful Brobdingnagians in the soaring temperatures of an extinct South African volcano.
> *The Guardian*, 1994

Colossus The Colossus of Rhodes, one of the seven ancient wonders of the world, was a huge bronze statue of the sun-god Helios standing beside the harbour entrance at Rhodes. According to Pliny the Elder it stood 30.5 m (100 ft) high. The Colossus was built *c.*292–280 BC and was destroyed in an earthquake in 224 BC. The familiar image of a statue so vast that its legs were either side of the harbour, used by Cassius in *Julius Caesar*, is not historically accurate. *Colossus* was Greek for 'gigantic statue'.

> Why, man, he doth bestride the narrow world
> Like a Colossus; and we petty men
> Walk under his huge legs, and peep about
> To find ourselves dishonourable graves.
> WILLIAM SHAKESPEARE *Julius Caesar*, 1623

> Richter has been called an intellectual Colossus.
> THOMAS CARLYLE *Tales by Musaeus, Tieck, Richter*, 1827

> I found the wall—it was only a foot or two beyond my reach. With a heave I had my foot on the spike, and turning, I had both hands on the opposite wall. There I stood, straddling like a Colossus over a waste of white waters, with the cave floor far below me in the gloom.
> JOHN BUCHAN *Prester John*, 1910

Gargantua Gargantua (whose name means 'gullet') is a prince of gigantic proportions and prodigious appetite in Rabelais's satire *Gargantua* (1534), from whom we derive the word 'gargantuan'.

> She ... saw the two giant connecting rods churning round and round, a nightmare from Gargantua.
> PETER CAREY *Oscar and Lucinda*, 1988

> Broadway followed, and marriage the same year, at the age of 19. The birth of a daughter in this first, as in his two subsequent marriages, in no way slowed down his gargantuan promiscuity.
> BRENDA MADDOX in The *Observer*, 1996

Goliath Goliath was the Philistine giant in the Bible who issued a challenge to single combat to any opponent from the Israelite army. The challenge was accepted by the young David, who slew the ten-foot tall Goliath with a stone from a sling (1 Sam. 17). ▶ *See special entry* □ **DAVID** *on p. 90.*

Silas was impressed with the melancholy truth of this last remark; but his force of mind failed before the only two penal methods open to him, not only because it was painful to him to hurt Eppie, but because he trembled at a moment's contention with her, lest she should love him the less for it. Let even an affectionate Goliath get himself tied to a small tender thing, dreading to hurt it by pulling, and dreading still more to snap the cord, and which of the two, pray, will be master?
GEORGE ELIOT *Silas Marner*, 1861

You call him small? He's a regular Goliath compared with the shortest man in the Bible.
ROBERTSON DAVIES *World of Wonders*, 1975

Gulliver Although Gulliver is not himself a giant in Swift's satire *Gulliver's Travels* (1726), he seems so to the extremely small Lilliputians whom he encounters on his first journey. When mentioned in connection with Lilliputians, therefore, a Gulliver is a giant dwarfing those around him. ▶ *See special entry* □ GULLIVER'S TRAVELS *on p. 171.*

He found it ridiculously easy; the slight Javanese bodies he was dealing with were dwarfed by his own. A clumsy, foolish Gulliver, he looked around for fresh attackers.
CHRISTOPER J. KOCH *The Year of Living Dangerously*, 1978

Elly had risen to greet him, but still he towered above her. He must, I calculated, be at least 6' 4". Elly ... put out a hand towards me. 'J.T. this is Marla, a very old friend from England.'
I came up to his shoulder. It was not a usual experience for me. I caught a glimpse of myself miniaturised in his glasses. What next? A handshake seemed too formal, anything else too forward. I nodded. He almost did the same.
Formalities over, he bent down and scooped up our bags, Gulliver picking up Lilliputian boulders.
SARAH DUNANT *Snow Storms in a Hot Climate*, 1988

The smaller university presses such as Edinburgh and Manchester are but Lilliputians to Oxford's Gulliver.
The Daily Telegraph, 1995

Jotun In Scandinavian mythology, the Jotuns were a race of frost giants who fought against the gods for possession of the world. While the gods lived in Asgard, the home of the Jotuns was Jotunheim.

The Amphitheatre was a huge circular enclosure, with a notch at opposite extremities of its diameter north and south. From its sloping internal form it might have been called the spittoon of the Jotuns.
THOMAS HARDY *The Mayor of Casterbridge*, 1886

Leviathan A number of passages in the Bible (e.g. Job 41, Ps. 74: 14) allude to God's victory over a sea monster called Leviathan, identified by Biblical scholars as a whale or crocodile. Hobbes's title, *Leviathan*, refers to sovereign power in his treatise on political philosophy, published in 1651. The word can be used to describe anything immense or powerful, but especially a whale.

Listening ... from the upper rooms of the empty house only gigantic chaos streaked with lightning could have been heard tumbling and tossing, as the winds and waves disported themselves like the amorphous bulks of leviathans whose brows are pierced by no light of reason, and mounted one on top of another, and lunged and plunged in the darkness or the daylight.
VIRGINIA WOOLF *To the Lighthouse*, 1927

Captain Anderson had left the quarterdeck to Summers, who still stared forward with a tense face as if he expected the appearance of the enemy or Leviathan or the sea serpent.

WILLIAM GOLDING *Rites of Passage*, 1980

Now South America, as we have seen, was isolated during the period in which horses and cattle were evolving in other parts of the world. But South America has its own great grasslands, and it evolved its own separate groups of large herbivores to exploit the resource. There were massive rhino-like Leviathans that had no connection with true rhinos.

RICHARD DAWKINS *The Blind Watchmaker*, 1986

Procrustes In Greek mythology, Procrustes was a brigand who forced travellers who fell into his hands to lie on an iron bed. If they were longer than the bed, he cut off the overhanging length of leg; if they were shorter than the bed, he stretched them until they fitted it. He was eventually killed by Theseus, who attached him to his own bed and then, as he was too long for it, cut off his head. The adjective 'Procrustean' is sometimes used to describe the process of cutting something large down to size.

Given the Procrustean dimensions of film, the director and writer, Curtis Hanson and Brian Helgeland, have simplified the plot, timeline and character.

JOHN SUTHERLAND in The *Guardian*, 1997

Titan The Titans were the giant-sized older gods of Greek mythology who preceded the Olympians. They overthrew their father Uranus but were in turn defeated by their own children, the Olympians, led by Zeus. A very large or strong person can be described as a 'Titan'.

He let out a howl and stayed where he was, face down on the ground. He looked just as big prone as he had upright; a fallen Colossus, a toppled Titan.

ELIZABETH PETERS *Silhouette in Scarlet*, 1983

The Gods were dead, starved to death by lack of belief, and when the Gods died the Titans returned, and he was a Titan untrammelled. Dr Isadore Titan Holly, suffering from gigantism of the head.

FAY WELDON *The Cloning of Joanna May*, 1989

However thin and bedraggled he had become since he had gone to the front, Velisarios was still the biggest man that anyone had ever seen, and Carlo, despite his equivalent experiences on the other side of the line, was also the biggest man that anyone had ever seen. Both of these Titans had become accustomed to the saddening suspicion within themselves that they were freaks.

LOUIS DE BERNIÈRES *Captain Corelli's Mandolin*, 1994

Leaders

Most of the figures below are military or political leaders. Many other historical leaders are covered at the theme **Dictators and Tyrants.** ▶ *See also* **Power, Soldiers.**

Abraham Abraham, was a biblical leader, considered to be the father of the Hebrews. All Jews claim descent from him.

> Wendell went on carefully, considerately, 'Let me propose this. Has she ever smoked pot?' 'Not with me around. I'm an old-fashioned father figure. Two parts Abraham to one part Fagin.'
> JOHN UPDIKE *Bech: A Book*, 1970

Alfred the Great Alfred the Great (849–99) was king of Wessex, succeeding his brother in 871. He defeated the Danes and protected south-west England from Viking attacks. He negotiated a treaty with the Danes partitioning England, reformed the law, and promoted education and the arts.

> It is told of Matthias Corvinus, king of Hungary—the Alfred the Great of his time and people—that he once heard (once *only*) that some (only *some*, my lad?) of his peasants were over-worked and under-fed.
> WILLIAM MORRIS *News from Nowhere and Other Writings*, 1886

Napoleon Bonaparte Napoleon Bonaparte (1769–1821) was born in Ajaccio, Corsica and commissioned in the French army in 1785, where he quickly rose in seniority, being made commander of the army of Italy in 1796. He became involved in a coup d'état against the Directorate, the French political regime, and in the new regime became first consul of the three ruling consuls, later being elected first consul for life, and finally assuming the title of emperor in 1804. He conquered and ruled much of Europe until his final defeat at the battle of Waterloo in 1815. Napoleon can be alluded to as someone who wields great power.

> With his expertise, energy and international contacts, he could really put Rummidge on the map, and that would be kind of fun. Morris began to project a Napoleonic future for himself at Rummidge.
> DAVID LODGE *Changing Places*, 1975

> Gaëtan has very thickly fringed eyes with light-grey irises; into which, because of his height, one looks down. I always find being taller than him disconcerting. He knows it and uses it for his greater success, for he imposes himself, Napoleonically, on his surroundings.
> ELIZABETH IRONSIDE *Death in the Garden*, 1995

> Another, Orlando Figes, has accused him of being a man of 'Bonapartist ambitions.'
> *The Independent*, 1997

Boudicca Boudicca or Boadicea (d. AD 62) was queen of the Iceni tribe of Britons living in East Anglia. After her husband, Prasutagus, died in AD 60, the Romans broke the treaty he had made, annexing Iceni land. Boudicca led a revolt against the Romans, succeeding in sacking Colchester (Camulodonum) and London (Londinium), and razing St Albans (Verulamium) to the ground. The Iceni were defeated by the Roman governor of Britain, Suetonius Paulinus, and two legions. An enduring popular image of Boudicca is that of her standing, in armour, driving a chariot.

> 'I told that last woman I'd have her if I saw anything in the papers,' he said. 'Sue her for libel.' 'Which last woman?' 'That one came down from London. Boadicea type, waving banners and papers at me.'
> SUSAN MOODY *Grand Slam*, 1994

Caesar Caesar was the title given to Roman emperors from Augustus (63 BC–AD 14) to Hadrian (AD 76–138). The title is usually taken to refer to Julius

Caesar (100-44 BC), who established the First Triumvirate in ancient Rome with Pompey and Crassus and became consul in 59. He commanded large parts of Gaul, extending Roman rule to the west, and invaded Britain in 55-54. Against Roman law, he brought his army back to Rome (49-48), successfully fought Pompey and the Senate, and was made dictator of the Roman Empire.

> I remember that my head was full of a text from the Psalms about not putting one's trust in horses. I prayed that this one horse might be an exception, for he carried more than Caesar and his fortunes.
> JOHN BUCHAN *Prester John*, 1910

> He surveyed their business, unsmiling, like a stout imperious Caesar.
> P. D. JAMES *Devices and Desires*, 1989

> 'I thought your piece on corruption in the health service was first class,' said the figure at the bar. 'Praise from Caesar,' smiled the younger man beside him.
> KEN MCCLURE *Requiem*, 1992

Charlemagne
Charlemagne (742-814) was the king of the Franks 768-814. He defeated and Christianized the Lombards, Saxons, and Avars and created the Holy Roman Empire, which he ruled from 800 to 814. As well as encouraging commerce and agriculture, he also promoted the arts and education.

> 'And wherever ye go and show that button, the friends of Alan Breck will come around you.' He said this as if he had been Charlemagne and commanded armies.
> ROBERT LOUIS STEVENSON *Kidnapped*, 1886

Cleopatra
Cleopatra (69-30 BC) was the queen of Egypt 47-30 BC. She had a love affair with Julius Caesar, with whom she had a son. She followed him to Rome when he returned from Egypt in 46 BC, but left Rome after Caesar was assassinated. Cleopatra then had a love affair with Mark Antony (Marcus Antonius), by whom she had three children. Rome declared war on Cleopatra and she and Mark Antony were defeated at the Battle of Actium. They both committed suicide. Cleopatra's relationship with Caesar is the subject of George Bernard Shaw's play *Caesar and Cleopatra* (1901) and her affair with Mark Antony is the subject of Shakespeare's *Antony and Cleopatra* (1623).

Oliver Cromwell
Oliver Cromwell (1599-1658) was a prominent leader in the opposition forces to Charles I in the English Civil War, becoming commander of the New Model Army under Thomas Fairfax. After the war he became in 1653, as lord protector, the ruler of Scotland, Ireland, and England and Wales.

> A number of varied fellow-creatures, some happy, many serene, a few depressed, one here and there bright even to genius, some stupid, others wanton, others austere; some mutely Miltonic, some potentially Cromwellian.
> THOMAS HARDY *Tess of the D'Urbervilles*, 1891

> Where are the patriots in your following? They are all red Kaffirs crying for blood and plunder. Supposing you were Oliver Cromwell you could make nothing out of such a crew.
> JOHN BUCHAN *Prester John*, 1910

Fagin
Fagin is the leader of a gang of child thieves in Charles Dickens's novel *Oliver Twist* (1838). He is usually mentioned in the context of someone who

trains children to steal, especially one who takes a strict, semi-parental role with regard to the children.

> In their search for company they may be lucky enough to find a kindly outreach worker from a charity, or join a gang of other street children, but too often the overtly friendly offer of help turns out to come from a modern Fagin, or drug dealer, or pimp or paedophile.
> *Amnesty International Magazine,* 1999

Garibaldi Guiseppe Garibaldi (1807–82) was the hero of the movement for Italian independence and unification, leading a volunteer force, the 'Red Shirts', to victory in Sicily and Naples.

> Slowly Russo began to shake his head from side to side: this was no Capone, this was a Garibaldi!
> PHILIP ROTH *You Can't Tell a Man by the Song He Sings,* 1959

Hippolyta In Greek mythology, Hippolyta, also known as Antiope, was the queen of the Amazons, a race of fierce fighting women warriors.

> No one . . . could any longer doubt the speaker to be the British Hippolyta of her epoch, and so the earliest progenitress of Parliament's petticoated invaders.
> *Chambers Journal,* 1909

Joan of Arc St Joan of Arc (*c.*1412–31), also known as 'The Maid of Orléans', was the daughter of peasants and became a French heroine and martyr. As a teenager she heard voices she believed to be the voices of saints urging her to fight for the Dauphin against the English in the Hundred Years War. She led the French army to relieve the English siege of Orléans and then led the Dauphin through occupied territory to Reims, where he was crowned Charles VII. Unable to persuade the king to support further attacks on the English, Joan was captured by the Burgundians, who sold her to the English in 1430. The English tried her as a heretic and burnt her at the stake. She was canonized in 1920.

> So, slipping and sliding, with Jane now circling helplessly around them and now leading the way, like a big-arsed Joan of Arc, they reached Jane's pad.
> JAMES BALDWIN *Another Country,* 1963

> Her cheeks were flushed, her eyes sparkling, her question a battle cry. She had the simple, single-minded, passionate fervor of a Joan of Arc: This is right. It must be done. I must do it, whatever the cost.
> KAREN KIJEWSKI *Wild Kat,* 1994

Pantheon Pantheon means, in Greek, 'all the gods' (from *pan* meaning 'all' and *theion* meaning 'god'), and can be used to refer to a group of distinguished people or people who wield considerable influence.

> But his true fighting weight, his antecedents, his amours with other members of the commercial Pantheon—all these were as uncertain to ordinary mortals as were the escapades of Zeus. While the gods are powerful, we learn little about them. It is only in the days of their decadence that a strong light beats into heaven.
> E. M. FORSTER *Howards End,* 1910

Tamerlane Tamerlane or Tamburlaine (1336–1405) was born Timur Lenk and was the Mongol ruler of Samarkand from 1369 to 1405. With his force of Mongols and Turks he conquered a large area of Persia, northern India, and Syria and established his capital at Samarkand.

Xerxes Xerxes (c.519–465 BC) was the king of Persia, son of Darius I. He led the invasion of Greece, building a bridge from boats to allow his army to cross the Hellespont (now the Dardenelles) and winning the battles of Artemisium and Thermopylae. He was later defeated at the battle of Salamis and had to withdraw from Greece.

> Gina made it clear that Anstice had consistently portrayed Richard as a Lionheart, a Tamburlaine, a veritable Xerxes in the sack.
> MARTIN AMIS *The Information*, 1995

Life: Generation of Life

The bringing to life of something inanimate is a powerful theme in myth and storytelling. In the stories below the 'spark of life' is variously the breath of God, fire, and electricity. ▶ *See also* **Rebirth and Resurrection**.

....

Adam and Eve In the Bible, the Book of Genesis relates how, having created the world and everything in it, God 'formed man from the dust of the ground, and breathed into his nostrils the breath of life; and man became a living soul' (Gen. 2: 7). God later took one of Adam's ribs and made it into the first woman, Eve. Adam is the first man in both the Judaeo-Christian and Muslim traditions. ▶ *See special entry* □ **ADAM AND EVE** *on p. 5.*

> I felt like the Adam of the medieval legends; the world-compounded body of a man whose flesh was soil, whose bones were stones, whose blood water, whose hair was grass, whose eyesight sunlight, whose breath was wind, and whose thoughts were clouds.
> LAWRENCE DURRELL *Clea*, 1960

Frankenstein Mary Shelley's gothic novel *Frankenstein* (1818) relates the exploits of Victor Frankenstein, a Genevan student of natural philosophy, who builds a creature resembling a man and brings it to life. The creature, or monster, superhuman in size and strength and terrible in appearance, inspires horror in all who see it, but is miserably lonely and longs to be loved. When Frankenstein refuses to create a mate for his creature, it turns on him and murders both his bride and his brother. Frankenstein decides that he must destroy his own creation, but is himself killed by his monster, which then goes away to end its own life, distraught at the death of its creator.

> Oh, Lisa, stop looking at me as if you were Frankenstein, and the monster had just got away from you!
> MARY STEWART *The Ivy Tree*, 1964

> There are some things they don't share, however. Charles, for instance, is human (despite what he likes to think to the contrary) but Richard is possibly not. Possibly an extra-terrestrial experiment gone wrong in fact—an alien's idea of what a human is like, put together from spare parts, the creation of a Martian Frankenstein.
> KATE ATKINSON *Human Croquet*, 1997

Galatea Galatea was the name given to the statue brought to life by Aphrodite so that the sculptor Pygmalion could marry his creation. ▶ *See* **PYGMALION**.

> She hated Spielvogel for what Spielvogel had written about the Peter who was to *her* so inspirational and instructive, the man she had come to adore for the changes he was helping to bring about in her life. Spielvogel had demythologized her Pygmalion—of course Galatea was furious.
> PHILIP ROTH *My Life as a Man*, 1970

> Your motive was as strong as Hattie's—stronger, because your feelings for Valentine are as violent and perverse as Laurie's were. You've fallen in love with your Galatea, the image you and Hattie created to assume the role of Valerie Valentine, and if the truth came out you'd lose her.
> ELIZABETH PETERS *Die for Love*, 1984

Pinocchio Pinocchio is the famous puppet hero of the story *Le Avventure di Pinocchio* (1883) by G. Lorenzini, who wrote under the name of Carlo Collodi. According to the story, the puppet Pinocchio is made by the carpenter Geppetto from a piece of wood that magically laughs and cries like a child. Once created, Pinocchio has many strange adventures before finally becoming a real boy.

Prometheus In Greek mythology, Prometheus was a demigod, one of the Titans, said to have created the first men by making figures of clay which, with the help of the goddess Athene, he brought to life. He later stole fire from the gods and gave it to man, and according to some stories it was this fire that Prometheus used to breathe life into his figures of clay and so create the first men. The Promethean spark or fire is thus the spark of life or vitality. ▶ *See special entry* ☐ **PROMETHEUS** *on p. 311*.

> White necks, carmine lips and cheeks, clusters of bright curls, do not suffice for me without the Promethean spark which will live after the roses and lilies are faded, the burnished hair grown grey.
> CHARLOTTE BRONTË *The Professor*, 1857

Pygmalion In Greek legend, Pygmalion was the king of Cyprus who created a statue of a beautiful woman, according to Ovid, and then fell in love with it. He prayed to Aphrodite for a wife who resembled the statue, and Aphrodite responded by bringing it to life. The woman, who Pygmalion married, has come to be called Galatea.

> And he has gone about her rehabilitation with immense inventiveness. I should have thought it somewhat dangerous to play at Pygmalion, but only now I begin to understand the power of the image.
> LAWRENCE DURRELL *Clea*, 1960

Light

Light is closely associated with the sun, and most of the figures below are in fact sun deities although moon deities are also included. Some artists who are noted for their characteristic treatment of light, such as Turner, are covered under the theme **Artists**. ▸ *See also* **Darkness**.

....

Apollo In Greek mythology, Apollo, also known as Phoebus (literally 'the bright one') or Phoebus Apollo, was the son of Zeus and Leto. He became associated with the sun and later usurped Helios's place as the god who drove the sun's chariot across the sky each day. His name can be used to denote the sun. ▸ *See special entry* ❑ **APOLLO** *on p. 15.*

> Hark! Hark! The lark at heaven's gate sings,
> And Phoebus 'gins arise
> His steeds to water at those springs
> On chaliced flowers that lies.
> WILLIAM SHAKESPEARE *Cymbeline*, 1609–10

> He would never have survived the lash of Phoebus.
> UMBERTO ECO *The Island of the Day Before*, 1994

Balder In Scandinavian mythology, Balder was a son of Odin and Frigga, and god of light and the summer sun. His mother, Frigga, had made him invulnerable by making all things swear that they would not harm him. However, she overlooked mistletoe, and the god Loki used this to bring about his death.

Celestial City In John Bunyan's religious allegory *Pilgrim's Progress* (1678, 1684), Christian undertakes a pilgrimage to the Celestial City, encountering on the way such adversaries as Giant Despair and Apollyon, the foul fiend. When he finally arrives at the Celestial City, set on a hill, and the gates are opened, he sees that 'the City shone like the sun, the streets also were paved with gold'.

> Gold and purple clouds lay on the hilltops, and rising high into the ruddy light were silvery white peaks that shone like the airy spires of some Celestial City.
> LOUISA M. ALCOTT *Little Women*, 1868

Goshen Goshen was the fertile region in Egypt allotted to Jacob and the Israelites, where there was light during the Ninth Plague of Egypt, the plague of darkness: 'there was thick darkness in all the land of Egypt three days, but all the people of Israel had light where they dwelt' (Exod. 10: 23). ▸ *See special entry* ❑ **MOSES AND THE BOOK OF EXODUS** *on p. 264.*

Helios Helios was the Greek sun god, represented as a charioteer who each day drove the chariot of the sun pulled by four white horses across the sky from east to west. Helios was later supplanted by Apollo.

Mithras Mithras was a Persian god of light and truth who was also adopted as a god by the Romans, especially in the military world. He was usually represented in the act of sacrificing a bull.

Phoebe In Greek mythology, Phoebe 'the bright one' was a daughter of the Titans Uranus and Gaia, whose name became associated with the moon.

> Like Phoebe breaking through an envious cloud
> PHILIP MASSINGER *Bashful Lover*, 1655

Phoebus Phoebus was an epithet for the Greek god Apollo, meaning 'the bright one'. The name was used in contexts where the god was identified with the sun. ▶ *See* **APOLLO**.

Ra In ancient Egyptian mythology, Ra was the sun god and supreme deity, worshipped as the creator of all life and often portrayed with a falcon's head bearing the solar disc. He appears travelling in a ship with the other gods, crossing the sky by day and passing through the underworld, the land of the dead, by night.

Selene In Greek mythology, Selene was the moon goddess, the daughter of the Titans Hyperion and Theia.

Love and Marriage

This theme overlaps with the closely related theme of **Sex and Sexuality**. The entries covered below are largely concerned with romantic or idealized love and, in the case of **HYMEN**, with marriage. ▶ *See also* **Lovers, Seducers and Male Lovers**.

Aphrodite In Greek mythology, Aphrodite was the goddess of love, beauty, and fertility, corresponding to the Roman goddess Venus. She is supposed to have been born from the sea-foam on the shores of the island of Cythera.

> But the fact was that he knew very little of the sex; yet detecting a sort of resemblance in style between the effusions of the woman he worshipped and those of the supposed stranger, he concluded that Aphrodite ever spoke thus, whosesoever the personality she assumed.
> THOMAS HARDY *The Mayor of Casterbridge*, 1886

> And by one of those paradoxes in which love delights I found myself more jealous of him in his dying than I had ever been during his life. These were horrible thoughts for one who had been so long a patient and attentive student of love, but I recognized once more in them the austere mindless primitive face of Aphrodite.
> LAWRENCE DURRELL *Justine*, 1957

Arthurian King Arthur and his knights have been the focus of many romantic legends in various languages, recounted by authors such as Chrétien de Troyes and later Thomas Malory. Arthurian literature is associated with the romantic notions of chivalry and courtly love, in which the knight serves his lady and woos her honourably.

> They are drunk with the knightly love one reads about in the Arthurian legends—knight and rescued lady.
> LAWRENCE DURRELL *Clea*, 1960

Barbara Cartland Barbara Cartland (1901–2000) was an English writer of light romantic fiction, which she produced prolifically over many years. Her popular romances include *Bride to a Brigand* (1983) and *A Secret Passage to Love* (1992).

Cordelia When in Shakespeare's play *King Lear* (1623) the king asks his three daughters which of them loves him the best, the two older sisters, Goneril and Regan, flatter their father with extravagant declarations of their love. The youngest daughter, Cordelia, is the only one to speak truthfully, acknowledging that she loves her father according to her duty, but refusing to say that she will always love only him, for when she marries she must also love her husband. Lear is furious and punishes her for what he believes to be her lack of love for him. Later, however, when the king has lost his sanity, it is Cordelia, rather than either of her sisters, who takes him in and cares for him. Cordelia thus represents the ideal of a daughter's love for her father.

> Mrs. Whittaker was Cordelia-like to her father during his declining years. She came to see him several times a month, bringing him jelly or potted hyacinths. Sometimes she sent her car and chauffeur for him, so that he might take an easy drive through the town, and Mrs. Bain might be afforded a chance to drop her cooking and accompany him.
> DOROTHY PARKER *The Wonderful Old Gentleman*, 1944

Cupid In Roman mythology, Cupid was the god of love, corresponding to the Greek god Eros. He is often pictured as a beautiful naked boy with wings, carrying a bow and arrows, with which he wounds his victims and makes them fall in love.

> And off I started, cursorily glancing sideways as I passed the toilet-table, surmounted by a looking-glass: a thin irregular face I saw, with sunk, dark eyes under a large, square forehead, complexion destitute of bloom or attraction; something young, but not youthful, no object to win a lady's love, no butt for the shafts of Cupid.
> CHARLOTTE BRONTË *The Professor*, 1857

> Playing Cupid, I should have you know, isn't just a matter of flying around Arcadia and feeling your tiny winkle throb when the lovers finally kiss. It's to do with time-tables and street maps, cinema times and menus, money and organisation.
> JULIAN BARNES *Talking It Over*, 1991

Doris Day Doris Day, born Doris Kappelhoff (1924), is an American film actress and singer who became popular in the 1950s for her roles in musicals, comedies, and light romances such as *Calamity Jane* (1953) and *Pillow Talk* (1959). Her name is associated with the idea of a wholesome, girl-next-door romance.

> Maybe because I wanted to lend the moment that sort of corny Doris Day romance, make it more memorable than it otherwise would have been.
> NICK HORNBY *High Fidelity*, 1995

Eros In Greek mythology, Eros (called Cupid by the Romans) was the god of love, usually represented as a winged boy with a bow and arrows. Eros is now generally used to represent the idea of sexual love or the libido.

> Introduced as lymph on the dart of Eros, it eventually permeated and coloured her whole constitution.
> THOMAS HARDY *Far from the Madding Crowd*, 1874

> She had loved Private Dukes and spawned a false oath to save him—affronting solider deities for the sake of honeyed, treacherous Eros.
> THOMAS KENEALLY *The Playmaker*, 1987

Gone with the Wind Margaret Mitchell's novel *Gone With the Wind* (1936), made into a film in 1939 starring Clark Gable and Vivien Leigh, is set during the American Civil War. At its centre is the romance between Scarlett O'Hara and the dangerously dashing Rhett Butler. *Gone With the Wind* can be alluded to as an example of glamorous or overblown romanticism.

Gretna Gretna Green is a village in the Dumfries and Galloway region of Scotland just north of the English border. It was formerly a popular place for couples eloping from England to be married according to Scots law, without the parental consent required in England for those who were under age.

> 'Do not ask me, sir,' Remington says coldly. 'I am not here to give you the directions to Gretna. You will not from this moment see my niece nor are you to attempt to open any communication with her, open or clandestine.'
> TIMOTHY MO *An Insular Possession*, 1986

Miss Havisham Miss Havisham is a character in Dickens's *Great Expectations* (1861) who was jilted by her bridegroom on her wedding day and spent years afterwards sitting in her room alone, wearing her wedding dress.

> She'd also suffered the tragic history of having been jilted by the same man on two different wedding days, a condition that prompted Dr. Lowji Daruwalla to privately refer to her as 'the Miss Havisham of Bombay—times two'.
> JOHN IRVING *A Son of the Circus*, 1994

> I love Magda and Jeremy. Sometimes I stay at their house, admiring the crisp sheets and many storage jars full of different kinds of pasta, imagining that they are my parents. But when they are together with their married friends I feel as if I have turned into Miss Havisham.
> HELEN FIELDING *Bridget Jones's Diary*, 1996

Hymen The son of Dionysus and Aphrodite, Hymen was the Greek god of marriage, usually represented as a handsome young man crowned with flowers and carrying a torch.

> To such lengths, indeed, does an intemperate love of pleasure carry some prudent men, or worn out libertines, who marry to have a safe bedfellow, that they seduce their own wives. Hymen banishes modesty, and chaste love takes its flight.
> MARY WOLLSTONECRAFT *A Vindication of the Rights of Women*, 1792

> I myself sincerely hope that Captain Anderson, gloomiest of Hymens, will marry them aboard so that we may have a complete collection of all the ceremonies that accompany the forked creature from the cradle to the grave.
> WILLIAM GOLDING *Rites of Passage*, 1980

Mills and Boon Mills and Boon is the name of a publishing partnership formed by Gerald Mills (d.1927) and Charles Boon (1877-1943), which specializes in publishing popular romantic fiction.

> In some respects this is a Mills & Boonish story, with moments of cloying sentimentality and throbbing musical crescendoes.
> *The Independent*, 1995

> Ralph stopped himself abruptly. He hadn't come in here to sniff Jem's clothes and form elaborate Mills and Boon-style fantasies about her.
> LISA JEWELL *Ralph's Party*, 1999

Venus Venus, identified with the Greek Aphrodite, was the Roman goddess of love, beauty, and fertility. She was supposed to have been born from the seafoam and was herself the mother of Eros.

I have already said that I am not much of an actor, but I gave a powerful, if crude impersonation of the hero who is tremendous on the field of Mars but slighted in the courts of Venus.
ROBERTSON DAVIES *Fifth Business*, 1970

Wendy In J. M. Barrie's *Peter Pan* (1904), Wendy Darling is the girl who is taken with her brothers to the magical Never-Never Land and offers to become a mother to the Lost Boys there. When the Darling children finally return home, Wendy is allowed to go back once a year to the Never Never Land to do Peter's spring cleaning for him. Wendy represents an idealized vision of motherhood.

Oh, you know, she makes everything seem so snug and homey; she wants to be a dear little Wendy-mother to us all. Not being a Peter Pan myself, I don't like it.
ROBERTSON DAVIES *Tempest-Tost*, 1951

Lovers

One of the areas richest in allusive opportunities is pairs of lovers. The archetypes are, of course, **ROMEO AND JULIET**, but there are many other such couples in literature, legend, and history. ▶ *See also* **Love and Marriage, Sex and Sexuality**.

....

Abelard and Héloïse Peter Abelard (1079–1142), French theologian and philosopher, became tutor to the young Héloïse (1098–1164) at the request of her uncle, Fulbert, a canon of Notre Dame. They fell in love, and when the affair was discovered by Fulbert, the couple fled. Héloïse bore a son and they were secretly married in Paris. However, Héloïse's enraged relatives castrated Abelard, who then became a monk, and required Héloïse to become a nun. Abelard and Héloïse are buried together in Paris, and a book of their correspondence was published in 1616.

Therefore the mooning world is gratified,
Quoting how prettily we sigh and swear;
And you and I, correctly side by side,
Shall live as lovers when our bones are bare
And though we lie forever enemies,
Shall rank with Abelard and Héloïse
DOROTHY PARKER 'The Immortals' in *Enough Rope*, 1926

They are people, goddam it, not pneumatic hydraulic, terrace toys. Not necessarily Héloïse and Abelard, Romeo and Miss Capulet, or even Nappi and Joe. But just a crumb of some kind of love there, lad.
JOHN D. MACDONALD *The Quick Red Fox*, 1964

Antony and Cleopatra Mark Antony (c.83–30 BC), a Roman general and triumvir met Cleopatra (69–30 BC), the queen of Egypt, and followed her to Egypt, where he stayed with her during the winter of 41–40. He was recalled to Italy, where he took control of the eastern part of the Roman Empire and married Octavia, sister of the emperor, Augustus. After three years he left his wife and rejoined Cleopatra. Augustus eventually declared war on Cleopatra and the couple fled back to Egypt after their defeat at the battle of Actium in 31 BC. Antony, after being erroneously informed of Cleopatra's suicide, fell on his sword. Cleopatra is said to have committed suicide by being bitten by an asp. Their love affair forms the basis of Shakespeare's play *Antony and Cleopatra* (1623).

> Passion is destructive. It destroyed Antony and Cleopatra, Tristan and Isolde.
> W. SOMERSET MAUGHAM *The Razor's Edge*, 1944

> Sex has left the body and entered the imagination now; that is why Arnauti suffered so much with Justine, because she preyed upon all that he might have kept separate—his artist-hood if you like. He is when all is said and done a sort of minor Antony, and she a Cleo. You can read all about it in Shakespeare.
> LAWRENCE DURRELL *Justine*, 1957

> 'You could have telephoned.' 'I'm very sorry that I didn't.' As indeed he was, and he knew he was going to go on being sorry. 'But you forgot me.' 'Not exactly forgot, Stella. And I have apologized.' 'And I have accepted it,' Stella said with dignity, with the air of one whom to do less would be beneath her. So might Cleopatra have spoken to Antony.
> GWENDOLINE BUTLER *The Coffin Tree*, 1994

Aucassin and Nicolette Aucassin and Nicolette were the subjects of a popular late 13th-century French romance composed in alternating prose and songs. Aucassin, son of the count of Beaucaire, falls in love with Nicolette, a Saracen captive. They endure a number of misfortunes and adventures but are eventually reunited and married.

Beatrice and Benedick Beatrice and Benedick are the two chief characters in Shakespeare's romantic comedy *Much Ado about Nothing* (1600). At the start of the play Benedick is determined to remain a bachelor, and the characters engage in mutual barbed teasing. When their friends and relatives trick each of them into believing that the other is in love, each does, in fact, fall for the other. At the end of the play, still teasing each other, they agree to marry.

Cinderella and the prince In the fairy story, Cinderella is not allowed to go to the royal ball with her unpleasant stepsisters. Her fairy godmother, finding her in tears, transforms a pumpkin into a coach, mice into horses, her rags into suitable clothes, and provides her with a pair of glass slippers. At the ball, Cinderella meets the prince. They are so absorbed that she forgets she must leave by midnight, and when the clock strikes she runs off, leaving one of her slippers behind. The prince declares that he will marry whomever the slipper fits. When he comes to Cinderella's house she suggests that she try the slipper on, and when it fits perfectly she takes the other slipper out of her pocket. She and the prince marry. The prince in the fairy story has come to be known as Prince Charming. ▶ *See special entry* □ CINDERELLA *on p. 56*.

> Darling John, I know I'm not exactly Cinderella but you really have come into my life like Prince Charming and I just can't bear the thought—I won't bear it! I know I'm an old silly, doubting you like this, but you've no idea how lonely it is without you!
> JOAN SMITH *Full Stop*, 1995

Cupid and Psyche Cupid (or Eros, as he was known to the Greeks) fell in love with the beautiful Psyche. He visited her only at night in the dark, insisting that she did not see what he looked like. When Psyche succumbed to curiosity and lit a lamp while he slept, a few drops of hot oil fell on him and woke him. He left her, and she wandered across the earth looking for him and accomplishing various tasks set for her by Venus. Eventually, Psyche was reunited with Cupid and married him in heaven.

> Ah, he doesn't know in the least what he is saying. This is not what he meant to say. His arm is stealing round the waist again, it is tightening its clasp; he is bending his face nearer and nearer to the round cheek, his lips are meeting those pouting child-lips, and for a long moment time has vanished. He may be a shepherd in Arcadia for aught he knows, he may be the first youth kissing the first maiden, he may be Eros himself, sipping the lips of Psyche—it is all one.
> GEORGE ELIOT *Adam Bede*, 1859

Dante and Beatrice Dante Alighieri (1265-1321) was an Italian poet and author of the *Divine Comedy*. His first book, *La Vita Nuova* (c.1290-4), details, in poetry and prose, his adoration for Beatrice Portinari (1265-90). He was platonically devoted to her all his life, although she did not apparently return his love and both were married to others.

> The way he was always pretending for the benefit of himself and everybody else that the world wasn't really the world, but either heaven or hell. And that going to bed with women wasn't really going to bed with them, but just two angels holding hands ... And all the time he was just a young schoolboy with a sensual itch like anybody else's, but persuading himself and other people that he was Dante and Beatrice rolled into one, only much more so.
> ALDOUS HUXLEY *Point Counter Point*, 1928

> At seventeen, however, he met his Beatrice, who was three years his senior. A lovely, laughing, big-legged girl who worked as a clerk in a Chinese department store.
> TONI MORRISON *The Bluest Eye*, 1970

> It was the purest, most selfless romantic devotion. It was Dante and Beatrice in a suburban key.
> DAVID LODGE *Therapy*, 1995

Daphnis and Chloe Daphnis and Chloe are the subjects of an ancient Greek pastoral romance, *Daphnis and Chloe* by Longus (AD 2-3). The story relates how the two young people meet, fall in love, and discover sexual desire, eventually marrying.

Darby and Joan Darby and Joan are alluded to as personifying an elderly but happily married couple. They were originally described in a poem in the *Gentleman's Magazine* (1735):

'Old Darby, with Joan by his side,
You've often regarded with wonder:
He's dropsical, she is sore-eyed,
Yet they're never happy asunder.'

> I can assure you I don't want any procession at all. I should be quite contented to go down with Alexandrina, arm in arm, like Darby and Joan, and let the clerk give her away.
> ANTHONY TROLLOPE *The Small House at Allington*, 1862

David and Bathsheba In the Bible, King David fell in love with Bathsheba, the wife of Uriah, when he saw her bathing from the roof of the palace. David sent for her, slept with her, and she became pregnant. David then arranged for Uriah to be sent into the front line of the battle in which the Israelites were beseiging Rabbah, and he was killed. After a period of mourning for Bathsheba, David married her (2 Sam. 11). ▶ *See special entry* □ **DAVID** *on p. 90.*

Dido and Aeneas Dido was the queen of Carthage, and the story of her love affair with Aeneas is recounted in Virgil's *Aeneid* (29-19 BC). Aeneas, on his way home from Troy, is shipwrecked off the coast of Carthage, where Dido falls in love with him. The affair is consummated when, during a storm while out hunting, they both take shelter in the same cave. Aeneas, however, is commanded by Jupiter to sail to Italy. Seeing the ships preparing to leave, Dido pleads with Aeneas, begging him to stay. When he has departed, she kills herself by building a pyre and throwing herself on it.

> In such a night
> Stood Dido with a willow in her hand
> Upon the wild sea-banks, and waft her love
> To come again to Carthage.
> WILLIAM SHAKESPEARE *The Merchant of Venice*, 1600

> True love is always despondent or tragical. Juliet loved, Haidee loved, Dido loved, and what came of it? Troilus loved and ceased to be a man.
> If destruction is their doomed lot, they perish worthily, and are burnt on a pyre, as Dido was of old. Of all the ladies of my acquaintance I think Lady Dido was the most absurd. Why did she not do as Cleopatra did? Why did she not take out her ships and insist on going with him? She could not bear to lose the land she had got by swindle; and then she could not bear the loss of her lover. So she fell between two stools. Whatever you do, my friend, do not mingle love and business. Either stick to your treasure and your city of wealth, or else follow your love like a true man. But never attempt both. If you do, you'll have to die with a broken heart as did poor Dido.
> ANTHONY TROLLOPE *Barchester Towers*, 1857

> Peter, on the other hand though not blind to its flaws, felt himself duty driven to work from within. A right pious little Aeneas, *Italiam non sponte sequor* and all that crap. Which made her . . . Odysseus? Fat, earthy, cunning old Odysseus? Hardly! That was much more Andy Dalziel. Then Dido? Come on! See her chucking herself on a pyre 'cos she'd been jilted. Helen? Ellie looked at herself in the mirror. Not today.
> REGINALD HILL *On Beulah Height*, 1998

Hero and Leander In the ancient Greek legend or folk tale, Hero lived on one side of the Hellespont (now named the Dardanelles) and her lover, Leander, lived on the other. Every night he would swim across to her, guided by a torch that she held for him. One night there was a storm, the torch went out, and Leander drowned. His body was washed up on the shore the next morning and Hero threw herself into the sea. The story was told in a poem by Musaeus (AD 5-6), and provides the subject matter for poems by Marlowe and Hood.

Isis and Osiris Isis was an ancient Egyptian goddess married to her brother, the god Osiris, who was king of Egypt. Together with their son Horus, they formed a trinity.

> They met once and then Michael began to write her letters as soon as he returned to college. In these letters he appointed her Isis and Arethusa, Iseult and the Seven

Muses. Djuna became the woman with the face of all women. With strange omis-
sions: he was neither Osiris nor Tristram, nor any of the mates or pursuers.
ANAÏS NIN *Children of the Albatross*, 1947

Jacob and Rachel In the Bible, Jacob, a son of Isaac, fell in love with Rachel,
the daughter of his uncle, Laban. He offered to work for seven years in return
for Rachel's hand in marriage. When the seven years were up, Jacob was
tricked into marrying Leah, Rachel's older sister, in place of Rachel. Laban
agreed that after a bridal week with Leah, Jacob could marry Rachel also, if he
would then work for another seven years, and Jacob complied (Gen. 29:
13–30).

> It's a deep mystery—the way the heart of man turns to one woman out of all the
> rest he's seen i' the world, and makes it easier for him to work seven year for her, like
> Jacob did for Rachel, sooner than have any other woman for th' asking.
> GEORGE ELIOT *Adam Bede*, 1859

Jane Eyre and Mr Rochester Jane Eyre is the heroine of Charlotte Brontë's
novel *Jane Eyre* (1847). Jane, an orphan, grows up to be an independent
woman who earns her living first as a teacher then as a governess. In the
latter occupation she meets Mr Rochester, father to her illegitimate pupil,
Adèle. The couple fall in love and, although Jane is initially resistant to the
idea, they eventually agree to marry. The ceremony is disrupted, however, and
it is revealed that Mr Rochester is already married to an insane Creole woman,
Bertha, who has been kept in an upstairs room in Mr Rochester's house. Jane
flees and nearly marries another man, but is eventually reunited with Mr
Rochester after his house has burned, his wife has been killed in the fire, and
he himself has been badly burned and injured.

Lancelot and Guinevere Sir Lancelot, son of King Ban, a king in Brittany,
was one of the greatest of King Arthur's knights of the Round Table. Unfortunately, he fell in love with Guinevere, Arthur's wife. When Arthur was
informed about their affair the lovers fled to Lancelot's castle. Arthur laid siege
to the castle and Guinevere returned to him while Lancelot went back to
Brittany. He returned to fight alongside Arthur in his battle with Mordred but
was too late to save the king and, finding that Guinevere had taken the veil,
became a priest.

Laon and Cythna Laon and Cythna are a brother and sister in Shelley's epic
poem *The Revolt of Islam* (1818). The pair attempt to organize a revolution
along the lines of Shelley's idea of the French revolution, and consummate
their success sexually. However, their success is short-lived.

> "Their supreme desire is to be together—to share each other's emotions, and fancies,
> and dreams."
> "Platonic!"
> "Well no. Shelleyan would be nearer to it. They remind me of—what are their
> names—Laon and Cythna. Also of Paul and Virginia a little ... "
> THOMAS HARDY *Jude the Obscure*, 1896

Merlin and Nimue In Arthurian legend, Merlin was the wizard who coun-
selled and guided King Arthur and his father, Uther, before him. Late in his life
he fell in love with Nimue. She tricked him into giving her the secrets of his
magic and then imprisoned him in the forest of Broceliande, near Brittany.
According to the legend, he never escaped and lies there still.

> And you know you were never much of a lover, Magnus. What does that matter? You were a great magician, and has any great magician ever been a great lover? Look at Merlin: his only false step was when he fell in love and ended up imprisoned in a tree for his pains. Look at Klingsor: he could create gardens full of desirable women, but he had been castrated with a magic spear.
> ROBERTSON DAVIES *The Deptford Trilogy*, 1975

Eugene Onegin and Tatiana In Pushkin's novel in verse form, *Eugene Onegin* (1823–31), Tatiana, a young country girl, falls in love with Eugene Onegin, the friend of her sister Olga's fiancé, Lensky. Onegin, who, though young, is cynical, disillusioned, and easily bored, is dismissive when Tatiana pours out her feelings to him in a letter. The following winter, Onegin flirts with Olga and Lensky challenges him to a duel in which Lensky is killed.

Some years later Tatiana meets and marries the middle-aged Prince Gremin. Onegin meets her at a ball, falls in love with her, and is subject to the same fevered passion as she had earlier experienced for him. Eventually he calls on her and manages to wring from her the admission that she does still love him. But she holds to her marriage and dismisses him.

Pushkin's poem is also the subject of Tchaikovsky's opera of the same name.

> I felt like Eugene Onegin listening to that tiresome Prince hymn his Tatyana.
> JULIAN BARNES *Talking It Over*, 1991

Othello and Desdemona In Shakespeare's play *Othello* (1622), Desdemona marries Othello, a Moor, who is asked to command the Venetian forces fighting the Turks in Cyprus. Mistakenly believing that his wife has been unfaithful to him, Othello, in a state of acute jealousy, smothers Desdemona in her bed. Desdemona is subsequently proved innocent and Othello, in despair, kills himself.

Paolo and Francesca Paolo and Francesca were lovers whose story was immortalized in Dante's *Inferno*. Francesca da Rimini was married to Giovanni Malatesta but fell in love with his brother, Paolo. When their affair was discovered they were both put to death in 1289.

Paul and Virginia Paul and Virginia are two children in the pastoral romance *Paul et Virginie* (1788) by Jacques-Henri Bernardin de Saint Pierre. The tale, inspired by Longus' *Daphnis and Chloe*, relates how the two are brought up by their respective mothers on a tropical island (Mauritius), as if brother and sister, under a regime designed to be in accordance with the laws of nature. They grow to adolescence in happy if frugal circumstances. Then Virginia moves to Paris to stay with a wealthy maiden aunt. On her return, some years later, she is shipwrecked off the Mauritian coast. She refuses to remove her clothing in order to save herself and drowns. In the shock and pain of bereavement, Paul and both mothers then also die.

> She had recovered from her emotion, and walked along beside him with a grave, subdued face. Bob did not like to assume the privileges of an accepted lover and draw her hand through his arm; for, conscious that she naturally belonged to a politer grade than his own, he feared lest her exhibition of tenderness were an impulse which cooler moments might regret. A perfect Paul-and-Virginia life had not absolutely set in for him as yet, and it was not to be hastened by force.
> THOMAS HARDY *The Trumpet Major*, 1880

Pelléas and Mélisande The story of Pelléas and Mélisande was initially told in the poetic drama by Maurice Maeterlinck (1892) and later in Debussy's opera of the same name (1902). Goland, the grandson of King Arkël, marries Mélisande, despite the fact that he knows little about her. They move to his father's gloomy, cold castle, where his younger half-brother, Pelléas, is staying, whereupon Pelléas and Mélisande fall in love. Golaud, on discovering them together, becomes jealous, even to the extent of trying to use his own infant son by his previous marriage to spy on them. Pelléas, who is planning to leave the castle, is forbidden to see Mélisande, but he feels that he must see her once more before leaving, and meets her outside the castle in the shadow of a tree. Golaud, on finding them again together, stabs and kills Pelléas and wounds himself and Mélisande. The latter dies giving birth to a child while Golaud is still torturing himself as to whether or not the lovers had slept together or were innocent of anything but embraces.

> Last night Gillian started quizzing me about one of the girls at the School. Talk about wide of the mark. Might as well accuse Pelleas of leg-over with Melisande. (Though I suppose they must have done it, mustn't they?)
> JULIAN BARNES *Talking It Over*, 1991

Petrarch and Laura Petrarch (1304–74) was an Italian Renaissance poet whose father had been expelled from Florence and with whom he moved to Avignon. He met Laura, the woman who was the inspiration for his love poetry, in Avignon in 1327. Her identity is not known.

> His love was as chaste as that of Petrarch for his Laura.
> THOMAS HARDY *The Return of the Native*, 1880

> Though he could not declare his doubts, he thought it more than probable that this Laura of the voiceless Petrarch was unworthy of such constancy, and that she had no intention whatever of rewarding it, even if the opportunity arrived.
> GEORGE GISSING *Born in Exile*, 1892

Pygmalion and Galatea In Greek mythology, Pygmalion was a legendary king of Cyprus who made a statue so beautiful that he fell in love with it and prayed to Aphrodite to give him a wife resembling the statue. Aphrodite responded by bringing the statue to life, and Pygmalion married the woman thus created, whose name was Galatea.

> How many lovers since Pygmalion have been able to build their beloved's face out of flesh, as Amaril has?
> LAWRENCE DURRELL *Balthazar*, 1958

Pyramus and Thisbe Pyramus and Thisbe are next-door neighbours in Babylon who are in love with each other. Their parents forbid them to marry, but they are able to talk to each other through a hole in the wall that divided their homes. Eventually they arrange to meet outside the city. Thisbe, arriving first, sees a lion fresh from the kill and flees, dropping her cloak. When Pyramus arrives and sees the cloak, now blood-stained having been mauled by the lion, he assumes that Thisbe has been killed by the lion and stabs himself to death. Thisbe returns as he is dying and also kills herself. Their story is told by Ovid and also, comically, by Bottom and his fellow workers in Shakespeare's *A Midsummer Night's Dream* (1600).

> Why Pia's brother had volunteered Jono was never clear; Jono had done so because he loved Charles and could not let him go alone. In the end they were parted early on, sent off to different regiments. Charles had fallen distressingly in love with Diana

whom he met on his last leave before his departure for France in 1915. She had kissed him and given him a photograph which he carried until his death four weeks later. Jono, too, had kissed her, chastely, as Pyramus had kissed the Wall, which she still represented for him, dividing him from and uniting him with the golden Charles who had ridden off to war like one of Edith's troubadours, carrying Diana's favour in his breast.
ELIZABETH IRONSIDE *Death in the Garden*, 1995

Romeo and Juliet The young lovers in Shakespeare's *Romeo and Juliet* (1599) are the offspring of two warring families, the Montagues and the Capulets. They meet at a feast given by the Capulets, are instantly attracted, and marry in secret. Juliet's family, unaware of her marriage, plan to marry her to Count Paris. Juliet takes a potion on the eve of the wedding which will make her appear dead for twenty-four hours. A message to Romeo goes astray. Romeo, hearing of Juliet's death, returns to Verona and to Juliet's body, takes poison, and dies. Juliet awakes, sees his body, and stabs herself.

I watched Duncan clipping his hedge this afternoon and could barely remember the handsome man he was. If I had been a charitable woman, I would have married him forty years ago and saved him from himself and Violet. She has turned my Romeo into a sad-eyed Billy Bunter who blinks his passions quietly when no one's looking.
MINETTE WALTERS *The Scold's Bridle*, 1994

Fleur's in love, I understand, with Phil Merrick—a Romeo-and-Juliet affair disapproved of by his grandfather; though his grandfather already has an Olympic bronze in disapproval.
STAYNES AND STOREY *Dead Serious*, 1995

Samson and Delilah The book of Judges in the Old Testament (Judg. 16: 4–22) relates that when Samson fell in love with Delilah, the Philistines asked her to discover the secret of his great strength. On three occasions when she asked him for the secret he lied to her. She continued to ask him, telling him that he could not love her as he claimed to if he did not tell her the truth. Eventually, Samson explained that the secret of his strength was in his hair, which had never been cut. Delilah arranged to have his hair shaved while he slept, and as a result Samson was captured by the Philistines. ▶ *See special entry* □ **SAMSON** *on p. 336.*

Scarlett O'Hara and Rhett Butler Scarlett O'Hara is a beautiful and egotistical Southern belle, the heroine of Margaret Mitchell's novel *Gone with the Wind* (1936), set during the American Civil War. The hugely successful 1939 film starring Vivien Leigh and Clark Gable further popularized the story of Scarlett and her stormy and ultimately unhappy love affair with the handsome Rhett Butler.

I found myself whistling Mozart under my breath as I got dressed. The Scarlett O'Hara syndrome. Rhett comes and spends the night and suddenly you're singing and happy again.
SARA PARETSKY *Guardian Angel*, 1992

Tristram and Iseult In the medieval legend, Tristram (or Tristan) is sent to seek the hand of Iseult (or Isolde) on behalf of his uncle, King Mark of Cornwall. During the voyage in which Tristram escorts Iseult to Cornwall, the couple mistakenly drink a love potion which had been intended for Iseult and

Mark on their wedding night. Tristram and Iseult fall hopelessly in love, although Iseult is contracted to marry Mark. In one version of the story, Tristram marries another woman but, when dying, sends for Iseult. He arranges a signal from the boat in which she would be travelling to let him know whether she is on board. If she is, a white flag will be flown; a black flag will be flown if she is not. When the boat arrives, the white flag is flying, but his wife tells him it is black and he dies in despair, believing that Iseult has not come. The relationship is the subject of Wagner's opera *Tristan and Isolde*, which ends after Tristan has died in Isolde's arms.

> Passion is destructive. It destroyed Antony and Cleopatra, Tristan and Isolde.
> W. SOMERSET MAUGHAM *The Razor's Edge*, 1944

Troilus and Cressida Troilus and Cressida are characters from Greek mythology, mentioned in Homer's *Iliad* although not as lovers. The main post-classical sources for their story, which is set against the background of the Trojan war, are Chaucer's *Troilus and Criseyde* (c.1385) and Shakespeare's play *Troilus and Cressida* (1609). Troilus, a son of the Trojan king Priam, falls in love with Cressida, and she is persuaded to start a love affair with him by Pandarus, her uncle. Cressida is then required to move to the Greek camp, either because her father has defected to the Greeks or as part of the war negotiations. Once in the Greek camp she betrays Troilus by falling in love with the Greek commander, Diomedes.

> In such a night
> Troilus methinks mounted the Troyan walls
> And sighed his soul toward the Grecian tents,
> Where Cressid lay that night.
> WILLIAM SHAKESPEARE *The Merchant of Venice*, 1600

> 'Troilus loved and was fooled,' said the more manly chaplain. 'A man may love and yet not be a Troilus. All women are not Cressids.'
> ANTHONY TROLLOPE *Barchester Towers*, 1857

Lying

The stories of **ANANIAS, MATILDA,** and **PINOCCHIO** each link lying with punishment. **BILLY LIAR** and **WALTER MITTY**, British and American respectively, are both fantasists. **BARON MÜNCHAUSEN**, the teller of tall tales, is, as the quotations illustrate, an apt name to invoke when it is difficult to believe what someone is saying. ▶ *See also* **Honesty and Truth, Hypocrisy**.

Ananias In the New Testament, Ananias was the husband of Sapphira, who lied in order to keep some money for himself. On being found out and accused of lying to God as well as to men he 'fell down, and gave up the ghost' (Acts 5: 5).

> Suddenly, catching the surgeon's arm convulsively, he exclaimed, pointing down to

the body, 'It is the divine judgement on Ananias! Look!'
HERMAN MELVILLE *Billy Budd*, 1924

Billy Liar Keith Waterhouse's 1959 novel *Billy Liar* tells the story of Billy Fisher, a compulsive day-dreamer who dreams of a better and more glamorous life. A Billy Liar is therefore a day-dreamer who lives in a fantasy world.

Joseph Goebbels Joseph Goebbels (1897-1945) became Hitler's minister of propaganda in 1933. He had control of the press and radio, and used these in order to control the flow of information to the German public and thus further the Nazi cause. He is sometimes mentioned as an archetypal propagandist.

Bhutto has rejected all these charges as politically motivated, saying that they were 'hatched up by the Goebbels of the Pakistani government'.
The *Observer*, 1997

I mean, let's face it, the propaganda that the car industry puts out would give Goebbels and Stalin a run for their money in terms of pure Utopian disinformation.
BEN ELTON *Inconceivable*, 1999

Matilda Hillaire Belloc's *Cautionary Tales* (1939) contains the story of *Matilda, Who Told Lies and Was Burned to Death*. Matilda, a young girl who 'told such Dreadful Lies', had called out the fire brigade as a joke, only to find herself a few weeks later at home when a real fire broke out. Despite her screams for help, no one would believe that there really was a fire:

'For every time She shouted 'Fire!'
They only answered 'Little Liar!' '

Matilda and the house were both burned.

Walter Mitty James Thurber's short story *The Secret Life of Walter Mitty* (1939) relates how a henpecked husband escapes his wife's nagging by retreating into his own world of daydreams in which he is the hero of many adventures. A Walter Mitty is someone who lives in a fantasy world, especially someone who has lost touch with reality.

A chauffeur described as a Walter Mitty character was jailed for a year yesterday for dishonestly trying to claim a share of the National Lottery's first jackpot of nearly 6m. Knightsbridge Crown Court in central London was told that James Madel had walked into the organiser Camelot's London offices on 21 November last year, amid a blaze of publicity, and handed officials a ticket he claimed had been ripped up by his dog but which nevertheless entitled him to £839,254.
The *Independent*, 1995

Baron Münchausen Baron Münchausen (sometimes spelled Munchhausen) is the hero of a book by Rudolf Erich Raspe entitled *Baron Münchausen's Narrative of his Marvellous Travels and Campaigns in Russia* (1785). The book recounts stories of the Baron's travels and adventures, which always emphasize the intelligence and prowess of the hero, and are far-fetched in the extreme. The original Baron Münchausen, believed to have lived 1720-97, is said to have served in the Russian army against the Turks and related wildly extravagant tales of his adventures.

And when in after days I lost my awe of Mr. Peter enough to question him myself, he laughed at my curiosity, and told me stories that sounded so very much like Baron

Münchausen's, that I was sure he was making fun of me.
ELIZABETH GASKELL *Cranford*, 1851–3

From that moment Blenkinthrope was tacitly accepted as the Münchausen of the party. No effort was spared to draw him out from day to day in the exercise of testing their powers of credulity, and Blenkinthrope, in the false security of an assured and receptive audience, waxed industrious and ingenious in supplying the demand for marvels.
SAKI 'The Seventh Pullet' in *Beasts and Super-Beasts*, 1914

Pinocchio Pinocchio is the puppet hero of the story *Le Avventure di Pinocchio* (1883) by G. Lorenzini, who wrote under the name of Carlo Collodi. According to the story, the puppet Pinocchio is made by the carpenter Geppetto from a piece of wood that magically laughs and cries like a child. Once created, Pinocchio has many strange adventures before finally becoming a real boy. During one of his adventures, his nose magically grows longer every time he tells a lie. Allusions to Pinocchio are often in the context of someone telling lies or being punished for doing so.

'Madonna Maria, Dottore, please tell me some lies.' 'I am not Pinocchio. The truth will make us free. We overcome by looking it in the eyes.'
LOUIS DE BERNIÈRES *Captain Corelli's Mandolin*, 1994

'I promise you, it's not a problem, it's been so long since Smith was even interested in a woman, it's a relief in a way.' Pinocchio, eat your heart out. 'I'm glad to see him happy. I've never seen him this happy before, you're very good for him.' But you'd be even better for me.
LISA JEWELL *Ralph's Party*, 1999

Macho Men

Cinema has provided us with a number of icons of high-testosterone violence, notably in the films of Clint Eastwood in the 1970s and those of Arnold Schwarzenegger and Sylvester Stallone in the 1980s. ▶ *See also* **Fierce Women**.

Dirty Harry Harry Callaghan, nicknamed Dirty Harry, is a tough San Francisco police inspector played by Clint Eastwood in several films including *Dirty Harry* (1971) and *Magnum Force* (1973). When violent criminals escape justice through lack of evidence, Callaghan resorts to his own brutal vigilante methods of law enforcement.

The 2,000 or so people who earn their living chasing bail jumpers are essentially unscreened, untrained, unlicensed and unregulated. They operate outside the laws that apply to everyone else, even laws that impose restrictions on the police, and it's a line of work that tends to appeal to those who have Dirty Harry fantasies and macho, self-dramatising visions of hunting down 'skippers' and returning them to justice in the boots of their cars.
The Observer, 1997

Ernest Hemingway Ernest Hemingway (1899–1961) was a US novelist, short story writer, and journalist, whose works include *For Whom the Bell Tolls* (1940) and *The Old Man and the Sea* (1952). He had a reputation for machismo and for celebrating such tough masculine pursuits as big-game hunting, bull-fighting, and deep-sea fishing.

> Cameron is what used to be quaintly called a man's man. For pleasure, he likes to race cars and shoot guns in the desert. But nothing, he'll tell you, is as 'hard, as physically demanding' as making films. Play sceptical and suggest, for mischief, that messing with images is hardly a proper manly pursuit and he'll turn into Hemingway with a lens.
> *The Observer*, 1998

Rambo Rambo is the hero of David Morrell's novel *First Blood* (1972), a Vietnam War veteran characterized as macho and bent on violent retribution, and popularized in three films in which the character is played by Sylvester Stallone. The name can be applied to any man who displays a great deal of physical violence or aggression.

> Times like that a mini fire-extinguisher isn't near as comforting as a sub-machine-gun, but it was the best I could do. I got ready to ram the button and kneed open the door—that's about the only advantage lever handles have, you don't need hands to use them. I felt a little silly crouching there like Rambo when there was no one in the place but me.
> SARAH LACEY *File under: Jeopardy*, 1995

> Dressed from head to toe in camouflage gear—the kind that so many fathers and sons wear on hunting expeditions in the surrounding countryside at weekends—they were firing Rambo-style with an array of weapons, including high-velocity rifles and handguns.
> *The Independent*, 1998

Tarzan Tarzan is a character in novels by Edgar Rice Burroughs and subsequent films and TV series. He is an English aristocrat, Lord Greystoke, who is abandoned as a small child in the African jungle and reared by apes. Tarzan is a very strong and fearless hero, often depicted as wrestling with wild animals or using liana vines to swing through the trees of the jungle.

> "The other side now, viejo," he shouted up to Anselmo and climbed across through the trestling, like a bloody Tarzan in a rolled steel forest.
> ERNEST HEMINGWAY *For Whom the Bell Tolls*, 1941

> I thought I recognized one of his buddies looking fetching in greasy styled hair and a stained T-shirt under a sports shirt he'd unbuttoned, son of an urban-Tarzan-gone-to-seed look.
> KAREN KIJEWSKI *Wild Kat*, 1994

Terminator In the film *The Terminator* (1984) and its sequel *Terminator 2: Judgment Day* (1991), Arnold Schwarzenegger plays an almost indestructible android sent from the future. Both films are extremely violent, and the Terminator destructively deploys an arsenal of massive weaponry.

> And I'd have to invest in martial arts coaching and learn some police techniques for subduing felons. I didn't want to turn myself into the Terminator, but I didn't want to continue to operate at my present Elmer Fudd level, either.
> JANET EVANOVICH *One for the Money*, 1994

John Wayne John Wayne (1907–79) was a US film actor, nicknamed 'the

Duke' and chiefly associated with his roles in such classic westerns as *Stage-coach* (1939), *Red River* (1948), and *The Searchers* (1956). His persona was usually that of the tough, strong, solitary hero.

> 'Don't threaten me, McGraw,' Thayer growled. John Wayne impersonation.
> SARA PARETSKY *Indemnity Only*, 1982

Magic

This theme comprises a selection of magicians, wizards, witches, and sorcerers. Some other instances of magic can be found within the themes **Disappearance and Absence** and **Invisibility**.

....

Aladdin's lamp In a story in the *Arabian Nights*, the poor youth Aladdin discovers in a cave a magic lamp. When he rubs the lamp he summons a genie (or jinn), the 'slave of the lamp', who must do his bidding.

Circe In Greek mythology, Circe was a beautiful enchantress who lived on the island of Aeaea. When Odysseus visited the island on his return from the Trojan War, she turned his men into swine. Odysseus protected himself with the mythical herb moly and forced her to break the spell and restore his men to human form. ▶ *See special entry* □ **ODYSSEUS** *on p. 283.*

> From the mountains comes the wind, bringing clear weather and falling temperatures. As a tribute to its dubious transforming powers it is called the Circe.
> *Oldie*, 1992

> Being pretty is no great matter. Any young lady with bright eyes and passable teeth can claim that much. Better to be clever, quick, and intrepid—to charm with your mind and enchant with your wit—in short, to be the one radiant Circe in a season of dreary Helens.
> KATE ROSS *Cut to the Quick*, 1993

Gandalf Gandalf is the white wizard in J. R. R. Tolkien's fantasy adventures *The Hobbit* (1937) and *The Lord of the Rings* (1954–5). At the start of the latter he is described as an old man wearing a tall pointed hat and a long grey cloak, with 'a long white beard and bushy eyebrows that stuck out beyond the brim of his hat'. He is renowned for his spectacular firework displays.

Merlin In Arthurian legend, Merlin was a wizard who acted as counsellor to King Arthur. According to one version of the legend, he was imprisoned in an oak tree for eternity by Nimue, a woman to whom he had revealed the secrets of his craft.

Morgan le Fay In Arthurian legend, Morgan le Fay was the half-sister of King Arthur. A former pupil of Merlin, she was an enchantress, possessed of magical powers. After Arthur's final battle, Morgan le Fay transported him to Avalon. In some versions of the legend, she was hostile to Arthur and endeavoured to kill him.

The largest mirage ever recorded was sighted in the Arctic . . . It included hills, valleys, and snow-capped peaks extending through at least 120 degrees of the horizon. It was the type of mirage known as the 'Fata Morgana', so called because such visions were formerly believed to be the nasty work of Morgan le Fay, King Arthur's evil fairy half-sister.
Queen's Quarterly, 1994

Prospero   In Shakespeare's *The Tempest* (1623), Prospero is the usurped duke of Milan, marooned on a remote enchanted island with his daughter Miranda. His knowledge of magic enables him to raise the storm at the beginning of the play and gives him power over the airy spirit Ariel. He finally resolves to renounce his 'rough magic', breaking his staff and burying his books, the sources of his powers.

You were Prospero enough to make her what she has become.
HENRY JAMES *Portrait of a Lady*, 1881

Witch of Endor   In the Book of Samuel, the Witch of Endor was the female medium consulted by Saul when he was threatened by the Philistine army. At his request she summoned up the ghost of the prophet Samuel, who prophesied the death of Saul and the destruction of his army by the Philistines.

Conjuration, sleight of hand, magic, witchcraft, were the subjects of the evening. Miss Pole was slightly sceptical, and inclined to think there might be a scientific solution found for even the proceedings of the Witch of Endor.
ELIZABETH GASKELL *Cranford*, 1853

Wizard of Oz   In L. Frank Baum's *The Wizard of Oz* (1900), Dorothy journeys with her companions to see the Wizard of Oz in the hope that he will help her return home. He turns out to be a fraud, not a wizard at all, but an old man who was blown to Oz from Omaha in a balloon.

Suddenly, as if by magic, like something from the Wizard of Oz, the huge doors behind Gayfryd start to open by themselves, very slowly.
IRENE DARIA *Fashion Cycle*, 1990

She squinted out the window some more, then came back to the table and picked up her glass. 'How can he see at night while he's wearing those sunglasses?'
I gave her a little shrug. There are some things even the great and wonderful Oz does not know.
ROBERT CRAIS *Lullaby Town*, 1992

Medicine

Pioneers in the history of the medical profession, together with legendary and biblical figures associated with the art of healing, are covered below.

....

Aesculapius   Aesculapius (or Asclepius), the son of Apollo and Coronis, was instructed in the art of medicine by the centaur Chiron. He was said to have been killed by Zeus after Hades had complained that Aesculapius' skills were keeping mortals from the underworld. After his death, he was honoured as the god of medicine and healing. He was represented holding a staff with a serpent wreathed around it, now the emblem of the medical profession.

> Carl Moss might be willing to protect Merle with the mantle of Aesculapius, up to a point.
> RAYMOND CHANDLER *The High Window*, 1943

> I looked round you see but I said, Wilmot, I said, this anatomy is not for you. No indeed, you have not the stomach for it. In fact as I said at the time, I abandoned Aesculapius for the Muse. Have I not said so to you, Mr Talbot?
> WILLIAM GOLDING *Rites of Passage*, 1980

Apollo Apollo was a Greek god, the son of Zeus and Leto and twin brother of Artemis. He was associated with the sun and a wide range of other attributes, including medicine. He was the father of Aesculapius, the god of medicine and healing. ▶ *See special entry* ☐ **APOLLO** *on p. 15*.

> He had only a nodding acquaintance with the Hippocratic oath, but was somehow aware that he was committed to Apollo the Healer to look upon his teacher in the art of medicine as one of his parents.
> JOHN MORTIMER *Paradise Postponed*, 1985

Bethesda In the Bible, Bethesda was a pool in Jerusalem that was supposed to have healing powers. It was there that Jesus healed a paralytic 'who had been ill for thirty-eight years'. Knowing that the man had been lying by the pool for some time, Jesus asked whether he wanted to be healed. The sick man answered: 'I have no man to put me into the pool when the water is troubled, and while I am going another steps down before me' (John 5: 7).

> She has sent her here to be healed, even as the Jews of old sent their diseased to the troubled pool of Bethesda.
> CHARLOTTE BRONTË *Jane Eyre*, 1847

> The new-comer stepped forward like the quicker cripple at Bethesda, and entered in her stead.
> THOMAS HARDY *The Mayor of Casterbridge*, 1886

Hippocrates Hippocrates (*c*.460–377 BC) is probably the most famous of all physicians, but in fact almost nothing is known about him. His name was attached to a body of ancient Greek medical writings which contained diverse opinions on the nature of illness and treatment. The Hippocratic oath, named after him, is an oath stating the duties of physicians, formerly taken by those taking up medical practice.

> The renowned British Hippocrates of the Pestle and Mortar.
> RICHARD STEELE *Spectator*, 1711

Hygiea Hygiea was the Greek goddess of health, the daughter of Aesculapius.

St Luke St Luke was an evangelist who is traditionally believed to be the author of the third Gospel and the Acts of the Apostles. He was a physician, thought to be the person referred to in Corinthians as 'Luke, the beloved physician' (Col. 4: 14).

Florence Nightingale An English nurse and medical reformer, Florence Nightingale (1820–1910) became famous during the Crimean War for improving sanitation and medical procedures, achieving a dramatic reduction in the mortality rate. She became known as the 'Lady of the Lamp' because of her nightly rounds of the wards carrying a lamp.

> Every woman loves an invalid. I bring out the Florence Nightingale in them.
> MARGARET ATWOOD *The Edible Woman*, 1969

> She got up, soaked a paper towel in warm water, came over and swabbed the wound. She poked around in one of the boxes and found sterile gauze, adhesive tape and hydrogen peroxide. Tending to me like Florence Nightingale, she bandaged the arm.
> JONATHAN KELLERMAN *When the Bough Breaks*, 1992

Paracelsus Paracelsus (*c.*1493–1541) was a Swiss physician who introduced a more scientific approach to medicine and saw illness as having an external cause rather than arising as a result of an imbalance in the body's humours.

> A recipe that an Indian taught me, in requital of some lessons of my own, that were as old as Paracelsus.
> NATHANIEL HAWTHORNE *The Scarlet Letter*, 1850

Memory

This theme covers both memory and forgetfulness.

....

Alfred Alfred (849–99), generally known as Alfred the Great, was the king of Wessex 871–99, who led the Saxons to victory over Danish invaders. The most famous story associated with Alfred is the legend that, when in hiding in Somerset, he forgot to watch a peasant woman's cakes, as he had been asked to do, with the result that they burnt.

> My word, Miriam! You're in for it this time. . . . You'd better be gone when his mother comes in. I know why King Alfred burned the cakes. Now I see it! 'Postle would fix up a tale about his work making him forget, if he thought it would wash. If that old woman had come in a bit sooner, she'd have boxed the brazen things' ears who made the oblivion, instead of poor Alfred's.
> D. H. LAWRENCE *Sons and Lovers*, 1913

Lethe In Greek mythology, Lethe was the river of forgetfulness, a river in the underworld, Hades, whose water when drunk made the souls of the dead forget their past life. ▶ *See special entry* ☐ HADES *on p. 172.*

> Minds that have been unhinged from their old faith and love, have perhaps sought this Lethean influence of exile, in which the past becomes dreamy because its symbols have all vanished, and the present too is dreamy because it is linked with no memories.
> GEORGE ELIOT *Silas Marner*, 1861

> In his seven-year voyage on the waters of Lethe (the north island of New Zealand

actually), Gordon forgot all about Eliza (not to mention us) and came back with a different wife altogether.
KATE ATKINSON *Human Croquet*, 1997

Lotus-eaters In Homer's *Odyssey*, the Lotus-eaters are a people who live only on the lotus fruit. When some of Odysseus' men taste the fruit they lose their desire to return home and 'their only wish was to linger there with the Lotus-eaters, to feed on the fruit and put aside all thought of a voyage home'. ▶ *See special entry* ☐ ODYSSEUS *on p. 283.*

Mnemosyne Mnemosyne was the mother of the Muses and goddess of memory in Greek mythology.

But the sight of old Mr Woodford standing in the entrance archway snapped his line of thought before Mnemosyne could come to his aid.
CHESTER HIMES *Headwaiter*, 1937

Nepenthe Nepenthe was an Egyptian drug believed to make people forget their sorrows. In the *Odyssey* it is used by Helen and described as 'a drug that dispelled all grief and anger and banished remembrance of every trouble'.

'I know not Lethe nor Nepenthe,' remarked he; 'but I have learned many new secrets in the wilderness, and here is one of them . . . '
NATHANIEL HAWTHORNE *The Scarlet Letter*, 1850

Proust Marcel Proust (1871–1922) was a French novelist, whose masterpiece, *À la Recherche du Temps Perdu* (1913–27), is usually translated into English with the title *Remembrance of Things Past*. In exploring its theme of recovery of the lost past, the novel repeatedly describes how a sensory stimulus in the present, such as the taste of a madeleine cake dipped into tea, can act as the unconscious trigger for a flood of memories from the past, especially from childhood.

Sam stood stropping his razor, and steam rose invitingly, with a kind of Proustian richness of evocation—so many such happy days, so much assurance of position, order, calm, civilization, out of the copper jug he had brought with him.
JOHN FOWLES *The French Lieutenant's Woman*, 1969

Settle for the cordite. That I am certain of. My nose tells the truth. I am the Proust of filth.
JOHN LAWTON *Black Out*, 1995

Messengers

This theme includes messengers, both human and divine, and carriers of mail, such as WELLS FARGO and the PONY EXPRESS. PHEIDIPPIDES and PAUL REVERE are both associated with carrying vital messages in wartime. ▶ *See also* **Communication**.

Gabriel In the Bible, Gabriel is one of the archangels closest to God and the one used by God to deliver revelations to men and women. Gabriel revealed to Zacharias that his wife Elisabeth would bear a son to be called John, who grew up to be John the Baptist (Luke 1: 8–20). He also appeared to the Virgin Mary to tell her that she would bear a son to be called Jesus (Luke 1: 26–38). In Islam, Gabriel appeared to Muhammad and revealed the Koran to him.

> 'She has revelations. All this stuff about Darcy's Utopia is dictated to her, she claims, by a kind of shining cloud.' I laughed. I couldn't help it. 'Like God appearing to Moses in a burning bush, or the Archangel Gabriel to Mohammed as a shining pillar?' I asked.
> FAY WELDON *Darcy's Utopia*, 1990

Hermes ▶ *See* MERCURY.

Iris In Greek mythology, Iris was the goddess of the rainbow, who acted as a messenger of the gods.

Mercury In Roman mythology, Mercury was the messenger of the gods, identified with the Greek Hermes. He is pictured as a herald wearing winged sandals which enable him to travel swiftly. Anyone who acts as a messenger can be described as doing the work of Mercury.

> The affair of the carriage was arranged by Mr Harding, who acted as Mercury between the two ladies.
> ANTHONY TROLLOPE *Barchester Towers*, 1857

> Viscount Trimingham said I was like Mercury—I run errands.
> L. P. HARTLEY *The Go-Between*, 1953

Pacolet In the early French romance *Valentine and Orson*, Pacolet is a dwarf messenger whose winged horse, made of wood, carries him instantly wherever he wishes.

> 'And pray how long, Miss Ashton,' said her mother, ironically, 'are we to wait the return of your Pacolet—your fairy messenger—since our humble couriers of flesh and blood could not be trusted in this matter?'
> WALTER SCOTT *The Bride of Lammermoor*, 1819

Pheidippides Pheidippides (5th century BC) was an Athenian messenger who was sent from Athens to Sparta to ask for help after the Persian landing at Marathon in 490. He is said to have covered 150 miles on foot in two days. The long-distance race known as the marathon derives its name from a later story that, after the Greeks had defeated the Persians, a messenger ran the twenty-two miles from Marathon to Athens with news of the Greek victory, but fell dead on arrival.

Pony Express The Pony Express was a system of mail delivery in the US in 1860–1. Relays of horse-riders covered a total distance of 1,800 miles between St Joseph in Missouri and Sacramento in California.

Paul Revere Paul Revere (1735–1818) was an American patriot, one of the demonstrators involved in the Boston Tea Party of 1773. In 1775 he rode through the night from Boston to Lexington to warn American revolutionaries of the approach of British troops.

Mrs Louderer drove, and Tam O'Shanter and Paul Revere were snails compared to us.
ELINORE PRUITT STEWART *Letters of a Woman Homesteader*, 1914

Wells Fargo Wells Fargo was the name of a US transportation company, founded in 1852, which carried mail to and from the newly developed West, founded a San Francisco bank, and later ran a stagecoach service.

Mischief

This theme comprises naughty or trouble-making children and mischievous spirits. ▶ *See also* **Cunning**, **Evil**.

....

Anansie Anansie is the trickster spider in West African folk tradition. In some stories he tricks the supreme god into allowing disease to enter the world.

Cautioning members about the 'Brer Anansi' arithmetic, Leacock asked them not to reduce the usefulness of the Federation because 'trade unions are becoming weaker in these parts.'
News (St. Vincent), 1994

Dennis the Menace Dennis the Menace is a trouble-making boy who first appeared in the British comic *The Beano* in 1951. Dennis has a shock of thick black hear, wears a red and black striped jumper, and has a dog called Gnasher. A character of the same name has appeared in US comic strips also since 1951, though he is blond and younger than the British Dennis.

Robin Goodfellow ▶ *See* PUCK.

Just William William Brown is the unruly, usually grubby-faced, schoolboy created by Richmal Crompton and featuring in a series of books (1922–70). Though well-intentioned, William has the knack of unwittingly producing chaos. He is the leader of a gang of friends known as the Outlaws.

Detective Superintendent Honeyman was a small, tidy man with a pale face and a repressed expression, which always made Slider think of Richmal Crompton's William scrubbed clean and pressed into his Eton suit for a party he didn't want to go to.
CYNTHIA HARROD-EAGLES *Blood Lines*, 1996

Loki In Scandinavian mythology, Loki was the god of mischief and discord. He caused the death of Balder by tricking the blind god Hodur into throwing at him a dart of mistletoe, the only thing that could harm Balder, who instantly died. Loki was punished by the gods by being bound beneath the earth.

On one flank Singer is a trickster, a prankster, a Loki, a Puck.
CYNTHIA OZICK *Art & Ardour*, 1984

Meddlesome Matty Meddlesome Matty appears in *Original Poems, for Infant*

Minds by Several Young Persons, a collection of poems for children by Ann and Jane Taylor and others, published in two volumes in 1804 and 1805. Matilda 'though a pleasant child' in other respects is a compulsive meddler.

> His passion for playing the literary Meddlesome Mattie was aroused.
> ROBERTSON DAVIES *The Deptford Trilogy*, 1975

Puck   Puck, also called Robin Goodfellow, is a mischievous sprite or goblin of popular folklore believed to roam the English countryside, playing pranks. He appears as a character in Shakespeare's *A Midsummer Night's Dream* (1600), where he is described as a 'shrewd and knavish sprite' who delights in frightening village girls, preventing butter from being churned, and leading people off the right path at night.

> She couldn't tell if he was smiling, or if his face always wore that puckish grin.
> DOUG BEASON and KEVIN J. ANDERSON *Assemblers of Infinity*, 1993

Miserliness

Among the literary skinflints who appear below, it is probably Ebenezer **SCROOGE** who is most readily used as an archetype of miserliness. Financial prudence is covered within the theme **Thrift**. ▶ *See also* **Wealth**.

Jean Paul Getty   Jean Paul Getty (1892–1976), an American oil billionaire, is more usually alluded to for his wealth, but he was also renowned for keeping a public pay phone for the use of his guests.

Harpagan   In Molière's comedy *L'Avare* (*The Miser*), Harpagon is a miser who, when forced to choose between the casket containing his treasure and the woman he loves, chooses the treasure.

> In old-fashioned times, an 'independence' was hardly ever made without a little miserliness as a condition, and you would have found that quality in every provincial district, combined with characters as various as the fruits from which we can extract acid. The true Harpagons were always marked and exceptional characters.
> GEORGE ELIOT *The Mill on the Floss*, 1860

Silas Marner   In George Eliot's novel *Silas Marner* (1861), Silas is a bitter, antisocial linen-weaver whose only consolation is the growing pile of gold coins he has accumulated. Only after his gold is stolen does he find new meaning to his life when he adopts, and comes to love, an abandoned village girl called Eppie.

> To answer this question, we must examine the intricate tapestry of meteorological dreariness, Silas Marnerian stinginess, Uriah Heepian creepiness and Ron Woodian slovenliness that coalesce to make Great Britain.
> *Spy*, 1993

Scrooge   The miserly Ebenezer Scrooge is a character in Dickens's *A Christmas*

Carol (1843), whose parsimony and lack of charity are most apparent at Christmas. On the night of Christmas Eve he is visited by the ghost of his late partner, Marley, and sees three spirits, the Ghost of Christmas Past, the Ghost of Christmas Present, and the Ghost of Christmas Yet to Come. These three ghosts allow Scrooge to revisit his childhood and to discover how he is now perceived by other people and the uncharitable response to his own death that the future holds. The experience shocks him into generous behaviour on Christmas Day. His name has come to denote any mean or tight-fisted person.

> Our genetic makeup permits a wide range of behaviours—from Ebenezer Scrooge before to Ebenezer Scrooge after. I do not believe that the miser hoards through opportunistic genes or that the philanthropist gives because nature endowed him with more than the normal complement of altruist genes.
> STEPHEN JAY GOULD *Ever Since Darwin*, 1978

> When, earlier this year, I decided finally to put my foot down and to ban party bags from my younger son's fifth birthday, there was a certain amount of agonising in the household over whether or not I would go down in local lore as the Scrooge of the reception class.
> *The Independent*, 1996

Shylock Shylock is the Jewish moneylender in Shakespeare's *The Merchant of Venice* (1600). He lends the sum of 3,000 ducats to the merchant, Antonio, on condition that if the sum is not repaid by the agreed date, Antonio will forfeit a pound of his flesh. When the time to pay falls due, Antonio is unable to refund Shylock, who insists on being paid his pound of flesh. Portia, the wife of Bassanio for whom Antonio has borrowed the money, disguises herself as a lawyer and conducts Bassanio's defence. When a plea for mercy fails, she outwits Shylock by insisting that, although he can take his pound of flesh, he must not spill a drop of blood in the process, since the bond allows only for flesh, not blood. Someone demanding or extorting repayment can be described as a Shylock.

> 'You want paying, that's what you want,' she said quietly, 'I know.' She produced her purse from somewhere and opened it. 'How much do you want, you little Shylock?'
> L. P. HARTLEY *The Go-Between*, 1953

Modernity

These allusions can all be used to describe an ultra-modern, futuristic office or other environment. ▶ *See also* **Outdatedness**, **Past**.

....

James Bond James Bond is the secret agent hero of the novels by Ian Fleming. Many of the films based on Fleming's novels include a scene in the villain's vast, often subterranean, high-tech headquarters or control room.

> In the far distance, stand large buildings where, presumably, workers in white space

suits wander around in rooms that look like something out of a James Bond film.
BILL BRYSON *The Lost Continent*, 1989

Nautilus Jules Verne's adventure classic *Twenty Thousand Leagues Under the Sea* (1869) describes the adventures on board the *Nautilus*, a giant submarine commanded by the mysterious Captain Nemo. The ship contains a library, drawing-room and dining-room, all elegantly furnished, and the captain's room, in which hang all manner of instruments for navigating the ship, including thermometers, barometers, hygrometers, chronometers, and manometers.

> Gwyn stepped into his study. . . . Here the two cultures, Gwyn believed, were attractively reconciled: the bright flame of human inquiry, plus lots of gadgets. Give Gwyn a palatinate smoking-jacket, as opposed to a pair of tailored jeans and a lumberjack shirt, and he could be Captain Nemo, taking his seat at the futuristic bridge of the sumptuous Nautilus.
> MARTIN AMIS *The Information*, 1995

Starship Enterprise In the TV science fiction series *Star Trek*, and the subsequent films, the Starship USS *Enterprise* is the spaceship captained by Captains Kirk and Picard. The bridge is dominated by computer monitors and other futuristic technology.

> Christ, the office will look like the Starship Enterprise by the time you've finished with it. Didn't we leaver Maher and Malcolm to escape the tyranny of computers?
> MARTIN EDWARDS *Yesterday's Papers*, 1994

Monsters

The quotations at **MINOTAUR** illustrate the writers' precision in their choice of allusion: both references exploit the details of the legend. Although the monsters grouped here mainly originate in folklore, legend, and gothic literature, some have become more widely known through their cinematic incarnations. ▶ *See also* **Evil**, **Fear**, **Horror**, **Large Size**.

....

Baba Yaga Baba Yaga is a witch in Russian folklore who lives in a house that stands on chicken legs, flies about in a mortar using a pestle for an oar, and eats children.

Dracula The famous Count Dracula, created by Bram Stoker in his 1879 novel *Dracula*, is a vampire, one of the Un-dead, who lies in his coffin by day and comes out at night to suck blood from the necks of his victims. He can only be destroyed by having a stake driven through his heart while he is resting.

> I knew I'd gone as white as a piece of chalk since coming in as if I'd been got at by a Dracula-vampire.
> ALAN SILLITOE *The Loneliness of the Long Distance Runner*, 1959

> 'I know some people believed that, coming from a family as old as ours, he should

have chosen a British girl. I've never been of that narrow way of thinking. We should always be ready to welcome new blood of the right kind.' I just stopped myself saying Count Dracula would agree with her.
GILLIAN LINSCOTT *Stage Fright*, 1994

Frankenstein Baron Victor Frankenstein is a character in Mary Shelley's gothic novel *Frankenstein* (1818). He is a scientist who creates a grotesque manlike monster out of corpses and brings it to life. The monster, unnamed in the novel but itself often now referred to as Frankenstein, eventually turns on its creator and brings about his ruin. A Frankenstein's monster (or a Frankenstein) is a creation that goes out of control so that it becomes frightening to, or destroys, its creator.

> Senator McDull contended that the government could not carry such a debt and remain a democratic nation, so he campaigned tirelessly and zealously against it. 'It will destroy the very foundations of the government which we are fighting to preserve,' he argued. 'Like a Frankenstein monster it would turn upon us and destroy us.'
> CHESTER HIMES *A Modern Fable*, 1939

Godzilla Godzilla is a huge dinosaur-like monster who was aroused from the sea-bed by an atomic explosion and threatened to destroy Tokyo. He first appeared in a 1955 film, and later in several sequels.

> I should have realised something unusual was up when my cat Hortense shot in from the garden with a tail like a flue-brush and disappeared into the cupboard in the upstairs loo. This was uncharacteristic of a cat who is second cousin to Godzilla.
> MICHÈLE BAILEY *Haycastle's Cricket*, 1996

Grendel The Old English poem *Beowulf* tells of the adventures of the Geatish hero Beowulf, and how he fights and destroys the monster Grendel, who has been terrorizing the court of the Danish king Hrothgar, and then Grendel's mother, who comes after him to avenge her son's death.

> The nest was like Grendel's lair: a bed of penguin feathers, broken eggshells, dried egg membranes, tufts of moss, decaying food, a few bones, excrement.
> D. G. CAMPBELL *Crystal Desert*, 1992

Minotaur In Greek mythology, the Minotaur was the creature with a bull's head and a man's body that was the offspring of Pasiphae (wife of King Minos of Crete) and a bull with which she fell in love. The Minotaur, confined in the Labyrinth built by Daedalus, devoured human flesh. Seven youths and seven girls from Athens were sacrificed to the Minotaur annually, until it was eventually killed by Theseus, with the aid of Ariadne.

> They sat opposite each other, on either side of the fire—the monumental matron . . . and the young, slim girl, so fresh, so virginal, so ignorant, with all the pathos of an unsuspecting victim about to be sacrificed to the minotaur of Time.
> ARNOLD BENNETT *The Old Wives' Tale*, 1908

> She remembered the sadness she had earlier noticed in his eyes. He was a man who had known both good and evil. She was sure of it now. His mind was a dark labyrinth, intricate and convoluted, with a Minotaur of some kind crouching at the core. There was something frightening as well as fascinating about him.
> JOHN SPENCER HILL *The Last Castrato*, 1995

Moses and the Book of Exodus

Exodus is the second book of the Bible, relating the departure of the Israelites under the leadership of Moses from their slavery in Egypt and their journey towards the promised land of Canaan.

Moses was born in Egypt at a time when Pharaoh had decreed that all male Hebrew children were to be killed at birth. After hiding the infant Moses for three months, his mother placed him in a basket made out of bulrushes amid the reeds of the Nile. He was discovered by Pharaoh's daughter, who took pity on him and decided to raise him as her own child, using the child's own mother for a nurse. So Moses was brought up at the court of Pharaoh.

When a grown man, he killed an Egyptian overseer whom he had seen beating a Hebrew, and was forced to flee to the land of Midian. Here Moses lived as a shepherd in the desert, until after forty years he was called by God, who appeared in the form of a bush that was in flames but was not consumed by them. God told him to return to Egypt and demand that Pharaoh set his people free.

Moses was accompanied by his brother Aaron, who acted as his spokesman. Together they confronted Pharaoh with God's demand 'Let my people go'. When Pharaoh persisted in refusing to allow Moses to lead the Israelites out of Egypt, God sent ten plagues to afflict the Egyptians: turning the Nile to blood; frogs; gnats; flies; death of cattle; boils; hail; locusts; darkness; and death of the Egyptian first-born. Pharaoh finally freed the Israelites from bondage and Moses led them out of Egypt. Changing his mind, Pharaoh sent his army in pursuit. The Israelites passed through the Red Sea, which God caused to part for them, but the pursuing Egyptians were drowned when the waters closed on them.

After three months the Israelites reached Mount Sinai. They camped at the foot of the mountain and it was at the top that God gave Moses the Ten Commandments. Led by Moses, the Israelites wandered through the Sinai desert for another forty years until they finally reached the borders of Canaan. Moses did not enter the Promised Land himself, but was allowed a glimpse of it from Mount Pisgah before he died, at the age of 120.

Throughout this book there are references to Moses and to the events described in the Book of Exodus.

▶ *See* ARK OF THE COVENANT *at* **Importance**
    BURNING BUSH *at* **Appearing**
    CANAAN *at* **Idyllic Places**
    DAN TO BEERSHEBA *at* **Distance**
    EXODUS *at* **Departure** *and* **Movement**

> **Moses and the Book of Exodus** *continued*

▶ *See* GOSHEN *at* **Abundance and Plenty, Light,** *and* **Idyllic Places**
HOLY OF HOLIES *at* **Importance**
ISRAELITES *at* **Poverty**
LAND OF MILK AND HONEY *at* **Abundance and Plenty**
MANNA *at* **Food and Drink**
MIRIAM *at* **Music**
MOSES *at* **Freedom, Safety and Protection**
NINTH PLAGUE OF EGYPT *at* **Darkness**
PHARAOH *at* **Dictators and Tyrants**
PLAGUES OF EGYPT *at* **Suffering**
PROMISED LAND *at* **Idyllic Places**
RED SEA *at* **Movement**.

Moustaches

As with images of hairstyles, those of distinctive types of moustache tend to be reinforced by the cinema, posters, and other forms of mass communication or popular culture. ▶ *See also* **Hair.**

Hitler Adolf Hitler (1889-1945) was the Austrian-born Nazi leader who became chancellor of Germany 1933-45. His face, with the little black moustache, is a familiar image in 20th-century iconography.

> 'You aren't going to shave off my moustache?' I spoke with feeling, for I loved the little thing. I had tended it in sickness and in health, raising it with unremitting care from a sort of half-baked or Hitler smudge to its present robust and dapper condition.
> P. G. WODEHOUSE *Laughing Gas*, 1936

> Dr Carl Moss was a big burly Jew with a Hitler moustache, pop eyes and the calmness of a glacier.
> RAYMOND CHANDLER *The High Window*, 1943

Lord Kitchener The face of the 1st Earl Kitchener of Khartoum (1850-1916), known as Lord Kitchener, is well known from a famous recruiting poster during the First World War that carried his large-moustached face and pointing finger above the slogan 'Your country needs you!'

> They stood next to each other, like pieces opposing each other on a chess board, oblivious of the interest of the ageing porter with the Lord Kitchener moustache.
> PETER CAREY *Illywhacker*, 1985

Adolph Menjou Adolph Menjou (1890-1963) was a dapper French-

American film actor who was always elegantly dressed and had a curly moustache, turned up at the ends.

> We took a Hungarian Airlines plane from East Berlin. The pilot had a handlebar mustache. He looked like Adolph Menjou. He smoked a Cuban cigar while the plane was being fueled. When we took off, there was no talk of fastening seat belts.
> KURT VONNEGUT *Slaughterhouse 5*, 1969

Zapata Emiliano Zapata (1879–1919) was a Mexican revolutionary leader who fought successive federal governments to repossess expropriated village lands. Probably because of the appearance of Marlon Brando in the film *Viva Zapata* (1952), the term 'Zapata' can be used to describe a type of moustache in which the two ends extend downwards to the chin.

> 'What's happened to your gaucho moustache?' 'I . . . I shaved it off.' 'Why?' 'In view of certain comments, your Honour, passed in the Station. It wasn't a gaucho. More a Viva Zapata, actually.'
> JOHN MORTIMER *Rumpole of the Bailey*, 1978

> He knew—he even hoped—this was probably false (and felt the formation, across his upper lip, of a Zapata moustache of sweat).
> MARTIN AMIS *London Fields*, 1989

Movement

This theme deals with the movement of people, particularly a large mass of people, from one place to another. Other accounts of journeys and voyages can be found within the closely related theme **Travellers and Wanderers**. ▶ *See also* **Ascent and Descent, Immobility**.

Birnam Wood In Shakespeare's *Macbeth* (1623), the witches assure Macbeth that he will not be defeated until Birnam Wood comes to Dunsinane Castle. Later, when the army of Malcolm and Macduff passes through Birnam Wood, Malcolm instructs every man to cut a branch, and under the camouflage of this 'leafy screen' the army marches on Dunsinane, giving the impression that the wood is indeed moving.

> When the curtain call came, some of the girls who had been serving as ushers rushed to the footlights like Birnam Wood moving to Dunsinane, loaded with bouquets.
> ROBERTSON DAVIES *The Manticore*, 1972

Exodus Exodus is the second book of the Bible, relating the departure of the Israelites under the leadership of Moses from their slavery in Egypt and their journey towards the promised land of Canaan. The word 'exodus' can now be applied to any mass departure of people, especially emigrants. ▶ *See special entry* □ **MOSES AND THE BOOK OF EXODUS** *on p. 264*.

Huns The Huns were a warlike nomadic people who originated in north-central Asia and overran Europe in the 4th–5th centuries. Led by Attila, they inflicted devastation on the eastern Roman empire, invaded Gaul, and threatened Rome.

> Various veterans had told him tales. Some talked of gray, bewhiskered hordes who were advancing with relentless curses and chewing tobacco with unspeakable valor; tremendous bodies of fierce soldiery who were sweeping along like the Huns.
> STEPHEN CRANE *The Red Badge of Courage*, 1895

Moses ▶ *See* RED SEA.

Muhammad According to legend, Muhammad (sometimes called Mahomet) summoned Mount Safa to come to him after being challenged to demonstrate his miraculous powers. When it failed to do so he attributed this to the mercy of Allah, for if it had come it would have crushed him and the bystanders. If the mountain would not come to him, said Muhammad, then he would go to the mountain. This phrase can be used in any context when a person or thing that you want is unwilling or unable to come to you, as a result of which you must make an effort to go yourself.

> The child scrambled up to the top of the wall and called again and again; but finding this of no avail, apparently made up his mind, like Mahomet, to go to the mountain, since the mountain would not come to him.
> ANNE BRONTË *The Tenant of Wildfell Hall*, 1848

Noah's dove In the biblical account of the flood, Noah sent out birds from the ark in the hope that they would bring back evidence of dry land: 'At the end of forty days Noah opened the window of the ark which he had made, and sent forth a raven; and it went to and fro until the waters were dried up from the earth. Then he sent forth a dove from him, to see if the waters had subsided from the face of the ground' (Gen. 8: 6-8). ▶ *See special entry* ☐ NOAH AND THE FLOOD *on p. 279*.

> He had research assistants, in fluctuating numbers, whom he despatched like Noah's doves and ravens into the libraries of the world, clutching numbered slips of paper, like cloakroom tickets or luncheon vouchers, each containing a query, a half-line of possible quotation, a proper name to be located.
> A. S. BYATT *Possession*, 1990

Peripatetic The word 'Peripatetic' (literally 'walking around') came to be applied to Aristotle's school at the Lyceum on account of his habit of walking up and down while teaching his students.

> A large group of buyers stood round the auctioneer, or followed him when, between his pauses, he wandered on from one lot of plantation-produce to another, like some philosopher of the Peripatetic school delivering his lectures in the shady groves of the Lyceum.
> THOMAS HARDY *The Woodlanders*, 1887

Red Sea According to the Old Testament Book of Exodus, Moses led the Israelites out of Egypt and through the Red Sea, which God caused to part for them to go through. The pursuing Egyptians were drowned when the waters closed on them. ▶ *See special entry* ☐ MOSES AND THE BOOK OF EXODUS *on p. 264*.

> They hurry after the Plenipo. Moses going through the Red Sea, thinks Gideon of Elliott's progress through the crowd.
> TIMOTHY MO *An Insular Possession*, 1986

Murderers

Most of the figures below are associated with the murder of a spouse, parent, or sibling. Other murderers are covered at the themes **Criminals** and **Outlaws**. ▶ *See also* **Evil**.

....

Bluebeard Bluebeard is a character in a tale by Charles Perrault's in the collection *Histoires et contes du temps passé* (1697). In the story, Bluebeard has a reputation for marrying women who subsequently disappear. He leaves his most recent wife, Fatima, in charge of their house while he is away, instructing her not to open a locked room in the house, although he leaves her the key. Overcome with curiosity, she opens the room, only to discover the bodies of his previous wives. Any murderous husband can be described as a Bluebeard.

> 'It'll be his wife,' said the woman, peering at the Doctor in awe and horror. 'Murdered his wife! You Bluebeard!'
> HUGH LOFTING *Dr Dolittle's Circus*, 1924

> This is one of the strangest cases this court may ever have heard. The case of a Bluebeard who kept his wife a virtual prisoner in their flat in Muswell Hill.
> JOHN MORTIMER *Rumpole of the Bailey*, 1978

Lizzie Borden Lizzie Borden (1860–1927) was an American woman acquitted in 1893 of the charge of murdering her father and stepmother the previous year. Nevertheless, many believed that she had killed them, giving rise to a popular rhyme:

'Lizzie Borden took an axe
And gave her mother forty whacks;
When she saw what she had done
She gave her father forty-one!'

Cain In the Bible, Cain was the eldest son of Adam and Eve. He killed his younger brother Abel, thus becoming, in the Judaeo-Christian tradition, the first recorded murderer. As a punishment for this crime, Cain was cursed to wander the earth for the rest of his life (Gen. 4: 2–16). God put a mark on him to indicate that no-one should kill him and thus shorten the punishment. The phrase 'mark of Cain' has come to stand for the sign of a murderer. ▶ *See special entry* □ **CAIN** *on p. 44.*

> Marks may not even have been his real name, she said; it should have been Mark, for the Mark of Cain, as he had a murderous look about him.
> MARGARET ATWOOD *Alias Grace*, 1996

Clytemnestra In Greek mythology, Clytemnestra was the wife of Agamemnon, king of Mycenae. During her husband's absence at the Trojan War she had taken a lover, Aegisthus. On Agamemnon's triumphant return from the war she and Aegisthus laid a trap for him, murdering him in his bath.

Dr Crippen Hawley Harvey Crippen (1862–1910), known as Dr Crippen, was an American-born British murderer. Crippen poisoned his wife, burying her remains in the cellar of their London home, for which crime he was later hanged. He nearly escaped, boarding an Atlantic liner with his secretary, but the suspicious captain of the ship contacted the police by radiotelegraphy, the first use of this medium in a criminal investigation, and he was apprehended.

> Gary's client, the Dr Crippen of fund management, was delirious with joy.
> REBECCA TINSLEY *Settlement Day*, 1994

Jack the Ripper Jack the Ripper is the name given to an unidentified English 19th-century murderer. From August to November 1888 at least six prostitutes were found brutally murdered, their bodies mutilated. The crimes were never solved, but the authorities received taunting notes from a person calling himself Jack the Ripper, who claimed to be the murderer.

Music

As can be seen below, there are a variety of classical and biblical figures who typify the sound of beautiful music-making. The idea of music so sweet that it can relieve a melancholic mood or charm wild animals seems to be a universal one.

Aeolian According to Greek mythology, Aeolus was a mortal who lived on the floating island of Aeolia. He was a friend of the gods, and Zeus gave him control of the winds. Aeolus was later regarded as the god of the winds. He has given his name to the Aeolian harp, a musical instrument that produces sounds when the wind passes through it. Aeolian music is thus music produced by the effect of the wind.

> Time to drink in life's sunshine—time to listen to the Aeolian music that the wind of God draws from the human heart-strings around us.
> JEROME K. JEROME *Three Men in a Boat*, 1889

Apollo In Greek mythology, Apollo, the son of Zeus and Leto, was the god of music and poetic inspiration. Although references are sometimes to the lute of Apollo, his instrument was in fact a seven-stringed lyre. ▶ *See special entry* ☐ **APOLLO** *on p. 15*.

> For valour, is not love a Hercules,
> Still climbing trees in the Hesperides?
> Subtle as Sphinx; as sweet and musical
> As bright Apollo's lute, strung with his hair.
> WILLIAM SHAKESPEARE *Love's Labour's Lost*, 1595
>
> I do not admire the tones of the concertina, as a rule; but oh! how beautiful the music seemed to us both then—far, far more beautiful than the voice of Orpheus or the lute of Apollo.
> JEROME K. JEROME *Three Men in a Boat*, 1889

Arcadia A mountainous district in the Peloponnese of southern Greece, Arcadia (or Arcady) in poetic fantasy represents an idealized region of rural contentment. It is the setting of Philip Sidney's prose romance *Arcadia*, published posthumously in 1590. The association of Arcadia with beautiful music may derive from the fact that Arcadia was the home of Pan, the god who frequented mountains, caves, and lonely places, and invented the Pan pipes.

> Oak would pipe with Arcadian sweetness.
> THOMAS HARDY *Far From the Madding Crowd*, 1874

> It was as though the wood and the strings of the orchestra played Arcadian melodies and in the bass the drums, softly but with forboding, beat a grim tattoo.
> W. SOMERSET MAUGHAM *The Painted Veil*, 1925

> I was wondering half-idly if there was a goat-herd with them, and if, perhaps, they had strayed from the troop, when I thought I heard, far away over the cliff-top, the sound of a pipe. Even as I heard it and strained my ears to catch the notes, it faded, and I dismissed it as fancy. The thin, broken stave had been purely pastoral, something from a myth of Arcady, nymphs and shepherds and Pan-pipes and green valleys.
> MARY STEWART *My Brother Michael*, 1960

Beethoven Ludwig van Beethoven (1770–1827) was a German composer, born in Bonn. His music is often said to have bridged the classical and romantic traditions. Although he began to be afflicted with deafness in 1802, an affliction which became total by 1817, his musical output was prodigious.

> I soon found out why Old Chong had retired from teaching piano. He was deaf. 'Like Beethoven!' he shouted to me. 'We're both listening only in our head!'
> AMY TAN *Two Kinds*, 1989

Blondel According to tradition, Blondel de Nesle, a French poet, was the friend of Richard I of England, known as Richard Coeur de Lion. Blondel set out to find the king after Richard, returning from the Holy Land in 1192, was imprisoned by the duke of Austria. Sitting under the castle window, Blondel sang a song in French that he and the king had composed together. Half-way through, Richard took the song up himself to reveal his whereabouts.

> Two ground-floor windows, three upstairs, all shuttered. . . . I felt like Blondel beneath Richard Coeur-de-Lion's window; but not even able to pass messages by song.
> JOHN FOWLES *The Magus*, 1977

St Cecilia St Cecilia (2nd or 3rd century) was a Roman martyr. According to legend, she took a vow of celibacy but was forced to marry a Roman. She converted her husband to Christianity, and both were martyred. She is frequently pictured playing the organ and is the patron saint of church music.

> They have combined their voices, such as they are, even if they could be supposed to be 'parlor voices', 'thin voices', 'poor voices' or any other kind of voice than St. Cecilia's own.
> *Harper's Monthly*, 1880

David David (d. *c*.962 BC) was king of Judah and Israel *c*.1000–*c*.962 BC. He was noted as a musician and is traditionally regarded as the author of the psalms. According to the Old Testament, the young David relieved King Saul's melancholy by playing the lyre: 'And whenever the evil spirit from God was upon Saul, David took the lyre and played it with his hand; so Saul was

refreshed, and was well, and the evil spirit departed from him' (1 Sam. 16:
23). ▶ *See special entry* ☐ **DAVID** *on p. 90.*

> That night when Beth played to Mr. Laurence in the twilight, Laurie, standing in the
> shadow of the curtain, listened to the little David, whose simple music always
> quieted his moody spirit.
> LOUISA M. ALCOTT *Little Women*, 1868

Euterpe Euterpe was one of the nine Muses in Greek mythology, associated
especially with lyric poetry and flute playing.

> He offended her by refusing to go into a dance-hall on the grounds that the music
> was so bad that it was a sacrilege against St Cecilia and Euterpe and Terpsichore,
> when she just wanted to go in and lose her unhappiness in dancing.
> LOUIS DE BERNIÈRES *Señor Vivo and the Coca Lord*, 1991

Gabriel According to the Bible, Gabriel was the archangel who acted as God's
messenger and foretold the birth of Jesus to Mary. In Christian tradition, he is
thought to be the archangel who will blow the trumpet to announce the
general resurrection: 'For the Lord himself shall descend from heaven with a
shout, with the voice of the archangel, and with the trump of God: and the
dead in Christ shall rise first' (1 Thess. 4: 16).

> Blowing harder than Gabriel's trumpet, it is, and enough snow already down to bury
> a whale.
> JOAN AIKEN *The Whispering Mountain*, 1968

Minerva Minerva, the Roman goddess of handicrafts and wisdom, was also
believed to have invented the flute. While she was playing the flute before Juno
and Venus, the goddesses laughed at the distorted face she made while blow-
ing the instrument, which caused Minerva to throw it indignantly away.

> 'Thank you very much', Said Oak, in the modest tone good manners demanded,
> thinking, however, that he would never let Bathsheba see him playing the flute; in
> this resolve showing a discretion equal to that related of its sagacious inventress, the
> divine Minerva herself.
> THOMAS HARDY *Far from the Madding Crowd*, 1874

Miriam In the Bible, Miriam was the sister of Aaron, who went with Moses
when he led his people across the Red Sea and out of Egypt. When they had
crossed the Red Sea safely, Miriam 'took up a timbrel in her hand' and said
'Sing ye to the Lord, for he hath triumphed gloriously' (Exod. 15: 20-1). This
is sometimes referred to as the 'Song of Miriam'. Miriam can therefore be
alluded to as someone who sings, especially for joy. (The reference to hiding
her little brother in the Forster quotation depends upon the assumption that it
was Miriam who was the sister who watched the infant Moses in his basket in
the bulrushes in Exod. 2. 4.) ▶ *See special entry* ☐ **MOSES AND THE BOOK OF EXODUS** *on
p. 264.*

> A new little brother is a valuable sentimental asset to a schoolgirl, and her school
> was then passing through an acute phase of baby-worship. Happy the girl who had
> her quiver full of them, who kissed them when she left home in the morning, who
> had the right to extricate them from mail-carts in the interval, who dangled them at
> tea ere they retired to rest! That one might sing the unwritten song of Miriam,
> blessed above all schoolgirls, who was allowed to hide her baby brother in a squashy
> place, where none but herself could find him!
> E. M. FORSTER *Where Angels Fear to Tread*, 1905

Orpheus According to Greek mythology, Orpheus was a poet who sang and played with his lyre so beautifully that he could charm wild beasts. He married Eurydice, a dryad, and when she died from a snake bite Orpheus went down to the Underworld to try to recover her. He used his music to persuade the goddess Persephone to let Eurydice return with him, to which Persephone agreed on condition that Orpheus should not look back as he left the Under-world. Violating this condition to assure himself that Eurydice was still follow-ing him, Orpheus did look back, whereupon she vanished forever.

> Orpheus with his lute made trees,
> And the mountain-tops that freeze,
> Bow themselves when he did sing.
> WILLIAM SHAKESPEARE *Henry VIII*, 1613

> 'What do you think of our modern Orpheus?' 'If you're referring to Tolley, I don't think he can conduct Beethoven.'
> ALDOUS HUXLEY *Point Counter Point*, 1928

Pan Pan was the Greek god of shepherds and flocks, a native of rural Arcadia. Usually represented as having a human torso and arms but the legs, ears, and horns of a goat, Pan frequented mountains, caves, and lonely places. On one occasion he pursued the nymph Syrinx, who escaped him by turning into a reed. As he could not distinguish her from among all the other reeds, he cut several and made them into the Pan pipes which still bear his name. Pan can be alluded to as a player of sweet music.

> He could cut cunning little baskets out of cherry-stones, could make grotesque faces on hickory nuts, or odd-jumping figures out of elder-pith, and he was a very Pan in the manufacture of whistles of all sizes and sorts.
> HARRIET BEECHER STOWE *Uncle Tom's Cabin*, 1852

Quasimodo Quasimodo is the ugly, deaf, hunchbacked bell-ringer of the Cath-edral of Notre Dame in Victor Hugo's novel *Notre-Dame de Paris*, usually trans-lated as *The Hunchback of Notre Dame* (1831). The popular image of the character has been largely formed by Charles Laughton's 1939 film portrayal in which a hauntingly pitiful Quasimodo finds comfort and solace in the bell tower of the cathedral with his beloved bells.

> Birchfield Place had relied, like most stately homes, on a state-of-the-art mix of hard-wired detectors on doors and windows, passive infrared detectors at all key points and pressure-activated alert pads in front of any items of significance. Given the fail-safes I'd put in place, I couldn't for the life of me see how anyone could have got through my system undetected without setting off enough bells to drive Quasimodo completely round the bend.
> VAL MCDERMID *Clean Break*, 1995

Terpsichore Terpsichore was one of the nine Muses in Greek mythology, asso-ciated especially with dancing and the singing that accompanies it.

Tin-Pan Alley Tin-Pan Alley is the name given to a district in New York (28th Street, between 5th Avenue and Broadway) where many songwriters, ar-rangers, and publishers of popular music were based. The district gave its name to the American popular music industry between the late 1880s and the mid-20th century.

> All this litter lies amid the desert's natural untidiness, the endless scatter of bony apparently lifeless scrub that speckles it from horizon to horizon. The only clear

spaces are the tracks along which wind the occasional line of trucks or armoured cars, the 'Tin-Pan Alleys' defined by petrol cans.
PENELOPE LIVELY *Moon Tiger*, 1988

Mystery

This theme concentrates on occurrences and stories that cannot easily be explained or understood. A number of famous real-life mysteries, such as the Bermuda Triangle and the Mary Celeste, involve unexplained disappearances. These have been included within the theme **Disappearance and Absence**. ▶ *See also* **Concealment** *and* **Disclosure**.

....

Agatha Christie Agatha Christie (1890–1976) was an English writer of detective fiction, in particular 'whodunits'. Many of her novels feature one or other of her two most famous creations, the Belgian Hercule Poirot and Miss Jane Marple.

> Gripping stuff from the Parisian software developer. An Agatha Christie-style murder mystery using the fantastic Cinematique system.
> *CU Amiga*, 1992

Wilkie Collins Wilkie Collins (1824–89) was an English novelist, chiefly remembered as the writer of the first full-length detective stories in English, notably *The Woman in White* (1860) and *The Moonstone* (1868).

> Suppose the servant really killed the master, or suppose the master isn't really dead, or suppose the master is dressed up as the servant, or suppose the servant is buried for the master; invent what Wilkie Collins's tragedy you like, and you still have not explained a candle without a candlestick, or why an elderly gentleman of good family should habitually spill snuff on the piano.
> G. K. CHESTERTON *The Honour of Israel Gow*, 1911

Eleusinian mysteries The Eleusinian mysteries were the most famous of the 'mysteries', or religious ceremonies, of ancient Greece, held at the city of Eleusis near Athens. They were dedicated to the corn goddess Demeter and her daughter Persephone, and were thought to celebrate the annual cycle of death and rebirth in nature. Such mysteries or mystery religions were secret forms of worship, and were available only to people who had been specially initiated.

> Been playing golf? I thought so. Wonderful game, so fascinating, such a challenge, as much intellectual as physical, I understand. I wish I had time for it myself. One feels so much at sea when talk turns to mashie-niblicks, cleeks, and mid-irons. Quite an Eleusinian mystery.
> LOUIS DE BERNIÈRES *Captain Corelli's Mandolin*, 1994

House of Usher 'The Fall of the House of Usher' (1839) is the title of one of Edgar Allan Poe's *Tales of Mystery and Imagination*, set in an eerie mansion in the vault of which Roderick Usher has buried his sister alive.

She motioned frantically to him not to make a noise. . . . 'My dear, why all this Fall-of-the-House-of-Usher stuff?'
STELLA GIBBONS *Cold Comfort Farm*, 1932

My hair is hanging along my cheeks, my skirt is swaddling about me. I can feel the cold damp of my brow. I must look like something out of 'The Fall of the House of Usher.'
DOROTHY PARKER *The Waltz*, 1944

Mona Lisa *Mona Lisa* is the title of a painting by Leonardo da Vinci, perhaps the most famous painting in the world. The painting is also known as *La Gioconda* because the sitter was the wife of Francesco di Bartolommeo del Giocondo di Zandi. Her enigmatic smile has become one of the most famous images in Western art.

She declined to express an opinion, answering only with a Mona Lisa smile.
A. S. BYATT *Possession*, 1990

Sphinx In Greek mythology, the Sphinx was a winged monster with a woman's head and a lion's body. It lay outside Thebes and asked travellers a riddle, killing anyone who failed to solve it. When Oedipus gave the right answer, the Sphinx killed itself. The sphinx asked what animal walked on four legs in the morning, two legs at noon, and three in the evening. Oedipus correctly answered that man crawls on all fours as a child, walks on two legs as an adult, and is supported by a stick in old age. In ancient Egypt, a sphinx was a stone figure with a lion's body and the head of a man, ram, or hawk. An enigmatic or mysterious person can be described as a sphinx or as sphinx-like.

This human mind wrote history, and this must read it. The Sphynx must solve her own riddle.
RALPH WALDO EMERSON 'History' in *Essays*, 1841

Ian persevered, hauling the rib cage up and down, trying to get air into the lungs mechanically. Stephen and I watched in silence for what seemed a very long time. I didn't try to stop him. Stopping had to be his own decision. And I suppose some quality in Malcolm's total lack of response finally convinced him, because he reluctantly laid the arms down to rest, and turned to us a blank and Sphinx-like face.
DICK FRANCIS *Trial Run*, 1978

He was without doubt the Raj's most sphynxian figure, the guardian of the secret of its final and most decisive deed.
The Observer, 1997

Udolpho Ann Radcliffe's *The Mysteries of Udolpho* (1794) is a gothic novel set at the end of the 16th century. Most of the action takes place in the sinister castle of Udolpho in which the sliding panels, secret passages, and apparently supernatural occurrences are all typical of the genre.

Was there a 'secret' at Bly—a mystery of Udolpho or an insane, an unmentionable relative kept in unsuspected confinement?
HENRY JAMES *The Turn of the Screw*, 1898

Veil of Isis Isis was an ancient Egyptian nature and fertility goddess, wife and sister of Osiris and mother of Horus. She is usually depicted as a woman with cow's horns, between which was the disc of the sun. Statues of her often carried the inscription: 'I am all that is, has been, and shall be, and none among mortals has lifted my veil'. Hence the phrase 'to lift the veil of Isis' means to penetrate a great mystery.

> That Fitzpiers would allow himself to look for a moment on any other creature than Grace filled Melbury with grief and astonishment. In the simple life he had led it had scarcely occurred to him that after marriage a man might be faithless. That he could sweep to the heights of Mrs. Charmond's position, lift the veil of Isis, so to speak, would have amazed Melbury by its audacity if he had not suspected encouragement from that quarter.
> THOMAS HARDY *The Woodlanders*, 1887

Naivety

This theme covers the idea of innocent simplicity or unworldliness, often associated with childhood. ▶ *See also* **Innocence, Wholesomeness**.

....

Arcadia A mountainous district in the Peloponnese of southern Greece, Arcadia in poetic fantasy represents an idealized region of innocence, simplicity, and rural contentment.

> What he wanted was an English bride of ancient lineage and Arcadian innocence.
> EDITH WHARTON *The Buccaneers*, 1938

> Some, who did not regard themselves as preachers, appeared to think of themselves as simple, shrewd old farmers; they wrote nostalgically of a bygone Arcadian era, when everybody was near enough to the farm to have a little manure on his boots.
> ROBERTSON DAVIES *Leaven of Malice*, 1954

> Their little valley in the mountains was densely wooded and well watered, and the guerrillas live a life of Arcadian simplicity and leisure, only venturing forth when one of them had a good idea about what to blow up next.
> LOUIS DE BERNIÈRES *The War of Don Emmanuel's Nether Parts*, 1990

Babes in the Wood Originally 'The Children in the Wood', an old ballad written in 1595, 'The Babes in the Wood' is the story of two infants, brother and sister, abandoned in a wood by their uncle who wants their property. The children die and a robin covers them with leaves. The wicked uncle loses his own sons and his property, and dies in jail. A reference to the Babes in the Wood usually signifies innocent suffering or unsophisticated innocence.

> He could not deplore . . . that he had not a blank page to offer his bride in exchange for the unblemished one she was to give to him. He could not get away from the fact that if he had been brought up as she had they would have been no more fit to find their way about than the Babes in the Wood.
> EDITH WHARTON *The Age of Innocence*, 1920

Enid Blyton Enid Blyton (1897–1968) was a prolific author of children's books, including the 'Noddy' books, series such as 'The Famous Five' and 'The Secret Seven', and school stories such as the 'Malory Towers' series. The majority of her books were published in the 1940s and 1950s, and they can now be alluded to as depicting an era of idealized childhood innocence.

Candide Candide is the naive young hero of Voltaire's satire *Candide*, published in 1759. Accompanied by his tutor, Pangloss, who assures him repeatedly that 'all is for the best in the best of all possible worlds', Candide has many adventures and suffers many mishaps, often as a result of his ingenuous and trusting nature. Candide has become synonymous with youthful innocence and naivety.

> He plunged into the heart of Mayfair. The mist thickened, not so much to obscure all but sufficiently to give what he passed a slightly dreamlike quality; as if he was a visitor from another world, a Candide who could see nothing but obvious explanations.
> JOHN FOWLES *The French Lieutenant's Woman*, 1969

Dickensian The novels of Charles Dickens contain many young heroines whose kind, sweet, open nature contrasts with the harshness and wickedness of the world around them.

> Hilda kept up all the appearance of Dickensian young-girlishness, but contrived at the same time to make all the advances, create all the opportunites and lead the conversation into all the properly amorous channels.
> ALDOUS HUXLEY *Point Counter Point*, 1928

Happy Hooligan The Happy Hooligan was an American comic strip character who appeared from 1900 to 1932, an Irish tramp with a red nose and a tin can for a hat. He was an innocent and an unconquerable optimist despite the fact that his attempts to help himself and others often ended with his falling into the hands of the law.

> Never tol' you 'bout him. Looked like Happy Hooligan. Harmless kinda fella. Always was gonna make a break. Fellas all called him Hooligan.
> JOHN STEINBECK *The Grapes of Wrath*, 1939

Daisy Miller Daisy Miller is the heroine of a short novel with the same name by Henry James, published in 1879. She is a naive young American woman who is touring Europe with her mother and brother and finds herself in compromising situations because of her trusting nature and ignorance of social conventions. When she is found viewing the Colosseum one evening with a young Italian and no chaperone, she is criticized for her lack of social decorum. She returns hurt to her hotel, where she contracts malaria and is dead within a week.

Miranda Miranda is the beautiful and innocent daughter of Prospero in Shakespeare's play *The Tempest* (1623). Brought up on a deserted island with only her father for company, Miranda has never seen the deceit, wickedness, and corruption of the world, and on becoming acquainted with men who have been shipwrecked on the island she utters the famous lines:

'How beauteous mankind is! O brave new world,
That has such people in't!'

Ironically, the people she is speaking of are the very ones who deposed and exiled Prospero many years before. Miranda's name can suggest a young innocent unaware of the darker side of human nature and full of wonder and joy at the world and human society.

She found herself standing, in the character of hostess, face to face with a man she had never seen before—moreover, looking at him with a Miranda-like curiosity and interest that she had never yet bestowed on a mortal.

THOMAS HARDY *A Pair of Blue Eyes*, 1873

He escorted them to their box with a sort of pompous humility, waving his fat jewelled hands, and talking at the top of his voice. Dorian Gray loathed him more than ever. He felt as if he had come to look for Miranda and had been met by Caliban.

OSCAR WILDE *The Picture of Dorian Gray*, 1891

noble savage ▶ *See* ROUSSEAU.

Arthur Rackham Arthur Rackham (1867–1939) was a British illustrator. Because he is best remembered for his illustrations of well-known children's books, his name has become associated with the idea of childhood innocence and simplicity.

How could this Arthur Rackham nymph, his English Alice, be Pete Curtis's 'very good lay'?

CHRISTOPHER J. KOCH *The Year of Living Dangerously*, 1978

Rousseau Jean-Jacques Rousseau (1712–78) was a French philosopher and writer, born in Switzerland. His belief in the fundamental goodness of human nature and the corrupting influence of modern society is most clearly expressed in his descriptions of the 'noble savage', an idealized man living a natural life, free from the influences of civilization.

She was all loving to me at first, but then she got sarcastic and said she couldn't stand the sight of me. 'Here comes the noble savage,' she called out when I came home, and used longer words I didn't know the meaning of when I asked her where my tea was.

ALAN SILLITOE *The Loneliness of the Long Distance Runner*, 1959

Shirley Temple Shirley Temple (b. 1928) was an American child star, appearing in a succession of films in the 1930s, in which she sang and danced. She is remembered for her sweet, innocent good looks, especially her mop of golden curls.

He made a chirping noise and patted his knee invitingly, and Hortense immediately leapt on his lap and starting rubbing her head against his chest, purring like mad. He tickled her under the chin, murmuring idiotic blandishments into her black velvet ears. 'Don't be fooled by the Shirley Temple routine,' I said sourly. 'That cat is four kilos of cunning in a black fur coat.'

MICHÈLE BAILEY *Haycastle's Cricket*, 1996

Beside McConnachie's massive bulk, Fizz looked like a kitten smiling up at a Rottweiler. Sun-bleached tendrils of hair framed a face that made Shirley Temple look depraved and her denim-blue eyes rested on Duncan with absolute faith and affection.

JOYCE HELM *Foreign Body*, 1997

Waltons *The Waltons* was the title of an American television series (1972–81). It portrayed the life and problems of a family living in the rural Appalachian mountains at the time of the Great Depression. Although they were poor and suffered hardships, the Waltons remained a close, devoutly religious family, supportive of each other, and their name has come to represent an idealized view of a family life in which simple, innocent pleasures are enjoyed together.

> Stewart's early life, I learnt, was rather sweet and Waltons-like. He loved his father and mother. He went to church.
> WILLIAM LEITH in *The Observer*, 1997

Wild Boy of Aveyron The Wild Boy of Aveyron was an 11-year-old boy who was found running wild and naked in a wood near Aveyron in the south of France in the early part of the 19th century. The French physician Jean Itard tried to train and educate him and published an account of his experiences in *Rapports sur le Sauvage d'Aveyron* (1807). 'The Wild Boy of Aveyron' can be used to describe someone who has absolutely no experience of the ways of the world, society, or people.

> 'People divide writers into two categories,' she went on, deeply embarrassed by his silence. 'Those who are preternaturally wise, and those who are preternaturally naïve, as if they had no real experience to go on. I belong in the latter category,' she added, flushing at the truth of what she said. 'Like the Wild Boy of the Aveyron.'
> ANITA BROOKNER *Hotel du Lac*, 1984

Nakedness

There is a common theme to the stories of **ACTAEON**, **LADY GODIVA**, and **SUSANNA**, that of a man catching sight of a naked woman and ultimately being punished for it.

Actaeon In Greek mythology, Actaeon was a hunter who, because he accidentally saw Artemis (the virgin goddess of the hunt) bathing naked, was changed into a stag and torn to pieces by his own hounds.

Adam and Eve Adam and Eve lived naked in the Garden of Eden 'and were not ashamed' (Gen. 2: 25). Only after they ate the forbidden fruit from the tree of knowledge did they become self-conscious: 'Then the eyes of both were opened, and they knew they were naked; and they sewed fig leaves together and made themselves aprons.' ▶ *See special entry* ☐ **ADAM AND EVE** *on p. 5*.

> So there they were, naked as Adam and Eve.
> PHILIP ROTH *Epstein*, 1959

Lady Godiva Lady Godiva (d. 1080) was an English noblewoman, wife of Leofric, earl of Mercia. According to a 13th-century legend, she rode naked through the market-place of Coventry, clothed only in her long, golden hair, to persuade her husband to reduce the heavy taxes he had imposed on the people. All the townspeople stayed indoors and shut up their windows, except for Tom the Tailor, who looked at her through a window as she rode past (and was consequently known thereafter as Peeping Tom). He was struck blind as a consequence of his action.

> To say I was cold would be like saying Lady Godiva was underdressed.
> KATHY REICHS *Death du Jour*, 1999

Susanna In the Apocrypha, Susanna was a beautiful and virtuous woman of Babylon who was lusted after by two elders who secretly spied on her when she was bathing naked in a garden. When she subsequently repelled their advances, they falsely accused her of adultery and she was condemned to death. She was proved innocent by Daniel, who exposed inconsistencies in her accusers' accounts, and the elders were themselves executed.

> 'I went for a walk. It was warm and I was aching to be outside.' 'Did you leave the island?' 'No. I hiked to the pond and wound up skinny-dipping.' 'Anybody see you?' 'You mean paddling around in my birthday suit like Susanna and the Elders?'
> MICHAEL MEWSHAW *True Crime*, 1991

Noah and the Flood

The Book of Genesis in the Bible relates how God, seeing that 'the wickedness of man was great in the earth', decided to send a great flood to destroy the whole of mankind. Only Noah 'found grace in the eyes of the Lord' and so God warned him of the coming flood and instructed him to build an ark (a large boat about 133 m. long) in which to save himself and his family and also two of every species of creature on the earth. Apart from those in the ark, all inhabitants of the earth drowned in the Flood, which lasted for forty days and forty nights. The floodwaters rose high with the ark on their surface, and after the rain stopped gradually receded. The ark came to rest on Mount Ararat. Noah sent out birds from the ark in the hope they would bring back evidence of dry land. First he sent out a raven, and then a dove. After a week the dove returned with an olive leaf so Noah knew the waters had completely receded. When Noah and his family were able to walk again on land, God blessed them, saying: 'Be fruitful, and multiply, and replenish the earth.' God promised Noah that he would never again send a flood to destroy all living things and produced a rainbow as 'a token of a covenant between me and the earth'. Noah lived to the age of 950 and his sons, Ham, Shem, and Japhet, became the ancestors of many nations.

Throughout this book there are references to the story of Noah and the Flood.

▶ *See* ARK *at* **Outdatedness**
  FLOOD *at* **Danger** *and* **Past**
  NOAH *at* **Escape and Survival** *and* **Past**
  NOAH'S DOVE *at* **Movement**
  NOAH'S FLOOD *at* **Water**.

Nonconformity

Most of the entries below typify the rebelliousness of adolescence. The other major strand is the idea of heresy. ▶ *See also* **Conformity** *and* **Rebellion and Disobedience**.

Bohemia Bohemia was formerly a central European kingdom, now forming the western part of the Czech Republic. The name is often applied to any district frequented by artists, writers, and other socially unconventional people.

> This, in the social order, is the diversion, the permitted diversion, that your original race has devised: a kind of superior Bohemia, where one may be respectable without being bored.
> EDITH WHARTON *The Custom of the Country*, 1913

Holden Caulfield Holden Caulfield is the adolescent hero of J. D. Salinger's novel *The Catcher in the Rye*, published in 1951. He is an archetypal adolescent rebel, full of angst and disaffection and rebelling against all that is 'phoney', 'corny', and 'old bull'. After being expelled from an expensive private school, Caulfield goes to New York but after a series of unsuccessful adventures, including an encounter with a prostitute and an abortive reunion with an old girlfriend, he is forced to go back home and is sent by his parents for psychiatric treatment.

James Dean James Dean (1931-55) was an American actor best remembered for his role in the 1955 film *Rebel Without a Cause*. The film opened just weeks after Dean's death in a car crash, and he became strongly associated with the character he played in the film, a confused, rebellious, and self-destructive adolescent.

> The one riding shotgun had the James Dean look, dark, wavy hair over a fuck-you pout. They thought they were badasses and I was an old fart. That made two surprises they had coming.
> JOHN DUNNING *The Bookman's Wake*, 1995

Huckleberry Finn Huckleberry Finn is the main character in *The Adventures of Huckleberry Finn* (1884) by Mark Twain. He is a spirited, self-reliant, and unconventional boy who fakes his own death in order to escape from his drunken, brutal father and he has many adventures.

Galileo Galileo Galilei (1564-1642) was an Italian astronomer and physicist. He accepted the Copernican system, a theory stating that the sun is the centre of the universe, although it was strenuously opposed by the Catholic Church. Under threat of torture he publicly recanted his views, but is later reported as declaring 'Eppur si muove' ('but it does move'). His name is now associated with the defiant upholding of scientific truth and integrity.

> Remember Galilyo. Always stick up for yourself!
> V. S. NAIPAUL *A House for Mr Biswas*, 1969

But a man does not attain the status of Galileo merely because he is persecuted; he must also be right.

STEPHEN JAY GOULD *Ever Since Darwin*, 1977

Rebel Without a Cause ▶ *See* JAMES DEAN.

Tom Sawyer Tom Sawyer is the hero of Mark Twain's novel *The Adventures of Tom Sawyer*, published in 1876. Tom is a bold, independent, mischievous boy who rejects the conventional values of hard work, honesty, and cleanliness.

I was the winner, Miss Illinois. All I could do was laugh. I'm twenty-two, standing up there in a borrowed evening gown, thinking: What am I doing here? This is like Tom Sawyer becomes an altar boy.

STUDS TERKEL *American Dreams: Lost and Found*, 1980

Socrates Socrates (469–399 BC) was a Greek philosopher concerned with the search for truth and reason in questions of morality and ethics. Through his discourse and careful questioning, he challenged accepted beliefs and attempted to expose foolishness, irrationality, and error. He wrote nothing himself, but is known through the works of one of his pupils, Plato, who recorded his dialogues and teachings. Socrates was charged with impiety and corrupting the young, and condemned to die by taking hemlock.

I hope that you will be glad to know that I have decided to make my own dowry. I think that my father has no sense of shame, and sometimes I feel very angry with him for refusing the very thing that is normal for every other girl. He is not fair because he is too rational. He thinks that he is a Socrates who can fly in the face of custom.

LOUIS DE BERNIÈRES *Captain Corelli's Mandolin*, 1994

Noses

As can be seen from the entries below, notable noses tend to be either long, large, or bright red.

Bardolph In Shakespeare's *Henry IV* and *Henry V*, Bardolph is one of Falstaff's companions. His bright red nose inspires Falstaff to say to him: 'Thou art our admiral, thou bearest the lantern in the poop, but 'tis in the nose of thee; thou art the Knight of the Burning Lamp' (*Henry IV*, *Part 1*).

If beauty is a matter of fashion, how is it that wrinkled skin, grey hair, hairy backs and Bardolph-like noses have never been 'in fashion'?

Frontiers: Penguin Popular Science, 1994

Cyrano de Bergerac Cyrano de Bergerac (1619–55) was a French soldier, duellist, and writer of comedies and satires. He is supposed to have had a prodigiously long nose. He is celebrated in the play that bears his name by Edmond Rostand (1897).

Derek Griffiths is a young coloured comedian with a face like crushed rubber . . . and a hooter to rival Cyrano de Bergerac.
The Times, 1972

Jimmy Durante Jimmy Durante (1893–1980) was a US pianist-comedian who had a long career in vaudeville, nightclubs, and films. He referred to his splendid nose as his 'schnozzola'.

Even Jimmy Durante's famous schnozzola, which Keith had had a chance to see up close . . . was a peanut compared to Sperry's.
VINCE STANTON *Keith Partridge Master Spy*, 1971

Pinocchio Pinocchio is the puppet hero of the story *Le Avventure di Pinocchio* (1883) by G. Lorenzini, who wrote under the name of Carlo Collodi. Made by the carpenter Geppetto, Pinocchio is a wooden puppet that comes to life and eventually becomes a real boy. His nose magically grows longer every time he tells a lie.

Also, the characters can be transformed or 'morphed' on screen. For example, when Mario tells lies to a viewer, his nose can be made to grow like Pinocchio's.
New Scientist, 1993

Rudolph According to the popular song, Rudolph the Red-nosed Reindeer, despite being ridiculed by the other reindeer because of his shiny red nose, is chosen to pull Santa Claus's sledge.

Odysseus

Odysseus, known to the Romans as Ulysses, is one of the best-known figures in Greek mythology. He was the king of Ithaca, son of Laertes and Anticlea. His wife was Penelope and his son Telemachus. Odysseus was noted in particular for his guile.

As one of the suitors of Helen of Troy, Odysseus proposed that when she married, she and whoever she finally chose to be her husband would be defended by all the other suitors. She chose Menelaus, and when she was abducted by Paris, the Greeks mounted an expedition to bring her back from Troy. Odysseus was a member of this expedition.

Homer's epic poem the *Odyssey* is an account of Odysseus' ten-year journey home to Ithaca after the fall of Troy. His adventures included encounters with:

the Lotus-Eaters, whose lotus flowers when eaten made Odysseus' crew lose all memory of past events and their homes and made them wish never to leave;

the one-eyed giant Polyphemus, one of the Cyclopes, who was eventually blinded by Odysseus and his men;

the Laestrygones, a tribe of cannibalistic giants;

Circe, a beautiful enchantress who lived on the island of Aeaea. After she turned half his men into swine, Odysseus protected himself with the mythical herb moly and forced her to break the spell and restore his men into human form. Odysseus was detained on Circe's island for a year;

the Sirens, whose singing had the power to lure sailors to their deaths on dangerous rocks. Odysseus had himself tied to the mast of his ship in order to hear their song safely, having first ordered his crew to plug their ears with wax;

the nymph Calypso, who detained him on her island for seven years. He refused her offer to make him immortal.

When Odysseus finally reached Ithaca after an absence of twenty years, he found Penelope beseiged by suitors. Waiting patiently and faithfully for her husband to return home, Penelope had warded off these suitors by promising that she would marry only when she had finished the piece of weaving that she had started. Each night she unravelled the work that she had done during the day. Athene disguised Odysseus as an old beggar so that he could arrive secretly at his palace. Assisted by his son Telemachus and two faithful retainers, he slew all the suitors and was finally reunited with Penelope.

Throughout this book there are references to the *Odyssey* and to many of the figures and episodes mentioned in the above account.

▶ *See* CALYPSO *at* **Danger**
    CIRCE *at* **Danger***,* **Magic***, and* **Sirens**
    LOTUS-EATERS *at* **Happiness** *and* **Memory**

Odysseus *continued*

▶ *See* ODYSSEUS *at* **Destiny and Luck, Disguise, Returning,** *and* **Travellers and Wanderers**
ODYSSEY *at* **Travellers and Wanderers**
PENELOPE *at* **Patience**
SIRENS *at* **Danger, Destruction,** *and* **Sirens**.

Old Age

By far the most commonly used archetype of longevity is **METHUSELAH**. The idea of longevity is coupled in a number of cases below with that of immortality. This appears to be generally presented as a curse rather than a blessing. The figure of **ELLI** from Norse mythology is unusual in representing old age as an overpowering force, quite distinct from the physical frailty that it confers. ▶ *See also* **Youth**.

....

Cumaean Sibyl The Cumaean Sibyl was the prophetess (or Sibyl) of the Temple of Apollo at Cumae in south Italy who guided Aeneas through the underworld in the *Aeneid*. It was said that in her youth Apollo had been enamoured of her and had offered to give her whatever she wished. She took a handful of sand and asked to live as many years as there were grains of sand in her hand, but she forgot to ask for health and youth as well. So she grew old and decrepit and had already lived 700 years by the time Aeneas encountered her. To equal the number of sand grains she still had another three centuries to live.

Elli In a story from Scandinavian mythology, Elli is the personification of old age who in the form of Utgard, Loki's foster-mother, a toothless old crone, wrestles the mighty Thor to the ground. The episode illustrates the point that no one, not even the strongest, can withstand old age.

Father Time Father Time is the personification of time, usually depicted as an old bearded man with a scythe and hourglass.

> Little Father Time is what they always called me. It is a nickname; because I look so aged, they say.
> THOMAS HARDY *Jude the Obscure*, 1895

> The American portion of our community 'saw in' the greatest day of their national calendar in a fittingly splendid style and circumstances today a fortnight previous. As our issue of that very date proceeded to the press some days earlier, not possessing mastery of Old Father Time and his scythe, we were unavoidably prevented from commenting on those happy rites.
> TIMOTHY MO *An Insular Possession*, 1986

Father William In Lewis Carroll's *Alice's Adventures in Wonderland* (1865), the Caterpillar instructs Alice to recite the poem 'You are old, Father William'. She begins:

'You are old, Father William,' the young man said,
'And your hair has become very white;
And yet you incessantly stand on your head—
Do you think, at your age, it is right?'

Father William is also sprightly enough to turn back-somersaults and balance an eel on the end of his nose. ▶ *See special entry* ▢ **ALICE IN WONDERLAND** *on p. 10.*

Jared According to the Book of Genesis, Jared was one of the patriarchs and is supposed to have lived to be 962 years old (Gen. 5: 20). He was the grandfather of Methuselah (who lived seven years longer).

> It was one of those faces which convey less the idea of so many years as its age than of so much experience as its store. The number of their years may have adequately summed up Jared, Mahalaleel, and the rest of the antediluvians, but the age of a modern man is to be measured by the intensity of his history.
> THOMAS HARDY *The Return of the Native*, 1880

Mahalalel According to the Book of Genesis, Mahalalel was one of the patriarchs and lived to the age of 895 (Gen. 5: 17). He was the great-grandfather of Methuselah.

Methuselah In the Bible, Methuselah was the oldest of the patriarchs, grandfather of Noah. He is supposed to have lived 969 years (Gen. 5: 27). His name is now proverbial for longevity.

> I would rather travel with an excursion party of Methuselahs than have to be changing ships and comrades constantly, as people do who travel in the ordinary way.
> MARK TWAIN *An Innocent Abroad*, 1869

> The throne, being lowered, was placed before the altar as it has been every year since the oldest Methuselah in the habitation can remember.
> JULIAN BARNES *A History of the World in 10½ Chapters*, 1989

> So around Richard were arrayed a few tattoo-bespattered warthogs and authentic thirty-year-old Methuselahs fingering their earrings as they applied themselves to their tabloids.
> MARTIN AMIS *The Information*, 1995

Struldbrug In Jonathan Swift's *Gulliver's Travels* (1726), the Struldbrugs are inhabitants of Luggnagg, a race endowed with immortality but who become increasingly infirm and decrepit. After the age of 80 they are regarded as legally dead. The term can be used to describe a person who is incapacitated by age or infirmity. ▶ *See special entry* ▢ **GULLIVER'S TRAVELS** *on p. 171.*

> Yet which of us in his heart likes any of the Elizabethan dramatists except Shakespeare? Are they in reality anything else than literary Struldbrugs?
> SAMUEL BUTLER *The Way of All Flesh*, 1903

Tithonus In Greek mythology, Tithonus was a Trojan prince who was so beautiful that the goddess Aurora fell in love with him. She asked Zeus to grant him immortality but forgot to ask for eternal youth, and he became very old and decrepit although he talked perpetually. Tithonus pleaded with Aurora to remove him from this world and she changed him into a grasshopper.

Optimism

The allusions that make up this theme all typify a tendency to look on the bright side of a situation or event, or to expect the best possible outcome. A **MICAWBER** is confident that the future will turn out well; a **PANGLOSS** has the capacity to interpret any misfortunes favourably; a **POLLYANNA** is excessively cheerful. ▶ *See also* **Pessimism**.

....

Aunt Chloe In Harriet Beecher Stowe's *Uncle Tom's Cabin* (1851), Uncle Tom, a negro slave, is about to be sold to a slave trader and separated from his family. When his wife, Chloe, protests at how unfair this is, Uncle Tom urges her to look on the bright side: 'Let's think on our marcies!'. Aunt Chloe then repeats this advice to their children.

> We needed that lesson, and we won't forget it. If we do, you just say to us, as old Chloe did in Uncle Tom, 'Tink ob yer marcies, chillen! Tink ob yer marcies!'
> LOUISA M. ALCOTT *Little Women*, 1868

Mr Micawber Mr Wilkins Micawber, in Dickens's novel *David Copperfield* (1850), dreams up elaborate schemes for making money which never materialise, but remains undaunted, always hoping for something to 'turn up'.

> No good news yet, but I have a Micawber-faith that something will turn up.
> GEORGE ELIOT *Letters*, 1852

> 'Christ, no!' said Lomas angrily. 'All that crap about running his car off the road because his company was collapsing was just gutter press garbage. He beat Micawber for optimism!'
> REGINALD HILL *Child's Play*, 1987

Pangloss In Voltaire's *Candide* (1759), Dr Pangloss is the tutor who imbues Candide with his guiding philosophy that all is for the best in the best of all possible worlds. No matter what misfortunes they each suffer on their travels—disease, shipwreck, earthquake, flogging, and even attempted hanging and dissection—Pangloss confidently and complacently assures Candide that things could not be otherwise.

> Of course it would be naive to expect the Chancellor to draw attention to the failings of government policy. None the less, the rest of us notice them, and find them hard to reconcile with the distinctly Panglossian tone that Mr Clarke adopted yesterday.
> *The Daily Telegraph*, 1996

> Nor do the proposals even address the preoccupations of economic under-performance, poor training, underinvestment and growing inequality. Instead there is an explicit Panglossian view that all in the economic garden is flourishing.
> *The Observer*, 1997

Pollyanna The heroine of stories for children written by the American author Eleanor H. Porter (1868-1920), Pollyanna is a perpetually cheerful girl who teaches everyone she meets to play the 'just being glad' game: 'the game was to just find something about everything to be glad about—no matter what 'twas'. The name Pollyanna has come to stand for an unflagging (and often excessively saccharine) cheerfulness, an ability to find apparent cause for happiness in the most unpromising situations. The term often seems to be accompanied by a sense of apology, a recognition that such optimism may seem to others rather naive.

> Hadn't they been happy here? After all the bedsits and borrowed apartments and shitty pensiones, hadn't this been the dream place? . . . Had he lived in some Pollyanna blur all this time? Was he missing something? Was she miserable and bored? And worse?
> TIM WINTON *The Riders*, 1994

> I don't want to sound too Pollyanna-ish, but anyone getting autumn state-of-the-world blues might tune in to BBC Radio's 1995 Young Writers' Festival, First Bite, which has just ended its first week. If the pieces I heard are any gauge of the creativity to come, then the grounds for optimism are abundant.
> *The Guardian*, 1995

Oratory

This theme is chiefly concerned with the content of what is said. Another theme, **Speech**, deals with the distinctive qualities of a person's speaking voice.

....

Cato Marcus Porcius Cato (234-149 BC) was a Roman statesman, orator, and writer. After visiting Carthage in 175 BC, he was so impressed by the dangerous power of the Carthaginians that he afterwards ended every speech in the Senate with the words 'Delenda est Carthago' ('Carthage must be destroyed').

> Other editors, who were disguised neither as preachers nor as farmers, donned news-print togas and appeared as modern Catos, ready to shed the last drop of their ink in defence of those virtues which they believed to be the exclusive property of the party not in power.
> ROBERTSON DAVIES *Leaven of Malice*, 1954

Winston Churchill Winston Churchill (1874-1965) was a British politician and prime minister who led the coalition government during the Second World War. He was a gifted orator whose wartime speeches included many famous passages such as: 'We shall fight on the beaches, we shall fight on the landing grounds, we shall fight in the fields and in the streets, we shall fight in the hills; we shall never surrender.'

> 'Yes. The truth is the last repository of youth. And while a man is prepared to look truth in the face and see the mirror of his defects, let no man call him old' And

having delivered himself of this phrase so redolent of Churchill, Beaverbrook and possibly even Baldwin at his most meaningless, Lord Petrefact blew a smoke ring from his cigar with great expertise.
TOM SHARPE *Ancestral Vices*, 1980

Cicero Marcus Tullius Cicero (106–43 BC) was a Roman orator, statesman, and writer. Cicero's name and the adjective 'Ciceronian' are sometimes mentioned to suggest eloquence or oratory.

You'd scarce expect one of my age
To speak in public on the stage;
And if I chance to fall below
Demosthenes or Cicero,
Don't view me with a critic's eye,
But pass my imperfections by.
Large streams from little fountains flow,
Tall oaks from little acorns grow,
DAVID EVERETT *Lines Written for a School Declamation*, 1776

'Except', said Dalziel. And paused. There was something splendidly Ciceronian about Dalziel's 'except'. A single word left hanging, ungrammatically, in the air. And amidst the serried ranks of senators a small sough of intaken breath, then utter silence as they concentrated all their attention on the next eloquent weighty sentence to emerge from that eloquent weighty figure, statuesque at the centre of the tessellated floor. 'Except it's all balls', said Dalziel.
REGINALD HILL *A Pinch of Snuff*, 1978

Demosthenes Demosthenes (384–322 BC) was an Athenian orator and statesman, famous for a series of orations attacking the rising power of Philip of Macedon.

The explorer waxes eloquent as Antony, Demosthenes and the Speaker of the House all rolled into one.
T. CORAGHESSAN BOYLE *Water Music*, 1981

Hamlet Hamlet, a legendary prince of Denmark, is the hero of Shakespeare's play of the same name (1604). Hamlet is a tormented character, devastated by the death of his father and remarriage of his mother, and uncertain as to what action to take. He is obsessively introspective and delivers long soliloquies expressing his mental anguish, most famously his contemplation of suicide in the speech beginning 'To be, or not to be: that is the question'. Hamlet can be alluded to as someone who talks at length, expressing anxieties, doubts, or unhappiness.

I said I wanted to be best man, I said I wanted a church wedding. I went on about it. I started shouting. I came the Hamlets a bit. I was drunk at the time, if you must know.
JULIAN BARNES *Talking It Over*, 1991

John the Baptist John the Baptist was a Jewish preacher and prophet, who preached at the time of Jesus, demanding that his hearers repent of their sins and be baptized.

He was a John the Baptist who took ennoblement rather than repentance for his text.
THOMAS HARDY *The Return of the Native*, 1880

Abraham Lincoln Abraham Lincoln (1809–65) was an American Republican statesman and the 16th president of the United States from 1861 to 1865. He was noted for his eloquent speeches, including his speech of 1863 during the American Civil War at the dedication of the cemetery of those killed in the battle of Gettysburg, known as the Gettysburg Address.

Pericles Pericles (c.495–429 BC) was an Athenian statesman and general noted for his oratory.

> Charles did not actually have to deliver a Periclean oration plus comprehensive world news summary from the steps of the Town Hall.
> JOHN FOWLES *The French Lieutenant's Woman*, 1969

Sermon on the Mount In the Bible, the Sermon on the Mount is the long sermon given by Jesus to his disciples on a mountain, recorded in Matt. 5–7. It contains the Beatitudes and the Lord's Prayer. ▶ *See special entry* ❑ **JESUS** *on p. 223*.

> They listened to the words of the man in their midst, who was preaching, while they abstractedly pulled heather, stripped ferns, or tossed pebbles down the slope. This was the first of a series of moral lectures or Sermons on the Mount, which were to be delivered from the same place every Sunday afternoon as long as the fine weather lasted.
> THOMAS HARDY *The Return of the Native*, 1880

John Wesley John Wesley (1703–91) was an English preacher and one of the founders of Methodism. He travelled throughout Britain, preaching and gaining converts.

Outdatedness

Writers use the allusions below mostly to describe something, often a belief or attitude, that is so old-fashioned as to seem anachronistic. ▶ *See also* **Modernity**, **Past**.

Ark The Book of Genesis relates how God warned Noah that he was going to send a great flood to destroy the world and instructed him to build the Ark, a huge ship, to save his family and a pair of every species of animal and bird. References to Noah and expressions such as 'out of the Ark' can be used in connection with something that is very antiquated or out of date. ▶ *See special entry* ❑ **NOAH AND THE FLOOD** *on p. 279*.

> Then he sat down near his brief-case on the far side of a scarred oak table that came out of the Ark. Noah bought it second-hand.
> RAYMOND CHANDLER *The Long Goodbye*, 1953

> And it would balance her table, thought Mair, although that was hardly likely to have been a consideration. She despised the Noah's Ark convention which decreed

that a superfluous man, however unattractive or stupid, was acceptable; a superfluous woman, however witty and well-informed, a social embarrassment.
P. D. JAMES *Devices and Desires*, 1989

Dark Ages The term 'the Dark Ages' has sometimes been used to designate
the period in the West between the fall of the Roman Empire and the high
Middle Ages (that is, from about the 5th to the 11th century), so called because it used to be regarded as a time of relative unenlightenment and obscurity. In other contexts the term can suggest any unenlightened or ignorant
period or, when used humorously, any little-regarded period before the present. To 'live in the Dark Ages' is to be old-fashioned or prejudiced in one's
behaviour and attitudes.

> Jim's brow darkened. 'Look, old son. The law's no place for Luddites. We're in busi-
> ness, remember? We need to compete, to provide a decent service.' 'I haven't heard
> Kevin or Jeannie Walters complaining.' 'You've done a superb job, I'm the first to say
> so. But we must move with the times. We can't keep living in the Dark Ages.'
> MARTIN EDWARDS *Yesterday's Papers*, 1994

Forth Bridge The Forth Bridge is a cantilevered railway bridge built in 1890
across the Forth of Firth, linking Fife and Lothian on the east coast of Scotland.
The bridge requires constant maintenance and the expression 'painting the
Forth Bridge' alludes to the idea that as soon as workers have finished painting
the bridge, they immediately have to start repainting it.

> So a treaty that took ten years to negotiate is out of date before it even comes into
> force. What you might call the Forth Bridge theory of arms control.
> *BBC Radio 4*, 1995

Jurassic In geology, the Jurassic period lasted from about 213 to 144 million
years ago. Dinosaurs were abundant and attained their maximum size.
Popularized by Steven Spielberg's blockbuster dinosaur film *Jurassic Park*
(1992), the term is sometimes used informally to mean 'extremely out of date
or antiquated'.

> Call me Jurassic, but I couldn't care less about authenticity and immediacy when I'm
> engrossed in a good story.
> *The Observer*, 1997

Noah's Ark ▶ *See* ARK.

Rip Van Winkle The hero of Washington Irving's story *Rip Van Winkle*
(1820), Rip falls asleep in the Catskill mountains in New York State, and
wakes after twenty years to find the world completely changed. He has, for
example, completely missed the War of American Independence. Someone
who has remained oblivious to social and political changes over an extended
period can be said to be 'Rip-Van-Winkleish'.

> A political Rip van Winkle who had never watched television and read neither
> newspapers nor books until the last years of his term, Kim cannot believe, even less
> comprehend, this changed world. His only reading material until 1990 had been the
> Bible.
> ANDREW HIGGINS in *The Observer*, 1997

Outlaws

There is a long tradition of the criminal outlaw being celebrated as a folk hero, a tradition exemplified in Britain by such figures as **ROBIN HOOD** and **DICK TURPIN**, in Australia by **NED KELLY**, and in the US by **BILLY THE KID**, **BONNIE AND CLYDE**, and others. ▶ *See also* **Criminals, Murderers**.

....

Billy the Kid William H. Bonney (1859–81), known as Billy the Kid, was an American bandit and bank robber, involved in the Lincoln County cattle war in New Mexico. He allegedly committed his first murder at the age of 12. He was finally shot by sheriff Pat Garrett.

Bonnie and Clyde Bonnie Parker (1911–34) and Clyde Barrow (1909–34) were the leaders of a gang in the US who conducted a series of robberies and murders. They were shot dead in their car by police in Louisiana in 1934. A film presenting a rather glamorized version of their lives, *Bonnie and Clyde* (1967), ends with a memorable slow motion sequence depicting their bodies jerking and falling in a barrage of gunfire.

> Determined to defend her honour, the couple are soon on the run pursued by all and sundry—a modern day Bonnie and Clyde.
> *Film Focus*, 1994

> These wackos are attention-seekers. Serial show-offs. I mean, for Christ's sake, making out against a Slurpy Pup in front of a bunch of bullet-riddled shoppers! They think they're some kind of twenty-first-century Bonnie and Clyde.
> BEN ELTON *Popcorn*, 1996

Butch Cassidy Butch Cassidy, whose real name was Robert Leroy Parker (1866–1937?), formed a gang called the Wild Bunch which was responsible for numerous train and bank robberies and murders in the US. Cassidy and his partner, the Sundance Kid, went to South America and it is not known what then happened to them or how they died. The film *Butch Cassidy and the Sundance Kid* (1969), starring Paul Newman and Robert Redford, romanticized their lives and showed them dying by running from a hiding-place into a hail of bullets.

Jesse James Jesse Woodson James (1874–82) was a US bank and train robber who formed a gang of outlaws with his brother Frank. In 1882 a member of the gang shot Jesse in order to claim the reward on his head.

> But that night he hadn't pitied himself, he had been imbued with all the self-complacency of the man behind the gun. He had thought condescendingly of Jesse James—such a cheap, two-bit chiseler compared with himself.
> CHESTER HIMES *Prison Mass*, 1933

Ned Kelly Ned Kelly (1855–80) was an Australian outlaw whose father had been transported from Ireland. Kelly headed a four-man gang of bandits, notorious for killing three policemen in 1878. After an attempted train ambush,

Kelly tried to escape in a homemade suit of armour, but was apprehended and hanged.

> And you're game, Monny. Game as Ned Kelly, and you'll get on your feet again.
> ROBERTSON DAVIES *A Mixture of Frailties*, 1951

Robin Hood The legend of Robin Hood probably began in the 12th or 13th centuries and was well established by the 14th. According to the stories, Robin Hood was an English medieval outlaw, who is reputed to have lived with his band of fellow outlaws in Sherwood Forest in Nottinghamshire and robbed the rich to help the poor.

> The idea that she was among thieves prevented her from feeling any comfort in the revival of deference and attention towards her—all thieves, except Robin Hood, were wicked people.
> GEORGE ELIOT *The Mill on the Floss*, 1860

Dick Turpin Dick Turpin (1705-35) was a famous English highwayman who started his career as a smuggler and cattle and horse thief. He was hanged at York for horse-stealing and murder.

Past

The emphasis in this theme is on things that have existed for an extremely long time. This idea dovetails with that of being behind the times in some way, covered at the theme **Outdatedness**. ▶ *See also* **Modernity**.

Adam and Eve According to the account in the Book of Genesis, Adam and Eve were the first man and woman to inhabit the earth. Anything that is said to have existed before the time of Adam and Eve must therefore have existed in the very distant past. ▶ *See special entry* □ **ADAM AND EVE** *on p. 5*.

> Perhaps their ancestors had danced like this in the moonlight ages before Adam and Eve were so much as thought of.
> ALDOUS HUXLEY *Crome Yellow*, 1921

King Arthur According to tradition, Arthur was an ancient king of Britain, whose life and adventures have become the focus for many legends involving romance, magic, and chivalrous heroism. Stories about Arthur and his Knights of the Round Table were developed and written down by writers such as Chrétien de Troyes and Thomas Malory.

Beowulf Beowulf was a legendary Scandinavian hero celebrated in the Old English epic poem *Beowulf*. The poem describes Beowulf's killing first of the monster Grendel in King Hrothgar's hall, then of Grendel's mother in an underwater cave, and finally Beowulf's own death in combat with a dragon. The poem is set in the Scandinavia of the fifth and sixth centuries, but the poem itself is believed to have been composed in the eighth century.

We were on a beach, and someone . . . suggested we engrave our names in big letters upon the sand, then one of us would mount the promenade and photograph inscription plus inscriber. A cliché in Beowulf's time, I know, but you can't keep coming up with new games.
JULIAN BARNES *Talking It Over*, 1991

Caesars The name Caesar was used by successive Roman emperors from Augustus to Hadrian, becoming a title of the Roman rulers. The reigns of the Caesars spanned from 27 BC to AD 138.

Within the space of a mile from its outskirts every irregularity of the soil was prehistoric, every channel an undisturbed British trackway; not a sod having been turned there since the days of the Caesars.
THOMAS HARDY *Tess of the D'Urbervilles*, 1891

Creation The Creation is the name given to the account in the Book of Genesis of God's creating of the universe and the first people, Adam and Eve.

This has been a key principle of taxation since the Creation.
The Observer, 1997

Cyclopean In Greek mythology, the Cyclops (or Cyclopes) were a race of savage one-eyed giants who were said to have lived as shepherds or to have made thunderbolts for Zeus. The building of massive prehistoric structures was supposed to have been the work of the Cyclops.

From time to time he came upon the great smooth stones, remains of the ancient wall, which had once separated two kingdoms, and touching their smooth surfaces with his hands he could not help thinking that there was something eerie about them. They seemed left over from some forgotten Cyclopean age.
LAWRENCE DURRELL *White Eagles over Serbia*, 1957

Flood In the biblical story related in Genesis, God brought a great flood upon the earth in the time of Noah because of the wickedness of the human race. Apart from Noah, his family, and the animals he was instructed to shelter on the ark, all inhabitants of the earth perished in the Flood, which lasted for forty days and forty nights. There are similar flood myths in other traditions, such as in the epic Gilgamesh and in the Greek legend of Deucalion. References to a time before the Flood are intended to suggest the very distant past. ▶ *See special entry* ☐ **NOAH AND THE FLOOD** *on p. 279.*

Putting an arm around his sopping half-sleeve shirt, I say, 'I bet if you set your mind to it you could go back before the Flood.'
PHILIP ROTH *The Professor of Desire*, 1978

Merlin In Arthurian legend, Merlin was a wizard who served as a mentor and counsellor to King Arthur.

And truly if the glass has lain here for all these centuries past and has not lost its brightness, then it is more ancient and more wonderful than anything Merlin devised.
PETER ACKROYD *The House of Doctor Dee*, 1993

Noah According to the biblical story related in Genesis, Noah and his family were chosen by God to be spared when he sent a great flood to destroy all people, because of the wickedness of the human race. As with the Flood, references to the time of Noah can suggest the very distant past.

> What I have written so far makes us sound like something from a dubious old melodrama—which would not be far wrong, because the family is as old as Noah, and I suppose you could say it's as rotten as a waterlogged Ark.
> MARY STEWART *Touch Not the Cat*, 1976

Patience

Two meanings of 'patience' are covered below: the calm endurance of hardship or suffering and the capacity for calm, self-possessed waiting.

Enoch Arden In Tennyson's poem of the same name (1864), Enoch Arden is shipwrecked with two companions. When his fellow-survivors die, 'in those two deaths he read God's warning "wait"'. So Enoch patiently waits to be rescued and after ten years a ship finally does appear. When he returns home he finds his wife, Annie, has remarried and resolves not to reveal his identity to her in order to preserve her new happiness.

> I knew I could outwait them. I could outwait Enoch Arden if I had to. But it would be nice if, when they finally got sick of waiting, I knew which way they'd exit.
> ROBERT B. PARKER *Walking Shadow*, 1994

Estragon ▶ *See* GODOT.

Godot In Samuel Beckett's play *Waiting for Godot* (1952), two tramps, Estragon and Vladimir, discuss philosophical issues while they await the arrival of the mysterious character Godot. Godot never appears, despite the promises of a young boy who comes on at the end of each act claiming to be his emissary.

> I approached the Audi and passed it. Fielding was reading a paper and seemed to be waiting. They were great lads for waiting. They could have out-waited Estragon.
> RICHARD HALEY *Thoroughfare of Stones*, 1995

Griselda Griselda is the heroine of the last tale of Boccaccio's *Decameron* (1353), used by Chaucer for 'The Clerk's Tale' (c.1387) in *The Canterbury Tales*. Her husband, the Marquis Walter, subjects her to various cruelties to test her love and patience, including making her believe that her children have been murdered and that he intends to divorce her and remarry. Griselda bears his cruelty to the end, when her children are restored to her and her husband accepts her again as his wife. Griselda represents the ideal of patience and wifely obedience.

> Monica made no reply. She had made several resolutions as she worked, and one of them was that she would never draw attention to anything she did for him, or seem to seek praise. Patient Griselda was only one of the parts she meant to play in the

life of Giles Revelstoke and it was certainly not the principal one.
ROBERTSON DAVIES *A Mixture of Frailties*, 1951

Clifford didn't look happy but he went. I waited, hands folded in my lap like patient Griselda.
SARAH LACEY *File Under Deceased*, 1992

Jacob In the Bible, Jacob was a son of Isaac. He fell in love with his cousin Rachel and offered to work for her father, Laban, for seven years to win her hand in marriage: 'And Jacob served seven years for Rachel; and they seemed unto him but a few days, for the love he had to her' (Gen. 29: 20). At the end of the seven years Jacob was tricked into marrying Leah, Rachel's older sister. He was given Rachel a week later, after promising to work for a further seven years.

'Croft's going to marry Bell!' exclaimed Eames, thinking almost with dismay of the doctor's luck in thus getting himself accepted all at once, while he had been suing with the constancy almost of a Jacob.
ANTHONY TROLLOPE *The Small House at Allington*, 1862

Six years were a long time, but how much shorter than never, the idea he had for so long been obliged to endure! Jacob had served twice seven years for Rachel: what were six for such a woman as this?
THOMAS HARDY *Far from the Madding Crowd*, 1874

Job The Old Testament Book of Job tells the story of Job, a prosperous man whose patience and piety are tried by dire and undeserved misfortunes. In spite of all his suffering, he remains confident in the goodness and justice of God, and his patience is finally rewarded with wealth and long life. He is alluded to as the epitome of forbearance.

'And I suppose you're Job himself.' 'I'd have to be. To put up with you.'
JOHN MORTIMER *Rumpole of the Bailey*, 1978

Amiable as the old man was, prolonged exposure to him would test anyone's patience. But Dolly Harris would have made Job seem like a chain-smoking neurotic.
MARTIN EDWARDS *Yesterday's Papers*, 1994

Penelope In Greek mythology, Penelope was the wife of Odysseus who waited patiently and faithfully for her husband to return home after the end of the Trojan war. She put off her many suitors by saying that she would marry only when she had finished the piece of weaving that she had started. Each night she unravelled the work that she had done during the day. ▶ *See special entry* □ ODYSSEUS *on p. 283.*

'There is always about you,' he said, 'a sort of waiting. Whatever I see you doing, you're not really there: you are waiting—like Penelope when she did her weaving.' He could not help a spurt of wickedness. 'I'll call you Penelope,' he said.
D. H. LAWRENCE *Sons and Lovers*, 1913

She feared in her heart that back home he would dismiss her, . . . that she would be left forever, faithful and forgotten, waiting like Penelope for a man who never came.
LOUIS DE BERNIÈRES *Captain Corelli's Mandolin*, 1994

Vladimir ▶ *See* GODOT.

Peace

Two ideas are covered in this theme: freedom from war or conflict and mental calm or serenity. ▶ *See also* **Conflict, War**.

Abraham's bosom Abraham is one of the earliest biblical characters, and is regarded as the father of the faithful. In the parable of the rich man and Lazarus, when Lazarus dies he is 'carried by the angels into Abraham's bosom', whereas the rich man goes to hell. 'And in hell he lift up his eyes, being in torments, and seeth Abraham afar off, and Lazarus in his bosom' (Luke 16: 23). Abraham's bosom is thus a place where the good rest in peace when they die.

Buddha The Buddha, born Siddhartha Guatama (*c*.563–*c*.480 BC), was an Indian religious teacher and the founder of Buddhism. Statues or pictures represent him in a state of tranquil meditation.

> The gorilla . . . sat like a hairy mystified Buddha on the shallow ledge.
> ALICE WALKER *Entertaining God*, 1994

> Now his face was as serene as a Buddha.
> BARBARA PARKER *Suspicion of Guilt*, 1995

Neville Chamberlain Neville Chamberlain (1869-1940) was a British Conservative statesman and Prime Minister 1937-40. In 1938 he signed the Munich Agreement ceding the Sudetenland to Germany, and returned to Britain triumphantly waving a copy of the agreement which he claimed would bring 'peace in our time'.

> 'I was never one for rows and trouble, you know that. Peace is more my line.' She made a joke at which we both laughed. 'Like that bloke Chamberlain!'
> ALAN SILLITOE *The Loneliness of the Long Distance Runner*, 1959

Concordia Concordia was the Roman goddess of peace and harmony.

Gandhi Mohandas Karamchand Gandhi (1869-1948), usually called Mahatma ('Great Soul') Gandhi, was an Indian nationalist and spiritual leader who pursued a policy of passive resistance and non-violent civil disobedience in opposition to British rule. He was influential in the Indian National Congress and was regarded as the country's supreme political and spiritual leader and the principal force in achieving India's independence. He was assassinated by a Hindu nationalist following his agreement to the creation of the state of Pakistan. Gandhi is sometimes referred to as the epitome of a pacifist.

> Anna was attempting a Zen-like state and failing miserably. The heat, the boredom, and Rick were a combination that would have gotten Gandhi's loincloth in a bundle.
> NEVADA BARR *Endangered Species*, 1997

Irene Irene was the Greek goddess of peace and conciliation.

Madonna The Madonna (literally 'my lady') is a name for the Virgin Mary, the mother of Jesus Christ, used especially when she is represented in a painting or sculpture, usually as a woman of serene and saintly beauty.

> Elizabeth was very beautiful, more beautiful perhaps than he had ever realized. Her straight clean hair was shining. Her face was softer, glowing and serene. It was a madonna loveliness, dependent on the family ambience.
> CARSON MCCULLERS *The Sojourner*, 1951

> As she stitches away at her sewing, outwardly calm as a marble Madonna, she is all the while exerting her passive stubborn strength against him.
> MARGARET ATWOOD *Alias Grace*, 1996

Pax In classical times, Pax was the allegorical figure personifying peace. She was represented by the Athenians as holding Plutus, the god of wealth, in her lap to demonstrate that peace gives rise to prosperity and opulence. The Romans represented her with the horn of plenty and carrying an olive branch in her hand.

Perseverance

This theme is closely linked with **Difficulty**, but here the emphasis is on a refusal to give up a course of action rather than the effort needed to accomplish a task. ▶ *See also* **Patience, Problems**.

Ancient Mariner The Ancient Mariner is the narrator of Samuel Taylor Coleridge's poem 'The Rime of the Ancient Mariner' (1798). Stopping a wedding guest at the door of the church where a wedding is about to take place, he insists on recounting his tale to the guest. He relates how he shot an albatross at sea, and the misfortune and suffering that subsequently befell the crew. The term 'Ancient Mariner' can describe someone who bores a reluctant listener or can denote a compulsive speaker, irresistible to his or her audience, as illustrated by Coleridge's lines:

'He holds him with his glittering eye—
The Wedding-Guest stood still,
And listens like a three years' child:
The Mariner hath his will.'

> Suddenly I remembered that Trimingham or no Trimingham he was much younger than I was and I could claim an older person's freedom of speech. At the same time I was aware of an Ancient Mariner in me who might be trying his patience.
> L. P. HARTLEY *The Go-Between*, 1953

> Like the Ancient Mariner, they cannot resist buttonholing strangers in order to inform them of the facts.
> LOUIS DE BERNIÈRES *Captain Corelli's Mandolin*, 1994

Little Engine That Could The *Little Engine that Could* is the title of a children's picture-book by Watty Piper (1945), illustrated by Lois Lenski. It tells the story of a small railway engine that pants encouragingly as it struggles up a slope: 'I think I can—I think I can—I think I can.'

> The plane rolled away from the terminal and taxied out onto the runway. There was a pause, and then the plane began to surge forward, picking up speed with much earnest intent. We rumbled and bumbled like the little engine that could. The plane lifted off into the night sky, the lighted buildings below becoming rapidly smaller until only a hapless grid of lights remained.
> SUE GRAFTON *L Is for Lawless*, 1995

Old Man of the Sea The Old Man of the Sea is a character in 'Sinbad the Sailor', one of the tales in the *Arabian Nights*. He persuades Sinbad to carry him on his shoulders, whereupon he twines his legs round him so that Sinbad cannot dislodge him. Sinbad is forced to carry him on his shoulders for many days and nights, until he manages to shake him off. The term can be used to refer to irritating persistence.

> He is the bore of the age, the old man whom we Sinbads cannot shake off.
> ANTHONY TROLLOPE *Barchester Towers*, 1857

Robert the Bruce Robert I (1274–1329), known as Robert the Bruce, was a Scottish king who led the campaigns against Edward I and Edward II, culminating in the Scottish victory at Bannockburn in 1314. According to tradition, Robert spent some time hiding in a cave after suffering a defeat at the hands of the English. After watching a spider fail many times in its attempt to spin a web but persevere until it finally succeeded, he was inspired to fight on against the English.

Tortoise Aesop's fable 'The Hare and the Tortoise' relates how a hare, jeering at the slow pace of a tortoise, challenged the latter to a race. On the day of the race the hare, confident of his greater speed, lay down to rest and fell asleep. The tortoise plodded on and won the race, leading to the moral that 'slow and steady wins the race'. The tortoise can be alluded to as an example of patient perseverance.

Pessimism

The tendency to expect things to turn out badly is covered here. Loss or absence of hope are covered at **Despair**. ▶ *See also* **Optimism**, **Prophecy**.

....

Samuel Beckett The plays of Irish writer and playwright Samuel Beckett (1906–89), such as *Waiting for Godot*, *Krapp's Last Tape*, and *Play*, express the author's bleak view of the vanity and futility of human endeavour in the face of man's inevitable death and oblivion.

> It is a joy sufficiently muted to accord with prevailing moods that range from

Chekhovian-autumnal to Beckettian-wintry.
New York Review of Books, 1997

Eeyore Eeyore is the gloomy old grey donkey in A. A. Milne's books about Winnie the Pooh.

> Eeyore of the Year was, as usual, a toss-up between Peter Owen ('If anything, it is getting worse') and Tom Rosenthal ('Among those books which sold less badly').
> *The Bookseller*, 1995

> Everyone had warned me rather gloomily about interviewing Glenda Jackson. I was told by journalists who knew her that she was 'very prickly' and 'hates talking about her acting career'. One of these Eeyores added: 'The problem is to stop her banging on about Labour transport policy and get her to talk about Hollywood.'
> *The Independent on Sunday*, 1997

Heraclitus Heraclitus (*c*.500 BC) was an early Greek philosopher who maintained that all things in the universe are in a state of constant change and that the mind derives a false idea of permanence of the external world from the passing impressions of experience. His gloomy view of the fleeting character of life led to him being called 'the weeping philosopher'.

> He laments, like Heraclitus the Maudlin Philosopher, at other Men's Mirth.
> SAMUEL BUTLER *Remains*, 1759

Jeremiah Jeremiah was an Old Testament prophet whose prophecies are contained in the Book of Jeremiah. These concern the unhappy fate that awaits the Israelites because they have rebelled against God. The Book of Lamentations, foretelling the destruction of Jerusalem, is traditionally attributed to him. Jeremiah's name can be applied to someone who predicts doom or disaster.

> Since we have so far emerged comparatively unscathed from all these predicted plagues and catastrophes, it is hard to take too seriously the latest Jeremiah-like pronouncements of Lacey and his colleagues about beef.
> *The Observer*, 1996

> 'Yes, it's nice to have it back,' he said, running his hands over the familiar steering wheel in an arch gesture. 'The start of something good, eh?' said Salt. 'I doubt it,' said Kavanagh. 'Jeremiah,' she said. 'That's what I like about you, Frank: even when your glass is three-quarters full, it's half-empty!'
> DAVID ARMSTRONG *Thought for the Day*, 1997

Marvin Marvin, referred to as 'the Paranoid Android', is a gloomy and depressed robot in Douglas Adams's book *The Hitch-Hiker's Guide to the Galaxy* and its sequels. He takes a universally pessimistic view about everything and is prone to complain that he has a pain down all the diodes on his left side.

Schopenhauer Arthur Schopenhauer (1788–1860) was a German philosopher whose pessimistic philosophy, embodied in his chief work *The World as Will and Idea* (1819), argued that attempts to understand the world rationally are doomed to failure.

> So we should not go around moping, looking as miserable as Schopenhauer when the toast has landed marmalade-down in the Wilton.
> *The Guardian*, 1998

Poverty

In some of the quotations below there is an explicit contrast drawn between poverty (**JOB, LAZARUS**) and wealth (Midas, Dives). **CINDERELLA** may be considered to represent the transition from pennilessness to prosperity, while Job's journey is in the opposite direction. ▶ *See also* **Failure**, **Wealth**.

Brer Rabbit Brer Rabbit is the trickster hero of many of the tales told by Uncle Remus in Joel Chandler Harris's various volumes of folklore tales published between 1881 and 1910. He can be alluded to as someone who is used to enduring hardships and deprivation and will use their wits to survive.

> Dusty ride, isn't it? I don't mind it myself; I'm used to it. Born and bred in de briar patch, like Br'er Rabbit.
> WILLA CATHER *A Death in the Desert*, 1905

Cinderella Cinderella, in the traditional fairy story, finds herself living with a stepmother and two stepsisters after her father's remarriage. She is kept in poverty, dressed in rags, and maltreated by the other women in the family who force her to carry out menial tasks in the house. Her fortunes change, however, once, with the aid of her fairy godmother, she is able to go to the ball and meet the prince who has come to be known as Prince Charming. ▶ *See special entry* ☐ **CINDERELLA** *on p. 56*.

> We were driven home—in a hired Rolls—to think it over. You know, to a pokey top-floor flat in Belsize Park. Like two Cinderellas.
> JOHN FOWLES *The Magus*, 1977

> Stephen Spiro, professor of respiratory medicine at University College London Hospital, believes lung cancer has long been perceived as a Cinderella disease. 'It is seen as a disease of the working classes. Everyone knows the cause. It has connotations of guilt so patients are not demanding enough.'
> *The Independent*, 1998

Bob Cratchit Bob Cratchit is Ebenezer Scrooge's clerk in Dickens's *A Christmas Carol* (1843). He is poorly paid (15 shillings a week), and the father of five living in a small four-roomed house in Camden Town. His youngest son, Tiny Tim, is weak and crippled. Despite his poverty, Cratchit is a devoted husband and father.

St Francis of Assisi Francis of Assisi (1181-1226) was born the son of a wealthy merchant but converted to a more pious life after a severe illness, founding both the Franciscan order, a mendicant order of friars, and the 'Poor Clares', the Franciscan order for women. The Franciscan orders were devoted to chastity, poverty, and obedience, with the emphasis on poverty.

Great Depression The Great Depression was a prolonged period of economic depression in the United States, Europe, and elsewhere during the 1930s following the Wall Street stock market crash in 1929.

In the exhausted car the two of us must have looked like nothing so much as belated
refugees from the platteland of the Great Depression.
J. M. COETZEE *Age of Iron*, 1990

Hooverville A Hooverville was a shanty town built by impoverished un-
employed people in the United States during the Great Depression. The shanty
towns were named after the president of the time, Herbert C. Hoover.

And now in my mind I stood upon the walk looking out across the hole past a
Hooverville shanty of packing cases and bent tin signs, to a railroad yard that lay
beyond.
RALPH ELLISON *Invisible Man*, 1952

Israelites The Israelites were the Hebrew people who were living in slavery in
Egypt at some period during the second millennium BC. They were rescued
from their plight by Moses, who led them to the land of Canaan, the biblical
name for an area of ancient Palestine west of the River Jordan, which had
been promised to the descendants of Abraham by God. ▶ *See special entry*
□ **MOSES AND THE BOOK OF EXODUS** *on p. 264.*

'If I go furze-cutting we shall be fairly well off.' 'In comparison with slaves, and the
Israelites in Egypt, and such people!'
THOMAS HARDY *The Return of the Native*, 1880

Job In the Bible, Job was a god-fearing and prosperous man whose piety God
tested by first taking away his wealth and then heaping other misfortunes
upon him. In the US, extreme poverty is sometimes described by mention of
'Job's house cat' or 'Job's turkey'. If Job is poor, how much worse off, presumably, must be an animal in his care.

'But stop nets do stop fish,' I said, enjoying the novelty of his position enough to play
devil's advocate. 'Well, of course they do. But if they stopped *all* the fish, crews on the
east would be richer'n Midas and those working the westernmost part of Bogue Banks
would be poorer'n Job's house cat.'
MARGARET MARON *Shooting at Loons*, 1994

Now he was as poor as Job, without a cob to scratch his arse.
ANDRÉ BRINK *Imaginings of Sand*, 1996

Lazarus In the Bible, Lazarus was the name of the ailing beggar who sat at the
gate of the rich man (traditionally named Dives) in the parable of the rich man
and Lazarus (Luke 16: 19–31). Lazarus was covered with sores and begged for
crumbs from the rich man's table. He was rewarded for his misfortunes in life
by being taken to Heaven by Abraham after death.

Others toil and moil all their lives long—and the very dogs are pitiful in our days, as
they were in the days of Lazarus.
ELIZABETH GASKELL *North and South*, 1854–5

The earl living down at Guetwick did not understand that the Income-tax Office in
the City, and the General Committee Office at Whitehall, were as far apart as Dives
and Lazarus, and separated by as impassable a gulf.
ANTHONY TROLLOPE *The Small House at Allington*, 1862

Little Match Girl The little match girl is the character in a story of the same
name by Hans Christian Andersen (1848). She is so poor that she tries to
warm herself by lighting the matches that she was intending to sell. Her body

is found the next morning, frozen to death in the snow.

> I tripped through the sleet like the little match girl.
> *The Observer*, 1996

Skid Row Skid Row is believed to be derived from 'skid road', originally a track for hauling logs and later used to refer to a part of town frequented by loggers. The term is used to refer to a part of town where the poorest people live, the haunt of drunks and vagrants.

Oliver Twist In Charles Dickens's novel *Oliver Twist* (1837–8), Oliver is born a pauper in a workhouse and suffers the cruel and restrictive conditions of the regime under the parish beadle, Mr Bumble. Inadequately fed, he infuriates the authorities by asking for more food. He later runs away to London, where he falls into the hands of a gang of pickpockets.

> This is the worst Christmas Day I have ever spent. . . . I feel like Oliver Twist in the workhouse.
> V. S. NAIPAUL *A House for Mr Biswas*, 1961

> Poor Davey! How you have starved! A real little work-house boy, an Oliver Twist of the spirit!
> ROBERTSON DAVIES *The Manticore*, 1972

Power

This theme concentrates on the political or institutional power that makes it possible to control other people's lives, and also on other types of influence over people, as illustrated by the figures of **MESMER**, the **PIED PIPER**, **PETRUCHIO**, and **SVENGALI**. Other powerful figures are included in the themes **Dictators and Tyrants** and **Leaders**. ▶ *See also* **Strength**.

Big Brother Big Brother is a character in George Orwell's novel *Nineteen Eighty-Four* (1949). He is the head of the totalitarian Party and dictator of the state in which Winston Smith lives. His portrait, with the caption 'Big Brother is watching you', is ubiquitous. ▶ *See also* **ORWELL**.

> It's a world I don't know. The world of the computer and the microwave oven. . . . Younger people growing up will find it easier to contend with, but I doubt it. They'll conform because it's the only way to go. Big Brother is there. I think they will become digits. I don't see myself as a digit, but I know I'm becoming one. It's necessary for me to have my Social Security number available or my driver's licence, because I don't have credit cards. It's un-American. Anywhere I gotta pay cash. You see, I'm not a digit yet.
> STUDS TERKEL *American Dreams: Lost and Found*, 1980

> He censored our reading, selected our playmates—we weren't allowed many—and watched us like Big Brother.
> BARBARA MICHAELS *Search the Shadows*, 1988

Labour's Shadow Social Security Secretary rules it out as a Big Brother scheme. Jack Straw reiterated Labour's long-standing objection to compulsory ID cards, but supports a voluntary scheme.
The Independent, 1996

Faust Faust is the subject of a medieval legend and subsequently of dramas by Marlowe, *Dr Faustus* (1604), and Goethe, *Faust* (1808, 1832). In the Marlowe version, Faustus, greedy for earthly power, sells his soul to Mephistopheles in exchange for twenty-four years during which Mephistopheles will provide anything he wants.

The object of the exercise . . . was not to enhance others' enjoyment and understanding of Jane Austen, still less to honour the novelist herself, but to put a definitive stop to the production of any further garbage on the subject. . . . The thought gave him deep satisfaction. In Faustian moments he dreamed of going on, after fixing Jane Austen, to do the same job on the other major English novelists, then the poets and dramatists.
DAVID LODGE *Changing Places*, 1975

Kafka The novels of Franz Kafka (1883-1924), a Czech novelist who wrote in German, portray the individual's isolation, bewilderment, and anxiety in a nightmarish, impenetrably oppressive world. In *The Trial* (1925), Joseph K. is arrested and subjected to a baffling ordeal by sinister figures of authority. The corresponding adjective is 'Kafkaesque'.

When she brought them in, he understood her apprehensiveness at once. He could see that they were men of tremendous authority. He had never read Kafka, but if he had he would have recognized them. They wore black suits, and did not smile when they greeted him, or offer to shake hands.
ALAN PATON *Ah, But Your Land Is Beautiful*, 1981

Mesmer Franz Anton Mesmer (1734-1815) was an Austrian physician who had a successful practice in Vienna, where he used a number of novel treatments. He is chiefly remembered for the introduction of hypnotism, known as mesmerism, as a therapeutic technique.

Like some magical Mesmer, he has persuaded his people to feel well about themselves.
The Observer, 1997

Moloch Moloch was a Canaanite deity referred to in several books of the Old Testament, to whom worshippers sacrificed their children. The Israelites moving into the land of Canaan were expressly forbidden to worship Moloch (Lev. 18: 21). Anything that has great power and demands a terrible sacrifice can be described as a Moloch.

The reduction of the Premier League to 20 teams will help by easing the fixture list but certain dates should still be declared no-go areas for that insatiable Moloch, television.
The Guardian, 1994

Orwell In George Orwell's novel *Nineteen Eighty-Four*, the character referred to as Big Brother is a dictator whose portrait with the caption 'Big Brother is watching you' can be found everywhere. Orwell's own name can now be used to allude to the power and omnipresence of a dictatorial state. The related adjective is 'Orwellian'. ▶ *See also* **BIG BROTHER.**

Parliament contains MPs and Ministers who know about the necessity for openness. They can be aware that security cameras and interlinked computers raise the Orwellian prospect that everything about their constituents, from their phone calls to what they buy on credit cards, can now be discovered with relative ease.
The Observer, 1997

Ozymandias Ozymandias is the name of the imaginary ancient king in Shelley's poem *Ozymandias* (1819), who enjoyed great power in his lifetime but whose power and works have all decayed over time. The inscription on the remains of a great stone carving of him reads:

'My name is Ozymandias, king of kings:
Look on my works, ye Mighty, and despair!'

> Wield gave what Pascoe had once described as his Ozymandias sneer and made a gesture which took in the car-packed garage.
> REGINALD HILL *A Killing Kindness*, 1980

Petruchio In Shakespeare's comedy *The Taming of the Shrew* (1623), Petruchio is the suitor for Katherina, the ill-tempered shrew of the title. After marrying Katherina, Petruchio tames her by devising a series of humiliations, including preventing her from eating or sleeping. At the end of the play, he is able to win a bet on which is the most submissive of three wives.

> In truth, Mrs Proudie was all but invincible; had she married Petruchio, it may be doubted whether that arch wife-tamer would have been able to keep her legs out of those garments which are presumed by men to be peculiarly unfitted for feminine use.
> ANTHONY TROLLOPE *Barchester Towers*, 1875

Pied Piper The Pied Piper is the subject of Robert Browning's poem 'The Pied Piper of Hamelin' (1842). The Piper undertakes to rid the town of Hamelin of the rats that have been plaguing its citizens. The Mayor and Corporation agree to pay a thousand guilders for this service. The Piper plays his pipe and the rats follow him to the river where all but one perish. The Mayor then reneges on the payment; in revenge, the Piper starts to play his pipe again and this time is followed by all the children. He marches to the mountain where

'A wondrous portal opened wide,
As if a cavern was suddenly hollowed;
And the Piper advanced and the children followed,
And when all were in to the very last,
The door in the mountain side shut fast.'

One child, lame and unable to keep up, remains outside. The citizens of Hamelin never see their children again.

> We passed the first houses, and children began to follow us, scampering along the banks till I felt like the Pied Piper.
> WILFRED THESIGER *The Marsh Arabs*, 1974

> Some fall in behind her, and follow her to the lecture theatre, so that she appears to be leading a little procession, a female Pied Piper.
> DAVID LODGE *Nice Work*, 1988

Sir Humphrey Sir Humphrey Appleby is the senior civil servant in the television series *Yes, Minister* (1980–82) and *Yes, Prime Minister* (1986–8). Whilst appearing to defer to his minister and later prime minister, Jim Hacker, Sir

Humphrey in fact aims to run things behind the scenes as Whitehall deems appropriate.

> It is good to know that Sir Humphrey survived the fallout on 1 May and that policy is still in the same old safe pair of hands.
> *The Observer*, 1997

Svengali Svengali is a musician in George du Maurier's novel *Trilby* (1894) who trains Trilby's voice and makes her a famous singer. His control over her is so great that when he dies, she loses her ability to sing. The name Svengali has come to be used of someone who establishes considerable or near-total influence over someone else.

> The idea of the hypnotist as an all-powerful demon, like Svengali, who could make anybody do anything, he pooh-poohed.
> ROBERTSON DAVIES *World of Wonders*, 1975

> Suddenly the spirit of that evil man is haunting this house. He has become your Svengali!
> JOHN KENNEDY TOOLE *A Confederacy of Dunces*, 1980

> Academics like myself are labelled as trendy progressives, not believing in structure, the Svengali figures to whom thousands of poor dears in the teaching profession are in ideological thrall, a patronising and laughable view.
> *The Observer*, 1997

Thought Police In George Orwell's novel *Nineteen Eighty-Four*, the thought police are the secret police whose job is to control and change the thoughts of anyone who dares to think independently, using brainwashing and torture.

Pride

In several of the allusions below the idea of pride was originally associated with offence against God, though they can also be applied in more general contexts. ▶ *See also* **Ambition, Humility, Vanity**.

....

Ahab In the Bible, Ahab (*c.*875–54 BC) was the king of Israel who married Jezebel and converted to the worship of the pagan god Baal. When he was finally killed, 'the dogs licked up his blood' (1 Kgs. 22: 38). Ahab can be alluded to for his wicked pride in refusing to believe in God but choosing rather to worship Baal.

> 'Does Judith or either of the boys ever come down to hear you preach?' . . . 'Nay, they struts like Ahab in their pride, and their eyes drip fatness, nor do they see the pit digged beneath their feet by the Lord.'
> STELLA GIBBONS *Cold Comfort Farm*, 1932

hubris In Greek tragedy, hubris was excessive pride or defiance of the gods, which led to total failure or destruction, brought about by the avenging goddess Nemesis.

In both Japan and the West, the fall of the tiger economies has been read as a simple tale of hubris and nemesis.
The Observer, 1997

Lucifer According to Christian tradition, Lucifer, also known as Satan or the Devil, was cast out of heaven for his pride in daring to rebel against God. Lucifer represents pride that leads to one's own destruction.

The shining Bull's Eye of the Court was gone, or it would have been the mark for a hurricane of national bullets. It had never been a good eye to see with—had long had the mote in it of Lucifer's pride.
CHARLES DICKENS *A Tale of Two Cities*, 1859

She knows now what it was. It was Pride, deadliest of the Seven Deadlies; the sin of Lucifer, the wellspring of all the others.
MARGARET ATWOOD *The Robber Bride*, 1993

But the Fontclairs are an old Norman family, and proud as Lucifer.
KATE ROSS *Cut to the Quick*, 1993

Ozymandias Ozymandias is the name of an imaginary ancient king in Shelley's poem *Ozymandias* (1819). He enjoyed great power in his lifetime, but his power and works have all decayed over time. The inscription on the remains of a great stone carving of him warns others not to fall into the trap of pride in their earthly achievements because all will crumble to dust after their death:

'My name is Ozymandias, king of king:
Look on my works, ye Mighty, and despair!'

Ozymandias can be used to represent hubris.

Maybe he [Orson Welles] suffered from an Ozymandias complex—he wanted to bequeath the world a vast, scattered ruin in order to imply a lost glory. It's true that no ruins were ever so magisterially bewildering.
The Guardian, 1997

Prisons

The names of such 20th-century prisons as **ALCATRAZ**, **COLDITZ**, the **GULAG ARCHIPELAGO**, and **ROBBEN ISLAND** have entered common usage to describe not only another prison but also any institution that resembles a prison in its regime or level of security. ▶ *See also* **Captives**, **Escape and Survival**.

Alcatraz Alcatraz was a notorious American prison on the island of Alcatraz in San Francisco Bay. Built in 1868, it was originally a prison for military offenders, but was later used for civilian prisoners. From 1934 it held the most dangerous criminals, including the gangster Al Capone. Alcatraz was closed in 1963. Its name has come to symbolize a prison from which escape is impossible.

> Conditions are awful inside a new £3m unit designed to hold the country's most
> dangerous prisoners, says Sir David Ramsbotham, the Chief Inspector of Prisons. The
> Close Supervision Centre at Woodhill Prison in Milton Keynes was labelled Britain's
> Alcatraz when it opened earlier this year.
> *The Independent*, 1998

Andersonville Andersonville is a village in SW Georgia in the United States. It
was the site of a notorious Confederate prison, where dreadful conditions led to
the death of over 12,000 Union soldiers.

Bastille The Bastille was a fortress in Paris, built as a royal castle by Charles V,
and completed in 1383. Used as a prison in the 17th and 18th centuries, it
became a symbol of repression. It was stormed and sacked by the Parisian mob
in 1789 on 14 July, now commemorated as Bastille Day, marking the beginning of the French Revolution.

> I would fain unite the duties of existence and have my mother at home with me, but
> alas, fate has arranged it otherwise, and here we are imprisoned as completely as if
> we were in the Bastille.
> CELIA THAXTER *Letters*, 1873

Black Hole of Calcutta The Black Hole of Calcutta was a dungeon in Fort
William, Calcutta. In June 1756, Siraj-ud-Dawlah, nawab of Bengal, reputedly
imprisoned some 146 British prisoners there in a narrow cell, 6m square. Only
twenty-three people survived, all the others suffocating. The expression is now
used to refer to any small, cramped place in which people are trapped.

> As I passed Erskine-Brown's open door I could see his room was bursting at the
> seams, and, as I hung up my hat and coat in the hallway, I heard the voice of the
> Erskine-Brown say he supposed they'd have to hang on in that Black Hole of Cal-
> cutta a little longer.
> JOHN MORTIMER *Rumpole of the Bailey*, 1978

Bloody Tower The Bloody Tower is a nickname for a part of the Tower of
London, built 1377–99. It derived its name from the belief that it was the place
where the Princes in the Tower were murdered. It also housed famous prisoners such as Sir Walter Ralegh.

Colditz Colditz is a medieval castle near Leipzig in eastern Germany. It was
used as a top-security prison camp during the Second World War, particularly
for prisoners who were known as likely escapees, and became famous as a
camp from which escape was considered almost impossible.

> Former residents described Bryn Estyn as the 'Colditz of residential care'.
> *The Observer*, 1996

Dartmoor Dartmoor is a high-security prison on Dartmoor, a moorland district in Devon, originally built to hold French prisoners of war during the
Napoleonic Wars.

Devil's Island Devil's Island is a small island off the coast of French Guiana. It
was used as a convict settlement, initially for prisoners with contagious diseases but later for political prisoners. Its most famous prisoner was Albert

Dreyfus (1859-1935), the French army officer of Jewish descent who was falsely accused of passing secrets to the Germans. His trial, imprisonment, and eventual release caused a major political crisis in France.

> Each of these transgressions isolated the club and its devotees further and further from the lip-pursing, right-thinking, Arsenal-hating mainland; Highbury became a Devil's Island in the middle of north London, the home of no-goods and miscreants.
> NICK HORNBY *Fever Pitch*, 1993

Gulag Archipelago The Gulag Archipelago is the name of the system of forced-labour camps in the Soviet Union, specifically in the period 1930-55, in which hundreds of thousands, perhaps millions, died. The term can be now be used in a more general sense.

> Much has been made by commentators about Delia's celebrated dullness. We are told repeatedly that she was once exiled to the TV equivalent of the Gulag Archipelago because she wasn't 'sexy enough'.
> *The Guardian*, 1995

Newgate Newgate is London's famous historic prison. Originally the gate-house of one of the city gates, Newgate was first used as a prison in the early Middle Ages, and the last prison on the site was closed in 1880 and demolished in 1902. The prison housed many notorious criminals as well as debtors, and became notorious in the eighteenth century for the wretched conditions in which the inmates lived.

> The Royal Palace . . . resembles Newgate whitewashed and standing on a sort of mangy desert.
> WILLIAM MAKEPEACE THACKERAY *Punch*, 1844

Reading Gaol Oscar Wilde spent time in Reading Gaol (1895-7) for homosexual offences, and wrote his poem *The Ballad of Reading Gaol* based on his experiences there. The poem highlights the harsh conditions in the prison and the despair of the prisoners.

> And by the end of the evening, Reading Gaol would have felt like the George V.
> JULIAN BARNES *Talking It Over*, 1991

Robben Island A small island off the coast of South Africa, Robben Island is the site of a prison in which political prisoners, including Nelson Mandela, were formerly held.

Sun City Sun City was the name given by political prisoners to Diepkloof Prison, near Johannesburg in South Africa. Sun City is actually a South African casino resort.

> It's a better place than Sun City. Better conditions.
> NADINE GORDIMER *My Son's Story*, 1990

Tower of London The Tower of London is a fortress in central London, used as a royal residence and later as a state prison.

Problem

The emphasis here is on a dilemma or predicament that needs resolving by contrast with the closely linked theme **Difficulty**, which is concerned more with a task requiring considerable effort to accomplish. ▶ *See also* **Danger**.

....

Buridan's ass Buridan, a French scholastic philosopher of the end of the 12th century, is credited with the following sophism: if a hungry ass were placed exactly between two hay-stacks in every respect equal, it would starve to death, because there would be no motive why it should go to one rather than to the other. 'Like Buridan's ass between two bundles of hay' is said of a person who cannot decide between two courses of action and who adopts neither.

> So she continued to brood and suffer, standing flat as Buridan's Ass between equal bundles of hay . . .
> ALEXANDER THEROUX *Adultery*, 1987

Catch-22 Joseph Heller's 1961 novel *Catch-22* deals with the dilemma of an American airforce bombardier who wishes to avoid combat duty. In order to do so, he has to be adjudged insane, but since anyone wishing to avoid combat duty is obviously sane, he must therefore be fit for duty. A Catch-22 is therefore any situation or dilemma from which there is no escape because of two mutually incompatible conditions.

> 'Our particular problem is that until we can find some witnesses, we can't prove it was murder and not suicide, and we can't get the manpower to do the sort of investigation we need to find witnesses until we can show that it was murder.' 'Catch twenty-two,' Mackay said triumphantly.
> CYNTHIA HARROD-EAGLES *Blood Lines*, 1996

> Some say debt relief undermines a country's credit worthiness. This is a classic Catch 22 because we know that while countries remain heavily indebted they find it hard to attract investment.
> *The Observer*, 1997

Gordian knot Gordius was a peasant who was chosen king of Phrygia, whereupon he tied the pole of his wagon to the yoke with an intricate knot. An oracle prophesied that whoever undid it would become the ruler of all Asia. Alexander the Great is said to have simply cut through the knot with his sword. Hence a Gordian knot is a complex problem or task, and 'to cut the Gordian knot' is to solve a seemingly inextricable problem by force or by evading the conditions that caused the problem in the first place.

> The book rang with the courage alike of conviction and of the entire absence of conviction; it appeared to be the work of men who had a rule-of-thumb way of steering between iconoclasm on the one hand and credulity on the other; who cut Gordian knots as a matter of course when it suited their convenience.
> SAMUEL BUTLER *The Way of All Flesh*, 1903

Pandora's box In Greek mythology, Pandora, the first mortal woman, created out of clay by Hephaestus, was given by the gods a jar (or box) that she was forbidden to open. Out of curiosity she disobeyed, and released from it all the evils and illnesses that have afflicted mankind ever since, with only Hope remaining at the bottom. The phrase 'a Pandora's box' is thus used for a source of many unforeseen and unmanageable problems.

> Hardy was the first to try to break the Victorian middle-class seal over the supposed Pandora's box of sex.
> JOHN FOWLES *The French Lieutenant's Woman*, 1969

> The anthropic principle opens a Pandora's box of smart worlds when it tries to explain just one.
> BART KOSKO *Fuzzy Thinking*, 1993

Scylla and Charybdis In Greek mythology, Scylla was a ferocious sea-monster whose cave was situated in the Straits of Messina opposite Charybdis, a whirlpool. Sailors had to navigate their way between these two dangers. Someone who is 'between Scylla and Charybdis' is in a predicament in which avoiding one of two dangers or pitfalls increases the risk of the other.

> Between the Scylla of Skullion and the Charybdis of Lady Mary, not to mention the dangers of the open sea in the shape of the Fellows at High Table, the Bursar led a miserable existence.
> TOM SHARPE *Porterhouse Blue*, 1974

> But none of them has soothed us, held our hands, led us past the Scylla and Charybdis of cookery cock-ups, better than Delia.
> *The Guardian*, 1995

Serpent The Book of Genesis in the Bible relates how the serpent tempted Eve to eat the forbidden fruit from the tree of the knowledge of good and evil. She in turn tempted Adam to eat, and as a result of this disobedience they were banished from the Garden of Eden. A serpent is therefore something that is a source of problems in an otherwise happy situation. ▶ *See special entry* ☐ ADAM AND EVE *on p. 5*.

> The fresh hill air had exhilarated my mind, and the aromatic scent of the evening gave the last touch of intoxication. Whatever serpent might lurk in it, it was a veritable Eden I had come to
> JOHN BUCHAN *Prester John*, 1910

> Nothing sends you straight back to childhood quicker than getting an unexpected insight into how things—relationships—really were when you lived in Eden, a child oblivious to the Serpent.
> MARGARET MARON *Shooting at Loons*, 1994

tar baby In one of Joe Chandler Harris's stories of Uncle Remus, Brer Fox, in one of his many attempts to catch Brer Rabbit, makes a baby out of tar and places it by the side of the road. When Brer Rabbit comes along, he tries to talk to the tar baby and, receiving no reply, becomes angry and hits out at it, whereupon he sticks fast. A tar baby is something that is to be avoided, because it will cause problems for anyone who touches it.

Turning to Salinas, she smiled again. 'No matter how you play him, Victor, Ricardo's sort of a tar baby. I suggest that you consider him more carefully before you imagine the jury weeping.'
RICHARD NORTH PATTERSON *Eyes of a Child*, 1995

The trouble is that both men are tar babies, contaminating anyone who deals with them.
The Observer, 1996

Prometheus

In Greek mythology, Prometheus was a Titan, the brother of Atlas, seen in many legends as the champion of humankind against the gods. In some stories he actually made the first men by making figures of clay which, with the help of Athene, he brought to life. He first angered Zeus when he was asked to arbitrate in a dispute between men and gods over which portion of a sacrificial bull should be given to the gods and which portion should be kept by men. Prometheus divided the carcass into two bags, one containing the flesh, which he made unappealing by covering it with the bull's stomach, the other containing the bones, which he covered with fat to make it look like meat. He thus tricked Zeus into choosing the bag containing the bones, which would thereafter be the gods' portion. In anger Zeus withheld fire from men, saying that they could eat their flesh raw. Prometheus responded by going to Olympus himself and stealing some fire hidden in a stalk of fennel, which he gave to men. He also improved their lives by teaching them arts and sciences. To avenge himself on men, Zeus instructed Hephaestus to make a clay woman, Pandora, who brought to earth all the evils and diseases that have since plagued man. As a punishment for his disobedience to the gods, Zeus had Prometheus chained to a rock, where each day an eagle tore out his liver, which grew again each night. He was eventually rescued by Hercules, who shot the eagle with his bow and arrow.

Various aspects of the Prometheus story are dealt with throughout the book.

▶ *See* **Cunning, Life: Generation of Life, Punishment, Rebellion and Disobedience,** *and* **Suffering.**

Prophecy

Prophecy is a central element in both the Old Testament and the classical world. Prophecies are not always believed and, when enigmatic, not always interpreted correctly. In the majority of cases, when names such as **BELSHAZZAR**, **CASSANDRA**, and **JEREMIAH** are invoked, it is bad news that is being predicted, usually death or disaster. By contrast, allusions to **NOSTRADAMUS** can be fairly neutral. ▶ *See also* **Dreams, Pessimism**.

....

Belshazzar Belshazzar, King of Babylon, gave a great banquet for a thousand of his lords (Dan. 5: 1–28). During the banquet they drank from goblets taken from the temple and praised the gods of gold, silver, bronze, iron, wood, and stone. Suddenly the fingers of a human hand appeared and wrote on the wall the words 'Mene, Mene, Tekel, Upharsin'. Daniel translated the words, explaining to Belshazzar that his reign was over, that he had been weighed in the balance and found wanting, and that his kingdom would be divided and given to the Medes and the Persians. The writing on the wall is thus a herald of doom. ▶ *See special entry* ☐ **DANIEL** *on p. 86*.

> This inexplicable incident, this reversal of my previous experience, seemed, like the Babylonian finger on the wall, to be spelling out the letters of my judgment.
> ROBERT LOUIS STEVENSON *The Strange Case of Dr Jekyll and Mr Hyde*, 1886

> And there at the centre of his desk was a large buff envelope with his name printed on it in a hand which was unmistakably Dalziel's. Why did the name Belshazzar suddenly flit into his mind?
> REGINALD HILL *Child's Play*, 1987

Calamity Jane Calamity Jane was a nickname given to Martha Jane Burke (c.1852–1903), the famous American frontierswoman, because she is said to have warned that 'calamity' would come to any man who tried to court her. Often dressing in men's clothes, she was renowned for her skill at riding and shooting. Her name can be applied to any female prophet of disaster.

> A crepe-hanger is the ultimate in depressing persons; 'wet-blankets', 'gloomy Gus's', 'calamity Janes'.
> *Notes & Queries*, 1930

Calpurnia Calpurnia was the wife of Julius Caesar. In Shakespeare's play *Julius Caesar* (1623), Calpurnia begs Caesar not to go out because many strange or horrible portents have occurred and she believes he is in danger. She has dreamed of his statue

'Which, like a fountain with an hundred spouts,
Did run pure blood.'

Caesar refuses to heed her warning and is assassinated.

Cassandra In Greek mythology, Cassandra was a daughter of Priam, king of Troy. Apollo loved her and gave her the gift of prophecy. When she resisted his advances, he turned the gift into a curse by ensuring that, although her prophecies were true, they would not be believed. Cassandra foretold the fall of Troy and the death of Agamemnon, fulfilled when his wife, Clytemnestra, murdered him. The name Cassandra can be used to describe anyone whose warnings go unheeded.

> Times of change, disruption, and revolution are naturally times of hope also, and not seldom the hopes of something better to come are the first tokens that tell people

that revolution is at hand, though commonly such tokens are no more believed than Cassandra's prophecies.
WILLIAM MORRIS *News from Nowhere and Other Writings*, 1886

He said, 'In the Civil Service, I work in a small unacknowledged off-shoot department which was set up sometime ago to foretell the probable outcome of any high political appointment. We also predict the future inevitable consequences of pieces of proposed legislation.' He paused and went on wryly, 'We call ourselves the Cassandra outfit. We see what will happen and no one believes us.'
DICK FRANCIS *Come to Grief*, 1995

Delphi Delphi was the site of the Delphic Oracle on the slopes of Mount Parnassus in ancient Greece. The pronouncements of the Oracle were made by the Priestess of Apollo, Pythia. They were unclear, often in riddles, and had to be interpreted. A delphic prediction or warning is one that is enigmatic or difficult to interpret.

As for the second prediction, it's not quite so Delphic, but perhaps I can permit myself to claim as foretelling the use of just such enclosures in places like present-day leisure park complexes.
New Scientist, 1994

Isaiah Isaiah was an Old Testament prophet whose prophecies are contained in the Book of Isaiah. He warned the Israelites that they had adopted foreign or unacceptable religious practices and that they should return to their former religious rites. Isaiah predicted the fall of Jerusalem and of Judah.

Jeremiah Jeremiah was an Old Testament prophet whose prophecies are contained in the Book of Jeremiah, and to whom the Book of Lamentations is also traditionally attributed. His prophecies concern the unhappy fate that awaits the Israelites because they have rebelled against God. The name Jeremiah can be applied to someone who predicts doom or disaster.

His was a soft world, fuzzy with private indecisions masked by the utterance of public verities which gave him the appearance of a lenient Jeremiah.
TOM SHARPE *Porterhouse Blue*, 1974

Test win knocks Jeremiahs for six. [headline]
The Guardian, 1995

Laocoön In Greek mythology, Laocoön was a Trojan priest who warned the Trojans not to let the Wooden Horse into Troy: 'Do not trust the horse, Trojans. Whatever it is, I fear the Greeks even when they bring gifts.' As a punishment from the gods for this attempted intervention, he and both his sons were crushed to death by two enormous sea serpents. ▶ *See special entry* □ **TROJAN WAR** *on p. 392*.

Nostradamus Nostradamus is the Latinized name by which Michel de Nostredame (1503–66) is generally known. He was a French astrologer and physician and the author of *Centuries* (1555), a collection of prophecies written in rhyming quatrains. Although cryptic and obscure, Nostradamus's verses have been interpreted as foretelling prominent global events over a span of more than 400 years.

I spoke last week to the science ficion writer Arthur C. Clarke, the Nostradamus of

space, whose predictions, among other things, have included the development of the communication satellite.
The Observer, 1997

Sibyl The Sibyls were prophetesses in ancient Greece. They included the Cumaean Sibyl, who guided Aeneas through the underworld. The term can be applied to someone who can prophesy the future.

Tiresias In Greek mythology, Tiresias was a blind prophet from Thebes who was renowned for his wisdom. He played a prominent part in the Oedipus legend.

writing on the wall ▶ *See* BELSHAZZAR.

Prostitutes

It is likely that the use of classical allusions provided writers in the past with a conveniently euphemistic term for an occupation they may well have been reluctant to refer to directly.

Aspasia Aspasia was a famous Greek courtesan, daughter of Axiochus of Miletus. She came to Athens, where she acquired fame by her beauty, culture, and wit. She so captivated Pericles that he made her his lifelong companion.

> The athenian virgins . . . grew up into wives who stayed at home . . . and looked after the husband's dinner. And what was the consequence of that, sir? that they were such very insipid persons that the husband would not go home to eat his dinner, but preferred the company of some Aspasia or Lais.
> THOMAS LOVE PEACOCK *Crotchet Castle*, 1831

> Mr. Valera is merely describing what all men desire in a woman, an Aspasia, the captivating femme galante, indifferent to morality, who was the adoring mistress and adviser to Pericles of ancient Greece.
> ALFRED BESTER *Galatea Galante, the Perfect Popsy*, 1980

Jezebel Jezebel was a Phoenician princess of the 9th century BC, the wife of Ahab, king of Israel. She was denounced by Elijah for promoting the worship of the Phoenician god, Baal, and trying to destroy the prophets of Israel. Her idolatry and her use of cosmetics led to the use of her name to represent female depravity, shamelessness, and wickedness.

> I have been a Jezebel, a London prostitute, and what not.
> SAMUEL RICHARDSON *Pamela*, 1740

> 'Mr Slope', said Mrs Proudie, catching the delinquent at the door, 'I am surprised that you should leave my company to attend on such a painted Jezebel as that'.
> ANTHONY TROLLOPE *Barchester Towers*, 1857

> He was going to an evening at his Lodge. You know what this Jezebel did? Only snipped off the ends of his evening trousers. With nail scissors.
> JOHN MORTIMER *Rumpole of the Bailey*, 1978

Lais Lais was a celebrated Greek courtesan, a Sicilian, carried to Corinth at the time of the Athenian expedition to Sicily. Popular with philosophers like Demosthenes, Xenocrates, and Diogenes, she was killed by the townswomen, who were jealous of her beauty.

Mary Magdalene In the New Testament, Mary Magdalene was a follower of Jesus, who cured her of evil spirits (Luke 8: 2). She is traditionally identified with the 'sinner' of Luke 7: 37, and can typify the reformed prostitute.

> 'Trying to help women who've come to grief.' Old Jolyon did not quite understand. 'To grief?' he repeated; then realised with a shock that she meant exactly what he would have meant himself if he had used that expression. Assisting the Magdalenes of London! What a weird and terrifying interest!
> JOHN GALSWORTHY *A Man of Property*, 1906

Phryne Phryne was a celebrated Greek courtesan of the 4th century BC, said to have been the model for such beautiful statues as the Cnidian Venus of Praxiteles and the Venus Anadyomene of Apelles. Phryne became so wealthy that she offered to pay for the rebuilding of the walls of Thebes.

> Her underclothes are positively Phrynean.
> ALDOUS HUXLEY *Point Counter Point*, 1928

Whore of Babylon The (Scarlet) Whore of Babylon is referred to in the Book of Revelation. She is described as a woman sitting on a scarlet beast with seven heads and ten horns: 'The woman was arrayed in purple and scarlet colour, and decked with gold and precious stones and pearls, having a golden cup in her hand full of abominations and filthiness of her fornication'. On her forehead was written: 'Babylon the great, mother of harlots and abominations of the earth' (Rev. 17: 3–5). The term was applied to the Roman Catholic Church by the early Puritans.

> Now there was Valentine—toute belle—and Mrs O'Connor, who at her best mightily resembled the Whore of Babylon.
> ALICE THOMAS ELLIS *The 27th Kingdom*, 1982

Punishment

As can be seen from the allusions grouped here, punishment for misdeeds is a fundamental concept in classical mythology and in the Old Testament, particularly the Book of Genesis. The punishments meted out to wrongdoers in the underworld have always fascinated poets and writers, providing them with a macabre descriptive set piece of collective punishment. In the *Odyssey*, for example, Odysseus observes the sufferings of SISYPHUS, TANTALUS, and TITYUS during his visit to the land of the dead. There is a similar episode in Spenser's *Faerie Queen*. ▶ *See also* **Curse**, **Revenge**.

Abelard Peter Abelard (1079-1142) was a French scholar, theologian, and philosopher. After secretly marrying one of his pupils, Heloïse, Abelard was castrated as a punishment at the instigation of her uncle, Canon Fulbert of Notre-Dame. Abelard became a monk and Heloïse a nun.

> By the end of the winter I was pregnant, but with Albert's access to black-market goods it was easy for us to find in Stuttgart a highly qualified obstetrician to help us out. Neither of us liked the idea, but Albert knew that if things were not arranged this way it was likely that some of father's huskier Staroviche cops would fall on him one night and at best leave him neutered. Pressure was perhaps increased by the fact that he called me Heloise, and even though he was no Abelard, he remembered what Heloise's uncle ... had done to the body of that great philosopher out of jealousy and vengeance.
> THOMAS KENEALLY *A Family Madness*, 1985

Actaeon In Greek mythology, Actaeon was a hunter who, because he accidentally saw Artemis (the virgin goddess of the hunt) bathing naked, was changed into a stag and torn to pieces by his own hounds.

> 'Rash man!' she said; 'like Actaeon, thou hast had thy will; be careful lest, like Actaeon, thou too perish miserably, torn to pieces by the ban-hounds of thine own passions.'
> H. RIDER HAGGARD *She*, 1887

Adam and Eve The Book of Genesis relates how Adam and Eve, the first man and woman, disobeyed God and ate the forbidden fruit from the tree of the knowledge of good and evil. As a punishment for this offence they were banished from the Garden of Eden. Furthermore, because Eve had eaten first and then tempted Adam, God told her that henceforth woman would always suffer in childbirth: 'I will greatly multiply thy sorrow and thy conception; in sorrow thou shalt bring forth children.' Man for his part would be forced to toil for his livelihood: 'In the sweat of thy face thou shalt eat bread, till thou return unto the ground.' ▶ *See special entry* □ ADAM AND EVE *on p. 5.*

Avenger of Blood In ancient Israel, a man who had the right to avenge the death of one of his kinsmen was called the Avenger of Blood or the Revenger of Blood. The practice is mentioned several times in the Bible, for example in Num. 35: 19: 'The revenger of blood himself shall slay the murderer; when he meeteth him, he shall slay him.'

> [They] footed it as if the Avenger of Blood had been behind them.
> WALTER SCOTT *The Bride of Lammermoor*, 1819

Avenging Angel The Angels of Vengeance or Avenging Angels is one term for the first angels created by God. Traditionally there are twelve Avenging Angels, of which six are known by name: Satanel, Michael, Gabriel, Uriel, Raphael and Nathanael. They are sometimes associated with the role of punishing wrongdoers.

> He thought of himself as an heroic avenging angel of death, not as a wandering boy with a rifle that would bruise his shoulder every time he fired it.
> LOUIS DE BERNIÈRES *The War of Don Emmanuel's Nether Parts*, 1990

St Bartholomew St Bartholomew was an Apostle who is said to have been martyred in Armenia by being flayed alive, and is hence regarded as the patron saint of tanners.

If they knew how old I am they would flay me with their terrible brushes—flay me like St Bartholomew.
ROBERTSON DAVIES *Fifth Business,* 1970

Battus In Greek mythology, Battus was a shepherd of Arcadia, who saw the god Hermes steal the flocks of Admetus. He was bribed by the god not to tell and pointing to a stone declared: 'Sooner will that stone tell of your theft than I.' When he was tricked into breaking his promise, Hermes turned him into a stone.

Bedonebyasyoudid In Charles Kingsley's children's story *The Water-Babies* (1863), Mrs Bedonebyasyoudid is a character encountered by Tom after he becomes a water-baby. She rewards good behaviour and punishes bad, illustrating the moral lesson that you reap what you sow.

Any qualms I might have had about deceiving Anita, disappeared completely on her wedding day. She had turned into Mrs Be-Done-By-As-You-Did.
FAY WELDON *Life Force,* 1992

Erinyes ▶ *See* FURIES.

Eve ▶ *See* ADAM AND EVE.

Furies In Greek mythology, the Furies (also known as the Erinyes) were the avenging spirits of punishment, often represented as three winged goddesses with snakes twisted in their hair. Their names were Alecto, Megaera, and Tisiphone, and they relentlessly pursued and punished wrongdoers who had otherwise escaped punishment, often when there was no human avenger left alive. Among the crimes they were particularly concerned with were the killing by one member of a family of another, blasphemy against the gods, and treachery to a host or guest. They were sometimes called the Eumenides, 'the kindly ones', a euphemism intended to placate them.

The Vengeance, uttering terrific shrieks, and flinging her arms about her head like all the forty Furies at once, was tearing from house to house, rousing the women.
CHARLES DICKENS *A Tale of Two Cities,* 1859

Gilderoy's kite Gilderoy was a famous Scottish highwayman, said to have been hanged higher than other criminals because of the wickedness of his crimes. To be hanged higher than Gilderoy's kite is to be punished more severely than the very worst criminal.

Ixion In Greek mythology, Ixion was a Thessalian king who tried to seduce Hera, for which he was punished by being bound to a fiery wheel that revolved unceasingly through the underworld. ▶ *See special entry* ☐ HADES *on p. 172.*

Jezebel Jezebel was a Phoenician princess of the 9th century BC, the wife of Ahab, king of Israel. She was denounced by Elijah for promoting the worship of the Phoenician god Baal, and trying to destroy the prophets of Israel. At the command of Jehu she was thrown out of a window and killed. Her carcass was eaten by dogs, so that when they went to bury her, 'they found no more of her than the skull, and the feet, and the palms of her hands'. It was decreed that 'in the portion of Jezreel shall dogs eat the flesh of Jezebel: And the carcase of Jezebel shall be dung upon the face of the field in the portion of Jezreel; so that they shalt not say This is Jezebel' (2 Kgs. 9: 32–37).

> Red flames will lick round their feet like the dogs lickin' Jezebel's blood in the Good Book.
> STELLA GIBBONS *Cold Comfort Farm*, 1932

Lot's wife According to Gen. 19: 24, God destroyed the towns of Sodom and Gomorrah by fire and brimstone as a punishment for the depravity and wickedness of their inhabitants. Lot, the nephew of Abraham, was allowed to escape from the destruction of Sodom with his family. His wife disobeyed God's order not to look back at the burning city and she was turned into a pillar of salt.

> 'I shall walk out of the office and never step into it again. I shall not even bestow the backwardest of glances upon it. Let Sodom and Gomorrah be razed—but I shall not be turned into a pillar of salt.' 'Is it Macao and Hong Kong you mean, when you talk of Sodom and Gomorrah? Or perhaps Canton? I trust I am not to be cast in the role of Lot's wife.'
> TIMOTHY MO *An Insular Possession*, 1986

Marsyas In Greek mythology, Marsyas was a satyr who was a skilful flute-player. He challenged Apollo to a musical contest and was flayed alive for his presumption when he lost.

> 'His present indigence is a sufficient punishment for former folly; and I have heard my pappa himself say, that we should never strike our unnecessary blow at a victim over whom providence holds the scourge of its resentment.'—'You are right, Sophy,' cried my son Moses, 'and one of the ancients finely represents so malicious a conduct, by the attempts of a rustic to flay Marsyas, whose skin, the fable tells us, had been wholly stript off by another.'
> OLIVER GOLDSMITH *The Vicar of Wakefield*, 1766

Midas Midas was a legendary king of Phrygia, who, according to one story, was granted by Dionysius his desire that everything he touched should turn into gold. When he found that he was unable to eat or drink, Midas begged to be released from the gift and was instructed to wash in the River Pactolus.

Nemesis Nemesis was the Greek goddess of retribution and vengeance, the agent of divine punishment for wrongdoing and especially for hubris, the presumptuous defiance of the gods.

> Arthur would so gladly have persuaded himself that he had done no harm! And if no one had told him the contrary, he could have persuaded himself so much better. Nemesis can seldom forge a sword for herself out of our consciences—out of the suffering we feel in the suffering we may have caused: there is rarely metal enough there to make an effective weapon.
> GEORGE ELIOT *Adam Bede*, 1859

> 'I've never seen anyone jump on a horse like you did,' Stephen said, as we set off to the Intourist. 'One second on the ground, the next, galloping.' 'You never know what you can do until Nemesis breathes down your neck.'
> DICK FRANCIS *Trial Run*, 1978

Peeping Tom According to legend, Tom the Tailor was said to have peeped at Lady Godiva when she rode naked through the streets of Coventry, as a result of which he was struck blind. He was thereafter known as Peeping Tom.

Prometheus In Greek mythology, Prometheus was a demigod, one of the

Titans. As punishment for stealing fire from the gods for the human race, Zeus had Prometheus chained to a rock where an eagle fed each day on his liver, which grew back each night. He was eventually rescued from this torment by Hercules, who shot the eagle with his bow and arrow. ▶ *See special entry* □ **PROMETHEUS** *on p. 311.*

Sisyphus In Greek mythology, Sisyphus was a king of Corinth, punished in Hades for his misdeeds in life by being condemned to the eternal task of rolling a huge stone to the top of a hill. Every time he approached the summit, the stone slipped and rolled down to the bottom again. ▶ *See special entry* □ **HADES** *on p. 172.*

Tantalus In Greek mythology, Tantalus was the king of Phrygia who was punished for his misdeeds (including killing his son Pelops and offering his cooked flesh to the gods) by being condemned in Hades to eternal thirst and hunger. Tantalus stood up to his chin in water which receded whenever he tried to drink it and under branches of fruit which drew back when he tried to reach them.

> It may condemn us, Tantalus-like, to reach evermore after some far-off, unattainable good.
> *Harper's Monthly*, 1858

Tartarus In Greek mythology, Tartarus was the lowest region of Hades which was reserved for the punishment of the wicked for their misdeeds, especially those such as Ixion and Tantalus who had committed some outrage against the gods. ▶ *See special entry* □ **HADES** *on p. 172.*

> Your soul gets judged, then it's punishment or reward. Tartarus or the Elysian fields.
> CHARLES HIGSON *Getting Rid of Mr Kitchen*, 1996

Thyestes In Greek mythology, Thyestes was the brother of Atreus, with whose wife he committed adultery. In revenge, Atreus invited him to a banquet and served him the flesh of Thyestes' own children to eat. Thyestes fled in horror, laying a curse on the house of Atreus.

Tityus Tityus was a giant of Greek mythology, punished with eternal torture in the underworld for attempting to rape Leto, the mother of Apollo and Artemis. Vultures continually devoured his liver.

Quest

The quest, universal in storytelling and myth, has evolved from the idea of a journey or expedition in search of a rare object to that of the pursuit of some elusive goal or intellectual discovery. ▶ *See also* **Adventure**.

Captain Ahab Captain Ahab is the captain of the whaling ship *Pequod* in

Herman Melville's *Moby Dick* (1851). ▶ *See* **MOBY DICK**.

Argonauts The Argonauts were the group of heroes who accompanied Jason on board the ship *Argo* in the quest for the Golden Fleece. ▶ *See* **GOLDEN FLEECE**.
▶ *See also special entry* ❑ **JASON AND THE ARGONAUTS** *on p. 220.*

El Dorado El Dorado (literally 'the gilded one') was the name of a fabled country (or city) abounding in gold, believed to exist somewhere in the region of the Orinoco and Amazon rivers. It was sought by 16th-century explorers, including the Spanish conquistadors and Sir Walter Ralegh.

> Thousands of mushroom pickers . . . stomp through British Columbia forests every fall looking for the mushroom picker's El Dorado: a bed of Canadian matsutake, or pine mushrooms—massive white mushrooms for which Japanese buyers are willing to pay $55 a pound.
> *Equinox*, 1989

Fermat's Last Theorem Pierre de Fermat (1601–65) was a French mathematician, a founder of probability theory and number theory. In 1640 he formulated the proposition: 'There do not exist positive integers x, y, z, n such that $x^n + y^n = z^n$ when n is greater than 2.' Intriguingly, Fermat noted that he had 'a truly wonderful proof of this proposition but it does not fit into the margin of this page'. For the next 350 years mathematicians tried to furnish a proof for what became known as Fermat's last theorem (or Fermat's theorem), until Andrew Wiles finally succeeded in 1995.

> You know this infallible system I have for becoming very rich by judicially investing in the velocity and stamina of horses with legal names? Ascot was going to provide the ultimate proof of its validity, a sort of Fermat's Last Theorem for racing.
> MARCEL BERLINS in The *Guardian*, 1997

Fountain of Youth The Fountain of Youth was a legendary spring which was supposed to have the power of rejuvenation and in which Alexander the Great and his army were said to have bathed. In the early 16th century it was sought by the Spanish explorer Juan Ponce de Leon.

Golden Fleece The Golden Fleece was the fleece of pure gold taken from the ram that carried Phrixus through the air to Colchis. It hung from an oak tree in a sacred grove in Colchis and was guarded by an unsleeping dragon. Jason set out with the Argonauts to find and recover the Golden Fleece, which he did with the help of Medea. ▶ *See special entry* ❑ **JASON AND THE ARGONAUTS** *on p. 220.*

> All along, the company's engineers pursued TV's Golden Fleece, the elusive 'passive' audience meter, a device capable of recognizing each TV viewer and recording even his briefest exit, without his having to lift a finger.
> *Atlantic*, 1992

Holy Grail The Holy Grail was an object of quest in medieval legend. It was supposed to be the dish or cup used by Christ at the Last Supper and in which Joseph of Arimathea had caught some of the blood of the crucified Christ. By the early 13th century it was closely associated with the Arthurian cycle of legends as a symbol of perfection sought by the knights of the Round Table. The term 'Holy Grail' is often applied to the object of a long and difficult quest.

> How many months he will be away we don't know yet, but he is setting out with all

the air of a knight in search of the holy Grail.
LAWRENCE DURRELL *Mountolive*, 1958

I've won the America's Cup. It's considered the Holy Grail of yachting.
STUDS TERKEL *American Dreams: Lost and Found*, 1980

There was a widening picture of me looking young and in racing colours: a piece of old film taken years ago of me weighing-in after winning the Grand National. I was holding my saddle in two hands and my eyes were full of the mystical wonder of having been presented with the equivalent of the Holy Grail.
DICK FRANCIS *Come to Grief*, 1995

Mecca Mecca (in Arabic, Makkah) is a city in western Saudi Arabia, an oasis town in the Red Sea region of Hejaz, east of Jiddah. It was the birthplace in AD 570 of the prophet Muhammad. Mecca is held to be the holiest city of the Islamic world and is the destination for Muslims undertaking the hadj pilgrimage. In general usage, a 'Mecca' is hence any place which attracts many visitors or the enthusiasts of a particular activity.

'But here we are at the Mecca of English cricket', said Lord Ickenham, suspending his remarks as the cab drew up at the entrance of Lord's.
P. G. WODEHOUSE *Cocktail Time*, 1958

Where 125th Street crossed Seventh Avenue is the Mecca of Harlem. To get established there, an ordinary Harlem citizen has reached the promised land.
CHESTER HIMES *Blind Man With a Pistol*, 1969

Moby Dick In Herman Melville's *Moby Dick* (1851), the great white whale of that name is the object of Captain Ahab's passionate and obsessional quest, driven by revenge for the loss of his leg in a previous encounter with the whale.

Philosopher's Stone The Philosopher's Stone was an imaginary substance, sought after by alchemists, that was supposed to have the power of changing base metals into gold and sometimes of curing all diseases and prolonging life indefinitely. The term can be used to describe a universal cure or solution that proves elusive.

Any opiate that relieves pain is habit forming, and the more effectively it relieves pain the more habit forming it is. The habit forming molecule, and the pain killing molecule of morphine are probably identical, and the process by which morphine relieves pain is the same process that leads to tolerance and addiction. Non habit forming morphine appears to be a latter day Philosopher's Stone.
WILLIAM BURROUGHS *The Naked Lunch*, 1959

Snark In Lewis Carroll's nonsense poem 'The Hunting of the Snark' (1876), the snark is a fabulous animal, the quarry of the expedition undertaken by the Bellman and his crew. The word can be applied to any elusive goal.

If Truth is the Snark of Westminster, it is most effectively pursued by those ambitious journalists who will seek to scoop each other and make their names by peddling the spin, delivered to favoured trusties by spokespeople, spin-doctors, sources and 'friends'.
SHEENA MCDONALD in *The Guardian*, 1998

Yellow Brick Road In L. Frank Baum's children's story *The Wizard of Oz* (1900), Dorothy follows the Yellow Brick Road to Oz in the hope that the

Wizard will help her to get home. She is joined on her journey by three companions she meets on the way: the Scarecrow, who wants a brain; the Cowardly Lion, who wants courage; and the Tin Man, who wants a heart.

For this group of divers their 'yellow brick road' will take them along a professional route towards the PADI Divemaster and PADI Open Water Scuba Instructor ratings.
Sport Diver, 1999

Realization

ARCHIMEDES and his cry of 'Eureka' have become synonymous with a sudden discovery or revelation. Other stories in which there occurs a similar moment of realization involve **ISAAC NEWTON** and St Paul on the **ROAD TO DAMASCUS**. ▶ *See also* **Detectives**, **Explorers**, **Knowledge**.

Archimedes Archimedes (*c.*287–212 BC) was a Greek mathematician and inventor, born in Syracuse in Sicily. There is a famous story relating to his discovery of the principle of fluid displacement. He had been given the task of finding a method for determining whether a crown was pure gold or alloyed with silver. He is supposed to have made the crucial discovery when taking a bath and seeing the water overflow. Archimedes ran naked through the streets shouting 'Eureka! Eureka!' ('I have found it! I have found it!').

I did not jump up and shout 'Eureka!' like Archimedes did.
BART KOSKO *Fuzzy Thinking*, 1993

Damascus (the road to) According to the Bible, Saul of Tarsus, a committed persecutor of Christians, set out on the road to Damascus planning to take prisoner any Christians he found there. On the way he suddenly found himself the centre of a blinding light and, falling to the ground, heard God's voice crying 'Saul, Saul, why persecutest thou me?' (Acts 9: 4). Saul, later known as Paul, became a powerful and influential Christian. Saul's conversion on the road to Damascus can be alluded to in the context of a sudden realization or change of opinion or belief.

There was no Damascus experience for me, no great leap for mankind (or womankind for that matter), only a series of small shifts, each insignificant in its own right, but each making possible the next.
ANDRÉ BRINK *Imaginings of Sand*, 1996

Mum had been to church and suddenly realized in a St Paul-on-road-to-Damascus-type blinding flash that the vicar is gay.
HELEN FIELDING *Bridget Jones's Diary*, 1996

Isaac Newton Isaac Newton (1642–1727) was an English mathematician and physicist, considered to be one of the greatest scientists of all time. According to a famous story, first told by Voltaire, in 1665 or 1666 Newton watched an apple fall from a tree in a garden, which inspired him to begin formulating the law of gravitation.

Rebellion and Disobedience

This theme deals chiefly with historical episodes of rebellion and mutiny and with other examples, especially from the Bible, of disobedience shown to authority. Prometheus is the embodiment *par excellence* of rebelliousness, he who would defy the gods. ▶ *See also* **Conformity, Nonconformity**.

....

Absalom In the Bible, Absalom was the third son of King David. He killed David's oldest son, Amnon, and later raised an army and rose against his father, chasing David out of Jerusalem. In the subsequent battle, David ordered his men to 'deal gently for my sake with the young man, even with Absalom' (2 Sam. 18: 5), but his commander, Joab, ignored this command and slew Absalom. On hearing of the death of his son, David wept, 'O my son, Absalom, my son, my son Absalom! Would God I had died for thee, O Absalom, my son, my son!' (2 Sam. 18: 33). Absalom is alluded to as the ultimate rebellious son. In Dryden's satire *Absalom and Achitophel*, the character of Absalom represents the duke of Monmouth, the illegitimate son of Charles II who led a rebellion against James II in 1685. ▶ *See special entry* □ **DAVID** *on p. 90*.

> Sometimes, the worthy gentleman would reprove my mother for being overindulgent to her sons, with a reference to old Eli, or David and Absalom, which was particularly galling to her feelings.
> ANNE BRONTË *The Tenant of Wildfell Hall*, 1848

> 'This business of love between father and son sounds like something in the Bible.' 'The patterns of human feeling do not change as much as many people suppose. King David's estimate of his rebellious son Absalom was certainly in masculine terms. But I suppose you recall David's lament when Absalom was slain?' 'I have been called Absalom before, and it isn't a comparison I like.'
> ROBERTSON DAVIES *The Manticore*, 1972

Adam and Eve The Book of Genesis in the Bible relates how Adam and Eve disobeyed God and ate the forbidden fruit from the tree of knowledge. Eve ate first, tempted by the Serpent, and she in turn tempted Adam to eat. As a result of this disobedience they were banished from the Garden of Eden. ▶ *See special entry* □ **ADAM AND EVE** *on p. 5*.

Bastille The Bastille was a fortress in Paris, built as a royal castle by Charles V, and completed in 1383. Used as a prison in the 17th and 18th centuries, it became a symbol of repression. It was stormed and sacked by the Parisian mob in 1789 on 14 July, now Bastille Day, marking the beginning of the French Revolution.

Boston Tea Party The Boston Tea Party is the name given to a violent demonstration by American colonists in 1773, prior to the War of American Independence. As a protest against the imposition of a tax on tea by the British parliament, in which they had no representation, the colonists dressed as American Indians, boarded three British ships moored in the harbour of Boston, Massachusetts, and threw overboard their cargo of tea.

Bounty The *Bounty* was a British navy ship which, in 1789, was bound from Tahiti to the Cape of Good Hope and the West Indies under the command of Captain Bligh. Some members of the crew, led by Fletcher Christian, mutinied and set the captain and eighteen companions adrift in an open boat. The mutineers returned to Tahiti and from there some of them went on to Pitcairn Island, where they formed a colony. Bligh and his companions managed to reach Timor in the East Indies, nearly 4,000 miles away. The episode was popularized by two films, made in 1935 and 1962, both called *The Mutiny on the Bounty*.

Oliver Cromwell Oliver Cromwell (1599–1658) was the English general who led the parliamentary forces, or Roundheads, against Charles I in the English Civil War. After the Roundhead victory, Cromwell helped to arrange the trial and execution of Charles I and set up a republican government. He can be alluded to as an anti-royalist revolutionary.

> The pity of it is, I hear such stuff from my peers. Elegant ideas for a social re-ordering. Pleasing plans for a *community of reason*. And Louis is weak. Let him give an inch, and some Cromwell will appear. It'll end in revolution. And that'll be no tea party.
> HILARY MANTEL *A Place of Greater Safety*, 1992

Daniel The Old Testament Book of Daniel relates how King Darius appointed Daniel as sole administrator over all the other presidents and princes. In an attempt to bring about Daniel's downfall, they asked the king to establish a decree saying that for thirty days no one should pray to any God or man except the king. Daniel ignored this command and 'his windows being open in his chamber toward Jerusalem, he kneeled upon his knees three times a day, and prayed, and gave thanks before his God, as he did aforetime' (Dan. 6: 10). As a result of this disobedience, Daniel was cast into the lions' den. ▶ *See special entry* □ **DANIEL** *on p. 86*.

> Boldwood's had begun to be a troublesome image—a species of Daniel in her kingdom who persisted in kneeling eastward when reason and common sense said that he might just as well follow suit with the rest.
> THOMAS HARDY *Far from the Madding Crowd*, 1874

Guy Fawkes Guy Fawkes (1570–1606) was a Catholic extremist who, with a small group of colleagues, was involved in the Gunpowder Plot, a conspiracy to blow up James I and his parliament on 5 November 1605. After being discovered in the cellar of the House of Lords with barrels of gunpowder, Fawkes, together with seven of his co-conspirators, was tried and executed. Guy Fawkes is alluded to as a clever schemer or secret conspirator, and the Gunpowder Plot as an unsuccessful attempt to remove someone from power.

> Missis was, she dared say, glad enough to get rid of such a tiresome, ill-conditioned child, who always looked as if she were watching everybody, and scheming plots underhand. Abbot, I think, gave me credit for being a sort of infantile Guy Fawkes.
> CHARLOTTE BRONTË *Jane Eyre*, 1847

He went forward, tiptoeing down the stairs more conspiratorially than ever—Guy Fawkes discovered, but yet irrationally hoping that he might escape notice by acting as though the Gunpowder Plot were still unrolling itself according to plan.
ALDOUS HUXLEY *Point Counter Point*, 1928

He'd have called in the Dean, the Treasurer, the Seneschal and these other fellows in the Cathedral, and they'd have put the Box in the Cathedral treasure vaults. And you know what kind of vaults those are: Guy Fawkes and his powder wouldn't get through those, as we know from bitter experience.
JOHN MASEFIELD *The Box of Delights*, 1935

Gunpowder Plot ▶ *See* GUY FAWKES.

Robin Hood
Robin Hood, the legendary English medieval outlaw, rebelled against the harsh government and high taxation of his time, robbing the rich to help the poor.

Lula repeated the word. 'Vigilante.' 'Someone who takes the law into his own hands,' I said. 'Hunh. I guess I know what it means. You're telling me Mo is like Zorro and Robin Hood.'
JANET EVANOVICH *Three to Get Deadly*, 1997

Lucifer ▶ *See* SATAN.

Prometheus
In Greek mythology, Prometheus was a demigod, one of the Titans, seen in many legends as the champion of humankind against the gods. When Zeus withheld fire from men, Prometheus responded by going to Olympus himself and stealing some fire, which he gave to men. He also improved their lives by teaching them arts and sciences. To avenge himself on men, Zeus bade Hephaestus make a clay woman, Pandora, who brought to earth all the evils and diseases that have since plagued man. To punish Prometheus for his disobedience to the gods, Zeus had him chained to a rock, where each day an eagle tore out his liver, which grew again each night. He was eventually rescued by Hercules, who shot the eagle with his bow and arrow. Prometheus is the archetype of the courageous rebel who dares to challenge the power of the gods and of fate. ▶ *See special entry* ☐ PROMETHEUS *on p. 311*.

Moreover to light a fire is the instinctive and resistand act of man when, at the winter ingress, the curfew is sounded throughout Nature. It indicates a spontaneous, Promethean rebelliousness against the fiat that this recurrent season shall bring foul times, cold darkness, misery and death.
THOMAS HARDY *The Return of the Native*, 1880

She sees the victimized character. She sees one long set of attacks on him. She would never take account of the self-inflicted wrong—the chap who breaks his own arm to avoid going back to school, then says some big bully has done it for him; the chap who lashes himself to his bedroom chair so as not to have to go and cope with the burglar—oh, she'd think he was Prometheus.
ELIZABETH BOWEN *The Death of the West*, 1938

He remembered Holy Week in the old days when a stuffed Judas was hanged from the belfry and boys made a clatter with tins and rattles as he swung out over the door. Old staid members of the congregation had sometimes raised objections: it was blasphemous, they said, to make this guy out of Our Lord's betrayer; but . . . it seemed to him a good thing that the world's traitor should be made a figure of fun.

It was too easy otherwise to idealise him as a man who fought with God—a Prometheus, a noble victim in a hopeless war.
GRAHAM GREENE *The Power and the Glory*, 1940

Satan According to Christian tradition, Satan, also known as Lucifer or the Devil, rebelled against God and as punishment was cast out from heaven: 'And there was war in heaven: Michael and his angels fought against the dragon; and the dragon fought and his angels, and prevailed not; neither was their place found any more in heaven. And the great dragon was cast out, that old serpent, called the Devil, and Satan, which deceiveth the whole world; he was cast out into the earth, and his angels were cast out with him' (Rev. 12: 7–9).

Vashti The Old Testament Book of Esther relates how King Ahasuerus ordered that his wife, Queen Vashti, should come before him, 'But the queen Vashti refused to come at the king's commandment by his chamberlains: therefore was the king very wroth, and his anger burned in him' (Esther 1: 12). As a result of this disobedience, Vashti was banished and the king married Esther in her place.

Zorro Zorro is the masked hero of Hollywood films of the 1930s to 1960s, who first appeared in a comic strip in 1919. Don Diego de la Vega belongs to a wealthy Spanish family but in secret is Zorro (The Fox), who rights wrongs and protects the weak, leaving his calling card, a letter Z cut into the clothing or body of his enemies, wherever he goes. He can be alluded to in the same way as Robin Hood, as someone who defies unjust rulers and stands up for the weak and helpless.

Rebirth and Resurrection

The **PHOENIX** and **LAZARUS** have become powerful symbols of regeneration. This theme complements **Life: Generation of Life**, where the idea is of something being brought to life for the first time. ▶ *See also* **Death**, **Returning**.

Hydra In Greek mythology, the Hydra was a many-headed snake of the marshes of Lerna in the Peloponnese, whose heads grew again as they were cut off. As one of his labours, Hercules had to kill the Hydra. With the help of his companion Iolaus, he did this by searing each neck with a burning torch as he cut off the head. ▶ *See special entry* ☐ **HERCULES** *on p. 182.*

His letters were usually all common form and padding, for . . . if he wrote about anything that really interested him, his mother always wanted to know more and more about it—every fresh answer being as the lopping off of a hydra's head and giving birth to half a dozen or more new questions.
SAMUEL BUTLER *The Way of All Flesh*, 1903

Lazarus Lazarus, the brother of Mary and Martha, was a friend of Jesus who was raised from the dead by Jesus in a miracle described in the New Testament. Lazarus had already been dead for four days when Jesus arrived at the tomb: 'He cried with a loud voice, Lazarus, come forth. And he that was dead came forth, bound hand and foot with graveclothes: and his face was bound about with a napkin' (John 11: 43-44). Lazarus is alluded to in the context of a literal or metaphorical resurrection. ▶ *See special entry* □ JESUS *on p. 223.*

> If her absence was a cause of well exercised tongues, then her Lazarus-like resurrection must have created much oral fatigue.
> MIKE NICOL *The Powers That Be*, 1989

Phoenix The Phoenix was a mythical bird of gorgeous plumage, the only one of its kind. After living for five or six centuries in the Arabian desert, it burnt itself on a funeral pyre ignited by the sun and fanned by its own wings, and rose from the ashes with renewed youth to live through another life-span. Anything that has been restored to a new existence after apparent destruction can be said to be like the Phoenix. It has come to symbolize resurrection.

> The house's character had changed much with the fire that had wrecked it and the several stages of reconstruction that renewed it; phoenix-like, the place seemed reborn of itself.
> RUSSELL HOBAN *The Mouse and His Child*, 1967

> Here in person was a sign, Alexander thought, if a hard sign to interpret, female by sex, male by gender, undergoing a positively Attic self-mutilation to become an analogue of the first Elizabeth's emblem, the renewed Phoenix.
> A. S. BYATT *The Virgin in the Garden*, 1978

Rescue

The hero rescuing someone, usually a beautiful woman, from imprisonment or danger has proved a staple of storytelling from PERSEUS to JAMES BOND. The image of the heroic knight coming to the rescue, as exemplified by GALAHAD, ST GEORGE, and others, is also reflected less specifically in the modern expressions 'knight in shining armour' and 'white knight'. ▶ *See also* **Danger, Escape and Survival, Safety**.

Andromeda In Greek mythology, Andromeda was chained to a rock and left to be devoured by a sea monster. She was saved by Perseus, who flew to her rescue on the winged horse, Pegasus, and slew the monster. ▶ *See* PERSEUS.

James Bond James Bond is the secret agent hero of the novels by Ian Fleming. In both the novels and the films based on them, the resourceful Bond repeatedly effects daring and audacious rescues.

> This is particularly true following the manager's decision to make a playing comeback at the age of 40. There are already signs it could produce a Coventry rescue act

of which any James Bond would be proud.
The Observer, 1997

Grace Darling Grace Darling (1815–42), the daughter of a lighthouse keeper on the Farne Islands off the coast of Northumberland, became a national heroine when in September 1838 she and her father rowed through a storm to rescue the survivors of the wrecked *Forfarshire*.

Sir Galahad In Arthurian legend, Sir Galahad was a knight of immaculate purity who was destined to find the Holy Grail. His name is a byword for chivalrous heroism, and the image of him riding up on his charger to rescue a maiden in distress is a common one.

> The usher called her again. I dropped the remnants of the small cigar on the marble floor of the Shire Hall and ground it underfoot. The lance was in the rest, Sir Galahad Rumpole was about to do battle for the damsel in distress, or words to that effect.
> JOHN MORTIMER *Rumpole of the Bailey*, 1978

> 'I guess it shocked me', he said. 'There I was, the naïve romantic, thinking of myself as Sir Galahad saving the damsel from the dragon, and I find out the damsel is out partying with the dragon'.
> TONY HILLERMAN *The Fallen Man*, 1997

St George St George is the patron saint of England, and is popularly portrayed as the archetypal dragon slayer and rescuer of fair maidens.

Sir Lancelot In Arthurian legend, Sir Lancelot (or Launcelot) was one of the knights of the Round Table, traditionally portrayed as the lover of Arthur's queen, Guinevere. As with other knights, he can be alluded to as a heroic and chivalrous rescuer of fair maidens in distress.

> 'You must have fainted. You slid forward off the lounger and nearly fell in the pool. *He*', Kat made up by emphasis for not knowing his name, 'came along just at the right moment and got you out. Sir Lancelot'.
> STAYNES AND STOREY *Dead Serious*, 1995

Perseus In Greek mythology, Perseus was the son of Zeus and Danae, a hero celebrated for many accomplishments. Riding on the winged horse, Pegasus, he killed the gorgon Medusa by cutting off her head. He also rescued Andromeda, who had been chained to a rock and left to be devoured by a monster. Perseus slew the sea monster, rescued Andromeda, and married her.

> He seemed to see her like a lovely rock-bound Andromeda, with the devouring monster Society careering up to make a mouthful of her; and himself whirling down on his winged horse—just Pegasus turned Rosinante for the nonce—to cut her bonds, snatch her up, and whirl her back into the blue.
> EDITH WHARTON *The Custom of the Country*, 1913

Red Cross Knight In Edmund Spenser's *The Faerie Queen*, the Red Cross Knight, almost certainly meant to be St George, is sent by the queen to slay a dragon that is ravaging the country of the princess Una. The Red Cross Knight does indeed destroy the dragon and marries Una.

> He himself isn't quite what Simon has been expecting; no heroic delivering Perseus, no Red Cross Knight.
> MARGARET ATWOOD *Alias Grace*, 1996

SAS The Special Air Service, or SAS, is a specialist British army regiment trained in commando techniques of warfare. It was formed during the Second World War and is used in clandestine operations, especially against terrorists and most dramatically in several high-profile rescues of hostages.

Scarlet Pimpernel 'The Scarlet Pimpernel' is the name assumed by the English nobleman, Sir Percy Blakeney, hero of Baroness Orczy's novel *The Scarlet Pimpernel* (published in 1905). Blakeney uses ingenious disguises to outwit his opponents and rescue French aristocrats from the guillotine during the French Revolution. He reveals his true identity to no one, not even to those he rescues, but leaves the sign of a small red flower, the scarlet pimpernel, as his calling-card whenever he has effected a rescue.

> One fifteen-year-old was kept isolated for three years in her bedroom. Sometimes all they want is higher education. Legends keep them going. Like the true story of a runaway who is now a graduate and successful businesswoman. Philip Balmforth, Bradford Police's community officer, is the indefatigable local scarlet pimpernel who rescues these girls and who arranges new lives, new identities.
> *The Independent*, 1998

US cavalry In many old American Western films, the US cavalry arrives just in time to save the heroes from certain death. Someone who arrives to help out in the nick of time can be described as being like the US cavalry.

> Put a roadblock at the other end of the lane. If I don't contact you within five minutes, send in the cavalry.
> PAUL JOHNSTON *Body Politic*, 1997

Returning

Most of the allusions below relate to the idea of returning after a long absence, sometimes associated with the notion of recognition. Returning to base and returning from the dead are represented by **ANTAEUS** and **LAZARUS** respectively.

....

Antaeus In Greek mythology, Antaeus was a giant, son of the sea-god Poseidon and the earth-goddess Gaia. He was invincible as long as he touched the earth (enabling him to draw new strength from his mother). When he wrestled Hercules, the latter lifted Antaeus into the air and crushed him to death in his arms.

> Still I knew I hadn't come out to Westport just to escape the phone and the doorbell. It was more that I needed to touch base, so to speak. Antaeus coming to earth so he might renew his strength. And I needed to visit the brightest man I know, my brother, Tim.
> ROBERT A. CARTER *Written in Blood*, 1992

Enoch Arden In Tennyson's poem of the same name, published in 1864, Enoch Arden is shipwrecked and presumed dead. After ten years he returns home, only to find that his wife, Annie, has remarried. Observing from afar the couple's happiness, Enoch decides not to ruin it by making himself known.

Bonnie Prince Charlie Charles Edward Stuart (1720–88), known as 'the Young Pretender' or 'Bonnie Prince Charlie', was the son of James Stuart and pretender to the British throne. After spending some time in exile in France, he returned to Scotland and led the Jacobite uprising of 1745–6, invading England and advancing as far as Derby. However, he was driven back to Scotland and defeated at the battle of Culloden. He again escaped to France and died later in exile in Rome. Bonnie Prince Charlie became the subject of much romantic literature, and his supporters always hoped that he would one day return again and defeat the English.

> But they would never find a leader. If there was some exiled prince of Chaka's blood, who came back like Prince Charlie to free his people, there might be danger; but their royalties are fat men with top hats and old frock coats, who live in dirty locations.
> JOHN BUCHAN *Prester John*, 1910

Doctor Foster According to the nursery rhyme,

> 'Doctor Foster went to Gloucester
> In a shower of rain.
> He stepped in a puddle right up to his middle,
> And never went there again'.

Doctor Foster can be alluded in the context of refusing or being reluctant to return to a place.

E.T. In the 1982 Steven Spielberg film *E.T.—The Extraterrestrial*, an alien being accidentally left behind by a mission to Earth befriends a lonely suburban boy. The boy helps him to build a makeshift radio transmitter after E.T. has expressed his desire to make contact with his home planet with the phrase: 'E.T. phone home'. At the end of the film a spaceship comes to take E.T. back home.

fatted calf ▶ *See* PRODIGAL SON.

Martin Guerre Martin Guerre was a 16th-century Gascon peasant who disappeared from his village for nine years. Subsequently a certain Arnaud du Thil, bearing a close resemblance to Guerre, presented himself as the missing man and was accepted by Guerre's wife as her husband. He was later revealed as an impostor by the true Martin Guerre. The story is the subject of the film *Le Retour de Martin Guerre* (1982).

Jonah Jonah was a Hebrew minor prophet who was called by God to preach in Nineveh, but disobeyed and tried to escape by sea. After being swallowed by 'a great fish' (traditionally a whale) and spending three days in its belly, Jonah finally emerged when he was vomited out onto dry land; he then went to preach to the Ninevites.

> I am back: again and again I am back, from the belly of the whale disgorged.
> J. M. COETZEE *Age of Iron*, 1990

Lazarus Lazarus, the brother of Mary and Martha, was a friend of Jesus who was raised from the dead by Jesus in a miracle described in the New Testament

(John 11: 1-45). Although Lazarus had already been dead for four days, Jesus called for him to 'come forth' out of the tomb, which Lazarus did, still wrapped in his grave bindings. Lazarus is alluded to in the context of a resurrection or come-back. ▶ *See special entry* ☐ **JESUS** *on p. 223.*

> He placed himself protectively by his mother. He was a lanky lad, as tall as she was, with bright blue eyes and a crest of reddish hair. Otherwise they were not alike, and he prided himself on taking after his dead father. If he was dead, he cherished the idea that what Alfreda had told him of the death in an accident was a lie, and that Dad would turn up, rich and famous. He had to be both or need not bother acting Lazarus.
> GWENDOLINE BUTLER *A Dark Coffin*, 1995

Odysseus Homer's epic poem the *Odyssey* recounts the story of Odysseus' return to his homeland, Ithaca, at the end of the Trojan War. When he eventually reaches Ithaca after an absence of twenty years he finds his wife Penelope besieged by suitors. Disguised as a beggar, Odysseus slays all the suitors and is finally reunited with Penelope. Odysseus is the model of the returning hero. ▶ *See special entry* ☐ **ODYSSEUS** *on p. 283.*

Prodigal Son In a parable told by Jesus, a young man squandered the property his father gave him 'with riotous living'. He is traditionally known as the Prodigal Son, meaning one who is spendthrift or recklessly extravagant. When, repenting his behaviour, the son returned home, he was received with compassion and forgiveness by his father: 'Bring forth the best robe, and put it on him; and put a ring on his hand, and shoes on his feet: And bring hither the fatted calf, and kill it; and let us eat, and be merry: For this my son was dead, and is alive again; he was lost, and is found' (Luke 15: 11-32). The terms 'prodigal' and 'prodigal son' are now generally used to refer to a repentant sinner or a returned wanderer.

> 'Aye, she'll git tired of deh life atter a while an' den she'll wanna be a-comin' home, won' she, deh beast! I'll let 'er in den, won' I?' 'Well, I didn't mean none of dis prod'gal bus'ness anyway', explained Jimmie. 'It wa'n't no prod'gal dauter, yeh fool', said the mother. 'It was prod'gal son, anyhow'.
> STEPHEN CRANE *Maggie: A Girl of the Streets*, 1893

> He waved to Atwood. 'Hello, Frank. Look who's back! The prodigal returns!'
> ROBERT HARRIS *Enigma*, 1995

Rip Van Winkle Rip Van Winkle is the hero of Washington Irving's story *Rip Van Winkle* (1820). Rip falls asleep in the Catskill Mountains in New York State, and wakes up twenty years later. When he returns to his home town, he finds many changes, including the death of his wife and the marriage of his daughter.

> Rip Van Winkle is pretty much who they will both feel like whenever they get to see Macao again.
> TIMOTHY MO *An Insular Possession*, 1986

> Having been incarcerated for most of the last forty-five years, he was probably feeling like Rip van Winkle, marveling at all the changes in the world at large.
> SUE GRAFTON *L Is for Lawless*, 1995

> Lots of people commented on how long it had been, and Trish began to feel as

though she were Rip van Winkle, coming alive again to a world she had not seen for decades.
NATASHA COOPER *Fault Lines*, 1999

Revenge

The allusions that we use to talk about revenge are chiefly drawn from the classical world. ▶ *See also* **Anger, Curse, Punishment**.

....

Erinyes ▶ *See* **FURIES**.

Eumenides In Greek mythology, Eumenides was an alternative name for the Furies. It was considered unwise to mention the Furies, or Erinyes, by name and so they were often referred to euphemistically as the Eumenides, meaning 'Kindly Ones'.

Furies In Greek mythology, the Furies, or Erinyes, were the avenging spirits of punishment, represented as three winged goddesses with snakes instead of hair. Named Tisiphone, Alecto, and Megaera, they mercilessly pursued and punished all transgressors. They are often portrayed as wild creatures pursuing a person, bent on revenge.

> He eyed them with distaste, resenting this universal calm at a time when he himself was feeling like a character in a Greek tragedy pursued by the Furies.
> P. G. WODEHOUSE *Cocktail Time*, 1958

Mafia The Mafia is a secret society of organized criminals, which originated in Sicily in the 13th century and now operates internationally, especially in the US, where it developed among Italian immigrants under the name of 'cosa nostra'. Mafia families are known for sticking together and ruthlessly avenging wrongs done to any member of the family.

> Lucas bought me a penknife. He is trying to bribe me into liking him again. Hard luck, Lucas! Us Moles never forget. We are just like the Mafia, once you cross us we bear a grudge all our lives.
> SUE TOWNSEND *The Secret Diary of Adrian Mole aged 13¾*, 1982

Medea In Greek mythology, Medea, princess of Colchis, was a sorceress who fell in love with Jason and helped him to obtain the golden fleece. When Jason later abandoned her to marry the daughter of Creon, king of Corinth, she was so enraged that she took revenge by murdering their two children as well as Jason's young bride. ▶ *See special entry* ☐ **JASON AND THE ARGONAUTS** *on p. 220*.

> Few of us wish to disturb the mother of a litter of puppies when mouthing a bone in the midst of her young family. Medea and her children are familiar to us, and so is the grief of Constance.
> ANTHONY TROLLOPE *Barchester Towers*, 1857

Count of Monte Cristo In Alexandre Dumas's novel *The Count of Monte*

Cristo (1844), Edmond Dantès, having escaped from the Château d'If after fourteen years of incarceration, begins a long campaign of revenge against those who betrayed him and brought about his imprisonment.

Nemesis In Greek mythology, Nemesis was a goddess of vengeance, usually portrayed as the agent of punishment for wrongdoing or excessive pride (hubris), and a personification of retribution or righteous anger.

> A Nemesis attends the woman who plays the game of elusiveness too often, in the utter contempt for her that, sooner or later, her old admirers feel.
> THOMAS HARDY *Jude the Obscure*, 1895

Ruthlessness

Most of the figures below are associated with physical cruelty or with unrelentingly harsh regimes. ▶ *See also* **Dictators and Tyrants**, **Evil**.

Captain Bligh William Bligh (1754–1817) was a British naval officer. In 1787 he was chosen as captain of HMS *Bounty* on a voyage to Tahiti and the West Indies. In 1979 part of the crew, under the first mate, Fletcher Christian, mutinied, setting Bligh and eighteen crew adrift in an open boat with few supplies and no charts. They succeeded in sailing to Timor, a journey of nearly 4,000 miles. Two films about this event, both titled *The Mutiny on the Bounty* (1935, 1962), have depicted Bligh as a domineering tyrant.

> According to Peasemarch, his butler, with whom I correspond, his manner towards her is still reminiscent of that of Captain Bligh of the Bounty displeased with the behaviour of one of the personnel.
> P. G. WODEHOUSE *Cocktail Time*, 1958

Dotheboys Hall ▶ *See* WACKFORD SQUEERS.

Draco Draco (7th century BC) was an Athenian legislator. The notorious severity of his codification of Athenian law has given rise to the English adjective 'draconian'.

> Since time immemorial the forces of Draco have massed in such stillness, and they were massing again behind the door.
> MIKE NICOL *The Powers That Be*, 1989

> The CBI has condemned the measures as 'Draconian'. But Beckett is convinced that tough action is needed.
> *The Observer*, 1997

Gestapo The Gestapo were the secret police in Germany under the Nazis. They were founded by Goering in 1933 and were feared for their ruthlessness.

> Harlan Potter is a cold-hearted son of a bitch. All Victorian dignity on the outside. Inside he's as ruthless as a Gestapo thug.
> RAYMOND CHANDLER *The Long Goodbye*, 1953

> Given what she had learned from Liz, Lolly's so-called strength of character was beginning to degenerate into Gestapo-like cruelty. She appeared to have ditched a husband, kept two daughters entirely ignorant of their background and family ties, lied over and over again.
> SUSAN MOODY *Sacrifice Bid*, 1997

inquisitor An inquisitor was an officer of the Inquisition, a court set up by the Catholic Church, originally in the thirteenth century, to determine whether individuals were heretics. The inquisitors of both the original Inquisition and the later Spanish Inquisition were known for their ruthlessness and use of torture.

> 'The wearing of dark glasses,' she said, 'is a modern psychological phenomenon. It signifies the trend towards impersonalization, the weapon of the modern Inquisitor.'
> MURIEL SPARK 'The Dark Glasses' in *The Collected Stories*, 1961

Jehovah Jehovah is an Old Testament name for God used by Christians. The name is sometimes used in the context of the severity of divine retribution.

> Standing as she stood in Grammer Oliver's shoes, he was simply a remorseless Jehovah of the sciences, who would not have mercy, and would have sacrifice; a man whom save for this, she would have preferred to avoid knowing.
> THOMAS HARDY *The Woodlanders*, 1887

> You placate him like Jehovah. That's no good.
> A. S. BYATT *The Virgin in the Garden*, 1978

Simon Legree Simon Legree is the cotton plantation owner in Harriet Beecher Stowe's *Uncle Tom's Cabin* (1851–2) to whom Tom is sold and who beats Tom to death.

> I don't mind him. He's a pretty good sort of old stiff. It's his sister Beulah. She was the one who put him up to it. She's the heavy in the sequence. As tough as they come. Ever hear of Simon Legree?
> P. G. WODEHOUSE *Laughing Gas*, 1936

Senator McCarthy Joseph Raymond McCarthy (1909–57) was an American Republican senator. He became chairman of the Permanent Subcommittee on Investigations in 1953 and carried out a campaign against supposed communists, which resulted in many citizens who were suspected of being members of the Communist Party being blacklisted and facing discrimination.

Wackford Squeers Wackford Squeers is the cruel headmaster of Dotheboys Hall, the Yorkshire school in Dickens's *Nicholas Nickleby* (1839). He systematically beats and starves the boys in his charge, especially Smike, a half-witted boy who is employed as a general drudge.

Safety

The main idea that links the allusions grouped below is that of being hidden from danger, being safe from harm. Figures who survive a dangerous situation, like Jonah or Lot, are covered in the theme **Escape and Survival**. ▶ *See also* **Danger, Rescue**.

....

Adullam In the Bible, when David was fleeing from Saul because Saul wanted to kill him, he took refuge in the cave Adullam. When others heard that he was there, they went to join him: 'And every one that was in distress, and every one that was in debt, and every one that was discontented, gathered themselves unto him' (I Sam. 22: 2). Adullam can be mentioned in the context of a place where those in trouble can seek refuge.

> Mixen Lane was the Adullam of all the surrounding villages. It was the hiding-place of those in distress, and in debt, and trouble of every kind.
> THOMAS HARDY *The Mayor of Casterbridge*, 1886

Alsatia In the 17th century, Alsatia was an area around Whitefriars, London, which became a sanctuary for criminals and debtors. The name is taken from Alsace, the much disputed territory between France and Germany.

> But Maggie always appeared in the most amiable light at her aunt Moss's: it was her Alsatia, where she was out of reach of law—if she upset anything, dirtied her shoes, or tore her frock, these things were matters of course at her aunt Moss's.
> GEORGE ELIOT *The Mill on the Floss*, 1860

Jehoshabeath According to the Bible, Ahaziah was a king of Judah who followed Ahab in his worship of Baal instead of God. He was killed by Jehu, and after his death his mother 'arose and destroyed all the seed royal of the house of Judah' (2 Chron. 22: 10). However, her daughter, Jehoshabeath, took one of the sons, Joash, and hid him in a bedchamber to keep him safe.

Joash ▶ *See* JEHOSHABEATH.

Linus blanket Linus is a character in the *Peanuts* cartoon strip, created in 1950 by Charles M. Schultz. The cartoons feature a group of children, including Charlie Brown with his dog, Snoopy. Linus is always shown carrying a piece of old blanket as a comforter, and the term 'Linus blanket' has come to represent anything that provides reassurance and a feeling of security.

> Roy went to the closet for a jacket. He gave it to his brother who laid his bible down and put on the coat, then picked up the bible again. It was his Linus blanket, I figured. He never went anywhere without it.
> TED WOOD *A Clean Kill*, 1995

Moses Moses (c.14th–13th centuries BC) was a Hebrew prophet and lawgiver. According to the Bible, he was born at a time when Pharaoh had decreed that all male Hebrew children were to be killed at birth. His mother hid him for three months and then, when she could hide him no longer, made him a small

basket out of bulrushes and placed him in the basket amid the reeds of the Nile. Moses was discovered by Pharaoh's daughter who took pity on him and decided to raise him as her own child, using the child's own mother for a nurse.
▶ *See special entry* ❏ **MOSES AND THE BOOK OF EXODUS** *on p. 264.*

> But going back to what's fundamental, Vic, it seems to me you guard everything you do like you were protecting baby Moses from the Pharaoh.
> SARA PARETSKY *Tunnel Vision*, 1994

Samson

In the Bible, the Book of Judges relates how Samson, an Israelite leader known for his great strength, was betrayed to the Philistines by his lover, Delilah. She discovered that the secret of Samson's strength lay in his long hair and had it cut off while he slept. Delilah delivered Samson up to the Philistines, who blinded him and imprisoned him in Gaza. During his captivity, his hair grew back and, being brought out to make sport for the Philistines during a religious celebration, he called on God for strength and pulled down the pillars supporting the temple, destroying himself and a large number of Philistines.

Various aspects of the Samson story are dealt with throughout the book.

▶ *See* DELILAH *at* **Betrayal** *and* **Cunning**
   PHILISTINES *at* **Enemy**
   SAMSON *at* **Blindness**, **Captives**, **Hair**, **Strength**, *and* **Weakness**
   SAMSON AND DELILAH *at* **Lovers**.

Sculptors

Literary allusions to sculptors have tended to be to those of antiquity or classical legend, typically in order to describe the seeming perfection of a person's physical beauty.

Galatea In Greek mythology, Galatea was the name of the ivory statue of a woman carved by the sculptor Pygmalion. He fell in love with his creation which, in answer to his prayer, the goddess Aphrodite brought to life. ▶ *See* **PYGMALION**.

Myron Myron (*c.*480–440 BC) was a Greek sculptor who produced very lifelike sculptures of people, most famously the *Discobolus*, a figure of a man throwing a discus.

Phidias Phidias (or Pheidias) was a 5th-century BC Athenian sculptor, celebrated for his colossal gold-and-ivory Athena Parthenos at Athens and for his vast statue of Zeus at Olympia. He also designed many of the sculptures of the Parthenon and Acropolis.

> In Clym Yeobright's face could be dimly seem the typical countenance of the future. Should there be a classical period to art hereafter, its Pheidias may produce such faces.
> THOMAS HARDY *The Return of the Native*, 1880

Praxiteles Praxiteles (4th century BC) was an Athenian sculptor. Although only one of his works survives, a sculpture of Hermes carrying the infant Dionysus, he is considered to be one of the foremost Greek sculptors. One of his most famous works was a statue of Aphrodite, which is known through later copies.

> She had bared her plump neck, shoulders, and arms to the moonshine, under which they looked as luminous and beautiful as some Praxitelean creation.
> THOMAS HARDY *Tess of the D'Urbervilles*, 1891

> He stood up slowly and went over to close the curtains. His silhouette against the window was like something Praxiteles might have knocked up for personal consumption.
> LAUREN HENDERSON *The Black Rubber Dress*, 1997

Pygmalion In Greek mythology, Pygmalion was a legendary king of Cyprus who made a statue so beautiful that he fell in love with it and prayed to Aphrodite to give him a wife resembling the statue. Aphrodite responded by bringing the statue to life, and Pygmalion married the woman thus created, whose name was Galatea.

> You see, he is after all building a woman of his own fancy, a face to a husband's own specifications; only Pygmalion had such a chance before!
> LAWRENCE DURRELL *Mountolive*, 1958

Seducers and Male Lovers

Most of the allusions covered below epitomize male promiscuity or sexual predatoriness. The idea of a male lover free of such connotations can be represented by **PRINCE CHARMING** and, sometimes, **ROMEO**. ▶ *See also* **Lovers**, **Sex and Sexuality**.

Casanova Giovanni Jacopo Casanova de Seingalt (1725–98) was an Italian adventurer, spy, gambler, and librarian who, according to his *Memoirs*, engaged in a prodigious number of promiscuous love affairs.

> Everybody looked like a broken-down movie extra, a withered starlet; disenchanted stunt-men, midget auto-racers, poignant California characters with their end-of-the-continent sadness, handsome, decadent, Casanova-ish men, puffy-eyed motel

blondes, hustlers, pimps, whores, masseurs, bellhops—a lemon lot, and how's a man going to make a living with a gang like that?
JACK KEROUAC *On the Road*, 1957

She had satisfied herself that there was no Lady Chatterley situation in progress and that was all that interested her. She would have been quite staggered if the reverse had proved to be the case since, not only did Alistair have very little going for him in the Casanova department, but Rowena would need major surgery to uncross her legs.
JOYCE HELM *Foreign Body*, 1997

Don Juan Don Juan Tenorio was a legendary Spanish nobleman famous for his seductions. The character appears in various works of literature and music, such as Mozart's opera *Don Giovanni*, Byron's poem *Don Juan*, and the 'Don Juan in Hell' section of Shaw's play *Man and Superman*. The term 'Don Juan' is now often used to describe a man with a reputation for seducing women.

It was a highly original, rather overwritten piece of sustained description concerned with a Don Juan of the New York slums.
F. SCOTT FITZGERALD *The Beautiful and the Damned*, 1922

'Marigold's taken up choral singing. They're doing the *Saint Matthew Passion*.' 'Oh yes. And what passion are you doing, Featherstone?' Miss Trant looked at her host with some suspicion. Featherstone, thinking he was being treated like a dangerous Don Juan, was flattered.
JOHN MORTIMER *Rumpole's Return*, 1980

Lothario Lothario is a character from Nicholas Rowe's play *The Fair Penitent* (1703), 'that haughty, gallant, gay Lothario'. As with those of Casanova and Don Juan, his name is now a byword for libertinism.

And yet Eleanor understood him as thoroughly as though he had declared his passion with all the elegant fluency of a practised Lothario.
ANTHONY TROLLOPE *Barchester Towers*, 1857

But what of the men they choose to live out their fantasies with? All too often men who work in tourist resorts are condemned as lecherous Lotharios interested only in sex.
The Independent, 1997

The difference is, when you see somebody here going from hotel room to hotel room at 3am, they're not Lotharios out for a couple of shags—they're doing business deals.
The Observer, 1997

Lovelace In Samuel Richardson's *Clarissa* (1747-8), Robert Lovelace is the dashing but unscrupulous womanizer who seduces the virtuous Clarissa.

Mr Dagonet's notion of the case was almost as remote from reality. All he asked was that his grandson should 'thrash' somebody, and he could not be made to understand that the modern drama of divorce is sometimes cast without a Lovelace.
EDITH WHARTON *The Custom of the Country*, 1913

Prince Charming Prince Charming is the hero of the fairy story *The Blue Bird* (*L'Oiseau Bleu*) by Mme d'Aulnoy. Having fallen in love with a king's daughter, he falls foul of her wicked stepmother and is condemned to spend seven years in the form of a blue bird. At the end of the seven years, he regains his proper shape and all turns out well. The name, which has come to be erroneously associated with other fairy stories, particularly with the prince in the

Cinderella story, can also be applied to any idealized young lover or suitor.

> You have made me understand what love really is. My love! my love! Prince Charming! Prince of life!
> OSCAR WILDE *The Picture of Dorian Gray*, 1891

> It always happens this way. The right bridegroom turns up verily like the Prince Charming all of a sudden when the time comes.
> R. K. NARAYAN *Under the Banyan Tree*, 1985

Romeo Romeo is the passionate and faithful young lover in Shakespeare's tragedy *Romeo and Juliet* (1599). His name can be used to denote a young man in love, though it is now frequently, and somewhat unjustly, applied to a womanizer, as in the phrase 'the office Romeo'.

> His personal feeling that loving Phoebe Wilson was a thing beyond the scope of the most determined Romeo he concealed. It could, apparently, be done.
> P. G. WODEHOUSE *Cocktail Time*, 1958

> It's that middle stretch of the night, when the curtains leak no light, the only street-noise is the grizzle of a returning Romeo, and the birds haven't begun their routine yet cheering business.
> JULIAN BARNES *A History of the World in 10½ Chapters*, 1989

Zeus The greatest of the Greek gods, identified by the Romans with Jupiter, Zeus was the protector and ruler of mankind, the dispenser of justice, and the god of weather (whose most famous weapon was the thunderbolt). Although he was the husband of Hera, there are many stories of him amorously pursuing other goddesses and, usually having assumed a disguise, mortal women. For example, Zeus visited Danae in the form of a shower of gold, Leda as a swan, and Europa as a bull.

Sex and Sexuality

This theme overlaps with the closely related theme **Love and Marriage**. The entries below are largely concerned with sexual desire, and in some cases with lechery or debauchery. More specific aspects of human sexuality are associated with such names as **LOLITA, OEDIPUS, MARQUIS DE SADE** and **SAPPHO**. ▶ *See also* **Prostitutes, Seducers and Male Lovers, Sirens**.

Adam According to the Book of Genesis, Adam was the first man on earth who, with Eve, the first woman, disobeyed God and was expelled from the Garden of Eden. The term 'old Adam' refers to the evil or sinfulness that is supposed to be inherent in human nature and is often used in the context of sexual desire. ▶ *See special entry* □ **ADAM AND EVE** *on p. 5.*

> As he put his arms around her again the still small voice of his conscience whispered

'Rachel'; it was answered by the robust voice of the Old Adam pointing out that he had never claimed to be a saint.
RUTH DUDLEY EDWARDS *Matricide at St Martha's*, 1994

Alcibiades Alcibiades (*c*.450–404 BC) was an Athenian general and statesman who had a reputation for debauchery. He had been a student and perhaps a lover of Socrates.

Aphrodite In Greek mythology, Aphrodite was the goddess of beauty, sexual love, and fertility, corresponding to the Roman goddess Venus. She is supposed to have been born from the sea-foam on the shores of the island of Cythera.

Who is this goddess who comes in a vision with uncovered breast cutting the air? It is Aphrodite, but not smile-loving Aphrodite, patroness of pleasures: an older figure, a figure of urgency, of cries in the dark, short and sharp, of blood and earth, emerging for an instant, showing herself, passing.
J. M. COETZEE *Age of Iron*, 1990

Ashtoreth ▶ *See* ASTARTE.

Astarte Astarte was the Phoenician goddess of sexual love and fertility, corresponding to the Babylonian Ishtar, the Egyptian Isis, the Greek Aphrodite, and others. In the Bible she is referred to as Ashtoreth or Ashtaroth, and her worship is linked with that of the male god Baal.

Bacchus Bacchus was another name for the Greek god Dionysus, the son of Zeus and Semele. Originally a god of the fertility of nature, associated with wild and ecstatic religious rites, in later traditions he is a god of wine who loosens inhibitions and inspires creativity in music and poetry. The adjectives 'Bacchic' and 'Bacchanalian' usually describe orgiastic or drunken revelry.

She was shaken by a Bacchic and bawdy mood.
GRAHAM GREENE *Brighton Rock*, 1938

Her dreams began to become scenes of entangled limbs and uninhibited bacchanalia. People copulated and cavorted in improbable positions with superhuman gusto.
LOUIS DE BERNIÈRES *The War of Don Emmanuel's Nether Parts*, 1990

Byron George Gordon, Lord Byron (1788–1824) was an English romantic poet, famous for his passionate love affairs as much as for his poetry. His major works include *Childe Harold's Pilgrimage* (1812–18) and *Don Juan* (1819–24). The term 'Byronic' can suggest both passionate romanticism and libertinism.

It appeared that he had been a Lincolnshire country doctor of Cornish extraction, striking appearance, and Byronic tendencies.
JOHN GALSWORTHY *The Man of Property*, 1906

Dionysian In Greek mythology, Dionysus (also called Bacchus) is a Greek god, the son of Zeus and Semele. Originally a god of the fertility of nature, associated with wild and ecstatic religious rites, in later traditions he is a god of wine who loosens inhibitions and inspires creativity in music and poetry. 'Dionysian' and 'Dionysiac' usually describe frenzied and unrestrained abandon or ecstasy.

Someone dimmed the lights and turned up the sitar music. They swayed and pressed and wriggled against each other in the twanging, orange, smoky twilight, it was a

kind of dance, they were all dancing, he was dancing—at last: the free, improvised, Dionysian dancing he'd hankered after.
DAVID LODGE *Changing Places*, 1975

Electra In Greek mythology, Electra was the daughter of Agamemnon and Clytemnestra. She persuaded her brother Orestes to kill Clytemnestra and her lover, Aegisthus, in revenge for the murder of Agamemnon. In psychoanalytical theory, an Electra complex is a daughter's subconscious sexual attraction to her father and hostility towards her mother, corresponding to the Oedipus complex in a son.

Do all fathers think their daughters are so beautiful?' It's a line that Arthur quotes approvingly to his beloved, thus snaring the movie in an Electra complex.
New Yorker, 1995

Eros In Greek mythology, Eros (called Cupid by the Romans) was the god of love, usually represented as a winged boy with a bow and arrows. Eros is now generally used to represent the idea of sexual love or the libido.

The dark tides of Eros, which demand full secrecy if they are to overflow the human soul, burst out during carnival like something long dammed up.
LAWRENCE DURRELL *Balthazar*, 1958

Freudian Sigmund Freud (1856–1939) was an Austrian neurologist and psychotherapist, the founder of psychoanalysis as both a theory of personality and a therapeutic practice. He emphasized the importance of sex as a prime motive force in human behaviour.

His service has been all on that most commonplace of battlefields, the domestic front; and he has the baggy eyes and saddened heart to prove it. He has known the Freudian hungers, received, at the age of twenty, a sound education in complicated misery from a bouncy-breasted Swedish girl friend, which still haunts his middle life, felt the desire for change and complication, but never satisfied it.
MALCOLM BRADBURY *Rates of Exchange*, 1983

Ganymede In Greek mythology, Ganymede (or Ganymedes) was a Trojan youth who was so beautiful that he was carried off by an eagle to be Zeus' cupbearer. He is the archetype of a beautiful and desirable youth.

He was always on the look-out for promising young men who could be advanced in his service. . . . I do not suggest that Boy ever recognized these young men as anything but business associates; but they were business associates with an overtone of Jove's cup-bearer that I, at least, could not ignore. Corporation Ganymedes, they did not know their role and were thus disappointments.
ROBERTSON DAVIES *Fifth Business*, 1970

Ishtar Ishtar was the Babylonian and Assyrian goddess of sexual love, fertility, and war.

Jezebel Jezebel was a Phoenician princess of the 9th century BC, the wife of Ahab, king of Israel. She was denounced by Elijah for promoting the worship of the Phoenician god Baal, and trying to destroy the prophets of Israel. Her use of cosmetics led to the use of her name to mean a shameless or immoral woman.

> Certainly, she had not seduced him; had not vamped him like some wicked Jezebel.
> RANDALL KENAN *Let the Dead Bury their Dead*, 1992

Lesbos Lesbos is a Greek island in the eastern Aegean. Its artistic golden age of the late 7th and early 6th centuries BC produced the poet Sappho, whose love poems express her passionate friendships with women. This explains the association of the island with female homosexuality and the derivation of the words 'lesbian' and 'Sapphic'.

> Most of the men I know are defective. Most of them are vain. My good friend and mentor Peggy O'Reggis lives in a universe in which men are only marginally visible. Ditto my lawyer, Virginia Goodchild, a committed citizen of Lesbos.
> CAROL SHIELDS *Mary Swann*, 1990

Lolita Vladimir Nabokov's novel *Lolita* (1958) concerns the obsession of the middle-aged Humbert Humbert with his 12-year-old stepdaughter Lolita, whom Humbert describes as a 'nymphet'. The word 'Lolita' can be used to describe any sexually precocious young girl.

> My present wife. I didn't 'seduce' her, she didn't do a Lolita act on me. We met (out of school as it happens), and bang, that was that.
> JULIAN BARNES *Talking It Over*, 1991

> One thing's for sure, if anyone would have been immune to the charms of a Liverpudlian Lolita, Benny's the man. Now if you'd been talking about a pretty schoolboy, things would have been different.
> MARTIN EDWARDS *Yesterday's Papers*, 1994

Lucretia In Roman legend, Lucretia (or Lucrece) was a woman who was raped by Sextus, a son of Tarquinus Superbus, king of Rome, and took her own life. According to tradition, this incident led to the expulsion of the Tarquins from Rome by a rebellion under Brutus, and the introduction of republican government. The story is told in Shakespeare's poem *The Rape of Lucrece* (1594).

> He then, though I struggled against him, kissed me and said, 'Who ever blamed Lucretia? The shame lay on the ravisher only.'
> SAMUEL RICHARDSON *Pamela*, 1740

Maenad In Greek mythology, maenads were female participants in the orgiastic rites of Dionysus. They were also known as Bacchae.

> I do not think I shall ever forget the impression she made on me at the party at which I first saw her. She was like a maenad. She danced with an abandon that made you laugh, so obvious was her intense enjoyment of the music and the movement of her young limbs.
> W. SOMERSET MAUGHAM *The Human Element*, 1951

Oedipus In Greek mythology, Oedipus was the son of Jocasta and of Laius, king of Thebes. The infant Oedipus was left to die on a mountainside by Laius, who had been warned by an oracle that his own son would kill him. Found by a shepherd, Oedipus was subsequently adopted by the king of Corinth and his wife, whom he grew up believing to be his parents. When an adult, Oedipus heard the oracle's prophecy and fled to Thebes, where he unwittingly killed his father and married Jocasta, by whom he had four children. On discovering what he had done he blinded himself in a fit of madness and left Thebes as an outcast, while Jocasta hanged herself. In psychoanalytical theory, the Oedipus complex is a son's subconscious sexual attraction to his mother and hostility towards his father. Oedipus is thus alluded to especially in the context of the incestuous love of a son for his mother.

> The last time I saw you, when I was passing through from Mississippi, you were in pretty bad shape. You've probably regressed completely by now living in that sub-standard old house with only your mother for company. Aren't your natural impulses crying for release? A beautiful and meaningful love affair would transform you, Ignatius. I know it would. Great Oedipus bonds are encircling your brain and destroying you.
> JOHN KENNEDY TOOLE *A Confederacy of Dunces*, 1980

Pan In Greek mythology, Pan was a god of nature, fecundity, flocks, and herds, usually represented with the horns, ears, and legs of a goat on a man's body. He invented and played a flute of seven reeds, called a syrinx. Pan is often portrayed as lecherous and many stories involve his amorous pursuit of nymphs.

> They coughed as they danced, and laughed as they coughed. Of the rushing couples there could barely be discerned more than the high lights—the indistinctness shaping them to satyrs clasping nymphs—a multiplicity of Pans whirling a multiplicity of Syrinxes; Lotis attempting to elude Priapus, and always failing.
> THOMAS HARDY *Tess of the D'Urbervilles*, 1891

Potiphar's wife Joseph was a Hebrew patriarch, son of Jacob. The wife of Potiphar, an Egyptian officer, tried to seduce him but Joseph repeatedly refused her advances because of his loyalty to his master, her husband. Finally when Potiphar's wife found herself alone in the house with Joseph, she grabbed hold of him, saying 'Lie with me'. Joseph fled from the house, leaving a piece of his clothing in her hand. She subsequently made a false accusation that he had attempted to rape her (Gen. 39). ▶ *See special entry* ☐ **JOSEPH** *on p. 224.*

> So pressing an issue is it [the sexual harassment of men by women] . . . that the European Union considered it necessary to produce a 93-page booklet on what it described as 'the Potiphar's wife syndrome'.
> *The Guardian*, 1994

Priapus In Greek mythology, Priapus was a god of fertility and procreation, represented as an ugly human figure with enormous genitals. He was also a god of gardens and vineyards. His name is sometimes used in the context of male libido; the adjective derived from his name 'priapic' means 'phallic'.

> Then she touched him. King Priapus, he who had been scared to death, now rose up from the dead.
> TOM WOLFE *The Bonfire of the Vanities*, 1987

Marquis de Sade Donatien Alphonse François, Comte de Sade (1740-1814), known as the Marquis de Sade, was a French writer and soldier. He was frequently imprisoned for sexual offences. While in prison he wrote a number of sexually explicit works, which include *Les 120 Journées de Sodome* (1784), *Justine* (1791), and *La Philosophie dans le boudoir* (1795). Sadism, the deriving of sexual pleasure from inflicting pain or suffering on others, is named after him.

Sappho Sappho, born in Lesbos, was a celebrated Greek lyric poet of the early

7th century BC. The poetry that survives consists mainly of love poems, many expressing her passionate friendships with women. This explains her association with female homosexuality and the derivation of the words 'lesbian' and 'Sapphic'.

> She was one of the group known as the 'Dorm 5 Co' who were suspected of active homosexual relations which, if the stories were true, left the school's more normal Sapphic romances looking almost Christian.
> PETER CAREY *Illywhacker*, 1985

Satyr In classical mythology satyrs were lustful woodland spirits associated with Dionysian revelry. In Greek art they were represented with the tail and ears of a horse, whereas Roman sculptors represented them with the ears, horns, tail, and legs of a goat.

> The looseness of his lower lip and the droop of his upper eyelids combined with the V's in his face to make his grin lewd as a satyr's.
> DASHIELL HAMMETT *The Maltese Falcon*, 1930

> It was hard to imagine H. E. sniffing after some other country woman, or being discovered mounting one of the milking girls. H. E., even when he was twenty-seven, would not have made a credible farmyard satyr.
> THOMAS KENEALLY *The Playmaker*, 1987

Sodom Sodom and Gomorrah were towns in ancient Palestine, probably south of the Dead Sea. According to Gen. 19: 24, they were destroyed by fire and brimstone from heaven as a punishment for the depravity and wickedness of their inhabitants. In particular 'the sin of Sodom' is traditionally taken to refer to buggery.

> 'Be serious. It's not just the wife. Dunny, we have to face it. You're queer.' 'The sin of Sodom, you mean? If you knew boys as I do, you would not suggest anything so grotesque. If Oscar Wilde had pleaded insanity, he would have walked out of court a free man.'
> ROBERTSON DAVIES *Fifth Business*, 1970

Venus Venus, corresponding to the Greek Aphrodite, was the Roman goddess of love, beauty, and fertility. She was supposed to have been born from the sea-foam and was herself the mother of Eros.

> 'As for Justine,' said Pursewarden to me when he was drunk once, 'I regard her as a tiresome old sexual turnstile through which presumably we must all pass—a somewhat vulpine Alexandrian Venus.'
> LAWRENCE DURRELL *Balthazar*, 1958

Oscar Wilde The Irish writer Oscar Wilde (1854–1900), a dandy and a notorious homosexual, was imprisoned for two years in Reading gaol (1895–97) for homosexual offences. He has subsequently been revered as a martyr by the gay rights movement.

> 'Your brother Roderick, I think,' Colefax continued, 'had a fiancee and was engaged to be married?' 'Oh yes. They'd both dined with me that night at my club. There was absolutely none of the Oscar Wildes about Rory.'
> JOHN MORTIMER *Rumpole's Return*, 1980

Silence

Two ideas are covered here: soundless places and speechless people. ▶ *See also* **Sound**, **Speech**.

....

Harpo Marx Adolph Arthur Marx (1888–1964), known as Harpo, was one of the Marx Brothers, a family of American comedians who made comic films in the 1930s. In the films, Harpo is always mute, communicating by means of an old-fashioned car horn.

'How did you know about us?' 'Her mother mentioned it. Talkative woman.' 'Her mother? She's about as talkative as Harpo Marx.'
MAX MARQUIS *Written in Blood*, 1995

Mary Celeste The *Mary Celeste* was an American brig that set sail from New York for Genoa, but was found in the North Atlantic in December 1872 abandoned but in perfect condition. The fate of the crew was never discovered, and the abandonment of the ship remains one of the great mysteries of the sea. The *Mary Celeste* can be alluded to as a place that is eerily silent and empty.

Sleeping Beauty In the well known fairy tale, Sleeping Beauty is a princess who has a spell put on her by a wicked fairy. As a result of this spell, Sleeping Beauty and all those in her palace fall asleep for a hundred years. The instant she is finally wakened from her slumber by a prince's kiss, all life and bustle returns to the palace. Sleeping Beauty's palace can be mentioned as a place of complete silence.

The front door was opened. They entered. In the silent, empty hall three and a half centuries of life had gone to sleep … 'Like the Sleeping Beauty,' she said. but even as she spoke the words, the spell was broken. Suddenly, as though the ringing glass had called the house back to life, there was sound and movement.
ALDOUS HUXLEY *Point Counter Point*, 1928

Similarity

Of the pairs below, only **ROLAND AND OLIVER** are not twin brothers. The idea of twins can, of course, be used to express physical similarity but also any strong degree of affinity or association. References to **CHANG AND ENG** call to mind the additional notion of inseparability. ▶ *See also* **Duality**.

....

Castor and Pollux In Greek and Roman mythology, Castor and Pollux (also known as the Dioscuri, 'the sons of Zeus') were the twin sons born to Leda, wife of Tyndareus, after her seduction by Zeus. They were believed to have hatched from a single egg. Castor was the son of Tyndareus and was mortal; Pollux was the son of Zeus and was immortal. When Castor was killed, Pollux offered to share his immortality between them, spending half their time below the earth with Hades and the other half on Olympus. They were eventually transformed by Zeus into the constellation Gemini so that they would not be separated.

> They operated in perfect, entwined counterpoint—a diplomatic Castor and Pollux.
> ED VULLIAMY in The *Observer*, 1997

Chang and Eng Chang and Eng (1811–74) were the original Siamese twins, born in Siam and joined by a fleshy band in the region of the waist. They married sisters and each fathered several children. Their names, or the term 'Siamese twins', can be used to describe any two people or things that are always together or very closely associated.

> Now envy and antipathy, passions irreconcilable in reason, nevertheless in fact may spring conjoined like Chang and Eng in one birth.
> HERMAN MELVILLE *Billy Budd*, 1924

Roland and Oliver Roland was the legendary nephew of Charlemagne and one of his paladins, the twelve peers of Charlemagne's court. He is the hero of the *Chanson de Roland*, a 12th-century medieval romance, and of Ariosto's *Orlando Furioso* (1532). Roland is said to have become a close friend of Oliver, another paladin, after engaging him in a prolonged single combat which was so evenly matched that neither ever won. The expression 'a Roland for an Oliver' denotes a well-balanced combat or an effective retort or retaliation.

> He gave my termagant kinsman a *quid pro quo*—a Rowland for his Oliver, as the vulgar say.
> WALTER SCOTT *Antiquary*, 1816

Romulus and Remus According to Roman mythology, Romulus and Remus were the twin sons of Mars by the vestal virgin Rhea Silvia. Custom dictated that, because they had been born to a vestal, the twins had to be abandoned in infancy in a basket on the River Tiber, but they were found and suckled by a she-wolf and later raised by a shepherd family. They subsequently undertook to build a city on the banks of the Tiber; after a quarrel, however, Romulus killed his brother. He went on to found Rome, naming the city after himself.

Tweedledum and Tweedledee Tweedledum and Tweedledee were origin-ally names applied to the rival composers Handel and Bononcini in a 1725 satirical poem by John Byrom, making the point that the differences between them were so small as to be negligible. The names were later popularized when Lewis Carroll used them for two identical characters in *Through the Looking Glass* (1872). They are fat, quarrelsome twin brothers who fight a ridiculous battle with one another. Two people or things that are so alike that they are practically indistinguishable can be referred to as Tweedledum and Tweedle-dee.

> Coffin studied them, then drew the interview to an end. Won't get much more out of Tweedledum and Tweedledee just now, he thought.
> GWENDOLINE BUTLER *A Dark Coffin*, 1995

Sirens

In the stories below, men are lured to disaster and destruction by a woman's beauty. ▶ *See also* **Temptation**.

....

Circe In Greek mythology, Circe was a beautiful enchantress who lived on the island of Aeaea. When Odysseus visited the island on his return from the Trojan War, she turned his men into swine. Odysseus protected himself with the mythical herb moly and forced her to break the spell and restore his men to human form. Odysseus was detained on Circe's island for a year. Allusions to her are usually in the context of a bewitching, dangerously attractive woman or place. ▶ *See special entry* ☐ ODYSSEUS *on p. 283.*

> None of the books I had read explained this sinister-fascinating, this Circe-like quality of Greece; the quality that makes it unique.
> JOHN FOWLES *The Magus*, 1977

Lorelei In Germanic folklore, Lorelei is the name of a rock at the edge of the Rhine, held to be the home of a siren with long blonde hair whose song lures boatmen to destruction. The name can also be applied to the siren herself. A Lorelei is a dangerously fascinating woman, a siren.

> My parents lived deep in the burg in a narrow duplex that on a cold day like this would smell like chocolate pudding cooking on the stove. The effect was similar to Lorelei, singing to all those sailors, sucking them in so they'd crash on the rocks.
> JANET EVANOVICH *Three to Get Deadly*, 1997

Mata Hari Mata Hari (1876–1917), born Margaretha Geertruida Zelle, was a Dutch dancer, courtesan, and spy. She became a professional 'oriental' dancer in Paris in 1905 and probably worked for both French and German intelligence services during the Second World War, obtaining military secrets from high-ranking Allied officers. She was executed by the French for espionage in 1917. The term 'Mata Hari' can be applied to any beautiful, seductive woman.

> I had a bad time at the hands of male journalists during Julian's trial and in the period leading up to it: some residual paranoia sticks. They look for a *femme fatale*, a Mata Hari of world finance, a seductress. If a woman is to be taken seriously she must either be past the menopause or very plain, preferably both.
> FAY WELDON *Darcy's Utopia*, 1990

> A junior partner promoted by their lover can be seen as a Mata Hari.
> *The Observer*, 1997

Sirens In Greek mythology, the Sirens were sea creatures who lured seafarers to destruction on dangerous rocks by the beauty of their singing. They were usually depicted as women or as half woman and half bird. In the *Odyssey*, Odysseus had himself tied to the mast of his ship in order to hear their song safely, having first ordered his crew to plug their ears with wax. The word 'siren' is used to describe a seductive woman, who lures men to their doom.
▶ *See special entry* ☐ ODYSSEUS *on p. 283.*

Of course such a marriage was only what Newland was entitled to; but young men are so foolish and incalculable—and some women so ensnaring and unscrupulous—that it was nothing short of a miracle to see one's only son safe past the Siren Isle and in the haven of a blameless domesticity.
EDITH WHARTON *The Age of Innocence*, 1920

Faces flashed in front of me. I made out Caro's and Katherine's, then they were both replaced by the flawless mask of the murderess, her lips moving as she spoke. I opened my eyes with a start and she disappeared. But her voice still rang in my ears, sweeter and more deadly than any siren's song.
PAUL JOHNSTON *Body Politic*, 1997

Sleep

Many stories explore the idea of prolonged sleep. In those referred to below, the duration of sleep varies from twenty years to 100 years, 200 years, or even eternity.

King Arthur Arthur, historically perhaps a 5th or 6th-century Romano-British chieftan or general, is in legend the king of Britain who presided over the Knights of the Round Table at Camelot. After being fatally wounded by his nephew, Mordred, the dying king was borne away to the island of Avalon, where he was buried. In some versions of the legend it is said that Arthur is not dead but sleeping, ready to awaken and return in the hour of Britain's need.

Looka there!—is it a girl? Is it a, *sorry*, woman? No—It's the Phantom Nympho! And she's *raring* to go, as per! Like King Arthur, see, she wasn't really dead; just sleeping (around) till her people felt in need of her once more. And now she's back. Back!
JULIE BURCHILL 'The Phantom Nympho Rides Again' in *Sex and Sensibility*, 1989

Dormouse The Dormouse is one of the characters that Alice meets at the Mad Hatter's tea party in Lewis Carroll's *Alice's Adventures in Wonderland* (1865). The Dormouse snoozes all through the tea party, despite attempts to wake it by pinching it. ▶ *See special entry* □ **ALICE IN WONDERLAND** *on p. 10.*

Endymion In Greek mythology, Endymion was a very beautiful young man, loved by Selene, the moon goddess. According to one story, Zeus granted him eternal youth by causing him to sleep forever. This story is the basis of Keats's poem *Endymion* (1818).

Hypnos Hypnos was the Greek god of sleep, son of Nyx (night).

Land of Nod In the Bible, the Land of Nod was the land east of Eden to which Cain was banished after he had slain his brother Abel (Gen. 4: 16). Although *Nod* probably meant 'wandering', the phrase, inviting a pun on *nod* 'to fall asleep', has now come to refer to a mythical land of sleep.

At last I slid off into a light doze, and had pretty nearly made a good offing towards

the land of Nod, when I heard a heavy footfall in the passage, and saw a glimmer of light come into the room from under the door.
HERMAN MELVILLE *Moby Dick*, 1851

Lady Macbeth In a famous scene in Shakespeare's play *Macbeth* (1623), Lady Macbeth, troubled by guilt for urging her husband to commit murder, is found sleepwalking. She washes her hands in her sleep in an attempt to remove the spots of blood that she imagines to be on them.

Morpheus In Roman mythology, Morpheus was the god of dreams, son of Somnus, the god of sleep. To fall into the arms of Morpheus is thus to fall asleep.

Just begin a story with a phrase such as 'I remember Disraeli—poor old Dizzy!— once saying to me, in answer to my poke in the eye', and you will find me and Morpheus off in a corner, necking.
DOROTHY PARKER *Book Reviews*, 1927–33

After coffee I announced myself eager for the fleecy crook of Morpheus' shoulder, and they buggered off.
JULIAN BARNES *Talking It Over*, 1991

Keith, even more irritable than Cooper to be dragged from the arms of Morpheus far away in London, perked up a little to hear that Jack was under arrest.
MINETTE WALTERS *The Scold's Bridle*, 1994

Rip Van Winkle Rip Van Winkle is the main character in a story by Washington Irving (1820). During a walk in the Catskill Mountains, Rip falls asleep, and wakes some twenty years later to find that the world has changed considerably. His wife has died, his daughter has married, and he has completely missed the War of American Independence.

There are few more powerful images of traditionalism in English cricket than the elderly man in the striped Hove deckchair. But after snoozing through history with a determination that makes Rip van Winkle look like a cat-napper, he is showing disturbing signs of life.
The Guardian, 1997

She led him to the window and swung the panel so that it acted as a mirror.
'See that antique wreck standing next to that gorgeous woman? That's you. If Rosie opens her eyes and sees you first, she'll think she's done a Rip Van Winkle and slept for fifty years.'
REGINALD HILL *On Beulah Height*, 1998

Sandman In children's stories, the Sandman is a man who makes children feel sleepy by sprinkling sand in their eyes.

Now if you're a good little girl and sleep sound so the Sandman won't have to throw sand in your eyes, Santa Claus will bring you something nice for Christmas.
CHESTER HIMES *Christmas Gift*, 1944

Most people find it easy to sleep on trains, but for me it's particularly easy. In fact, I find it almost impossible to stay awake. I grew up in a house that backed on to a train line and night-time was when you'd notice the trains most. My version of the Sandman is the 12:10 from Euston.
ALEX GARLAND *The Beach*, 1996

Seven Sleepers In early Christian legend, the Seven Sleepers were seven

Christian youths of Ephesus who, while fleeing persecution, entered a cave and fell asleep. They slept for almost 200 years. The legend is also told in the Koran.

> I wonder by my troth, what thou and I
> Did, till we loved? Were we not weaned till then,
> But sucked on country pleasures, childishly?
> Or snorted we in the seven sleepers' den?
> JOHN DONNE *Songs and Sonnets, 'The Good Morrow',*

> We shouted back loud enough to wake the seven sleepers.
> JEROME K. JEROME *Three Men in a Boat,* 1889

Sleeping Beauty In the well known fairy tale, Sleeping Beauty is a princess who has a spell put on her by a wicked fairy. As a result of this spell, Sleeping Beauty and all those in her palace fall asleep for a hundred years. She is finally wakened from her slumber by a prince's kiss.

> Edith came in from the back drawing-room, winking and blinking her eyes at the stronger light, shaking back her slightly-ruffled curls, and altogether looking like the Sleeping Beauty startled from her dreams.
> ELIZABETH GASKELL *North and South,* 1854–5

Somnus Somnus was the Roman god of sleep, father of Morpheus.

Titania In Shakespeare's *A Midsummer Night's Dream*, Titania is the queen of the fairies, and wife of Oberon. While she sleeps in her 'flow'ry bed', Oberon drops on her eyelids the juice from a magic flower which will make her fall in love with the first creature she sees when she wakes. This turns out to be Bottom the weaver, who has been given an ass's head by the mischievous sprite Puck.

> She lay curled up on the sofa in the back drawing-room in Harley Street, looking very lovely in her white muslin and blue ribbons. If Titania had ever been dressed in white muslin and blue ribbons, and had fallen asleep on a crimson damask sofa in a back drawing-room, Edith might have been taken for her.
> ELIZABETH GASKELL *North and South,* 1854–5

Wee Willie Winkie Wee Willie Winkie is a nursery rhyme character who makes sure that all children are in bed and asleep:

'Wee Willie Winkie runs through the town
Upstairs and downstairs in his night gown,
Rapping at the window, crying through the lock,
Are the children all in bed, for it's past eight o'clock?'

Small Size

All the allusions below can be used to describe a diminutive person. **LILLI-PUTIAN** can also be used to signify something that is tiny in scale. ▶ *See also* **Large Size**.

....

Alice At the beginning of Lewis Carroll's *Alice's Adventures in Wonderland* (1865), Alice drinks from a little bottle labelled 'Drink me' and immediately starts to shrink: "'What a curious feeling!" said Alice, "I must be shutting up like a telescope." And so it was indeed: she was now only ten inches high'. ▶ *See special entry* □ **ALICE IN WONDERLAND** *on p. 10.*

Borrowers *The Borrowers* (1952) by Mary Norton is the story of Pod, Homily, and Arrietty, a family of tiny people living beneath the floors of an old country mansion. They 'borrow' everything they need from the household of the 'human beans' above them.

Lilliputian In Book I of Jonathan Swift's *Gulliver's Travels* (1726), Gulliver finds himself shipwrecked on the island of Lilliput. The tiny Lilliputians are only six inches tall and, as Gulliver discovers, are as small-minded as they are small-bodied, being petty, pretentious, and factious. ▶ *See special entry* □ **GULLIVER'S TRAVELS** *on p. 171.*

> The children fill the house with the Lilliputian din of drums, trumpets, and penny-whistles.
> WASHINGTON IRVING *The Sketch-Book*, 1819–20

> A Lilliputian chest-of-drawers no doubt containing sea-shells and locks of children's hair.
> KINGSLEY AMIS *Lucky Jim*, 1953

> The engines were laid out sort of like a giant car engine, with every piece exposed so it could be cared for quickly. If you were a Lilliputian you would climb up and down a car engine just this way.
> SARA PARETSKY *Deadlock*, 1984

Munchkin In L. Frank Baum's children's story *The Wizard of Oz* (1900), the Munchkins are little people who live in the land of Oz.

> Unfortunately, the chairs at Momo are of the children's bedroom variety and if you hang your jacket on the back, it dusts the floor. Meanwhile, waiters loom over you in their designer Momo T-shirts ... and in this unnecessarily authentic and uncomfortable Munchkin world, even for a regular-sized woman like me, scrunched-up Madam looked—and apparently felt—like the Wicked Witch of the West.
> *The Observer*, 1997

Thumbelina Thumbelina is a tiny girl in a fairy tale by Hans Christian Andersen who, after being rescued by a swallow, marries the equally tiny king of the Angels of the Flowers.

Tom Thumb Tom Thumb was the hero of an English folk tale, the son of a ploughman and his wife who was only as tall as his father's thumb. After many adventures he was knighted by King Arthur. General Tom Thumb was the name given to Charles Stratton (1838–83), an American midget exhibited in the Barnum and Bailey shows.

Smiles

The two most famous smiles could hardly be more different. The **CHESHIRE CAT** has an enormous grin, the **MONA LISA** a faint, almost imperceptible upturn at the corners of her mouth. ▶ *See also* **Happiness**.

....

Cheshire Cat In Lewis Carroll's *Alice's Adventures in Wonderland* (1865), Alice encounters a large cat grinning from ear to ear. When she asks the Duchess the reason for this, the Duchess replies 'It's a Cheshire Cat, and that's why'. Later Alice watches the Cheshire Cat vanish 'beginning with the end of the tail, and ending with the grin, which remained some time after the rest of it had gone'. The expression 'to grin like a Cheshire cat', meaning to grin fixedly and broadly, pre-dates Carroll's story. ▶ *See special entry* ◻ **ALICE IN WONDERLAND** *on p. 10*.

> He nodded and was gone. The unnatural brightness of his smile seemed to linger in the air after the door closed, like the smile of a Cheshire cat.
> RAYMOND CHANDLER *The High Window*, 1943

> He seated himself, dodged a lump of sugar which a friendly hand had thrown from a neighbouring table, and beamed on his friends like a Cheshire cat.
> P. G. WODEHOUSE *Cocktail Time*, 1958

> He disappeared, leaving a cackle hanging in the air behind him like the Cheshire cat's grin.
> MIKE PHILLIPS *Point of Darkness*, 1994

Gioconda ▶ *See* **MONA LISA**.

Jolly Green Giant The Jolly Green Giant is the trademark of the Green Giant food company, producers of sweetcorn and other tinned and frozen vegetables. He is a friendly green-skinned giant who booms, 'Ho, ho, ho!'

> My father sits at the head of the table, beaming like the Jolly Green Giant.
> MARGARET ATWOOD *Cat's Eye*, 1988

Mona Lisa The *Mona Lisa* is the title of a painting by Leonardo da Vinci, perhaps the most famous painting in the world. The painting is also known as *La Gioconda* because the sitter was the wife of Francesco di Bartolommeo del Giocondo di Zandi. Her enigmatic smile has become one of the most famous images in Western art. The painting is now in the Louvre, Paris.

> Time had wrought another change too; not for her the sly, complacent smile of la

Gioconda; the years had been more than 'the sound of lyres and flutes', and had saddened her.
EVELYN WAUGH *Brideshead Revisited*, 1945

She grinned a smile of pure gold; it was like seeing Mona Lisa break into a laugh.
CHESTER HIMES *Blind Man with a Pistol*, 1969

Billy's smile as he came out of the shrubbery was at least as peculiar as Mona Lisa's.
KURT VONNEGUT *Slaughterhouse 5*, 1969

wolf in Red Riding Hood In the traditional fairy story, Little Red Riding Hood is a young girl sent by her mother to take cakes to her sick grandmother's remote cottage. A wolf eats the grandmother and takes her place in the bed, impersonating her when Red Riding Hood arrives. 'What big teeth you have!', the little girl says to her 'grandmother', to which the wolf replies: 'All the better to eat you with!'

Carl May smiled and it seemed to Bethany that his teeth were fangs and growing as long as the wolf's ever were in 'Red Riding Hood'.
FAY WELDON *The Cloning of Joanna May*, 1989

Soldiers

The figures below are renowned military strategists. Other leaders are covered in the related theme **Leaders**. ▶ *See also* **Courage**, **War**.

Alexander Alexander the Great (356–323 BC), the son of Philip II of Macedon, became king at 19 when his father was assassinated (336 BC). He defeated the Persians in three major battles, at the River Granicus, at Issus in Cilicia, and at Gaugamela, freeing the Greek city states and Egypt from Persian rule. While in Egypt he founded Alexandria. He extended his empire eastwards as far as India before dying young of a fever. Alexander is often cited as one of the greatest generals of all time.

Had Philip's warlike son been intellectually so far ahead as to have attempted civilization without bloodshed, he would have been twice the godlike hero that he seemed, but nobody would have heard of an Alexander.
THOMAS HARDY *The Return of the Native*, 1880

Monday dawned, the sun rising into the inevitable blue sky with the radiant serenity of Alexander entering a conquered province.
REGINALD HILL *On Beulah Height*, 1998

Hannibal Hannibal (247–182 BC) was the Carthaginian general who precipitated the second Punic War by attacking the town of Saguntum in Spain, an ally of Rome. He crossed the Alps in 218 with an army of about 30,000 and forty elephants. In Italy Hannibal inflicted a series of defeats on the Romans over a period of sixteen years but failed to take Rome itself. After being recalled to Africa to defend Carthage he was defeated at Zama by Scipio Africanus in

202. Hannibal has subsequently enjoyed a reputation as one of history's great military geniuses.

> He is not the Caesar, but the Hannibal of French politics.
> *Century Magazine*, 1883

Napoleon Napoleon Bonaparte (1769–1821), born in Corsica, became commander-in-chief of the French army in Italy at the age of 27. A coup d'état three years later established him initially as first consul, then as consul for life, and finally, in 1804, as emperor of France. Napoleon conquered and ruled much of Europe, establishing an extensive European empire, until his final defeat at the battle of Waterloo in 1815. He is often cited as an example of a brilliant campaigner and strategist.

> 'Oh, shucks!' said the youth. 'You ain't the bravest man in the world, are you?' 'No, I ain't,' exclaimed the loud soldier indignantly, 'and I didn't say I was the bravest man in the world neither. I said I was going to do my share of fighting—that's what I said and I am, too. Who are you anyhow? You talk as if you thought you was Napoleon Bonaparte.'
> STEPHEN CRANE *The Red Badge of Courage*, 1895

General Patton George Smith Patton (1885–1945) was an American general who commanded US forces in the Second World War. Known as 'Old Blood and Guts', he pursued an aggressive military strategy, taking the 3rd Army across France and Germany as far as the Czech border.

Wellington The 1st Duke of Wellington (1769–1852) was a British soldier and statesman. His military victories included those against the French during the Peninsular War (1808–14) and in particular the defeat of Napoleon at the battle of Waterloo (1815).

> Well, I don't want to be a soldier, he thought. I know that. So that's out. I just want us to win this war. I guess really good soldiers are really good at very little else, he thought. That's obviously untrue. Look at Napoleon and Wellington. You're very stupid this evening, he thought.
> ERNEST HEMINGWAY *For Whom the Bell Tolls*, 1941

Solitude

This theme incorporates two main ideas: solitude and the state of being an exile or an outcast. **ADAM**, **ROBINSON CRUSOE**, and **JESUS** can all be used to represent solitude, being in a place without the company of other people. **GRETA GARBO** and **HOWARD HUGHES** are more recent examples of social recluses. The other group—**CAIN, HAGAR, ISHMAEL, MARIUS**, and the **WANDERING JEW**—are representative of outcasts or exiles, those shunned by other people or banished from their home.

Adam According to the Book of Genesis in the Bible, Adam was the first man, created by God from the dust of the ground. Adam lived alone in the Garden of Eden until God created a companion for him: this was the first woman Eve, made from one of Adam's ribs. ▶ *See special entry* □ **ADAM AND EVE** *on p. 5.*

> But here ... shut in by the stable hills, among which mere walking had the novelty of pageantry, any man could imagine himself to be Adam without the least difficulty.
> THOMAS HARDY *The Return of the Native*, 1880

Cain In the Bible, Cain was the eldest son of Adam and Eve who murdered his own brother Abel (Gen. 4: 1–16). For this crime God expelled him from his homeland so that he was forced to spend the rest of his life wandering the earth as an outcast. God put a mark on him to indicate that no one should kill him and thus shorten the punishment. ▶ *See special entry* □ **CAIN** *on p. 44.*

> 'If I had only got her with me—if I only had!' he said. 'Hard work would be nothing to me then! But that was not to be. I—Cain—go alone as I deserve—an outcast and a vagabond.'
> THOMAS HARDY *The Mayor of Casterbridge*, 1886

Robinson Crusoe The eponymous hero of Daniel Defoe's novel *Robinson Crusoe* (1719) survives a shipwreck and lives on an uninhabited island for twenty-four years, at first alone and later joined by Man Friday. Crusoe's adventures are based on those of Alexander Selkirk (1676–1721), a sailor who, at his own request, was put ashore on an island in the Pacific and survived there for over four years. One of the most memorable episodes in the novel is Crusoe's horrified discovery of a footprint on the beach.

> Once, like another Crusoe, by the edge of the river he came upon a track—the faint tracery of a snowshoe rabbit on the delicate snow-crust. It was a revelation. There was life in the Northland.
> JACK LONDON *In a Far Country*, 1900

> He must have found the recipe in the pages of Postlethwaite's Vade Mecum For Travellers in Foreign Lands, a book which he kept under lock and key in his trunk and by which he absolutely swore. It contained, he said, everything that a man in Robinson Crusoe's position ought to know—even how to make a fire by rubbing sticks together; it was a mine of marvellous information.
> LAWRENCE DURRELL *Clea*, 1960

Greta Garbo Greta Garbo (1905–90) was born in Sweden as Greta Gustafsson. She became a successful Hollywood actress, renowned for her beauty, and starred in films such as *Queen Christina* (1933), *Anna Karenina* (1935), and *Ninotchka* (1939). She gave up her film career in 1941 and remained a recluse from then until her death. The phrase 'I want to be alone', used by Garbo in the 1932 film *Grand Hotel*, became closely identified with her.

> Fischer withdrew completely from professional chess and entered a Garboesque seclusion, freezing in perpetuity the popular image of himself as the intense young man from Brooklyn who had triumphed so spectacularly at Reykjavik.
> *The Independent*, 1992

Ben Gunn Ben Gunn is the marooned pirate in Robert Louis Stevenson's adventure story *Treasure Island*. Abandoned on the island by his shipmates, he has spent three years alone, living on 'goats and berries and oysters', and dreaming of toasted cheese.

> 'Well, here I am, marooned', Kay said to himself; keeping well under cover lest they should send another cannon ball. 'Now I am like poor Ben Gunn in *Treasure Island*: unless I am able to run down the goats, if there are any, I am not likely to get much dinner.'
> JOHN MASEFIELD *The Box of Delights*, 1935

Hagar In the Bible, Hagar was the Egyptian maid of Abraham's wife Sarah. Hagar bore Abraham a son, Ishmael (Gen. 16: 21). She and Ishmael were driven away as outcasts after Sarah gave birth to Isaac.

> Beside the milk-bush sat the Kaffir woman still—like Hagar, he thought, thrust out by her mistress in the wilderness to die.
> OLIVE SCHREINER *The Story of an African Farm*, 1883

Howard Hughes Howard Hughes (1905-76) was an American millionaire businessman and film producer who became a recluse for the last twenty-five years of his life.

> But as Olazabal was producing his pyrotechnics, David Gilford was slipping surreptitiously around in 67. This excellent Staffordshire player is as determinedly anonymous as Howard Hughes and despite the presence of microphones in the press interview area, it was still difficult to make out what he was saying.
> *The Guardian*, 1995

Ishmael The biblical Ishmael was the son of Abraham by Hagar, the maid of Abraham's wife, Sarah. Ishmael was cast out when Sarah gave birth to Isaac. The name of Ishmael, like that of his mother, Hagar, is used allusively for an outcast. The name is used for the narrator of Herman Melville's *Moby Dick*, the opening words of which are 'Call me Ishmael'.

> I always did hate those people . . . and they always have hated and always will hate me. I am an Ishmael by instinct as much as by accident of circumstances, but if I keep out of society I shall be less vulnerable than Ishmaels generally are.
> SAMUEL BUTLER *The Way of All Flesh*, 1903

> They were a jumble of people wearing about every tinge of skin there is. Inman guessed them to be as outlaw and Ishmaelite as himself. Show folk, outliers, a tribe of Irish gypsy horse traders all thrown in together.
> CHARLES FRAZIER *Cold Mountain*, 1997

Jesus The episode in the life of Jesus that is being alluded to in the quotation below is his forty days' fast in the wilderness as related in the New Testament (Matt. 4: 1-11). ▶ *See special entry* ❑ JESUS *on p. 223.*

> 'I been thinkin', he said. 'I been in the hills thinkin', almost you might say like Jesus went into the wilderness to think His way out of a mess of troubles.'
> JOHN STEINBECK *The Grapes of Wrath*, 1939

Lone Ranger The Lone Ranger is a masked law-enforcer in the American West, created in 1933 by George W. Trendle and Fran Striker for a radio series and popularized in a later TV series (1956-62). In the stories he is sometimes accompanied by an American Indian called Tonto. The Lone Ranger's name, though, is generally applied to an individual who acts alone in undertaking a rescue mission of some kind.

> 'I don't think of myself as an opera director', insists Jonathan Miller, 'I can't read music and I don't even go to the opera very much'. But for 25 years Dr Miller has been the Lone Ranger of the international opera world, the outsider whose productions strip away the cliches and hammy performances imposed by tradition.
> *The Daily Telegraph*, 1997

> 'I thought it was about time I reciprocated in this life-saving business. I had a deal with Rob. We agreed that whichever of us you called first would tell the other and join forces in the rescue'.
> 'How did you know there'd be a rescue?' Mark asked, his head muzzy and hurtling, his voice slurred.
> 'Just call me Mystic Meg. Come on Mark. The days of the Lone Ranger are far behind. Everybody needs their Tonto'.
> MEL STEIN *White Lines*, 1997

Marius Gaius Marius (157–86 BC), the great Roman general, was overcome by his rival, Sulla, and fled to Africa, landing at Carthage. When the Roman governor there sent word that he had to leave the country, Marius's reply was: 'Tell the praetor you have seen Gaius Marius a fugitive sitting among the ruins of Carthage.'

> And here Bartleby makes his home; sole spectator of a solitude which he has seen all populous—a sort of innocent and transformed Marius brooding among the ruins of Carthage!
> HERMAN MELVILLE *Bartleby*, 1856

Pied Piper Robert Browning's narrative poem 'The Pied Piper of Hamelin' (1842) tells how the Piper agrees to rid the town of Hamelin of rats by piping them to their destruction in the river. When the Mayor then reneges on his payment for this service, the Piper gets his revenge by leading the town's children away. They follow the exciting promise of his piping into an opened portal in the mountain-side. One child, however, is lame and cannot keep up with the rest. He explains his subsequent lifelong sadness and solitude towards the end of the poem:

'And just as I became assured
My lame foot would be speedily cured,
The music stopped and I stood still,
And found myself outside the hill,
Left alone against my will,
To go now limping as before,
And never hear of that country more!'

> It is a thought that has occurred to Rio di Angelo, a former member of Heaven's Gate, the suicide cult whose membership checked out en masse in March after announcing their departure on the Internet. Like the last child, too lame to follow the Pied Piper into the mountain, di Angelo was left behind.
> *The Observer*, 1997

Wandering Jew In medieval legend, the Wandering Jew was a man condemned to roam the earth until the Day of Judgement, as a punishment for having taunted Christ on the way to the Crucifixion, urging him to go faster.

> He would slouch out, like Cain or the Wandering Jew, as if he had no idea where he was going and no intention of ever coming back.
> CHARLES DICKENS *Great Expectations*, 1861

Sound

In the quotations below the sound that is being described is human in origin, whether it is that of voices or applause. ▶ *See also* **Music**, **Oratory**, **Silence**, **Speech**.

....

Babel According to the Book of Genesis in the Bible, there was a time near the beginning of the world when all men lived in one place and all spoke the same language. They built a tall tower, the Tower of Babel, in an attempt to reach up to heaven. On seeing the tower, God was concerned that man was becoming too powerful and so decided to thwart him by introducing different languages. He therefore went down to 'confound their language, that they may not understand one another's speech' (Gen. 11: 7). Once different languages were introduced and men no longer understood one another, the building of the tower stopped. The Tower of Babel can be alluded to as a place where people disagree with each other in a noisy way, and a Babel or babel is a confused noise of many voices.

> Discipline prevailed: in five minutes the confused throng was resolved into order, and comparative silence quelled the Babel clamour of tongues.
> CHARLOTTE BRONTË *Jane Eyre*, 1847

> He woke to a babel the next morning, and when he went down to the hall found the sisters getting their children ready for school.
> V. S. NAIPAUL *A House for Mr Biswas*, 1961

Judgement Day In Christian tradition, the Day of Judgement is the day when God will judge all the living and the dead and reward or punish them accordingly. The quotation below refers to the sound of all the people gathered together to be judged by God.

> At that there was a great outcry in the courtroom, like the uprush of voices at the Judgement Day; and I knew I was doomed.
> MARGARET ATWOOD *Alias Grace*, 1996

Krakatoa Krakatoa is a small volcanic island in Indonesia. An eruption in 1883 destroyed most of the island.

> He took the lectern to a Krakatoa of applause.
> MARTIN AMIS *The Information*, 1995

Speech

This theme concentrates on distinctive ways of speaking. Examples of eloquence and oratory are dealt with in the theme **Oratory**.

....

Bluebottle Bluebottle was a character in *The Goon Show*, an extremely popular BBC radio comedy series which ran from 1952 to 1960. Bluebottle, played by Peter Sellers, spoke in a comical high-pitched, whiny voice.

Lady Bracknell In Oscar Wilde's comedy *The Importance of Being Earnest* (1895), Lady Bracknell is Gwendolen Fairfax's mother. In a famous scene Gwendolen's suitor, Jack Worthing, explains that he was discovered as a baby in a handbag, to which Lady Bracknell responds 'A handbag?' The incredulous, withering delivery of this line by Edith Evans in the 1952 film of Wilde's play is well known and often imitated.

> 'Why are you walking around with it in your handbag?' he demanded, giving Lady Bracknell a run for her money.
> VAL MCDERMID *Clean Break*, 1995

Marlon Brando Marlon Brando (b. 1924) is an American actor whose films include *A Streetcar Named Desire* (1951), *On the Waterfront* (1954), and *The Godfather* (1972). A leading exponent of method acting, he is particularly associated with a mumbling delivery of his lines.

> Colin the Englishman is distrusted because he talks not too much but too well. Real painters grunt, like Marlon Brando.
> MARGARET ATWOOD *Cat's Eye*, 1988

Miss Jean Brodie Muriel Spark's novel *The Prime of Miss Jean Brodie*, first published in 1961, tells the story of Miss Jean Brodie, an Edinburgh schoolmistress during the 1930s. She is a spinster with firm views on the education of young women, remembered for saying: 'I am putting old heads on your young shoulders . . . all my pupils are the crème de la crème'. She speaks in a distinctive polite, precise, and authoritative voice.

> He left his post long enough to walk me to the gate. 'Sarge!' he yelled. One of the men by the door looked up. 'This is the Thayer girl's governess!' he called, cupping his hands. 'Thank you, Officer', I said, imitating Miss Jean Brodie's manner.
> SARA PARETSKY *Indemnity Only*, 1982

Winston Churchill Winston Churchill (1874–1965) was a British politician and prime minister who led the coalition government during the Second World War. He is remembered for his leadership qualities and his gifts as an orator. During the war he made several now-famous speeches, broadcast over the radio in his deep, slightly rasping voice.

> The last phrase he pronounced in the strange (man-sawing-wood) delivery of Churchill.
> LAWRENCE DURRELL *Clea*, 1960

Donald Duck Donald Duck is a cartoon character created by Walt Disney who has a distinctive high-pitched, quacking voice.

> Besides, he was kind of a sweet kid and had a voice like Donald Duck.
> JOSEPH WAMBAUGH *The Glitter Dome*, 1981

Eccles Eccles was a character in *The Goon Show*, an extremely popular BBC radio comedy series which ran from 1952 to 1960. Eccles, played by Spike Milligan, spoke in a slow, foolish-sounding voice.

God ▶ See JEHOVAH.

Jehovah Jehovah is used as a name for God in the Old Testament. The voice of God or Jehovah is imagined to be loud and booming.

> The thousand voices burst out with that almost supernatural sound which choral singing always has. Enormous, like the voice of Jehovah.
> ALDOUS HUXLEY *Point Counter Point*, 1928

Abraham Lincoln Abraham Lincoln (1809-65) was an American Republican statesman and the 16th president of the United States from 1861 to 1865. He was noted for his eloquent speeches, including the Gettysburg address of 1863, and the sincere tone of his voice.

> What a technique that guy had. What he'd do was, he'd start snowing his date in this very quiet, *sincere* voice—like as if he wasn't only a very handsome guy but a nice, *sincere* guy, too. I damn near puked, listening to him. His date kept saying, 'No— please. Please, don't. *Please*.' But old Stradlater kept snowing on her in this Abraham Lincoln, sincere voice, and finally there'd be this terrific silence in the back of the car.
> J. D. SALINGER *The Catcher in the Rye*, 1951

Mrs Malaprop In Sheridan's *The Rivals* (1775), Mrs Malaprop is the aunt and guardian of Lydia Languish. She is noted for her aptitude for misusing long words, responsible for such remarks as 'Illiterate him, I say, quite from your memory' and 'She's as headstrong as an allegory on the banks of the Nile'. Solecisms of this kind are now of course known as malapropisms.

Mickey Mouse Mickey Mouse, a cartoon character created by Walt Disney, first appeared in 1928. He has a squeaky, high-pitched voice.

> I began to repeat this sentence in a variety of tones, stresses and dialects, ranging from a rapid Mickey Mouse squeak to a bass drawl.
> KEITH WATERHOUSE *Billy Liar*, 1959

Punch and Judy Punch (also called Punchinello) and Judy are two characters in a traditional English seaside puppet-show. Punch, the quarrelsome and violent buffoon, and his wife Judy both talk in strained, high-pitched voices.

> Yakimov's normal voice was thin, sad and unvarying, the voice of a cultured Punchinello.
> OLIVIA MANNING *The Great Fortune*, 1960

Punchinello ▶ See **PUNCH AND JUDY.**

Stentor Stentor was a Greek herald in the Trojan War, supposed to have the voice of fifty men combined. He was unwise enough to challenge Hermes to a shouting match and when he lost paid the penalty for his presumption by being put to death. His name, and the word 'stentorian', can be used to describe a person with a powerful voice.

> And his voice rang out into the night like that of Stentor as he bawled.
> RICHARD BUTLER *Against Wind*, 1979

Speed

Most of the figures included here are swift runners. **BEN HUR** and **JEHU** both drove chariots at great speed, and their names have come to be applied to drivers of other vehicles.

Atalanta In Greek mythology, Atalanta was a huntress who was extremely fleet-footed. She had been warned against marriage by the Delphic oracle and so refused to marry any man unless he first defeated her in a race. If the runner lost, he was put to death. Many suitors tried to outrun her, but all failed until one, variously identified as Hippomenes or Melanion, asked Aphrodite for help and was given three golden apples by her. When he dropped these at intervals during the race, Atalanta was unable to resist the apples' beauty and stopped to pick them up.

> Laurie reached the goal first and was quite satisfied with the success of his treatment, for his Atalanta came panting up with flying hair, bright eyes, ruddy cheeks, and no signs of dissatisfaction in her face.
> LOUISA M. ALCOTT *Little Women*, 1868

> Even in the early days when she had lived with her parents in a ragged outskirt of Apex, and hung on the fence with Indiana Frusk, the freckled daughter of the plumber 'across the way', she had cared little for dolls or skipping ropes, and still less for the riotous games in which the loud Indiana played Atalanta to all the boyhood of the quarter.
> EDITH WHARTON *The Custom of the Country*, 1913

Ben Hur Ben Hur is the hero of Lew Wallace's novel *Ben-Hur, a Tale of the Christ* (1880). Set in Rome at the time of Christ, the novel tells the story of Ben Hur, a Jew who converts to Christianity. The story was popularized by two Hollywood epics, a 1925 silent film and a 1959 remake starring Charlton Heston. Both films featured memorably exciting scenes of a chariot race.

> Leslie Beck's Life Force is the energy not so much of sexual desire as of sexual discontent: the urge to find someone better out there, and thereby something better in the self, the one energy working against the other, creating a fine and animating friction: or else racing along side by side, like the Chariots in *Ben Hur*, wheels

colliding, touching, hell-bent, sparking off happiness and unhappiness.
FAY WELDON *Life Force*, 1992

Camilla Camilla was a Volscian princess, dedicated when young to the service of Diana. A huntress and warrior, Camilla was so fast a runner she could run over a field of corn without crushing it, and over the surface of the sea without her feet getting wet.

Not so, when swift Camilla scours the Plain,
Flies o'er th'unbending Corn, and skims along the Main.
ALEXANDER POPE *An Essay on Criticism*, 1711

Margaret ran, swift as Camilla, down to the window.
ELIZABETH GASKELL *North and South*, 1854–5

Hermes In Greek mythology, Hermes was the messenger of the gods, identified with the Roman god Mercury. ▶ *See* **MERCURY**.

Jehu Jehu, a king of Israel (841–815 BC), was known for driving his chariot very fast and recklessly. According to the Old Testament Book of Kings: 'he driveth furiously' (2 Kgs. 9: 20).

And at last away he drove, Jehu-like, as they say, out of the court-yard.
SAMUEL RICHARDSON *Pamela*, 1740

A drunken postilion . . . who frightened her by driving like Jehu the son of Nimshi, and shouting hilarious remarks at her.
GEORGE ELIOT *Adam Bede*, 1859

Those who only ever saw him behind a desk supposed the Mercedes was a status symbol. But Sale learnt his trade before mobile phones, when the ability to drive like Jehu could mean the difference between hold-the-front and a page-two filler, and when the need arose he could still burn rubber like a Hollywood stuntman.
JO BANNISTER *The Primrose Switchback*, 1999

Laelaps In Greek mythology, Laelaps was a hound so swift it always caught its quarry.

Mercury In Roman mythology, Mercury was the messenger of the gods, identified with the Greek god Hermes. He wore a wide-brimmed winged cap and winged sandals, which enabled him to travel very swiftly.

I know the height of your ambition and your unrest, but it is given to you to encompass all your ends. Remember that no moss may stick to the stone of Sisyphus, no, nor grass hang upon the heels of Mercury.
PETER ACKROYD *The House of Dr Dee*, 1993

Red Queen In an episode in Lewis Carroll's *Through the Looking-Glass* (1871), Alice finds herself running hand in hand with the Red Queen, who repeatedly urges them on with the words 'Faster! Faster!' But 'however fast they went, they never seemed to pass anything'. As the Queen observes to Alice: 'it takes all the running you can do to keep in the same place'.

The principle of zero change in success *rate*, no matter how great the evolutionary progress in *equipment*, has been given the memorable name of the 'Red Queen effect' by the American biologist Leigh van Valen. In *Through the Looking Glass*, you will remember, the Red Queen seized Alice by the hand and dragged her, faster and

faster, on a frenzied run through the countryside, but no matter how fast they ran they always stayed in the same place.
RICHARD DAWKINS *The Blind Watchmaker*, 1986

Roadrunner Roadrunner is an American cartoon character, a bird that can run extremely fast and always manages to outrun its arch-enemy, a coyote called Wile E. Coyote.

Speedy Gonzalez Speedy Gonzalez is a Mexican mouse in a series of Warner Brothers cartoons, noted for his ability to run very fast.

White Rabbit In Lewis Carroll's *Alice's Adventures in Wonderland* (1865), the White Rabbit is perpetually in a hurry, always scurrying away from her and anxiously consulting his watch because he is so late. ▶ *See special entry* ☐ **ALICE IN WONDERLAND** *on p. 10.*

Sternness

Descriptions of a person's forbidding appearance, severe demeanour, or strict behaviour often invoke the names of renowned puritans such as **CALVIN** and **KNOX**. ▶ *See also* **Anger**, **Disapproval**.

....

John Calvin John Calvin (1509-64) was a French Protestant theologian and reformer, a leader of the Protestant Reformation in France and Switzerland. His name has come to be closely identified with strict puritanism and a rigid moral code.

Hell and damnation: he knew about the very unofficial tapes. And Teddy with a puritan conscience that made Messrs Knox and Calvin look flexible, even soft. Not the moment to be precipitate myself. Not the occasion for the full and frank admission.
RAYMOND FLYNN *Busy Body*, 1998

John Knox John Knox (c.1505-72) was a Scottish Protestant reformer and preacher, greatly influenced by Calvin. He is alluded to as someone who is stern and disapproving.

The handsome sergeant's features were during this speech as rigid and stern as John Knox's in addressing his gay young queen.
THOMAS HARDY *Far From the Madding Crowd*, 1874

Well, let's say that John Knox would have been happy with it. It lasted twenty minutes, went on a lot about sacred duties, home-making, nest-building, nurturing, emotionally supporting, understanding that God had placed man and woman in their respective spheres and no man should mess around with that and then touched quite a lot on wicked secular ideas that were turning our womenfolk into fit candidates for Sodom and Gomorrah along with all the emasculated perverts that are today's menfolk.
RUTH DUDLEY EDWARDS *Matricide at St Martha's*, 1994

Rhadamanthus Rhadamanthus was the son of Zeus and Europa, and brother of Minos, who, as a ruler and judge in the underworld, was renowned for his justice. The term 'Rhadamanthine' has come to mean stern and incorruptible in judgement.

> Women at forty do not become ancient misanthropes, or stern Rhadamanthine moralists, indifferent to the world's pleasures—no, even though they be widows.
> ANTHONY TROLLOPE *The Small House at Allington*, 1862

Storytellers

References to famous literary storytellers can be applied to people recounting a story or anecdote or indeed giving any kind of account.
▶ *See also* **Oratory**.

....

Ancient Mariner The Ancient Mariner is the central character and narrator in Samuel Coleridge's poem 'The Rime of the Ancient Mariner' (1798). He stops a wedding guest at the door of the church where a wedding is about to take place, and insists on recounting the tale of how he shot an albatross at sea and the misfortune and suffering that subsequently befell the crew. The term 'Ancient Mariner' can be can be used to describe either a compulsive speaker, irresistible to his audience, as someone boring a reluctant listener, or as someone who insists on telling their tale of woe.

> In Oily's demeanour as he took another sip of his cocktail and prepared to speak there was a suggestion of that Ancient Mariner of whom the poet Coleridge wrote. Like him, he knew he had a good story to relate, and he did not intend to hurry it.
> P. G. WODEHOUSE *Cocktail Time*, 1958

> Gentle reader, I fain would spare you this, but my pen hath its will like the Ancient Mariner.
> WILLIAM BURROUGHS *Naked Lunch*, 1959

> It's not that I subscribe to The Most Horrific Pain You Can Imagine manifesto of the Ancient Mariner-style experienced mother, who takes pleasure in traumatising women about to give birth for the first time.
> *The Independent*, 1994

Demodocus Demodocus was a blind bard at the Phaeacian court of Alcinous who, according to Homer's *Odyssey*, entertained Odysseus with his songs telling of the adulterous love of Ares and Aphrodite and of the famous story of the Wooden Horse of Troy.

> It was quite impossible—recounting tales in the presence of people who knew them already. She wondered how Taliesin, Demodocus and all the other storytellers had coped.
> ALICE THOMAS ELLIS *The 27th Kingdom*, 1982

Scheherazade Scheherazade is the narrator of the *Arabian Nights*, the bride of

King Shahriyar who, after discovering his first wife's infidelity, has sworn to marry a new wife each day and execute her the next morning. Scheherazade escapes this fate by telling him stories in instalments, always breaking off at an interesting point, promising to resume the story the next night. After 1,001 nights of her storytelling, King Shahriyar cancels his threat.

> At my next appointment, feeling rather like Scheherazade unfolding one of her never-ending, telescopic tales to king Schahriar, I took up where I had left off.
> ROBERTSON DAVIES *The Manticore*, 1972

> Her voice fills in the intervals between nurses and consultant's rounds, visitors and sleep. After days, possibly weeks, maybe years, I realize that she's telling me a story. She is my own Scheherazade, she knows everything, she must be the storyteller from the end of the world.
> KATE ATKINSON *Human Croquet*, 1997

Taliesin Taliesin was a 6th-century Welsh bard, to whom a considerable quantity of poetry has been ascribed. He is the supposed author of the *Book of Taliesin* (14th cent.), a collection of heroic poems.

> If the Obie thing broke, the famed cottage (therapeutic oratory, refuge and sacrarium, Brentwood's own confessional Taliesin of above-the-line tears, fears and renewal) would be the sudden locus of *Hard Copy* helicopters, *Vanity Fair* layouts and O.J.ish lookie-loos.
> BRUCE WAGNER *I'm Loosing You*, 1997

Strangeness

Surrealism is, of course, a 20th-century movement and this theme does seem to have a much stronger 20th-century stamp to it than many others in this book.

Alice in Wonderland Lewis Carroll's children's story *Alice's Adventures in Wonderland* (1865) is an account of a young girl's encounters with a collection of strange animals and people in a surreal, illogical, dream-like world. The phrase 'Alice-in-Wonderland' can be used to describe a puzzling, seemingly illogical situation. ▶ *See special entry* □ **ALICE IN WONDERLAND** *on p. 10.*

> It is easy, though, to lose the track in the confusion of tyre-marks and rough signposts, and when this happens the driver, a small wiry Londoner baked to the colour of burned custard, navigates by a combination of map-reading and guesswork. He drove a taxi before the war, it emerges, and treats the desert with contemptuous familiarity, as though it were some Alice-in-Wonderland inversion of London topography.
> PENELOPE LIVELY *Moon Tiger*, 1998

Arabian Nights The *Arabian Nights* are a collection of exotic and fantastic stories written in Arabic, also called *Arabian Nights' Entertainments* or *The*

Thousand and One Nights. The stories are set in the following framework: Shahriyar, the king of Samarkand, has executed all his wives following the wedding night until he marries Scheherazade, who saves her life by entertaining him with a story each night for 1,001 nights. The tales include the stories of Aladdin, Ali Baba, and Sinbad the Sailor.

> My father had brought me out of Scotland at the age of six, and I had never been home since; so England was a sort of Arabian Nights to me, and I counted on stopping there for the rest of my days.
> JOHN BUCHAN *The Thirty Nine Steps*, 1915

> A great tale of marvels. Real Arabian Nights stuff.
> ROBERTSON DAVIES *World of Wonders*, 1975

> As I talked I was aware that it sounded like some horrible Arabian Nights fairy tale, and yet it was actually happening to us.
> ZANA MUHSEN *Sold*, 1991

Dada Dada was an early 20th-century artistic and literary movement which rejected traditional moral and aesthetic values and emphasized the illogical and absurd. The movement was started in Zurich in 1916 by the poet Tristan Tzara and others, and soon spread to New York, Paris, and Cologne. Artists associated with Dada included Jean Arp, André Breton, Max Ernst, Man Ray, and Marcel Duchamp. One of the most famous works produced was Duchamp's version of the *Mona Lisa* decorated with a moustache and an obscene caption.

> Nevertheless, his dreams continue, and are, if anything, more varied, more vivid, more Dadaist in their narration, and more persistent in their reaching after odd tossed chunks of history.
> CAROL SHIELDS *Mary Swan*, 1990

Salvador Dali Salvador Dali (1904–89) was a Spanish painter and prominent member of the surrealist movement, who was greatly influenced by Sigmund Freud's writings on dreams and the unconscious. Many of his paintings depict fantastic dream images painted with almost photographically realist detail and set in arid Catalan landscapes. *The Persistence of Memory* (1931) features the famous image of limp, melting watches.

> I am a breast. A phenomenon ... took place within my body between midnight and 4 am on February 18, 1971, and converted me into a mammary gland disconnected from any human form, a mammary gland such as could only appear, one would have thought, in a dream or a Dali painting.
> PHILIP ROTH *The Breast*, 1972

Dickensian Many of the vividly portrayed characters in Charles Dickens's novels are eccentric or grotesque, and hence the term 'Dickensian' can suggest a person's almost caricature-like oddness in behaviour, mannerisms, or appearance.

> I wanted to go back and leer at my strange Dickensian mother in the hash joint.
> JACK KEROUAC *On the Road*, 1957

Kafkaesque The novels of Franz Kafka (1883–1924), a Czech novelist who wrote in German, portray the individual's isolation, bewilderment, and anxiety in a nightmarish, impenetrably oppressive world. The corresponding adjective is 'Kafkaesque'.

Toiling up the slope from Falmer railway station, you had the Kafkaesque sensation of walking into an endlessly deep stage set where apparently three-dimensional objects turned out to be painted flats, and reality receded as fast as you pursued it.
DAVID LODGE *Nice Work*, 1988

When I asked why, the spokesman, a decent man just trying to earn a crust like the rest of us, tried his best to explain the Government's Kafkaesque logic.
The Observer, 1997

René Magritte René Magritte (1898–1967) was a Belgian Surrealist painter. His paintings have a dream-like quality, juxtaposing the ordinary, the strange, and the erotic, all depicted with meticulous realism.

Monty Python *Monty Python's Flying Circus* was a popular British TV comedy series of the 1970s, noted for the surreal absurdity of many of its sketches. The word 'Pythonesque' is used to describe humour of a similarly bizarre or zany kind.

At Brize Norton, at least, someone seemed to be making attempts to set up a kind of rapport between the local and the military presences. There were notices advertising a camp car boot sale and a summer fete, besides the one cheerfully alerting the villagers to the dangers of 'RAF police dogs on patrol'. A sort of surreal, Monty-Pythonish charm hangs over these juxtapositions.
The Observer, 1997

Narnia Narnia is the name of the imaginary land in which C S Lewis set his children's fantasy *The Lion, the Witch and the Wardrobe* (1950) and six subsequent stories. Narnia's inhabitants include talking beasts (notably the lion Aslan), giants, centaurs, and witches.

The first chapter of *Amelior Regained* consisted of a discussion between one of the men and one of the women, in a forest, about social justice. In other words, here was some Narnian waterbaby or other and some titless Hobbit or other, with her foot on a log, talking freedom.
MARTIN AMIS *The Information*, 1995

Piranesi Giovanni Battista Piranesi (1720–78) was an Italian engraver and architect famous for his views of the ruins of Rome and fantastic etchings of imaginary prisons (1745–61).

When it was time for the first train in the morning, he would go back to the mysteriously deserted, Piranesi perspectives of the station, discoloured by dawn.
ANGELA CARTER *Fireworks*, 1974

Sinbad The hero of one of the tales in the *Arabian Nights*, Sinbad is a rich young man of Baghdad who relates the fantastic adventures he meets with in his seven voyages. Among these are his encounter with the Old Man of the Sea and his being carried aloft by the Roc, a giant bird.

He delighted the rustics with his songs, and, like Sinbad, astonished them with his stories of strange lands, and shipwrecks, and sea-fights.
WASHINGTON IRVING *The Sketch-Book*, 1819–20

Twilight Zone *The Twilight Zone* was an American television series (1959–65) which told a different supernatural or science fiction story every week. The title of the series is sometimes alluded to in the context of a seemingly supernatural occurrence or a highly improbable coincidence.

Wonderland ▶ *See* ALICE IN WONDERLAND.

Strength

The biblical **SAMSON** and the classical **HERCULES** have proved the most durable archetypes of the strong man. Several of the figures included below also appear within the theme **Weakness**. ▶ *See also* **Large Size**, **Power**.

....

Muhammad Ali Born Cassius Clay in 1942, Muhammad Ali, the American boxer, won the world heavyweight title for the first time in 1964, regaining it in 1974 and 1978, to become the only boxer to be world champion three times. He retired in 1981. Ali frequently boasted 'I am the greatest'.

> Gimme a cup of coffee as strong as Muhammad Ali.
> CHESTER HIMES *Blind Man with a Pistol*, 1969

Amazon In Greek mythology, the Amazons were a race of female warriors alleged to exist on the borders of the known world. They are said to have cut off their right breasts to make it easier for them to draw their bows, hence their name, which means 'without a breast'. Any strong, tall, or athletic woman can be described as an Amazon. The corresponding adjective is 'Amazonian'.

> Sofia right about her sisters. They all big strong healthy girls, look like amazons.
> ALICE WALKER *The Color Purple*, 1983

> The image I lingered on the longest was, unsurprisingly, of Francoise. Francoise as an Amazon, frozen, with a spear poised above her head, concentrating fiercely on the shapes beneath the water.
> ALEX GARLAND *The Beach*, 1996

Atlas Atlas was one of the Titans in Greek mythology, punished for rebelling against Zeus by being made to support the heavens on his shoulders. The image of Atlas holding up the sky, or sometimes the earth itself, is a common one in art and literature.

> When she heard from a neighbour that there was a strongman in the square performing wonders and prodigies worthy of Atlas himself, she put up the broom with which she had been sweeping the yard and hurried out to join the gaggle of inquisitive and impressionable that had gathered near the well.
> LOUIS DE BERNIÈRES *Captain Corelli's Mandolin*, 1994

Charles Atlas Charles Atlas was the name adopted by the body-builder Angelo Siciliano (1894–1974), a '98-pound weakling' who became 'the world's strongest man'. The advertisements for his body-building course carried the famous slogan: 'You too can have a body like mine.'

Paul Bunyan Paul Bunyan is an American folk hero, a giant lumberjack of tremendous strength, who was accompanied on his travels by Babe, a gigantic blue ox.

> The total aroma profile of the full malolactic wine . . . is huge. This is no wimp wine. It's Paul Bunyan, overalls and all.
> *Wine and Spirits*, 1991

Hercules In Greek mythology, Hercules was a hero of superhuman strength and courage who performed twelve immense tasks or 'labours' imposed on him by Eurystheus, king of Argos. After his death he was ranked among the gods. Any exceptionally strong or muscular man can be described as a 'Hercules', or by the adjective 'Herculean'. ▶ *See special entry* □ **HERCULES** *on p. 182.*

> He was a mild, good-natured, sweet-tempered, easy-going, foolish, dear fellow—a sort of Hercules in strength, and also in weakness.
> CHARLES DICKENS *Great Expectations*, 1861

> A man entered who could hardly have been less than six feet in height, with the chest and limbs of a Hercules.
> ARTHUR CONAN DOYLE *A Scandal in Bohemia*, 1892

> He was strong and sturdy and this appealed to me, for one of my ambitions was to become a kind of Hercules.
> L. P. HARTLEY *The Go-Between*, 1953

Hulk The Incredible Hulk is a US comic book character. The scientist Bruce Banner is exposed to gamma ray radiation which causes him to be transformed periodically into the Hulk, a huge green-skinned man-like monster of extraordinary strength.

Leviathan Leviathan, a sea monster, is mentioned in several passages in the Bible (e.g. Job 41, Ps. 74: 14) and the name is generally considered to refer to a whale or crocodile. Anything very large or powerful, especially a whale, can be described as a Leviathan.

> I wish to be a better man than I have been; than I am—as Job's leviathan broke the spear, the dart and the habergeon, hinderances which others count as iron and brass, I will esteem but straw and rotten wood.
> CHARLOTTE BRONTË *Jane Eyre*, 1847

Polydamas In Greek legend, Polydamus was a celebrated athlete who imitated Hercules in whatever he did. He killed a lion with his fist and is said to have stopped a speeding chariot with his hand. He died attempting to catch a falling boulder.

Popeye The cartoon character Popeye the Sailor Man was created by Elzie Segar for the comic strip *Thimble Theater* in 1919. Eating a can of spinach gave Popeye prodigious strength. He was depicted with hugely bulging forearms, one eye, and a pipe clenched between his teeth. His girlfriend was the skinny Olive Oyl and his arch-enemy Bluto.

> The overall impression was of a powerhouse. Lennie had been a seaman for years, and he still had the rolling gait. In fact, with his muscular build he resembled a pumped-up Popeye.
> NORMAN PARKER *Parkhurst Tales*, 1994

Samson In the Bible, Samson was an Israelite leader (probably 11th century

BC) famous for his strength. He was said to have slain 1,000 Philistines with the jawbone of an ass. After his betrayal, capture, and blinding, he took his revenge by pulling down the pillars of a house, destroying himself and a large gathering of Philistines: 'And Samson took hold of the two middle pillars upon which the house stood . . . And he bowed himself with all his might; and the house fell upon the lords and upon all the people that were therein' (Judg. 16: 29–30). ▶ *See special entry* □ **SAMSON** *on p. 336.*

> Well, Miss Matty! men will be men. Every mother's son of them wishes to be considered Samson and Solomon rolled into one—too strong ever to be beaten or discomfited—too wise ever to be outwitted.
> ELIZABETH GASKELL *Cranford*, 1851–3

> He had awakened that morning from a sleep deep as annihilation; and during those first few moments in which the brain, like Samson shaking himself, is trying its strength, he had some dim notion of an unusual nocturnal proceeding.
> THOMAS HARDY *Tess of the D'Urbervilles*, 1891

> 'We have been assuming Inman was struck hand to hand. Couldn't he have had something thrown at him?' 'By a professional darts-player with muscles like Samson,' said Cox.
> KINGSLEY AMIS *The Riverside Villas Murder*, 1973

Spartan The Spartans, natives of the ancient Greek city state Sparta in the southern Peloponnese, were famous for their toughness in enduring pain and hardship.

> A Spartan matron, iron-hearted, bearing warrior-sons for the nation.
> J. M. COETZEE *Age of Iron*, 1990

> The water temperature would have struck even a Spartan as low and the soap was as carbolic as Hamilton's temper, but I felt better afterwards.
> PAUL JOHNSTON *Body Politic*, 1997

Superman Superman is a US comic book superhero character who possesses prodigious strength, the ability to fly, and other powers. Born on the planet Krypton, Superman conceals his identity by adopting the alter ego of mild-mannered reporter Clark Kent. Superman was created by writer Jerry Siegel and artist Joe Shuster.

Tarzan Tarzan is a character in novels by Edgar Rice Burroughs and subsequent films and television series. He is the son of an English noble (Lord Greystoke by birth) who is orphaned in West Africa in his infancy and reared by apes in the jungle. The name can be applied to any man of great physical strength and agility.

> Putting me to silence by brute strength? Okay, Tarzan. Then you'll never hear the rest—which is also the best.
> ROBERTSON DAVIES *The Manticore*, 1972

Thor In Scandinavian mythology, Thor, the son of Odin and Frigga, was the god of thunder and war. He was also the god of the weather, agriculture, and the home. He was usually represented as a man of enormous strength armed with a hammer called Mjollnir which returned to his hand after he had thrown it. Thor also wore iron gloves to help him grasp his hammer and belt, which doubled his strength.

Titan The Titans were the older gods who preceded the Olympians and were the children of Uranus (Heaven) and Gaia (Earth). Led by Cronus, they over-threw Uranus. When Cronus' son Zeus rebelled against his father, most of the Titans supported Cronus, but they were eventually defeated by Zeus. A person of very great strength and size can be described as a Titan.

> Laputa was in truth a Titan, who in the article of death could break down a bridge which would have taken any three men an hour to shift.
> JOHN BUCHAN *Prester John*, 1910

> We were wrapped in mist, enveloped in snow, and an accursed Arctic wind sprang up from the north that flung itself upon us like the bunched fist of a Titan.
> LOUIS DE BERNIÈRES *Captain Corelli's Mandolin*, 1994

Struggle

The idea of a struggle can strikingly be suggested by reference to an account of a wrestling match or other physical tussle.

Hercules In Greek mythology, Hercules was a hero of superhuman strength and courage who performed twelve immense tasks or 'labours' imposed on him by Eurystheus, king of Argos. The first of these was to kill the Nemean lion, which ravaged the country near Mycenae. After failing to subdue it with his club and arrows, Hercules choked the lion to death with his bare hands. He carried it back to Mycenae on his shoulders and thereafter clothed himself in its skin. ▶ *See special entry* ☐ **HERCULES** *on p. 182.*

> He had nought but four or five white scratches on the left side of his open and amiable countenance as if like Hercules he had struggled with a wild beast! (Hercules, you know, was fabled to have wrestled with the Nemaean Lion.)
> WILLIAM GOLDING *Rites of Passage*, 1980

Jacob In the Bible, Jacob was the younger of Isaac's twin sons, who became his heir. According to one story concerning him, one night he wrestled with a man until the break of day, refusing to release him until he blessed Jacob. The man eventually revealed himself to be an angel, who then changed Jacob's name: 'Your name shall no more be called Jacob, but Israel, for you have striven with God and with men, and have prevailed' (Gen. 32: 28). The name Israel literally means 'he that strives with God'. The episode is a popular sub-ject in art.

> Sometimes their hearts failed them and they felt that they could not resist the passion that burned the marrow of their bones. They resisted. They wrestled with evil as Jacob wrestled with the angel of God and at last they conquered.
> W. SOMERSET MAUGHAM *The Judgment Seat*, 1951

> But finally it is impossible to escape those monsters that devour from the inner depths, and the only ways to vanquish them are either to wrestle with them like Jacob with his angel or Hercules with his serpents, or else ignore them until they give up and disappear.
> LOUIS DE BERNIÈRES *Captain Corelli's Mandolin*, 1994

Laocoön Laocoön was a Trojan priest who, with his two sons, was crushed to death by two huge sea serpents as a punishment for warning the Trojans to reject the Wooden Horse left by the Greeks. A classical marble sculpture (c.50 BC) of the death-struggle of Laocoön and his sons, with the serpents coiled around their limbs, was rediscovered in the Renaissance and is now in the Vatican Museum. It is, in fact, this sculpture rather than the story that is often being alluded to. ▶ See special entry □ **TROJAN WAR** on p. 392.

> 'And seeing it's you, I'll give you a hint: the way the string's tied, you can get loose at once if he lies down flat and you crawl right up over his head; then the string drops off without untying the knots. Bye now.' And she was off to encourage other strugglers, who lay in Laocoon groups about the floor.
> ROBERTSON DAVIES Leaven of Malice, 1954

Stupidity

The names below denote foolishness and stupidity, even the ironically titled **WISE MEN OF GOTHAM**. ▶ See also **Intelligence, Judgement and Decision, Knowledge, Wisdom**.

Abdera Abdera was an ancient Greek city on the coast of Thrace whose inhabitants were proverbial for their stupidity.

Boeotian Boeotia was a district of ancient Greece, known for the stupidity of its inhabitants. Hence a Boeotian can mean a stupid person.

> An opportunity ... which I should have been a Bœotian indeed had I neglected.
> JOHN GIBSON LOCKHART Valerius, 1821

Philistine The ancient Philistines were the traditional enemies of the Israelites, regarded by them as hostile barbarians. Their name has come to be applied to people who are indifferent to culture and the arts and have uncultivated tastes.

> When I was a young man, though his books sold but little and one or two were banned by the libraries, it was very much a mark of culture to admire him. He was thought boldly realistic. He was a very good stick to beat the Philistines with.
> W. SOMERSET MAUGHAM Cakes and Ale, 1930

> Five hundred copies of The Voice of Youth were on sale in the dinner hall today. Five hundred copies were locked in the games cupboard by the end of the afternoon. Not one copy was sold! My fellow pupils are nothing but Philistines and Morons!
> SUE TOWNSEND The Secret Diary of Adrian Mole Aged 13¾, 1982

Scarecrow In L. Frank Baum's children's story The Wizard of Oz (1900), the Scarecrow is one of the companions who joins Dorothy on the Yellow Brick Road on her journey to find Oz. He does not have, and wants to find, a brain.

Simple Simon Simple Simon is a character in a children's nursery rhyme and the name can be applied to any foolish person or simpleton.

Wise Men of Gotham Gotham is a village in Nottinghamshire which is associated with the English folk tale 'The Wise Men of Gotham', in which the inhabitants of the village demonstrated cunning by feigning stupidity. Gotham was proverbial in the Middle Ages for folly, and the phrase 'wise man of Gotham' used to mean a fool.

Bertie Wooster Bertie Wooster is the amiable but vacuous young man about town in *The Inimitable Jeeves* (1924) and the subsequent series of novels by P. G. Wodehouse. He relies on his resourceful valet, Jeeves, to rescue him from the predicaments his dim-wittedness lands him in.

> At the time the Tory press was portraying Tony Blair as a sort of upper-class twit, a Bertie Wooster figure with an idiotic grin.
> *The Observer*, 1997

Success

Each of the figures included here embodies the 'rags-to-riches' progression from humble status to prosperity or eminence. ▶ *See also* **Failure**, **Victory**, **Wealth**.

Cinderella Cinderella, in the traditional fairy story, finds herself living with a stepmother and two stepsisters after her father's remarriage. She is maltreated by her family, who force her to do menial tasks in the house. When a royal ball is planned, Cinderella does not expect to be able to attend but her fairy godmother turns a pumpkin into a coach and provides suitable clothes and glass slippers. At the ball she meets the prince. Rushing away from the ball at the stroke of midnight, she leaves behind a glass slipper. The prince announces that he will marry whoever can wear the slipper and it fits only Cinderella. The name Cinderella is sometimes shortened to Cinders.

> 'Suppose I try,' said Mr. Hale. 'Everybody else has had their turn at this great difficulty. Now let me try. I may be the Cinderella to put on the slipper after all.'
> ELIZABETH GASKELL *North and South*, 1854

> In fact, in the beginning, I was just as excited as my mother, maybe even more so. I pictured this prodigy part of me as many different images, trying each one on for size . . . I was Cinderella stepping from her pumpkin carriage with sparkly cartoon music filling the air.
> AMY TAN *Two Kinds*, 1989

> The story of how she was cast is a delightful one, and adds to the Cinders quality of her tale. Her fairy godmother was the director Joel Schumacher, who happened to walk past her in a corridor at Universal. He says he saw 'this incredible-looking girl coming towards me like a young Arabian racehorse. I told my assistant to follow her and find out if she was an actress.'
> *The Observer*, 1997

Jacob In the Bible, Jacob was sent to Padan-Aram by his father, Isaac, to find a wife among his cousins. Jacob worked for his uncle Laban for many years, marrying his daughters, Leah and Rachel, and fathering twelve sons who became the founders of the twelve tribes of ancient Israel. Eventually Jacob wished to stop working for his uncle and set up his own flock. In lieu of wages, he agreed with Laban to take from his uncle's flocks any sheep, lambs, or goats that were dark-coloured, spotted, or speckled. Gradually, Jacob built up his own flocks from these animals until he was prosperous with large flocks, servants, camels, and asses (Gen. 27: 28–30: 43).

> The fact remained that whatever he touched he prospered in. Like Jacob in Padan-Aram, he would no sooner humbly limit himself to the ringstraked-and-spotted exceptions of trade than the ringstraked-and-spotted would multiply and prevail.
> THOMAS HARDY *The Mayor of Casterbridge*, 1886

Sir Joseph Porter, KCB Sir Joseph Porter KCB is a character in Gilbert and Sullivan's *H.M.S. Pinafore* (1878) who boasts that he has achieved the exalted status of 'ruler of the Queen's Navee' by his industry as an office boy, junior clerk, articled clerk, lawyer and MP without any experience in the Navy. His song ends with the instruction that if you want to 'rise to the top of the tree', you should:

'Stick close to your desks and never go to sea,
And you all may be rulers of the Queen's Navee!'.

Suffering

This theme encompasses both mental anguish and physical torment. ▶ *See also* **Grief**.

Acheron In Greek mythology, Acheron ('the river of woe') was one of the rivers of Hades, sometimes used to mean Hades itself. ▶ *See special entry* ☐ **HADES** *on p. 172.*

> Throughout that night Boldwood's dark form might have been seen walking about the hills and downs of Weatherbury like an unhappy Shade in the Mournful Fields by Acheron.
> THOMAS HARDY *Far from the Madding Crowd*, 1874

Ajax Ajax was a Greek hero of the Trojan War, proverbial for his size and strength. When Agamemnon awarded the armour of the dead Achilles to Odysseus and not to him, Ajax went mad with rage, slaughtered a flock of sheep, and then committed suicide in shame. ▶ *See special entry* ☐ **TROJAN WAR** *on p. 392.*

> She sat as helpless and despairing among her black locks as Ajax among the slaughtered sheep.
> GEORGE ELIOT *The Mill on the Floss*, 1860

Babes in the Wood Originally 'The Children in the Wood', an old ballad written in 1595, 'The Babes in the Wood' is the story of two infants, brother and sister, abandoned in a wood by their uncle, who wants their property. The children subsequently die. A reference to the Babes in the Wood usually signifies innocent suffering.

> Everything looked strange and different in the darkness. We began to understand the sufferings of the Babes in the Wood.
> JEROME K. JEROME *Three Men in a Boat*, 1889

St Bartholomew St Bartholomew was an Apostle who is said to have been martyred in Armenia by being flayed alive, and is hence regarded as the patron saint of tanners.

> The last of them, excoriated like a Saint Bartholomew, held up in his right hand his still-bleeding skin limp as an unused cape.
> UMBERTO ECO *The Island of the Day Before*, 1994

Calvary Calvary, also known as Golgotha (both of which come from words, in Latin and Aramaic respectively, meaning 'the place of the skull'), was the hill just outside Jerusalem where Jesus was crucified. The word can be applied to any experience of intense mental suffering. ▶ *See special entry* ☐ **JESUS** *on p. 223*.

> In a very special, very private sense DeQuincey is your Cross and your marriage is your Calvary.
> EDMUND WHITE *A Boy's Own Story*, 1982

> Of course, the FA Cup could still prove United's Calvary this season, as it nearly did in the third round against Sunderland, who led at Old Trafford and Roker Park.
> *The Guardian*, 1996

Dickensian The novels of Charles Dickens are filled with slums, workhouses, debtors' prisons, and other examples of social deprivation. The term 'Dickensian' can thus be used to suggest conditions of poverty, squalor, and hardship. It can likewise denote a corrupt and brutal educational regime like that at Dotheboys Hall in Dickens's *Nicholas Nickleby*.

> So Eddie and his older brother, Mark, were suddenly dispatched to boarding school when they were six and eight respectively—unfortunately, a Dickensian school which rang to the thwack of the cane.
> *The Observer*, 1997

Gethsemane Gethsemane was a garden lying in the valley between Jerusalem and the Mount of Olives, where Jesus went with his disciples to pray on the night before his Crucifixion and which was the scene of his agony and betrayal by Judas (Matt. 26: 36–46). The name Gethsemane is sometimes used to typify a scene of mental or spiritual anguish, as is the phrase 'agony in the garden'. ▶ *See special entry* ☐ **JESUS** *on p. 223*.

> It was a night which led the traveller's thoughts instinctively to dwell on nocturnal scenes of disaster in the chronicles of the world, on all that is terrible and dark in history and legend—the last plague of Egypt, the destruction of Sennacherib's host, the agony in Gethsemane.
> THOMAS HARDY *The Return of the Native*, 1878

Golgotha Golgotha, also known as Calvary (both of which come from words, in Aramaic and Latin respectively, meaning 'the place of the skull'), was the hill, just outside Jerusalem, where Jesus was crucified. The word can be applied to any experience of intense mental suffering. ▶ *See special entry* □ **JESUS** *on p. 223.*

> Billy dozed, awakened in the prison hospital again. The sun was high. Outside were Golgotha sounds of strong men digging holes for upright timbers in hard, hard ground. Englishmen were building themselves a new latrine.
> KURT VONNEGUT *Slaughterhouse 5*, 1969

> Gladiators, Wellingtons and Blenheims began to appear in the sky over our heads, and so the British added their strength to the Greek daggers twisting in our wounds. General Soddu inspected us and compared us to granite. 'Does granite bleed', asked Francesco, 'on Golgotha?'
> LOUIS DE BERNIÈRES *Captain Corelli's Mandolin*, 1994

Hades In Greek mythology, Hades was the underworld, the abode of the spirits of the dead, though the name was originally applied to the god, known also as Pluto, who ruled there, rather than to his kingdom. The underworld was guarded by Cerberus, a three-headed dog. Five rivers, including the Styx, separated Hades from the land of the living. The lowest region of Hades, where the wicked were punished, was called Tartarus. ▶ *See special entry* □ **HADES** *on p. 172.*

> He stood motionless, undecided, glaring with his eyes, thinking of the pains and penalties of Hades.
> ANTHONY TROLLOPE *Barchester Towers*, 1857

Ixion In Greek mythology, Ixion was a Thessalian king who tried to seduce Hera, for which he was punished by being bound to a fiery wheel that revolved unceasingly through the underworld. The phrase 'Ixionian wheel' can be used to mean endless torment. ▶ *See special entry* □ **HADES** *on p. 172.*

> So, floating on the margin of the ensuing scene, and in full sight of it, when the half-spent suction of the sunk ship reached me, I was then, but slowly, drawn towards the closing vortex. . . . Round and round, then, and ever contracting towards the button-like black bubble at the axis of that slowly wheeling circle, like another Ixion I did revolve.
> HERMAN MELVILLE *Moby Dick*, 1851

Joan of Arc St Joan of Arc (*c*.1412–31), known as 'the Maid of Orleans', was a French national heroine. Inspired by supernatural voices, she dressed as a man and led the French armies against the English, relieving the besieged city of Orleans in 1429. After being captured, she was convicted of heresy and witchcraft, and burnt at the stake in Rouen.

> Think of how many Western heroes died bravely in excruciating pain—Saint Joan burned, Saint Sebastian transfixed with arrows, other martyrs racked, drawn, and quartered.
> STEPHEN J. GOULD *Ever Since Darwin*, 1978

Job In the Old Testament book that bears his name, Job was a prosperous man whose patience and piety were tried by dire and undeserved misfortunes, including 'loathsome sores from the sole of his foot to the crown of his head' (Job 2: 7). In spite of suffering these afflictions, his confidence in the goodness and justice of God was not shaken.

> 'That's splendid. One feels a certain pang of pity for whoever it is he's starting to work for, but that's splendid. The family were worried about him.' 'I don't wonder. I

can't imagine anybody more capable of worrying a family than Eggy. Just suppose if Job had had him as well as boils!'
P. G. WODEHOUSE *Laughing Gas*, 1936

Laocoön Laocoön was a Trojan priest who, with his two sons, was crushed to death by two huge sea serpents as a punishment for warning the Trojans to reject the Wooden Horse left by the Greeks. A classical marble sculpture (*c*.50 BC) depicts Laocoön and his sons dying in agony, with the serpents coiled around their limbs. Hardy alludes to this sculpture in the quotation below.
▶ *See special entry* □ **TROJAN WAR** *on p. 392.*

If he had been a woman he must have screamed under the nervous tension which he was now undergoing. But that relief being denied to his virility, he clenched his teeth in misery, bringing lines about his mouth like those in the Laocoön, and corrugations between his brows.
THOMAS HARDY *Jude the Obscure*, 1895

St Lawrence St Lawrence (d. 258) was a Roman martyr and deacon of Rome. According to tradition, Lawrence was ordered by the prefect of Rome to hand over the church's treasure, in response to which he assembled the poor people of the city and presented them to the prefect. For this he was put to death by being roasted on a gridiron.

It is very easy to talk of repentance, but a man has to walk over hot ploughshares before he can complete it; to be skinned alive as was St Bartholomew; to be stuck full of arrows as was St Sebastian; to lie broiling on a gridiron like St Lorenzo!
ANTHONY TROLLOPE *Barchester Towers*, 1857

Melpomene Melpomene was the Muse of tragedy in Greek and Roman mythology.

His face is like the tragic mask of Melpomene.
THOMAS HARDY *Jude the Obscure*, 1895

Philoctetes Philoctetes was a Greek hero of the Trojan War. He was with Hercules when he died and received from him Hercules' bow and poisoned arrows. On his way to the war Philoctetes was bitten by a serpent and abandoned by his companions on the island of Lemnos owing to a foul-smelling wound on his foot. When in the tenth year of the war the Greeks were informed by an oracle that only with Hercules' arrows could Troy be taken, Odysseus and Diomedes came back to fetch him to Troy, where he killed Paris.
▶ *See special entry* □ **TROJAN WAR** *on p. 392.*

Arresting for a moment the wave of memories, Roberto realized he had evoked his father's death not with the pious intention of keeping open that Philoctetes' wound, but by mere accident.
UMBERTO ECO *The Island of the Day Before*, 1994

plagues of Egypt In the Book of Exodus, God sent ten plagues to afflict the Egyptians (Exod. 7–12). The plagues were: turning the Nile to blood; frogs; gnats; flies; death of cattle; boils; hail; locusts; darkness; death of the Egyptian first-born. As a result of these plagues, Pharaoh freed the Israelites from bondage. ▶ *See special entry* □ **MOSES AND THE BOOK OF EXODUS** *on p. 264.*

If Mr Thurle's so ready to take farms under you, it's a pity but what he should take this, and see if he likes to live in a house wi' all the plagues o' Egypt in't—wi' the cellar full o' water, and the frogs and toads hoppin' up the steps by dozens—and the

floors rotten, and the rats and mice gnawing every bit o' cheese, and runnin' over our heads as we lie i' bed till we expect 'em to eat us up alive.
GEORGE ELIOT *Adam Bede*, 1859

Prometheus In Greek mythology, Prometheus was a demigod, one of the Titans. As punishment for stealing fire from the gods for the human race, Zeus had Prometheus chained to a rock where an eagle fed each day on his liver, which grew back each night. He was eventually rescued from this torment by Hercules. ▶ *See special entry* □ **PROMETHEUS** *on p. 311.*

Raft of the Medusa *The Raft of the Medusa* (1819) is the most famous work by the French painter Theodore Géricault. It depicts with harrowing realism the sufferings of survivors of an actual shipwreck, who had been cut adrift and left to drown. Some of the figures are based on Géricault's study of corpses and sickness.

St Sebastian St Sebastian was a Roman martyr of the 3rd century. According to legend, he was a soldier who was shot with arrows on the orders of Diocletian, and, after surviving this ordeal, was then clubbed to death. The scene of St Sebastian being shot by archers was a popular subject among Renaissance painters.

He was so preoccupied with an inner life that he took little notice of the humiliations and slights that pushed and jabbed at him the moment he ventured outside the community. If, like the rest of his kind, he was a Sebastian, the arrows did not penetrate his sense of self.
NADINE GORDIMER *My Son's Story*, 1990

Sisyphus In Greek mythology, Sisyphus was a king of Corinth, punished in Hades for his misdeeds in life by being condemned to the eternal task of rolling a huge stone to the top of a hill. Every time he approached the summit, the stone slipped and rolled down to the bottom again. A seemingly endless ordeal can be described as Sisyphean. ▶ *See special entry* □ **HADES** *on p. 172.*

Mandras made Pelagia read all the letters, handing them to her one by one, so that, with tears in her eyes, her voice quavering, she endured a purgatorial hour of utter panic, each letter a torment of Sisyphus, the sweat pouring down her face and stinging her eyes.
LOUIS DE BERNIÈRES *Captain Corelli's Mandolin*, 1994

St Stephen St Stephen (d. *c.*35) was the first Christian martyr, stoned to death in Jerusalem.

It was so kind and tender of you to give up half a day's work to come and see me! ... You are Joseph the dreamer of dreams, dear Jude. And a tragic Don Quixote. And sometimes you are St. Stephen, who, while they were stoning him, could see Heaven opened.
THOMAS HARDY *Jude the Obscure*, 1895

Tantalus In Greek mythology, Tantalus was the king of Phrygia who was punished for his misdeeds (including killing his son Pelops and offering his cooked flesh to the gods) by being condemned in Hades to stand up to his chin in water which receded whenever he tried to drink it and under branches of fruit which drew back when he tried to reach them. ▶ *See special entry* □ **HADES** *on p. 172.*

> That must be it, it was all planned from the beginning, I was never to have her, always to be tormented, mocked like Tantalus.
> JOHN FOWLES *The Magus*, 1977

> This is not the first time ill luck has befallen one of her projects: in fact her career has been punctuated by similar misfortunes. It's an architectural version of the torments of Tantalus: a competition is held; against all the odds Hadid wins; the photographers, the 15 minutes of fame ensue; then before one spade of earth can be turned, fate intervenes and kills the thing off.
> *The Independent on Sunday*, 1996

Tartarus In Greek mythology, Tartarus was the lowest region of Hades where the wicked were punished for their misdeeds, especially those such as Ixion and Tantalus who had committed some outrage against the gods. ▶ *See special entry* □ **HADES** *on p. 172.*

Werther In Goethe's romance *The Sorrows of Young Werther* (1774), Werther falls in love with Charlotte, who is betrothed to Albert, and gives himself up to a few weeks' happiness in Albert's absence. Then he tears himself away. Albert and Charlotte are married, and despair gradually comes over Werther, who finally takes his own life. 'Wertherian' can be used to describe morbidly sentimental, emotional distress.

> He should have spent this afternoon among the poor at St Ewold's, instead of wandering about at Plumstead, an ancient love-lorn swain, dejected and sighing, full of imaginary sorrows and Wertherian grief.
> ANTHONY TROLLOPE *Barchester Towers*, 1857

> Only one thing was clear. Even if Maud would never again consider marrying him—which was no more than he deserved—he must get down on his knees and beg her pardon for the monstrous things he had said. After that, it did not matter what became of him. And he went away to dress for dinner, with the air of young Werther on his way to his suicide chamber.
> KATE ROSE *Cut to the Quick*, 1993

Superiority

This theme covers the idea of rising above the mundane and petty aspects of human life and the human character. The arrogant sense of one's own superiority to others is covered at **Arrogance**.

Homeric Homer (8th century BC) was a Greek epic poet, traditionally held to be the author of the *Iliad* and the *Odyssey*. The adjective 'Homeric' is used to denote actions and events that happen on a grand, superhuman scale or people who perform such actions.

> The papers in South Africa eulogised them [the Springboks rugby team] in Homeric terms.
> *The Daily Telegraph*, 1995

Nietzsche Friedrich Wilhelm Nietzsche (1844-1900) was a German philosopher whose works include *Also Sprach Zarathustra* ('Thus Spoke Zarathustra') (1883-5) and *Jenseits von Gut and Böse* ('Beyond Good and Evil') (1886). Themes in his writings include contempt for Christian ethics and for democracy and admiration of the 'will to power', the Ubermensch (superman), and the 'master class', the small group of superior people who dominate the mass of inferior people, the 'herd'. Nietzsche's Ubermensch was an ideal being whose superior physical and mental qualities represent the goal of human evolution.

> Because she was brave, because she was 'spoiled', because of her outrageous and commendable independence of judgment, and finally because of her arrogant consciousness that she had never seen a girl as beautiful as herself, Gloria had developed into a consistent, practising Nietzschean.
> F. SCOTT FITZGERALD *The Beautiful and the Damned*, 1922

> 'I should like some coffee,' she announced, with what she hoped was Nietzschean directness.
> ANITA BROOKNER *Hotel du Lac*, 1984

Olympian Mount Olympus, in Greece, is traditionally held to be the home of the Greek gods. An Olympian or Olympian figure is someone godlike in his or her superiority over lesser mortals.

> I think I shall have a lofty throne for you, godmamma, or rather two, one on the lawn and another in the ballroom, that you may sit and look down upon us like an Olympian goddess.
> GEORGE ELIOT *Adam Bede*, 1859

> 'Indeed!' Mr Barbecue-Smith smiled benignly, and looking up at Denis with an expression of Olympian condescension, 'And what sort of things do you write?'
> ALDOUS HUXLEY *Crome Yellow*, 1921

> Ruth can hardly keep still and Philip Drummond has to tell her to sit down and await her turn, and when her turn comes she tears Molteno to pieces for his equivocal espousal of justice. Molteno looks at her as though her were some Olympian Judge of Appeal, astonished and mystified that a lawyer could exhibit such passion.
> ALAN PATON *Ah, But Your Land Is Beautiful*, 1981

Titan In Greek mythology, the Titans were the older gods who preceded the Olympians. They were the children of Uranus (Heaven) and Gaia (Earth). They rebelled against and overthrew Uranus and were in turn defeated by their own children, the Olympians, led by Zeus.

> Grace was his, and the white purity of boyhood, and beauty such as old Greek marbles kept for us. There was nothing that one could not do with him. He could be made a Titan or a toy. What a pity it was that such beauty was destined to fade!
> OSCAR WILDE *The Picture of Dorian Gray*, 1891

Teachers

Among the teachers included here, **MR CHIPS** and **WACKFORD SQUEERS** represent the opposite poles of their profession.

....

Miss Jean Brodie Muriel Spark's novel *The Prime of Miss Jean Brodie*, first published in 1961, tells the story of Miss Jean Brodie, an Edinburgh school-mistress during the 1930s. She is a spinster with firm views on the education of young women, remembered for saying: 'I am putting old heads on your young shoulders . . . all my pupils are the crème de la crème'.

> Kevin would exclaim, 'Yoghurt! Steamed vegetables! Lots of fruit!—this is Miss Jean Brodie warning you!' Gabe would just smile feebly, sleep sand in his eyes.
> EDMUND WHITE *Farewell Symphony*, 1997

Mr Chips In James Hilton's *Goodbye, Mr Chips* (1935), Mr Chipping is a classics teacher at Brookfield School. Known to his pupils as Mr Chips, he devotes himself to teaching generations of boys at the school until his retirement. He is the archetype of the dedicated schoolmaster.

> Opposite Bruce sat Professor Chambers, a sad-looking, dusty old Mr Chips whom the students had asked to chair the occasion.
> BEN ELTON *Popcorn*, 1996

Chiron In Greek mythology, Chiron was a learned centaur who acted as tutor to many heroes in their youth, including Jason, Hercules, and Achilles.

> Something less unpleasingly oracular he tried to extract; but the old sea Chiron, thinking perhaps that for the nonce he had sufficiently instructed his young Achilles, pursed his lips, gathered all his wrinkles together, and would commit himself to nothing further.
> HERMAN MELVILLE *Billy Budd*, 1924

Wackford Squeers Wackford Squeers is the ignorant headmaster of the Yorkshire school Dotheboys Hall in Dickens's *Nicholas Nickleby* (1839). Squeers presides over a cruel regime, starving and bullying his miserable pupils under pretence of education.

> Trembling first-formers (secretaries) huddled over their work like Dickensian pupils, fearing the inevitable moment when a toothy, strigine, six-foot Wackford Squeers of a Headmistress would come screaming into the room.
> *Time Out*, 1991

Temperature

This theme covers both extremes of temperature: bitter cold, as represented by the **HYPERBOREANS** and **SCOTT OF THE ANTARCTIC,** and intense heat, as associated with the fires of **HELL** and **SHADRACH**'s fiery furnace.

Hell According to Christian, Jewish, and Islamic tradition, Hell is the place of punishment where the souls of the damned are condemned after death. It is sometimes pictured as a place of great heat and fire, and the souls of the wicked are 'cast into hell fire' (Matt. 18: 9).

Hyperborean In Greek mythology, the Hyperboreans were a fabled race worshipping Apollo and living in a land in a distant northerly land 'beyond the north wind'. This was in fact a land of perpetual sunshine and happiness, but because of its location the term 'Hyperborean' has come to denote cold northern climes.

> It's the unnatural combat of the four primal elements.—It's a blasted heath.—It's a Hyperborean winter scene.—It's the breaking-up of the ice-bound stream of Time.
> HERMAN MELVILLE *Moby Dick,* 1851

Phoebus Phoebus (literally 'bright one') was an epithet of the Greek god Apollo, used in contexts where the god was identified with the sun.

> He would never have survived the lash of Phoebus.
> UMBERTO ECO *The Island of the Day Before,* 1994

Scott of the Antarctic Robert Falcon Scott (1868-1912) was an English explorer and naval officer, who led two expeditions to Antarctica. On the second expedition (1910-12) Scott and four companions reached the South Pole by sled, only to discover that the Norwegian explorer Amundsen had beaten them to their goal by a month. Scott and his companions died on the return journey.

> With low pressure sweeping in from the Bay of Biscay, you'd have to be Scott of the Antarctic to go out collecting conkers.
> *The Observer,* 1998

Shadrach, Meshach, and Abednego The Bible relates a famous episode during Nebuchadnezzar's reign, in which the king set up a golden idol and commanded all to worship it. When three Jews, Shadrach, Meshach, and Abednego, refused to do so, the king ordered some of his soldiers to throw them into a 'fiery furnace'. Although the soldiers were consumed by the flames, Shadrach, Meshach, and Abednego miraculously came out unharmed: 'these men, upon whose bodies the fire had no power, nor was an hair of their head singed, neither were their coats changed, nor the smell of fire had passed on them.' ▶ *See special entry* ☐ **DANIEL** *on p. 86.*

> Left to its own devices, the class tied Eunice Ann Simpson to a chair and placed her in the furnace room. We forgot her, trooped upstairs to church, and were listening quietly to the sermon when a dreadful banging issued from the radiator pipes,

persisting until someone investigated and brought forth Eunice Ann saying she didn't want to play Shadrach any more—Jem Finch said she wouldn't get burnt if she had enough faith, but it was hot down there.
HARPER LEE *To Kill a Mockingbird*, 1960

Temptation

The entries below include not only those subjected to temptation (**JESUS** and **PERSEPHONE**), but also the tempters or agents of temptation. ▶ *See also* **Sirens**.

....

Devil The Devil is another name for Satan, the arch-tempter in the Bible.

> I am very sure I had no manner of design in my head, when I went out; I neither knew, or considered where to go, or on what business; but as the devil carried me out, and laid his bait for me, so he brought me to be sure to the place, for I knew not whither I was going, or what I did.
> DANIEL DEFOE *Moll Flanders*, 1722

Eve According to the Book of Genesis, Eve, the first woman on earth, persuaded Adam to eat the forbidden fruit from the Tree of Knowledge. Her name is sometimes used in the context of a woman tempting a man. ▶ *See special entry* □ **ADAM AND EVE** *on p. 5.*

> I was firm as a man could be till I saw those eyes and that mouth again—surely there never was such a maddening mouth since Eve's!
> THOMAS HARDY *Tess of the D'Urbervilles*, 1891

Evil One The Evil One is another name for Satan, the arch-tempter in the Bible.

> Where, to what distance apart, had her father wandered, led by doubts which were to her temptations of the Evil One?
> ELIZABETH GASKELL *North and South*, 1854–5

forbidden fruit According to the account in the Book of Genesis, God commanded Adam and Eve not to eat the fruit of the Tree of Knowledge but, tempted by the serpent, they disobeyed him: 'So when the woman saw that the tree was good for food, and that it was a delight to the eyes, and that the tree was to be desired to make one wise, she took of its fruit and ate; and she also gave some to her husband, and he ate' (Gen. 3: 6). The phrase 'forbidden fruit' can be used to describe something that is desired or enjoyed all the more because it is not allowed, especially illicit sexual pleasure. ▶ *See special entry* □ **ADAM AND EVE** *on p. 5.*

> Later, we had to sneak. I'd hired on at Rent-a-Back by then, and she would ride along on my jobs—spend the day with me while her parents thought she was swimming at their club. 'Oh forbidden fruit! No wonder you two were attracted', Sophia said.
> ANNE TYLER *A Patchwork Planet*, 1998

Jesus Jesus was tempted by Satan in the wilderness. ▶ *See* **SATAN**.

Mephistopheles Mephistopheles is the evil spirit to whom Faust in German legend sold his soul, especially as represented in Marlowe's *Doctor Faustus* (*c.*1590) and Goethe's *Faust* (1808, 1832). Mephistopheles entraps Faust with wit, charm, and rationality. His name, and the adjective 'Mephistophelean', are often used to describe a fiendish but urbane tempter.

> [The show's] core [is] the Faustean pact between a young college teacher and the Mephistopheles of NBC television desperate for a hero with whom they believed the viewers could identify.
> *The Guardian*, 1995

Persephone In Greek mythology, after Persephone had been abducted by Hades to be his queen in the underworld, she was granted the opportunity to return to the earth on condition that no food had passed her lips in the underworld. However while wandering in the gardens she had eaten some pomegranate seeds from a tree, and this fact was revealed by Ascalaphus. Persephone was ordered by Zeus to remain six months with Hades and to spend the rest of the year on the earth with her mother, Demeter. ▶ *See special entry* □ **HADES** *on p. 172.*

> It must just be a question of what you're used to, she thought, picturing Persephone, resolutely anorexic in the Halls of Dis until the pomegranate proved too much for her will power.
> ALICE THOMAS ELLIS *The 27th Kingdom*, 1982

Satan Satan, or the Devil, is characterized as the arch-tempter in the Bible. At the end of Jesus' 40-day fast in the wilderness he challenged Jesus with a series of temptations: to relieve his hunger by turning stones into loaves of bread; to prove his divine power by throwing himself from the temple-top; to gain absolute earthly power 'if you will fall down and worship me'. Jesus rejected each of these temptations (Matt. 4: 1–11). The famous words 'Get thee behind me, Satan!' were spoken by Jesus as a rebuke to Peter for suggesting that Jesus ought not to be crucified (Matt. 16: 23; Mark 8: 33). The phrase is commonly used now when any kind of temptation is being renounced. ▶ *See special entry* □ **JESUS** *on p. 223.*

> Charles felt himself, under the first impact of this attractive comparison, like Jesus of Nazareth tempted by Satan. He too had had his days in the wilderness to make the proposition more tempting.
> JOHN FOWLES *The French Lieutenant's Woman*, 1969

Thinness

A common literary device when describing a thin person is to do so with reference to the work of **EL GRECO**, **GIACOMETTI**, or **MODIGLIANI**, all noted for their exaggeratedly thin figures. ▶ *See also* **Fatness**.

Ichabod Crane In Washington Irving's short story *The Legend of Sleepy Hollow* (1820), Ichabod Crane is the village schoolmaster, suitor to the local girl Katrina Van Tass. He is skinny and gangly, with a nose 'like a snipe'. His rival suitor, Brom Bones, disguises himself as a ghostly headless horseman and scares the timid Ichabod out of the village.

> 'Tall chap with exophthalmic eyes, prominent nose. Walks with a stoop', Ecco said out of the blue, remembering.
> Cordelia blushed. The bluntness of the description—which was deadly accurate—took her by surprise. Among undergraduates back home, Wain was known affectionately behind his back as Ichabod.
> JOHN SPENCER HILL *The Last Castrato*, 1995

> He had an Ichabod Crane body and a wild thatch of Einstein-like white hair. His sunken, permanently sad eyes and big, expressive hands had held many a courtroom spellbound as he's pled for the rights of underdogs of all shapes, colors and sizes through the years in a booming evangelistic voice.
> DEANNIE MILLS FRANCIS *Trap Door*, 1995

Don Quixote Don Quixote is the hero of a romance (1605–15) by Miguel de Cervantes, a satirical account of chivalric beliefs and conduct. He is described in the opening chapter as being 'of a hale and strong complexion, lean-bodied, and thin-faced'. He has his wits disordered by his devoted reading of chivalric romances and sets out in search of knightly adventures with his companion, Sancho Panza, whose short, fat appearance contrasts with that of Don Quixote. ▶ *See special entry* □ **DON QUIXOTE** *on p. 00.*

> A tall, thin, Don Quixote-looking old man came into the shop for some woollen gloves.
> ELIZABETH GASKELL *Cranford*, 1851–3

> The short jacket and the low, round hat he assumed . . . brought out wonderfully the length of his grave, brown face. He stepped back into the full light of the room, looking like the vision of a cool, reflective Don Quixote, with the sunken eyes of a dark enthusiast and a very deliberate manner.
> JOSEPH CONRAD *The Secret Agent*, 1907

El Greco El Greco (1541–1614) was a Spanish painter, born in Crete as Domenikos Theotokopoulos. His portraits and religious works are characterized by elongated and distorted figures and solemn facial expressions. Among his famous works are the altarpiece *The Assumption of the Virgin* (1577–9) and the painting *The Burial of Count Orgaz* (1586).

> They're like the hands in El Greco's portraits.
> SOMERSET MAUGHAM *The Razor's Edge*, 1944

> Senor Aguirre joined his El Greco hands and looked at me over the spire of his fingertips.
> JOHN BANVILLE *The Book of Evidence*, 1989

Alberto Giacometti Alberto Giacometti was a Swiss sculptor (1901–66) noted for the exaggerated length and thinness of his figures.

> Their Giacometti-like thinness is a withering by pitiless experience.
> CAMILLE PAGLIA *Sexual Personae*, 1990

Abraham Lincoln Abraham Lincoln (1809–65) was an American Republican statesman and the 16th president of the United States (1861–5). Lincoln was a tall man, standing over six feet, and had a gaunt face with sunken, wrinkled cheeks.

I looked at him, at the long, bony, almost Lincolnesque face.
RALPH ELLISON *Invisible Man*, 1952

Inside was the church pew, as straight and spare as Abe Lincoln lying down.
ALICE WALKER *Advancing Luna—and Ida B. Wells*, 1980

Amedeo Modigliani Amedeo Modigliani (1884-1920) was an Italian painter and sculptor. Influenced by African sculpture, his portraits and nudes have boldly simplified features and distinctively elongated forms.

She was . . . waiting like a longbodied emaciated Modigliani surrealist woman in a serious room.
JACK KEROUAC *On the Road*, 1957

It was enough, however, for Mayo to see everything that needed to be seen: a longer shadow depending from one of the newel posts, a Modigliani figure, grotesquely elongated, its own shadow dancing alongside as it gently swung, a heavy, carved-oak upright chair kicked away and lying on its back.
MARJORIE ECCLES *A Species of Revenge*, 1996

Olive Oyl In Elzie Segar's comic strip *Popeye the Sailor Man*, Olive Oyl is Popeye's skinny girlfriend.

The nice thing about leggings is they fit anybody from Olive Oyl to a lapsed Weightwatcher.
SARAH LACEY *File under: Arson*, 1995

She stood tall, straight and thin, like a tense Olive Oyl gone blonde.
LINDA MATHER *Gemini Doublecross*, 1995

Twiggy Twiggy (born Leslie Hornby, 1949) was an English fashion model of the 1960s. She began her modelling career in 1966, becoming famous for her short-haired, thin-bodied boyish look. Twiggy later appeared in films such as *The Boyfriend* (1971) and *The Blues Brothers* (1980).

He looked over at waiflike Louise, a Twiggy lookalike with her cropped hair and miniskirt.
EILEEN GOUDGE *Such Devoted Sisters*, 1992

Thrift

This theme encompasses the general idea of carefulness with money. The more negative and extreme version of this attribute is covered at the theme **Miserliness**.

....

Mr Micawber The ever-impecunious Mr Wilkins Micawber, in Dickens's novel *David Copperfield* (1850), famously encapsulates the principle of balancing income and expenditure as follows: 'Annual income twenty pounds, annual expenditure nineteen nineteen six, result happiness. Annual income twenty pounds, annual expenditure twenty pounds ought and six, result misery.'

'My father now, he preferred to patronize the turf accountant. But he was generally sorry after. Great one for confessing, he was. A regular Mr Micawber.' He paused and looked at Llewellyn. 'Yes, a regular Mr Micawber. Only with him it wasn't the money he liked to balance out, it was the sins. Like the sensible Dubliner he was, he made sure he got the current week's sins cleared away at confession before he got started on the next lot. That way he could be certain he'd only have one week's sins to account for when he met his maker. Balancing the heavenly books, he called it.'
GERALDINE EVANS *Death Line*, 1995

If a government can pilot its way to a budget surplus, the economic and political results are very happy, especially for the Left. Our highly political Chancellor has noted and learned; financial Micawberism brings substantial rewards.
WILL HUTTON in The *Observer*, 1999

Samuel Smiles Samuel Smiles (1812–1904) was a Scottish doctor who wrote several works of advice. His books include *Self Help* (1859) and *Thrift* (1875). The name can be used to allude to financial prudence.

British banks and finance houses, their fingers so badly burnt by colossal debt write-offs, have behaved with the caution of Samuel Smiles in their lending policies.
WILL HUTTON in The *Observer*, 1997

Spartan The Spartans were the inhabitans of an ancient Greek city state in the southern Peloponnese. They were known for their austerity and self-discipline. Frugality or austerity can now be described as Spartan.

Pearl and he ate heartily upon these occasions, not knowing what Spartan nastiness the preoccupied Mrs. Vambrace might have left in the refrigerator for them at home.
ROBERTSON DAVIES *Tempest-Tost*, 1951

Time

This theme covers various aspects of the passing of time. Other related themes are **Outdatedness** and **Past**.

Connecticut Yankee In Mark Twain's satirical fantasy *A Connecticut Yankee in King Arthur's Court* (1889), Hank Morgan is a Connecticut mechanic who is knocked unconscious in a fight and awakens to find himself transported back to 6th-century Camelot. Using his 19th-century knowledge of technology and history, he determines to introduce to Arthur's kingdom the supposed benefits of advanced civilization.

Father Time Father Time is the personification of time, usually in the form of an old bearded man with a scythe and hourglass.

The American portion of our community 'saw in' the greatest day of their national calendar in a fittingly splendid style and circumstances today a fortnight previous. As our issue of that very date proceeded to the press some days earlier, not possessing mastery of Old Father Time and his scythe, we were unavoidably prevented from commenting on those happy rites.
TIMOTHY MO *An Insular Possession*, 1986

White Rabbit In Lewis Carroll's *Alice's Adventures in Wonderland* (1865), Alice follows the White Rabbit as he hurries along, constantly muttering to himself 'Oh dear! Oh dear! I shall be so late!' and 'Oh my ears and whiskers, how late it's getting!' ▶ *See special entry* □ ALICE IN WONDERLAND *on p. 10.*

'Look, a student!' my friend cried, and we watched as he rolled by, wearing khaki shorts, a Stanford logo T-shirt and baseball hat, muttering like the white rabbit about being late for class.
The Independent, 1997

Travellers and Wanderers

The long journey, voyage, or series of wanderings has proved a staple motif of world literature, with Homer's ODYSSEY the acknowledged paradigm. Some journeys, like those of the ARGONAUTS and ODYSSEUS, have an end; others, like those of CAIN and the WANDERING JEW, do not. ▶ *See also* Adventure, Quest, Walk.

....

Ahasuerus ▶ *See* WANDERING JEW.

Ancient Mariner In Samuel Taylor Coleridge's poem 'The Rime of the Ancient Mariner' (1798), the Ancient Mariner, as penance for killing an albatross, is forever condemned to travel from land to land, relating his story and teaching by his example love and reverence to all God's creatures.

Argonauts In Greek mythology, the Argonauts were the group of heroes who accompanied Jason on board the ship *Argo* in the quest for the Golden Fleece. The Argonauts included Hercules, Orpheus, Theseus, Nestor, and Castor and Pollux. Among the dangers they faced on their perilous voyage were the Symplegades, or clashing cliffs, which clashed together and crushed ships as they passed between them. ▶ *See special entry* □ JASON AND THE ARGONAUTS *on p. 220.*

'Come along, Captain Robinson,' he shouted, with a sort of bullying deference under the rim of the old man's hat; the Holy Terror gave a submissive little jump. The ghost of a steamer was waiting for them. Fortune on that fair isle! They made a curious pair of Argonauts. Chester strode on leisurely, well set up, portly, and of conquering mien; the other, long, wasted, drooping, and hooked to his arm, shuffled his withered shanks with desperate haste.
JOSEPH CONRAD *Lord Jim*, 1900

Leopold Bloom James Joyce's novel *Ulysses* (1922) charts the wanderings of Leopold Bloom, a Jewish advertisement canvasser, and Stephen Dedalus, a young poet, around Dublin on 16 June 1904. The various chapters roughly correspond to the episodes of Homer's *Odyssey*, with Bloom representing Odysseus and Stephen Telemachus. In the course of the story, a public bath, a cemetery, a newspaper office, a library, public houses, a maternity hospital, and a brothel are visited.

> As a youth, he worked variously as a bricklayer, coffin-polisher and artist's model at the local college of art. The milk round, however, was special; it offered him a daily, Bloom-like odyssey of Edinburgh and he grew to know its streets so well that even when he had left it far behind, he would be able to trace its contours in his head.
> *The Guardian*, 1998

George Borrow George Borrow (1803-81) was an English writer and traveller. His travels in England, Europe, Russia, and the Far East provided material for his narrative of gypsy life *Lavengro* (1851), and its sequel, *The Romany Rye* (1857). These works present a partly factual, partly fictional account of his travels.

> Staggering along the path like some lost shepherd, doubtless living out his own private dreams as Dr Johnson or George Borrow or somebody, came Councillor Duxbury himself, dabbing his streaming eyes and clutching his gnarled old stick.
> KEITH WATERHOUSE *Billy Liar*, 1959

Cain In the Bible, Cain was the eldest son of Adam and Eve who murdered his own brother Abel (Gen. 4: 1-16). For this crime he was cast out from his homeland and forced to live a life of vagrancy as an outcast. ▶ *See special entry* □ CAIN *on p. 44.*

> He never even seemed to come to his work on purpose, but would slouch in as if by mere accident; and when he went to the Jolly Bargemen to eat his dinner, or went away at night, he would slouch out, like Cain or the Wandering Jew, as if he had no idea where he was going and no intention of ever coming back.
> CHARLES DICKENS *Great Expectations*, 1861

Cook's tour Thomas Cook (1808-92) was an English travel agent who founded the travel firm Thomas Cook in 1841 and originated the guided tour. A Cook's tour is a tour or journey in which many places are visited, often briefly.

> The cars and petrol will be requisitioned by the army and the trains'll be packed with troops. I doubt if anyone'll get away, but if you do, you'll go empty-handed, and it won't be no Cook's tour.
> OLIVIA MANNING *The Great Fortune*, 1960

Dionysus Dionysus in Greek mythology was the god of fertility and wine. He was said to have made an expedition to eastern lands including India, spreading his cult and teaching mankind the elements of civilization and the use of wine. On his travels Dionysus is frequently represented drawn in a chariot by tigers and accompanied by Pan, Silenus, and a rowdy retinue of satyrs and maenads. ▶ *See special entry* □ DIONYSUS *on p. 117.*

> In his wanderings he resembled the Dionysos of the *Bacchae*.
> A. S. BYATT *The Virgin in the Garden*, 1978

Gulliver Gulliver is the hero of Jonathan Swift's satire *Gulliver's Travels* (1726), who in the course of the book visits many strange lands including Lilliput, Brobdingnag, Laputa, Lagado, and the land of the Houyhnhnms. ▶ *See special entry* □ **GULLIVER'S TRAVELS** *on p. 171.*

Homer Homer (8th century BC) was a Greek epic poet, to whom the *Odyssey* and the *Iliad* are traditionally attributed. The adjective 'Homeric' can be used to describe an epic journey or voyage.

> Songdogs by Colum McCann . . . Sublimely written Homeric story traces the nomadic narrator's search across Mexico, the USA and Ireland for his missing mother.
> *The Big Issue*, 1995

Kon-Tiki The *Kon-Tiki* is the name of the raft made of balsa logs in which, in 1947, the Norwegian anthropologist Thor Heyerdahl sailed from Peru to the islands of Polynesia in order to prove that ancient people could have migrated in this way.

Odysseus ▶ *See* **ODYSSEY**.

> It had been demoralising to wander like Odysseus from place to place, far from home, improvising a resistance that never seemed to amount to anything.
> LOUIS DE BERNIÈRES *Captain Corelli's Mandolin*, 1994

Odyssey In Greek mythology, Odysseus was the son of Laertes, king of Ithaca, and central figure of the *Odyssey*. He was known to the Romans as Ulysses. Homer's epic poem the *Odyssey* recounts the ten-year voyage of Odysseus during his years of wandering after the fall of Troy, and of his eventual return home to Ithaca and his killing of the suitors of his faithful wife, Penelope. His adventures include encounters with the Cyclops, Circe, the Lotus-Eaters, and the Sirens. Any long series of wanderings or long, adventurous journey can be described as an odyssey. ▶ *See special entry* □ **ODYSSEUS** *on p. 283.*

> I took a walk down by the Mississippi River and watched the logs that came floating from Montana in the north—grand Odyssean logs of our continental dream.
> JACK KEROUAC *On the Road*, 1957

Ossian Ossian is the anglicized form of Oisin, the name of a legendary Irish warrior and bard, the son of Finn MacCool. Ossian's name became well known in 1760–3 when the Scottish poet James Macpherson published what was later discovered to be his own verse as an alleged translation of 3rd-century Gaelic tales. Ossian's wanderings are the subject of a poem by W. B. Yeats.

Marco Polo Marco Polo (*c.*1254–*c.*1324) was a Venetian traveller and writer. Between 1271 and 1275 he accompanied his father and uncle on a trading expedition east into central Asia, eventually reaching China and the court of Kublai Khan. After entering diplomatic service with the emperor and travelling widely in the empire for a decade and a half, Polo returned home to Venice (1292–5) via Sumatra, India, and Persia. His written account of his travels was the West's primary source of knowledge of the Far East until the 19th century, though doubt has subsequently been cast on its veracity.

> The commonest ailment experienced by modern-day Marco Polos is an intestinal attack known as gyppy tummy.
> *New Scientist*, 1970

Sinbad Sinbad the Sailor is the hero of one of the tales in the *Arabian Nights*.

He is a rich young man of Baghdad who undertakes seven extraordinary sea-voyages during which he meets with various fantastic adventures, including encounters with the Old Man of the Sea and the Roc, a giant bird.

> 'I don't know how soon I be goin' to settle down,' proclaimed the rustic sister of Sinbad.
> SARAH ORNE JEWETT 'The Flight of Betsey Lane' (1893) in *Stories*, 1896

Ulysses Ulysses is the Roman name for Odysseus. ▶ *See* ODYSSEY.

> Her father was a romantic wanderer—a sort of Greek Ulysses.
> THOMAS HARDY *The Return of the Native*, 1880

Wandering Jew In medieval legend, the Wandering Jew was a man condemned to roam the earth until the Day of Judgement, as a punishment for having taunted Christ on the way to the Crucifixion, urging him to go faster. In some versions of the legend he is given the name Ahasuerus.

> But her thoughts soon strayed far from her own personality; and, full of a passionate and indescribable solicitude for one to whom she was not even a name, she went forth into the amplitude of tanned wild around her, restless as Ahasuerus the Jew.
> THOMAS HARDY *The Return of the Native*, 1880

Trojan War

The seeds of the Trojan War lay in an incident at the wedding of the mortal Peleus and the immortal sea-nymph Thetis. All the gods and goddesses were invited to the wedding feast with the exception of Eris, the goddess of discord. Angered at her exclusion, Eris threw a golden apple inscribed with the words 'for the fairest' at the feet of the wedding guests, causing disagreement between three goddesses, Hera, Athene, and Aphrodite, who each claimed the prize for herself. When Zeus appointed the Trojan prince Paris, the son of King Priam, to judge them, each goddess in turn tried to bribe him. Athene promised him wisdom and victory in war; Hera promised him dominion over mankind; Aphrodite promised him the most beautiful woman on earth as his wife. Paris chose Aphrodite as the winner of the contest and in so doing earned Troy the hostility of Hera and Athene.

Helen was the daughter of Zeus and Leda and grew into the most beautiful woman in the world. She had numerous suitors, but eventually married Menelaus, the king of Sparta. As one of her former suitors, Odysseus proposed that she and her husband would always be defended by the other suitors, and they all pledged to do so if occasion arose. Paris visited Sparta and abducted Helen, taking her back to Troy. Menelaus enlisted the help of his brother Agamemnon, king of Mycenae, to recover his wife. Under the command of Agamemnon, the Greeks, including Helen's former suitors, raised a fleet and mounted an expedition to rescue Helen from Troy. Warriors on the Greek side included such heroes as Achilles, Ajax, Diomedes, Odysseus, and Nestor.

The first nine years of the war were taken up by a siege of the city of Troy. Homer's *Iliad* recounts an episode in the tenth year of the siege during which Achilles quarrelled with his commander, Agamemnon. Furious that he had to return a captive Trojan girl to her father to appease the god Apollo, Agamemnon agreed to do so, but demanded that Achilles hand over to him his concubine Briseis to take her place. Achilles retired in anger to his tent, refusing to fight any longer. This enabled the Trojans to drive the Greeks back to the shore. Achilles' great friend, Patroclus, persuaded Achilles to let him borrow his armour but was killed by the Trojan hero Hector. Filled with grief and rage, Achilles finally emerged and returned to the battle. In revenge, he killed Hector in single combat and dragged his body behind the wheels of his chariot round the walls of Troy. Achilles himself was wounded in the heel by a poisoned arrow shot by Paris, Hector's brother, and died of this wound.

After the death of Achilles the Greeks devised a ruse to capture the city of Troy. They constructed a large wooden horse, built by a craftsman called Epeius, and left it outside the walls of the city. They then sailed out of sight, leaving behind just one man, Sinon, who pretended

Trojan War *continued*

to be a Greek deserter and reported to the Trojans that the horse was an offering to Athene, which, if brought within the city walls, would render Troy impregnable. Cassandra warned that the horse was a trick, but was not believed. Laocoön, a Trojan priest, also warned the Trojans not to let the horse into the city but was ignored. The horse was in fact full of Greek warriors, and once it had been brought into Troy and night had fallen, these warriors came out and took the city. Troy was sacked and razed by fire. Priam and his remaining sons were killed.

Throughout this book there are references to the Trojan War and to many of the figures mentioned in the above account.

▶ See ACHILLES *at* **Anger, Disguise**, *and* **Weakness**
    ACHILLES AND PATROCLUS *at* **Friendship**
    AGAMEMNON *at* **Anger**
    AJAX *at* **Suffering**
    APPLE OF DISCORD *at* **Conflict**
    ATREUS *at* **Curse**
    EPEIUS *at* **Craftsmen**
    HECUBA *at* **Grief and Sorrow**
    HELEN *at* **Beauty: Female Beauty**
    JUDGEMENT OF PARIS *at* **Judgement and Decision**
    LAOCOÖN *at* **Prophecy, Struggle**, *and* **Suffering**
    NESTOR *at* **Wisdom**
    PHILOCTETES *at* **Suffering**
    TROJAN HORSE *at* **Cunning**.

Ugliness

In a number of the quotations below, there is an explicit contrast made between ugliness and beauty: **CHARON** and a Greek god, **BORIS KARLOFF** and Marilyn Monroe, **VULCAN** and Apollo, and, of course, **BEAUTY AND THE BEAST**.

Antiphates' wife Antiphates was the chief of the Laestrygonians, a tribe of flesh-eating giants encountered by Odysseus and his companions on their journey back to Ithaca. According to Homer's account, his wife was repulsive-looking.

> Mandras' mother was one of those perplexing creatures as ugly as the mythical wife

of Antiphates, of whom the poet wrote that she was 'a monstrous woman whose ill-aspect struck men with horror'.
LOUIS DE BERNIÈRES *Captain Corelli's Mandolin*, 1994

Beauty and the Beast *Beauty and the Beast* is the title of a fairy tale in which a beautiful young woman, Beauty, is forced to live with the Beast, an ugly monster, in order to save her father's life. She comes to pity and love the Beast and finally consents to marry him. Beauty's love frees the beast from a magic spell and he is transformed into a handsome prince. Any couple of unequal physical attractiveness can be described as Beauty and the Beast.

When he was about fifteen they used to call him Beauty about the College, and me they nicknamed the Beast.
H. RIDER HAGGARD *She*, 1887

They were looking at each other, not touching, looking long and quiet at each other. The girl entirely wrapped in furs, so it was hard to tell where her own glossy hair began and ended, and the poor beast, with his rough and yellow hide—Beauty and her Beast, in this guise, but Beauty was so close to her Beast now, wrapped in beast's clothing, as sharp and wary as a beast, surviving as one.
DORIS LESSING *The Memoirs of a Survivor*, 1974

Hieronymus Bosch Hieronymus Bosch (c. 1450–1516) was a Flemish painter whose allegorical works are filled with grotesque monsters and horribly ugly people. Bosch's caricature-like faces are typically deformed, bloated, cadaverous, or disease-ridden.

Hardcastle fixed me with her reptilian eyes. If Hieronymus Bosch had turned his talents to gargoyles, Hilary Hardcastle would have been one of his most treasured creations.
DEXTER DIAS *False Witness*, 1995

Charon In Greek mythology, Charon was the ferryman who ferried the souls of the dead across the rivers Styx and Acheron to Hades. He was described as an old but vigorous man, with a hideous countenance, long white beard, and piercing eyes. His clothes were tattered and filthy. ▶ *See special entry* □ **HADES** *on p. 172*.

Then when he was a little older the undergraduates found fresh names for us. They called me Charon, and Leo the Greek God!
H. RIDER HAGGARD *She*, 1887

Dickensian Many of the novelist Charles Dickens's characters, such as Wackford Squeers and Daniel Quilp, are physically grotesque, and hence the term 'Dickensian' can be used to suggest a person's repulsive appearance.

I can't help describing him as if he were some sort of Dickensian freak.
ROBERTSON DAVIES *The Manticore*, 1972

Duessa In Spenser's allegory *The Faerie Queene* (1590; 1596), Duessa, representing Falsehood, assumes the appearance of a beautiful girl, Fidessa, but is later revealed to be in reality a hideous hag.

Elephant Man John Merrick (1863–90), born with severe facial deformities caused by a rare disease, was exhibited in Victorian times as a fairground freak, the Elephant Man, until he was rescued by a doctor.

If either party ... does not wish to continue the relationship, they must clearly and

considerately state this in a manner that reassures the other party that they are not the Elephant Man/Woman without being patronising.
BRIDGET JONES'S DIARY in The *Independent*, 1997

frog prince In *The Frog Prince*, a fairy story by the Brothers Grimm, the frog who helps out the princess is eventually restored to his true human form, that of a handsome prince who has been placed under an enchantment. Various children's fairy stories concern the character of an ugly frog who is really a handsome prince who has been put under such a spell. In some versions the spell can only be broken if a beautiful girl or princess kisses the frog.

> He would park on the road above the pier and give me a shilling and slope off, leaving me to what he called my own devices. I see myself, the frog prince, enthroned on the high back seat of the Morris Oxford, consuming a cornet of ice cream, licking the diminishing knob of goo round and round with scientific application, and staring back that the passing promenaders, who blanched at the sight of my baleful eye and flickering, creamy tongue.
> JOHN BANVILLE *The Book of Evidence*, 1989

Gorgon In Greek mythology, the Gorgons were three sisters, Stheno, Euryale, and Medusa (the only mortal one), who had snakes for hair and the power to turn anyone who looked at them to stone. A gorgon is a frightening or repulsive woman.

> She was an unnatural-looking being—so young, fresh, blooming, yet so Gorgon-like. Suspicion, sullen ill-temper were on her forehead, vicious propensities in her eye, envy and panther-like deceit about her mouth.
> CHARLOTTE BRONTË *The Professor*, 1857

> She was wearing something very like a man's evening suit, made in dark velvet, and looked remarkably elegant. I was beginning not to notice her Gorgon face.
> ROBERTSON DAVIES *The Manticore*, 1972

Hunchback of Notre Dame ▶ *See* QUASIMODO.

Boris Karloff Boris Karloff (1887–1969), born William Henry Pratt, was a British-born American actor. His gaunt looks made him particularly well suited to roles in horror films, and his most memorable performance was as the monster in *Frankenstein* (1931).

> The people protecting you have morticians who could make Boris Karloff look like Marilyn Monroe.
> TOM SHARPE *Grantchester Grind*, 1995

Macbeth's witches In Shakespeare's *Macbeth* (1623), the three weird sisters, or witches, encountered by Macbeth and Banquo on the blasted heath are described as

'So wither'd, and so wild in their attire,
That look not like th'inhabitants o' th'earth'
and later as 'you secret, black, and midnight hags'.

> She stood there, by that beech trunk—a hag like one of those who appeared to Macbeth on the heath of Forres.
> CHARLOTTE BRONTË *Jane Eyre*, 1847

Medusa ▶ *See* GORGON.

Quasimodo Quasimodo is the name of the hunchbacked bell-ringer in Victor Hugo's novel *Notre-Dame de Paris*, usually translated as *The Hunchback of Notre Dame* (1831). Though grotesque in appearance, Quasimodo is gentle and tender-hearted and becomes devoted to Esmeralda, a gypsy dancer.

> Close beside the bed, a bed Kudzuvine had never been in before and in a room he didn't begin to recognize, there sat the most malevolent creature he had ever seen since Quasimodo in a reshowing of The Hunchback of Notre Dame.
> TOM SHARPE *Grantchester Grind*, 1995

Ugly Duckling In the children's fairy story *The Ugly Duckling* (1846) by Hans Christian Andersen, a cygnet in a brood of ducklings is mocked by them for his drab appearance but turns into a beautiful swan. The term 'ugly duckling' can be applied to a person, initially thought ugly, who turns out to be extremely beautiful.

Ugly Sisters In the children's fairy story, Cinderella has two ugly stepsisters who despise and ill-treat her. They are usually depicted as being vain and completely unaware of their unprepossessing appearance. ▶ *See special entry* ☐ CINDERELLA *on p. 56.*

> 'Ma's got this cousin with a flat near the Colosseum.' 'And is this cousin young, male, gorgeous and loaded?' 'As a matter of fact, she's ninety-two and looks like a cross between the Hunchback of Notre Dame and one of the ugly sisters.'
> SUSAN MOODY *The Italian Garden*, 1994

Vulcan Vulcan was the Roman god of fire and metalworking, corresponding to the Greek Hephaestus. He was lame as a result of having interfered in a quarrel between his parents (Juno and Jupiter). Ugly in appearance, he was married to the most beautiful of the goddesses, Venus (who had many affairs). Vulcan is often depicted at the forge.

> The picture you have just drawn is suggestive of a rather too overwhelming contrast. Your words have delinated very prettily a graceful Apollo: he is present to your imagination,—tall, fair, blue-eyed, and with a Grecian profile. Your eyes dwell on a Vulcan,—a real blacksmith, brown, broad-shouldered: and blind and lame into the bargain.
> CHARLOTTE BRONTË *Jane Eyre*, 1847

> She considered the name her personal affair. She had arrived at it first purely on the basis of its ugly sound and then the full genius of its fitness had struck her. She had a vision of the name working like the ugly sweating Vulcan who stayed in the furnace and to whom, presumably, the goddess had to come when called.
> FLANNERY O'CONNOR *Good Country People*, 1955

Unpleasant or Wicked Places

There are two main groups among the entries below. Unpleasant places include, for example, the **BLACK HOLE OF CALCUTTA**, the **CHAMBER OF HORRORS**, and **DANTE'S INFERNO**. Wicked places include, for example, **BABYLON**,

GIN LANE, and SODOM AND GOMORRAH. ▶ *See also* **Horror, Idyllic Places**, **Suffering**.

....

Acheron In Greek mythology, Acheron ('the river of woe') was one of the rivers in Hades over which the souls of the dead were ferried by Charon. The name can also be used to mean the underworld or Hades. ▶ *See special entry* □ **HADES** *on p. 172*.

> [They] then made their way across the river, which under the grey and growing light looked as desolate as Acheron.
> G. K. CHESTERTON *The Man Who Was Thursday*, 1908

Admah and Zeboiim According to Deut. 29: 23, the cities of Admah and Zeboiim suffered the same fate as Sodom and Gomorrah, namely destruction by God as a punishment for their citizens' sinfulness.

Avernus Avernus is the name of a lake near Cumae and Naples. Close to the lake was the cave through which Aeneas descended to the underworld. The name means literally 'without birds', from the belief that its poisonous waters would cause any bird that attempted to fly over it to fall into the water.

Babylon Babylon was an ancient city in Mesopotamia which lay on the Euphrates and was first settled around 3000 BC. Hammurabi made Babylon the capital of the Babylonian empire and it became renowned for its grandeur and decadence. The Jews were exiled there from 597 to about 538 BC. The name of the city is now often applied to a place or group that is considered to be materialistic, corrupt, and associated with the pursuit of sensual pleasure.

> Imagine! Him! The budding star of the McCoy case—and no place—no place at all!—in the very Babylon of the twentieth century!—to take a lovely willing girl with brown lipstick.
> TOM WOLFE *The Bonfire of the Vanities*, 1987

> Tell me why is Nunes here? Why does he beat old women? Why does he lock up someone who has done no wrong? What have we done, what horrible sin lies buried in this village that these poor people must be made to live in such mortal terror? It is enough to make me stop believing. Here is no Sodom, no Gomorrah, no Babylon. This is an ordinary village with ordinary people.
> MIKE NICOL *The Powers That Be*, 1989

Black Hole of Calcutta The Black Hole of Calcutta was a dungeon in Fort William, Calcutta. Following the capture of Calcutta by Siraj-ud-Dawlah, nawab of Bengal, 146 English prisoners were said to have been confined there in a narrow cell for the night of 20 June 1756, with only twenty-three of them surviving to the morning. A severely overcrowded place can be described as a Black Hole of Calcutta.

> As I passed Erskine-Brown's open door I could see his room was bursting at the seams, and, as I hung up my hat and coat in the hallway, I heard the voice of the Erskine-Brown say he supposed they'd have to hang on in that Black Hole of Calcutta a little longer.
> JOHN MORTIMER *Rumpole of the Bailey*, 1978

Bluebeard's castle Bluebeard is a character in a tale by Charles Perrault, in the collection *Histoires et contes du temps passé* (1697). He kills several wives in turn for disobeying his instruction not to open a locked room in the castle. The terrible secret the room contains is the bodies of his previous wives.

> I lingered in the long passage to which this led, separating the front and back rooms of the third story: narrow, low, and dim, with only one little window at the far end, and looking, with its two rows of small black doors all shut, like a corridor in some Bluebeard's castle.
> CHARLOTTE BRONTË *Jane Eyre*, 1847

Chamber of Horrors The Chamber of Horrors is a section of the Madame Tussaud's waxworks in London which contains a macabre series of tableaux of notorious murderers at their work and of scenes of torture.

> Flora was trying to decide just what the kitchen looked like, and came to the conclusion it was the Chamber of Horrors at Madame Tussaud's.
> STELLA GIBBONS *Cold Comfort Farm*, 1932

Dante's Inferno The term 'Dante's Inferno' refers to the part of Dante's epic poem *The Divine Comedy* (c.1309–20) that depicts the poet's journey through Hell. Any hell-like vision or scene can be described as being like Dante's Inferno.

> Bored, she stepped outside, on to a steel gallery overlooking the factory floor. She surveyed the scene, feeling more than ever like Dante in the Inferno. All was noise, smoke, fumes and flames.
> DAVID LODGE *Nice Work*, 1988

Gehenna Gehenna is the Hebrew name for the Valley of Hinnom, a valley to the south of Jerusalem. Hinnom was known as the 'Valley of Slaughter' (Jer. 7: 31–2), and was used for idolatrous worship, with children being burnt alive as sacrifices to the idol Moloch. The name came to be associated with the fires of Hell.

> Down to Gehenna or up to the Throne,
> He travels fastest who travels alone
> RUDYARD KIPLING *The Story of the Gadsbys*, 1890

Gin Lane *Gin Lane* (1751), depicting a scene of drunkenness and squalor, is one of the most famous prints by William Hogarth, the English painter, engraver, and satirist. Gin-drinking was widespread at the time, and regarded by many as a cause of crime and other social problems.

> In his intrepid trip down the stairs he encountered every sort of vice: fornication, crack smoking, heroin injecting, dice games and three-card monte, and more fornication. . . . 'It's bloody Hogarth,' said Steiner. 'Gin Lane. Except that it's vertical.'
> TOM WOLFE *The Bonfire of the Vanities*, 1987

Gomorrah ▶ *See* SODOM AND GOMORRAH.

Gulag Archipelago The Gulag Archipelago is the name of the system of forced-labour camps in the Soviet Union, specifically in the period 1930–55, in which hundreds of thousands, perhaps millions, died. The term can be now be used in a more general sense.

> Much has been made by commentators about Delia's celebrated dullness. We are

told repeatedly that she was once exiled to the TV equivalent of the Gulag Archipelago because she wasn't 'sexy enough'.
The Guardian, 1995

Hades In Greek mythology, Hades was the underworld, the abode of the spirits of the dead. Originally the name Hades referred only to the ruler of the underworld, also known as Pluto, rather than to the place. ▶ *See special entry* ☐ **HADES** *on p. 172.*

He stood motionless, undecided, glaring with his eyes, thinking of the pains and penalties of Hades.
ANTHONY TROLLOPE *Barchester Towers*, 1857

On we went for many minutes in absolute awed silence, like lost souls in the depths of Hades.
H. RIDER HAGGARD *She*, 1887

Hell In the Christian, Jewish, and Islamic faiths, Hell is the place of punishment where the souls of the damned are confined after death. It is described in the Bible as 'everlasting fire, prepared for the devil and his angels' (Matt. 26: 41) and 'a lake of fire, burning with brimstone' (Rev. 19: 20).

Hinnom The Valley of Hinnom to the south of Jerusalem was known as the 'Valley of Slaughter' (Jer. 7: 31-2). It was used for idolatrous worship, with children being burnt alive as sacrifices to the idol Moloch, and there is a strong association between the name and the fires of Hell.

The lightning had struck the tree. A sulphurous smell filled the air; then all was silent, and black as a cave in Hinnom.
THOMAS HARDY *Far from the Madding Crowd*, 1874

Hyrcania Hyrcania was an ancient mountainous region bordering the Caspian Sea, noted for its rough wooded terrain full of serpents and wild beasts.

Pandemonium Pandemonium is the abode of all the demons, originally the capital of Hell in Milton's *Paradise Lost* (1667). The word 'pandemonium' is usually applied to a place of utter confusion and uproar, but is sometimes used to suggest a place of vice and wickedness.

It presented to me then as exquisite and divine a retreat as Pandemonium appeared to the devils of hell after their sufferings in the lake of fire.
MARY SHELLEY *Frankenstein*, 1831

Siberia Siberia, the vast region of northern Russia noted for its severe winters, was traditionally used as a place of banishment and exile. Its name typifies a cold, inhospitable place of exile.

She and her family are still living in the projects—exiled to an urban Siberia where shop, banks, and other amenities of city living are few and far between.
Washington City Paper, 1992

Sodom and Gomorrah Sodom and Gomorrah were towns in ancient Palestine, probably south of the Dead Sea. According to Gen. 19: 24, they were destroyed by fire and brimstone from heaven as a punishment for the depravity and wickedness of their inhabitants. Lot, the nephew of Abraham, was allowed to escape from the destruction of Sodom with his family. His wife disobeyed God's order not to look back at the burning city and was turned into a pillar of salt.

'The village', she said in her quiet voice, 'the village grows worse and worse every day'. 'What has happened now?' asked Mr Bodiham, feeling suddenly very weary. 'I'll tell you.' She pulled up a brown varnished chair and sat down. In the village of Crome, it seemed, Sodom and Gomorrah had come to a second birth.
ALDOUS HUXLEY *Crome Yellow*, 1921

The landslip had swept away a whole Sodom and Gomorrah of private fantasies and unacted desires. He felt a new man in the calm, initially sexless atmosphere of Desiree Zapp's luxurious eyrie high up on the peak of Socrates Avenue.
DAVID LODGE *Changing Places*, 1975

In front of me is the Pacific, which sends up sunset after sunset, for nothing; at my back are the improbable mountains, and beyond them an enormous barricade of land. Toronto lies behind it, at a great distance, burning in thought like Gomorrah.
MARGARET ATWOOD *Cat's Eye*, 1988

Tammany Hall Tammany Hall was the headquarters of a US Democratic Party organization that was very influential in New York City during the 19th and early 20th centuries. The organization was notorious for corruption and for maintaining power by the use of bribes, and the name Tammany Hall can now be used to denote any place of political corruption.

He had been a legendary President of the Union, succeeding in getting elected in spite of being at Magdalen, a college with little or no history of involvement in the Union. He did this by creating what became known as 'the Magdalen Machine', a ruthless Tammany Hall-style operation that propelled several other Magdalen students to the presidency, including a hardline Communist called Malcolm Bull.
The Observer, 1997

Tartarus In Greek mythology, Tartarus was the lowest region of Hades where the wicked suffered punishments for their misdeeds on earth, especially those such as Tantalus and Ixion who had offended the gods. ▶ *See special entry* ☐ **HADES** *on p. 172.*

Tophet Tophet was the name of a place in the Valley of Hinnom to the south of Jerusalem. Hinnom was known as the 'Valley of Slaughter' (Jer. 7: 31–2), and was used for idolatrous worship, with children being burnt alive as sacrifices to the idol Moloch. Later Tophet was used for burning refuse, and bonfires were kept burning there for this purpose. Hence there is a strong association between the name and the fires of Hell.

It seemed the great Black Parliament sitting in Tophet. A hundred black faces turned round in their rows to peer; and beyond, a black Angel of Doom was beating a book in a pulpit.
HERMAN MELVILLE *Moby Dick*, 1851

The careless sergeant smiled within himself, and probably too the devil smiled from a loop-hole in Tophet, for the moment was the turning-point of a career.
THOMAS HARDY *Far from the Madding Crowd*, 1874

Vanity

As with some of the other themes in this book, a single figure dominates this theme. The name of **NARCISSUS** has become synonymous in English with the idea of excessive self-admiration. ▶ *See also* **Arrogance, Pride**.

....

Narcissus In Greek mythology, Narcissus was a youth of extraordinary beauty who cruelly spurned many admirers, including the nymph Echo. On bending down to a pool one day to drink, he fell in love with his own reflection. There are various versions of the fate that subsequently befell Narcissus. According to one version, he fell into the pool as he tried to embrace his own reflection and drowned. Another version relates how, having tried to kiss and embrace his reflection and failed, Narcissus simply pined away and died. After his death, the gods turned his body into the white flower that bears his name. Narcissus is the epitome of excessive vanity, and his name has given us the word 'narcissism'.

> A feeling of pain crept over him as he thought of the desecration that was in store for the fair face on the canvas. Once, in boyish mockery of Narcissus, he had kissed, or feigned to kiss, those painted lips that now smiled so cruelly at him.
> OSCAR WILDE *The Picture of Dorian Gray*, 1891

> There were gilt cherubs in the bathroom holding white towels through rings in their mouths, and the walls and ceiling were made of looking-glass. Narcissus could lie in his nacreous bath and, gazing upward, see all of himself reflected.
> ALICE THOMAS ELLIS *The 27th Kingdom*, 1982

Snow White's stepmother In the traditional fairy story, Snow White's step-mother is proud and vain, and regularly demands of her magic mirror:

'Mirror, mirror on the wall,
Who is the fairest of them all?'

When Snow White grows to be more beautiful than her, she orders her step-daughter to be taken into the forest and killed.

Ugly Sisters In the fairy tale of *Cinderella*, Cinderella's two stepsisters have both been invited to the prince's ball and spend days fussing over what they are going to wear to the ball and how beautiful they are going to look. In pantomime versions of the tale, the stepsisters are presented as the Ugly Sisters, played by men and made grotesquely ugly so that their vanity becomes ridiculous and comical.

Victory

This theme deals with victory in a battle or contest. Other kinds of attainment are covered in the theme **Success**. ▶ *See also* **Defeat**.

....

Agincourt Agincourt (now Azincourt), a village in France, is close to the site of a battle between the French and the English in 1415 during the Hundred Years War. Although the English were heavily outnumbered, the terrain, a muddy valley, suited the English forces, largely archers, rather than the French who had armoured cavalry and infantry fighting in massed formations. The English lost only about 200 men to French losses of over 5,000. The battle is remembered chiefly because of its prominence in Shakespeare's *Henry V*.

Bull Run During the American civil war, two battles were fought between the Union and Confederate armies at Manassas Junction in Virginia, near a stream named Bull Run. In the first battle in 1861, General Jackson's Confederate Army held off Union troops until relieved by reinforcements, in the process earning for Jackson the nickname 'Stonewall'. In the second battle, General Robert E. Lee defeated the Union army, driving them from the battleground and forcing them to retreat to Washington, DC.

David In the Bible, the shepherd boy David accepted the challenge to fight the Philistine warrior Goliath (1 Sam. 17). Although Goliath was nine feet tall, David killed him armed only with a sling and pebbles. David's triumph in overcoming Goliath is the more remarkable because of the inequality in their relative status. ▶ *See special entry* □ **DAVID** *on p. 90*.

> Every day we hear of more Italian armies driven back or defeated, and we feel the jubilation of David with Goliath dead at his feet.
> LOUIS DE BERNIÈRES *Captain Corelli's Mandolin*, 1994

Nike Nike was the Greek goddess of victory, usually represented as a winged figure. Statues of Nike are often referred to as 'Winged Victories', such as the Nike of Samothrace (c.200 BC), preserved in the Louvre in Paris.

> She's a Nike . . . on the prow of a Greek ship.
> ANNA DOUGLAS SEDGWICK *Little French Girl*, 1924

Pyrrhic victory Pyrrhus (c.318–272 BC) was king of Epirus c.307–272. In defeating the Romans at Asculum in 279, he sustained heavy losses, commenting 'Such another victory and we are ruined'. Hence a 'Pyrrhic victory' is one gained with terrible loss of life or at too great a cost.

Walk

This theme covers distinctive types of gait.

....

Agag Agag was the king of the Amalekites, whom Saul defeated in battle. Although Saul wanted to spare Agag's life, the prophet Samuel ordered Agag to be brought to him: 'Then said Samuel, Bring ye hither to me Agag the king of the Amalekites. And Agag came unto him delicately' (1 Sam. 15: 32). Samuel then 'hewed Agag in pieces' as retribution for Agag's brutality. As can be seen from the quotations below, the word 'delicately' is forever associated with the name of Agag.

> So as I lay on the ground with my ear glued close against the wall, who should march round the church but John Trenchard, Esquire, not treading delicately like King Agag, or spying, but just come on a voyage of discovery for himself.
> J. M. FAULKNER *Moonfleet*, 1898

> If they were not rendered completely immobile, they certainly walked as delicately as Agag, the King of the Amalekites, is supposed to have done according to 1 Samuel xv.32.
> *The Independent on Sunday*, 1997

Charlie Chaplin Charlie Chaplin (1889-1977) was an English film actor and director. In many of his silent comedies, such as *The Kid* (1921) and *The Gold Rush* (1925), he portrayed a little tramp who wore a bowler hat and baggy trousers, twirled a cane, and had a comical wide-legged, tottering walk.

> There was a soldier who crossed his eyes and folded down his lower lip, another who pouted and blew her a kiss, another who converted his marching into a Charlie Chaplin walk.
> LOUIS DE BERNIÈRES *Captain Corelli's Mandolin*, 1994

Dr Johnson Samuel Johnson (1709-84), often referred to as 'Dr Johnson', was an English lexicographer, writer, critic, and celebrated conversationalist. In 1773 he undertook a journey with James Boswell to the Scottish Highlands and Hebrides, recorded in his *A Journey to the Western Islands of Scotland* (1775) and in Boswell's *Journal of a Tour to the Hebrides* (1785). The image of Johnson striding purposefully along while engaged in witty conversation is an enduring one.

> Even Dr Johnson could not have carried on a conversation when he was walking down Fleet Street at the speed of an express train.
> W. SOMERSET MAUGHAM *Cakes and Ale*, 1930

Long John Silver Long John Silver is the one-legged ship's cook who is the leader of the mutinous pirates among the crew of the *Hispaniola* in R. L. Stevenson's *Treasure Island* (1883).

> But I do play a bit of tennis still, wearing a kind of brace on the knee which keeps it more or less rigid. I have to sort of drag the right leg like Long John Silver when I hop around the court, but it's better than nothing.
> DAVID LODGE *Therapy*, 1995

Groucho Marx Groucho Marx (Julius Henry Marx, 1890–1977) was one of the US comedy team, the Marx Brothers. His urgent, crouching walk was as distinctive as his wisecracking one-liners and his facial appearance, complete with painted black moustache, glasses, and cigar.

> He rushed out of the car like Groucho Marx to get cigarettes—that furious, ground-hugging walk with the coattails flying.
> JACK KEROUAC *On the Road*, 1957

Ministry of Silly Walks The Ministry of Silly Walks appears in a well-known sketch from *Monty Python's Flying Circus*, a popular British TV comedy series of the 1970s. A spoof government department, the Ministry employs bowler-hatted civil servants each of whom has an outlandish style of walking.

War

Of the war deities grouped here, **MARS** is the best known and the one most commonly used to represent the concept of war.

....

Ares In Greek mythology, Ares, the son of Zeus and Hera, was the god of war, corresponding to the Roman god Mars.

Athene In Greek mythology, Athene was the goddess of wisdom, handicrafts, and also of war. She is usually represented in sculpture and paintings in armour. She is supposed to have sprung, fully armed and uttering her war-cry, from the head of Zeus.

Brynhild In Scandinavian mytholgy, Brynhild was a Valkyrie whom Sigurd won by penetrating the wall of fire behind which she lay in an enchanted sleep, from which he revived her. She corresponds in the *Nibelungenleid* to Brunhild, the wife of Gunther, who instigated the murder of Siegfried. As Brunnhilde she is one of the main characters in Wagner's operatic cycle *The Ring of the Nibelungs*.

Mars In Roman mythology, Mars was the god of war, corresponding to the Greek god Ares.

> 'Ha, ha!—you must have your joke; well, I'll think o' that. And so they expect Buonaparty to choose this very part of the coast for his landing, hey? And that yeomanry be to stand in front as the forlorn hope?' 'Who says so?' asked the florid son of Mars, losing a little redness.
> THOMAS HARDY *The Trumpet Major*, 1880

> I have already said that I am not much of an actor, but I gave a powerful, if crude impersonation of the hero who is tremendous on the field of Mars but slighted in the courts of Venus.
> ROBERTSON DAVIES *Fifth Business*, 1970

Minerva In Roman mythology, Minerva was the goddess of wisdom, handicrafts, and also of war. She corresponds to the Greek goddess Athene.

> There was, as I have said, a Minerva fully armed.
> MARILYNNE ROBINSON *Mother Country*, 1989

Tyr In Scandinavian mythology, Tyr was the god of battle, corresponding to the Roman Mars.

Valkyries In Scandinavian mythology, the Valkyries (literally 'choosers of the slain') were Odin's twelve handmaidens who hovered over battlefields, selected the most valiant warriors to die in battle, and escorted them to Valhalla, the hall of heroes. They appear in Wagner's opera *Die Walküre* (1854–56).

> Dorothy Thompson seemed to me an overpowering figure in a Wagnerian opera, a Valkyrie, deciding with careless pointing of her spear who should die on the battlefield.
> JOHN HERSEY 'Sinclair Lewis' in *Life Sketches*, 1987

> Martya ducked the tub aimed at her; the second exploded at Kareen's feet. Muno's attempt to lay down a covering fire for his party's retreat backfired when Enrique dropped to his knees and scrambled away down the hall toward his screaming Valkyriesque protectors.
> LOIS MCMASTER BUJOLD *A Civil Campaign*, 1999

Water

The entries here all relate to the sea and mainly comprise sea-deities or their children.

Neptune In Roman mythology, Neptune was the god of the sea, identified with the Greek god Poseidon.

> Flying fish. These extraordinary creatures, actually scaly denizens of the deep and subjects of Neptune, are possessors, like the members of the feathered tribe, of wings.
> TIMOTHY MO *An Insular Possession*, 1986

> He was not an athlete, but he was at the water's hissing edge when his father emerged, like a matted red–lipped Neptune, blue–nosed, encased in dripping wet wool and shining burnt toast.
> PETER CAREY *Oscar and Lucinda*, 1988

Nereid The Nereids were sea nymphs in Greek mythology, daughters of Nereus. They include Galatea and Thetis, the mother of Achilles.

> Mandras was too young to be a Poseidon, too much without malice. Was he a male sea-nymph, then? Was there such a thing as a male Nereid or Potamid?
> LOUIS DE BERNIÈRES *Captain Corelli's Mandolin*, 1994

Nereus In Greek mythology, Nereus was an old god of the sea and a son of

Gaia. He and his wife, Doris, had fifty daughters, the Nereids.

> And finally the storme impetuous
> Sunke up these riches, second unto none,
> Within the gulfe of greedie Nereus.
> EDMUND SPENSER *Complaints*, 1591

Noah's flood The Book of Genesis in the Bible relates how God sent a great Flood to destroy the whole of mankind because of their wickedness. The Flood lasted for forty days and forty nights, and drowned all inhabitants of the earth apart from Noah and his family, whom God had warned and instructed to build an ark, in which he was to save two of each species of creature. ▶ *See special entry* ❑ **NOAH AND THE FLOOD** *on p. 279.*

> The Nantucketer, he alone resides and riots on the sea; he alone, in Bible language, goes down to it in ships; to and fro ploughing it as his own special plantation. There is his home; there lies his business, which a Noah's flood would not interrupt, though it overwhelmed all the millions in China.
> HERMAN MELVILLE *Moby Dick*, 1851

Poseidon Poseidon was the god of the sea and water in Greek mythology. He was the son of Cronus and Rhea and is usually pictured holding or hurling a trident. Poseidon corresponds to the Roman god Neptune.

Triton Triton was the son of Poseidon and Amphitrite, in Greek mythology. He was half man and half fish, having a fish's tail.

> Sometimes diving under her and merging the other side, spouting water like a Triton.
> PATRICK O'BRIAN *Treason's Harbour*, 1983

Weakness

Weakness here is taken mainly to mean vulnerability, though the idea of fragility or puniness is also covered. The idea of the mighty, seemingly invincible hero with a single vulnerable point or source of weakness has been an enduring one in storytelling and literature. **ACHILLES** and his heel have, of course, become proverbial, but are paralleled by **SAMSON** and his hair, **BALDER** and mistletoe, **SIEGFRIED** and the linden leaf, and even **SUPER-MAN** and kryptonite. Ironically, the vulnerable point is often the direct result of the process that confers invulnerability. ▶ *See also* **Strength**.

Achilles Achilles was a hero of the Trojan War, son of Peleus and Thetis. During his infancy his mother dipped him in the River Styx, thus making his body invulnerable except for the heel by which she held him. Achilles was wounded in the heel during the Trojan War by a poisoned arrow shot by Paris, and died of this wound. A person's 'Achilles' heel' is thus their only weak or vulnerable point. ▶ *See special entry* ☐ **ACHILLES** *on p. 3.*

> It reveals a curious Achilles heel in the master spindoctor: brilliant as he is at selling Labour, he is strangely bad at selling himself.
> *The Observer*, 1997

Antaeus In Greek mythology, Antaeus was a giant, son of the sea-god Poseidon and the earth-goddess Gaia. He forced all comers to wrestle with him and overcame and killed them until he was defeated by Hercules. Antaeus was invincible as long as he touched the earth (enabling him to draw new strength from his mother), but was lifted into the air by Hercules and crushed to death in his arms.

Balder In Scandinavian mythology, Balder was the son of Odin. Beautiful and popular, he was the god of light. When Balder had a dream that he would die, his mother, Frigga, exacted a promise from all things that they would not harm him, but she overlooked the mistletoe. Loki tricked the blind god Hodur into throwing a branch of mistletoe at Balder, and this killed him.

Delilah ▶ *See* **Samson**.

Goliath David's slaying of the Philistine giant Goliath with a stone from a sling (I Sam. 17) can be alluded to, as in the quotation below, in the context of something apparently impregnable or invincible being breached or overcome because of the discovery of a weak point. ▶ *See special entry* ☐ **DAVID** *on p. 90.*

> They were unable to bar the door to those diabolic bestioles which crawl through the smallest hole even as David found the chink in Goliath's armour.
> JULIAN BARNES *A History of the World in 10½ Chapters*, 1989

Humpty Dumpty Humpty Dumpty is a nursery rhyme character whose name is taken to refer to an egg:

'Humpty Dumpty sat on a wall,
Humpty Dumpty had a great fall.
All the king's horses, and all the king's men
Couldn't put Humpty together again.'

The name can be applied to anything fragile, especially something that once damaged cannot be restored.

> It would be hundreds of years before any emergent Amazons would ever grasp the fact that a man is vulnerable only in his pride, but delicate as Humpty-Dumpty once that is meddled with.
> F. SCOTT FITZGERALD *Tender Is the Night*, 1934

> It is, we would remind our readers ... impossible to make an omelette without first breaking eggs. We ... cannot wait to see the great Chinese Humpty Dumpty given a forceful shove off his wall of secrecy and deceit and broke all to pieces. Not all the Emperor's men shall put him together again.
> TIMOTHY MO *An Insular Possession*, 1986

> We should not bang on about Gascoigne throwing it away because in our hearts we always knew that this was a footballer as fragile as Humpty Dumpty with a bout of vertigo.
> PAUL WEAVER in The *Guardian*, 1998

Caspar Milquetoast Caspar Milquetoast was a timid comic strip character created by the American cartoonist H. T. Webster in 1924. A Milquetoast is thus any meek, submissive, or timid person.

> And UN Secretary General Kofi Annan, momentarily abandoning his customary Caspar Milquetoast approach, actually has gone to NATO and said a credible threat of force was 'essential' to make diplomacy effective.
> *Chicago Tribune*, 1999

Samson In the Bible, Samson was an Israelite leader (prob. 11th century BC) famous for his strength. He fell in love with Delilah and confided to her that his strength lay in his hair: 'There hath not come a razor upon my head . . . if I be shaven, then my strength will go from me, and I shall become weak, and be like any other man' (Judg. 16: 17). Delilah did indeed have Samson's hair cut off while he slept and betrayed him to the Philistines. Samson's hair can be alluded to when referring to a strong or powerful person rendered weak and vulnerable. ▶ *See special entry* ☐ **SAMSON** *on p. 336.*

> Arabella ascended the stairs, softly opened the door of the first bedroom, and peeped in. Finding that her shorn Samson was asleep she entered to the bedside and started regarding him.
> THOMAS HARDY *Jude the Obscure*, 1895

> 'Lassiter!' Jane whispered, as she gazed from him to the black, cold guns. Without them he appeared shorn of strength, defenseless, a smaller man. Was she Delilah?
> ZANE GREY *Riders of the Purple Sage*, 1912

> This is the very dilemma that once confronted a young Hick. Hailed as great before he'd achieved it, he lost the glow of youth with frightening rapidity. With the erosion of innocence went his power, weakened like Samson at the barber's shop.
> *The Observer*, 1998

Siegfried In Germanic legend, Siegfried, equivalent to the Sigurd of Norse legend, was a prince of the Netherlands and the hero of the first part of the *Nibelungenlied*. He was treacherously slain by Hagen, who discovered that Siegfried was vulnerable in only one spot on his back. Siegfried had become invulnerable after being bathed in the hot blood of a dragon he had slain, but a linden leaf had fallen between his shoulder-blades, preventing that part from being covered in the blood.

Superman Superman is a US comic book superhero who possesses prodigious strength, the ability to fly, and other powers. He is invulnerable except when exposed to pieces of the green rock kryptonite, fragments of the planet of his birth, Krypton.

Wealth

There are three main strands to this theme: traditional archetypes of wealth, drawn principally from mythology and the Bible (e.g. **CROESUS**, **DIVES**, and **MIDAS**); more modern examples of extremely rich people (e.g. **HOWARD HUGHES**, **ARISTOTLE ONASSIS**, **ROCKEFELLER**); and places of fabulous wealth (e.g. **ALADDIN'S CAVE**, **EL DORADO**, **SOLOMON'S TEMPLE**). ▶ *See also* **Avarice, Miserliness, Poverty**.

....

Aladdin's cave (or palace) Aladdin, the hero of a story in the *Arabian Nights*, is born the son of a poor tailor and is too lazy after his father's death to help out his mother. A magician tricks him into a cave filled with treasure, in order to retrieve a magic lamp. When the magician discovers that Aladdin has stolen as much of the treasure as he can hide in his clothes, he shuts him into the cave, whereupon Aladdin discovers the secret of the lamp, a jinnee who must do his bidding. He is able to escape the cave, and the 'slave of the lamp' makes him and his mother rich. Eventually the slave of the lamp builds a magnificent palace for Aladdin and the daughter of the Sultan whom he marries.

> The brilliancy might have befitted Aladdin's palace rather than the mansion of a grave old Puritan ruler.
> NATHANIEL HAWTHORNE *The Scarlet Letter*, 1850

> She thought . . . of the Aladdin's cave she had perceived in the Pusey's suite, with its careless deployment of pleasurable attributes.
> ANITA BROOKNER *Hotel du Lac*, 1984

> Ever since then the place has remained in my memory the Mecca of fashion, an Aladdin's cave of incomparable splendour.
> ANDRÉ BRINK *Imaginings of Sand*, 1996

Croesus Croesus (6th century BC) was the last king of Lydia, a country on the east coast of the Aegean Sea in what is now Turkey. He was famed for his great wealth. The phrase 'as rich as Croesus' has become proverbial.

> 'This girl's father,' said William, 'is as rich as Croesus. He owns property without end.'
> D. H. LAWRENCE *Sons and Lovers*, 1913

> It did not seem quite fair to Marion, but Marion was as rich as Croesus, everyone knew, and Marion had sold Leslie Beck's baby and perhaps didn't deserve too much.
> FAY WELDON *Life Force*, 1992

> Here is a man barely into his forties who has already amassed riches beyond Croesus (he owns 141 million shares in Microsoft, currently trading at 83.37 apiece). Last year the rise in the value of his stock meant that he earned about 30 million a day.
> *The Observer*, 1997

Daddy Warbucks Daddy Warbucks is a rich businessman in the American comic strip *Little Orphan Annie*, who takes care of Annie. As his name suggests, he was originally a munitions manufacturer.

Dives Dives (from the Latin for 'rich') is the name traditionally given to the rich man in the parable of the rich man and Lazarus (Luke 16: 19-31). The rich man lived in great luxury whilst Lazarus was a beggar at his gate, covered with sores and longing even for the crumbs from the rich man's table. When both died, Dives found himself in hell and, looking up, saw Lazarus being taken up to Heaven by Abraham. Abraham explained to him that he had already had good things in his lifetime whereas Lazarus had not. Consequently, Lazarus received comfort in the afterlife whilst the rich man endured agony.

> Remember, we are bid to work while it is day—warned that 'the night cometh when no man shall work'. Remember the fate of Dives, who had his good things in this life. God give you strength to choose that better part which shall not be taken from you!
> CHARLOTTE BRONTË *Jane Eyre*, 1847

El Dorado El Dorado (literally 'the gilded one') was the fabled city or country of gold sought in the 16th century by Spanish conquistadors, who believed it existed somewhere in the area of the Orinoco and Amazon rivers. Hence, any place of fabulous wealth can be described as an El Dorado.

> A year ago, I finally weaned myself off office life and took to working from home. It is far more productive, of course, but I still feel a little pang when I hear words such as coffee machine or stationery cupboard—stationery cupboard, in particular, sounds like El Dorado now I have to buy my own Jiffy bags.
> *The Sunday Times*, 1994

> One should have thought a transfer to a continental club would have made more sense, even though Italian fooball is no longer the El Dorado it used to be.
> *The Sunday Telegraph*, 1995

Fort Knox Fort Knox is a building in north Kentucky, part of a military reservation, which houses the US gold reserves in the form of bullion.

> It's important to chip away at Ford's defences here because they seem to be protecting the Fort Knox of his imagination.
> *The Observer*, 1997

Jean Paul Getty Jean Paul Getty (1892–1976) was an American oil billionaire who became allegedly the world's richest man.

Golden Fleece In Greek mythology, the Golden Fleece was the fleece of pure gold taken from the ram which carried Phrixus to Colchis on the Black Sea. Phrixus sacrificed the ram to Zeus and offered its fleece to Aeetes, king of Colchis, who hung it from an oak tree guarded by a dragon that never slept. It was eventually recovered by Jason. ▶ *See special entry* ☐ **JASON AND THE ARGONAUTS** *on p. 220*.

> The birth of Jason had not been a happy day for Dominique. The little bastard was just over a year old now. Wrapped in his golden fleece, his birth had signalled a new wave of excessive behaviour from Dominique.
> MEL STEIN *White Lines*, 1997

Howard Hughes Howard Hughes (1905–76) was an American millionaire who produced films and designed and flew aircraft. He became a recluse in his later years.

Maecenas Gaius Cilnius Maecenas (d. 8 BC) was a wealthy Roman statesman and patron of Virgil, Horace, and other poets.

> When Mrs Felpham asked him to tea, Rampion wanted to refuse the invitation—but to refuse it without being boorish or offensive. After all, she meant well enough, poor woman. She was only rather ludicrous. The village Maecenas, in petticoats,

patronizing art to the extent of two cups of tea and a slice of plum cake.
ALDOUS HUXLEY *Point Counter Point*, 1928

But let's just say for the moment that Saatchi was a Maecenas to an important generation of British artists, and that even if he never buys another painting, or mounts another show, we should be grateful to him for giving us Sensation.
LYNN BARBER in The *Observer*, 2000

Mammon Deriving from the Aramaic word for 'riches', Mammon is sometimes used in the Bible to mean wealth when considered as an idol whose worship is in opposition to that of God. The most familiar reference is probably Jesus's teaching that 'No man can serve two masters: for either he will hate the one and love the other; or else he will hold to the one, and despise the other. Ye cannot serve God and mammon' (Matt. 6: 24). Mammon was taken by medieval writers as the proper name of the devil of covetousness, and this use was revived by Milton in *Paradise Lost*. The name is now used as the personification of wealth, seen as greedy and selfish materialism.

I know poetry is not dead, nor genius lost; nor has Mammon gained power over either, to bind or slay: they will both assert their existence, their presence, their liberty and strength again one day.
CHARLOTTE BRONTË *Jane Eyre*, 1847

Carling is so closely identified with the increasing commercialisation of rugby union it's as if he personally got hold of the compass and swung the game in the direction of Mammon. He didn't.
The Guardian, 1995

Midas In Greek mythology, Midas was the king of Phrygia, a country in what is now part of Turkey. He was granted a wish by Dionysus and wished that everything he touched should be turned to gold. However, when even the food in his mouth turned to gold, he was allowed to lose the gift by bathing in the River Pactolus. The name of Midas is thus used for someone very rich, and the 'Midas touch' is a gift for making money, seemingly without effort.

Custom dictates that carolers be asked in and offered a cookie ... and so must any person who comes to your door, otherwise the spirit of Christmas will leave your house, and even if you be as rich as Midas, your holiday will be sad and mean.
GARRISON KEILLOR *Lake Wobegon Days*, 1985

Ferguson's inspired signing of Cantona, and other purchases of his, have shown him to have a bit of a transfer Midas touch. Once he has ventured money on a player, the Manchester United manager usually manages to get the best out of him.
The Sunday Telegraph, 1995

John Pierpoint Morgan John Pierpoint Morgan (1837–1913) was an American banker whose wealth was sufficient to enable him to stabilize the American economy in 1895.

I bought a dozen volumes on banking and credit and investment securities and they stood on my shelf in red and gold like new money from the mint, promising to unfold the shining secrets that only Midas and Morgan and Maecenas knew.
F. SCOTT FITZGERALD *The Great Gatsby*, 1925

Nibelung In Germanic mythology, Nibelung was the king of a race of Scandinavian dwarves, also called the Nibelung, who owned a hoard of treasure and gold. In the 13th-century epic German poem the *Nibelungenlied*, the treasure is guarded by the dwarf Alberich and later taken by Siegfried, the hero of the poem.

Aristotle Onassis Aristotle Socrates Onassis (1906–75) was a Greek ship owner who built up an extensive independent shipping empire and founded the Greek national airline, Olympic Airways.

> Chilcott rubbed his hands together. 'Wickham's something in the City and as rich as Onassis, according to Sir Peter. Could do me a lot of good, business-wise, if I play my cards right.'
> SUSAN MOODY *Grand Slam*, 1994

Kerry Packer Kerry (Francis Bullimore) Packer (b. 1937) is an Australian media tycoon who became famous for creating 'World Series Cricket' in 1977, a series of unofficial one-day matches in Australia for which he paid top cricketers high fees to play. He obtained exclusive television rights for his own TV channel to cover the series.

> 'I wouldn't worry,' Margin told Delaney. 'It's probably only a box number somewhere, and no one can watch a box number twenty-four hours a day. You'd have to be Kerry Packer to afford it.'
> THOMAS KENEALLY *A Family Madness*, 1985

Plutus Plutus was the son of Demeter and the god of wealth in Greek mythology. The Greeks represented him as blind because he distributed riches indiscriminately, as lame because riches come slowly, and with wings because riches disappear more quickly than they come.

> It would be difficult for the most jealous and eager devotee at the shrine of Plutus to devise any securities for property.
> *Harpers Monthly*, 1880

Rockefeller John Davison Rockefeller (1839-1937) was an American oil magnate who founded the Standard Oil Company, gaining increasing control of all aspects of the oil industry in the 1870s. He later used his fortune for philanthropic projects.

> The agent says, There's plenty of work for willing men. You can work overtime till you drop and if you save it up, mate, you'll be Rockefeller at the end of the war.
> FRANK MCCOURT *Angela's Ashes*, 1997

> If Edward's hours were billable, she thought, he'd be as rich as Rockefeller.
> NORA KELLY *Old Wounds*, 1998

Rothschild Meyer Amschel Rothschild (1743-1812), a German Jew, founded a banking house in Frankfurt and a dynasty. His five sons set up banks throughout Europe. His third son, Nathan (1777-1836), who founded the London bank, made a £1 million profit on the Stock Exchange having staked his fortune on the outcome of the battle of Waterloo.

> If she wanted a new hat, he'd say hadn't he bought her a hat only five or six years ago and get off nasty cracks about women who seemed to think they'd married into the Rothschild family.
> P. G. WODEHOUSE *Cocktail Time*, 1958

> 'I said I was your housekeeper,' replied that lady . . . 'Oh good,' said Aunt Irene. 'He'll think I'm Rothschild.'
> ALICE THOMAS ELLIS *The 27th Kingdom*, 1982

Solomon's temple In 957 BC King Solomon built the Israelites' first temple on Mount Zion, Jerusalem (1 Kgs. 5–7 and 2 Chron. 3–4). The magnificence of this temple became legendary. Each room had walls panelled with cedar wood, carved with palm trees and cherubim, and overlaid with gold.

> In this process the chamber and its furniture grew more and more dignified and luxurious; the shawl hanging at the window took upon itself the richness of tapestry; the brass handles of the chest of drawers were as golden knockers; and the carved bed-posts seemed to have some kinship with the magnificent pillars of Solomon's temple.
> THOMAS HARDY *Tess of the D'Urbervilles*, 1891

Sun King Louis XIV (1638–1715), known as the Sun King (Le Roi Soleil), whose palace, Versailles, was richly furnished, surrounded himself with wealth. He can stand for the embodiment of rich, lavish, and sumptuous splendour.

> These two small tables were surrounded and bedecked by a buildup of objects, fabrics, and bibelots so lush it would have made the Sun King blink.
> TOM WOLFE *The Bonfire of the Vanities*, 1987

Vanderbilt Cornelius Vanderbilt (1794–1877) was a US businessman and philanthropist who amassed a fortune from shipping and railroads. Subsequent generations of his family increased the family wealth and continued his philanthropy.

> The word 'mural' suggests to most people either the wall spaces of Rockefeller Center or the wealth of a Vanderbilt.
> *American Home*, 1936

Wholesomeness

This theme is dominated by the American celebration of homely small-town values as depicted in many films of the 1940s and 1950s. In a number of the quotations below the apparent wholesomeness being encountered is considered to be superficial or illusory. ▶ *See also* **Goodness**, **Naivety**.

Frank Capra Frank Capra (1897–1991) was an Italian-born US film director. Many of his films, such as *Mr Deeds Goes to Town* (1936), *Mr Smith Goes to Washington* (1939), and *It's a Wonderful Life* (1946), celebrate the idea of the humble common man whose idealism, honesty, and goodness always triumph over materialism, deceit, and selfishness. Such a rose-tinted view of the world is sometimes referred to as 'Capraesque'.

> But all the activity went on without raised voices, and even the cars that circled the square did it quietly. There wasn't a loud muffler to be heard anywhere. The town

was a Norman Rockwell painting come to life; a Frank Capra movie in 3-D and color.

JOHN MADDOX ROBERTS *A Typical American Town*, 1995

Doris Day The US actress and singer Doris Day (b. Doris Kappelhoff in 1924) played the cheerful, freckle-faced girl-next-door in numerous musicals and comedies in the late 1940s and early 1950s. In the late 1950s and early 1960s she appeared in a series of innocent sex comedies such as *Pillow Talk* (1959), in which she habitually played the virginal heroine. Groucho Marx claimed to have 'been around so long I can remember Doris Day before she was a virgin'.

What feminism does not need . . . is an endless recycling of Doris Day Fifties clichés about noble womanhood.

CAMILLE PAGLIA 'Big Udder: Suzanne Gordon's 'Prisoners of Men's Dreams'' in *Sex, Art, & American Culture*, 1991

Andy Hardy The Hardy family appeared in a series of Hollywood films between 1937 and 1947. They were portrayed as a typical all-American family who embodied homely small-town values. In 1942 the films were accorded a special Academy Award 'for representing the American Way of Life'. The clean-living teenager Andy Hardy was played by Mickey Rooney.

It is difficult now to say why the book was so 'sensational', but we can make a guess: the town—Peyton Place, that is—is exactly like the Carvel of the Andy Hardy picture, a prim and proper little apple-pie town whose major occasions are the senior prom, graduation and the Labor Day picnic.

The Independent, 1992

Mary Poppins Mary Poppins is the name of the Edwardian nanny with magical powers who appears in a series of children's books by P. L. Travers. It is probably Julie Andrews's portrayal of the character in the film musical *Mary Poppins* (1964) that has caused the character's name to become a byword for unfailing cheerfulness and somewhat saccharine wholesomeness.

We were never happy. Gavin was a public schoolboy who never grew up. Like many men with that background, he was uneasy with women. Some end up treating us like whores, others decide we're madonnas. Gavin was the madonna type. Unfortunately I'm not. I found the strain of playing Mary Poppins just too much. In the end I told him to bugger off and be done with it.

KEN MCCLURE *Requiem*, 1992

Donna Reed Donna Reed (b. Donna Mullenger, 1921–86) was a US film actress, closely identified with wholesome girl-next-door roles in such films as Frank Capra's *It's a Wonderful Life* (1946). In her long-running TV show *The Donna Reed Show* (1958-66) she personified the perfect and devoted wife and mother.

Janie, Trish, and Kay had graduated from Dobbs High School together and had then married Cotton Grove boys within two years of each other, which brought them back into the same social orbit where two incomes weren't a necessity quite yet. The 'Donna Reed' syndrome lasted a bit longer in the South than elsewhere, and none of the three had held down real jobs back then.

MARGARET MARON *Bootlegger's Daughter*, 1992

Poor Luis! she thought. Sitting at home in front of the television, he had invented

just the kind of Donna Reed mother a lonely little boy would invent.
ROBERT B. PARKER *Thin Air*, 1995

So far, they had not. She had visions of an eternally smiling Donna Reed gliding among the congregation like a ministering angel, but she still found herself standing awkwardly at Will's side, wondering if she was overdressed and trying without notable success to think of something she could possibly discuss with these people who seemed neither to read nor travel.
SHARYN MCCRUMB *The Hangman's Beautiful Daughter*, 1996

Cliff Richard Cliff Richard (b. Harry Webb, 1940) is a British pop singer whose many successful recordings include 'Living Doll' and 'The Young Ones'. He became a born-again Christian in the 1970s and since then has combined his pop career with evangelism. Cliff Richard is sometimes mentioned with reference to his clean-living image and his youthful looks.

'And I suppose you got nowhere at Brown's?' 'Squeaky clean.' 'Same here, this pair. They've got Cliff Richard in the front office and Mother Theresa doing the books.'
ALEX KEEGAN *Kingfisher*, 1995

Norman Rockwell Norman Rockwell (1894–1978) was a US illustrator and cartoonist best known for his covers for the magazine the *Saturday Evening Post*. These were typically idealized scenes of everyday small-town American life of the kind described in the Elizabeth Peters quotation below.

The charm was more than visual, however. It was equally compounded of nostalgia for a way of life that had not so much vanished as never really existed. Freckle-faced boys riding bikes and healthy, pink-cheeked nuclear families dressed in their Sunday best, walking hand in hand toward a white, steepled church … A Norman Rockwell cover, flimsy as the paper on which it was printed, with ugly things hidden behind the pretty facade.
ELIZABETH PETERS *Naked Once More*, 1989

He reminded me of a Norman Rockwell *Saturday Evening Post* cover, the rural general practitioner about to remove a splinter from a tearful boy's finger. Kindly, gentle, wise, competent.
WILLIAM G. TAPPLY *Tight Lines*, 1992

Waltons *The Waltons* was a popular US television series (1972–81) based on the life of its creator, Earl Hamner Jr. Set in a poor area of Virginia during the Depression and the Second World War, the stories, often fairly sentimental, concerned the struggles and trials of a good-natured, honest family. The usual closing sequence, in which each member of the family called goodnight to the others, is much parodied. The Waltons can be alluded to in the context of a family that seems just too good to be true.

Stewart's early life, I learnt, was rather sweet and Waltons-like. He loved his father and mother. He went to church.
WILLIAM LEITH in *The Observer*, 1997

Wisdom

Among the various wise teachers, counsellors, and judges grouped here, it is the name of **SOLOMON** that has been most widely regarded as synonymous with wisdom, now proverbially so. ▶ *See also* **Intelligence, Judgement and Decision, Knowledge, Stupidity**.

....

Athene Athene (also called Pallas Athene) was the Greek goddess of wisdom and practical skills, known to the Romans as Minerva. In classical times the owl was regularly associated with her.

> It did not do to think, nor, for the matter of that, to feel. She gave up trying to understand herself, and joined the vast armies of the benighted, who follow neither the heart nor the brain, and march to their destiny by catchwords. . . . They have sinned against passion and truth, and vain will be their strife after virtue. . . . They have sinned against Eros and Pallas Athene, and not by any heavenly intervention, but by the ordinary course of nature, those allied deities will be avenged.
> E. M. FORSTER *A Room with a View*, 1908

Confucius Confucius (551–479 BC) was a Chinese philosopher and teacher of ethics. He spent much of his life as a moral teacher of a group of disciples, expounding his ideas about the importance of practical codes of personal morality, etiquette, and statesmanship which formed the basis of the philosophy of Confucianism. His teachings and sayings were collected by his pupils after his death.

> You would be better off at the present time to imagine yourself as one of the great shots of the day, or even a competent one, rather than as Confucius.
> TIMOTHY MO *An Insular Possession*, 1986

Daniel Daniel was a Hebrew prophet (6th century BC) whose prophecies are contained in the Book of Daniel in the Bible. In the apocryphal Book of Susanna he is portrayed as a wise judge, proving the falsely accused Susanna to be innocent. In Shakespeare's *The Merchant of Venice*, Shylock praises Portia, who is disguised as a lawyer, with the words:

'A Daniel come to judgment! Yea, a Daniel!
O wise young judge, how I do honour thee!'

▶ *See special entry* ☐ **DANIEL** *on p. 86.*

> Weigh me the two, you Daniel, going to judgement, when your day shall come!
> CHARLES DICKENS *The Chimes*, 1844

> You nearly caught me, Major Scobie, that time. It was a matter of import duties, you remember. You could have caught me if you had told your policeman to say something a little different. I was quite overcome with astonishment, Major Scobie, to sit in a police court and hear true facts from the mouths of policemen. . . . I said to myself, Yusef, a Daniel has come to the Colonial Police.
> GRAHAM GREENE *The Heart of the Matter*, 1948

Ganesha In Hinduism, Ganesha, the son of Siva and Parvati, is the elephant-headed god of wisdom and prudence. He is worshipped as the remover of obstacles and the patron of learning.

Magi The Magi were the 'three wise men from the East' (Matt. 2: 1) who travelled to Bethlehem to pay homage to the infant Jesus and bring him gifts of gold, frankincense, and myrrh. Later tradition identified them as kings and named them Caspar, Melchior, and Balthazar.

Merlin In Arthurian legend, Merlin was a wizard who served as a mentor and counsellor to King Arthur. His name can be used to typify a wise counsellor.

> The Blair government is well aware of this, which is why it has embarked on a wholesale overhaul of our constitutional arrangements. In this light, the plan for a London mayor is distinct from the soccer and drugs appointments. We need a new democratic framework that can engage an active citizenry who can then dispense, for the most part, with the ministrations of modern Merlins.
> *The Observer*, 1997

Mimir In Scandinavian mythology, Mimir was a giant who guarded the well of wisdom near the roots of the great ash tree, Yggdrasil.

> Allfadir did not get a drink of Mimir's spring.
> RALPH WALDO EMERSON *The Conduct of Life*, 1860

Minerva Minerva was the Roman goddess of wisdom and practical skills, corresponding to the Greek Athene.

> The Thing itself is no better than a Minerva of his own fertile Brain.
> R. NORTH *Examen*, 1734

Nestor In Greek mythology, Nestor was a king of Pylos, the oldest and wisest of the Greek chieftains in the Trojan War. Nestor's name can be used to typify a wise old man or mentor. ▶ *See special entry* □ **TROJAN WAR** *on p. 392.*

> Another attempt to refute atheistic pluralism, which carried more weight than this statement by an educated amateur, was that made by the Nestor of English science and cofounder of the theory of evolution, Alfred Russel Wallace.
> H. ATKINS trans. KARL GUTHKIE *Last Frontier*, 1983

Odin In Scandinavian mythology, Odin (corresponding to the Germanic god Woden or Wotan) was the supreme god and creator, the husband of Frigga and the father of Thor and Balder. He was worshipped as the god of wisdom, war, poetry, and the dead. Odin obtained his wisdom by drinking from Mimir's well but had to sacrifice an eye to do so, and is consequently usually represented as one-eyed, often attended by two black ravens, Hugin (thought) and Munin (memory).

Seven Sages of Greece The Seven Sages was the name given in ancient times to the following wise men: Solon of Athens, Thales of Miletus, Bias of Priene, Chilo of Sparta, Cleobulus of Lindus, Pittacus of Mitylene, and Periander of Corinth.

Solomon Solomon, the son of David and Bathsheba, was the king of ancient Israel c.970–c.930 BC. He was famed for his wisdom and justice. The phrase 'the Judgement of Solomon' refers to his arbitration in a dispute about a baby claimed by each of two women (I Kgs. 3: 16–28). Solomon proposed dividing the baby in half with his sword, and then gave it to the woman who showed concern for its life: 'And all Israel heard of the judgement which the king had rendered; and they stood in awe of the king, because they perceived that the wisdom of God was in him, to render justice.' Anyone demonstrating great wisdom can be described as a Solomon.

> I, who am all-powerful, I, whose loveliness is more than the loveliness of that Grecian Helen, of whom they used to sing, and whose wisdom is wider, ay, far more wide and deep than the wisdom of Solomon the Wise.
> H. RIDER HAGGARD *She*, 1887

> 'All women are thus.' Kim spoke as might have Solomon.
> RUDYARD KIPLING *Kim*, 1900

Solon Solon (*c*.630–*c*.560 BC) was an Athenian statesman and lawgiver, noted for his economic, constitutional, and legal reforms. He was one of the supposed **SEVEN SAGES OF GREECE**. A wise statesman can be described as a Solon.

> Are you Socrates or Solon, always right?
> BARBARA MICHAELS *The Wizard's Daughter*, 1980

Thoth In Egyptian mythology, Thoth was the god of the moon, wisdom, writing, and the sciences. He is usually represented with the head of an ibis.

> He was an important man. He wielded power: power of appointment, power of disappointment, power of the cheque book, power of Thoth and the Mercurial access to the Arcana of the Stant Collection.
> A. S. BYATT *Possession*, 1990

Wise Men ▸ *See* MAGI.

Writers

There are many writers covered in this book. For example, Kafka is included at **Strangeness**, Conan Doyle at **Adventure**, Orwell at **Power**, and Smiles at **Thrift**. The writers grouped below are those who have been regarded as archetypes of 'the great writer'.

....

Francis Bacon Francis Bacon (1561–1626) was a philosopher and essayist, best known as the author of *The Advancement of Learning* (1605) and many essays. He is sometimes mentioned as an exemplar of a beautiful, often epigrammatic, English writing style.

> For his orations convulsed his hearers and his contributions were excellent, being patriotic, classical, comical, or dramatic, but never sentimental. Jo regarded them as worthy of Bacon, Milton, or Shakespeare.
> LOUISA M. ALCOTT *Little Women*, 1868

Dante Dante Alighieri (1265–1321) was an Italian poet, born in Florence. His reputation as a major figure of world literature rests on his masterpiece, *The Divine Comedy* (*c*.1309-20), an epic poem that relates his spiritual journey though Hell and Purgatory guided by the poet Virgil, and Paradise, guided by his beloved Beatrice.

> We talk of literature as a trade, not of Homer, Dante, and Shakspeare.
> GEORGE GISSING *New Grub Street*, 1891

Edward Gibbon Edward Gibbon (1737-94) was an English historian and author of *The History of the Decline and Fall of the Roman Empire* (1776-88), generally regarded as a monumental work of literature as well as historical analysis. Ranging from the 2nd century AD to the fall of Constantinople in 1453, Gibbon's work covers the founding of Christianity, the movement and settlement of the Teutonic tribes, the conquests of the Muslims, and the Crusades. The famous remark, 'Another damned, thick, square book! Always scribble, scribble, scribble! Eh! Mr Gibbon?' is usually attributed to the duke of Gloucester.

> It is my ambition to out-Gibbon Mr Gibbon.
> WILLIAM GOLDING *Rites of Passage*, 1980

Homer Homer (8th century BC) was a Greek epic poet, held to be the author of the *Iliad* and the *Odyssey*, though it is probable that these were based on much older stories which had been passed on orally. According to tradition, he was blind. In later antiquity Homer was regarded as the greatest and unsurpassable poet.

Milton John Milton (1608-74) was a major English poet of the 17th century whose works include *Lycidas* (1638), *Paradise Lost* (1667), *Paradise Regained* (1671), and *Samson Agonistes* (1671).

Samuel Pepys Samuel Pepys (1633-1703) is chiefly remembered for his diary (1660-9) in which he vividly describes life in the early Restoration period and records such contemporary events as the Great Plague, the Fire of London, and the sailing of the Dutch fleet up the Thames.

Shakespeare William Shakespeare (1564-1616), the English dramatist and poet, is habitually cited as the epitome of the literary or theatrical genius.

> The appointed day came. ... Rampion presented himself. ... Mrs Felpham tried to rise to the occasion. The village Shakespeare, it was obvious, must be interested in the drama.
> ALDOUS HUXLEY *Point Counter Point*, 1928

Youth

Most of the entries below are concerned not simply with the idea of being young, but with the ever-intriguing fantasies of having one's youth restored or being granted the gift of eternal youth. These stories contrast with some of those at the theme **Old Age** in which immortality is accompanied by perpetual aging.

....

Cagliostro Count Alessandro Cagliostro (1743–95), whose real name was Giuseppe Balsamo, was a charlatan and adventurer born in Palermo. He claimed to be able to grant everlasting youth to anyone who would pay him for his secret. Cagliostro was imprisoned for life by the Inquisition on the grounds of his association with freemasonry.

> Marat has a family? I mean a mother and a father and the usual things? The ordinary arrangement, the cook said. Odd, really, I never thought of Marat having a beginning. I thought he was thousands and thousands of years old, like Cagliostro. Can I see him?
> HILARY MANTEL *A Place of Greater Safety*, 1992

Dorian Gray In Oscar Wilde's novel *The Picture of Dorian Gray* (1890), Dorian is an extraordinarily handsome young man who remains youthful-looking while the portrait he has had painted ages on his behalf and reflects Dorian's inner moral corruption. A person who is described as a 'Dorian Gray' or who is said to have 'a portrait in the attic' is someone who looks unnaturally young, especially if in addition they are suspected of having a somewhat dissipated lifestyle.

> Attenborough has grown from a young man into an old one on television. At the same time, the natural history programme—a genre which he helped invent—has done a Dorian Gray. Infra-red, slo-mo, 'Starlight' cameras: with every year, the genre is fresher, more agile and has a bigger stash of tricks up its sleeve.
> *The Observer*, 1998

Endymion In Greek mythology, Endymion was a young man of surpassing beauty, whom Zeus granted eternal sleep so that he would remain perpetually youthful. He was loved by the moon goddess Selene.

> But your Endymion, your smooth, Smock-fac'd Boy . . . shall a Beauteous Dame enjoy.
> JOHN DRYDEN *Juvenal Satires x*, 1693

Hebe In Greek mythology, Hebe, the daughter of Zeus and Hera, was the goddess of youth. She had the power of restoring the aged to youth and beauty. Hebe attended on Hera and was the cup-bearer of the gods, in which role she was later succeeded by Ganymede. Her Roman name was Juventus.

> Girlhood just ripening into womanhood . . . Upon my word—a very Hebe!'
> ANNE BRONTË *Tenant of Wildfell Hall*, 1848

Peter Pan Peter Pan is the hero of J. M. Barrie's play of the same name (1904), a boy with magical powers who never grew up. He takes the Darling children on an adventure to Never-Never Land, where they encounter Captain Hook and his pirate gang. The term 'Peter Pan' can be applied to a man who never seems to grow older or who is immature.

> Only Rainger would want to dance and skylark in the shadow of the prison door. He wasn't really wicked, he was Peter Pan. He simply could not cope with the responsibilities of the adult world, could not connect his actions in the drug trade with the human wreckage that floated in its wake, nor begin to comprehend why his light-

hearted infidelities had brought his wife to the edge of serious mental disorder.
RICHARD HALEY *Thoroughfare of Stones*, 1995

Britain's music industry was toasting more than the knighthood for Cliff Richard, the pop world's Peter Pan, following the release of figures yesterday which showed that sales have powered ahead by more than a fifth in the first six months of the year.
The Guardian, 1995

The computer games industry never grows up. This does not mean an idyllic Peter Pan-style childhood but rather a perpetual adolescence.
The Independent, 1998

Index

007	Adventure
Abaddon	Destruction, Devil
Abdera	Stupidity
Abelard	Punishment
Abelard and Héloïse	Lovers
Abraham	Fertility, Leaders
Abraham's bosom	Peace
Absalom	Death, Rebellion and Disobedience
Achates	Friendship
Acheron	Suffering, Unpleasant or Wicked Places
Achilles	Abundance and Plenty, Anger, Disguise, Weakness
Achilles and Patroclus	Friendship
Acres, Bob	Cowardice
Actaeon	Hunters, Nakedness, Punishment
Actium	Defeat
Adam	Sex and Sexuality, Solitude
Adam and Eve	Actors, Happiness, Innocence, Life: Generation of Life, Nakedness, Past, Punishment, Rebellion and Disobedience
Admah and Zeboiim	Unpleasant or Wicked Places
Adonis	Beauty: Male Beauty
Adullam	Safety
Aegeus	Despair
Aeneas	Gesture
Aeolian	Music
Aeschylus	Baldness
Aesculapius	Medicine
Agag	Walk
Agamemnon	Anger
Aganippe	Inspiration
Agincourt	Victory
Aglaia	Beauty: Female Beauty
Agnes, St	Chastity and Virginity
Ahab	Evil, Pride
Ahab, Captain	Hatred, Insanity, Quest
Ahasuerus (Persian King)	Anger
Ahasuerus (Wandering Jew)	Travellers and Wanderers
Ahriman	Devil
Ajax	Suffering

Aladdin's cave (or palace)	Wealth
Aladdin's lamp	Magic
Alamo	Courage, Defeat
Albatross	Curse
Alberich's cloak	Invisibility
Albion	Idyllic Places
Alcatraz	Prisons
Alcibiades	Sex and Sexuality
Alexander	Soldiers
Alfred	Memory
Alfred the Great	Leaders
Ali, Muhammad	Strength
Ali Baba	Concealment
Alice	Ascent and Descent, Hair, Height, Small Size
Alice in Wonderland	Strangeness
Alsatia	Safety
Amalekite	Enemy
Amalthea	Food and Drink
Amazon	Fierce Women, Strength
ambrosia	Food and Drink
Amin, Idi	Dictators and Tyrants
Anak	Large Size
Ananias	Lying
Anansie	Mischief
Ancient Mariner	Curse, Perseverance, Storytellers, Travellers and Wanderers
Andersonville	Prisons
Andromeda	Captives, Rescue
Angel of Death	Death
Antaeus	Returning, Weakness
Antiphates' wife	Ugliness
Antisthenes	Disapproval
Antony and Cleopatra	Lovers
Anubis	Death
Aphrodite	Appearing, Beauty: Female Beauty, Fertility, Love and Marriage, Sex and Sexuality
Apocalypse	Destruction
Apollo	Animals, Love of, Beauty: Male Beauty, Inspiration, Light, Medicine, Music
Apollyon	Devil
Apple of Discord	Conflict
Apples of Sodom	Illusion
Appleseed, Johnny	Abundance and Plenty
Arabian Nights	Strangeness
Arachne	Change
Arcadia	Idealism, Idyllic Places, Music, Naivety

Archimago	Hypocrisy
Archimedes	Realization
Arden	Idyllic Places
Arden, Enoch	Disappearance and Absence, Patience, Returning
Ares	War
Argonauts	Quest, Travellers and Wanderers
Argus	Craftsmen, Guarding, Knowledge
Ariadne	Complexity
Ariel	Indifference
Aristotle	Intelligence
Ark	Outdatedness
Ark of the Covenant	Importance
Armageddon	Destruction
Arnold, Benedict	Betrayal
Artemis	Beauty: Female Beauty, Chastity and Virginity, Hunters
Artful Dodger	Cunning, Escape and Survival
Arthur, King	Past, Sleep
Arthurian	Love and Marriage
Ascalaphus	Betrayal
Ashtoreth	Fertility, Sex and Sexuality
Aspasia	Prostitutes
Astaire, Fred	Dancing
Astarte	Fertility, Sex and Sexuality
Atalanta	Hunters, Speed
Athene	Appearing, Craftsmen, War, Wisdom
Atlantis	Disappearance and Absence, Distance
Atlas	Difficulty, Strength
Atlas, Charles	Strength
Atreus	Curse
Attila the Hun	Dictators and Tyrants
Aucassin and Nicolette	Lovers
Augean stables	Difficulty
Augustine, St	Intelligence
Aunt Chloe	Optimism
Austerlitz	Defeat
Autolycus	Cunning
Avalon	Idyllic Places
Avenger of Blood	Punishment
Avenging Angel	Punishment
Avernus	Unpleasant or Wicked Places
Azrael	Death
Baba Yaga	Monsters
Babel	Chaos and Disorder, Communication, Sound
Babel, Tower of	Communication, Height
Babes in the Wood	Naivety, Suffering

Babylon	Unpleasant or Wicked Places
Bacchanalia	Food and Drink
Bacchante	Chaos and Disorder, Food and Drink
Bacchus	Fertility, Food and Drink, Sex and Sexuality
Bach	Complexity
Bacon, Francis	Writers
Baggins, Bilbo	Adventure, Invisibility
Balboa	Explorers
Balder	Light, Weakness
Banquo's ghost	Appearing
Bardolph	Noses
Bardot, Brigitte	Animals, Love of
Barmecide's Feast	Illusion
Bartholomew, St	Punishment, Suffering
Barton, Dick	Detectives
basilisk	Hatred
Bastille	Prisons, Rebellion and Disobedience
Bates, Norman	Fear
Bathsheba	Beauty: Female Beauty
Batman and Robin	Heroes
Battus	Punishment
Beardsley	Artists
Beatrice and Benedick	Lovers
Beau Geste	Deserted Places
Beauty and the Beast	Beauty: Female Beauty, Ugliness
Beckett, Samuel	Pessimism
Bedlam	Chaos and Disorder, Insanity
Bedonebyasyoudid	Punishment
Beelzebub	Devil
Beethoven	Music
Belch, Sir Toby	Gluttony
Belle Dame Sans Merci	Indifference
Belshazzar	Food and Drink, Prophecy
Ben Hur	Speed
Bennet, Mrs	Ambition
Beowulf	Past
Bergerac, Cyrano de	Noses
Bermuda Triangle	Disappearance and Absence
Bethesda	Medicine
Beulah	Idyllic Places
Big Brother	Power
Big-Endians and Little-Endians	Conflict
Biggles	Heroes
Billy the Kid	Outlaws
Birnam Wood	Movement
Black Beauty	Horses

Black Death	Death
Black Hander	Concealment
Black Hole of Calcutta	Prisons, Unpleasant or Wicked Places
Blaise, Modesty	Heroes
Blake	Artists
Bligh, Captain	Ruthlessness
Blimp, Colonel	Lack of Change
Blind Pew	Blindness
Blondel	Music
Bloody Tower	Prisons
Bloom, Leopold	Travellers and Wanderers
Bluebeard	Murderers
Bluebeard's castle	Danger, Unpleasant or Wicked Places
Bluebottle	Speech
Blyton, Enid	Naivety
Boeotian	Stupidity
Bohemia	Nonconformity
Bonaparte, Napoleon	Leaders, Soldiers
Bond, James	Adventure, Modernity, Rescue
Bones, Brom	Disguise
Bonnie and Clyde	Outlaws
Book of Kells	Importance
Borden, Lizzie	Murderers
Borgia, Cesare	Evil
Borgia, Lucrezia	Evil
Borgias	Conflict, Cunning, Evil
Borrow, George	Travellers and Wanderers
Borrowers	Small Size
Bosch, Hieronymus	Horror, Ugliness
Boston Tea Party	Rebellion and Disobedience
Botticelli	Artists, Beauty: Female Beauty
Boudicca	Leaders
Bountiful, Lady	Generosity
Bounty	Rebellion and Disobedience
Bovary, Emma	Adultery
Boy's Own	Adventure
Bracknell, Lady	Speech
Brando, Marlon	Speech
Bray, Vicar of	Change
Brendan, St	Explorers
Brer Rabbit	Poverty
Britomart	Chastity and Virginity
Brobdingnagian	Large Size
Brodie, Miss Jean	Speech, Teachers
Brown, John	Freedom
Bruegel	Artists

Brutus	**Betrayal**
Brynhild	**War**
Brynner, Yul	**Baldness**
Buchan, John	**Adventure**
Buddha	**Peace**
Bull Run	**Victory**
Bunker Hill	**Courage**
Bunter, Billy	**Fatness, Gluttony**
Bunyan, Paul	**Strength**
Buridan's ass	**Problem**
Burne-Jones	**Artists**
burning bush	**Appearing**
Butch Cassidy	**Outlaws**
Butler, Rhett	**Heroes**
Byron	**Hair, Heroes, Sex and Sexuality**
Byzantine	**Complexity**
Caesar	**Betrayal, Leaders**
Caesars	**Past**
Caesar's wife	**Innocence**
Cagliostro	**Youth**
Cain	**Blindness, Curse, Guilt, Murderers, Solitude, Travellers and Wanderers**
Calamity Jane	**Prophecy**
Calchas	**Envy**
Caliban	**Evil**
Caligula	**Dictators and Tyrants**
Calliope	**Inspiration**
Calpurnia	**Prophecy**
Calvary	**Suffering**
Calvin, John	**Disapproval, Sternness**
Calydonian boar hunt	**Hunters**
Calypso	**Danger**
Camilla	**Speed**
Canaan	**Idyllic Places**
Candide	**Naivety**
Canute	**Failure, Lack of Change**
Cape Horn	**Danger**
Capone, Al	**Criminals**
Capra, Frank	**Wholesomeness**
Capulet	**Anger**
Caravaggio	**Darkness**
Carry On films	**Comedy and Humour**
Cartland, Barbara	**Love and Marriage**
Casanova	**Seducers and Male Lovers**
Casey	**Failure**
Cassandra	**Doubt, Prophecy**

Castalia	Inspiration
Castor and Pollux	Similarity
Catch-22	Problem
Cato	Disapproval, Oratory
Caulfield, Holden	Nonconformity
Cecilia, St	Music
Celestial City	Idyllic Places, Light
Centaur	Duality
Cephalus	Jealousy
Cerberus	Guarding
Challenger, Professor	Intelligence
Chamberlain, Neville	Peace
Chamber of Horrors	Unpleasant or Wicked Places
Chang and Eng	Similarity
Chaplin, Charlie	Walk
Chappaquiddick	Failure
Charlemagne	Leaders
Charley's Aunt	Disguise
Charlie, Bonnie Prince	Returning
Charon	Death, Ugliness
Chaucer	Comedy and Humour
Cheshire Cat	Disappearance and Absence, Smiles
Chips, Mr	Teachers
Chiron	Teachers
Christ	Goodness
Christian	Goodness
Christie, Agatha	Mystery
Christmas, Father	Generosity
Churchill, Winston	Oratory, Speech
Cicero	Oratory
Cimmerian	Darkness
Cinderella	Change, Chastity and Virginity, Conformity, Poverty, Success
Cinderella and the prince	Lovers
Circe	Danger, Magic, Sirens
Claude	Artists
Cleopatra	Beauty: Female Beauty, Leaders
Clio	Inspiration
Cloud Cuckoo Land	Idyllic Places
Clouseau	Failure
Clytemnestra	Murderers
Cockaigne	Idyllic Places
Colditz	Prisons
Collins, Wilkie	Mystery
Colossus	Large Size
Columbus	Explorers

Concordia	Peace
Confucius	Wisdom
Connecticut Yankee	Time
Constance	Grief and Sorrow
Cook, Captain	Explorers
Cook's tour	Travellers and Wanderers
Cooper, Gary	Courage
Corcoran, Captain	Doubt
Cordelia	Honesty and Truth, Love and Marriage
Coriolanus	Arrogance and Pomposity
Cornucopia	Abundance and Plenty, Food and Drink
Correggio	Happiness
Cortés	Explorers
Cowardly Lion	Cowardice
Cox and Box	Duality
Crane, Ichabod	Thinness
Cratchit, Bob	Poverty
Creation	Past
Crippen, Dr	Murderers
Croesus	Wealth
Cromwell, Oliver	Leaders, Rebellion and Disobedience
Cruella de Vil	Evil
Crusoe, Robinson	Solitude
Cumaean Sibyl	Old Age
Cupid	Love and Marriage
Cupid and Psyche	Lovers
Custer's last stand	Courage
Cyclopean	Past
Dada	Strangeness
Daddy Warbucks	Wealth
Daedalus	Craftsmen
Daley, Arthur	Criminals
Dali, Salvador	Strangeness
Damascus (the road to)	Change, Realization
Damon and Pythias	Friendship
Dan Dare	Heroes
Dan to Beersheba	Distance
Daniel	Courage, Danger, Rebellion and Disobedience, Wisdom
Daniel in the lions' den	Danger
Dante	Horror, Writers
Dante and Beatrice	Lovers
Dante's Inferno	Unpleasant or Wicked Places
Daphne	Change, Chastity and Virginity, Immobility
Daphnis and Chloe	Lovers
Darby and Joan	Lovers

Darcy, Mr	Heroes
Dark Ages	Outdatedness
Darkest Africa	Distance
Darling, Grace	Rescue
Darth Vader	Evil
Dartmoor	Prisons
Darwin	Intelligence
David	Chastity and Virginity, Darkness, Music, Victory
David and Bathsheba	Lovers
David and Jonathan	Friendship
Day, Doris	Love and Marriage, Wholesomeness
Dead Sea Fruit	Illusion
Dean, James	Nonconformity
Death	Death
Degas	Artists
Deianira	Jealousy
Deimos	Fear
Deirdre	Grief and Sorrow
Delectable Mountains	Idyllic Places
Delilah	Betrayal, Cunning, Weakness
Delphi	Prophecy
Delphic Oracle	Communication
Demeter	Fertility
Demodocus	Storytellers
Demosthenes	Oratory
Dennis the Menace	Mischief
Desdemona	Innocence
Deucalion	Escape and Survival
Devil	Cunning, Devil, Temptation
Devil's Island	Prisons
Diana	Beauty: Female Beauty, Hunters
Dickensian	Naivety, Strangeness, Suffering, Ugliness
Dido and Aeneas	Lovers
Dillinger, John	Criminals
Dimmesdale, Arthur	Concealment
Diogenes	Disapproval, Honesty and Truth
Dionysiac	Happiness
Dionysian	Happiness, Sex and Sexuality
Dionysus	Chaos and Disorder, Difficulty, Fertility, Travellers and Wanderers
Dirty Harry	Macho Men
Disney, Walt	Animals, Love of
Dives	Wealth
Doctor Foster	Returning
Dodge City	Chaos and Disorder
Dolittle, Doctor	Animals, Love of, Communication
Don Juan	Seducers and Male Lovers

Don Quixote	Distance, Idealism, Illusion, Insanity, Thinness
Don Quixote and Sancho Panza	Friendship
Donald Duck	Speech
Dorian Gray	Youth
Dormouse	Sleep
Dotheboys Hall	Ruthlessness
Doubting Thomas	Doubt
Doyle, Arthur Conan	Adventure
Draco	Ruthlessness
Dracula	Monsters
Drake, Sir Francis	Explorers
Dresden	Destruction
Drew, Nancy	Detectives
Dreyfus	Innocence
Drummond, Bulldog	Heroes
Duessa	Ugliness
Dufy	Artists
Dulcinea	Inspiration
Duncan, Isadora	Dancing
Dunkirk	Courage
Durante, Jimmy	Noses
Earhart, Amelia	Disappearance and Absence
Eccles	Speech
Eden	Idyllic Places
Eden, Garden of	Abundance and Plenty
Edsel	Failure
Eeyore	Pessimism
Einstein	Intelligence
El Dorado	Idyllic Places, Quest, Wealth
El Greco	Artists, Thinness
Electra	Sex and Sexuality
Elephant Man	Ugliness
Eleusinian mysteries	Mystery
Elijah	Ascent and Descent
Elisha	Gesture
Elli	Old Age
Elysium	Idyllic Places
Emperor's New Clothes	Illusion
end of the rainbow	Distance
Endor, Witch of	Appearing, Magic
Endymion	Beauty: Male Beauty, Sleep, Youth
Epeius	Craftsmen
Epicurus	Happiness
Erato	Inspiration
Erebus	Darkness

Erinyes	Punishment, Revenge
Eris	Conflict
Eros	Love and Marriage, Sex and Sexuality
Esau	Hair, Hatred
Esau and Jacob	Bargain
Escher	Complexity
Esther	Beauty: Female Beauty
Estragon	Patience
E.T.	Returning
Etty	Artists
Eumenides	Revenge
Euphrosyne	Beauty: Female Beauty
Euterpe	Inspiration, Music
Eve	Betrayal, Evil, Punishment, Temptation
Evil One	Devil, Temptation
Excalibur	Difficulty
Exodus	Departure, Movement
Facing-both-ways, Mr	Duality
Fagin	Criminals, Leaders
fairy godmother	Change
Falernian	Food and Drink
Falstaff	Fatness
Fat Controller	Fatness
Fate	Destiny and Luck
Fates	Destiny and Luck, Indifference
Father Time	Old Age, Time
Father William	Old Age
fatted calf	Food and Drink, Returning
Faust	Bargain, Despair, Power
Fawkes, Guy	Rebellion and Disobedience
Fawlty, Basil	Anger
Fell, Dr	Hatred
Fermat's Last Theorem	Quest
fiddle while Rome burns	Indifference
Finn, Huckleberry	Nonconformity
Flash Gordon	Heroes
Flood	Past
Flora	Fertility
Flying Dutchman	Curse
Flynn, Errol	Heroes
Fogg, Phileas	Adventure
Fonda, Jane	Hair
Fonteyn, Margot	Dancing
forbidden fruit	Temptation
Fort Knox	Wealth
Forth Bridge	Outdatedness

Fortuna	Destiny and Luck
Fortunate Isles	Idyllic Places
Fountain of Youth	Quest
Francis of Assisi, St	Animals, Love of, Goodness, Poverty
Frankenstein	Life: Generation of Life, Monsters
Freudian	Disclosure, Sex and Sexuality
Freyja	Fertility
Friday, Man	Friendship
frog prince	Change, Ugliness
Furies	Punishment, Revenge
Gabriel	Appearing, Goodness, Messengers, Music
Galahad, Sir	Goodness, Rescue
Galatea	Appearing, Life: Generation of Life, Sculptors
Galileo	Honesty and Truth, Nonconformity
Gandalf	Magic
Gandhi	Peace
Ganesha	Wisdom
Ganymede	Ascent and Descent, Beauty: Male Beauty, Sex and Sexuality
Garbo, Greta	Hair, Solitude
Gargantua	Gluttony, Large Size
Garibaldi	Leaders
Garm	Guarding
Garrick, David	Actors
Gehenna	Unpleasant or Wicked Places
Genghis Khan	Dictators and Tyrants
George, St	Rescue
George III	Insanity
Gestapo	Ruthlessness
Gethsemane	Suffering
Getty, Jean Paul	Miserliness, Wealth
Giacometti, Alberto	Thinness
Giant Despair	Despair
Gibbon, Edward	Writers
Gibson Girl	Beauty: Female Beauty
Gilderoy's kite	Punishment
Gin Lane	Unpleasant or Wicked Places
Ginnungagap	Darkness
Gioconda	Smiles
Giotto	Artists
Gloucester	Blindness
God	Speech
Godfather	Criminals
Godiva, Lady	Hair, Nakedness
Godot	Patience
Godzilla	Monsters

Goebbels, Joseph	Lying
Goldberg, Rube	Complexity
Golden Fleece	Quest, Wealth
Goldilocks	Hair
Golgotha	Suffering
Goliath	Large Size, Weakness
Gomorrah	Unpleasant or Wicked Places
Gone with the Wind	Love and Marriage
Good Samaritan	Goodness
Goodfellow, Robin	Mischief
Goody Two-Shoes	Goodness
Goons	Comedy and Humour
Gordian knot	Complexity, Problem
Gorgon	Ugliness
Goshen	Abundance and Plenty, Idyllic Places, Light
Goth	Destruction
Götterdämmerung	Destruction
Goya	Artists, Horror
Grable, Betty	Hair
Graces	Beauty: Female Beauty
Gradgrind	Conformity
Great Depression	Poverty
Great Divide	Distance
Greatheart	Courage
Grendel	Monsters
Gretna	Love and Marriage
Grim Reaper	Death
Grimm	Fear
Griselda	Patience
Grünewald	Horror
Grundy, Mrs	Disapproval
Guerre, Martin	Returning
Gulag Archipelago	Prisons, Unpleasant or Wicked Places
Gulliver	Captives, Guilt, Immobility, Large Size, Travellers and Wanderers
Gunn, Ben	Insanity, Solitude
Gunpowder Plot	Rebellion and Disobedience
Gyges	Invisibility
Hades	Darkness, Guilt, Suffering, Unpleasant or Wicked Places
Hagar	Solitude
Haggard, Rider	Adventure
Hamadryad	Beauty: Female Beauty
Hamlet	Doubt, Oratory
Hannibal	Soldiers
Hansel and Gretel	Fear

Happy Hooligan	Naivety
Happy Islands	Idyllic Places
Hardy, Andy	Wholesomeness
Harpagan	Miserliness
harpy	Fierce Women
Harvey	Invisibility
Havisham, Miss	Love and Marriage
Hawking, Stephen	Intelligence
Hayworth, Rita	Dancing
Heathcliff	Beauty: Male Beauty, Hair
Heath Robinson	Complexity
Hebe	Beauty: Female Beauty, Youth
Hecuba	Grief and Sorrow
Heep, Uriah	Gesture, Humility, Hypocrisy
Helen	Beauty: Female Beauty
Helicon	Inspiration
Helios	Light
Hell	Temperature, Unpleasant or Wicked Places
Hemingway, Ernest	Macho Men
Henry, Patrick	Freedom
Hephaestus	Craftsmen
Heraclitus	Pessimism
Hercules	Difficulty, Height, Strength, Struggle
Hermes	Messengers, Speed
Hero and Leander	Lovers
Herod	Evil
Herod and Salome	Bargain
Herriot, James	Animals, Love of
Hesperus, wreck of the	Chaos and Disorder
Hinnom	Unpleasant or Wicked Places
Hippocrates	Medicine
Hippocrene	Inspiration
Hippolyta	Leaders
Hiroshima	Destruction
Hitchcock, Alfred	Fear
Hitler	Dictators and Tyrants, Moustaches
Hoffa, Jimmy	Disappearance and Absence
Hogarth	Artists, Evil
Holmes, Sherlock	Detectives, Intelligence
Holocaust	Death
Holy Grail	Quest
Holy of Holies	Importance
Homer	Blindness, Travellers and Wanderers, Writers
Homeric	Adventure, Superiority
Hood, Robin	Generosity, Outlaws, Rebellion and Disobedience
Hooverville	Poverty

Hopper	Artists
Horatius	Courage
Horn of Plenty	Abundance and Plenty, Food and Drink
Hotspur	Anger
Houdini	Escape and Survival
House of Usher	Mystery
Houyhnhnms	Intelligence
hubris	Pride
Hughes, Howard	Solitude, Wealth
Hulk	Strength
Humpty Dumpty	Weakness
Hunchback of Notre Dame	Ugliness
Huns	Movement
Hyde, Mr	Evil
Hydra	Appearing, Rebirth and Resurrection
Hygiea	Medicine
Hymen	Love and Marriage
Hyperborean	Temperature
Hyperboreans	Happiness
Hypnos	Sleep
Hyrcania	Unpleasant or Wicked Places
Iago	Cunning, Envy, Evil, Honesty and Truth
Icarus	Ambition, Ascent and Descent, Failure
Ingres	Artists
inquisitor	Ruthlessness
Invisible Man	Invisibility
Io	Change
Irene	Peace
Iris	Messengers
Isaac	Escape and Survival
Isaiah	Prophecy
Ishmael	Solitude
Ishtar	Sex and Sexuality
Isis and Osiris	Lovers
Islands of the Blest	Idyllic Places
Israelites	Poverty
Ithuriel	Gesture
Ivan the Terrible	Dictators and Tyrants
Ixion	Punishment, Suffering
Jack and the beanstalk	Height
Jack the Ripper	Murderers
Jacob	Cunning, Disguise, Patience, Struggle, Success
Jacob and Rachel	Lovers
Jacob's ladder	Ascent and Descent

Jacob's pottage — Food and Drink
Jain — Animals, Love of
James, Jesse — Outlaws
Jane Eyre and Mr Rochester — Lovers
Janus — Duality, Knowledge
Jared — Old Age
Jason — Adventure, Invisibility
Jehoshabeath — Safety
Jehovah — Ruthlessness, Speech
Jehu — Speed
Jekyll and Hyde — Change, Duality
Jephthah's daughter — Chastity and Virginity
Jeremiah — Pessimism, Prophecy
Jericho — Destruction
Jeroboam — Curse
Jesuit — Intelligence
Jesus — Forgiveness, Goodness, Humility, Jealousy, Solitude, Temptation
Jezebel — Prostitutes, Punishment, Sex and Sexuality
Jim — Freedom
Joan of Arc — Leaders, Suffering
Joash — Safety
Job — Humility, Patience, Poverty, Suffering
John O'Groats to Land's End — Distance
Johnson, Dr — Walk
John the Baptist — Oratory
Jolly Green Giant — Smiles
Jolly Miller — Indifference
Jonah — Curse, Escape and Survival, Returning
Jones, Indiana — Adventure, Heroes
Joseph — Chastity and Virginity, Dreams, Envy, Goodness, Jealousy
Joshua — Immobility
Jotun — Large Size
Judas — Betrayal, Guilt, Hair
Judgement Day — Sound
Juggernaut — Destruction
Juno — Anger
Jurassic — Outdatedness
Jurassic Park — Danger
Just William — Mischief

Kafka — Power
Kafkaesque — Strangeness
Karenina, Anna — Adultery

Karloff, Boris	Ugliness
Karma	Destiny and Luck
Karnac	Deserted Places
Kelly, Ned	Outlaws
Kent, Clark and Superman	Change
Keystone Kops	Comedy and Humour
King, Martin Luther	Goodness
Kitchener, Lord	Moustaches
Klimt	Artists
Knox, John	Disapproval, Sternness
Kojak	Baldness
Kon-Tiki	Travellers and Wanderers
Krakatoa	Sound
Labyrinth	Complexity
Lady in Red	Betrayal
Laelaps	Speed
Lais	Prostitutes
Lake, Veronica	Hair
Lamb of God	Innocence
Lancelot, Sir	Heroes, Rescue
Lancelot and Guinevere	Lovers
land of milk and honey	Abundance and Plenty
Land of Nod	Sleep
Land of Promise	Idyllic Places
Laocoön	Prophecy, Struggle, Suffering
Laodicean	Indifference
Laon and Cythna	Lovers
Laurel and Hardy	Comedy and Humour
Lautrec	Artists
Lawrence, St	Suffering
Lawrence of Arabia	Heroes
Lazarus	Poverty, Rebirth and Resurrection, Returning
Lear, King	Insanity
Legree, Simon	Ruthlessness
Leonardo	Artists
Leontes	Jealousy
Lesbos	Sex and Sexuality
Lethe	Death, Memory
Leviathan	Large Size, Strength
Liar, Billy	Lying
Lilliputian	Importance, Small Size
Lincoln, Abraham	Freedom, Oratory, Speech, Thinness
Linus blanket	Safety
Little Bighorn	Defeat
Little Dutch boy	Courage

Little Engine That Could	Perseverance
Little Match Girl	Poverty
Little Orphan Annie	Hair
Lochinvar	Heroes
Loki	Cunning, Evil, Mischief
Lolita	Sex and Sexuality
Loman, Willy	Failure
Lone Ranger	Concealment, Solitude
Long John Silver	Walk
Lorelei	Danger, Sirens
Lot	Departure, Escape and Survival
Lothario	Seducers and Male Lovers
Lot's wife	Change, Punishment
Lotus-eaters	Happiness, Memory
Louis XIV	Arrogance and Pomposity
Lovelace	Seducers and Male Lovers
Lucan, Lord	Disappearance and Absence
Lucifer	Ascent and Descent, Cunning, Devil, Failure, Pride, Rebellion and Disobedience
Lucretia	Sex and Sexuality
Lucullus	Food and Drink
Luddites	Lack of Change
Luke, St	Medicine
Lysistrata	Chastity and Virginity
Macavity	Disappearance and Absence
Macbeth, Lady	Ambition, Cunning, Evil, Gesture, Sleep
Macbeth/Lady Macbeth	Guilt
Macbeth's witches	Ugliness
Machiavelli	Cunning
Mad Hatter	Insanity
Mad Hatter's Tea Party	Chaos and Disorder
Madonna	Beauty: Female Beauty, Goodness, Peace
Maecenas	Wealth
Maenad	Chaos and Disorder, Sex and Sexuality
Mafeking	Courage
Mafia	Revenge
Magdalene, Mary	Grief and Sorrow, Guilt, Prostitutes
Magi	Wisdom
Magritte, René	Strangeness
Mahalalel	Old Age
Malaprop, Mrs	Speech
Malvolio	Arrogance and Pomposity
Mambrino's helmet	Invisibility
Mammon	Avarice, Wealth
Man in the Iron Mask	Captives
manna	Food and Drink

Marat	Death
March Hare	Insanity
Marie Antoinette	Arrogance and Pomposity, Idealism, Indifference
Marius	Solitude
Marlowe, Philip	Detectives
Marner, Silas	Miserliness
Marple, Miss	Detectives
Mars	War
Marsyas	Punishment
Marvel, Captain	Heroes
Marvin	Pessimism
Marx, Groucho	Walk
Marx, Harpo	Silence
Marx Brothers	Comedy and Humour
Mary Celeste	Deserted Places, Disappearance and Absence, Silence
Mason, Perry	Detectives
Mata Hari	Sirens
Matilda	Lying
McCarthy, Senator	Ruthlessness
McLuhan	Communication
Mecca	Quest
Meddlesome Matty	Mischief
Medea	Jealousy, Revenge
Medes and Persians	Lack of Change
Medusa	Hair, Ugliness
Mekon	Baldness
Melpomene	Inspiration, Suffering
Menjou, Adolph	Moustaches
Mephistopheles	Devil, Temptation
Mercury	Messengers, Speed
Merlin	Magic, Past, Wisdom
Merlin and Nimue	Lovers
Mesmer	Power
mess of pottage	Bargain
Messiah	Freedom
Methuselah	Old Age
Micawber, Mr	Optimism, Thrift
Michelangelo	Artists, Beauty: Male Beauty
Mickey Mouse	Importance, Speech
Midas	Avarice, Disclosure, Punishment, Wealth
Midian, hosts of	Enemy
Miller, Daisy	Naivety
Millet	Artists
Mills and Boon	Love and Marriage
Milquetoast, Caspar	Weakness
Milton	Writers

Mimir	Wisdom
Minerva	Appearing, Craftsmen, Music, War, Wisdom
Ministry of Silly Walks	Walk
Minotaur	Monsters
Miranda	Naivety
Miriam	Music
Mithras	Light
Mitty, Walter	Illusion, Lying
Münchausen, Baron	Lying
Mnemosyne	Memory
Moby Dick	Quest
Modigliani, Amedeo	Thinness
Moloch	Evil, Power
Mona Lisa	Mystery, Smiles
Monroe, Marilyn	Beauty: Female Beauty
Montagues and Capulets	Conflict, Enemy
Monte Cristo, Count of	Captives, Revenge
Monty Python	Comedy and Humour, Strangeness
Morgan, John Pierpoint	Wealth
Morgan le Fay	Magic
Moriarty	Criminals
Morpheus	Dreams, Sleep
Moses	Appearing, Freedom, Movement, Safety
Mother Hubbard	Abundance and Plenty
Muhammad	Movement
Munchkin	Small Size
Muses	Inspiration
Mussolini	Dictators and Tyrants
Myron	Sculptors
Naboth's vineyard	Avarice
naiad	Hair
Napoleon	Leaders, Soldiers
Narcissus	Beauty: Male Beauty, Vanity
Narnia	Strangeness
Nautilus	Modernity
Nazirite	Hair
Nebuchadnezzar	Dreams, Hair, Insanity
nectar	Food and Drink
Nefertiti	Beauty: Female Beauty
Nelson	Blindness
Nemesis	Destiny and Luck, Punishment, Revenge
Nepenthe	Memory
Neptune	Water
Nereid	Water
Nereus	Water
Nero	Dictators and Tyrants, Indifference

Nestor	Wisdom
Never-Never Land	Idyllic Places
New Jerusalem	Idyllic Places
Newgate	Prisons
Newton, Isaac	Intelligence, Realization
Nibelung	Wealth
Nietzsche	Superiority
Niflheim	Darkness
Nightingale, Florence	Goodness, Medicine
Nightmare on Elm Street	Fear
Nijinsky	Dancing
Nike	Victory
Nimrod	Hunters
Nineveh	Destruction, Distance
Ninth Plague of Egypt	Darkness
Niobe	Grief and Sorrow
Nirvana	Happiness
Noah	Escape and Survival, Nakedness, Past
Noah's Ark	Outdatedness
Noah's dove	Movement
Noah's flood	Water
noble savage	Naivety
Noddy	Importance
Norns	Destiny and Luck
Nostradamus	Prophecy
Nureyev, Rudolph	Dancing
Nymph	Beauty: Female Beauty
Oates, Captain	Departure
Occam's razor	Intelligence
Odin	Wisdom
Odysseus	Destiny and Luck, Disguise, Noses, Returning, Travellers and Wanderers
Odyssey	Travellers and Wanderers
Oedipus	Blindness, Destiny and Luck, Jealousy, Sex and Sexuality
Old Harry	Devil
Old Man of the Sea	Difficulty, Perseverance
Old Nick	Devil
Olympian	Superiority
Olympus	Importance
Onassis, Aristotle	Wealth
Onegin, Eugene and Tatiana	Lovers
Ophelia	Death, Insanity
Ophir	Distance

Orion	Hunters
Orpheus	Music
Orwell	Power
Ossian	Travellers and Wanderers
Othello	Jealousy
Othello and Desdemona	Lovers
Outer Mongolia	Distance
Oyl, Olive	Thinness
Ozymandias	Power, Pride
Packer, Kerry	Wealth
Pacolet	Messengers
Pan	Chaos and Disorder, Music, Sex and Sexuality
Pandemonium	Chaos and Disorder, Unpleasant or Wicked Places
Pandora's box	Problem
Pangloss	Optimism
Pantagruel	Gluttony
Pantheon	Leaders
Paolo and Francesca	Lovers
Papa Doc	Dictators and Tyrants
Paracelsus	Medicine
Paradise	Idyllic Places
Parcae Sisters	Indifference
Paris	Judgement and Decision
Parnassus	Inspiration
Parthian	Departure
Patton, General	Soldiers
Paul and Virginia	Lovers
Pauline	Change
Pavlov	Conformity
Pavlova	Dancing
Pax	Peace
Pecksniff	Hypocrisy
Peeping Tom	Blindness, Punishment
Pegasus	Escape and Survival, Horses
Pelion on Ossa	Difficulty
Pelléas and Mélisande	Lovers
Penelope	Patience
Pepys, Samuel	Writers
Pericles	Oratory
Peripatetic	Movement
Persephone	Temptation
Perseus	Rescue
Peter Pan	Hair, Youth
Petra	Deserted Places
Petrarch and Laura	Lovers
Petruchio	Power

Phaethon	Failure
Pharaoh	Dictators and Tyrants, Dreams
Pharisee	Hypocrisy
Pheidippides	Messengers
Phidias	Sculptors
Philistine	Stupidity
Philistines	Enemy
Philoctetes	Suffering
Philosopher's Stone	Quest
Phobos	Fear
Phoebe	Light
Phoebus	Light, Temperature
Phoenix	Rebirth and Resurrection
Phryne	Prostitutes
Picasso	Artists
Pickwick, Mr	Fatness
Pied Piper	Power, Solitude
Pieria	Inspiration
Piggy, Miss	Fatness
Pilate, Pontius	Gesture, Guilt, Innocence
Pilate's wife	Dreams
Pillars of Hercules	Distance
Pinkerton's	Detectives
Pinocchio	Life: Generation of Life, Lying, Noses
Piranesi	Strangeness
plagues of Egypt	Suffering
Plato	Idealism, Intelligence
Pluto	Darkness
Plutus	Wealth
Pocahontas	Beauty: Female Beauty
Podsnap	Arrogance and Pomposity
Poirot, Hercule	Detectives
Pollock	Artists
Pollyanna	Optimism
Polo, Marco	Travellers and Wanderers
Polonius	Concealment
Polycrates	Destiny and Luck
Polydamas	Strength
Polyhymnia	Inspiration
Polyphemus	Jealousy
Pomona	Abundance and Plenty
Pompeii	Deserted Places, Destruction
Pony Express	Messengers
Pooh-Bah	Arrogance and Pomposity
Popeye	Strength
Poppins, Mary	Wholesomeness

Porter, KCB, Sir Joseph	Success
Portia	Disguise
Poseidon	Anger, Water
Potiphar's wife	Sex and Sexuality
pound of flesh	Bargain
Praxiteles	Sculptors
Pre-Raphaelite	Hair
Priapus	Sex and Sexuality
Prince Charming	Seducers and Male Lovers
Prince of Darkness	Devil
Princes in the Tower	Captives
Prisoner of Chillon	Captives
Prisoner of Zenda	Captives
Procrustes	Conformity, Large Size
Prodigal Son	Food and Drink, Forgiveness, Returning
Prometheus	Cunning, Life: Generation of Life, Problem, Punishment, Rebellion and Disobedience, Suffering
Promised Land	Idyllic Places
Prospero	Magic
Prospero's banquet	Disappearance and Absence
Proteus	Appearing, Change
Proust	Memory
Prynne, Hester	Adultery
Psycho	Fear
Puck	Mischief
Punch and Judy	Conflict, Speech
Punchinello	Speech
Pygmalion	Life: Generation of Life, Sculptors
Pygmalion and Galatea	Lovers
Pyramus and Thisbe	Lovers
Pyrrhic victory	Victory
Quasimodo	Music, Ugliness
Quatermain, Allan	Adventure
Ra	Light
Rabelais	Comedy and Humour
Rachel	Grief and Sorrow
Rackham, Arthur	Naivety
Raft of the Medusa	Suffering
Ragnarok	Destruction
Rambo	Macho Men
Rapunzel	Hair
Rasputin	Evil
Reading Gaol	Prisons
Reardon, Edwin	Failure
Rebel Without a Cause	Nonconformity

Red Cross Knight	Rescue
Red Queen	Speed
Red Sea	Movement
Red Shoes	Dancing
Reed, Donna	Wholesomeness
Rembrandt	Artists, Darkness
Revere, Paul	Messengers
Reynolds	Artists
Rhadamanthus	Judgement and Decision, Sternness
Richard, Cliff	Wholesomeness
Rip Van Winkle	Outdatedness, Returning, Sleep
Rivera	Artists
rivers of Babylon	Grief and Sorrow
Roadrunner	Speed
Robben Island	Prisons
Robert the Bruce	Perseverance
Robin Hood	Generosity, Outlaws, Rebellion and Disobedience
Rochester, Mrs	Concealment, Insanity
Rockefeller	Generosity, Wealth
Rockwell, Norman	Wholesomeness
Rogers, Ginger	Dancing
Roland and Oliver	Similarity
Romeo	Seducers and Male Lovers
Romeo and Juliet	Lovers
Romulus and Remus	Similarity
Roscius	Actors
Rosinante	Horses
Rothko	Artists
Rothschild	Wealth
Rousseau	Artists, Naivety
Rubens	Artists, Beauty: Female Beauty, Fatness
Rubicon	Change
Rudolph	Noses
Rumpelstiltskin	Change, Disclosure
Ruritania	Cunning
Sadduccee	Doubt
Sade, Marquis de	Sex and Sexuality
Salome	Dancing
Samaritan	Goodness
Samson	Blindness, Captives, Hair, Safety, Strength, Weakness
Samson and Delilah	Lovers
Samuel	Food and Drink
Sandman	Sleep
Santa Claus	Generosity
Sappho	Sex and Sexuality

SAS	Rescue
Satan	Cunning, Devil, Hair, Rebellion and Disobedience, Temptation
Saturnalian	Food and Drink
Satyr	Sex and Sexuality
Saul/Paul	Change
Savonarola	Disapproval
Sawyer, Tom	Cunning, Nonconformity
scapegoat	Guilt
Scaramouch	Cowardice
Scarecrow	Stupidity
Scarlet Pimpernel	Disappearance and Absence, Rescue
Scarlett O'Hara and Rhett Butler	Lovers
Scheherazade	Cunning, Storytellers
Schindler, Oskar	Goodness
Schopenhauer	Pessimism
Schwarzenegger, Arnold	Heroes
Schweitzer, Albert	Goodness
Scott, Walter	Adventure
Scott of the Antarctic	Temperature
Scrooge	Miserliness
Scylla and Charybdis	Danger, Problem
Sebastian, St	Suffering
Selene	Light
Sennacherib	Disappearance and Absence
Sermon on the Mount	Oratory
Serpent	Cunning, Problem
Seven Sages of Greece	Wisdom
Seven Sleepers	Sleep
Shadrach, Meshach, and Abednego	Temperature
Shakespeare	Writers
Shangri-la	Idyllic Places
Sharp, Becky	Cunning
Sheba, Queen of	Arrogance and Pomposity
Sheppard, Jack	Escape and Survival
Shylock	Bargain, Miserliness
Siberia	Distance, Unpleasant or Wicked Places
Sibyl	Communication, Knowledge, Prophecy
Siegfried	Heroes, Weakness
Silenus	Fatness, Food and Drink
Simeon Stylites, St	Height
Simple Simon	Stupidity
Sinbad	Adventure, Strangeness, Travellers and Wanderers
Sir Humphrey	Power
Sirens	Danger, Destruction, Sirens

Sisyphus	Difficulty, Failure, Punishment, Suffering
Skid Row	Poverty
Skywalker, Luke	Heroes
Sleeping Beauty	Silence, Sleep
Sleipnir	Horses
Slough of Despond	Despair
Smiles, Samuel	Thrift
Snark	Quest
Snow Queen	Indifference
Snow White	Beauty: Female Beauty
Snow White's stepmother	Envy, Vanity
Socrates	Intelligence, Nonconformity
Sodom	Sex and Sexuality
Sodom and Gomorrah	Destruction, Unpleasant or Wicked Places
Solomon	Judgement and Decision, Wisdom
Solomon's temple	Wealth
Solon	Wisdom
Somnus	Sleep
sorcerer's apprentice	Difficulty
Spade, Sam	Detectives
Spartan	Strength, Thrift
Speedy Gonzalez	Speed
Spenser	Chastity and Virginity
Sphinx	Mystery
Spock	Intelligence
Squeers, Wackford	Ruthlessness, Teachers
Stalin	Dictators and Tyrants
Stanislavsky	Actors
Starship Enterprise	Modernity
Steen	Artists
Stentor	Speech
Stepford Wives	Conformity
Stephen, St	Suffering
Struldbrug	Old Age
Stygian	Darkness
Styx	Death
Sun City	Prisons
Sun King	Wealth
Superman	Change, Heroes, Strength, Weakness
Susanna	Innocence, Nakedness
Svengali	Power
sword of Damocles	Danger
Symplegades	Danger
Taliesin	Storytellers
Tamerlane	Leaders

Tammany Hall	Unpleasant or Wicked Places
Tannhäuser	Forgiveness
Tantalus	Punishment, Suffering
tar baby	Problem
Tartarus	Darkness, Punishment, Suffering, Unpleasant or Wicked Places
Tartuffe	Hypocrisy
Tarzan	Macho Men, Strength
Taylor, Jeremy	Lack of Change
Teflon	Escape and Survival
Temple, Shirley	Hair, Naivety
Teresa, Mother	Goodness
termagant	Fierce Women
Terminator	Macho Men
Terpsichore	Dancing, Inspiration, Music
Thalia	Beauty: Female Beauty, Comedy and Humour, Inspiration
Thermopylae	Courage
Thespis	Actors
Thirty Pieces of Silver	Betrayal
Thor	Strength
Thoth	Wisdom
Thought Police	Power
Thraso	Arrogance and Pomposity
Three Musketeers	Friendship
Thumbelina	Small Size
Thyestes	Punishment
Timbuktu	Distance
Tinker Bell	Escape and Survival
Tin Man	Immobility, Lack of Change
Tin-Pan Alley	Music
Tiresias	Blindness, Prophecy
Titan	Importance, Large Size, Strength, Superiority
Titania	Sleep
Titanic	Danger
Tithonus	Old Age
Titian	Artists
Tityus	Punishment
Toad, Mr	Disguise
Tom Thumb	Small Size
Tophet	Unpleasant or Wicked Places
Topsy	Hair, Knowledge
Tortoise	Perseverance
Toulouse-Lautrec	Artists
Tower Hill	Death
Tower of London	Prisons
Tracy, Dick	Detectives

tree of knowledge	Knowledge
Tristram	Despair, Hunters
Tristram and Iseult	Lovers
Triton	Water
Troilus and Cressida	Lovers
Trojan Horse	Cunning
Turner	Artists
Turpin, Dick	Outlaws
Tutankhamun	Curse
Tutu, Archbishop	Goodness
Tweedledum and Tweedledee	Similarity
Twiggy	Thinness
Twilight Zone	Strangeness
Twist, Oliver	Poverty
Tyburn	Death
Typhoid Mary	Danger, Deserted Places
Tyr	War
Udolpho	Mystery
Ugly Duckling	Change, Ugliness
Ugly Sisters	Ugliness, Vanity
Ultima Thule	Distance
Ulysses	Travellers and Wanderers
Uncle Tom	Betrayal
Urania	Inspiration
Uriah	Betrayal
US cavalry	Rescue
Utopia	Idealism, Idyllic Places
Valhalla	Idyllic Places
Valkyries	War
Valley of (the Shadow of) Death	Death
Vandal	Destruction
Vanderbilt	Wealth
Van Dyck	Artists
Van Gogh	Artists
Vashti	Rebellion and Disobedience
Veil of Isis	Mystery
Velasquez	Artists
Venus	Appearing, Beauty: Female Beauty, Love and Marriage, Sex and Sexuality
Venus de Milo	Hair
Veronese	Artists
Vespucci, Amerigo	Explorers
Vesuvius	Anger

Victoria, Queen	Comedy and Humour
Vietnam	Defeat
Vitus, St	Dancing
Vladimir	Patience
Volpone	Cunning
Voltaire	Disapproval
Vulcan	Craftsmen, Ugliness
Waltons	Naivety, Wholesomeness
Wandering Jew	Solitude, Travellers and Wanderers
Warshawski, V. I.	Detectives
Washington, George	Honesty and Truth
Waterloo	Defeat
Wayne, John	Heroes, Macho Men
Wee Willie Winkie	Sleep
Wellington	Soldiers
Wells Fargo	Messengers
Wendy	Love and Marriage
Werther	Suffering
Wesley, John	Oratory
West Side Story	Dancing
White Rabbit	Speed, Time
Whore of Babylon	Evil, Prostitutes
Wild Boy of Aveyron	Naivety
Wilde, Oscar	Captives, Sex and Sexuality
Winnie the Pooh	Gluttony
Wise Men	Wisdom
Wise Men of Gotham	Stupidity
Witch of Endor	Appearing, Magic
Wizard of Oz	Magic
wolf in Red Riding Hood	Disguise, Smiles
wolf in sheep's clothing	Disguise
Wonderland	Strangeness
Woody Woodpecker	Hair
Wooster, Bertie	Stupidity
Would-Be, Lady	Ambition
writing on the wall	Communication, Prophecy
Xanadu	Idyllic Places
Xerxes	Leaders
Yahoo	Destruction
Yellow Brick Road	Quest
Yogi Bear	Gluttony
Zapata	Moustaches
Zeus	Change, Seducers and Male Lovers

Zeuxis	**Artists**
Zorba	**Dancing**
Zorro	**Concealment, Rebellion and Disobedience**